# 3rd Clinical Natural Language Processing Workshop (ClinicalNLP 2020)

Online
19 November 2020

ISBN: 978-1-7138-1989-9

Printed from e-media with permission by:

Curran Associates, Inc.
57 Morehouse Lane
Red Hook, NY  12571

Some format issues inherent in the e-media version may also appear in this print version.



Printed with permission by Curran Associates, Inc. (2021)

For permission requests, please contact the Association for Computational Linguistics
at the address below.

Association for Computational Linguistics
209 N. Eighth Street
Stroudsburg, Pennsylvania 18360


Phone:   1-570-476-8006
Fax:       1-570-476-0860

acl@aclweb.org

**Additional copies of this publication are available from:**

Curran Associates, Inc.
57 Morehouse Lane
Red Hook, NY 12571 USA
Phone: 845-758-0400
Fax:     845-758-2633
Email:   curran@proceedings.com
Web:    www.proceedings.com

EMNLP 2020

**The 3rd Clinical Natural Language Processing Workshop**

**Proceedings of the Workshop**

November 19, 2020

# Introduction

This volume contains papers from the 3rd Workshop on Clinical Natural Language Processing (ClinicalNLP), held at EMNLP 2020.

Clinical text offers unique challenges that differentiate it not only from open-domain data, but from other types of text in the biomedical domain as well. Notably, clinical text contains a significant number of abbreviations, medical terms, and other clinical jargon. Clinical narratives are characterized by nonstandard document structures that are often critical to overall understanding. Narrative provider notes are designed to communicate with other experts while at the same time serving as a legal record. Finally, clinical notes contain sensitive patient-specific information that raise privacy and security concerns that present special challenges for natural language systems. This workshop focuses on the work that develops methods to address the above challenges, with the goal of advancing state-of-the-art in clinical NLP.

This year, we received the total of 48 submissions, out of which 14 were accepted as oral presentations and 19 as posters.

**Organizers:**

Anna Rumshisky, UMass Lowell
Kirk Roberts, University of Texas Health Science Center at Houston
Steven Bethard, University of Arizona
Tristan Naumann, Microsoft Research

**Program Committee:**

John Aberdeen, The MITRE Corporation
Emily Alsentzer, Massachusetts Institute of Technology
Sabine Bergler, Concordia University
Parminder Bhatia, Amazon
William Boag, Massachusetts Institute of Technology
Cheryl Clark, The MITRE Corporation
Surabhi Datta, University of Texas Health Science Center at Houston
Murthy Devarakonda, Arizona State University
Dmitriy Dligach, Loyola University
Jungwei Fan, Mayo Clinic
Jason Fries, Stanford University
Travis Goodwin, National Library of Medicine
Yoan Gutiérrez, University of Alicante
Sadid Hasan, CVS Health
Saeed Hassanpour, Dartmouth University
Djoerd Hiemstra, Radboud University
Eben Holderness, Brandeis University
Baotian Hu, Harbin Institute of Technology
Di Jin, Massachusetts Institute of Technology
Alistair Johnson, Massachusetts Institute of Technology
Yoshinobu Kano, Shizuoka University
Egoitz Laparra, University of Arizona
Chen Lin, Boston Children's Hospital
Sijia Liu, Mayo Clinic
Matthew McDermott, Massachusetts Institute of Technology
Bridget McInnes, Virginia Commonwealth University
Timothy Miller, Boston Children's Hospital
Yifan Peng, Weill Cornell Medicine
Hoifung Poon, Microsoft Research
Preethi Raghavan, IBM Research
Frank Rudzicz, University of Toronto
Allen Schmaltz, Harvard University
Thomas Searle, King's College London
Chaitanya Shivade, Amazon
Yuqi Si, University of Texas Health Science Center at Houston
Sarvesh Soni, University of Texas Health Science Center at Houston
Karin Verspoor, The University of Melbourne
Byron Wallace, Northeastern University
Yanshan Wang, Mayo Clinic
Ben Wellner, The MITRE Corporation
Stephen Wu, University of Texas Health Science Center at Houston
Dongfang Xu, University of Arizona
Rui Zhang, University of Minnesota

**Invited Speaker:**

Hong Yu, UMass Lowell

Talk Title: Deep Learning is Conquering Human Tasks. How Far Can it Go in Medicine? Advances, Challenges, and Future Directions

Biography: Hong Yu is faculty at the Department of Computer Science and Director of Biomedical and Health Research in Data Sciences, University of Massachusetts Lowell. She is also a Research Health Scientist at the Edith Nourse Rogers Memorial Veterans Hospital. She holds adjunct faculty positions at UMass Amherst and UMass Medical School. She is an elected fellow of the American College of Medical Informatics. She has published over 200 peer-reviewed articles in natural language processing and applied machine learning.

# Table of Contents

# Conference Program

**19 Nov 2020**

**09:00–10:00   Opening Session**

09:00–09:45   *Keynote Talk: Deep Learning is Conquering Human Tasks. How Far Can it Go in Medicine? Advances, Challenges, and Future Directions*
Hong Yu

09:45–10:00   *Keynote Q&A*
Hong Yu

**10:00–10:40   Oral Session 1**

10:00–10:05   *Various Approaches for Predicting Stroke Prognosis using Magnetic Resonance Imaging Text Records*
Tak-Sung Heo, Chulho Kim, Jeong-Myeong Choi, Yeong-Seok Jeong and Yu-Seop Kim

10:05–10:15   *Multiple Sclerosis Severity Classification From Clinical Text*
Alister D'Costa, Stefan Denkovski, Michal Malyska, Sae Young Moon, Brandon Rufino, Zhen Yang, Taylor Killian and Marzyeh Ghassemi

10:15–10:25   *BERT-XML: Large Scale Automated ICD Coding Using BERT Pretraining*
Zachariah Zhang, Jingshu Liu and Narges Razavian

**10:25–10:40   *Oral Session 1: Q&A***

10:40–10:50    **Coffee Break**

10:50–11:40    **Oral Session 2**

10:50–10:55    *Incorporating Risk Factor Embeddings in Pre-trained Transformers Improves Sentiment Prediction in Psychiatric Discharge Summaries*
Xiyu Ding, Mei-Hua Hall and Timothy Miller

10:55–11:05    *Information Extraction from Swedish Medical Prescriptions with Sig-Transformer Encoder*
John Pougué Biyong, Bo Wang, Terry Lyons and Alejo Nevado-Holgado

11:05–11:15    *Evaluation of Transfer Learning for Adverse Drug Event (ADE) and Medication Entity Extraction*
Sankaran Narayanan, Kaivalya Mannam, Sreeranga P Rajan and P Venkat Rangan

11:15–11:25    *BioBERTpt - A Portuguese Neural Language Model for Clinical Named Entity Recognition*
Elisa Terumi Rubel Schneider, João Vitor Andrioli de Souza, Julien Knafou, Lucas Emanuel Silva e Oliveira, Jenny Copara, Yohan Bonescki Gumiel, Lucas Ferro Antunes de Oliveira, Emerson Cabrera Paraiso, Douglas Teodoro and Cláudia Maria Cabral Moro Barra

11:25–11:40    *Oral Session 2: Q&A*

11:40–12:00    **Poster Teasers**

11:40–11:41    *Dilated Convolutional Attention Network for Medical Code Assignment from Clinical Text*
Shaoxiong Ji, Erik Cambria and Pekka Marttinen

11:41–11:42    *Classification of Syncope Cases in Norwegian Medical Records*
Ildiko Pilan, Pål H. Brekke, Fredrik A. Dahl, Tore Gundersen, Haldor Husby, Øystein Nytrø and Lilja Øvrelid

11:42–11:43    *Comparison of Machine Learning Methods for Multi-label Classification of Nursing Education and Licensure Exam Questions*
John Langton, Krishna Srihasam and Junlin Jiang

11:43–11:44    *Clinical XLNet: Modeling Sequential Clinical Notes and Predicting Prolonged Mechanical Ventilation*
Kexin Huang, Abhishek Singh, Sitong Chen, Edward Moseley, Chih-Ying Deng, Naomi George and Charolotta Lindvall

11:56–11:57 *Where's the Question? A Multi-channel Deep Convolutional Neural Network for Question Identification in Textual Data*
George Michalopoulos, Helen Chen and Alexander Wong

11:57–11:58 *Learning from Unlabelled Data for Clinical Semantic Textual Similarity*
Yuxia Wang, Karin Verspoor and Timothy Baldwin

11:58–11:59 *Joint Learning with Pre-trained Transformer on Named Entity Recognition and Relation Extraction Tasks for Clinical Analytics*
Miao Chen, Ganhui Lan, Fang Du and Victor Lobanov

12:00–13:20 **Poster Session & Lunch**

13:20–14:10 **Oral Session 3**

13:20–13:25 *Extracting Semantic Aspects for Structured Representation of Clinical Trial Eligibility Criteria*
Tirthankar Dasgupta, Ishani Mondal, abir naskar and Lipika Dey

13:25–13:35 *An Ensemble Approach to Automatic Structuring of Radiology Reports*
Morteza Pourreza Shahri, Amir Tahmasebi, Bingyang Ye, Henghui Zhu, Javed Aslam and Timothy Ferris

13:35–13:45 *Utilizing Multimodal Feature Consistency to Detect Adversarial Examples on Clinical Summaries*
Wenjie Wang, Youngja Park, Taesung Lee, Ian Molloy, Pengfei Tang and Li Xiong

13:45–13:55 *Advancing Seq2seq with Joint Paraphrase Learning*
So Yeon Min, Preethi Raghavan and Peter Szolovits

13:55–14:10 *Oral Session 3: Q&A*

**19 Nov 2020 (continued)**

**14:10–14:55    EMNLP Findings Session 1**

14:10–14:15    *Learning to Generate Clinically Coherent Chest X-Ray Reports*
Justin Lovelace, Bobak Mortazavi

14:15–14:20    *Learning Visual-Semantic Embeddings for Reporting Abnormal Findings on Chest X-rays*
Jianmo Ni, Chun-Nan Hsu, Amilcare Gentili, Julian McAuley

14:20–14:30    *Characterizing the Value of Information in Medical Notes*
Chao-Chun Hsu, Shantanu Karnwal, Sendhil Mullainathan, Ziad Obermeyer, Chenhao Tan

14:30–14:40    *PharmMT: A Neural Machine Translation Approach to Simplify Prescription Directions*
Jiazhao Li, Corey Lester, Xinyan Zhao, Yuting Ding, Yun Jiang, V.G.Vinod Vydiswaran

**14:40–14:55    *EMNLP Findings Session 1: Q&A***

**14:55–15:05    Coffee Break**

**15:05–15:50    EMNLP Findings Session 2**

15:05–15:15    *A Dual-Attention Network for Joint Named Entity Recognition and Sentence Classification of Adverse Drug Events*
Susmitha Wunnava, Xiao Qin, Tabassum Kakar, Xiangnan Kong, Elke A. Rundensteiner

15:15–15:25    *Dr. Summarize: Global Summarization of Medical Dialogue by Exploiting Local Structures*
Anirudh Joshi, Namit Katariya, Xavier Amatriain, Anitha Kannan

15:25–15:35    *Generating Accurate Electronic Health Assessment from Medical Graph*
Zhichao Yang, Hong Yu

**15:35–15:50    *EMNLP Findings Session 2: Q&A***

**15:50–16:35    Best Paper Session**

15:50–16:00    *On the diminishing return of labeling clinical reports*
Jean-Baptiste Lamare, Oloruntobiloba Olatunji and Li Yao

16:00–16:10    *The Chilean Waiting List Corpus: a new resource for clinical Named Entity Recognition in Spanish*
Pablo Báez, Fabián Villena, Matías Rojas, Manuel Durán and Jocelyn Dunstan

16:10–16:20    *Analyzing Text Specific vs Blackbox Fairness Algorithms in Multimodal Clinical NLP*
John Chen, Ian Berlot-Attwell, Xindi Wang, Safwan Hossain and Frank Rudzicz

**16:20–16:35    *Best Paper Session: Q&A***

**16:35–16:50    Concluding Session**

# Various Approaches for Predicting Stroke Prognosis using Magnetic Resonance Imaging Text Records


**Tak-Sung Heo[1], Chulho Kim[2], Jeong-Myeong Choi[1], Yeong-Seok Jeong[3], Yu-Seop Kim[3]**
[1]Department of Convergence Software, Hallym University, Republic of Korea
[2]Department of Neurology, College of Medicine, Hallym University, Republic of Korea
[3]College of Software, Hallym University, Republic of Korea
`gjxkrtjd221@gmail.com` `gumdol52@naver.com` `jeong5905@gmail.com`
`dnfkdi1995@gmail.com` `yskim01@hallym.ac.kr`



## Abstract

Stroke is one of the leading causes of death and disability worldwide. Stroke is treatable, but it is prone to disability after treatment. To grasp the degree of disability caused by stroke, we use magnetic resonance imaging text records to predict stroke and measure the performance according to the document-level and sentence-level representation. As a result of the experiment, the document-level representation shows better performance.


## 1 Introduction

Stroke is a neurologic disorder that is characterized by an acute disruption of cerebral blood flow and corresponding symptoms lasting more than 24 hours. Stroke is one of the leading causes of death and disability worldwide (Sacco et al., 2013; Campbell et al., 2019). As the incidence of stroke is increasing and proportion of stroke survivors with a disability is also increasing recently, there are increasing demands of proper diagnosis and long-term treatment strategy to reduce the global burden of stroke (Ekker et al., 2019). Among the diagnostic tools for stroke, the most important imaging methods are brain computed tomography (CT) and magnetic resonance image (MRI). We can obtain vascular images and various functional images by brain MRI. Its usefulness can change recent paradigm of the stroke treatment (Wang et al., 2016; Atchaneeyasakul et al., 2020).

Stroke is treatable, but it is prone to disability after treatment and must be prevented in advance (Park et al., 2018). To grasp the degree of disability caused by stroke, many studies have been conducted to predict stroke prognosis in recent years (Shrestha et al., 2015; Pack et al., 2018; Monteiro et al., 2018).

Park et al. (2018) used the medical examination results of 3,605 patients as input features. For input features, a total of 76 features are extracted as results of medical tests such as 12-lead electrocardiography, chest x-ray, lipid profiles, standard blood tests, and other diagnoses. Among these features, only 19 features were used through feature selection, and these features were input to the Bayesian network to predict the prognosis of stroke.

Monteiro et al. (2018) used several medical examination records, such as CT and MRI, from admission to discharge of 425 patients, as input features. These features are input into machine learning models such as logistic regression, decision tree, support vector machine, random forest, and extreme gradient boosting (XGB) model to predict stroke prognosis.

Previous studies have predicted the prognosis of stroke using various diagnostic results. Since a vast number of tests are required for these prediction methods, a burden of a lot of time and cost may occur from the patient's point of view. In this study, the prognosis of stroke is predicted using only MRI text records created after radiologists analyze MRI images.

Stroke prognosis prediction using MRI texts corresponds to the text classification task. Recently, the text classification task is showing good performance through a convolutional neural network (CNN) which extracts local information of adjacent words, long short-term memory (LSTM), which is good in the sequential data processing, bi-directional LSTM (Bi-LSTM), which has forward-backward LSTM structure, XGB, which is level-wise tree-based learning algorithms of gradient boosting method, and light gradient boosting machine (LGBM), which is leaf-wise tree-based learning algorithms of gradient boosting method




*Proceedings of the 3rd Clinical Natural Language Processing Workshop*, pages 1–6
November 19, 2020. ©2020 Association for Computational Linguistics

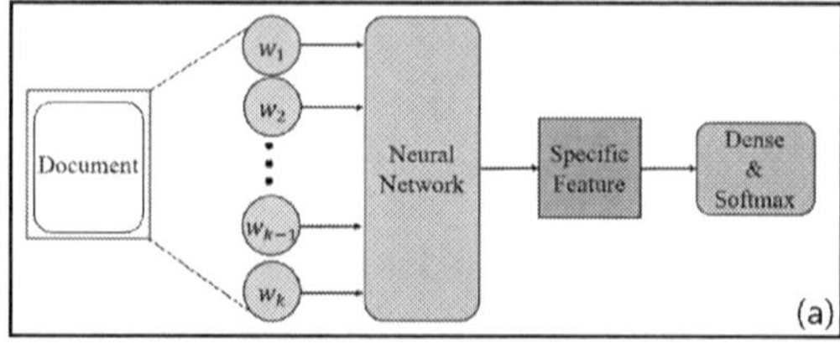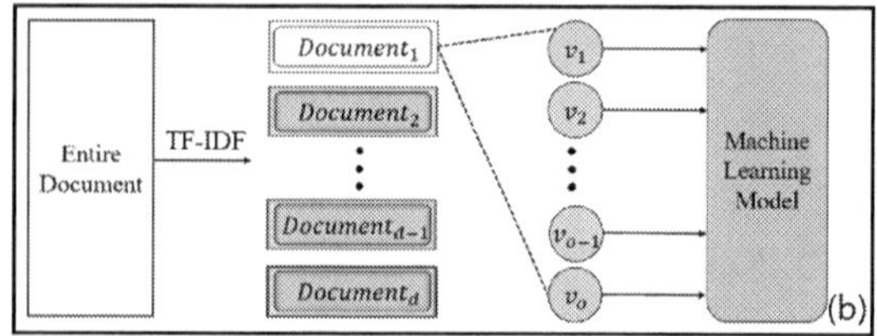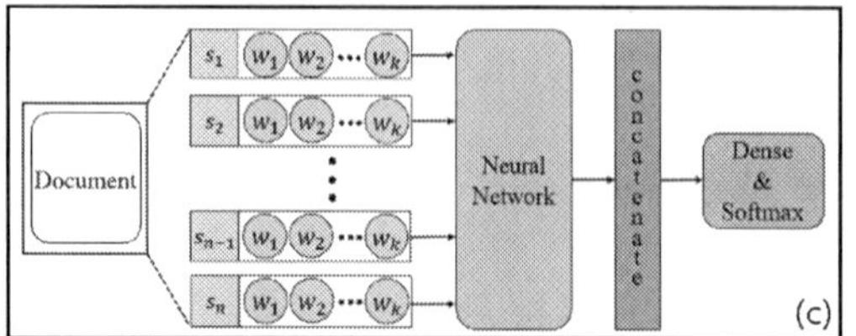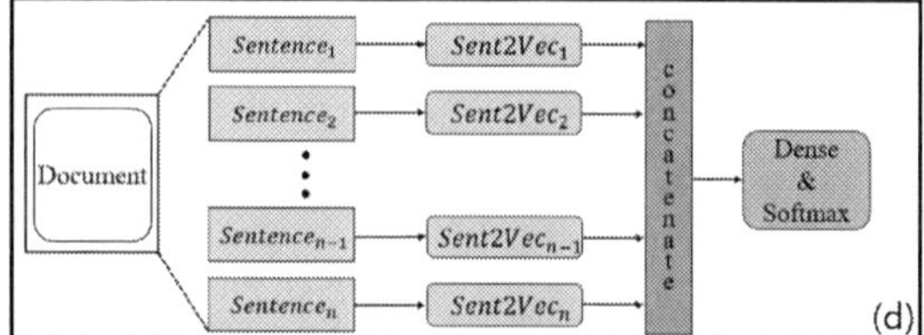

Figure 1: (a). Representation of document-level, (b). Representation of TF-IDF, (c). Representation of sentence-level using word embedding, (d). Representation of sentence-level using sentence embedding

(Kim, 2014; Zhou et al., 2015; Alzamzami et al., 2020).

Few widely known studies have used MRI text recordings to predict stroke prognosis. In this study, rather than improving the performance, the performance difference according to the document representation method is identified and analyzed. In this paper, MRI text is represented at the document level or sentence level.

Document-level representation is an approach that represents the entire document as a vector and considers it as an input and analyzes it. And sentence-level representation is an approach that analyzes the entire document by representing each sentence constituting the document as individual vectors and inputting them.

This paper is composed as follows. Section 2 is about a dataset and describes the MRI text records used in this study. Section 3 describes the architecture of the model corresponding to each representation regarding Figure 1. Section 4 shows experimental results, including the hyperparameters used in the experiment, and compares and analyzes the results of various representation levels. Section 5 describes a conclusion, which outlines the summary and plans for this study.

## 2 Dataset

MRI text records used in this study are collected from people hospitalized with acute ischemic stroke at Hallym University Chuncheon Sacred

| ID | Text of MRI | Label |
|----|-------------|-------|
| A | 1. focal old petechial hemorrhage in left parietal subcortical WM<br>2. No diffusion restriction<br>3. magnetic resonance angiography: No gross abnormal finding. | 0 |
| B | 1. multiple diffusion restriction in left temporo-parietal subcortical WMs. ; multiple acute infarction.<br>2. Old small infarct in left parietal cortex. | 1 |

Table 1: Examples of MRI text records

Heart Hospital [1] from February 2010 to October2019. Patients performed MRI scans several times during hospitalization. However, we only used here for text reports of brain MRI that were examined immediately after hospitalization. Text of MRI in Table 1 means text records of MRI images analyzed by radiologists, and the order of sentences shown here is meaningless. A label is determined according to the score of modified rankin scale[2] (mRS) which is a clinical outcome measure of the degree of disability. The mRS used in this study is the prognostic score of stroke patients after 3 months, defined as 0-6 points. Patients with scores of 0-2 mRS are grouped as 'good outcome', and patients with a score of 3-6 are grouped as 'poor outcome' (Powers et al., 2015; Rangaraju et al., 2017). In this study, label 0 is defined as 'good outcome' and label 1 as 'poor outcome'.

The total number of MRI text records collected is 2,071. In MRI text records, the number of MRI

---

[1] https://chuncheon.hallym.or.kr

[2] https://en.wikipedia.org/wiki/Modified_Rankin_Scale

text records with label 0 is 1,317, and the number of MRI text records with label 1 is 754. In the MRI text record, the average number of sentences is 10, the minimum number of sentences is 1, and the maximum number of sentences is 40.

## 3  Document Representation

In this study, two document representation methods, document-level and sentence-level, are used to predict the prognosis of stroke.

### 3.1  Document-Level Representation

In the document-level representation, the document's entire contents are represented like a single sentence and entered into the model. In this representation, word embedding and TF-IDF are used. The model structure using word embedding is shown in (a) of Figure 1, and the model structure using TF-IDF is shown in (b) of Figure 1.

**Document-Level using Word Embedding**  Word vectors extracted through word embedding can be inputs of CNN, multi-filter CNNs, LSTM, or Bi-LSTM, and the structures of these models can be described as follow:

- When CNN is used, the features of adjacent words are entered into global max-pooling to extract the most prominent features. Finally, these features predict the prognosis of stroke through the softmax layer.

- When multi-filter CNNs are used, the features of adjacent words for each filter size are centered into global max-pooling to extract the most prominent features, and then these features are concatenated into one vector. Finally, concatenated one vector predicts the prognosis of stroke using the softmax.

- When LSTM is used, the last hidden state that contains the entire information of the document predicts the prognosis of stroke using the softmax layer.

- When Bi-LSTM is used instead of LSTM, the last hidden states of forward LSTM and backward LSTM are concatenated. The concatenated hidden states predict the prognosis of stroke using the softmax layer.

**Document-Level using TF-IDF**  The weights of the words extracted from each document through TF-IDF are finally entered into the level-wise tree-based learning algorithm XGB[3] or the leaf-wise tree-based learning algorithm LGBM[4] to predict the prognosis of the stroke.

### 3.2  Sentence-Level Representation

In the sentence-level representation, a document is divided into sentences and represented with several sentences. Since these divided sentences need to use information about the entire document to predict stroke prognosis, all the sentences about the document are entered into the model at once. In this representation, word embedding and sentence embedding are used. The model structure using word embedding is shown in (c) of Figure 1, and the model structure using sentence embedding is shown in (d) of Figure 1.

**Sentence-Level using Word Embedding**  When word embedding is used, to make information about divided sentences into the document, LSTM is applied to each sentence, then hidden states about each sentence are concatenated into one vector. Finally, the concatenated one vector predicts the prognosis of stroke using the softmax layer. LSTM used in this representation uses the siamese network that shares weights (Mueller and Thyagarajan, 2016). In the siamese network, weights are learned to approximate the prediction values by sharing the weights to several unordered sentences. When using Bi-LSTM instead of LSTM, the last hidden states of forward LSTM and backward LSTM are concatenated, and the method after that is the same as LSTM.

**Sentence-Level using Sentence Embedding**  When sentence embedding is used, to make information about divided sentences into entire information about the document, sentence vectors about each sentence are concatenated into one vector. Finally, concatenated one vector predicts the prognosis of stroke using the softmax layer.

## 4  Experiments

In this study, MRI text records remove all non-

---

[3] https://github.com/dmlc/xgboost

[4] https://github.com/microsoft/LightGBM

| No. | Model | Precision | Recall | F1-Score | Accuracy |
|-----|-------|-----------|--------|----------|----------|
| a.1 | CNN + Dense | 0.796 | 0.7577 | 0.7689 | 79.81% |
| a.2 | Multi-Filter CNNs + Dense | 0.8045 | 0.761 | 0.7733 | 80.29% |
| a.3 | LSTM + Dense | 0.7525 | 0.7292 | 0.7329 | 76.53% |
| a.4 | Bi-LSTM + Dense | 0.7643 | 0.7373 | 0.7458 | 77.5% |
| b.1 | XGB | 0.7846 | 0.7468 | 0.7578 | 78.85% |
| b.2 | LGBM | 0.7682 | 0.742 | 0.7506 | 77.88% |
| c.1 | LSTM + Dense | 0.7732 | 0.7291 | 0.7404 | 77.6% |
| c.2 | Bi-LSTM + Dense | 0.7196 | 0.7052 | 0.7096 | 73.85% |
| d | Dense | 0.7333 | 0.7012 | 0.7089 | 74.62% |

Table 2: Performance comparison according to various representations

English alphabet and stopwords, and all the texts are changed to lower case letters and then experimented. For the experiment, the entire data is divided in the ratio of training set: test set = 9: 1, and the training set is again divided into 5-fold. Among the training set divided into folds, four folds learn a model, and the other fold validates a trained model. The performance of the model is measured by applying the test set to the trained model.

## 4.1 Hyperparameters

Word embedding uses BioWordVec, a pre-trained FastText model that represents the meaning of words in 200 dimensions (Zhang et al., 2019), and sentence embedding uses BioSentVec, a pre-trained Sent2Vec model that represents the meaning of sentences in 700 dimensions (Chen et al., 2019). These models are pre-trained models for large clinical corpus.

In CNN, the number of filters is 256, the filter size is 3, and the stride is 1. In multi-filter CNNs, all hyperparameters are the same as CNNs, except that the filter sizes are 3, 4, and 5. LSTM is used as the number of units of 100. Bi-LSTM is used as the number of units of 200. And XGB uses the basic hyperparameters provided by the Distributed Machine Learning Community[5], and LGBM uses the basic hyperparameters provided by Microsoft[6]. Moreover, the loss function uses binary-cross entropy, and the optimizer uses Adam.

## 4.2 Results

Table 2 shows the performance comparison of various representation methods and shows the experiments' results with various models of each representation method. In the first column, a is a document-level representation, b is the TF-IDF representation, c and d are sentence-level representations through word embedding and sentence embedding, respectively. Moreover, precision, recall, F1-score, and accuracy are Marco-Averaged scores and mean average values of 5 experiment results.

As a result of the experiment, a.2, which considers the relationships of adjacent word representations in the document-level, shows the best performance. And, b, which is a method that uses the frequency of words appearing in the documents, was expected to show lower performance than a, but it is visible that the performance is higher than a.3 and a.4. With these results, a.3 and a.4 consider word orders for each sentence, but due to the characteristic of MRI text records, the order of sentences was irregular, so we can infer that the performance was relatively low. c and d, which are sentence-level representations that sufficiently consider sentence's information, expected to show better performance than a and b, but they show low performance. Through this, we can infer that in MRI text records, which do not have the order of sentences, it does not mean much to reconstruct documents into sentences. Based on these analyses, we confirm that the document-level representation method showed better performance in predicting the prognosis of stroke when using MRI text records and that the relationship of adjacent words is more important than the sequential information.

## 5 Conclusion

In this study, the performance is compared and analyzed according to the document-level and the sentence-level representation methods using MRI

[5] https://github.com/dmlc/xgboost/blob/master/doc/parameter.rst

[6] https://github.com/Microsoft/LightGBM/blob/master/docs/Parameters.rst

text records to predict stroke prognosis. In the document-level representation, the entire document is used as an input value of the model using word embedding and TF-IDF, and in the sentence-level representation, the document is divided into sentences and used as the input value of the model using word embedding and sentence embedding. As a result of the experiment, it is better to consider the information of adjacent words using the document-level representation compared to the sentence-level representation.

Since the number of datasets used in this study is unbalanced, it may adversely affect performance improvements. Therefore, in future studies, we will include data used by other hospitals in the data used by this study to make more exquisite models. Also, based on the results of this study, we will investigate studies that detect a variety of diseases using neural networks based on a document-level representation. Accordingly, we will apply the latest language model and various neural networks to improve performance for stroke prognosis prediction.

## Acknowledgements

This work was supported by the National Research Foundation of Korea (NRF) grant funded by the Korea government (MSIT) (No. 2019R1A2C2 006010) and the National Research Fund of Korea (NRF-2019R1G1A1097707).

## References

Fatimah Alzamzami, Mohamad Hoda, and Abdulmotaleb El Saddik. 2020. Light Gradient Boosting Machine for General Sentiment Classification on Short Texts: A Comparative Evaluation. *IEEE Access*. https://doi.org/10.1109/access.2020.2997330.

Kunakorn Atchaneeyasakul, Ty Shang, Diogo Haussen, Gustavo Ortiz, and Dileep Yavagal. 2019. Impact of MRI selection on triage of endovascular therapy in acute ischemic stroke: the MRI in Acute Management of Ischemic Stroke (MIAMIS) Registry. *Interventional Neurology*, 8(2-6): 135-143. https://doi.org/10.1159/000490580.

Bruce C. V. Campbell, Deidre A. De Silva, Malcolm R. Macleod, Shelagh B. Coutts, Lee H. Schwamm, Stephen M. Davis, and Geoffrey A. Donnan. 2019. Ischemic stroke. *Nature Reviews Disease Primers*, 5(1):70. https://doi.org/10.1038/s41572-019-0118-8.

Qingyu Chen, Yifan Peng, and Zhiyong Lu. 2019. BioSentVec: creating sentence embeddings for bio-medical texts. In *2019 IEEE International Conference on Healthcare Informatics (ICHI)*, pages 1-5. https://doi.org/10.1109/ichi.2019.8904728.

Merel S. Ekker, Jamie I. Verhoeven, Ilonca Vaartjes, Koen M. van Nieuwenhuizen, Catharina J.M. Klijn, and Frank-Erik de Leeuw. 2019. Stroke incidence in young adults according to age, subtype, sex, and time trends. *Neurology*, 92(21): e2444-e2454. https://doi.org/10.1212/wnl.0000000000007533.

Yoon Kim. 2014. Convolutional Neural Networks for Sentence Classification. In *Proceedings of the 2014 Conference on Empirical Methods in Natural Language Processing (EMNLP)*, pages 1746-1751. https://www.aclweb.org/anthology/D14-1181/.

Miguel Monteiro, Ana Catarina Fonseca, Ana Teresa Freitas, Teresa Pinho e Melo, Alexandre P. Francisco, José M. Ferro, Arlindo L. Oliveira. 2018. Using machine learning to improve the prediction of functional outcome in ischemic stroke patients. *IEEE/ACM transactions on computational biology and bioinformatics*, 15(6): 1953-1959. https://doi.org/10.1109/tcbb.2018.2811471.

Jonas Mueller and Aditya Thyagarajan. 2016. Siamese Recurrent Architectures for Learning Sentence Similarity. In *thirtieth AAAI conference on artificial intelligence*. https://dl.acm.org/doi/10.5555/3016100.3016291.

Eunjeong Park, Hyuk-jae Chang and Hyo Suk Nam. 2018. A bayesian network model for predicting post-stroke outcomes with available risk factors. *Frontiers in neurology*, 9. https://doi.org/10.3389/fneur.2018.00699.

William J. Powers, Colin P. Derdeyn, José Biller, Christopher S. Coffey, Brian L. Hoh, Edward C. Jauch, Karen C. Johnston, S. Claiborne Johnston, Alexander A. Khalessi, Chelsea S. Kidwell, James F. Meschia, Bruce Ovbiagele, and Dileep R. Yavagal. 2015. 2015 American Heart Association/American Stroke Association focused update of the 2013 guidelines for the early management of patients with acute ischemic stroke regarding endovascular treatment: a guideline for healthcare professionals from the American Heart Association/American Stroke Association. *Stroke*, 46(10):3020-3035. https://doi.org/10.1161/str.0000000000000074.

Srikant Rangaraju, Diogo Haussen, Raul G. Nogueira, Fadi Nahab, and Michael Frankel. 2017. Comparison of 3-Month Stroke Disability and Quality of Life across Modified Rankin Scale Categories. *Interventional neurology*, 6(1-2):36-41. https://doi.org/10.1159/000452634.

Ralph L. Sacco, Scott E. Kasner, Joseph P. Broderick, Louis R. Caplan, J.J. (Buddy) Connors, Antonio Culebras, Mitchell S.V. Elkind, Mary G. George, Allen D. Hamdan, Randall T. Higashida, Brian L. Hoh, L.

Scott Janis, Carlos S. Kase, Dawn O. Kleindorfer, Jin-Moo Lee, Michael E. Moseley, Eric D. Peterson, Tanya N. Turan, Amy L. Valderrama, and Harry V. Vinters. 2013. An Updated Definition of Stroke for the 21st Century. *Stroke*, 44(7): 2064-2089. https://doi.org/10.1161/str.0b013e318296aeca.

Shakti Shrestha, Ramesh Sharma Poudel, Dipendra Khatiwada, and Lekhjung Thapa. 2015. Stroke subtype, age, and baseline NIHSS score predict ischemic stroke outcomes at 3 months: a preliminary study from Central Nepal. *Journal of multidisciplinary healthcare*. 8: pages 443-448. https://doi.org/10.2147/jmdh.s90554.

Shanshan Wang, Zhenghang Su, Leslie Ying, Xi Peng, Shun Zhu, Feng Liang, Dagan Feng, and Dong Liang. 2016. Accelerating magnetic resonance imaging via deep learning. In *2016 IEEE 13th International Symposium on Biomedical Imaging (ISBI)*, pages 514-517. https://doi.org/10.1109/isbi.2016.7493320.

Yijia Zhang, Qingyu Chen, Zhihao Yang, Hongfei Lin, and Zhiyong Lu. 2019. BioWordVec, improving biomedical word embeddings with subword information and MeSH. *Scientific data*, 6(1): 1-9. https://doi.org/10.1038/s41597-019-0055-0.

Chunting Zhou, Chonglin Sun, Zhiyuan Liu, and Francis C.M. Lau. 2015. A C-LSTM neural network for text classification. *arXiv preprint arXiv:1511.08630*. https://arxiv.org/abs/1511.08630.

# Multiple Sclerosis Severity Classification From Clinical Text


**Alister D'Costa**[1,2*], **Stefan Denkovski**[1,3*], **Michal Malyska**[1*],
**Sae Young Moon**[1,3*], **Brandon Rufino**[1,4*],
**Zhen Yang**[5], **Taylor Killian**[1,6], **Marzyeh Ghassemi**[1,6]
[1]University of Toronto, [2]Ontario Institute for Cancer Research,
[3]Toronto Rehabilitation Institute, [4]Bloorview Research Institute,
[5]Unity Health Toronto, [6]Vector Institute
[*]Equal Contribution

{alister.dcosta, stefan.denkovski, michal.malyska, sally.moon, brandon.rufino,
t.killian, marzyeh.ghassemi}@mail.utoronto.ca, zhen.yang@unityhealth.to



## Abstract

Multiple Sclerosis (MS) is a chronic, inflammatory and degenerative neurological disease, which is monitored by a specialist using the Expanded Disability Status Scale (EDSS) and recorded in unstructured text in the form of a neurology consult note. An EDSS measurement contains an overall 'EDSS' score and several functional subscores. Typically, expert knowledge is required to interpret consult notes and generate these scores. Previous approaches used limited context length Word2Vec embeddings and keyword searches to predict scores given a consult note, but often failed when scores were not explicitly stated. In this work, we present MS-BERT, the first publicly available transformer model trained on real clinical data other than MIMIC. Next, we present MSBC, a classifier that applies MS-BERT to generate embeddings and predict EDSS and functional subscores. Lastly, we explore combining MSBC with other models through the use of Snorkel to generate scores for unlabelled consult notes. MSBC achieves state-of-the-art performance on all metrics and prediction tasks and outperforms the models generated from the Snorkel ensemble. We improve Macro-F1 by 0.12 (to 0.88) for predicting EDSS and on average by 0.29 (to 0.63) for predicting functional subscores over previous Word2Vec CNN and rule-based approaches.


## 1 Introduction

Recent advancements of deep learning models with electronic health records (EHR) have shown a great deal of success in many clinical applications (Shickel et al., 2017), such as disease detection (Choi et al., 2016b), diagnostics (Choi et al., 2017), risk predictions (Futoma et al., 2015) and patient subtyping (Che et al., 2017a; Baytas et al., 2017). However, when the data within the EHR is presented in the form of narrative, unstructured clinical notes, extensive work is required by a profes-

sional to diagnose and generate labels for a patient (PRATT, 1973).

The development of pre-trained language models, namely Bidirectional Encoder Representations from Transformers (BERT), have significantly improved natural language processing (NLP) tasks within the general language domain (Devlin et al., 2018). However, in specialized domains such as the clinical one, the vocabulary, syntax and semantics differ significantly from general language (Liu et al., 2012) and thus pretraining a language model on domain-specific texts is critical to improving performance. This is supported by the observed increase in performance on domain-specific NLP tasks when pretraining a BERT model on domain-specific texts (Lee et al., 2019; Peng et al., 2019; Alsentzer et al., 2019; Beltagy et al., 2019). Take for example BlueBERT (Peng et al., 2019), which has been further pretrained on over 4 billion words from PubMed abstracts and 500 million words from MIMIC-III (Johnson et al., 2016) and has been shown to outperform BERT on multilabel classification from the Hallmarks of Cancers corpus (Peng et al., 2019).

Domain-specific language models, such as Blue-BERT, still face several challenges for clinical NLP tasks. First, clinical texts must be de-identified of sensitive information, with the replacement of key tokens reducing the model's ability to interpret the text (Meystre et al., 2014). Second, texts from a specific clinical application may contain unique sub-language that the model was not trained on, hindering the model's performance. Third, transformer models have a fixed context length of 512 tokens that is significantly shorter than the average length of clinical texts (Devlin et al., 2018). As a result of truncating the text to fit the context length, the model is unable to analyze the entire text and may miss important information. These are the challenges of applying

7


*Proceedings of the 3rd Clinical Natural Language Processing Workshop*, pages 7–23
November 19, 2020. ©2020 Association for Computational Linguistics

existing BERT models to specific clinical NLP tasks, which we have addressed through our contributions applied to a multiple sclerosis (MS) dataset.

**Our contributions are as follows:**

[1] A publicly available BERT based model pre-trained on over 70,000 MS consult notes, which we call MS-BERT.

[2] A comprehensive pipeline for target predictions that integrates MS-BERT into a classifier, which we call MSBC. We apply MSBC to two tasks: (I) prediction of EDSS and functional subscores from neurological consult notes of MS patients and (II) generation of labels for an unlabelled consult note cohort.

[3] Methods for data de-identification that preserves contextual information, optimized for fixed-context length models.

[4] A novel approach to generate encounter level embeddings for documents larger than the BERT context window.

[5] Semi-supervised labelling pipeline using the Snorkel framework (Ratner et al., 2017) that increased the training data available for EDSS prediction and provided a quantitative analysis of silver-labelling strategies on real clinical applications.

## 2    Methods

**De-identification of clinical text.** The consult notes used in this study contained sensitive information such as patient's name, phone numbers, physician's name and address. We de-identified the data using a curated database of patient and doctor information and regular expression matching. We replaced identifying pieces of information with specific tokens that met the following criteria: (1) the token was within the current BERT vocabulary, (2) the token had a similar semantic meaning to the word it replaced, and (3) the token was not found in the original data set. For example, all last names were replaced with "Salamanca". In doing so, we aimed to limit the loss of contextual information that results from de-identification. We also overcame challenges with sub-optimal placeholder replacements often present in clinical datasets, like

MIMIC-III (Johnson et al., 2016). As an example, MIMIC-III may replace a patient's last name with "[**LAST NAME PLACEHOLDER**]", which is tokenized by BERT into at least 7 tokens (one for each square bracket, one for each star and at least one for the place holder within the brackets). A list of our de-identification replacements can be found within the appendices (contribution [3]).

**MS-BERT.** We used the de-identified consult notes to pre-train a language model optimized for NLP tasks related to MS, namely MS-BERT. MS-BERT is a BERT model that uses BlueBERT (Peng et al., 2019) as its starting point, where BlueBERT is a BERT model pre-trained on PubMed abstracts & MIMIC III note cohorts (Johnson et al., 2016). We used a masked language modeling (MLM) pre-training task (Devlin et al., 2018) over all de-identified consult notes. The task used the bi-directional nature of the BERT model to predict a series of randomly selected masked tokens in a piece of text, allowing the model to learn the contextual meaning of the words in a sentence. This resulted in a language model that is optimized for understanding MS consult notes. The MS-BERT language model has been made available for use and is publicly accessible. The pretrained MS-BERT model can be found here (contribution [1]).

**Encounter Level Embedding.** We generated encounter level embeddings for each consult note to address issues related to the limited context length of transformer models. Most transformer models have a context length limited to a number of sub-word tokens (512 in case of BERT (Devlin et al., 2018)); however, the consult notes are often significantly longer. We separated consult notes longer than the context length into chunks of the maximum context length (in our case the length was 512 tokens). We then used MS-BERT to embed each chunk, resulting in a variable length output sequence of 768 dimensional vectors.

We explored 3 methods of converting the sequence of chunk level embeddings into a singular encounter level embedding: (1) taking the average across the sequence; (2) taking the max across the sequence; and (3) using a convolutional neural network (CNN) encoder based on Zhang and Wallace (2015) included in the AllenNLP library. For more details see Figure 1.

In preliminary testing, the first two options under-performed the CNN encoder by a large margin ($\sim$60%), thus we proceeded with the third option. Our final CNN encoder consists of six 1D convolutions with kernels of size [2, 3, 4, 5, 6, 10] and 128 filters each for a total of 768 dimensions in the output. This output is our final note embedding. We compared these full-length encounter level embeddings to embeddings that were generated using only a single context window (i.e. 512 tokens) and found that encounter level summaries were critical to model performance.

[1] **MSBC**. Finally, we developed a custom classifier named MSBC (Multiple Sclerosis BERT CNN) to predict MS severity labels (EDSS or a functional subscore) using MS-BERT. MSBC is built using the AllenNLP (Gardner et al., 2017) framework. A breakdown of MSBC is as follows. MSBC first reads in a consult note, tokenizes the text using the BERT vocabulary and then splits the tokens into chunks of size 512. MS-BERT weights are applied to each token chunk and all chunks for a note are then passed into the CNN based sequence to vector (Seq2Vec) encoder described above to pool the chunks and generate an encounter level embedding (i.e. a 1D vector of 768). This encounter level embedding is passed through 2 linear feed forward layers, acting as a dimension reduction step, before finally being passed to a linear classification layer to predict a label for the note. Figure 1 shows an overview of MSBC's architecture.

We trained and optimized MSBC for variables of interest, namely EDSS and functional subscores. Each note in the training set was passed through MSBC as described above. The resulting label was compared to the target label and a loss was computed. We used an AdamW optimizer to propagate errors back through the model, with a learning rate of 0.0005, weight decay of 0.01 and bias correction on a binary cross entropy loss function. We treat this as a classification problem instead of regression because EDSS is not uniform i.e. the difference between 3 and 4 is not the same as 4 and 5. We trained each model over 50 epochs using a batch size of 5 with 4 gradient accumulation steps. The model was saved at the end of each epoch if it had the best value for the validation metric. If during training the best validation metric was not beaten within 5 epochs, the trainer stopped early. A model for each prediction task was generated using MSBC and the train and validation sets described above. Once trained, we evaluated performance on

the held out test set.

**Semi-Supervised Labelling**. Due to the costs of manually reviewing and labelling clinical texts, a significant majority of clinical texts in EHRs remain unlabelled (Garla et al., 2013). To leverage the full potential of all clinical text available and generate pseudo-labels for unlabelled data, we explored semi-supervised labelling using the Snorkel framework (v 0.9.3) (Ratner et al., 2017). Snorkel facilitates weak supervision of unlabelled data given weak heuristics and classifiers (i.e. labelling functions or LFs) (Ratner et al., 2016, 2017). Snorkel's Label Model, a generative model, combines the predictions and generates a single confidence weighted label per data point. Snorkel does this by using the LFs' observed agreement and disagreement rates to estimate the unknown accuracy of the LF's. Snorkel then learns and models the accuracies of the LFs to combine the labels and generate the final label per data point (Ratner et al., 2019). To identify the optimal combination of LFs to label the unlabelled notes, we evaluated the performance of task predictions on various Snorkel ensembles. The model that yielded the highest performance on our validation-set was chosen to be used to label the unlabelled notes.

We created two additional models using the MSBC architecture: MSBC+, trained on a combination of labelled and pseudo-labelled data and MSBC-silver, which is a model trained on only pseudo-labelled data. We pursued the development of MSBC-silver as an attempt to see if we could reconstruct our model without access to the original labelled data, similarly to Krishna et al. (2020).

## 3 Experiments

Multiple sclerosis (MS) is one of the most common non-traumatic disabling neurological condition among young adults worldwide (Ploughman et al., 2014; Wade, 2014). Onset of MS typically occurs between the ages of 20 to 40 years, with women more often affected than men (Ploughman et al., 2014). MS is a disease that impacts the central nervous system (CNS) (Goldenberg, 2012), leading to the degradation of myelin sheathing and axons within the nervous system. This degradation is highly varied and unpredictable in both location and intensity within the body. Resulting symptoms include but are not limited to: visual impairment, loss of balance, numbness, bladder dysfunction and fatigue (Calabresi, 2004).

---

[1] Code for our pipeline and experiments are available here (contributions [2,4,5])

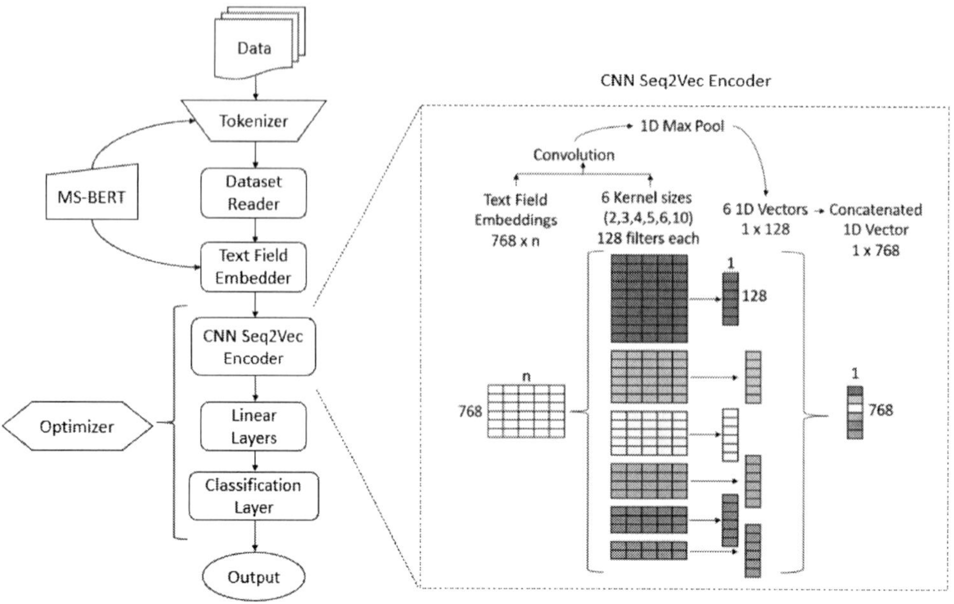

Figure 1: The MSBC architecture. We used a CNN described by Zhang and Wallace (2015) to generate encounter level embeddings.

MS is typically monitored by the Expanded Disability Status Scale (EDSS) (Kurtzke, 1983). EDSS is used to evaluate the degree of CNS impairment on a scale from 0 to 10. EDSS also includes eight functional subscores (Kurtzke, 1983) such as an ambulation score and a visual score. A full list of functional subscores is found within Table 2 and their respective descriptions can be found in the appendices.

EDSS and functional subscores are discussed in a patient's consult note, dictated by a physician and manually transcribed. EDSS is determined by a combination of functional subscores and is typically stated within consult notes. However, functional subscores are not typically stated within a consult note and need to be derived from contextual information about the patient's health. Traditionally, both EDSS and functional subscores are manually derived by an expert within the field and logged into the patient's health record. Minute differences in patient descriptions can correspond to different EDSS and functional subscore values. Through consultation with MS healthcare professionals we expect the qualitative descriptions of MS symptoms contained within the clinical notes to remain uniform across healthcare systems.

## 3.1   Data

The dataset, compiled by a leading MS research hospital, contains approximately 70,000 MS consult notes for about 5,000 patients, totaling over 35.7 millon words. These notes were collected from patients who visited this hospital's MS clinic between 2015 to 2019. Of the 70,000 notes approximately 16,000 are manually labeled by a research assistant for EDSS and functional subscores. The gender split within the dataset was observed to be 72% female and 28% male as shown in Figure 2 and reflecting the natural discrepancy in MS (Harbo et al., 2013).

Once de-identified, data was separated into labelled and unlabelled sets. The labelled set was further separated into test ($\sim$30%), train ($\sim$50%) and validation ($\sim$20%) subsets. When designing the splits for our data, we wanted to ensure that we could accurately predict EDSS and functional subscores on new notes for both current and new patients and to reduce any gender bias that may occur from population discrepancy. First we stratified by gender. Then we either fully contained the notes of one patient within a subset or divided the patients notes across subsets chronologically. This allowed for earlier notes to be used for training, and later notes for validation and test. Due to

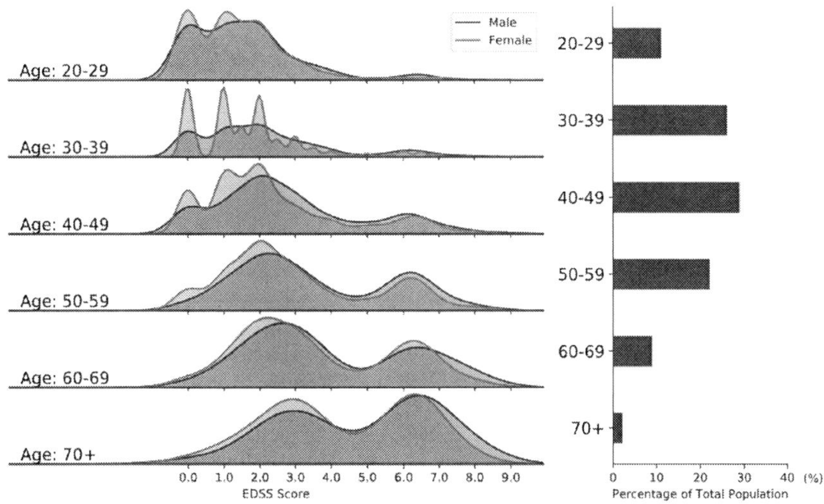


Figure 2: Distribution of EDSS scores varied by age and gender.

de-identification of notes the risk of information leakage between subsets is minimized.

## 3.2 Experiment 1: EDSS and Functional Subscore Prediction

**Previous Work**. Previous approaches to extract information from MS consult notes have typically relied on keyword searches (Davis and Haines, 2015; Damotte et al., 2019). We refer to the collection of these searches as the rule-based (RB) approach. Word2Vec embeddings used with a convolutional neural network (CNN), have been shown to be successful in clinical tasks such as creating explainable predictions of medical codes from clinical text (Mullenbach et al., 2018). Previous work done at our affiliated MS hospital used Word2Vec embeddings and a CNN model to generate EDSS predictions. Best results were achieved by incorporating the RB approach with the Word2Vec CNN. This method first used the RB approach to extract keywords and phrases that infer EDSS scores. If the RB approach was unable to predict a score, then the prediction from the Word2Vec CNN model was used. More information on the development of the CNN model can be found in the appendices. In this work, we compared the performance on predicting EDSS and functional subscores between the: (1) Word2Vec CNN, (2) a sequential approach using RB plus Word2Vec CNN, (3) MSBC, and (4) a sequential approach using RB plus MSBC.

Additional baselines were established with term frequency-inverse document frequency (tf-idf) features. These features have been successful in var-

ious clinical NLP tasks (Bhattarai et al., 2009; Narayan Shukla and Marlin, 2020; Boag et al., 2018). A number of baseline models were developed on top tf-idf features such as: support vector machines (SVM), logistic regression (LR) and linear discriminant analysis (LDA). Due to a lack of performance on the easier task of predicting EDSS scores (see Table 1), they were not evaluated for the prediction of functional subscores.

**Results**. Our results for EDSS prediction are summarized in Table 1 and functional scores in Table 2. MSBC achieves top performance in both tasks in all metrics. For EDSS prediction, Macro-F1 and Micro-F1 are improved upon by 0.11 and 0.043 respectively. For functional subscore prediction, we see a significant improvement of over 0.35 in Macro-F1 and almost 0.15 in Micro-F1.

**Discussion**. The significant improvement of MSBC, especially in Macro-F1, indicates that MS-BERT is better able to distinguish nuances within text that characterize different EDSS and functional subscores. Interestingly, the Word2Vec CNN outperformed BlueBERT, which is likely attributed to the fact that Word2Vec was pre-trained on our corpus of text. Also, our different method of de-identifying data from MIMIC-III (which Blue-BERT was pre-trained on), may have reduced Blue-BERT's effectiveness. However, the contextually similar token replacement should limit this impact.

We see a strong improvement in functional subscore predictions over the baselines. While EDSS is stated directly in notes, functional subscores are

Table 1: EDSS prediction performance for all models. Higher values indicate stronger performance and highest values are bolded.

| Model | Macro-F1 | Micro-F1 |
|---|---|---|
| Multiple Sclerosis Bert Classifier (MSBC) | **0.88296** | **0.94177** |
| MSBC Truncated (only first 512 tokens) | 0.74680 | 0.90086 |
| Rule-Based (RB) + Word2Vec CNN | 0.76817 | 0.89668 |
| RB + MSBC | 0.86625 | 0.92987 |
| Word2Vec CNN | 0.66475 | 0.88144 |
| RB | 0.76694 | 0.83761 |
| BlueBERT CNN | 0.51000 | 0.81000 |
| Linear SVC | 0.48503 | 0.74452 |
| LDA | 0.50122 | 0.74390 |
| SVC RBF | 0.45877 | 0.72428 |
| Log Reg | 0.45763 | 0.71175 |

Table 2: Sub-score prediction performance differences between baseline and MSBC. Higher values indicate stronger performance. Highest values are bolded. It should be noted that low to no support for the highest levels of sub-scores impacted Macro-F1.

| Models | MSBC | | RB | | RB + Word2Vec | |
|---|---|---|---|---|---|---|
| Subscore | Macro-F1 | Micro-F1 | Macro-F1 | Micro-F1 | Macro-F1 | Micro-F1 |
| Ambulation | 0.6980 | 0.88797 | 0.2710 | 0.5627 | 0.2674 | 0.5155 |
| Bowel Bladder | 0.6039 | 0.86619 | 0.2773 | 0.5525 | 0.2027 | 0.5209 |
| Brain Stem | 0.5842 | 0.90356 | 0.4174 | 0.5694 | 0.3712 | 0.6598 |
| Cerebellar | 0.6437 | 0.85707 | 0.4927 | 0.6120 | 0.4188 | 0.5908 |
| Mental | 0.5496 | 0.79470 | 0.3643 | 0.5586 | 0.3003 | 0.5499 |
| Pyramidal | 0.7192 | 0.87755 | 0.4173 | 0.5128 | 0.4028 | 0.5598 |
| Sensory | 0.5570 | 0.87518 | 0.4082 | 0.4173 | 0.3485 | 0.5603 |
| Visual | 0.7153 | 0.93855 | 0.5020 | 0.4082 | 0.4207 | 0.6986 |
| **Mean** | **0.6339** | **0.8751** | 0.3937 | 0.5737 | 0.3416 | 0.5820 |

typically referenced indirectly. This makes it more difficult for a rule based approach and simple models to learn the contextual information required to assess scores. Furthermore, EDSS and functional subscores also suffer from a high level of disagreement among clinicians, particularly for the sensory and mental categories (Piri Cinar and Guven Yorgun, 2018). The level of disagreement typical is lower for EDSS scores greater than 5.5 and in general does not exceed 1. At two clinics, examined EDSS scores differed by 0.5 for up to 29% of patients and by 1 for up to 50% of patients. This level of subjectivity and variability within the true labels may make it difficult for the model to predict accurately. That said, due to the contextual awareness brought by MS-BERT, MSBC shows strong improvement from previous work when predicting functional subscores. Additionally, the labels for functional subscores were generated post-examination by trained clinicians based on the contents of notes. Therefore, missing information from notes led to missing labels for certain functional subscores, resulting in varying levels of support for different scores.

MSBC under-performed on classes with low support. The bottom 25% of classes in terms of support averaged an F1 score of 0.78, which was 0.1 lower than the mean for all classes. However, classes with low support are typical of EDSS due to its bi-modal distribution (Meyer-Moock et al., 2014). This is a result of the non-linear method of determining EDSS based on certain heuristics and conditions (i.e. the difference between an EDSS score of 3 to 4, is not the same as 4 to 5).

To help understand why and when rule based approaches failed, we looked at performance of the models only on notes that rule based approaches were not able to label EDSS scores (see appendices). This accounted for around 12% of the notes and we see very poor performance for all other models with F1 scores below 0.36 (and very high F1-scores for those rule based were able to label), while MSBC is still able to achieve an F1 score above 0.6. This may indicate that a certain portion of notes that contain poor quality information and may be "trickier" to label. These "tricky" notes could be notes that state "no change" or "similar" results to past notes, without restating those scores for example. However, it is predicted that MSBC was still able to outperform other models through its ability to understand contextual information embedded in the text.

### 3.3 Experiment 2: Semi-Supervised Labelling of EDSS

We evaluated the effectiveness of the Snorkel ensembles and compared the performance of: (1) MSBC (which has been observed in Experiment 1), (2) MSBC+, and (3) MSBC-silver.

We hereon refer to two types of labels: (1) gold labels (n~16,000), which were manually obtained by a professional at our MS clinic and are considered truth in our experiments, and (2) silver labels (n~54,000), which were generated from the model chosen for EDSS labelling.

**Results**. Various Snorkel ensembles were evaluated as presented in Table 3. Only the LF combinations that included MSBC were evaluated as MSBC had the best EDSS prediction performance. From the F1 scores, we observe that MSBC alone outperforms all ensembles that contain MSBC by at least 0.02 on Macro-F1. The addition of weaker classifiers consistently decreased the ensemble's performance. Furthermore, we observe that the amount of conflict for MSBC (i.e. fraction of data MSBC disagrees with for at least one other LF) increases as weaker classifiers are added to the ensemble.

From the above analysis, we concluded that MSBC alone, out of all Snorkel ensembles, performs the best and therefore was chosen to generate silver-labels for the unlabelled neurology notes. Various models were trained using the MSBC architecture and are presented in Table 4. The best version of MSBC was the model trained solely on gold label data (our original MSBC). Macro-F1 score and Micro-F1 score are observed to drop in MSBC+. MSBC-silver was the worst out of the 3 variations with a Macro-F1 of 0.83 and Micro-F1 of 0.91 but is still observed to outperform the previous best baseline (RB+Word2Vec CNN presented in Table 1) by an approximate Macro and Micro-F1 of 0.06 and 0.02 respectively.

**Discussion**. MSBC alone performs better than all Snorkel ensembles. The performance of the ensembles consistently decreased as more weak classifiers and heuristics were added. We hypothesize that the drop in performance is due to the fact that the Snorkel's Label Model learns to predict the accuracy of the LFs based on observed agreements and disagreements. It also assumes conditional independence among the LFs (Ratner et al., 2019). This result is not surprising given that the qualitative analysis of errors showed that MSBC was almost strictly an improvement over the Rule-Based approach. MSBC only struggled with notes that had EDSS indicated in the roman numeral 'iv' (which could be misconstrued to be the lower-case acronym for intravenous) and notes where patient complaints of their symptoms were contained in a different note chunk than the physician findings which contradicted those symptoms. In all other cases, the model made no significant (off by no more than 0.5-1 on the EDSS scale) errors compared to the weak heuristics. Therefore in the presence of a strong LF, such as MSBC, we suspect that the addition of weaker LFs introduce disagreements with MSBC and thus decreased predictive performance. Furthermore, all LFs were developed based on the same labelled training data (for example, tf-idf models were trained on the same training set). Hence, it is likely that the LFs were correlated, which violated the conditional independence assumption made by Snorkel and compromised prediction accuracy.

Our model trained on silver labeled data, MSBC-silver, performs worse than MSBC by 0.03-0.06. This small decrease in performance indicates that our model is able to relearn its own distribution and helps validate its performance. MSBC-silver outperformed all previous baselines on the EDSS prediction task. The strong results of MSBC-silver helps show the effectiveness of using MSBC as a labelling function. This work shows potential to reduce tedious hours required by a professional to read through a patient's consult note and manually generate an EDSS score.

## 4 Concluding Thoughts

In this work we present methods to overcome the challenges that arise when applying a modern transformer model on a specific clinical NLP task, specifically MS severity prediction. We did this through: (1) de-identifying clinical texts in a

Table 3: EDSS predictions results for Snorkel ensembles containing MSBC. Conflicts reflect the fraction of data that MSBC disagrees with at least one other LF. Highest values are bolded.

| Ensemble combinations | Macro-F1 | Micro-F1 | Conflicts |
|---|---|---|---|
| MSBC | **0.88296** | **0.94177** | N/A |
| MSBC + Rule Based LFs (RB LFs) | 0.86617 | 0.93363 | 0.23471 |
| MSBC + RB LFs + Word2Vec | 0.78582 | 0.91901 | 0.33229 |
| MSBC + RB LFs + Word2Vec + LDA | 0.77004 | 0.88917 | 0.46796 |
| MSBC + RB LFs + Word2Vec + TFIDFs | 0.55728 | 0.82592 | **0.55145** |

Table 4: Performance of MSBC predicting EDSS using different label types. Gold labels (n=16,000) were manually obtained by a professional at our MS clinic and are considered truth in our experiments. Silver labels (n=54,000) were generated from MSBC predictions which was trained on gold labels. Higher values indicate stronger performance. Highest values are bolded.

| Model | Trained on | Macro-F1 | Micro-F1 |
|---|---|---|---|
| MSBC | Gold Labels | **0.88296** | **0.94177** |
| MSBC+ | Silver + Gold Labels | 0.86238 | 0.92569 |
| MSBC-silver | Silver Labels | 0.82922 | 0.91442 |

way that preserves contextual meaning; (2) generating encounter level embeddings to eliminate loss of information resulting from the limited context length of transformer models; (3) further pretraining a BERT model on MS consult notes to build a language model (MS-BERT) with better understanding of MS clinical notes; (4) developing a classifier (MSBC) that uses MS-BERT to achieve state of the art performance on predicting EDSS and functional subscores; and (5) using our classifier to generate labels for previously unlabelled data, showing its effectiveness as a labelling model.

We believe that the MS-BERT language model and its improved ability to understand MS consult notes will aid clinicians in the diagnosis and treatment of MS. Furthermore, we believe that being trained on more clinical text, MS-BERT has the potential to improve other NLP tasks within the clinical domain.

### 4.1 Future Work

First, we are in the process of implementing an interpretability module that would provide per-word attentions instead of the per-sub-word-token attentions available out-of-the-box. Second, we want to evaluate MS-BERT's performance on other language tasks such as relation extraction, sentence similarity, inference tasks, and question answering within the clinical space. Third, we would like to experiment with other note-level embeddings and model architectures, such as the CNN presented by Kim 2014 (Kim, 2014). While we are pleased with the performance of MSBC, we would like to demonstrate that our approach (the methods for de-identifying data, fine-tuning a language model, the generation of encounter level embeddings and our custom classifier) can be applied on other clinical datasets. Also, we would like to pre-train longer context transformer models such as the Reformer (Kitaev et al., 2020) which targets longer context windows and compare it to Clinical BERT which is tailored for the clinical domain (Alsentzer et al., 2019). Finally, we would like to see if using token level embeddings as inputs to our CNN encoder, along with replacing some tokens with more clinically relevant ones in the base BERT vocabulary could improve encounter level embedding quality.

## 5   Acknowledgments

We would like to thank the researchers and staff at the Data Science and Advanced Analytics (DSAA) team at St. Michael's Hospital, for providing consistent support and guidance throughout this project. We would also like to thank Dr. Marzyeh Ghassemi, and Taylor Killan for providing us the opportunity to work on this exciting project. Lastly, we would like to thank Dr. Tony Antoniou and Dr. Jiwon Oh from the MS clinic at St. Michael's Hospital for their support on the neurological examination notes.

## References

Emily Alsentzer, John Murphy, William Boag, Wei-Hung Weng, Di Jin, Tristan Naumann, and Matthew McDermott. 2019. Publicly available clinical BERT embeddings. In *Proceedings of the 2nd Clinical Natural Language Processing Workshop*, pages 72–78, Minneapolis, Minnesota, USA. Association for Computational Linguistics.

Inci M Baytas, Cao Xiao, Xi Zhang, Fei Wang, Anil K Jain, and Jiayu Zhou. 2017. Patient subtyping via time-aware lstm networks. In *Proceedings of the 23rd ACM SIGKDD international conference on knowledge discovery and data mining*, pages 65–74.

Iz Beltagy, Kyle Lo, and Arman Cohan. 2019. Scibert: Pretrained language model for scientific text. In *EMNLP*.

Archana Bhattarai, Vasile Rus, and Dipankar Dasgupta. 2009. Classification of Clinical Conditions : A Case Study on Prediction of Obesity and Its Comorbidities. *Science*, pages 183–194.

Willie Boag, Dustin Doss, Tristan Naumann, and Peter Szolovits. 2018. What's in a Note? Unpacking Predictive Value in Clinical Note Representations. *AMIA Joint Summits on Translational Science proceedings. AMIA Joint Summits on Translational Science*, 2017:26–34.

Peter A. Calabresi. 2004. Diagnosis and management of multiple sclerosis. *American Family Physician*, 70(10):1935–1944.

Chao Che, Cao Xiao, Jian Liang, Bo Jin, Jiayu Zho, and Fei Wang. 2017a. An rnn architecture with dynamic temporal matching for personalized predictions of parkinson's disease. In *Proceedings of the 2017 SIAM International Conference on Data Mining*, pages 198–206. SIAM.

Zhengping Che, Yu Cheng, Zhaonan Sun, and Yan Liu. 2017b. Exploiting Convolutional Neural Network for Risk Prediction with Medical Feature Embedding.

Edward Choi, Mohammad Taha Bahadori, Elizabeth Searles, Catherine Coffey, and Jimeng Sun. 2016a. Multi-layer Representation Learning for Medical Concepts. *Proceedings of the ACM SIGKDD International Conference on Knowledge Discovery and Data Mining*, 13-17-August-2016:1495–1504.

Edward Choi, Mohammad Taha Bahadori, Jimeng Sun, Joshua Kulas, Andy Schuetz, and Walter Stewart. 2016b. Retain: An interpretable predictive model for healthcare using reverse time attention mechanism. In *Advances in Neural Information Processing Systems*, pages 3504–3512.

Edward Choi, Andy Schuetz, Walter F Stewart, and Jimeng Sun. 2017. Using recurrent neural network models for early detection of heart failure onset. *Journal of the American Medical Informatics Association*, 24(2):361–370.

Francois Chollet et al. 2015. Keras.

Vincent Damotte, Antoine Lizée, Matthew Tremblay, Alisha Agrawal, Pouya Khankhanian, Adam Santaniello, Refujia Gomez, Robin Lincoln, Wendy Tang, Tiffany Chen, Nelson Lee, Pablo Villoslada, Jill A Hollenbach, Carolyn D Bevan, Jennifer Graves, Riley Bove, Douglas S Goodin, Ari J Green, Sergio E Baranzini, Bruce Ac Cree, Roland G Henry, Stephen L Hauser, Jeffrey M Gelfand, and Pierre-Antoine Gourraud. 2019. Harnessing electronic medical records to advance research on multiple sclerosis. *Multiple sclerosis (Houndmills, Basingstoke, England)*, 25(3):408–418.

Mary F. Davis and Jonathan L. Haines. 2015. The intelligent use and clinical benefits of electronic medical records in multiple sclerosis. *Expert Review of Clinical Immunology*, 11(2):205–211.

Jacob Devlin, Ming-Wei Chang, Kenton Lee, and Kristina Toutanova. 2018. BERT: Pre-training of Deep Bidirectional Transformers for Language Understanding.

Joseph Futoma, Jonathan Morris, and Joseph Lucas. 2015. A comparison of models for predicting early hospital readmissions. *Journal of Biomedical Informatics*, 56:229–238.

Matt Gardner, Joel Grus, Mark Neumann, Oyvind Tafjord, Pradeep Dasigi, Nelson F. Liu, Matthew Peters, Michael Schmitz, and Luke S. Zettlemoyer. 2017. Allennlp: A deep semantic natural language processing platform.

Vijay Garla, Caroline Taylor, and Cynthia Brandt. 2013. Semi-supervised clinical text classification with laplacian svms: An application to cancer case management. *Journal of Biomedical Informatics*, 46(5):869–875.

Marvin M. Goldenberg. 2012. Multiple sclerosis review. *P and T*, 37(3):175–184.

Hanne F. Harbo, Ralf Gold, and Mar Tintora. 2013. Sex and gender issues in multiple sclerosis. *Therapeutic Advances in Neurological Disorders*, 6(4):237–248.

Alistair EW Johnson, Tom J Pollard, Lu Shen, H Lehman Li-wei, Mengling Feng, Mohammad Ghassemi, Benjamin Moody, Peter Szolovits, Leo Anthony Celi, and Roger G Mark. 2016. MIMIC-III, a freely accessible critical care database. *Scientific data*, 3:160035.

Yoon Kim. 2014. Convolutional neural networks for sentence classification. In *EMNLP 2014 - 2014 Conference on Empirical Methods in Natural Language Processing, Proceedings of the Conference*, pages 1746–1751.

Nikita Kitaev, Lukasz Kaiser, and Anselm Levskaya. 2020. Reformer: The efficient transformer. In *International Conference on Learning Representations*.

Kalpesh Krishna, Gaurav Singh Tomar, Ankur P. Parikh, Nicolas Papernot, and Mohit Iyyer. 2020. Thieves on sesame street! model extraction of bert-based apis. In *International Conference on Learning Representations*.

John F. Kurtzke. 1983. Rating neurologic impairment in multiple sclerosis: An expanded disability status scale (EDSS). Technical Report 11.

Jinhyuk Lee, Wonjin Yoon, Sungdong Kim, Donghyeon Kim, Sunkyu Kim, Chan Ho So, and Jaewoo Kang. 2019. Biobert: a pre-trained biomedical language representation model for biomedical text mining. *Bioinformatics*.

Peng Li and Heng Huang. 2016. Clinical Information Extraction via Convolutional Neural Network.

F Liu, H Yu, C Weng, Feifan Liu, Chunhua Weng, and Hong Yu. 2012. Natural Language Processing, Electronic Health Records, and Clinical Research. *Clinical Research Informatics*, pages 293–310.

Sandra Meyer-Moock, You Shan Feng, Mathias Maeurer, Franz Werner Dippel, and Thomas Kohlmann. 2014. Systematic literature review and validity evaluation of the Expanded Disability Status Scale (EDSS) and the Multiple Sclerosis Functional Composite (MSFC) in patients with multiple sclerosis. *BMC Neurology*, 14(1):1–10.

Stéphane M. Meystre, Óscar Ferrández, F. Jeffrey Friedlin, Brett R. South, Shuying Shen, and Matthew H. Samore. 2014. Text de-identification for privacy protection: A study of its impact on clinical text information content. *Journal of Biomedical Informatics*, 50:142–150.

Tomas Mikolov, Ilya Sutskever, Kai Chen, Greg Corraudo, and Jeffrey Dean. 2013. Distributed representations ofwords and phrases and their compositionality. In *Advances in Neural Information Processing Systems*. Neural information processing systems foundation.

James Mullenbach, Sarah Wiegreffe, Jon Duke, Jimeng Sun, and Jacob Eisenstein. 2018. Explainable Prediction of Medical Codes from Clinical Text. pages 1101–1111.

Satya Narayan Shukla and Benjamin M. Marlin. 2020. Integrating Physiological Time Series and Clinical Notes with Deep Learning for Improved ICU Mortality Prediction. Technical report.

Yifan Peng, Shankai Yan, and Zhiyong Lu. 2019. Transfer Learning in Biomedical Natural Language Processing: An Evaluation of BERT and ELMo on Ten Benchmarking Datasets. pages 58–65.

Bilge Piri Cinar and Yuksel Guven Yorgun. 2018. What We Learned from The History of Multiple Sclerosis Measurement: Expanded Disease Status Scale. *Archives of Neuropsychiatry*, 55(Suppl 1):S69.

M Ploughman, S Beaulieu, C Harris, S Hogan, O J Manning, P W Alderdice, J D Fisk, A D Sadovnick, P O'Connor, S A Morrow, L M Metz, P Smyth, N Mayo, R A Marrie, K B Knox, M Stefanelli, and M Godwin. 2014. The Canadian survey of health, lifestyle and ageing with multiple sclerosis: methodology and initial results.[Erratum appears in BMJ Open. 2015;5(3):e005718; PMID: 25757943]. *BMJ Open*, 4(7):e005718.

A.W. PRATT. 1973. Medicine, Computers, and Linguistics. In *Advances in Biomedical Engineering*, pages 97–140. Elsevier.

Alexander Ratner, Stephen H. Bach, Henry Ehrenberg, Jason Fries, Sen Wu, and Christopher Re. 2017. Snorkel: Rapid training data creation with weak supervision. *Proceedings of the VLDB Endowment*, 11(3):269–282.

Alexander Ratner, Christopher De Sa, Sen Wu, Daniel Selsam, and Christopher Ré. 2016. Data Programming: Creating Large Training Sets, Quickly. Technical report.

Alexander Ratner, Braden Hancock, Jared Dunnmon, Frederic Sala, Shreyash Pandey, and Christopher Ré. 2019. Training complex models with multi-task weak supervision. *Proceedings of the AAAI Conference on Artificial Intelligence*, 33:4763–4771.

Sunil Kumar Sahu, Ashish Anand, Krishnadev Oruganty, and Mahanandeeshwar Gattu. 2016. Relation extraction from clinical texts using domain invariant convolutional neural network. pages 206–215.

Benjamin Shickel, Patrick James Tighe, Azra Bihorac, and Parisa Rashidi. 2017. Deep ehr: a survey of recent advances in deep learning techniques for electronic health record (ehr) analysis. *IEEE journal of biomedical and health informatics*, 22(5):1589–1604.

Brett J. Wade. 2014. Spatial Analysis of Global Prevalence of Multiple Sclerosis Suggests Need for an Updated Prevalence Scale. *Multiple Sclerosis International*, 2014:1–7.

Yonghui Wu, Min Jiang, Jun Xu, Degui Zhi, and Hua Xu. 2017. Clinical Named Entity Recognition Using Deep Learning Models. *AMIA ... Annual Symposium proceedings. AMIA Symposium*, 2017:1812–1819.

Ye Zhang and Byron C. Wallace. 2015. A sensitivity analysis of (and practitioners' guide to) convolutional neural networks for sentence classification. *CoRR*, abs/1510.03820.

## A De-identification of Clinical Text

Table 5: Full breakdown of word and category replacements for note de-identification.

| Value | Replacement |
|---|---|
| Last / Family Names | Salamanca |
| Female First Names | Lucie |
| Male First Names | Ezekiel |
| Phone/Fax | 1718 |
| MRN/PID | 999 |
| Dates / DOB | 2010s |
| Time | 1610 |
| Addresses | Silesia |
| Location/Hospital/Clinics | Troy |

## B Functional Subscores for EDSS

Table 6: Functional subscores for EDSS.

| Functional Scores | Description |
|---|---|
| Visual Function | Ability to read of eye chart at 20 feet |
| Brainstems | Eye movement, balance, hearing, numbness, swallowing, speech |
| Pyramidal | Reflexes, limb strength, motor performance |
| Cerebellar | Muscle coordination and control (ataxia) |
| Sensory | Ability to detect light touch or vibration |
| Bowl and Bladder | Control and correct function of bladder and bowl functions |
| Cerebral | Depression, mental alertness (mentation) |
| Ambulation | Ability to walk unimpaired |

## C Baseline Models

### Term Frequency-Inverse Document Frequency

We trained a number of baseline models on top of our tf-idf features, finding that our max feature space was optimal at 1500 tokens. After hyper-parameter tuning our tf-idf baseline models, we observed that the following performed best for predicting EDSS scores:

- Support vector classification (SVC) with tuned regularization parameter 'C' equal to 1. Both linear and radial basis function (RBF) kernels were generated based on their strong performance in this classification task.

- Linear discriminate analysis (LDA) with a singular value decomposition solver.

- Logistic regression (LR) using a limited-memory BFGS (lbfgs) solver with 'l2' regularization and inverse regularization strength, 'C', equal to 100. This model also considered class weights within the training set.

### Word2Vec and Convolution Neural Networks

Word2Vec models (Mikolov et al., 2013; Choi et al., 2016a) take a corpus of text and learn vector representations, called embeddings, for each word (Che et al., 2017b). Words with similar context have been observed to have close embeddings in the vector space.

CNNs have been observed to work well in a variety of clinical tasks. For example, CNN architectures have proved successful in relation extraction (Sahu et al., 2016), risk prediction (Che et al., 2017b), the extraction of medical events from clinical notes (Li and Huang, 2016), and clinical named entity recognition (Wu et al., 2017).

Previous work done at our collaborating hospital used a 200-dimensional Word2Vec embedding trained on all MS consult notes (n=75,009) with a window size of 10 and a minimum count of 2. Next, they converted all tokenized notes into their word vector representations. While doing so, they set a maximum note length of 1,000 tokens and zero padded notes as necessary. They then designed a 3-dimensional input sequence (batch size x 1000 x 200). This input sequence was fed into a Keras (Chollet et al., 2015) implementation of the CNN architecture described by Kim 2014 (Kim, 2014). Finally, using convolutional layers (with max pooling), and fully connected layers (with softmax output), they trained their CNN model using the RMSProp optimizer with early stopping.

## D Detailed Breakdown of MSBC prediction on EDSS

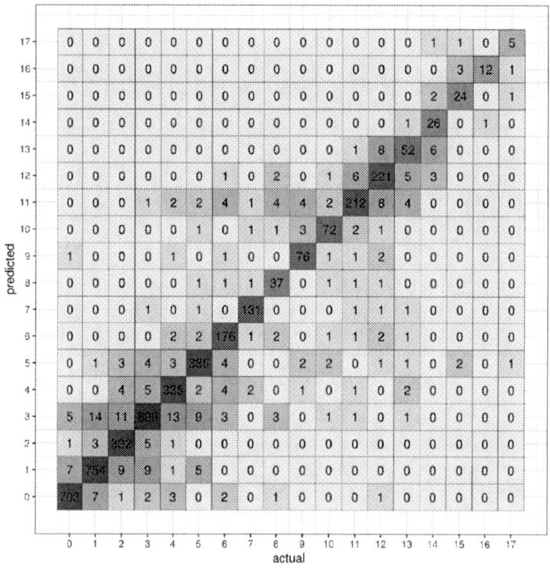

Figure 3: Heat map showing the distribution of predictions from our model compared to true values. Tight grouping is noticed in high levels of support, and less grouping where there is less support.

## E Performance of MSBC on 'Tricky' Notes

Table 7: Performance of MSBC across all values for EDSS.

| MSBC's Breakdown | | | | |
| --- | --- | --- | --- | --- |
| EDSS | Precision | Recall | F1 | Support |
| 0 | 0.9764 | 0.9805 | 0.9784 | 717 |
| 1.0 | 0.9605 | 0.9679 | 0.9642 | 779 |
| 1.5 | 0.9751 | 0.9333 | 0.9534 | 420 |
| 2.0 | 0.9365 | 0.9708 | 0.9533 | 926 |
| 2.5 | 0.9410 | 0.9280 | 0.9344 | 361 |
| 3.0 | 0.9413 | 0.9436 | 0.9425 | 408 |
| 3.5 | 0.9362 | 0.8980 | 0.9167 | 196 |
| 4.0 | 0.9632 | 0.9562 | 0.9597 | 137 |
| 4.5 | 0.8605 | 0.7400 | 0.7957 | 50 |
| 5.0 | 0.9157 | 0.8837 | 0.8994 | 86 |
| 5.5 | 0.8889 | 0.8889 | 0.8889 | 81 |
| 6.0 | 0.8689 | 0.9339 | 0.9002 | 227 |
| 6.5 | 0.9247 | 0.8984 | 0.9113 | 246 |
| 7.0 | 0.7761 | 0.7647 | 0.7704 | 68 |
| 7.5 | 0.9286 | 0.6842 | 0.7879 | 38 |
| 8.0 | 0.8889 | 0.8000 | 0.8421 | 30 |
| 8.5 | 0.7500 | 0.9231 | 0.8276 | 13 |
| 9.0 | 0.7143 | 0.6250 | 0.6667 | 8 |
| **Mean** | 0.8970 | 0.8734 | 0.8830 | 4791 |
| **Weighted Mean** | 0.9420 | 0.9417 | 0.9414 | 4791 |

Table 8: EDSS prediction across notes that were not found via a key word search. Bolded scores represent best model performance.

| EDSS Prediction on Samples that Rules were Unable to Label | | | |
| --- | --- | --- | --- |
| Model | Macro-F1 | Micro-F1 | Weighted-F1 |
| MSBC | **0.49942** | **0.61268** | **0.60340** |
| RB + Word2Vec (Bench Mark) | 0.19297 | 0.33275 | 0.32934 |
| Word2Vec CNN | 0.19297 | 0.33275 | 0.32934 |
| SVC RBF | 0.26748 | 0.40493 | 0.36611 |
| Log Reg Baseline | 0.24783 | 0.35916 | 0.34876 |
| LDA | 0.23374 | 0.33627 | 0.32295 |
| Linear SVC | 0.18703 | 0.30634 | 0.29474 |

Table 9: EDSS prediction across notes that were found via a key word search. Bolded scores represent best model performance.

| EDSS Predictions on Samples that Rules were Able to Label | | | |
| --- | --- | --- | --- |
| Model | Macro-F1 | Micro-F1 | Weighted-F1 |
| MSBC | **0.95363** | **0.98603** | **0.98599** |
| RB + Word2Vec CNN (Bench Mark) | 0.93298 | 0.97253 | 0.97259 |
| Word2Vec CNN | 0.79170 | 0.95525 | 0.95393 |
| LDA | 0.53302 | 0.79872 | 0.80062 |
| Linear SVC | 0.52528 | 0.80346 | 0.80861 |
| SVC RBF | 0.48367 | 0.76723 | 0.75366 |
| Log Reg Baseline | 0.48057 | 0.75918 | 0.75845 |

## F Exploratory Data Analysis

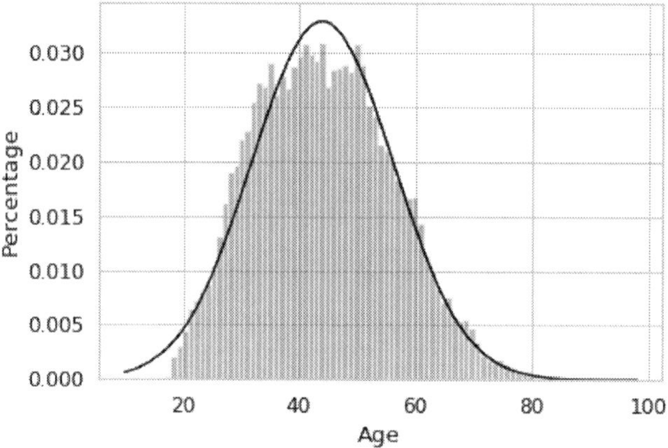


Figure 4: Distribution of age within the data set.

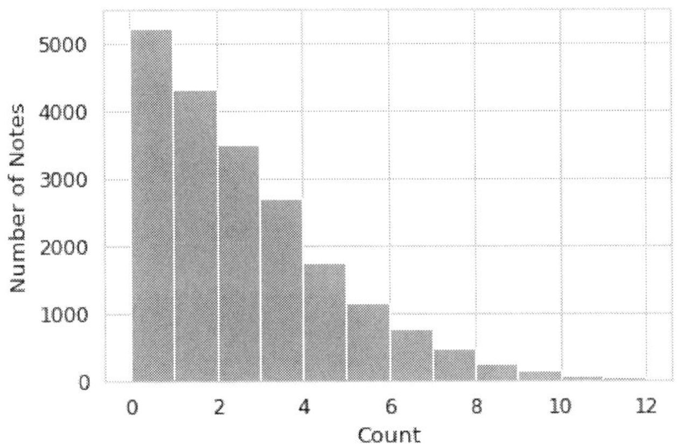

Figure 5: Histogram showing the number of notes per patient.

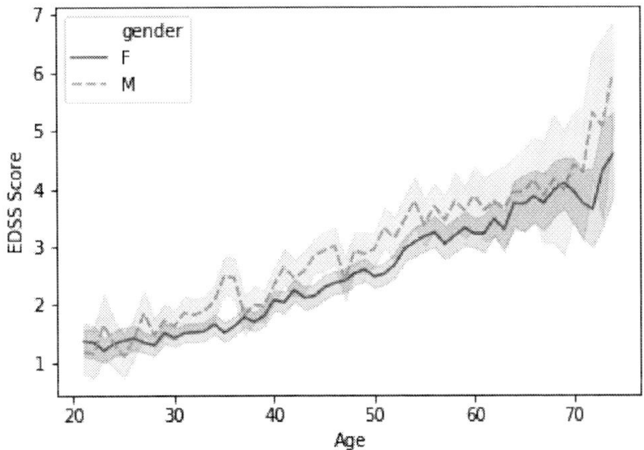

Figure 6: Plot of mean EDSS score vs age.

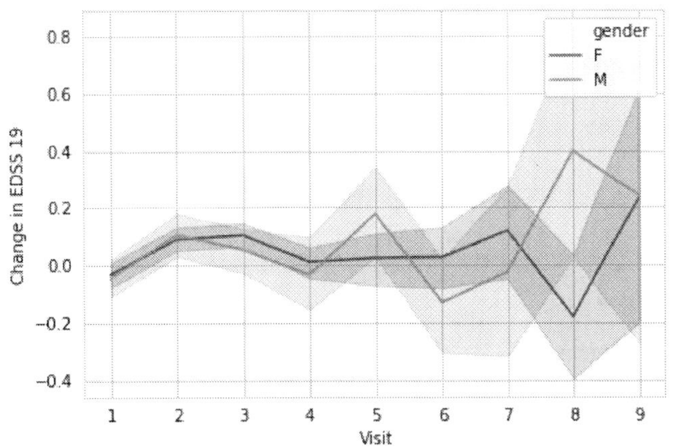

Figure 7: Change of EDSS score in subsequent visits.

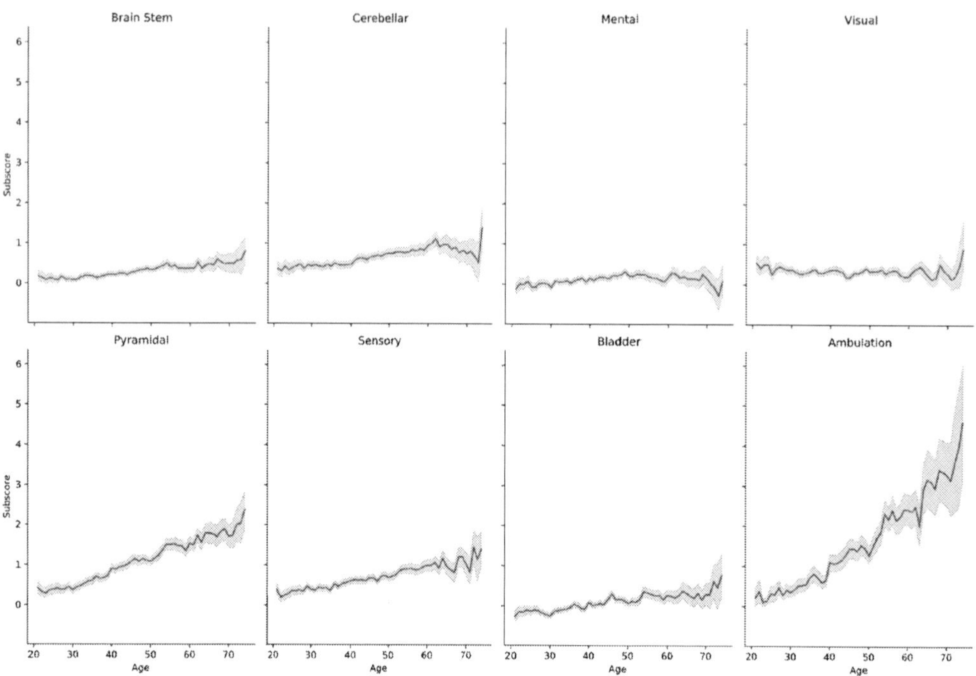

Figure 8: Change of functional subscores with age.

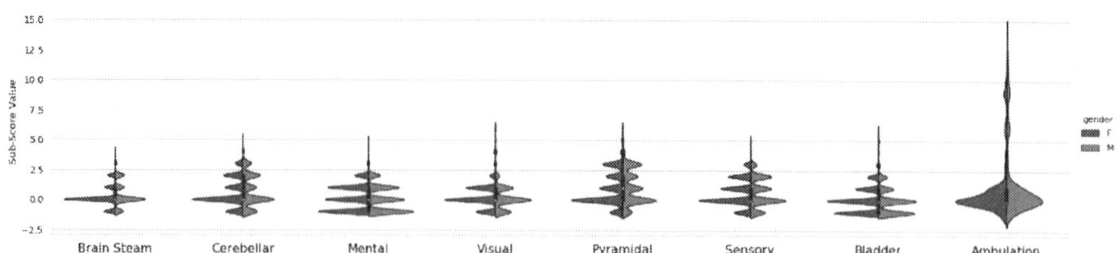

Figure 9: Distribution of functional subscores across gender.

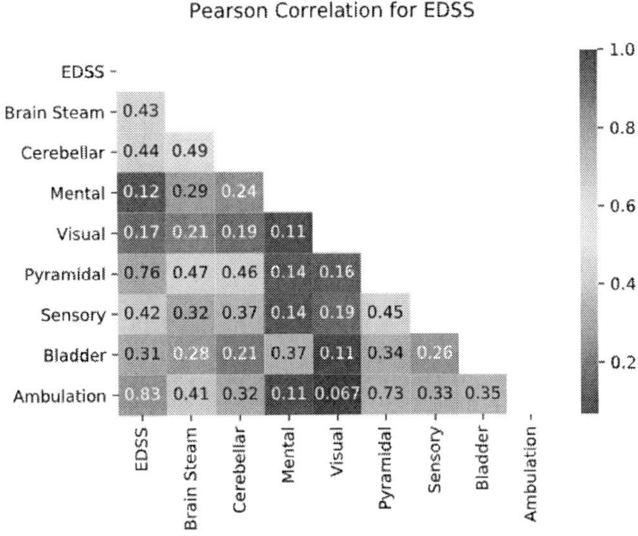


Figure 10: Correlation matrix between functional subscores and EDSS. Strong correlations between EDSS and ambulatory and pyramidal subscores as expected.

# BERT-XML: Large Scale Automated ICD Coding Using BERT Pretraining


**Zachariah Zhang**
NYU Langone Health
zz1409@nyu.edu

**Jingshu Liu**
NYU Langone Health
jl7722@nyu.edu

**Narges Razavian**
NYU Langone Health
narges.razavian@nyumc.org



## Abstract

ICD coding is the task of classifying and coding all diagnoses, symptoms and procedures associated with a patient's visit. The process is often manual, extremely time-consuming and expensive for hospitals as clinical interactions are usually recorded in free text medical notes. In this paper, we propose a machine learning model, BERT-XML, for large scale automated ICD coding of EHR notes, utilizing recently developed unsupervised pretraining that have achieved state of the art performance on a variety of NLP tasks. We train a BERT model from scratch on EHR notes, learning with vocabulary better suited for EHR tasks and thus outperform off-the-shelf models. We further adapt the BERT architecture for ICD coding with multi-label attention. We demonstrate the effectiveness of BERT-based models on the large scale ICD code classification task using millions of EHR notes to predict thousands of unique codes.


## 1 Introduction

Information embedded in Electronic Health Records (EHR) have been a focus of the healthcare community in recent years. Research aiming to provide more accurate diagnose, reduce patients' risk, as well as improve clinical operation efficiency have well-exploited structured EHR data, which includes demographics, disease diagnosis, procedures, medications and lab records. However, a number of studies show that information on patient health status primarily resides in the free-text clinical notes, and it is challenging to convert clinical notes fully and accurately to structured data (Ashfaq et al., 2019; Guide, 2013; Cowie et al., 2017).

Extensive prior efforts have been made on extracting and utilizing information from unstructured EHR data via traditional linguistics based methods in combination with medical metathesaurus and semantic networks (Savova et al., 2010; Aronson and Lang, 2010; Wu et al., 2018a; Soysal et al., 2018). With rapid developments in deep learning methods and their applications in Natural Language Processing (NLP), recent studies adopt those models to process EHR notes for supervised tasks such as disease diagnose and/or ICD[1] coding (Flicoteaux, 2018; Xie and Xing, 2018; Miftahutdinov and Tutubalina, 2018; Azam et al., 2019; Wiegreffe et al., 2019).

Yet to the best of our knowledge, applications of recently developed and vastly-successful self-supervised learning models in this domain have remained limited to very small cohorts (Alsentzer et al., 2019; Huang et al., 2019) and/or using other sources such as PubMed publication (Lee et al., 2020) or animal experiment notes (Amin et al., 2019) instead of clinical data sets. In addition, many of these studies use the original BERT models as released in (Devlin et al., 2019), with a vocabulary derived from a corpus of language not specific to EHR.

In this work we propose BERT-XML as an effective approach to diagnose patients and extract relevant disease documentation from the free-text clinical notes with little pre-processing. BERT (Bidirectional Encoder Representations from Transformers) (Devlin et al., 2019) utilizes unsupervised pretraining procedures to produce meaningful representation of the input sequence, and provides state of the art results across many important NLP tasks. BERT-XML combines BERT pretraining with multi-label attention (You et al., 2018), and outperforms other baselines without self-supervised pretraining by a large margin. Ad-

---

[1]ICD, or International Statistical Classification of Diseases and Related Health Problems, is the system of classifying all diagnoses, symptoms and procedures for a patient's visit. For example, I50.3 is the code for Diastolic (congestive) heart failure. These codes need to be assigned manually by medical coders at each hospital. The process can be very expensive and time consuming, and becomes a natural target for automation.




*Proceedings of the 3rd Clinical Natural Language Processing Workshop*, pages 24–34
November 19, 2020. ©2020 Association for Computational Linguistics

ditionally, the attention layer provides a natural mechanism to identify part of the text that impacts final prediction.

Compare to other works on disease identification, we demonstrate the effectiveness of BERT-based models on automated ICD-coding on a large cohort of EHR clinical notes, and emphasize the following aspects: 1) **Large cohort pretraining and EHR Specific Vocabulary.** We train BERT model from scratch on over 5 million EHR notes and with a vocabulary specific to EHR, and show that it outperforms off-the-shelf or fine-tuned BERT using off-the-shelf vocabulary. 2) **Minimal pre-processing of input sequence.** Instead of splitting input text into sentences (Huang et al., 2019; Savova et al., 2010; Soysal et al., 2018) or extracting diagnose related phrases prior to modeling (Azam et al., 2019), we directly model input sequence up to 1,024 tokens in both pre-training and prediction tasks to accommodate common EHR note size. This shows superior performance by considering information over longer span of text. 3) **Large number of classes.** We use the 2,292 most frequent ICD-10 codes from our modeling cohort as the disease targets, and shows the model is highly predictive of the majority of classes. This extends previous effort on disease diagnose or coding that only predict a small number of classes. 4) **Novel multi-label embedding initialization.** We apply an innovative initialization method as described in Section 3.3.2, that greatly improves training stability of the multi-label attention.

The paper is organized as follows: We summarize related works in Section 2. In Section 3 we define the problem and describe the BERT-based models and several baseline models. Section 4 provides experiment data and model implementation details. We also show the performances of different model and examples of visualization. The last Section concludes this work and discusses future research areas.

## 2 Related Works

### 2.1 CNN, LSTM based Approaches and Attention Mechanisms in ICD-coding

Extensive work has been done on applying machine learning approaches to automatic ICD coding. Many of these approaches rely on variants of Convolutional Neural Networks (CNNs) and Long Short-Term Memory Networks (LSTMs). Flicoteaux (2018) uses a text CNN as well as lexical matching to improve performance for rare ICD labels. In Xu et al.(2019), authors use an ensemble of a character level CNN, Bi-LSTM, and word level CNN to make predictions of ICD codes. Another study Xie and Xing (2018) proposes a tree-of-sequences LSTM architecture to simultaneously capture the hierarchical relationship among codes and the semantics of each code. Miftahutdinov and Tutubalina (2018) propose an encoder-decoder LSTM framework with a cosine similarity vector between the encoded sequence and the ICD-10 codes descriptions. A more recent study Azam et al. (2019) compares a range of models including CNN, LSTM and a cascading hierarchical architecture in prediction class with LSTM and show the hierarchical model with LSTM performs best.

Many works further incorporates the attention mechanisms as introduced in Bahdanau et al. (2015), to better utilize information buried in longer input sequence. In Baumel et al. (2018), the authors introduce a Hierarchical Attention bidirectional Gated Recurrent Unit(HA-GRU) architecture. Shi et al. (2017) use a hierarchical combination of LSTMs to encode EHR text and then use attention with encodings of the text description of ICD codes to make predictions.

While these models have impressive results, some fall short in modeling the complexity of EHR data in terms of the number of ICD codes predicted. For example, Shi et al. (2017) limit their predictions to the 50 most frequent codes and Xu et al. (2019) predict 32. In addition, these works do not utilize any pretraining and performance can be limited by size of labeled training samples.

### 2.2 Transformer Modules

Unsupervised methods to learn word representations has been well established within the NLP community. Word2vec (Mikolov et al., 2013) and GloVe (Pennington et al., 2014) learn vector representations of tokens from large unsupervised corpora in order to encode semantic similarities in words. However, these approaches fail to incorporate wider context into account as the pretraining only considers words in the immediate neighbourhood.

Recently, several approaches are developed to learn unsupervised encoders that produce contextualized word embedding such as ElMo (Peters et al., 2018) and BERT (Bidirectional Encoder Representations from Transformers) (Devlin et al., 2019).

These models utilize unsupervised pretraining procedures to produce representations that can transfer well to many tasks. BERT uses self-attention modules rather than LSTMs to encode text. In addition, BERT is trained on both a masked language model task as well as a next sentence prediction task. This pretraining procedure has provided state of the art results across many important NLP tasks.

Inspired by the success in other domains, several works have utilized BERT models for medical tasks. Shang et al. (2019) use a BERT style model for medicine recommendation by learning embeddings for ICD codes. Sänger et al. (2019) use BERT as well as BioBERT (Lee et al., 2020) as base models for ICD code prediction. Clinical BERT (Alsentzer et al., 2019) uses a BERT model fine-tuned on MIMIC III (Johnson et al., 2016) notes and discharge summaries and apply to downstream tasks. Si et al. (2019) compare traditional word embeddings including word2vec, GloVe and fastText to ELMo and BERT embeddings on a range of clinical concept extraction tasks.

Transformer based architectures have led to a large increase in performance on clinical tasks. However, they rely on fine tuning off-the-shelf BERT models, whose vocabulary is very different from clinical text. For example, while clinical BERT (Alsentzer et al., 2019) fine-tune the model on the clinical notes, the authors did not expand the base BERT vocabulary to include more relevant clinical terms. Cui et al. (2019) show that pretraining with many out of vocabulary words can degrade quality of representations as the masked language model task becomes easier when predicting a chunked portion of a word. Si et al. (2019) show BERT models pretrained on the MIMIC-III data dominate those pretrained on non-clinical datasets on clinical concept extraction tasks. This further motivates our hypothesis that pretraining on clinical text will improve the performance on ICD-coding task.

Moreover, existing BERT implementations often require segmenting the notes. For example, Clinical BERT caps at a length of 128 and Sänger et al. (2019) truncate note length to 256. This poses question on how to combine segments from the same document in down-stream prediction tasks, as well as difficulty in learning long-term relationship across segments. Instead, we extend the maximum sequence length to 1,024 and can accommodate common clinical notes as a single input sequence.

## 3  Methods

### 3.1  Problem Definition

We approach the ICD tagging task as a multi-label classification problem. We learn a function to map a sequence of input tokens $x = [x_0, x_1, x_2, ..., x_N]$ to a set of labels $y = [y_0, y_1, ...y_M]$ where $y_j \in [0, 1]$ and $M$ is the number of different ICD classes. Assume that we have a set of $N$ training samples $\{(x_i, y_i)\}_{i=0}^N$ representing EHR notes with associated ICD labels.

### 3.2  BERT Pre-training

In this work, we use BERT to represent input text. BERT is an encoder composed of stacked transformer modules. The encoder module is based on the transformer blocks used in (Vaswani et al., 2017), consisting of self-attention, normalization, and position-wise fully connected layers. The model is pretrained with both a masked language model task as well as a next sentence prediction task.

Unlike many practitioners who use BERT models that have been pretrained on general purpose corpora, we trained BERT models from scratch on EHR Notes to address the following two major issues. Firstly, healthcare data contains a specific vocabulary that leads to many out of vocabulary(OOV) words. BERT handles this problem with WordPiece tokenization where OOV words are chunked into sub-words contained in the vocabulary. Naively fine tuning with many OOV words may lead to a decrease in the quality of the representation learned as in the masked language model task as shown by Cui (Cui et al., 2019). Models such as Clinical BERT may learn only to complete the chunked word rather than understand the wider context. The open source BERT vocabulary contains an average 49.2 OOV words per note on our dataset compared with 0.93 OOV words from our trained-from-scratch vocabulary. Secondly, the off-the-shelf BERT models only support sequence lengths up to 512, while EHR notes can contain thousands of tokens. To accommodate the longer sequence length, we trained the BERT model with 1024 sequence length instead. We found that this longer length was able to improve performance on downstream tasks. We train both a small and large architecture model whose configurations are given in table 1. More details on pretraining are described in Section 4.2.1.

We show sample output from our BERT model

**Masked Language Model Example**

| |
|---|
| review of systems : gen : no weight loss or gain , good general state of health , no weakness , no fatigue , no fever , good exercise tolerance , able to do usual activities . heent : head : no headache , no dizziness , no lightheadness eyes : normal vision , no redness , no blind spots , no floaters . ears : no earaches , no fullness , normal hearing , no tinnitus . nose and sinuses : no colds , no stuffiness , no discharge , no hay fever , no nosebleeds , no sinus trouble . mouth and pharynx : no cavities , no bleeding gums , no sore throat , no hoarseness . neck : no lumps , no goiter , no neck stiffness or pain . ln : no adenopathy cardiac : no chest pain or discomfort no syncope , no dyspnea on exertion , no orthopnea , no pnd , no edema , no cyanosis , no heart murmur , no palpitations resp : no pleuritic pain , no sob , no wheezing , no stridor , no cough , no hemoptysis , no respiratory infections , no bronchitis . |

Figure 1: Example of masked language model task for BERT trained on EHR notes. Highlighted tokens are model predictions for [MASK] tokens

in Figure 1. Our model successfully learns the structure of medical notes as well as the relationships between many different types of symptoms and medical terms.

## 3.3 BERT ICD Classification Models

### 3.3.1 BERT Multi-Label Classification

The standard architecture for multi-label classification using BERT is to embed a [CLS] token along with all additional inputs, yielding contextualized representations from the encoder. Assume $H = \{h_{cls}, h_0, h_1, ...h_N\}$ is the last hidden layer corresponding to the [CLS] token and input tokens 0 through $N$, $h_{cls}$ is then directly used to predict a binary vector of labels.

$$\mathbf{y} = \sigma(\mathbf{W_{out}h_{cls}}) \tag{1}$$

where $y \in R^M$ , $W_{out}$ are learnable parameters and $\sigma()$ is the sigmoid function.

### 3.3.2 BERT-XML

**Multi-Label Attention**

One drawback of using the standard BERT multi-label classification approach is that the [CLS] vector of the last hidden layer has limited capacity, especially when the number of labels to classify is

large. We experiment with the multi-label attention output layer from AttentionXML (You et al., 2018), and find it improves performance on the prediction task. This module takes a sequence of contextualized word embeddings from BERT $H = \{h_0, h_1, ...h_N\}$ as inputs. We calculate the prediction for each label $y_j$ using the attention mechanism shown below.

$$\mathbf{a_{ij}} = \frac{\exp(\langle \mathbf{h_i, l_j} \rangle)}{\sum_{i=0}^{N} \exp(\langle \mathbf{h_i, l_j} \rangle)} \tag{2}$$

$$\mathbf{c_j} = \sum_{i=0}^{N} \mathbf{a_{ij}h_i} \tag{3}$$

$$\mathbf{y_j} = \sigma(\mathbf{W_a}\mathrm{relu}(\mathbf{W_b c_j})) \tag{4}$$

Where $l_j$ is the vector of attention parameters corresponding to label $j$. $W_a$ and $W_b$ are shared between labels and are learnable parameters.

**Semantic Label Embedding**

The output layer of our model introduces a large number of randomly initialized parameters. To further leverage our unsupervised pretraining, we use the BERT embeddings of the text description of each ICD code to initialize the weights of the corresponding label in the output layer. We take the mean of the BERT embeddings of each token in the description. We find this greatly increases the stability of the optimization procedure as well decreases convergence time of the prediction model.

## 3.4 Baseline Models

### 3.4.1 Logistic Regression

A logistic regression model is trained with bag-of-words features. We evaluated L1 regularization with different penalty coefficients but did not find improvement in performance. We report the vanilla logistic regression model performance in table 2.

### 3.4.2 Multi-Head Attention

We then trained a bi-LSTM model with a multi-head attention layer as suggested in (Vaswani et al., 2017). Assume $H = \{h_0, h_1, ..., h_n\}$ is the hidden layer corresponding to input tokens 0 through $n$ from the bi-LSTM, concatenating the forward and backward nodes. The prediction of each label is calculated as below:

$$\mathbf{a_{ik}} = \frac{\exp(\langle \mathbf{h_i, q_k} \rangle)}{\sum_{i=0}^{n} \exp(\langle \mathbf{h_i, q_k} \rangle)} \tag{5}$$

$$\mathbf{c_k} = (\sum_{i=0}^{n} \mathbf{a_{ik}h_i})/\sqrt{\mathbf{d_h}} \tag{6}$$

$$\mathbf{c} = concatenate[\mathbf{c_0}, \mathbf{c_1}, ..., \mathbf{c_K}] \qquad (7)$$

$$\mathbf{y} = \sigma(\mathbf{W_a c}) \qquad (8)$$

$k = 0, ..., K$ is the number of heads and $d_h$ is the size of the bi-LSTM hidden layer. $q_k$ is the query vector corresponding to the $k$th head and is learnable. $W_a \in R^{M \times K d_h}$ is the learnable output layer weight matrix. Both the query vectors and the weight matrices are initialized randomly.

### 3.4.3 Other EHR BERT Models

We compare the BERT model pretrained on EHR data (EHR BERT) with other models released for the purpose of EHR applications, including BioBERT (Lee et al., 2020) and clinical BERT (Alsentzer et al., 2019). We compare to the BioBERT v1.1 (+ PubMed 1M) version of the BioBERT model and Bio+Discharge Summary BERT for Clinical BERT. We use the standard multi-label output layer described in section 3.3.1. We choose to compare only with Alsentzer et al. (2019) and not Huang et al. (2019) as they are trained on very similar datasets derived from MIMIC-III using the same BERT initialization.

## 4 Experiments

### 4.1 Data

We use medical notes and diagnoses in ICD-10 codes from the NYU Langone Hospital EHR system. These notes are de-identified via the Physionet De-ID tool (Neamatullah et al., 2008), with all personal identifiable information removed such as names, phone numbers, and addresses of both the patients and the clinicians. We exclude notes that are erroneously generated, student generated, belongs to miscellaneous category, as well as notes that contain fewer than 50 characters as these are often not diagnosis related. The resulting data set contains a total of 7.5 million notes corresponding to visits from about 1 million patients, with a median note length of around 150 words and 90th percentile of around 800 tokens. Overall about 50 different types of notes presents in the data. Over 50% of the notes are progress notes, following by telephone encounter (10%) and patient instructions (5%).

This data is then randomly split by patient into 70/10/20 train, dev, test sets. For the models with a maximum length of 512 tokens, notes exceeding the length are split into segments of every 512 tokens until the remaining segment is shorter than the maximum length. Shorter notes, including the ones generated from splitting, are padded to a length of 512. Similar approach applies to models with a maximum length of 1,024 tokens. For notes that are split, the highest predicted probability per ICD code across segments is used as the note level prediction.

We restrict the ICD codes for prediction to all codes that appear more than 1,000 times in the training set, resulting in 2,292 codes in total. In the training set, each note contains 4.46 codes on average. For each note, besides the ICD codes assigned to it via encounter diagnosis codes, we also include ICD codes related to chronic conditions as classified by AHRQ (Friedman et al., 2006; Chi et al., 2011), that the patient has prior to a en- counter. Specifically, if we observe two instances of a chronic ICD code in the same patient's records, the same code would be imputed in all records since the earliest occurrence of that code. Notes without the in-scope ICD codes are still kept in the dataset, with all 2,292 classes labeled as 0.

### 4.2 BERT-Based Models

### 4.2.1 BERT Pretraining

We trained two different BERT architectures from scratch on EHR notes in the training set. Config- urations of both models are provided in Table 1. We use the most frequent 20K tokens derived from the training set for both models. Our vocabulary is select based on the most frequent tokens in the training set. In addition, we extended the max po- sitional embedding to 1024 to better model long term dependencies across long notes. More details given in sections 4.

Models are trained for 2 complete epochs with a batch size of 32 across 4 Titan 1080 GPUs and Nvidia Apex mixed precision training for a total training time of 3 weeks. We found that after 2 epochs the training loss becomes relatively flat. We utilize the popular HuggingFace[2] implementation of BERT. Training and development data splits are the same as the ICD prediction model. Number of epochs is selected based on dev set loss. We compare the pretrained models with those released in the original BERT paper (Devlin et al., 2019) in the downstream classification task, including the off-the-shelf BERT base uncased model and

---

[2]https://github.com/huggingface/pytorch-transformers

|  | **EHR BERT models** | |
| | **small** | **big** |
| hidden size | 512 | 768 |
| # layers | 8 | 12 |
| # attention heads | 8 | 12 |
| intermediate size | 2048 | 3072 |
| activation function | gelu | gelu |
| hidden dropout | .1 | .1 |
| attention dropout | .1 | .1 |
| max len | 1024 | 1024 |

Table 1: configurations for from scratch BERT models. Big configuration matches the base BERT configuration from original paper but has larger max positional embedding

that after fine-tuning on EHR data. The original BERT models only support documents up to 512 tokens in length. In order to extend these to the same 1024 length as other models, we randomly initialize positional embeddings for positions 512 to 1024.

### 4.2.2 BERT ICD Classification Models

Models are trained with Adam optimizer (Kingma and Ba, 2015) with weight decay and a learning rate of 2e-5. We use a warm-up proportion of .1 during which the learning rate is increased linearly from 0 to 2e-5. After which the learning rate decays to 0 linearly throughout training. We train models for 3 epochs using batch size of 32 across 4 Titan 1080 GPUs and Nvidia mixed precision training. Learning rate and number of epochs are tuned based on AUC of the dev set. All of the ICD classification models optimizes the Binary Cross Entropy loss with equal weights across classes.

### 4.3 Baseline Models

All baseline models use a max input length of 512 tokens. The multi-headed attention model utilizes pretrained input embeddings with the StarSpace (Wu et al., 2018b) bag-of-word approach. We use the notes in training set as input sequence and their corresponding ICD codes as labels and train embeddings of 300 dimensions. Input embeddings are fixed in prediction task because of memory limitation. Additionally, a dropout layer is applied to the embeddings with rate of 0.1. We use a 1-layer bi-LSTM encoder of 512 hidden nodes with GRU, and 200 attention heads.

The multi-headed attention model is trained with Adam optimizer with weight decay and an initial learning rate of 1e-5. We use a batch size of 8 and trained it up to 2 epochs across 4 Titan 1080 GPUs. Hyperparameters including learning rate, drop out rate and number of epochs are tuned based on AUC of the dev set.

### 4.4 Results

For each model we report macro AUC and micro AUC. We found that all BERT based models far outperform non-transformer based models. In addition, the big EHR BERT trained from scratch outperforms off-the-shelf BERT models. We believe this speaks to the benefit of pretraining using a vocabulary closer to the prediction task. In addition we find that adding multi-label attention outperforms the standard classification approach given the large number of ICD codes.

We analyze the performance by ICD in figure 2. We achieve very high performance in many ICD classes: 467 of them have an AUC of 0.98 or higher. On ICDs with a low AUC value, we notice that the model can have trouble delineating closely related classes. For example, ICD G44.029-"Chronic cluster headache, not intractable" has a rather low AUC of 0.57. On closer analysis, we find that the model commonly misclassifies this ICD code with other closely related ones such as G44.329-"Chronic post-traumatic headache, not intractable". In future iterations of the model we can better adapt our output layer to the hierarchical nature of the classification problem. Detailed performance of the EHR-BERT+XML model on the test set for the top 45 frequent ICD codes is included in Appendix A.

Furthermore, we find that models trained with max length of 1024 outperform those of 512. EHR notes tend to be long and this shows the value of modeling longer sequences for EHR applications. However, training time for the longer sequence models is roughly 3.5 times that of the shorter ones. In order to scale training and inference to longer patient histories with multiple notes it is necessary to develop faster and more memory efficient transformer models.

In addition, while the BERT based models do better than standard models on average, we see very pronounced gains in lower frequency ICDs. Table 3 compares the macro AUC for all ICD codes with fewer than 2000 training examples (757 ICDs in total) of the best BERT and non-BERT models. Note that the best non-BERT model does worse on

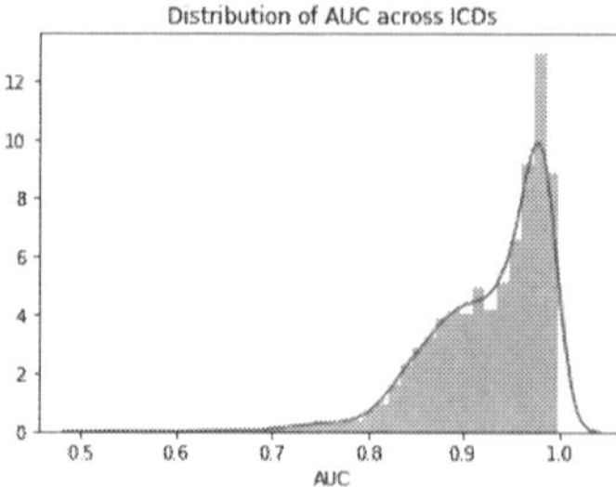


Figure 2: distributions of AUCs across ICD 10 codes

**Prediction Visualization : Right Hip Fracture**

physical therapy progress note ... right hip pain mnn . nnn nnn . nn treatment diagnosis : r hip pain , s / p labral repair with [UNK] primary insurance : [UNK] group subscriber number : @ subnum @ secondary insurance : n / a primary language spoken : english [UNK] nn [UNK] interpreter present : no any relevant changes to medical status : no recent falls : no precautions : see surgical protocol in media file , currently phase ii

Figure 3: visualization of XML-BERT attention layer. Darker colors correspond to higher attention weights.

this set compare to its performance on all ICDs, while the best BERT model performs better on average on the lower frequency ones. This further illustrates the value of the unsupervised pretraining and provides a good motivation to expand our analysis to even less frequent ICD codes in future works.

### 4.5 Visualization

For many machine learning applications, it is important to enable users to understand how the model comes to the predictions, especially in healthcare industry where decisions have serious implications for patients. To understand the model predictions, we can visualize the attention weights of the XML output layer of each of the classes. In figure 3 we show attention weights corresponding to a note coded with right hip fracture. The model successfully identify key terms such as 'right hip pain', 'hip pain' and 's/p labral'.

In addition, we examine the attention weights between tokens in the BERT encoder. In figure 4 we show the attention scores between each word of the note of the final layer of the BERT encoder of a note with 735 tokens. We observe that, while probability mass tends to concentrate between se-

quentially close tokens, a significant amount of probability mass also comes from far away tokens. In addition we see specialisation of different heads. For example, head 0 (row 1, column 1 in figure 4) tends to capture long range contextual information such as the note type and encounter type which are typically listed at the beginning of each note; while head 5 (row 1, column 1 in figure 4) tends to model local information. We believe the increase in performance can partially be attributed to the ability to model long range contextual information.

## 5 Conclusion

Automatic ICD coding from medical notes has high value to clinicians, healthcare providers as well as researchers. Not only does auto-coding have high potential in cost- and time-saving, but more accurate and consistent ICD coding is necessary to facilitate patient care and improve all downstream healthcare EHR based research.

We demonstrate the effectiveness of models leveraging the most recent developments in NLP with BERT as well as multi-label attention on ICD classification. Our model achieves state of the art results using a large set of real world EHR data across many ICD classes. In addition we find that domain specific pretrained BERT model outperforms BERT models trained on general purpose corpora. We note that the off-the-shelf WordPiece tokenizer can naively split domain-specific yet OOV words and resulting in a BERT model focusing on word completion, while using a specific EHR vocabulary seem to help overcome the problem. Lastly, we also observe the benefit of modeling longer sequences.

On the other hand, the current work has several limitations. Most importantly, while we have found that modeling longer term dependencies improves performance, it comes at a large cost of training time. Doubling the input length roughly triples the training and inference time. For many applications this increase in computational demand may offset the gain in model performance. This motivates further exploration on efficient variants of the self-attention modules to accommodate longer input length in similar tasks. Additionally, adding XML to the BERT architecture generates significant yet rather marginal performance improvement (Micro-AUC improvement of 0.002 for EHR BERT Big model with maximum input length of 1024). This also increases the computation complexity

|  | AUC | |
| --- | --- | --- |
|  | **Micro** | **Macro** |
| Logistic Reg (max length 512) | 0.932 | 0.815 |
| Multi-head Attn (max length 512) | 0.941 | 0.859 |
| BERT (max length 512) | 0.954 | 0.895 |
| BERT (max length 1024) | 0.955 | 0.898 |
| Finetuned BERT (max length 1024) | 0.958 | 0.903 |
| BioBERT | 0.960 | 0.908 |
| clinical BERT | 0.961 | 0.904 |
| EHR BERT Small (max length 512) | 0.959 | 0.897 |
| EHR BERT Small (max length 1024) | 0.965 | 0.918 |
| EHR BERT Small + XML (max length 1024) | 0.968 | 0.924 |
| EHR BERT Big (max length 512) | 0.964 | 0.917 |
| EHR BERT Big (max length 1024) | 0.968 | 0.925 |
| EHR BERT Big + XML (max length 512) | 0.967 | 0.919 |
| EHR BERT Big + XML (max length 1024) | **0.970** | **0.927** |

Table 2: Test set model performance. The largest confidence interval calculated was only 4e-5 so all results shown are statistically significant.

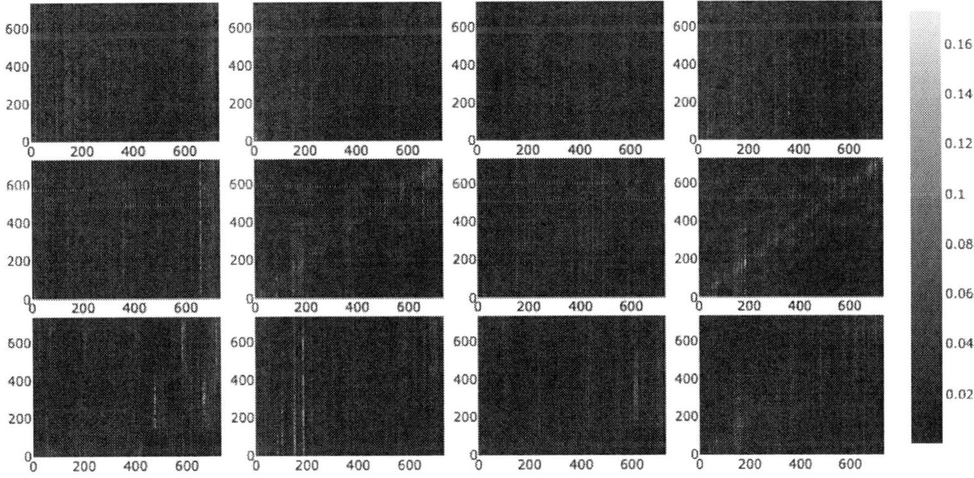



Figure 4: The attention weights of each head for each head in the last layer of the BERT encoder. Brighter color denotes higher attention score. We see some heads specialize in modeling local information(row 2, column 2) while some specialize in passing global information (row 1, column 1). Suggest print in color.

Macro AUC - Low Frequency ICDS

| | |
|---|---|
| Multi-head Att | 0.825 |
| Big EHR BERT + XML | 0.933 |

Table 3: Macro AUC of the best non transformer model and the best BERT model compared using only ICDs with fewer than 2000 examples. Note that the non pretrained model performs worse on this section of the dataset while the BERT model performs just as good.

and more efficient alternatives, such as hierarchical based methods as evaluated in Azam et al. (2019), are promising candidates.

For future works, we plan on expanding our model to more classes with fewer records as we observe the model performing as well on low frequency ICD codes as on the high frequency ones. To address limitations discussed above, we plan on adapting our model to utilize the hierarchical nature of the ICD codes as well as developing memory efficient models that can support inference across long sequences.

## References


Emily Alsentzer, John Murphy, William Boag, Wei-Hung Weng, Di Jindi, Tristan Naumann, and Matthew McDermott. 2019. Publicly available clinical bert embeddings. In *Proceedings of the 2nd Clinical Natural Language Processing Workshop*, pages 72–78.

Saadullah Amin, Günter Neumann, Katherine Dunfield, Anna Vechkaeva, Kathryn Annette Chapman, and Morgan Kelly Wixted. 2019. Mlt-dfki at clef ehealth 2019: Multi-label classification of icd-10 codes with bert.

Alan R Aronson and François-Michel Lang. 2010. An overview of metamap: historical perspective and recent advances. *Journal of the American Medical Informatics Association*, 17(3):229–236.

Hamza A Ashfaq, Corey A Lester, Dena Ballouz, Josh Errickson, and Maria A Woodward. 2019. Medication accuracy in electronic health records for microbial keratitis. *JAMA ophthalmology*.

Sheikh Shams Azam, Manoj Raju, Venkatesh Pagidimarri, and Vamsi Chandra Kasivajjala. 2019. Cascadenet: An lstm based deep learning model for automated icd-10 coding. In *Future of Information and Communication Conference*, pages 55–74. Springer.

Dzmitry Bahdanau, Kyung Hyun Cho, and Yoshua Bengio. 2015. Neural machine translation by jointly learning to align and translate. 3rd International Conference on Learning Representations, ICLR 2015 ; Conference date: 07-05-2015 Through 09-05-2015.

Tal Baumel, Jumana Nassour-Kassis, Raphael Cohen, Michael Elhadad, and Noemie Elhadad. 2018. Multi-label classification of patient notes: case study on icd code assignment. In *Workshops at the Thirty-Second AAAI Conference on Artificial Intelligence*.

Mei-ju Chi, Cheng-yi Lee, and Shwu-chong Wu. 2011. The prevalence of chronic conditions and medical expenditures of the elderly by chronic condition indicator (cci). *Archives of gerontology and geriatrics*, 52(3):284–289.

Martin R Cowie, Juuso I Blomster, Lesley H Curtis, Sylvie Duclaux, Ian Ford, Fleur Fritz, Samantha Goldman, Salim Janmohamed, Jörg Kreuzer, Mark Leenay, et al. 2017. Electronic health records to facilitate clinical research. *Clinical Research in Cardiology*, 106(1):1–9.

Yiming Cui, Wanxiang Che, Ting Liu, Bing Qin, Ziqing Yang, Shijin Wang, and Guoping Hu. 2019. Pre-training with whole word masking for chinese bert. *arXiv preprint arXiv:1906.08101*.

Jacob Devlin, Ming-Wei Chang, Kenton Lee, and Kristina Toutanova. 2019. Bert: Pre-training of deep bidirectional transformers for language understanding. In *NAACL-HLT (1)*, pages 4171–4186.

Rémi Flicoteaux. 2018. Ecstra-aphp@ clef ehealth2018-task 1: Icd10 code extraction from death certificates. In *CLEF (Working Notes)*.

Bernard Friedman, H Joanna Jiang, Anne Elixhauser, and Andrew Segal. 2006. Hospital inpatient costs for adults with multiple chronic conditions. *Medical Care Research and Review*, 63(3):327–346.

Beacon Nation Learning Guide. 2013. Capturing high quality electronic health records data to support performance improvement. *Implementation Objective*, 2:16.

Kexin Huang, Jaan Altosaar, and Rajesh Ranganath. 2019. Clinicalbert: Modeling clinical notes and predicting hospital readmission. *CoRR*, abs/1904.05342.

Alistair EW Johnson, Tom J Pollard, Lu Shen, H Lehman Li-wei, Mengling Feng, Mohammad Ghassemi, Benjamin Moody, Peter Szolovits, Leo Anthony Celi, and Roger G Mark. 2016. Mimic-iii, a freely accessible critical care database. *Scientific data*, 3:160035.

Diederik P. Kingma and Jimmy Ba. 2015. Adam: A method for stochastic optimization. In *ICLR (Poster)*.

Jinhyuk Lee, Wonjin Yoon, Sungdong Kim, Donghyeon Kim, Sunkyu Kim, Chan Ho So, and Jaewoo Kang. 2020. Biobert: a pre-trained biomedical language representation model for biomedical text mining. *Bioinformatics*, 36(4):1234–1240.

Zulfat Miftahutdinov and Elena Tutubalina. 2018. Deep learning for icd coding: Looking for medical concepts in clinical documents in english and in french. In *International Conference of the Cross-Language Evaluation Forum for European Languages*, pages 203–215. Springer.

Tomas Mikolov, Ilya Sutskever, Kai Chen, Greg S Corrado, and Jeff Dean. 2013. Distributed representations of words and phrases and their compositionality. In *Advances in neural information processing systems*, pages 3111–3119.

Ishna Neamatullah, Margaret M Douglass, H Lehman Li-wei, Andrew Reisner, Mauricio Villarroel, William J Long, Peter Szolovits, George B Moody, Roger G Mark, and Gari D Clifford. 2008. Automated de-identification of free-text medical records. *BMC medical informatics and decision making*, 8(1):32.

Jeffrey Pennington, Richard Socher, and Christopher Manning. 2014. Glove: Global vectors for word representation. In *Proceedings of the 2014 conference on empirical methods in natural language processing (EMNLP)*, pages 1532–1543.

Matthew E Peters, Mark Neumann, Mohit Iyyer, Matt Gardner, Christopher Clark, Kenton Lee, and Luke Zettlemoyer. 2018. Deep contextualized word representations. In *Proceedings of NAACL-HLT*, pages 2227–2237.

Mario Sänger, Leon Weber, Madeleine Kittner, and Ulf Leser. 2019. Classifying german animal experiment summaries with multi-lingual bert at clef ehealth 2019 task 1. In *CLEF (Working Notes)*.

Guergana K Savova, James J Masanz, Philip V Ogren, Jiaping Zheng, Sunghwan Sohn, Karin C Kipper-Schuler, and Christopher G Chute. 2010. Mayo clinical text analysis and knowledge extraction system (ctakes): architecture, component evaluation and applications. *Journal of the American Medical Informatics Association*, 17(5):507–513.

Junyuan Shang, Tengfei Ma, Cao Xiao, and Jimeng Sun. 2019. Pre-training of graph augmented transformers for medication recommendation. In *Proceedings of the 28th International Joint Conference on Artificial Intelligence*, pages 5953–5959. AAAI Press.

Haoran Shi, Pengtao Xie, Zhiting Hu, Ming Zhang, and Eric P Xing. 2017. Towards automated icd coding using deep learning. *arXiv preprint arXiv:1711.04075*.

Yuqi Si, Jingqi Wang, Hua Xu, and Kirk Roberts. 2019. Enhancing clinical concept extraction with contextual embeddings. *Journal of the American Medical Informatics Association*, 26(11):1297–1304.

Ergin Soysal, Jingqi Wang, Min Jiang, Yonghui Wu, Serguei Pakhomov, Hongfang Liu, and Hua Xu. 2018. Clamp–a toolkit for efficiently building customized clinical natural language processing pipelines. *Journal of the American Medical Informatics Association*, 25(3):331–336.

Ashish Vaswani, Noam Shazeer, Niki Parmar, Jakob Uszkoreit, Llion Jones, Aidan N Gomez, Łukasz Kaiser, and Illia Polosukhin. 2017. Attention is all you need. In *Advances in neural information processing systems*, pages 5998–6008.

Sarah Wiegreffe, Edward Choi, Sherry Yan, Jimeng Sun, and Jacob Eisenstein. 2019. Clinical concept extraction for document-level coding. In *Proceedings of the 18th BioNLP Workshop and Shared Task*, pages 261–272.

Honghan Wu, Giulia Toti, Katherine I Morley, Zina M Ibrahim, Amos Folarin, Richard Jackson, Ismail Kartoglu, Asha Agrawal, Clive Stringer, Darren Gale, et al. 2018a. Semehr: A general-purpose semantic search system to surface semantic data from clinical notes for tailored care, trial recruitment, and clinical research. *Journal of the American Medical Informatics Association*, 25(5):530–537.

Ledell Yu Wu, Adam Fisch, Sumit Chopra, Keith Adams, Antoine Bordes, and Jason Weston. 2018b. Starspace: Embed all the things! In *AAAI*, pages 5569–5577.

Pengtao Xie and Eric Xing. 2018. A neural architecture for automated icd coding. In *Proceedings of the 56th Annual Meeting of the Association for Computational Linguistics (Volume 1: Long Papers)*, pages 1066–1076.

Keyang Xu, Mike Lam, Jingzhi Pang, Xin Gao, Charlotte Band, Piyush Mathur, Frank Papay, Ashish K Khanna, Jacek B Cywinski, Kamal Maheshwari, et al. 2019. Multimodal machine learning for automated icd coding. In *Machine Learning for Healthcare Conference*, pages 197–215. PMLR.

Ronghui You, Suyang Dai, Zihan Zhang, Hiroshi Mamitsuka, and Shanfeng Zhu. 2018. Attentionxml: Extreme multi-label text classification with multi-label attention based recurrent neural networks. *arXiv preprint arXiv:1811.01727*.

# A ICD Performance for frequent ICDs

| ICD-10 | Count | AUC | ICD-10 | Count | AUC | ICD-10 | Count | AUC |
|---|---|---|---|---|---|---|---|---|
| I10 | 391298 | 0.877 | M81.0 | 46528 | 0.868 | I73.9 | 24992 | 0.898 |
| E78.5 | 291430 | 0.863 | Z00.00 | 43136 | 0.988 | F41.1 | 26032 | 0.842 |
| I25.10 | 131280 | 0.904 | I48.0 | 40032 | 0.923 | E11.65 | 22912 | 0.882 |
| E11.9 | 132150 | 0.874 | Z51.11 | 42336 | 0.970 | F17.200 | 21408 | 0.849 |
| K21.9 | 133422 | 0.816 | G47.33 | 38592 | 0.846 | Z23 | 23296 | 0.977 |
| E55.9 | 114322 | 0.839 | N40.0 | 34688 | 0.896 | M17.0 | 19648 | 0.885 |
| E03.9 | 91072 | 0.840 | J45.909 | 34496 | 0.835 | M54.5 | 21296 | 0.973 |
| E66.9 | 80454 | 0.838 | E66.01 | 30080 | 0.877 | C50.912 | 21984 | 0.944 |
| E78.00 | 72740 | 0.862 | N18.3 | 28784 | 0.888 | M06.9 | 18160 | 0.913 |
| F41.9 | 71836 | 0.835 | I48.2 | 26592 | 0.936 | C50.911 | 22544 | 0.945 |
| F32.9 | 68172 | 0.824 | Z95.0 | 24592 | 0.930 | C50.919 | 22880 | 0.950 |
| I48.91 | 61056 | 0.922 | G62.9 | 25632 | 0.853 | R53.83 | 19616 | 0.968 |
| G89.29 | 49600 | 0.838 | M17.9 | 22992 | 0.854 | I35.0 | 17536 | 0.917 |
| J44.9 | 48224 | 0.881 | E78.2 | 24096 | 0.876 | Z51.12 | 20784 | 0.963 |
| M19.90 | 47968 | 0.830 | I34.0 | 21600 | 0.900 | J45.20 | 18848 | 0.856 |

Table 4: Individual ICD Performance for most frequent ICDs, Big EHR BERT + XML. Count is the total positive examples we have observed in our test set.

# Incorporating Risk Factor Embeddings in Pre-trained Transformers Improves Sentiment Prediction in Psychiatric Discharge Summaries


Xiyu Ding[1] and Mei-Hua Hall[2,3] and Timothy A. Miller[1,3]

[1]Computational Health Informatics Program, Boston Children's Hospital, Boston, MA
[2]Psychosis Neurobiology Laboratory, McLean Hospital, Belmont, MA
[3]Harvard Medical School, Boston, MA



## Abstract

Reducing rates of early hospital readmission has been recognized and identified as a key to improve quality of care and reduce costs. There are a number of risk factors that have been hypothesized to be important for understanding re-admission risk, including such factors as problems with substance abuse, ability to maintain work, relations with family. In this work, we develop RoBERTa-based models to predict the sentiment of sentences describing readmission risk factors in discharge summaries of patients with psychosis. We improve substantially on previous results by a scheme that shares information across risk factors while also allowing the model to learn risk factor-specific information.


## 1 Introduction

About 1 in 5 Medicare patients discharged from the hospital is rehospitalized within 30 days (Jencks et al., 2009). Four out of the top ten conditions with the largest number of readmissions among the Medicaid enrollees were mental health conditions or substance use disorders (Hines et al., 2014). Readmissions are harmful both in being disruptive to patients and families, and as a major driver of health-care costs in psychiatry (Wu et al., 2005; Mangalore and Knapp, 2007). Also, premature discharge of patients contributes not only to rehospitalization but to increased risk of homelessness and the possibility of violent behavior or suicide. Thus, reducing rates of early hospital readmission has been recognized and identified as a key to improve quality of care and reduce costs.

There are a number of risk factors that previous work compiled from the literature (Holderness et al., 2018) to be important for understanding re-admission risk, including such factors as problems with substance abuse, ability to maintain work, relations with family. Studying readmission through

the use of explicit risk factors may go against prevailing trends in machine learning (black box models that take in raw signals), but has at least two potential benefits: 1) Allowing for descriptive study of, and thus better understanding of, the factors that are important for readmission; and 2) The possibility that a risk classifier that uses explicit risk factors will be more interpretable and trustworthy to providers, and thus more likely to be put into practical use.

In this work, we make use of a publicly available data set of sentences from discharge summary that is annotated for seven risk factors, along with the "sentiment," marked as *Positive*, *Negative*, or *Neutral* (more details in background). Previous work on this dataset showed that the task was approachable with neural methods, but performance suffered because of small dataset size (Holderness et al., 2019). Here, we address this issue with two advances. First, we show that transfer learning helps dramatically. While the previous work used smaller neural models trained from scratch, we start from pre-trained transformer models (RoBERTa (Liu et al., 2019)), and improve them for the task with architectural and data augmentation strategies.

Second, we show that sharing data between the different risk factor domains is better for performance than training separately, at least with pre-trained models. Previous work trained separate classifiers for each of the risk factor domains, due to the (legitimate) belief that there are significant differences in predicting sentiment in different risk factor domains (Holderness et al., 2019). Here, we demonstrate that a method that allows for sharing of information between different risk factor domains can improve performance. Because of a mismatch in the way training and test data were annotated, we introduce a data augmentation method for the training set that allows our method to improve over the vanilla RoBERTa baseline. The improvements

35


*Proceedings of the 3rd Clinical Natural Language Processing Workshop*, pages 35–40
November 19, 2020. ©2020 Association for Computational Linguistics

from this latter technique point in a direction that could allow for further improvements even without additional training data.

## 2 Background

The dataset we use was created in previous work (Holderness et al., 2018) and made publicly available. It consists of sentences extracted from discharge summaries of patients with psychosis at Boston-area hospitals. Previous work had examined two tasks on this dataset, the identification of the risk domain represented by the sentence (*Appearance*, *Mood*, *Interpersonal*, *Substance Use*, *Occupation*, *Thought Content* and *Thought Process*), and the sentiment of the sentence given the risk domain. In the training data, each sentence has only one risk factor, and thus one sentiment, but the test data allows for sentences to have multiple risk factors, and thus multiple different sentiments for a single sentence, conditioned on the risk factor domain. Both the previous work for risk factor classification (Holderness et al., 2018) and sentiment classification (Holderness et al., 2019) used multilayer neural networks in their experiments and found them to be the best-performing.

Despite the promise of the above work, the tasks are still unsolved. Recent work in contextualized embeddings has shown great success for sentence classification tasks. Specifically, BERT-based models (Devlin et al., 2019), based on the transformer architecture (Vaswani et al., 2017), showed that pre-training deep transformer encoders on massive text datasets with a language modeling objective could lead to improvements in a variety of tasks. The best performance is typically obtained by fine tuning, where a classifier head is attached to a special sentence token, and new tasks are learned via standard supervised learning, in which the weights of the classifier head are trained from scratch while the weights of the transformer encoder are allowed to update. In this work, we make use of the RoBERTa updates to BERT (Liu et al., 2019), which use the same architecture but pre-trained on a larger dataset and for a longer time.

## 3 Data

The training dataset contains 3500 sentence-length texts, 500 from each of the seven readmission risk factors mentioned above. The test dataset contains 1650 texts which can involve multiple risk factors and are more variable in length compared

with the training data, as described in the previous study (Holderness et al., 2019). We divided the training instances into training and development set with an 80%/20% split,[1] leaving us with 2800 training instances and 700 development instances.

Since we are focusing on sentiment prediction in this work, we take the risk factor domains as given, and for test sentences with multiple risk factor domains, we create multiple instances where the input pairs the sentence text with each domain, and the target is the gold sentiment label for that domain. This results in 2103 test instances. 750 of these are labeled as the *Other* domain, which does not have training instances nor reported results, so we discard these, leaving 1353 test instances.

## 4 Methods

We developed several variations of a risk factor sentiment classifier based on the RoBERTa architecture.

### 4.1 Baseline

We fine-tune seven independent RoBERTa models as the baseline, one for each of the risk factor domains. This follows previous work (Holderness et al., 2019), which suggested that positive or negative clinical sentiments might differ in different risk factor domains.

### 4.2 Plain RoBERTa

Instead of fine-tuning seven independent models, we fine-tune one RoBERTa model on all training texts to learn the shared representation of sentiments, ignoring the risk factor domain of the sentences during training and only learning sentiment labels. Since the test set allows for a sentence to have multiple risk factor domains, but this model can only make one sentiment prediction per sentence, the model is penalized on cases where a sentence has multiple risk factor domains with different sentiments.

### 4.3 Risk Factor Domain Embeddings

In this method, we modify the input representation to contain both the input sentence and the risk factor domain to be classified. In BERT-style models, this means using the special sentence-separating token ([SEP]) between the sentence tokens and the domain tokens. For example, the first sentence in

---

[1] Specifically, we use *iterative_train_test_split* from scikit-multilearn (Szymański and Kajdanowicz, 2017) to create a split that is stratified with respect to multiple labels.

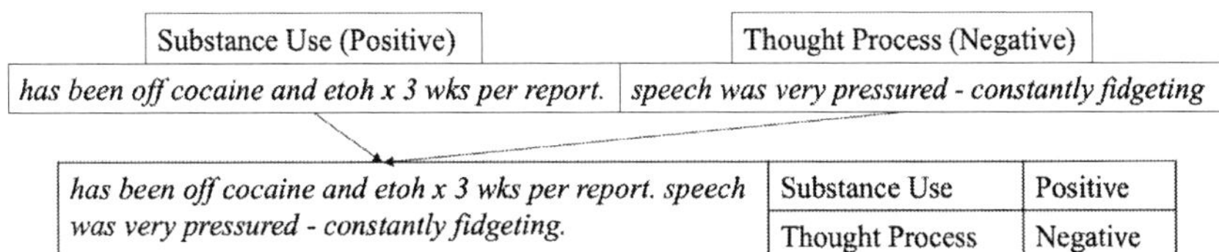


Figure 1: One example of the augmented sentences. Two randomly chosen sentences from the training data are concatenated to create two training instances with different risk factor domains.

Figure 1 would be represented as *[CLS] has been off cocaine and etoh x 3 wks per report. [SEP] substance use [SEP]*. Giving the domain as the second sentence allows the model to potentially learn what part of the input the classifier should focus on, and previous work has shown similar methods to be effective (Shi and Lin, 2019). In contrast to another possible approach with a separate input stream for domain feature, this method allows us to utilize the pre-trained contextual embeddings of the domain words and let the model learn to use its attention mechanism to relate the risk factor domains with the corresponding part of the sentences and make sentiment predictions about only that part.

## 4.4 Data Augmentation

The training data only has one risk factor domain and sentiment annotation per sentence, and so the above approach alone may fail on test data, because at training time the model may never need to use the domain embedding, because the whole sentence is relevant because of the way the data was constructed. Then when applied to the test data the risk factor domain embedding could be useful, but the model has never been trained to use it.

Therefore, we developed a data augmentation scheme that creates new synthetic training instances from pairs of existing instances, such that these synthetic instances more closely resemble test instances with multiple risk factor domain and sentiment labels. We concatenate two randomly sampled sentences in the training data from two different domains, and create two training instances from that concatenated input, with the two different domain and sentiment labels from the original instances. We add a period and space between sentences missing them to look more natural. Figure 1 shows an example of the augmented sentences. These synthetic instances are surely lacking discourse coherence that the real instances in the test set will have, but our hypothesis is that they will at least force the model to associate domain embeddings with specific parts of the input at training time and not just learn the sentiment for the whole

input sequence.

We created 2800 new training instances with this sampling procedure (1400 unique texts), for an augmented training data size of 5600 instances (this method is only use for augmenting training and is not applied to the test data). We then fine-tune the model from the previous section with this augmented data set, using the domain risk factor as the second sentence as above.

## 4.5 Training Details

We use the HuggingFace Transformer library (Wolf et al., 2019) for our RoBERTa implementations. We use grid search to find the optimal hyper-parameters (batch size, learning rate and max sequence length) for the RoBERTa fine-tuning process. We monitor the training and validation loss for each training epoch and save the model with the highest Macro-F1 score on the development set before testing on the test set. We use pandas for data processing (Wes McKinney, 2010) and scikit-learn for model evaluation (Pedregosa et al., 2011).

| Model | Neu F1 | Pos F1 | Neg F1 | Acc | Macro F1 |
|---|---|---|---|---|---|
| Baseline (Indep.) | 0.375 | 0.623 | 0.698 | 0.591 | 0.565 |
| Roberta | 0.445 | 0.727 | **0.789** | 0.690 | 0.653 |
| Roberta+D | 0.456 | 0.723 | 0.778 | 0.680 | 0.652 |
| Roberta+D+Aug | **0.468** | **0.743** | **0.789** | **0.699** | **0.666** |

Table 1: Modeling results for the four architectures with the highest score on each performance metric in bold.

## 5 Evaluation

We evaluated the four different architectures on this task to explore the importance of sharing information between different risk factor domains as well as learning the domain specific information.

We first evaluate at the instance level, computing precision and recall for each sentiment label, and combining to get an F1 score for each sentiment label, as well as overall accuracy (proportion of instances correctly predicted regardless of sentiment or risk factor domain). Table 1 summarizes the accuracy F1 score results, with Macro F1 also

| Model | Domain | Pos P | Pos R | Pos F1 | Neg P | Neg R | Neg F1 | Neu P | Neu R | Neu F1 |
|---|---|---|---|---|---|---|---|---|---|---|
| Holderness et al. (2019) | Average | 0.62 | 0.416 | 0.478 | 0.67 | 0.652 | 0.658 | 0.289 | 0.437 | 0.329 |
| **Roberta** | Average | 0.760 | 0.671 | 0.709 | 0.802 | **0.785** | **0.790** | 0.385 | 0.477 | 0.418 |
| | Interpersonal | 0.665 | 0.716 | 0.690 | 0.779 | 0.782 | 0.779 | 0.619 | 0.580 | 0.597 |
| | Mood | 0.846 | 0.738 | 0.787 | 0.750 | 0.818 | 0.780 | 0.510 | 0.528 | 0.518 |
| | occupation | 0.791 | 0.590 | 0.674 | 0.688 | 0.759 | 0.719 | 0.409 | 0.514 | 0.451 |
| | Substance Use | 0.646 | 0.605 | 0.620 | 0.808 | 0.765 | 0.789 | 0.392 | 0.468 | 0.423 |
| | Appearance | 0.854 | 0.647 | 0.735 | 0.852 | 0.868 | 0.857 | 0.395 | 0.565 | 0.465 |
| | Thought Content | 0.768 | 0.697 | 0.730 | 0.892 | 0.728 | 0.800 | 0.067 | 0.237 | 0.108 |
| | Thought Process | 0.748 | 0.706 | 0.728 | 0.842 | 0.772 | 0.807 | 0.306 | 0.447 | 0.362 |
| **Roberta+D+Aug** | Average | **0.779** | **0.708** | **0.735** | **0.860** | 0.713 | 0.768 | **0.404** | **0.581** | **0.459** |
| | Interpersonal | 0.654 | 0.822 | 0.724 | 0.896 | 0.646 | 0.748 | 0.653 | 0.720 | 0.682 |
| | Mood | 0.873 | 0.714 | 0.785 | 0.750 | 0.883 | 0.810 | 0.480 | 0.456 | 0.464 |
| | Occupation | 0.838 | 0.656 | 0.733 | 0.896 | 0.607 | 0.722 | 0.475 | 0.769 | 0.585 |
| | Substance Use | 0.680 | 0.556 | 0.606 | 0.833 | 0.824 | 0.829 | 0.415 | 0.489 | 0.446 |
| | Appearance | 0.882 | 0.776 | 0.824 | 0.893 | 0.491 | 0.626 | 0.313 | 0.762 | 0.438 |
| | Thought Content | 0.737 | 0.636 | 0.680 | 0.882 | 0.732 | 0.799 | 0.114 | 0.410 | 0.179 |
| | Thought Process | 0.787 | 0.798 | 0.790 | 0.872 | 0.811 | 0.840 | 0.381 | 0.463 | 0.416 |

Table 2: Results of Roberta and Roberta fine-tuned on augmented dataset (Roberta+D+Aug) with the highest score on each performance metric in bold. The top row is reported results of the "Fully Supervised MLP" system of Holderness et al. (2019). "Average" scores are computed by taking the average of 7 risk factor domains in the same column.

| Example input text | Domain | GOLD | Roberta | Roberta+D+Aug |
|---|---|---|---|---|
| A. Pt.'s **affect appeared** slightly brighter, **but** remains **flat** | Mood | Positive | Positive | Positive |
| at baseline. Her **mood** appears **slightly improved** as well. | Appearance | Neutral | Positive | Neutral |
| B. Discussed pt.'s **job** and recent episode of | Mood | Neutral | Neutral | Negative |
| "**crying** but not knowing why." | Occupation | Neutral | Neutral | Neutral |
| C. discussed **work dynamics**, **MI** for **substance abuse**, | Occupation | Neutral | Neutral | Neutral |
| processing the episode, medication planning | Substance Use | Negative | Neutral | Neutral |

Table 3: Three examples of the sentiment extraction results in the test data

reported as the average across sentiment labels. Table 2 shows detailed results of the plain RoBERTa and the augmented (RoBERTa+D+Aug) model, including precision and recall, and broken down by risk factor domain. The average across risk factor domains is substantially higher than the results reported in previous work.

The overall best performance was obtained by using domain embeddings with data augmentation (RoBERTa+D+Aug). Although fine-tuning seven independent RoBERTa models for each risk factor domain is the worst performing model, its baseline scores are still higher than the previous study which did not use pre-trained models (Holderness et al., 2019). Plain RoBERTa is surprisingly strong in this task despite the fact that it ignores the risk factor domain and is forced to make the same predictions for texts with multiple sentiment labels.

The improvement obtained by fine-tuning one single RoBERTa model instead of seven independent models suggests that the benefits of sharing information between risk factor domains outweigh the potential risks that the model will learn conflicting information. However, simply using domain as the second sentence during RoBERTa fine-tuning does not lead to improvement in the overall model performance. Augmenting the training data to look more like the test data was necessary in order for the domain embedding input to show benefits.

We tested the significance of the improvements in accuracy and Macro-F1 between RoBERTa and RoBERTa+D+Aug by fine-tuning with 20 randomly selected seeds, and performing a one-tail t-test, and results were found to be significant (p<0.05, p<0.005 for accuracy and Macro-F1).

## 6 Discussion and Conclusion

We selected instances from the test set where the system trained on augmented data (RoBERTa+D+Aug) did well, and others where it did not (see Table 3). Example A shows that the system is able to distinguish between the positive mood and neutral appearance, where plain RoBERTa was forced to select a single sentiment label. Example B shows where RoBERTa+D+Aug still makes mistakes – plain RoBERTa actually does better by picking the single sentiment for the sentence that fits best, while RoBERTa+D+Aug tries to pick two different sentiments and gets one wrong. In fact, in 66.5% of the 221 test sentences with multiple risk factor domains, the sentiment labels are the same, which means plain RoBERTa is usually not penalized for picking a single sentiment label. Example C shows an example where both models make errors, probably due to missing the complex inference that the patient has a substance abuse issue that requires treatment (MI=motivational interviewing).

Overall, our new approach shows major gains in performance over the existing state of the art for this problem. The biggest gains come from simply using large pre-trained models. However, the modified architecture and data augmentation technique lead to further gains, and have the ability to separate out multiple sentiments for a single sentence on new data. Future work may see larger benefit with methods for creating augmented training data that create more natural-looking sentence pairs. The source code used to fine-tune the model will be made publicly available [2].

## Acknowledgments

Research reported in this publication was supported by the National Library Of Medicine of the National Institutes of Health under Award Numbers R01LM012918 and R01LM012973. The content is solely the responsibility of the authors and does not necessarily represent the official views of the National Institutes of Health.

## References

Jacob Devlin, Ming-Wei Chang, Kenton Lee, and Kristina Toutanova. 2019. BERT: Pre-training of deep bidirectional transformers for language understanding. In *Proceedings of the 2019 Conference of the North American Chapter of the Association for Computational Linguistics: Human Language Technologies, Volume 1 (Long and Short Papers)*, pages 4171–4186, Minneapolis, Minnesota. Association for Computational Linguistics.

Anika L. Hines, Marguerite L. Barrett, Joanna Jiang, and Claudia A. Steiner. 2014. Conditions With the Largest Number of Adult Hospital Readmissions by Payer, 2011. HCUP Statistical Brief #172, Agency for Healthcare Research and Quality, Rockville, MD.

Eben Holderness, Philip Cawkwell, Kirsten Bolton, James Pustejovsky, and Mei-Hua Hall. 2019. Distinguishing clinical sentiment: The importance of domain adaptation in psychiatric patient health records.

In *Proceedings of the 2nd Clinical Natural Language Processing Workshop*, pages 117–123, Minneapolis, Minnesota, USA. Association for Computational Linguistics.

Eben Holderness, Nicholas Miller, Kirsten Bolton, Philip Cawkwell, Marie Meteer, James Pustejovsky, and Mei Hua-Hall. 2018. Analysis of risk factor domains in psychosis patient health records. In *Proceedings of the Ninth International Workshop on Health Text Mining and Information Analysis*, pages 129–138, Brussels, Belgium. Association for Computational Linguistics.

Stephen F. Jencks, Mark V. Williams, and Eric A. Coleman. 2009. Rehospitalizations among patients in the medicare fee-for-service program. *New England Journal of Medicine*, 360(14):1418–1428. PMID: 19339721.

Yinhan Liu, Myle Ott, Naman Goyal, Jingfei Du, Mandar Joshi, Danqi Chen, Omer Levy, Mike Lewis, Luke Zettlemoyer, and Veselin Stoyanov. 2019. Roberta: A robustly optimized BERT pretraining approach. *arXiv preprint arXiv:1907.11692*.

Roshni Mangalore and Martin Knapp. 2007. Cost of schizophrenia in England. *The journal of mental health policy and economics*, 10(1):23–41. Place: Italy.

Wes McKinney. 2010. Data Structures for Statistical Computing in Python. In *Proceedings of the 9th Python in Science Conference*, pages 56 – 61.

F. Pedregosa, G. Varoquaux, A. Gramfort, V. Michel, B. Thirion, O. Grisel, M. Blondel, P. Prettenhofer, R. Weiss, V. Dubourg, J. Vanderplas, A. Passos, D. Cournapeau, M. Brucher, M. Perrot, and E. Duchesnay. 2011. Scikit-learn: Machine learning in Python. *Journal of Machine Learning Research*, 12:2825–2830.

Peng Shi and Jimmy Lin. 2019. Simple BERT models for relation extraction and semantic role labeling.

P. Szymański and T. Kajdanowicz. 2017. A scikit-based Python environment for performing multi-label classification. *ArXiv e-prints*.

Ashish Vaswani, Noam Shazeer, Niki Parmar, Jakob Uszkoreit, Llion Jones, Aidan N Gomez, Łukasz Kaiser, and Illia Polosukhin. 2017. Attention is all you need. In *Advances in neural information processing systems*, pages 5998–6008.

Thomas Wolf, Lysandre Debut, Victor Sanh, Julien Chaumond, Clement Delangue, Anthony Moi, Pierric Cistac, Tim Rault, R'emi Louf, Morgan Funtowicz, and Jamie Brew. 2019. Huggingface's transformers: State-of-the-art natural language processing. *ArXiv*, abs/1910.03771.

Eric Q. Wu, Howard G. Birnbaum, Lizheng Shi, Daniel E. Ball, Ronald C. Kessler, Matthew Moulis,

---

[2]`https://github.com/Machine-Learning-for-Medical-Language/psychosis-sentiment-data-augmentation`

and Jyoti Aggarwal. 2005. The economic burden of schizophrenia in the United States in 2002. *The Journal of clinical psychiatry*, 66(9):1122–1129. Place: United States.

# Information Extraction from Swedish Medical Prescriptions with Sig-Transformer Encoder


**John Pougué Biyong**[1]    **Bo Wang**[2,3]    **Terry Lyons**[1,3]    **Alejo J Nevado-Holgado**[2]

[1]Mathematical Institute, University of Oxford, UK
[2]Department of Psychiatry, University of Oxford, UK
[3]The Alan Turing Institute, London, UK
`john.pougue-biyong@maths.ox.ac.uk, bo.wang@psych.ox.ac.uk`



## Abstract

Relying on large pretrained language models such as Bidirectional Encoder Representations from Transformers (BERT) for encoding and adding a simple prediction layer has led to impressive performance in many clinical natural language processing (NLP) tasks. In this work, we present a novel extension to the Transformer architecture, by incorporating signature transform with the self-attention model. This architecture is added between embedding and prediction layers. Experiments on a new Swedish prescription data show the proposed architecture to be superior in two of the three information extraction tasks, comparing to baseline models. Finally, we evaluate two different embedding approaches between applying Multilingual BERT and translating the Swedish text to English then encode with a BERT model pretrained on clinical notes.


## 1   Introduction

Medical prescription notes written by clinicians about patients contains valuable information that the structured part of electronic health records (EHRs) does not have. Manually extracting and annotating such information from large amount of textual fields in medical records such as prescription notes is time-consuming, and expensive since it has to be provided by domain specialists who are in high demand. Information extraction (IE), a specialised area in natural language processing (NLP), refers to the automatic extraction of structured information such as concepts, entities and events from free text (Wang et al., 2018). While rule-base IE systems are still widely used in healthcare (Banda et al., 2018; Davenport and Kalakota, 2019), machine learning-based data-driven approaches have gained much more interest due to their ability to scale and learn to recognise complex patterns. In this paper, we present a set of medical prescriptions written in Swedish and develop a neural network-based system that extracts important information from the textual data.

Recent advances in pretraining large-scale contextualised language representations, including ELMo (Peters et al., 2018) and BERT (Devlin et al., 2018), have proven to be a successful strategy for transfer learning and pushed the performance in many NLP tasks of general purpose. Clinical notes differ substantially to general-domain text and biomedical literature, in terms of its linguistic characteristics. Several studies have fine-tuned general-domain language models such as BERT on in-domain clinical text (e.g. electronic health records) (Si et al., 2019; Peng et al., 2019; Alsentzer et al., 2019; Huang et al., 2020) for downstream clinical NLP tasks. As summarised in (Gu et al., 2020) many such tasks can be formulated as a classification or regression task, wherein either a simple linear layer or sequential models such as LSTM or conditional random field (CRF) are added after the BERT encoding of the input text as task-specific prediction layer.

BERT's model architecture is based on the Transformer model (Vaswani et al., 2017), which employs the self-attention mechanism to attend to different positions of the input sequence. As it doesn't contain any recurrence or convolution, the model has to add positional encoding in order to model the order of the sequence (e.g. word order). Signature transform, initially introduced in rough path theory as a branch of stochastic analysis, is a non-parametric approach of encoding sequential data while capturing the order information in the data. It has shown successes in the recent years in a range of machine learning tasks involving sequential modelling (Arribas et al., 2018; Morrill et al., 2020; Toth and Oberhauser, 2020; Wang et al., 2020). We hypothesise the signature transform method can be integrated in the Transformer

41


*Proceedings of the 3rd Clinical Natural Language Processing Workshop*, pages 41–54
November 19, 2020. ©2020 Association for Computational Linguistics

model, in which its ability to naturally capture sequential ordering complements the ability of attending to important positions and learning long-range dependencies in self-attention.

As a preliminary study, our aim is to develop a machine learning-based system that extracts relevant information from the Swedish medical prescription notes[1], namely *quantity*, *quantity tag* and *indication*. The contributions of this work are as follows:

1. We experiment two different approaches of embedding the Swedish prescription notes. One encodes the Swedish text directly using Multilingual BERT (M-BERT) (Devlin et al., 2018) while for the other approach we translate the prescriptions and then apply Clinical-BERT (Huang et al., 2020) that is pretrained on clinical text in English.

2. We propose an extension to the Transformer model, named Sig-Transformer Encoder (STE), which integrates signature transform into the Transformer architecture so the order information in the prescription notes can be learnt in a more effective way. To the best of our knowledge, this is the first attempt to integrate signature transform in the Transformer architecture.

3. We demonstrate good performance in two of the three tasks, namely *quantity* and *quantity tag*. As for the *indication* task, we provide an analysis on why the models fail.

4. We show one of our proposed STE-based approaches, namely M-BERT+STE, outperforming other baseline models.

## 2 Background

Clinical language representation has attracted an increasing interest in the natural language processing (NLP) community (Kalyan and Sangeetha, 2020). More recently with the advent of Bidirectional Encoder Representations from Transformers (BERT) (Devlin et al., 2018), fine-tuning of general-domain language models has been widely adopted for many clinical NLP tasks[2]. Among them two clinicalBERT studies (Alsentzer et al., 2019; Huang

et al., 2020) have conducted fine-tuning from either BERT or BioBERT (Lee et al., 2020) using de-identified clinical notes from MIMIC-III (Johnson et al., 2016). In particular, Huang et al. (2020) showed the effectiveness of its ClinicalBERT-based model for predicting hospital readmissions.

Many NLP applications in the medical domain can be formulated as either token classification, sequence classification or sequence regression, in which a pretrained language model such as clinicalBERT can be used to encode the input token sequence (which returns either the encoding for every input token or just the [CLS] token) and then a task-specific prediction model is added on top to generate the final output (Gu et al., 2020). In this section, we describe the Transformer encoder and the signature transform, which are the bases of our proposed architecture.

### 2.1 Transformer Encoder

The Transformer model employs an encoder-decoder structure (Vaswani et al., 2017). Its encoder, which is the model architecture of BERT, is composed of a stack of $N$ identical layers. Each layer has a multi-head self-attention mechanism followed by a position-wise fully connected feed-forward network. The attention function used in the Transformer model takes three input vectors: query ($Q$), key ($K$) and value ($V$). It generates an output vector by computing the weighted sum of the values. The weights are computed by the dot products of the query and all keys, scaled and applied a softmax function.

$$\text{Attention}(Q, K, V) = \text{softmax}(\frac{QK^T}{\sqrt{d_k}})V \quad (1)$$

Multi-head attention splits $Q$, $K$ and $V$ into multiple heads by linearly projection, which allows the model to jointly attend to information at different positions from different representation subspaces. Each projected head goes through the scaled dot-product attention function, then concatenated and projected again to output the final values. The Transformer encoder does not explicitly model position information in its structure, and instead it requires adding representations of absolute positions (i.e. positional encoding) to its inputs. Shaw et al. (2018) presented an extension to self-attention, which incorporates relative position information

---

[1]Our ultimate goal is to apply such model to a much larger database. However, this is beyond the scope of this paper.

[2]Gu et al. (2020) have challenged this strategy and reported better performance for PubMed-based biomedical tasks by conducting domain-specific pretraining from scratch. However, it did not address the clinical domain and has left it for future work.

for the input data. In this work, we propose to integrate signature transform with self-attention given that path signatures have been proven to be an effective way of capturing the sequential order information in the data.

## 2.2 Signature Transform

The theory of rough paths, developed by Lyons (1998), can be thought of as a non-linear extension of the classical theory of controlled differential equations. *Path signature* or simply *signature*, is an infinite collection of statistics characterising the underlying path (a discretised version of a continuous path), and *signature transform* is the map from a path to its signature[3]. Consider a $d$-dimensional time-dependent path $P$ over the time interval $[0, T] \subset \mathbb{R}$, to a continuous map $P : [0, T] \to \mathbb{R}^d$. The signature $S(P)$ of this path $P$ over time interval $[0, T]$ is the infinite collection of all iterated integrals of $P$ such that every continuous function of the path may be approximated arbitrarily well by a linear function of its signature:

$$S(P)_{0,T} = (1, S(P)^1_{0,T}, \ldots, S(P)^d_{0,T}, S(P)^{1,1}_{0,T}, \ldots)$$

where the $0^{th}$ term is 1 by convention, and the superscripts of the terms after the $0^{th}$ term run along the set of all multi-index $\{(i_1, \ldots, i_k)|k \geq 1, i_1, \ldots, i_k \in [d]\}$ with the co-ordinate iterated integral being:

$$S(P)^{i_1,\ldots,i_k}_{0,T} = \int \cdots \int_{\substack{t_1 < \cdots < t_k \\ t_1,\ldots,t_k \in [0,T]}} dP^{i_1}_{t_1} \otimes \cdots \otimes dP^{i_k}_{t_k}$$

where $\forall k \geq 1$, $P_t \in R^d$, $\forall t \in [0, T]$. $S(P)^{i_1,\ldots,i_k}_{0,T}$ is termed as the $k$th level of the signature. In practice we truncate the signature to order $n$, where the degree of its iterated integrals is no greater than $n$. This ensures the path signature has finite dimensional representation. Let $TS(P)^n_{0,T}$ denote the truncated signature of $P$ of order $n$, i.e.

$$TS(P)^n_{0,T} = (1, S(P)^1_{0,T}, \ldots, S(P)^{k_n}_{0,T})$$

Therefore the dimensionality of the truncated path signature is $(d^{n+1} - d)(d - 1)^{-1}$. We describe signature transform in more (mathematical) details in Appendix A.2.

---

<sup></sup>[3]We refer the reader to (Lyons, 2014) for a rigorous introduction of signature transform, and (Chevyrev and Kormilitzin, 2016) for a primer on its use in machine learning.

In recent years using path signatures as features in a suitable neural network model has shown success in various applications, such as online handwritten Chinese character recognition (Yang et al., 2016; Xie et al., 2018), action recognition in videos (Yang et al., 2017) and speech emotion recognition (Wang et al., 2019). More recently, Kidger et al. (2019) proposed to use signature transform deeper within a network, rather than as a feature transformation. Kidger and Lyons (2020) developed differentiable computation of signature transform on both CPU and GPU. To the best of our knowledge, we are the first to incorporate signature transform in the Transformer architecture.

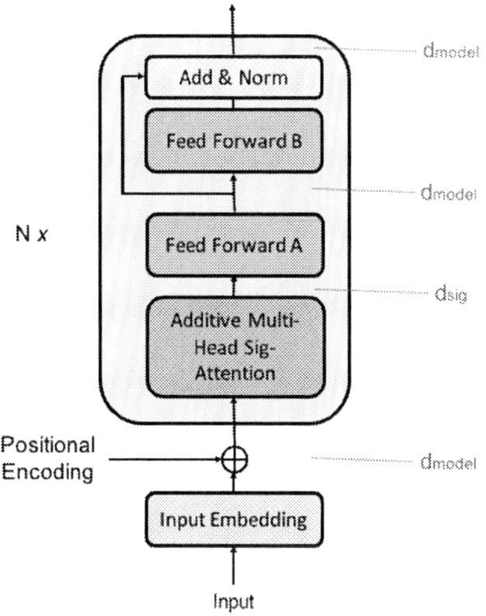



Figure 1: The Sig-Transformer Encoder. $d_{sig}$ is the dimension size in the truncated signature, and $d_{model}$ is the dimension size in the embedding layer as well as before and after the second feed-forward sub-layer.

## 3 Sig-Transformer Encoder

In this section, we present our proposed extension to the Transformer Encoder (TE), named Sig-Transformer Encoder (STE). As depicted in Figure 1, STE consists of a stack of $N$ identical layers, and each layer has three sub-layers. It replaces the multi-head self-attention sub-layer in TE with our Additive Multi-Head Sig-Attention mechanism, followed by two position-wise fully connected feed-forward sub-layers. Same as the Transformer model, we also employ a residual connection (He et al., 2016) at the last sub-layer, followed by layer normalisation (Ba et al., 2016). The two feed-forward sub-layers and the embed-

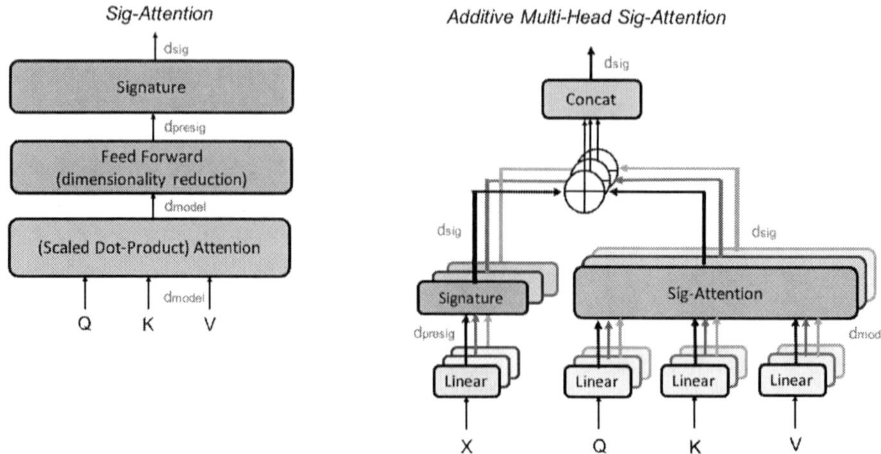


Figure 2: (left) Sig-Attention mechanism; (right) Additive Multi-Head Sig-Attention.

ding layers, produce output of the same dimension $d_{model} = 768$.

### 3.1 Sig-Attention

The core idea behind our proposed Additive Multi-Head Sig-Attention is the Sig-Attention mechanism (Figure 2 left). It takes the query ($Q$), key ($K$) and value ($V$) vectors as input, and performs three consecutive transformations: (1), scaled dot-product attention; (2), position-wise fully linear map, for dimensionality reduction; (3), signature transform. Its output is computed as follows:

$$\text{SigAttention}(Q, K, V) =$$
$$\text{ReducedSig}(\text{Attention}(Q, K, V))$$

where

- $\text{Attention}(Q, K, V)$ is as defined in Equation (1);

- $\text{ReducedSig}(x) = S^N(xW + b)$ for any $x$;

- $S^N$ is the signature truncated at a given order $N$;

- $W$ and $b$ are respectively the weight and bias matrices of the linear map.

As the size of the truncated signature increases exponentially with its input dimension, it is important to reduce the size of attended context vector before applying signature transform. We refer the readers to Table 5 for examples of how the size of the truncated signature ($d_{sig}$) is determined by its input dimension ($d_{presig}$) and the order of signature truncation ($order_{sig}$).

### 3.2 Additive Multi-Head Sig-Attention

In the proposed Additive Multi-Head Sig-Attention model, we combine the information from the input sequence with the output of Sig-Attention, in different representation subspaces (Figure 2 right). The model takes the embedding of an input sequence $X$ as well as the queries, keys and values as input:

$$\text{AdditiveMultiHead}(X, Q, K, V) =$$
$$\text{Concat}(\text{head}_1, ..., \text{head}_h)$$
$$\text{where head}_i = \text{ReducedSig}(X) +$$
$$\text{SigAttention}(QW_i^Q, KW_i^K, VW_i^V)$$

and $h$ is the number of parallel heads, the projections are parameter matrices $W_i^Q \in \mathbb{R}^{d_{model} \times d_k}$, $W_i^K \in \mathbb{R}^{d_{model} \times d_k}$, $W_i^V \in \mathbb{R}^{d_{model} \times d_k}$ and $d_k = d_{model}/h$.

As shown in Figure 2 (right), we linearly project the queries, keys and values as well as the input embeddings to $d_{model}$ and $d_{presig}$ dimensions. Then the query, key and value vectors will be fed into the Sig-Attention mechanism, while having been reduced its dimensions by the linear projection the input vector $X$ will be applied to signature transform. The two output signatures are added, resulting in one signature vector $s_i \in \mathbb{R}^{d_{sig}}$ for each head $i$. Finally all the signature vectors are concatenated and passed onto the next sub-layer.

### 3.3 Position-wise Feed-Forward Networks

The second sub-layer in Figure 1 is a linear transformation $W \in \mathbb{R}^{d_{sig} \times d_{model}}$ which is applied to each position separately and identically. It simply brings back the dimensions from $d_{sig}$ to $d_{model}$. The third sub-layer is a ReLU activation followed by another linear transformation. The dimensionality of its input and output is $d_{model}$.

## 3.4 Dropout

Dropout is applied to the output of the three sub-layers as well as after the ReLU activation in the third sub-layer. We use a rate of $P_{drop} = 0.1$, as is used in (Vaswani et al., 2017). Moreover, residual connection and layer normalisation are used only in the third sub-layer.

## 4 Data

Our proposed Sig-Transformer Encoder can be used for general purpose representation learning, and any classifier or regressor can be added on top of it to perform down-stream tasks. We conduct all of our experiments with a medical prescription data for the class of "beta-blockers (ATC code C07)", provided by the Karolinska University Hospital. It is sampled from a much larger database of 41 million medical prescription records. This dataset contains 3,852 non-duplicated prescriptions written in Swedish. Some examples of annotated prescriptions are shown in Table 1.

The medical practitioners at the hospital have annotated three labels, in which we use QUANTITY for regression while QUANTITY TAG and INDICATION as two classification tasks:

- QUANTITY: the total amount of tablets or capsules prescribed. The values are multiples of 0.5;
- QUANTITY TAG (5 classes): the label or tag of the quantity prescribed to the patient;
    1. *Not Specified*: the quantity was not specified in the prescription;
    2. *Complex* : a range of quantities was given. In that case, the quantity is an average between the minimum and the maximum quantities;
    3. *PRN* : prescription to take only if needed;
    4. *As Per Previous Prescription*: refers to guidance in previous prescription;
    5. *Standard*: standard prescription;
- INDICATION (5 classes): the purpose of the prescription. It originally had 44 classes where many account for only one record[4]. The

---

[4]The original 44 classes and the number of prescriptions per class, can be found in Figure 5.

medical practitioners have aggregated them into 5 medically meaningful classes: *Cardiac*, *Tremors*, *Migraine*, *Others*, and *NA* (Not Annotated).

One challenge of the data is the remarkable class imbalance in its labels, as shown in Table 2. It's still prominent in the INDICATION field after aggregating the original classes, where *Cardiac* and *NA* account for majority of the instances, while the other 3 classes are seldom annotated in the data. Another challenge, which is prevalent in electronic health record (EHR) datasets, is the free-form nature of its text and the writing styles vary considerably between different doctors.

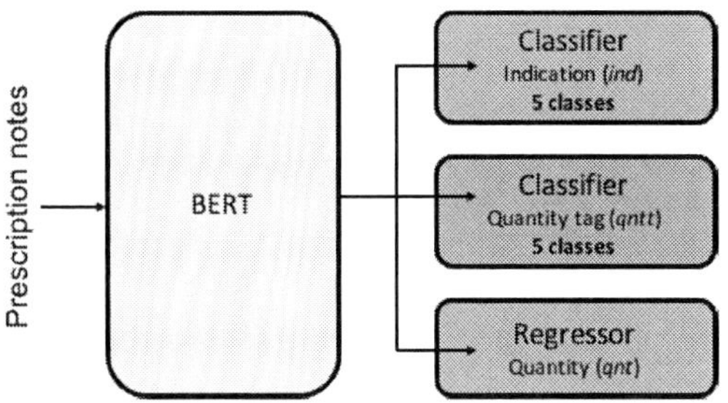


Figure 3: Multi-task learning architecture without Sig-Transformer Encoder (STE).

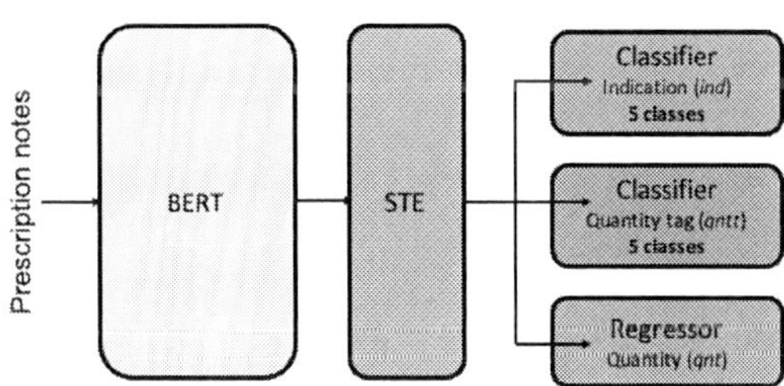


Figure 4: Our proposed multi-task learning architecture with Sig-Transformer Encoder (STE).

## 4.1 Data Preprocessing

As mentioned in Section 1 we experiment two different embedding models for the Swedish prescription records, in which one of them, namely Clinical-BERT (Huang et al., 2020), requires its input text to be English. We use the Google Translate API to obtain translated English prescriptions. Minimal text preprocessing was taken, and all prescription text including non-ASCII characters (e.g. å, ä, ö) was read with UTF-8 encoding.

| Swedish | Translated English | Indication | Quantity | Quantity Tag |
|---|---|---|---|---|
| 1 TABLETT FOREBYGGANDE MOT MIGRAN | 1 tablet prevention against migrain | Migraine | 1 | Standard |
| MOT HOGT BLODTRYCK OCHHJARTKLAPPNING 2 TABLETTER KLOCKGAN 08:00 1 TABLETT KLOCKAN 18:00. | Against high blood pressure and heart palpitations 2 tablets at 08:00, 1 tablet at 18:00. | Cardiac-hypertension | 3 | Standard |
| 2 TABLETTER KL. 08, 2 TABLETT KL. 20. DAGLIGEN. OBS KVALLSDOSEN HAR HOJTS JFRT MED 070427. | 2 tablets kl. 08, 2 tablet kl. 20. Daily. Note the evening box has hojts jfrt with 070427. | NA | 4 | Standard |
| 1 tablett vid behov mot stress | 1 tablet if needed against stress | Anxiety | 1 | PRN |
| FOR BLODTRYCK OCH HJARTRYTM - | For blood pressure and heart rhythm - | Cardiac-hypertension-dysrhythmia | 0 | Not Specified |
| 1 tabl pA morgonen och en halv tabl pA kvAllen fOr hjArtrytmen. | 1 table in the morning and a half table in the evening for the heart rhythem. | Cardiac-dysrhythmia | 1.5 | Standard |
| 1-2 tablett 2 gAnger dagligen | 1-2 tablets 2 times daily | NA | 3 | Complex |

Table 1: Example prescriptions with translations and annotations. The second column is the English translation obtained from Google Translate API. The last three columns are the labels of interest which we aim to extract automatically. Some longer example prescriptions can be viewed in Table 8.

| QUANTITY TAG | | | INDICATION | | |
|---|---|---|---|---|---|
| Standard | 3489 | 90.6% | Cardiac | 2980 | 77.4% |
| PRN | 89 | 2.3% | Tremors | 81 | 2.1% |
| APPP | 40 | 1.0% | Migraine | 69 | 1.8% |
| Complex | 29 | 0.8% | Other | 15 | 0.4% |
| NS | 205 | 5.3% | NA | 707 | 18.4% |

Table 2: Class distribution for QUANTITY TAG and INDICATION. APPP is an abbreviation for *As Per Previous Prescription*, NS stands for *Not Specified* and NA stands for *Not Annotated*.

## 5 Multi-Task Learning

Our objective is to automatically find the QUANTITY of prescribed medicine as well as QUANTITY TAG and INDICATION of the prescription, for each prescription note. We formulate this as a multi-task learning problem consisting of a regression task and two classification tasks. As depicted in Figure 3, such multi-task learning model uses BERT or any of its variants to encode each input prescription note represented by the respective [CLS] token, then we can add three separate predictors on top of it and all three jointly learn with the embedding layer. We use this architecture as one of our baseline approaches.

In our proposed multi-task learning architecture, we add Sig-Transformer Encoder (STE) in-between the embedding layer (BERT) and the three predictors in order to learn the sequential order informa-tion in the input text encoded by the token-level BERT representations (instead from [CLS]). The three predictors and STE are jointly trained. We compare the two architectures and other baseline models in Section 6.

## 6 Experiments

### 6.1 Experiment Setup

As described in Section 2, BERT and its variants have been used in a range of clinical machine learning tasks. Considering our data is in Swedish we explore two different approaches for encoding the prescription notes: (1), Apply Multilingual BERT (M-BERT) (Devlin et al., 2018) directly to the Swedish text; (2), Translate the prescriptions to English as described in Section 4.1, and then encode the translated text with ClinicalBERT (Huang et al., 2020). ClinicalBERT is fine-tuned on clinical notes, therefore it has embedded more domain knowledge and has proven to be more effective over BERT-base on several clinical tasks. However, any translation error would affect the performance of subsequent models.

We use the PyTorch implementation of Transformers by Hugging Face[5] for loading M-BERT and ClinicalBERT, and *Signatory*[6] (Kidger and Lyons, 2020) for differentiable computations of

---

[5]https://github.com/huggingface/transformers
[6]https://github.com/patrick-kidger/signatory

signatures on GPU. We use a linear layer as the classifier for QUANTITY TAG, and two-layer network for QUANTITY and INDICATION respectively. More details of the implementation choices are described in Appendix A.1. We use cross-entropy (CE) loss for the two classification tasks and mean-square error (MSE) for the regression task. The overall loss function is a weighted average of the loss functions of all three tasks:

$$\mathcal{L} =$$
$$\alpha_{qnt} \times MSE_{qnt} + \beta_{qntt} \times CE_{qntt} + \beta_{ind} \times CE_{ind}$$

where *qnt* stands for quantity, *qntt* stands for quantity tag, *ind* stands for indication, and $\alpha_{qnt} + \beta_{qntt} + \beta_{ind} = 1$. $\alpha_{qnt}$, $\beta_{qntt}$ and $\beta_{ind}$ are parameters to be optimised.

To compare model performance we use the simple multi-task learning models described in Section 5 without adding STE (Figure 3), as the baseline systems. We also replace STE with LSTM for comparison as both learn sequential information from the input data[7]. All experiments are conducted using 5-fold cross validation, where we use 3 folds for training, 1 fold for validation and 1 fold as the test set at each iteration. We repeat the experiments for each model with 10 different random seeds and average the scores as the final result.

## 6.2 Results

The results for all three tasks are summarised in Table 3. We first notice all models have failed to recognise the INDICATION classes, which we will discuss in Section 6.3. In this section we mainly discuss the performance for QUANTITY and QUANTITY TAG.

Among the three models without the use of LSTM or STE, both ClinicalBERT and Multilingual BERT (M-BERT) outperform the BERT-base model in all three tasks. As for the three LSTM-based models, using the BERT-base representations achieves the best performance while ClinicalBERT and M-BERT are comparable with each other. Among our proposed STE-based models, M-BERT+STE outperforms the other two variants.

Comparing the results across the board, adding LSTM or STE improves the model performance in most cases except for ClinicalBERT, where the

addition of LSTM or STE has worsened the performance for ClinicalBERT. We think the potential discrepancies in the translation of the Swedish prescriptions have possibly affected the working of LSTM and STE, as both models take all the translated token embeddings of each prescription as input where the simple ClinicalBERT baseline only takes the encoding of the [CLS] token as input. Comparing between the two different prescription embedding approaches, translating them then apply ClinicalBERT clearly beats using the multilingual-BERT when LSTM or STE is not added. When we incorporate LSTM or STE in the model, the multilingual embedding approach has obtained better results in most cases. Overall, one of our proposed models, M-BERT+STE, achieves the best performance for the QUANTITY and QUANTITY TAG tasks[8].

In Table 6 we present results obtained by each model across different classes of QUANTITY TAG. We can see the *Standard* class (i.e. standard prescription) followed by *PRN* (i.e. prescription to take only if needed) and *APPP* (i.e. as per previous prescription) have received better classifications by the three STE models. The models also performed well in the *Not Specified* class. The *Complex* class refers to a range of quantities given in the prescription. As expected, many models do not perform well in this class. The overall best performing model, M-BERT+STE, also performs consistently well across different classes of QUANTITY TAG.

## 6.3 The difficult case of Indication

The class imbalance is remarkable for QUANTITY TAG and INDICATION in this dataset, as described in Section 4. The strong results obtained from many models for QUANTITY TAG suggests albeit the class imbalance the boundaries between its classes are distinguishable and can be learnt from fewer examples. INDICATION is a more challenging task. The aggregation of the original 44 classes to the final 5 classes has reduced the severity of the class imbalance issue[9]. However, the new classification becomes much less distinguishable and the new classes are less distinct as each class now contains

---

[7]Unlike the Transformer model, recurrent neural networks (RNNs) such as LSTM, model relative and absolute positions along the time dimension directly through their sequential structure (Shaw et al., 2018).

[8]The results obtained by M-BERT+STE and ClinicalBERT are different at the significance level of 0.1, with p = 0.068 and 0.065 for QUANTITY and QUANTITY TAG respectively, using Wilcoxon signed-rank test.

[9]We have experimented with the original 44 classes, and obtained terrible results. We have also tried setting class weights to alleviate the class imbalance issue with no significant difference observed in the final results.

| Model | QUANTITY | QUANTITY TAG | INDICATION |
|---|---|---|---|
| Base | 0.50 | 0.60 | 0.08 |
| ClinicalBERT | 0.21 | 0.89 | 0.09 |
| M-BERT | 0.41 | 0.63 | **0.10** |
| Base + LSTM | 0.45 | 0.76 | 0.06 |
| ClinicalBERT + LSTM | 0.47 | 0.64 | **0.10** |
| M-BERT + LSTM | 0.50 | 0.68 | 0.02 |
| Base + STE | 0.23 | 0.78 | 0.03 |
| ClinicalBERT + STE | 0.36 | 0.77 | 0.06 |
| M-BERT + STE | **0.15** | **0.92** | 0.05 |

Table 3: Performance comparison between our proposed STE-based approaches and baseline models. The QUANTITY task is measured in mean squared error (MSE), while for QUANTITY TAG and INDICATION we use Macro F-1 score. Base refers the original BERT-base model, M-BERT is the Multilingual BERT model pretrained on Swedish text data. STE refers to Sig-Transformer Encoder.

a range of topics, as shown in Figure 5. Such low scores are also observed across different classes of INDICATION in Table 7.

### 6.4 Ablation Study

The positional encoding proposed in (Vaswani et al., 2017) is based on sinusoids of varying frequency, and the authors hypothesise this would help the model to generalise to sequences of variable lengths during training. Our proposed architecture has both the absolute positional representations of words and the signature transform that is also invariant to the sequence length for encoding order of events. Here we conduct ablation study by removing the positional encoding or the signature transform components from the best performing model, M-BERT+STE, and compare the results. As shown in Table 4, we obtain worse performance without positional encoding or without signature transform, for all three tasks, suggesting the contributions of using the absolute positional encoding and the proposed integration of signature transform.

| Model | Quantity | Quantity Tag | Indication |
|---|---|---|---|
| Full model | 0.15 | 0.92 | 0.05 |
| w/o PE | 0.38 | 0.81 | 0.01 |
| w/o ST | 0.31 | 0.77 | 0.02 |

Table 4: Ablation study of the best performing M-BERT + STE model, removing positional encoding (PE) or signature transform (ST).

## 7 Conclusions and Future Work

In this work, we propose a new extension to the Transformer architecture, named Sig-Transformer Encoder (STE), by incorporating signature transform with the self-attention mechanism. As a preliminary study, we aimed to automatically extract information related to *quantity*, *quantity tag* and the *indication* label from a Swedish medical prescription dataset. We demonstrated good performance in two of the three tasks in a multi-task learning framework. Lastly, we compared two embedding approaches between applying Clinical-BERT (on translated text) and Multilingual BERT (M-BERT). Although one of our proposed models, namely M-BERT+STE, reported the best performance for *quantity* and *quantity tag*, all models failed to perform on the *indication* task which we provided possible explanations.

For future work, we plan to apply the proposed STE models to the much larger prescription database and investigate ways to improve the labelling for *indication*. We also plan to benchmark our models on other clinical tasks such as predicting hospital readmission (Huang et al., 2020), as well as the more general NLP tasks evaluated in (Devlin et al., 2018). Moreover, a further investigation to better understand the contribution of signature transform and the interplay between signature and attentions would be very insightful.

## Acknowledgments

This work was supported by the MRC Mental Health Data Pathfinder award to the University of Oxford [MC_PC_17215], by the NIHR Oxford Health Biomedical Research Centre and by the The Alan Turing Institute under the EPSRC grant EP/N510129/1. We would like to thank Dr. Remus-Giulio Anghel and Dr. Yasmina Molero Plaza for providing the data and sharing information about the data.

## References

Emily Alsentzer, John Murphy, William Boag, Wei-Hung Weng, Di Jindi, Tristan Naumann, and Matthew McDermott. 2019. Publicly available clinical bert embeddings. In *Proceedings of the 2nd Clinical Natural Language Processing Workshop*, pages 72–78.

Imanol Perez Arribas, Guy M Goodwin, John R Geddes, Terry Lyons, and Kate EA Saunders. 2018. A signature-based machine learning model for distinguishing bipolar disorder and borderline personality disorder. *Translational psychiatry*, 8(1):1–7.

Jimmy Lei Ba, Jamie Ryan Kiros, and Geoffrey E Hinton. 2016. Layer normalization. *arXiv preprint arXiv:1607.06450*.

Juan M Banda, Martin Seneviratne, Tina Hernandez-Boussard, and Nigam H Shah. 2018. Advances in electronic phenotyping: from rule-based definitions to machine learning models. *Annual review of biomedical data science*, 1:53–68.

Ilya Chevyrev and Andrey Kormilitzin. 2016. A primer on the signature method in machine learning. *arXiv preprint arXiv:1603.03788*.

Thomas Davenport and Ravi Kalakota. 2019. The potential for artificial intelligence in healthcare. *Future healthcare journal*, 6(2):94.

Jacob Devlin, Ming-Wei Chang, Kenton Lee, and Kristina Toutanova. 2018. Bert: Pre-training of deep bidirectional transformers for language understanding. *arXiv preprint arXiv:1810.04805*.

Yu Gu, Robert Tinn, Hao Cheng, Michael Lucas, Naoto Usuyama, Xiaodong Liu, Tristan Naumann, Jianfeng Gao, and Hoifung Poon. 2020. Domain-specific language model pretraining for biomedical natural language processing. *arXiv preprint arXiv:2007.15779*.

Kaiming He, Xiangyu Zhang, Shaoqing Ren, and Jian Sun. 2016. Deep residual learning for image recognition. In *Proceedings of the IEEE conference on computer vision and pattern recognition*, pages 770–778.

Kexin Huang, Jaan Altosaar, and Rajesh Ranganath. 2020. Clinicalbert: Modeling clinical notes and predicting hospital readmission. In *Proc. ACM Conference on Health, Inference, and Learning (CHIL)*.

Alistair EW Johnson, Tom J Pollard, Lu Shen, H Lehman Li-Wei, Mengling Feng, Mohammad Ghassemi, Benjamin Moody, Peter Szolovits, Leo Anthony Celi, and Roger G Mark. 2016. Mimic-iii, a freely accessible critical care database. *Scientific data*, 3(1):1–9.

Katikapalli Subramanyam Kalyan and S Sangeetha. 2020. Secnlp: A survey of embeddings in clinical natural language processing. *Journal of biomedical informatics*, 101:103323.

Patrick Kidger, Patric Bonnier, Imanol Perez Arribas, Cristopher Salvi, and Terry Lyons. 2019. Deep signature transforms. In *Advances in Neural Information Processing Systems*, pages 3105–3115.

Patrick Kidger and Terry Lyons. 2020. Signatory: differentiable computations of the signature and logsignature transforms, on both CPU and GPU. *arXiv:2001.00706*.

Jinhyuk Lee, Wonjin Yoon, Sungdong Kim, Donghyeon Kim, Sunkyu Kim, Chan Ho So, and Jaewoo Kang. 2020. Biobert: a pre-trained biomedical language representation model for biomedical text mining. *Bioinformatics*, 36(4):1234–1240.

Terry Lyons. 2014. Rough paths, signatures and the modelling of functions on streams. In *Proceedings of the International Congress of Mathematicians*, pages 163–184.

Terry J Lyons. 1998. Differential equations driven by rough signals. *Revista Matemática Iberoamericana*, 14(2):215–310.

James H Morrill, Andrey Kormilitzin, Alejo J Nevado-Holgado, Sumanth Swaminathan, Samuel D Howison, and Terry J Lyons. 2020. Utilization of the signature method to identify the early onset of sepsis from multivariate physiological time series in critical care monitoring. *Critical Care Medicine*, 48(10):e976–e981.

Yifan Peng, Shankai Yan, and Zhiyong Lu. 2019. Transfer learning in biomedical natural language processing: An evaluation of bert and elmo on ten benchmarking datasets. In *Proceedings of the 18th BioNLP Workshop and Shared Task*, pages 58–65.

Matthew E Peters, Mark Neumann, Mohit Iyyer, Matt Gardner, Christopher Clark, Kenton Lee, and Luke Zettlemoyer. 2018. Deep contextualized word representations. In *Proceedings of NAACL-HLT*, pages 2227–2237.

Peter Shaw, Jakob Uszkoreit, and Ashish Vaswani. 2018. Self-attention with relative position representations. In *Proceedings of the 2018 Conference of the North American Chapter of the Association for Computational Linguistics: Human Language Technologies, Volume 2 (Short Papers)*, pages 464–468.

Yuqi Si, Jingqi Wang, Hua Xu, and Kirk Roberts. 2019. Enhancing clinical concept extraction with contextual embeddings. *Journal of the American Medical Informatics Association*, 26(11):1297–1304.

Csaba Toth and Harald Oberhauser. 2020. Bayesian learning from sequential data using gaussian processes with signature covariances. In *Proceedings of the International Conference on Machine Learning (ICML)*.

Ashish Vaswani, Noam Shazeer, Niki Parmar, Jakob Uszkoreit, Llion Jones, Aidan N Gomez, Łukasz Kaiser, and Illia Polosukhin. 2017. Attention is all you need. In *Advances in neural information processing systems*, pages 5998–6008.

Bo Wang, Maria Liakata, Hao Ni, Terry Lyons, Alejo J Nevado-Holgado, and Kate Saunders. 2019. A path signature approach for speech emotion recognition. In *Interspeech 2019*, pages 1661–1665. ISCA.

Bo Wang, Yue Wu, Niall Taylor, Terry Lyons, Maria Liakata, Alejo J Nevado-Holgado, and Kate EA Saunders. 2020. Learning to detect bipolar disorder and borderline personality disorder with language and speech in non-clinical interviews. In *Interspeech 2020*. ISCA.

Yanshan Wang, Liwei Wang, Majid Rastegar-Mojarad, Sungrim Moon, Feichen Shen, Naveed Afzal, Sijia Liu, Yuqun Zeng, Saeed Mehrabi, Sunghwan Sohn, et al. 2018. Clinical information extraction applications: a literature review. *Journal of biomedical informatics*, 77:34–49.

Zecheng Xie, Zenghui Sun, Lianwen Jin, Hao Ni, and Terry Lyons. 2018. Learning spatial-semantic context with fully convolutional recurrent network for online handwritten chinese text recognition. *IEEE transactions on pattern analysis and machine intelligence*, 40(8):1903–1917.

Weixin Yang, Lianwen Jin, and Manfei Liu. 2016. Deepwriterid: An end-to-end online text-independent writer identification system. *IEEE Intelligent Systems*, 31(2):45–53.

Weixin Yang, Terry Lyons, Hao Ni, Cordelia Schmid, Lianwen Jin, and Jiawei Chang. 2017. Leveraging the path signature for skeleton-based human action recognition. *arXiv preprint arXiv:1707.03993*.

## A  Appendices

### A.1  Implementation Details

Our classifier for INDICATION is a two-layer network, in which the first layer has the size of 50 and 5 for the second layer. ReLU activation and dropout are used in-between the two layers. The dropout rate is set to be 0.1. We also use a two-layer network for the QUANTITY regression task, in which the first layer has the size of 10 and its second layer predicts the value for *quantity*. We also add a dropout the rate 0.1 in-between the two layers. Our classifier for QUANTITY TAG has only one layer the size of 5.

We reduce the dimension of attended vector before signature transform from 768 to 32, as depicted in Figure 2 (left). We set the order of truncated signature to be 2, and employ 8 parallel attention layers (or heads). We ran grid-search over two choices of learning rate $lr : [0.00003, 0.00005]$, and 10 randomly sampled triplets of $\alpha_{qnt}$, $\beta_{qntt}$ and $\beta_{ind}$. Each value of $\alpha_{qnt}$, $\beta_{qntt}$ and $\beta_{ind}$ is between 0 and 1 respectively, while we make sure each combination of the three values sums to 1.

### A.2  Signature of paths

We begin with the definition of the signature, using more traditional notation of stochastic calculus.

**Definition 1.** *Let $X = (X^1, ..., X^d)$ be a path in $\mathbb{R}^d$. The signature of $X$ is defined as the infinite collection of iterated integrals:*

$$S(X) = \left( \int ... \int_{a<t_1<...<t_k<b} dX_{t_1} \otimes ... \otimes dX_{t_k} \right)_{k \geq 0}$$

$$= \left( \left( \int ... \int_{a<t_1<...<t_k<b} dX_{t_1}^{i_1}...dX_{t_k}^{i_k} \right)_{1 \leq i_1,...,i_k \leq d} \right)_{k \geq 0}$$

*where $dX_t = \frac{dX_t}{dt}dt$ and the $k = 0$ term is taken to be $1 \in \mathbb{R}$.*

**Definition 2.** *The truncated signature of order $N$ of $X$ is defined as:*

$$S^N(X) = \left( \int ... \int_{a<t_1<...<t_k<b} dX_{t_1} \otimes ... \otimes dX_{t_k} \right)_{0 \leq k \leq N}.$$

The dimension of the truncated signature explodes exponentially with the input path dimension:

**Proposition 1.** *For any $d \geq 1$, the truncated signature of order $N$ of a d-dimensional path has the dimension of:*

$$\sum_{k=0}^{N} d^k = \frac{d^{N+1} - 1}{d - 1}$$

In practice, the term of order 0 is dropped as it is always equal to 1. For clarity, we define:

$$S(X)^{i_1,...,i_k} = \int ... \int_{a<t_1<...<t_k<b} dX_{t_1}^{i_1}...dX_{t_k}^{i_k}$$

with $1 \leq i_1, ..., i_k \leq d$, so that:

$$S(X) = \left( \left( S(X)^{i_1,...,i_k} \right)_{1 \leq i_1,...,i_k \leq d} \right)_{k \geq 0}$$
$$= (1, S(X)^1, ..., S(X)^d, S(X)^{1,1}, S(X)^{1,2}, ...).$$

| $d_{presig}$ | order$_{sig}$ | $d_{sig}$ | $d_{presig}$ | order$_{sig}$ | $d_{sig}$ |
| --- | --- | --- | --- | --- | --- |
| 512 | 1 | 512 | 16 | 3 | 4K |
| 512 | 2 | 262K | 8 | 2 | 72 |
| 256 | 2 | 66K | 8 | 3 | 584 |
| 128 | 2 | 16K | 8 | 4 | 5K |
| 128 | 3 | 2M | 4 | 4 | 340 |
| 64 | 2 | 4K | 4 | 5 | 1365 |
| 64 | 3 | 266K | 4 | 6 | 5K |
| 32 | 2 | 1057 | 2 | 9 | 1022 |
| 32 | 3 | 34K | 2 | 10 | 2K |
| 16 | 2 | 272 | 2 | 12 | 8K |

Table 5: The number of dimensions ($d_{sig}$) of the truncated signature is determined by the size of its input ($d_{presig}$) and the order of truncation selected (order$_{sig}$).

| Model | QUANTITY TAG | | | | | QUANTITY |
| --- | --- | --- | --- | --- | --- | --- |
| | Standard | APPP | PRN | Complex | NS | |
| Base | 0.71 | 0.50 | 0.10 | 0.76 | 0.95 | 0.50 |
| ClinicalBERT | 0.83 | 0.97 | 0.89 | 0.99 | 0.79 | 0.21 |
| M-BERT | 0.94 | 0.41 | 0.04 | 0.81 | 0.98 | 0.41 |
| Base + LSTM | 0.93 | 0.36 | 0.99 | 0.77 | 0.74 | 0.45 |
| ClinicalBERT + LSTM | 0.90 | 0.23 | 0.99 | 0.61 | 0.49 | 0.47 |
| M-BERT + LSTM | 0.29 | 0.99 | 0.72 | 0.47 | 0.93 | 0.50 |
| Base + STE | 0.97 | 0.84 | 0.77 | 0.44 | 0.88 | 0.23 |
| ClinicalBERT + STE | 0.99 | 0.70 | 0.85 | 0.65 | 0.65 | 0.36 |
| M-BERT + STE | 0.86 | 0.97 | 1.00 | 0.89 | 0.86 | 0.15 |

Table 6: Model performance comparison for QUANTITY and also across different classes in QUANTITY TAG. APPP: As Per Previous Prescription; NS: Not Specified.

| Model | INDICATION | | | | |
| --- | --- | --- | --- | --- | --- |
| | Cardiac | Tremors | Migraine | Others | NA |
| Base | 0.03 | 0.05 | 0.02 | 0.27 | 0.03 |
| ClinicalBERT | 0.00 | 0.24 | 0.03 | 0.04 | 0.13 |
| M-BERT | 0.05 | 0.01 | 0.09 | 0.35 | 0.00 |
| Base + LSTM | 0.02 | 0.00 | 0.00 | 0.31 | 0.00 |
| ClinicalBERT + LSTM | 0.01 | 0.03 | 0.34 | 0.08 | 0.02 |
| M-BERT + LSTM | 0.05 | 0.00 | 0.00 | 0.04 | 0.03 |
| Base + STE | 0.00 | 0.00 | 0.02 | 0.08 | 0.05 |
| ClinicalBERT + STE | 0.00 | 0.26 | 0.05 | 0.02 | 0.00 |
| M-BERT + STE | 0.00 | 0.11 | 0.00 | 0.00 | 0.15 |

Table 7: Model performance comparison across different classes in INDICATION. NA: Not Annotated.

| Indication (44) | | | | |
|---|---|---|---|---|
| CARDIAC - HYPERTENSION - PALPITATIONS | 49 | ESOPHAGEAL VARICES | 1 |
| CARDIAC - PALPITATIONS - TREMORS | 1 | ANXIETY - CARDIAC - PALPITATIONS | 3 |
| CARDIAC - PALPITATIONS - ANGINA | 1 | ANXIETY | 6 |
| CARDIAC - PALPITATIONS - ATRIAL FIBRILLATION | 1 | ANXIETY - MIGRAINE | 1 |
| CARDIAC - ATRIAL FIBRILLATION | 57 | HYPERTHYROIDISM | 1 |
| CARDIAC - DYSRHYTHMIA | 101 | HYPERGLYCEMIA | 2 |
| CARDIAC - HEART FAILURE | 60 | CHEST PAIN | 1 |
| CARDIAC - HYPERTENSION - ANGINA - PALPITATIONS | 1 | | |
| CARDIAC - ATRIAL FIBRILLATION - DYSRHYTHMIA/RATE | 1 | | |
| CARDIAC - HYPERTENSION - DYSRHYTHMIA | 19 | TREMORS | 77 |
| CARDIAC - MIGRAINE | 1 | TREMORS - CARDIAC - HYPERTENSION | 1 |
| CARDIAC - DYSRHYTHMIA/RATE | 114 | TREMORS - ANXIETY | 1 |
| CARDIAC - HYPERTENSION - ESOPHAGEAL VARICES | 1 | TREMORS - CARDIAC - PALPITATIONS | 2 |
| CARDIAC - PALPITATIONS | 162 | | |
| CARDIAC - HYPERTENSION - HEART FAILURE | 4 | | |
| CARDIAC - HYPERTENSION - MIGRAINE | 12 | MIGRAINE | 69 |
| CARDIAC - HYPERTENSION - ANGINA | 28 | | |
| CARDIAC - TREMORS | 2 | | |
| CARDIAC - DYSRHYTHMIA - MIGRAINE | 1 | NA | 707 |
| CARDIAC - ANGINA - ATRIAL FIBRILLATION | 1 | | |
| CARDIAC - HEPATIC CIRCULATION | 1 | | |
| CARDIAC - ANGINA | 34 | | |
| CARDIAC - DYSRHYTHMIA/RATE - PALPITATIONS | 1 | | |
| CARDIAC - HYPERTENSION | 1655 | | |
| CARDIAC - HYPERTENSION - ATRIAL FIBRILLATION | 2 | | |
| CARDIAC - ESOPHAGEAL VARICES | 2 | | |
| CARDIAC | 608 | | |
| CARDIAC - ANGINA - DYSRHYTHMIA/RATE | 1 | | |
| CARDIAC - HYPERTENSION - DYSRHYTHMIA/RATE | 50 | | |
| CARDIAC - PALPITATIONS - MIGRAINE | 1 | | |
| CARDIAC - HYPERTENSION - TREMORS | 8 | | |

Figure 5: Number of prescriptions per indication class, where the indication label has the original 44 classes. *NA* stands for *Not Annotated*.

| Swedish | Translated English | Indication | Quantity | Quantity Tag |
|---|---|---|---|---|
| 0.5 TABLETTER 2 GANGER DAGLIGEN. FOR HJARTRYTMEN OCH SANKER BLODTRYCKET TABLETTERNA SVALJES HELA (KAN DELAS VID SVALJSVARIGHETER, MEN FAR EJ K | 0.5 tablets 2 times daily. For the heart rhythm and reduces blood pressure The tablets are swallowed whole (can be divided at swallowing durations, but don't k | Cardiac-hypertension | 1 | Standard |
| 1 TABLETT 1 GANG DAGLIGEN I 3 VECKOR. EVENTUELL HOJNING TILL 2 TABLETTER DAGLIGEN BEROENDE PA KONTROLLEN OCH SYMTOMLINDRING, MOT HJARTKLAPPNING | 1 table 1 time daily for 3 weeks. Successful increase for 2 tablets daily dependent on control and symptoms relief, against palpitations | Cardiac-palpitations | 1 | Complex |
| 1 TABLETT 1 GANG DAGLIGEN. EFTERHAND EVENTUELL OKNING TILL EN TABLETT MORGON OCH LUNCH MEN BORJA MED EN TABLETT TIDIG MORGON, MOT SKAKNINGAR. | 1 tbale 1 time daily. Previously opening to a tablet morning and lunch but begin with a tablet early morning, against shakes | NA | 1 | Standard |
| 1/2 TABLETT PA MORGONEN , 1/2 TABLETT PA LUNCHEN OCH 1/2 TABLETT PA KVALLEN MOT TREMOR, BLODTRYCKSREGLERANDE | 1/2 table on morning, 1/2 table on lunch and 1/2 table on evening against tremor, blood pressure control | NA | 1.5 | Standard |
| 1 TABLETT 1 GANG DAGLIGEN MOT HOGT BLODTRYCK DU BOR BESTALLA LAKARTIDLAMPLIGEN MAJ JUNI FOR KONTROLL BT DIABETES. | 1 tablet 1 time daily against high blood pressure you should order the painting lighting may june for control BT diabetes | Cardiac-hypertension | 1 | Standard |
| 2 depottabletter kl. 08, 1 depottablett kl. 20. Dagligen. Mot hOgt blodtryck | 2 prolonged-release tablets at. 08, 1 prolonged-release tablet at. 20. Daily. Against high blood pressure | Cardiac-hypertension | 3 | Standard |

Table 8: Longer example prescriptions with translations and annotations.

# Evaluation of Transfer Learning for Adverse Drug Event (ADE) and Medication Entity Extraction


**Sankaran Narayanan**
Amrita Vishwa
Vidyapeetham
Amritapuri, India
nsankaran@
am.amrita.edu

**Kaivalya Mannam**
Georgia Institute of
Technology
Atlanta, Georgia
kmannam3@
gatech.edu

**Sreeranga P. Rajan**
Alphabet Inc. and
Stanford University
California, USA
sree@
cs.stanford.edu

**P. Venkat Rangan**
Amrita Vishwa
Vidyapeetham
Amritapuri, India
venkat@
amrita.edu


## Abstract


We evaluate several biomedical contextual embeddings (based on BERT, ELMo, and Flair) for the detection of medication entities such as Drugs and Adverse Drug Events (ADE) from Electronic Health Records (EHR) using the 2018 ADE and Medication Extraction (Track 2) n2c2 data-set. We identify best practices for transfer learning, such as language-model fine-tuning and scalar mix. Our transfer learning models achieve strong performance in the overall task (F1=92.91%) as well as in ADE identification (F1=53.08%). Flair-based embeddings out-perform in the identification of context-dependent entities such as *ADE*. BERT-based embeddings out-perform in recognizing clinical terminology such as Drug and Form entities. ELMo-based embeddings deliver competitive performance in all entities. We develop a sentence-augmentation method for enhanced ADE identification benefiting BERT-based and ELMo-based models by up to 3.13% in F1 gains. Finally, we show that a simple ensemble of these models outpaces most current methods in ADE extraction (F1=55.77%).


## 1 Introduction

Adverse Drug Events (ADE) arising from the medical intervention of drugs account for 1.3 million visits to the emergency department in the United States alone (CDC, 2017). Randomized controlled trials (RCTs), the primary mechanism for monitoring and identifying ADEs, are hampered by insufficient sample sizes of clinical trials (Sultana et al., 2013). Pharmacovigilance databases such as the Food and Drug Administration's Adverse Event Reporting System (FAERS) strive to be authoritative sources for Physicians; however, they require regular manual data entry (Hoffman et al., 2014; Chedid et al., 2018).

Electronic Health Records (EHRs) contain valuable information about patient medication history: drugs prescribed, reasons for administration, dosages/strengths, and ADEs. Automated extraction of these medication entities by Natural Language Processing (NLP) techniques can facilitate wide-scale pharmacovigilance (Moore and Furberg, 2015; Liu et al., 2019a).

Incorporating such a predictive system within the clinical note-taking interface may help the Physician by alleviating the need to access external clinical decision support applications (Chen et al., 2016). For instance, if a physician notes down *'started on Dilantin for seizure prophylaxis for a few days'*, the text could be quickly parsed - highlighting *'Dilantin'* as a drug, *'seizure prophylaxis'* as the reason for administration, *'few days'* as the duration, and warnings of *'eye discharge'*, *'oral sores'*, etc. as potential ADEs. In the example given, *'seizure prophylaxis'* and *'few days'* may occur any where in the clinical text, but only in the context of *'Dilantin'* they indicate reason / duration for administration. Besides, such 'dynamic' interfaces can aid medical students to learn from their collective experiences.

Among medication entities, *ADE* and *Reason* are challenging to disambiguate (Henry et al., 2020). Frequently, the specific reason for drug administration may appear in a subsequent sentence (Dandala et al., 2020). Besides, ADE data-sets include gold-annotations for these entities, only if they are associated with a drug. Doing so leads to a significant reduction in the number of gold annotations (Wei et al., 2020).

As part of our work in uniting clinical decision support functions and note-taking interfaces, we needed to develop a high-performing medication extraction model using open-source NLP frameworks. Following (Miller et al., 2019), we modeled this as a named-entity recognition task (Uzuner




*Proceedings of the 3rd Clinical Natural Language Processing Workshop*, pages 55–64
November 19, 2020. ©2020 Association for Computational Linguistics

| S.No. | Author | Method | Overall F1 | ADE F1 |
| --- | --- | --- | --- | --- |
| 1. | Alibaba Inc. | BiLSTM-CRF | 94.18 | 58.73 |
|  | (Henry et al., 2020) | + ELMo embedding, Section Features |  |  |
| 2. | Dandala et al. (2020) | BiLSTM-CRF | 93.5 | 53.5 |
|  |  | Custom-trained ELMo using MIMIC-III |  |  |
|  |  | Knowledge-embeddings from FAERS |  |  |
|  |  | Custom pre-processing |  |  |
| 3. | Wei et al. (2020) | CRF + BiLSTM-CRF + Joint | 93.45 | 52.95 |
|  |  | 3-model NER ensemble; joint-relation classifier |  |  |
| 4. | Ju et al. (2020) | 4-layer tree-structured BiLSTM-CRF | 92.55 | 27.90 |
|  |  | Word, sub-word, and character embeddings |  |  |
|  |  | Three-groups of specialized features |  |  |
|  |  | Overlapping span handling |  |  |
| 5. | Kim and Meystre (2020) | CRF+CRFext+SEARN+BiLSTM ensemble | 92.66 | 27.11 |
|  |  | Glove embeddings |  |  |
|  |  | Inputs from MedEx and external corpora |  |  |
|  |  | Stanford CoreNLP for tokenization |  |  |
| 6. | Dai et al. (2020) | CRF + BiLSTM-CRF | 91.9 | 38.75 |
|  |  | Cascading BiLSTM architecture |  |  |
|  |  | Pre-trained domain-specific embeddings |  |  |
|  |  | Nested entity handling |  |  |
| 7. | Miller et al. (2019) | BiLSTM-CRF | 90* | 27* |
|  |  | Flair embeddings (general purpose corpora) |  |  |
|  |  | Default features and hyper-parameters |  |  |
|  |  | *: 50 epoch run, final performance could be higher |  |  |
| 8. | Chen et al. (2020) | BiLSTM-CRF | 84.97 | 43.29 |
|  |  | UMLS-based concept lookups |  |  |
|  |  | Specialized handling of temporal entities |  |  |
|  |  | Regular expressions and rules |  |  |

Table 1: Relevant related work.

et al., 2011; Si et al., 2019) and experimented with transfer learning using openly available biomedical contextual embeddings. It is in this context,

1. We evaluate transfer learning models incorporating: BioBERT (Lee et al., 2020), Clinical-BERT (Alsentzer et al., 2019), ELMo (Peters et al., 2018) and Flair (Akbik et al., 2018) contextual embeddings pre-trained on PubMed abstracts (Fiorini et al., 2018).

2. We evaluate embedding-specific methods to maximize performance: language-model fine-tuning, scalar mix, sub-word token aggregation.

3. Based on the performance of the transfer learning models, we develop procedures for enhanced *ADE* and *Reason* identification. Sentence-augmentation at prediction-time benefits *ADE* extraction by up to +3.13% in F1 gains. It also facilitates a deeper understanding of the behavior of the embeddings. Ensembling strategies help improve performance of all three challenging enities: *ADE, Duration, and Reason* with up to +2.63% in F1 gains for *ADE*.

Our main intention was to get a transfer learning pipeline working with these embeddings and therefore we did not perform any detailed hyper-parameter optimization. Despite this, we were able to achieve strong performance with all the embeddings. Standalone models achieved F1-scores of **53.08%** in ADE extraction and **92.91%** in the overall task with default features. A basic ensemble constructed from these standalone models achieved F1-scores of **55.77%** in ADE extraction and **92.82%** in the overall task confirming the viability of the overall strategy.

## 2 Related Work

Classical research in this area focused on rule-based systems (such as MedEx (Xu et al., 2010), ADEPt (Iqbal et al., 2017)) and CRF-based machine-learning leveraging hand-crafted features (Aramaki et al., 2010; Chapman et al., 2019; Nikfarjam et al., 2015).

The 2018 n2c2 Adverse Drug Events and Medication Extraction in EHR data-set (Buchan et al.) and Medications and Adverse Drug Events from Electronic Health Records (MADE 1.0) (Jagannatha et al., 2019) are instances of ClinicalNLP shared-tasks focused on medication entity extrac-

| corpus | notes | Drug | Strength | Form | Frequency | Route | Dosage | Reason | ADE | Duration |
|---|---|---|---|---|---|---|---|---|---|---|
| training | 303 | 16225 | 6691 | 6651 | 6281 | 5476 | 4221 | 3855 | 959 | 592 |
| test | 202 | 10575 | 4359 | 4230 | 4012 | 3513 | 2681 | 2545 | 625 | 378 |

Table 2: Dataset Characteristics.

tion. Most participants leveraged the BiLSTM-CRF neural model in their work (Chalapathy et al., 2016). We have listed the top performing methods from the 2018 n2c2 ADE challenge in Table 1.

Dandala et al. (2020) custom-trained biomedical ELMo embeddings using the MIMIC-III data-set (Johnson et al., 2016); they also used a rich set of sentence tokenization rules. Ju et al. (2020) leveraged a tree-architecture to detect overlapping spans in addition to lexical and knowledge features (e.g., word shapes, Human Disease Ontology / MedDRA side-effect database information).

Relationship association for medication entities is complementary to our work and can be implemented either jointly or in a pipeline. Such a joint architecture utilizes the signals from the relations task to filter out unwanted medication entities. Wei et al. (2020) adopted such a joint-approach with a three-classifier ensemble achieving 52.95% in *ADE* extraction. Chen et al. (2020) also used a joint-architecture supplemented by UMLS (Bodenreider, 2004) concept lookups and unique modeling of temporal entities.

Dai et al. (2020) cascaded classifiers sequentially to widen the contextual information available for *ADE* identification. This model also facilitates improved identification when spans overlap. They evaluated ten pre-trained embedding models: half of them were based on MIMIC-III while the rest were general-purpose. Kim and Meystre (2020) uniquely leveraged SEARN (Daumé et al., 2009), a search-based prediction algorithm for its preference of precision over recall.

Our work is most similar to Miller et al. (2019); they demonstrate that strong medication extraction models can be constructed with minimal engineering using contextual embeddings. The main differences from above mentioned studies are the evaluation of a broader array of contemporary biomedical embeddings, detailed study of fine-tuning strategies, and augmentation methods for *ADE* extraction.

## 3 Methods

### 3.1 Data and Pre-Processing

We use the 2018 n2c2 Adverse Drug Events and Medication Extraction (Track 2) data-set for our experiments. The data-set has a total of 505 clinical notes with nine medication-entities, as shown in Table 2. We convert these files into CoNLL 2000 BIO (Begin, Inside, Outside) format after pre-processing: split sentences into words, normalize numeric values, treat a subset of punctuation characters as word-boundary markers.

### 3.2 Transfer Learning Model

We formulate the medication extraction task as a standard NER task incorporating a single biomedical embedding from the list below:

1. BioBERT (BB) is a pre-trained version of BERT using PubMed abstracts. We used the Base version.

2. ClinicalBERT (CB) is also BERT-based, trained on clinical notes corpora.

3. ELMo-PubMed (EP) is based on ELMo, pre-trained on PubMed abstracts.

4. Flair-PubMed (FP) is a Flair contextual embedding pre-trained on PubMed abstracts.

We also incorporated the *Glove* (Pennington et al., 2014) classical word embedding as part of our model after a brief evaluation (Section 4.2). Our architectural formulation allows for experimenting with newer embeddings or combined embeddings with incremental effort.

### 3.3 Experimental Setup

We implement our models using the Flair open-source framework (Akbik et al., 2019). Flair, based on PyTorch, provides off-the-shelf BiLSTM+CRF model, a pluggable architecture for adding embeddings and data-sets. We have retained default hyperparameters and training procedures (details in Appendix A). During parameter selection, we train for 50 epochs. Final models are trained for 150 epochs or until convergence. We used the evaluation script provided as part of the data-set to appraise our models using the test-set. We report the 'Relaxed F1' score per prevailing practice.

## 4  Model Selection Procedures

In Transfer Learning, the linguistic-information encoded by contextual embedding acts as a primary input to the downstream task layer (BiLSTM). Fine-tuning is generally accepted to be beneficial. However, it requires familiarity with the scripts / associated frameworks specific to the embedding and data-set adaptation.

### 4.1  BERT Embeddings

BERT models have close to a dozen layers (heads). Understanding the linguistic information encoded by these layers and their relative contribution to downstream tasks is an active research area (Liu et al., 2019b; Kovaleva et al., 2019). Flair uses the last four layers of the BERT models to generate embeddings by default.

1. *Choice of Layers (4L vs All)*: The default setting of the end four transformer layers leads to sub-optimal performance (under-fitting) on the training set (Table 3, Row 1). Rather than choosing specific layers, we tried using all layers. This option generates a vast number of features (11 x 768), for the downstream task (Bi-LSTM), and causes training to run out-of-memory.

2. *Scalar Mix (SM)*: As an alternate, we adopted Scalar Mix (Peters et al., 2018), a pooling mechanism on the layer-generated representations. Scalar Mix results in a reasonable number of features (768) and performs optimally (Row 2).

3. *Mean-Pooling of sub-tokens (MP)*: BERT models uniquely use word-piece tokenization for out-of-vocabulary (OOV) words. Embeddings can be generated using first sub-token, or first and last sub-tokens, or using an aggregate (mean-pooling) of all sub-tokens. The latter provides best performance (Row 3).

These settings deliver optimal performance for the BERT-models.

### 4.2  Impact of adding Glove

Akbik et al. (2018) show that paired use of classic word embeddings (such as Glove) and contextual

| S.No | Method | Reason F1 | ADE F1 | Overall F1 |
|------|--------|-----------|--------|------------|
|      | **ClinicalBERT** | | | |
| 1. | Default (4L) | 62.87 | 11.83 | 91.50 |
| 2. | All + SM | 63.10 | 32.07 | 92.11 |
| 3. | All + SM/MP | 65.02 | 32.47 | 92.41 |
| 4. | 3. w/o Glove | 64.17 | 22.73 | 92.15 |
|      | **BioBERT (Base)** | | | |
| 5. | 4L + SM/MP | 63.27 | 39.73 | 92.11 |
| 6. | All + SM/MP | 64.04 | 43.07 | 92.20 |
| 7. | 6. w/o Glove | 64.65 | 43.74 | 92.17 |

Table 3: BERT Parameter Selection (50 epochs)

| Embedding | Standalone | +Glove | F1 $\Delta$ |
|-----------|-----------|--------|-------------|
| ClinicalBERT | 92.15 | 92.41 | +0.26 |
| BioBERT | 92.17 | 92.20 | +0.03 |
| ELMo-PubMed | 92.31 | 92.23 | -0.08 |
| Flair-PubMed | 92.39 | 92.92 | +0.53 |

Table 4: Impact of adding Glove (50 epochs)

embeddings enhance NER task performance. Table 4 shows the impact of adding Glove. For the CB model, the noticeable gains were *Reason* (+1.00 F1) and *ADE* (+9.00 F1). For the FP model, *ADE* reduction (-2.00 F1) was offset by gains in *Reason* (+1.00 F1), *Duration* (+0.50 F1), and *Drug* (+0.40 F1). The EP model did not show any meaningful difference. We used the paired method for the rest of our experiments.

### 4.3  Flair Embedding Fine-Tuning

Language-model fine-tuning aims to improve the performance of Flair-PubMed contextual embeddings on speciality corpora. We performed fine-tuning for 10 epochs using the 4391 clinical notes from the i2b2/n2c2 data-sets. While all entities exhibited gains, the prominent gainers are shown in Table 5. We used this fine-tuned model for the rest of our experiments.

| Entity | Prior F1 | Post F1 | F1 $\Delta$ |
|--------|----------|---------|-------------|
| Drug | 94.26 | 94.77 | +0.51 |
| Duration | 83.85 | 85.09 | +1.24 |
| Route | 94.80 | 95.40 | +1.08 |
| ADE | 40.92 | 47.00 | +6.08 |
| Reason | 65.33 | 68.46 | +3.13 |
| Overall (micro) | 92.22 | 92.92 | +0.70 |

Table 5: Flair-PubMed fine-tuning (50 epochs)

| Entity | BB-Pr | BB-Re | BB-F1 | CB-Pr | CB-Re | CB-F1 |
|---|---|---|---|---|---|---|
| Drug | 95.24 | 94.64 | $94.94_2$ | 95.78 | 94.24 | $95.00_1$ |
| Strength | 97.94 | 97.95 | $97.85_2$ | 97.30 | 97.99 | 97.64 |
| Duration | 88.86 | 80.16 | 84.28 | 90.32 | 81.48 | $85.67_1$ |
| Route | 95.59 | 94.93 | 95.26 | 95.69 | 94.79 | 95.24 |
| Form | 96.83 | 94.70 | $95.76_2$ | 97.20 | 94.75 | $95.96_1$ |
| ADE | 64.55 | 39.04 | 48.65 | 58.79 | 31.04 | 40.63 |
| Dosage | 93.05 | 93.92 | $93.48_2$ | 93.19 | 93.47 | 93.33 |
| Reason | 77.00 | 59.06 | 66.84 | 80.71 | 57.52 | $67.17_2$ |
| Frequency | 96.84 | 97.06 | 96.95 | 97.52 | 96.96 | $97.24_1$ |
| Overall | 94.32 | $91.34_2$ | **92.81** | $94.85_1$ | 90.93 | **92.85** |

Table 6: BB and CB Models

| Entity | EP-Pr | EP-Re | EP-F1 | FP-Pr | FP-Re | FP-F1 |
|---|---|---|---|---|---|---|
| Drug | 94.70 | 93.93 | 94.31 | 94.79 | 94.71 | 94.75 |
| Strength | 97.54 | 97.68 | 97.61 | 97.92 | 98.01 | $97.97_1$ |
| Duration | 89.37 | 82.28 | $85.67_1$ | 88.67 | 82.80 | $85.65_2$ |
| Route | 96.01 | 94.62 | $95.31_2$ | 95.89 | 94.88 | $95.38_1$ |
| Form | 97.23 | 94.31 | $95.75_2$ | 96.84 | 94.33 | 95.57 |
| ADE | 65.00 | 41.60 | $50.73_2$ | 65.12 | 44.80 | $53.08_1$ |
| Dosage | 93.71 | 93.36 | $93.54_1$ | 93.11 | 93.32 | 93.22 |
| Reason | 79.21 | 58.23 | 67.12 | 78.30 | 60.98 | $68.57_1$ |
| Frequency | 97.61 | 96.64 | $97.12_2$ | 96.71 | 97.48 | 97.10 |
| Overall | $94.49_2$ | 90.93 | **92.68** | 94.21 | $91.64_1$ | **92.91** |

Table 7: EP and FP Models

| Gold | Pred | BB | CB | EP | FP |
|---|---|---|---|---|---|
| ADE | Reason | 81.8% | 79.2% | 86.08% | 83.82% |
| Reason | ADE | 97.32% | 96.6% | 97.97% | 97.09% |
| A/R | Drug | 98.8% | 98.48% | 98.60% | 99.19% |
| Form | Route | 98.49% | 98.51% | 98.41% | 98.37% |
| Route | Form | 98.43% | 98.57% | 98.66% | 98.43% |
| Dosage | Strength | 99.01% | 98.30% | 98.61% | 98.61% |
| Dosage | Frequency | 99.21% | 99.84% | 99.87% | 99.36% |
| Duration | Frequency | 96.80% | 96.55% | 96.58% | 96.01% |

Table 8: Confusion Matrix

## 5 Discussion

Tables 6 and 7 show the overall performance of the various models. The prefixes (BB, CB, EP, FP) shows the contextual embedding used; and the suffix (Pr, Re, F1) shows the Precision, Recall, F1 metrics. The two highest F1 score for each entity are indicated via subscripts. The three most challenging entities are underlined. Table 8 shows the proportion of overlap between two entities. We use TP / (TP+FN) where TP is the number of 'Gold' entities identified correctly and FN is the number of mispredictions ('Pred'). Smaller values indicate higher overlap.

### 5.1 Error Analysis

1. *Drug*: BERT-models out-perform in the recognition of entities that are predominantly part of the clinical lexicon (e.g., *Drug* and *Form*) with CB model out-performing in both. We think that clinical note pre-training contributes to this out-performance. BERT-based models seem to misclassify *Drug* entities when special characters are involved. Consider the three sentences: 'CONTRAINDICA-TIONS FOR IV <u>CONTRAST</u>', 'C-SPINE WITHOUT <u>CONTRAST</u>', 'C-SPINE W/O <u>CONTRAST</u>'. 'CONTRAST'[1] is a gold *Drug* annotation. FP/EP models identify 'CONTRAST' in all the three sentences. BERT-models get the first and second one correctly while ignoring the last. Approximately 17 out of 31 references to 'CONTRAST' in the test-set are without special characters and hence recognized correctly by all models. The remaining ones are abbreviations such as 'W/O', 'WW/O', or terms such as 'NON CONTRAST'. These are ignored by the BERT models.

2. *Duration*: Having the fewest entities (378), *Duration* gets mislabeled maximally with *Frequency* and to a lesser degree with *Dosage*. Henry et al. (2020)'s observation that colloquial language use is a leading contributor to the confusion also implies the underlying context-sensitivity. In 'CLOBETASOL ... x up to <u>2 weeks per month</u>', '2 weeks per month' gets incorrectly tagged as *Frequency*. In Section 5.3 we show that ensembling FP model with any one of the other models delivers best overall *Duration* performance.

3. *Form and Route*: Unusual *Routes* ('take one tab <u>under your tongue</u>') were naturally ignored by all models. Commonly, the method of drug administration is used to describe the drug form also. In 'Heparin 5,000 unit/mL Solution Sig: One (1) Injection TID (3 times a day)', 'Injection' refers to the former and hence a *Route* while in 'EGD with epinephrine injection and BICAP cautery', it refers to the drug *Form*. Likewise, 'infusion' generates disagreement. BERT-models generally do well.

4. *Dosages and Strength*: *Dosages* were mislabeled most commonly for *Strengths* ('iron <u>0.5 ml</u> per day') by all models followed by *Frequency*. In 'lcvophcd @ 12 mcg/min', the FP model identifies 'mcg/min' as 'Strength' (correctly) while other models identify 'mcg/min' as 'Frequency'.

---

[1] 'contrast dye' is given to a patient to accentuate structures in the CT Scan (Cedars-Sinai)

| Entity | BB | CB | EP | FP |
|---|---|---|---|---|
| Drug | 29 (0.27%) | 21 (0.2%) | 27 (0.26%) | 55 (0.52%) |
| Strength | 4 (0.09%) | 10 (0.24%) | 2 (0.05%) | 12 (0.28%) |
| Duration | 2 (0.53%) | 1 (0.26%) | 2 (0.53%) | 6 (1.59%) |
| Route | 11 (0.31%) | 5 (0.14%) | 5 (0.14%) | 9 (0.26%) |
| Form | 5 (0.11%) | 6 (0.14%) | 7 (0.16%) | 6 (0.14%) |
| ADE | 11 (1.76%) | 12 (1.92%) | 24 (3.84%) | 46 (7.36%) |
| Dosage | 14 (0.52%) | 20 (0.75%) | 16 (0.6%) | 16 (0.6%) |
| Reason | 45 (1.77%) | 29 (1.14%) | 38 (1.49%) | 95 (3.73%) |
| Frequency | 3 (0.07%) | 6 (0.15%) | 2 (0.05%) | 9 (0.22%) |

Table 9: Unique Counts (Count / Total)

5. Each model uniquely detects several entities not detected by other models (Table 9). Consider the two sentences that occur next to each other in a clinical note: 'could affect your Coumadin??????/warfarin dosage.' 'Coumadin (Warfarin) and diet:'. The former contains '?' and '/' inter-mixed with the entities. All models detect the entities in the second sentence. However, for the first sentence, the FP model identifies a single *Drug* entity Coumadin??????/warfarin while the others ignore it altogether.

6. *ADE and Reason*: FP model out-performed in ADE recognition (F1=53.08%) followed by the EP model (F1=50.73%). Although the top three models (FP, EP, BB) differ only marginally in Precision (0.6%) they exhibit significant divergence in Recall (+5.76%). There are three significant factors:

Mislabeling between *ADE* and *Reason*: CB model generates the highest number of mislabels (low recall) while EP does the best as shown in Table 8.

Mislabeling of *ADE/Reason* with *Drug*: In 'Heme/onc was consulted regarding hemolysis and anticoagulation. ... Given her multiple indications for anticoagulation, decision was made to begin coumadin ...', the first reference to 'anticoagulation' is a *Drug* gold annotation ('blood thinners') while the latter is a *Reason* ('medical indication'). This example demonstrates the need for good contextual disambiguation. BB/FP models identify correctly. The EP model, ignores the former, and incorrectly identifies the latter as *Drug*. The CB model fails to identify both entities.

Incomplete word context: Often a *Drug* entity is needed to successfully infer the presence of an *ADE* or a *Reason* entity. However,

| S. No | Method | Precision | Recall | F1 |
|---|---|---|---|---|
| | **ClinicalBERT (CB)** | | | |
| 1. | Per-Sentence | 58.79 | 31.04 | 40.63 |
| 2. | 1. ∪ Look-ahead-1 | 46.13 | 40.00 | **42.84** |
| 3. | 2. ∪ Paragraph | 45.44 | 40.64 | 42.91 |
| | **BioBERT (BB)** | | | |
| 1. | Per-Sentence | 64.55 | 39.04 | 48.65 |
| 2. | 1. ∪ Look-ahead-1 | 54.31 | 49.44 | **51.76** |
| 3. | 2. ∪ Paragraph | 53.60 | 50.08 | 51.78 |
| | **ELMo-PubMed (EP)** | | | |
| 1. | Per-Sentence | 65.00 | 41.60 | 50.73 |
| 2. | 1. ∪ Look-ahead-1 | 54.19 | 50.72 | **52.40** |
| 3. | 2. ∪ Paragraph | 53.86 | 51.36 | 52.58 |
| | **Flair-PubMed (FP)** | | | |
| 1. | Per-Sentence | 65.12 | 44.80 | **53.08** |
| 2. | 1. ∪ Lookahead-1 | 52.82 | 50.88 | 51.83 |
| 3. | 2. ∪ Paragraph | 52.38 | 52.80 | 52.59 |

Table 10: ADE augmentation (150 epochs)

| |
|---|
| Reason (True Positive) |
| 1. - Hypothyroid. Continued **Synthroid** |
| 2. ... admitted ... due to H1N1 influenza A. |
| ... 6 days of **Tamiflu** and **Levaquin** ... |
| Reason (False Positive) |
| 3. You were ... right foot cellulitis and osteomyelitis. You were started on **antibiotics**. |
| ADE (True Positive) |
| 4. ... developed AMS and decreased respiratory rate. ... thought to be secondary to **methadone** overdose ... |
| ADE (False Positive) |
| 5. His AMS was due to pain ... He had significant altered mental status after one day when he appeared more somnolent after a dose of **Morphine** 2mg IV. |

Table 11: Augmentation TP / FP Examples

it may occur in a subsequent sentence creating a challenge for the model. To verify this hypothesis, we evaluated model behavior by combining a sentence with one or more of its subsequent sentences. This is discussed in the next section.

## 5.2 Prediction-time Sentence Augmentation

We evaluated model behavior by combining a sentence with one or more of its subsequent sentences. For example, the 'Look-ahead-1 strategy', pairs a sentence with the one immediately following it. We progressively increased the pairing length up to a paragraph. Table 10 shows the *ADE* performance resulting from this augmentation strategy. Table 11 lists several examples (*Drug* entities are marked **bold** when they occur in the subsequent sentence).

1. Reason: 'Hypothyroid' is detected by augmentation due to the co-occurrence of 'Syn-

| Ensemble | ADE F1 | Reason F1 | Overall F1 |
|---|---|---|---|
| FP+BB | 55.21 | 69.28 | 92.80 |
| FP+CB | 54.73 | 69.37 | 92.86 |
| FP+EP | **55.77** | **69.60** | 92.82 |

Table 12: Ensembles

| Entity | Precision | Recall | F1 | F1 $\Delta$ |
|---|---|---|---|---|
| Drug | 93.18 | 95.88 | 94.51 | -0.24 |
| Strength | 97.56 | 98.30 | 97.93 | -0.14 |
| Duration | **86.54** | **86.77** | **86.66** | **+1.01** |
| Route | 95.12 | 95.36 | 95.24 | -0.14 |
| Form | 96.50 | 94.98 | 95.73 | +0.16 |
| ADE | **58.90** | **52.96** | **55.77** | **+2.69** |
| Dosage | 92.26 | 94.67 | 93.45 | +0.23 |
| Reason | **74.25** | **65.50** | **69.60** | **+1.03** |
| Frequency | 96.27 | 97.86 | 97.06 | -0.04 |
| Overall | 92.74 | 92.89 | 92.82 | -0.10 |

Table 13: FP+EP Ensemble

throid'. In Ex. 3, 'osteomyelitis' is tagged by augmentation due to the co-occurrence of 'antibiotics'. However, interestingly, both are un-annotated despite a prior-occurrence of 'antibiotics' carrying a *Drug* annotation.

2. ADE: 'overdose' is identified correctly at sentence-level (Ex. 4). The remaining ones, namely, 'AMS' and 'decreased respiratory rate' are identified by augmentation.

3. In Ex. 5, *altered mental status* is identified at sentence-level but is un-annotated (despite 'somnolent' indicating the state of 'feeling drowsy'). 'AMS' is recognized by augmentation but is un-annotated probably because of its diagnostic nature.

The 'Look-ahead-1' strategy is the most effective: *ADE* F1 scores increase by +3.11%, +2.21%, +1.67% for the BB, CB, EP models despite a reduction in Precision. Recall gains for the FP model are offset by a higher reduction in Precision. For *Reason* entity, all models benefit by augmentation, with the gains ranging between 0.51% to 1.23%. This exercise basically shows that inter-sentence word context impacts *ADE* and *Reason* identification and is beneficial when the underlying model is unable to contextualize effectively.

### 5.3 Model Ensembles

We briefly evaluated model ensembling strategies for enhanced *ADE* performance. We generate predictions on the underlying models. We combine non-conflicting entities. In the case of a conflict, we prioritize ADE predictions; otherwise, we choose the entity using the confidence score. Table 12 shows three ensemble models based on their 'Overall F1' scores. Table 13 shows the entity-wise performance for the FP+EP ensemble model (selected based on the highest *ADE* F1 score). The ensemble model delivers the best performance in all three challenging entities: *ADE, Duration, and Reason* validating the feasibility of the strategy.

## 6 Limitations and Future Work

There are a few limitations in this study that we plan to address in future works:

1. We did not fine-tune BERT and ELMo-based embedding models. Doing so may alter the performance profile of these models. Hence, an apples-to-apples comparison between the models is not recommended.

2. Adoption of better tokenization methods (e.g., clinical text processing tools), and handling special-cases (such as abbreviations) may further enhance model robustness.

3. We also did not do an exhaustive survey of the available embeddings. There may be other more effective embeddings.

## 7 Conclusion

In this study, we presented strong performing transfer learning models for the extraction of medication entities using several biomedical contextual embeddings. Our experiments shed light on the strengths of the various embeddings: Flair-PubMed embedding out-performs in ADE extraction. BioBERT and ClinicalBERT embeddings out-perform in recognition of Drug and Form medication entities. ELMo-PubMed embedding delivers competitive performance in all medication entities. We showed that sentence-augmentation and ensembling are viable strategies to enhance ADE performance. Our approach is free of hand-generated features and built using off-the-shelf neural models, default hyper-parameters, and training procedures. These factors decrease the development effort. A detailed analysis of embedding-specific factors contributing to mis-classification and inclusion of fine-tuning procedures are part of our ongoing work.

# 8 Acknowledgements

We thank the anonymous reviewers for their valuable suggestions and feedback. This work was supported by the biomedical AI groups of Amrita Technologies, Amritapuri, India and Amrita Institute of Medical Sciences, Kochi, India.

# 9 Availability of Data and Materials

1. The 2018 n2c2 ADE and Medication Extraction (Track 2) data-set is protected by Data Usage Agreement. It can be obtained from Harvard DBMI Portal.

2. The code and setup instructions used for the experiments in this paper is available from Git.

# References


Alan Akbik, Tanja Bergmann, Duncan Blythe, Kashif Rasul, Stefan Schweter, and Roland Vollgraf. 2019. Flair: An easy-to-use framework for state-of-the-art nlp. In *Proceedings of the 2019 Conference of the North American Chapter of the Association for Computational Linguistics (Demonstrations)*, pages 54–59.

Alan Akbik, Duncan Blythe, and Roland Vollgraf. 2018. Contextual string embeddings for sequence labeling. In *Proceedings of the 27th International Conference on Computational Linguistics*, pages 1638–1649.

Emily Alsentzer, John Murphy, William Boag, Wei-Hung Weng, Di Jindi, Tristan Naumann, and Matthew McDermott. 2019. Publicly available clinical bert embeddings. In *Proceedings of the 2nd Clinical Natural Language Processing Workshop*, pages 72–78.

Eiji Aramaki, Yasuhide Miura, Masatsugu Tonoike, Tomoko Ohkuma, Hiroshi Masuichi, Kayo Waki, and Kazuhiko Ohe. 2010. Extraction of adverse drug effects from clinical records. *MedInfo*, 160:739–743.

Olivier Bodenreider. 2004. The unified medical language system (umls): integrating biomedical terminology. *Nucleic acids research*, 32(suppl_1):D267–D270.

Kevin Buchan, Kahyun Lee, Susanne Churchill, and Isaac Kohane. n2c2 2018—track 2: Adverse drug events and medication extraction in ehrs.

CDC. 2017. Adverse drug events in adults. https://www.cdc.gov/medicationsafety/adult_adversedrugevents.html, Last reviewed on 2017-10-17.

Cedars-Sinai. Ct scan of the abdomen. https://www.cedars-sinai.edu/Patients/Programs-and-Services/Imaging-Center/For-Patients/Exams-by-Procedure/CT-Scans/CT-Scan-of-the-Abdomen.aspx, Last Reviewed on.

Raghavendra Chalapathy, Capital Markets CRC, Ehsan Zare Borzeshi, and Massimo Piccardi. 2016. Bidirectional lstm-crf for clinical concept extraction. *ClinicalNLP 2016*, page 7.

Alec B Chapman, Kelly S Peterson, Patrick R Alba, Scott L DuVall, and Olga V Patterson. 2019. Detecting adverse drug events with rapidly trained classification models. *Drug safety*, 42(1):147–156.

Victor Chedid, Priya Vijayvargiya, and Michael Camilleri. 2018. Invited editorial: Advantages and limitations of faers in assessing adverse event reporting for eluxadoline. *Clinical gastroenterology and hepatology: the official clinical practice journal of the American Gastroenterological Association*, 16(3):336.

Jonathan H Chen, Mary K Goldstein, Steven M Asch, and Russ B Altman. 2016. Dynamically evolving clinical practices and implications for predicting medical decisions. In *Biocomputing 2016: Proceedings of the Pacific Symposium*, pages 195–206. World Scientific.

Long Chen, Yu Gu, Xin Ji, Zhiyong Sun, Haodan Li, Yuan Gao, and Yang Huang. 2020. Extracting medications and associated adverse drug events using a natural language processing system combining knowledge base and deep learning. *Journal of the American Medical Informatics Association*, 27(1):56–64.

Hong-Jie Dai, Chu-Hsien Su, and Chi-Shin Wu. 2020. Adverse drug event and medication extraction in electronic health records via a cascading architecture with different sequence labeling models and word embeddings. *Journal of the American Medical Informatics Association*, 27(1):47–55.

Bharath Dandala, Venkata Joopudi, Ching-Huei Tsou, Jennifer J Liang, and Parthasarathy Suryanarayanan. 2020. Extraction of information related to drug safety surveillance from electronic health record notes: Joint modeling of entities and relations using knowledge-aware neural attentive models. *JMIR medical informatics*, 8(7):e18417.

Hal Daumé, John Langford, and Daniel Marcu. 2009. Search-based structured prediction. *Machine learning*, 75(3):297–325.

Nicolas Fiorini, Robert Leaman, David J Lipman, and Zhiyong Lu. 2018. How user intelligence is improving pubmed. *Nature biotechnology*, 36(10):937–945.

Sam Henry, Kevin Buchan, Michele Filannino, Amber Stubbs, and Ozlem Uzuner. 2020. 2018 n2c2 shared task on adverse drug events and medication extraction in electronic health records. *Journal of the American Medical Informatics Association*, 27(1):3–12.

Keith B Hoffman, Andrea R Demakas, Mo Dimbil, Nicholas P Tatonetti, and Colin B Erdman. 2014. Stimulated reporting: the impact of us food and drug administration-issued alerts on the adverse event reporting system (faers). *Drug safety*, 37(11):971–980.

Ehtesham Iqbal, Robbie Mallah, Daniel Rhodes, Honghan Wu, Alvin Romero, Nynn Chang, Olubanke Dzahini, Chandra Pandey, Matthew Broadbent, Robert Stewart, et al. 2017. Adept, a semantically-enriched pipeline for extracting adverse drug events from free-text electronic health records. *PloS one*, 12(11):e0187121.

Abhyuday Jagannatha, Feifan Liu, Weisong Liu, and Hong Yu. 2019. Overview of the first natural language processing challenge for extracting medication, indication, and adverse drug events from electronic health record notes (made 1.0). *Drug safety*, 42(1):99–111.

Alistair EW Johnson, Tom J Pollard, Lu Shen, H Lehman Li-wei, Mengling Feng, Mohammad Ghassemi, Benjamin Moody, Peter Szolovits, Leo Anthony Celi, and Roger G Mark. 2016. Mimic-iii, a freely accessible critical care database. *Scientific data*, 3:160035.

Meizhi Ju, Nhung TH Nguyen, Makoto Miwa, and Sophia Ananiadou. 2020. An ensemble of neural models for nested adverse drug events and medication extraction with subwords. *Journal of the American Medical Informatics Association*, 27(1):22–30.

Youngjun Kim and Stéphane M Meystre. 2020. Ensemble method–based extraction of medication and related information from clinical texts. *Journal of the American Medical Informatics Association*, 27(1):31–38.

Olga Kovaleva, Alexey Romanov, Anna Rogers, and Anna Rumshisky. 2019. Revealing the dark secrets of bert. In *Proceedings of the 2019 Conference on Empirical Methods in Natural Language Processing and the 9th International Joint Conference on Natural Language Processing (EMNLP-IJCNLP)*, pages 4365–4374.

Jinhyuk Lee, Wonjin Yoon, Sungdong Kim, Donghyeon Kim, Sunkyu Kim, Chan Ho So, and Jaewoo Kang. 2020. Biobert: a pre-trained biomedical language representation model for biomedical text mining. *Bioinformatics*, 36(4):1234–1240.

Feifan Liu, Abhyuday Jagannatha, and Hong Yu. 2019a. Towards drug safety surveillance and pharmacovigilance: current progress in detecting medication and adverse drug events from electronic health records.

Nelson F Liu, Matt Gardner, Yonatan Belinkov, Matthew E Peters, and Noah A Smith. 2019b. Linguistic knowledge and transferability of contextual representations. In *Proceedings of NAACL-HLT*, pages 1073–1094.

Timothy Miller, Alon Geva, and Dmitriy Dligach. 2019. Extracting adverse drug event information with minimal engineering. In *Proceedings of the 2nd Clinical Natural Language Processing Workshop*, pages 22–27.

Thomas J Moore and Curt D Furberg. 2015. Electronic health data for postmarket surveillance: a vision not realized. *Drug safety*, 38(7):601–610.

Azadeh Nikfarjam, Abeed Sarker, Karen O'connor, Rachel Ginn, and Graciela Gonzalez. 2015. Pharmacovigilance from social media: mining adverse drug reaction mentions using sequence labeling with word embedding cluster features. *Journal of the American Medical Informatics Association*, 22(3):671–681.

Jeffrey Pennington, Richard Socher, and Christopher D Manning. 2014. Glove: Global vectors for word representation. In *Proceedings of the 2014 conference on empirical methods in natural language processing (EMNLP)*, pages 1532–1543.

Matthew Peters, Mark Neumann, Mohit Iyyer, Matt Gardner, Christopher Clark, Kenton Lee, and Luke Zettlemoyer. 2018. Deep contextualized word representations. In *Proceedings of the 2018 Conference of the North American Chapter of the Association for Computational Linguistics: Human Language Technologies, Volume 1 (Long Papers)*, pages 2227–2237.

Yuqi Si, Jingqi Wang, Hua Xu, and Kirk Roberts. 2019. Enhancing clinical concept extraction with contextual embeddings. *Journal of the American Medical Informatics Association*, 26(11):1297–1304.

Janet Sultana, Paola Cutroneo, and Gianluca Trifirò. 2013. Clinical and economic burden of adverse drug reactions. *Journal of pharmacology & pharmacotherapeutics*, 4(Suppl1):S73.

Özlem Uzuner, Brett R South, Shuying Shen, and Scott L DuVall. 2011. 2010 i2b2/va challenge on concepts, assertions, and relations in clinical text. *Journal of the American Medical Informatics Association*, 18(5):552–556.

Qiang Wei, Zongcheng Ji, Zhiheng Li, Jingcheng Du, Jingqi Wang, Jun Xu, Yang Xiang, Firat Tiryaki, Stephen Wu, Yaoyun Zhang, et al. 2020. A study of deep learning approaches for medication and adverse drug event extraction from clinical text. *Journal of the American Medical Informatics Association*, 27(1):13–21.

Hua Xu, Shane P Stenner, Son Doan, Kevin B Johnson, Lemuel R Waitman, and Joshua C Denny. 2010. Medex: a medication information extraction system for clinical narratives. *Journal of the American Medical Informatics Association*, 17(1):19–24.

## A  Appendices

### A.1  List of Hyper Parameters

1. LSTM: Single-Layer, Bi-Directional, 256 hidden states.

2. Locked dropout: 0.5.

3. Word dropout: 0.05.

4. SGD optimizer with initial learning rate: 0.1, annealing rate of 0.5, and patience of 3.

5. Batch Size: 16. For BERT experiments, we used a batch size of 8 to avoid GPU out-of-memory issues.

6. We train with both training and development data-set (train_with_dev=True).

7. All experiments were conducted on Google Colab GPU + High-RAM configuration.

# BioBERTpt - A Portuguese Neural Language Model for Clinical Named Entity Recognition

Elisa Terumi Rubel Schneider[1], João Vitor Andrioli de Souza[1], Julien Knafou[2],
Jenny Copara[2], Lucas E. S. e Oliveira[1], Yohan B. Gumiel[1], Lucas F. A. de Oliveira[1],
Douglas Teodoro[2], Emerson Cabrera Paraiso[1] and Claudia Moro[1]

[1]Pontifícia Universidade Católica do Paraná, Brazil
[2]University of Applied Sciences and Arts of Western Switzerland
{elisa.rubel, joao.souza}@pucpr.edu.br, paraiso@ppgia.pucpr.br, c.moro@pucpr.br

## Abstract

With the growing number of electronic health record data, clinical NLP tasks have become increasingly relevant to unlock valuable information from unstructured clinical text. Although the performance of downstream NLP tasks, such as named-entity recognition (NER), in English corpus has recently improved by contextualised language models, less research is available for clinical texts in low resource languages. Our goal is to assess a deep contextual embedding model for Portuguese, so called BioBERTpt, to support clinical and biomedical NER. We transfer learned information encoded in a multilingual-BERT model to a corpora of clinical narratives and biomedical-scientific papers in Brazilian Portuguese. To evaluate the performance of BioBERTpt, we ran NER experiments on two annotated corpora containing clinical narratives and compared the results with existing BERT models. Our in-domain model outperformed the baseline model in F1-score by 2.72%, achieving higher performance in 11 out of 13 assessed entities. We demonstrate that enriching contextual embedding models with domain literature can play an important role in improving performance for specific NLP tasks. The transfer learning process enhanced the Portuguese biomedical NER model by reducing the necessity of labeled data and the demand for retraining a whole new model.

## 1  Introduction

Despite recent increases in the availability of machine learning methods, extracting structured information from large amounts of unstructured and noisy clinical documents, as available in electronic health record (EHR) systems, is still a challenging task. Patient's EHR are filled with clinical concepts, often misspelled, abbreviated and represented by a variety of synonyms. Nevertheless, they contain valuable and detailed patient information (Lopes et al., 2019). Natural language processing (NLP) tasks, such as Named Entity Recognition (NER), are used for acquiring knowledge from unstructured texts, by recognizing meaningful entities in text passages. In the clinical domain, NER can be used to identify clinical concepts, such as diseases, signs, procedures and drugs, supporting other data analysis as prediction of future clinical events, summarization, and relation extraction between entities (e.g., drug-to-drug interaction).

Rule-based NER approaches, supported by dictionary resources, perform well in simple contexts (Eftimov et al., 2017). However, they are limited to work with the complexity of clinical texts. For complex corpora, machine learning approaches, such as conditional random fields (CRF) (Lafferty et al., 2001) and, lately, a combination with Bidirectional Long Short-Term Memory (BiLSTM) models, have been proposed (Lample et al., 2016). These supervised approaches have a considerable performance gain when trained on huge amounts of labeled data. Neural network language models introduced the idea of deep learning into language modeling by learning a distributed representation of words. These distributed word representations, trained on massive amounts of unannotated textual data, have been proved to provide good lower dimension feature representations in a wide range of NLP tasks (Wang et al., 2020). The Continuous Bag-of-Words and Skip-gram models



*Proceedings of the 3rd Clinical Natural Language Processing Workshop*, pages 65–72
November 19, 2020. ©2020 Association for Computational Linguistics

proposed to reduce the computational complexity were considered as a milestone in the development of the so-called word embeddings (Mikolov et al., 2013), followed by the Global Vector (GloVe) (Pennington et al., 2014) and the fastText (Bojanowski et al., 2016) models.

While these approaches work with a single global representation for each word, several context-dependent representations models have been recently proposed, such as embeddings from language models (ELMo) (Peters et al., 2018), flair embeddings (Akbik et al., 2018), the Universal Language Model Fine-tuning (ULMFit) (Howard and Ruder, 2018) and bidirectional encoder representations from transformers (BERT) (Devlin et al., 2018). Contextual embedding models pretrained on large-scale unlabelled corpora, particularly those supported by the transformer architecture (Vaswani et al., 2017), reached the state-of-the-art performance on many NLP tasks (Liu et al., 2020). Nevertheless, when applying the general word representation models in healthcare text mining, the characteristics of clinical texts are not considered, known to be noisy, with a different vocabulary, expressions, and word distribution (Knake et al., 2016). Therefore, contextual word embedding models, like BERT, can be fine-tuned, i.e., have their last layers updated to adapt to a specific domain, like clinical and biomedical, using domain-specific training data. These transfer learning process allows the training of a general domain model with medical domain corpus, proving to be a viable technique to medical NLP tasks (Ranti et al., 2020).

Despite the low availability of clinical narratives, given the sensitive nature of health data and privacy concerns (Berman, 2002), several models were trained on clinical and biomedical corpora. In 2013, the word2vec model was trained on biomedical corpora (Pyysalo et al., 2013), creating a language model with high-quality vector space representations. BioBERT (Lee et al., 2019) is a BERT model trained from scratch using PubMed and PubMed Central (PMC) scientific texts, reaching the state-of-the-art results on some biomedical NLP tasks. Clinical BERT (Alsentzer et al., 2019) demonstrated that the pre-trained model with clinical data improved performance in three common clinical NLP tasks. Li et al. (2019) reached state-of-the-art for biomedical and clinical entity normalization with a model trained using EHR data.

Despite the essential contributions of contextual word embeddings on clinical NER, all these studies used English corpora. Indeed, there are few studies in lower resources languages for the clinical domain. In Portuguese, Lopes et al. (2019) proposed a fastText model trained with clinical texts, which achieved higher results when compared to out-of-domain embeddings. In a recent work, de Souza et al. (2019) explored the CRF algorithm for the NER task on SemClinBr (Oliveira et al., 2020), the same annotated corpus we used in this work. They classified three clinical entities (*Disorders*, *Procedures* and *Chemicals and Drugs*) and some medical text abbreviations, achieving promising results. A Portuguese clinical word embedding model were trained using Skip-gram with negative sampling and evaluated on a downstream biomedical NLP task for Urinary Tract Infection disease identification (Oliveira et al., 2019). Their results showed that larger, coarse-grained models achieve a slightly better outcome when compared with small, fine-grained models in the proposed task.

Although these previous works achieved relevant results, we have not found studies for clinical Portuguese using attention-based architectures, such as BERT, which have been achieving the state-of-the-art for most of English NLP tasks. Even with the existence of multilingual models, like BERT-multilingual, it is important to investigate what can be the contribution in creating a domain fine-tuned model for a lower-resource language. As demonstrated in the work of Peng et al. (2019), pre-trained BERT models with biomedical and clinical data achieves better results in the BLUE benchmark for English. This leads us to believe that the same is valid for Portuguese. Thus, the objective of this work is to assess the performance of a domain specific attention-based model, BioBERTpt, to support NER tasks in Portuguese clinical narratives. We intend to investigate how an in-domain model can influence the performance of BERT-based models for NER in clinical data. Also, as knowledge encoded in transformer-based language models can be leveraged to several downstream NLP tasks, we release publicly the first BERT-based model trained on clinical data for Portuguese [1].

## 2 Methods

In this section, we first describe how BioBERTpt was developed using clinical notes and scientific

---

[1] https://github.com/HAILab-PUCPR/BioBERTpt

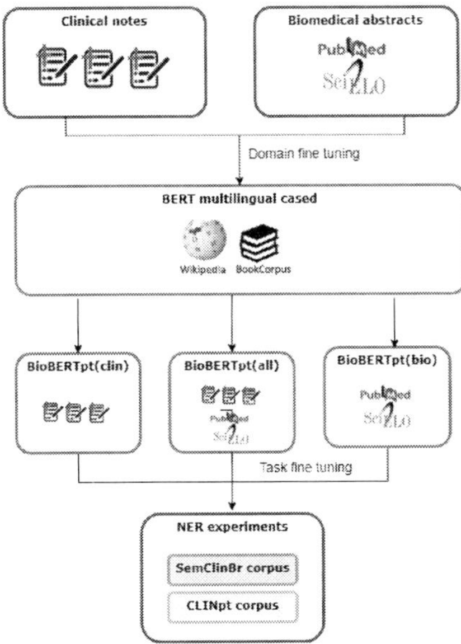

Figure 1: Clinical notes and scientific biomedical abstracts are fed to a pre-trained BERT multilingual model to create BioBERTpt(clin), BioBERTpt(bio) and BioBERTpt(all). These models are then used to extract information from Portuguese clinical notes, evaluated in the clinical NER corpora SemClinBr and CLINpt.

abstracts. Next, we introduce the corpora used for the NER tasks and the evaluation metrics used in our experiments.

## 2.1 Development of BioBERTpt

In this paper, we fine-tuned three BERT-based models on Portuguese clinical and biomedical corpora, initialized with multilingual BERT weights provided by Devlin et al. (2018).

With the approval from the PUCPR Research Ethics Committee with CAAE (Certificate of presentation for Ethical Appreciation), number 51376015.4.0000.0020, we collected 2,100,546 clinical notes from Brazilian hospitals, from 2002 to 2018. All the clinical text have been properly de-identified, to respect patient's privacy. This corpus contains multi specialty information, including cardiology, nephrology and endocrinology, from different types of clinical texts (narratives), such as discharge summaries, nurse notes and ambulatory notes. In total, the clinical notes contain 3.8 million sentences with 27.7 million words. Our clinical model was trained with this corpus, benefiting from the weights already trained in the multilingual BERT model.

We also trained a biomedical model, using titles and abstracts from Portuguese scientific papers published in Pubmed and in the Scielo (Scientific Electronic Library Online)[2], an integrated database that contains Brazilian's scientific journal publications in multidisciplinary areas such as health. These texts were obtained from the Biomedical Translation Task in the First Conference on Machine Translation (WMT16), which evaluated the translation of scientific abstracts between English, French, Spanish and Portuguese (Bojar et al., 2016). In this work, we used only the Portuguese part, composed by documents from Scielo and Pubmed databases about biological and health, resulting in 16.4 million words. The text corpora used for training our models are listed in Table 1.

In the preprocessing step, we split the notes and abstracts into sentences and tokenize them with the default BERT wordpiece tokenizer (Devlin et al., 2018). All models were trained for 5 epochs on a GPU GTX2080Ti Titan 12 GB, with the hyperparameters: batch size as 4, learning rate as 2e-5 and block size as 512. We used the PyTorch implementation of Bert proposed by Hugging Face[3].

To investigate how the domain can influence the task performance, we trained: a) a model with the clinical data, from the narratives of Brazilian hospitals, b) a model with the biomedical data, from the scientific papers abstracts, and c) a full version, i.e., using both clinical and biomedical data. Throughout this paper, we will refer to these corresponding models as BioBERTpt(clin), BioBERTpt(bio) and BioBERTpt(all), respectively.

## 2.2 NER experiments

**Corpora:** In our first NER experiment, we use SemClinBr (Oliveira et al., 2020), a semantically annotated corpus for Portuguese clinical NER, containing 1,000 labeled clinical notes. This corpus comprehended 100 UMLS semantic types, summarized in 13 groups of entities: *Disorders, Chemicals and Drugs, Medical Procedure, Diagnostic Procedure, Disease Or Syndrome, Findings, Health Care Activity, Laboratory or Test Result, Medical Device, Pharmacologic Substance, Quantitative Concept, Sign or Symptom* and *Therapeutic or Preventive Procedure*. Although SemClinBr supports IOB2 (aka BIO) and IOBES (aka BILOU) tagging schemes, we report our experiment in IOB2, widely

---

[2]https://scielo.org/
[3]https://github.com/huggingface/transformers

67

Table 1: List of text corpora used for BioBERTpt

| Corpus | Source | N° of sentences | N° of words | Domain |
| --- | --- | --- | --- | --- |
| Clinical notes | EHR from Brazilian hospitals | 3.8 million | 27.7 million | Clinical |
| Scielo: Health area | Literature titles and abstracts | 532,920 | 12.4 million | Biomedical |
| Scielo: Biological area | Literature titles and abstracts | 130,098 | 3.2 million | Biomedical |
| Pubmed | Literature titles | 74,451 | 812,711 | Biomedical |

used in the literature.

For the second NER experiment, we run our models in a small dataset with IOBES format, proposed by Lopes et al. (2019). This corpus is a collection of 281 Neurology clinical case descriptions, with manually-annotated named entities, from now on called CLINpt. These cases were collected from a clinical journal published by the Portuguese Society of Neurology.

**Execution:** Our experiments were performed with holdout using a corpus split of 60% for training, 20% for validation and 20% for test. We used the Hugging Face API, which provides the BertForTokenClassification class. This class adds a token-level classifier, a linear layer that uses the last hidden state of the sequence. For both NER tasks we used this configuration: AdamW optimizer, weight decay as 0.01, batch size as 4, maximum length as 256, learning rate as 3e-5, maximum epoch as 10, and the linear schedule that decreases the learning rate throughout the epochs with warmup as 0.1.

**Evaluation criteria:** We evaluate the results using precision, recall and F1-score metrics. As in SemClinBr each entity can have more than one semantic type associated (similar to a multi-label classification), we used the label-based metrics, an adaptation of existing single-label problem metrics, to measure the model general performance. We calculated the micro-average metric, when the score is computed globally over all instances and then over all class labels (Sorower, 2010).

In addition, we also analyzed statistical significance between the F1-score of the models for all entities in SemClinBr. We defined seven samples, where each one corresponds to a set of the F1-score values of all entities in the corpus, calculated for each respective model. As the Friedman test only indicates if there is a difference between the means of the samples, without identifying which sample(s) is(are) different from the set, we applied a Wilcoxon signed-ranks pair-wise as post-test. The Wilcoxon signed-rank test was calculated between pairs of samples, in order to show which pairs of samples have different means. The results are considered statistically significant for $P$ value $<.05$.

We compare BioBERTpt with the already existing contextual models: BERT multilingual uncased, BERT multilingual cased, Portuguese BERT base and Portuguese BERT large. Both BERT multilingual are large versions and provide Portuguese language support, called in this work BERT multi(u) for the uncased version and BERT multi(c) for the cased version. The Portuguese BERT models, proposed by Souza et al. (2019), are BERT-models trained on the BrWaC (Brazilian Web as Corpus), a large Portuguese corpus, with whole-word mask. We used both base and large versions, called here BERT PT(b) and BERT PT(l), respectively. All these word embeddings are out-of-domain, i.e., trained in general context corpora, like Wikipedia and books.

## 3 Results

Table 2 shows the average precision, recall and F1-score values for all BERT models on SemClinBr and CLINpt corpora, where our in-domain models outperformed in the average scores.

In the SemClinBr corpus, BioBERTpt(bio) improved 0.1 in precision, BioBERTpt(all), 2.0 in recall and 1.6 in F1-score, over the out-of-domain model with better performance. Full F1-score values for each entity are provided on our repository. Analyzing the performance by entity, the in-domain models in general were better at recall and F1-score. Our models obtained better results in precision for 4 entities, recall for 8 and F1-score for 11. The out-of-domain models obtained better results for 9 entities in precision, 5 in recall and 2 in F1-score. The results of the Friedman test evidenced that there is a difference between some models. The post-test Wilcoxon signed-ranks pair-wise showed the statistical relevance between models over all entities, as shown in Figure 2.

Table 2: The average scores of the NER tasks, for each model evaluated. In bold, the best results

| Corpus / model | Precision | Recall | F1 |
|---|---|---|---|
| **SemClinBr** | | | |
| BERT multi (u)[a] | 0.623 | 0.566 | 0.588 |
| BERT multi (c)[b] | 0.604 | 0.567 | 0.582 |
| BERT PT(b)[c] | 0.595 | 0.587 | 0.585 |
| BERT PT(l)[d] | 0.563 | 0.531 | 0.541 |
| BioBERTpt(bio) | **0.624** | 0.586 | 0.602 |
| BioBERTpt(clin) | 0.609 | 0.603 | 0.602 |
| BioBERTpt(all) | 0.608 | **0.607** | **0.604** |
| **CLINpt** | | | |
| BiLSTM-CRF [e] | 0.753 | 0.745 | 0.749 |
| BERT multi (u) | 0.903 | 0.921 | 0.912 |
| BERT multi (c) | 0.912 | 0.931 | 0.921 |
| BERT PT(b) | 0.910 | 0.922 | 0.916 |
| BERT PT(l) | 0.898 | 0.927 | 0.912 |
| BioBERTpt(bio) | **0.917** | 0.925 | 0.921 |
| BioBERTpt(clin) | **0.917** | **0.935** | **0.926** |
| BioBERTpt(all) | 0.912 | 0.929 | 0.920 |

[a]BERT multilingual uncased
[b]BERT multilingual cased
[c]Portuguese BERT base
[d]Portuguese BERT large
[e]Baseline from previous work Lopes et al. (2019), where the authors used Fastext as word embeddings.

BioBERTpt(all) had statistically higher results on F1-score than BERT multilingual uncased (*P* value as 0.04640), Portuguese BERT large (*P* value as 0.00298) and Portuguese BERT base (*P* value as 0.01750). BioBERTpt(clin) had its performance statistically higher in relation to Portuguese BERT large (0.00713) and Portuguese BERT base (*P* value as 0.01075), and BioBERTpt(bio), in relation to Portuguese BERT large (*P* value as 0.01750). Also, BERT multilingual uncased had a significant higher performance in relation to Portuguese BERT large (*P* value as 0.03305).

The results on the CLINpt corpus, also presented in table 4, shows that BioBERTpt(clin) improved precision in 0.5, recall in 0.4 and F1-score in 0.5.

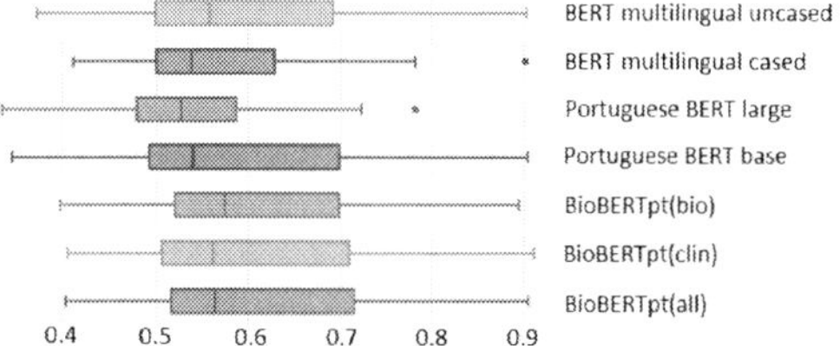


Figure 2: F1-scores of all entities from SemClinBr for evaluation of the models (Wilcoxon signed-ranks pairwise post-test).

Despite CLINpt cases are not representative of the usual clinical notes and narratives found in EHRs, our clinical model presented the best results. Although with little improvement compared to BERT multilingual cased, BioBERTpt(clin) reached the state-of-the-art on this corpus for these three metrics.

## 4  Discussion

### 4.1  Effect of domain

Our results show that the in-domain models outperform the general models in average precision, recall and F1-score on the two Portuguese corpora. These results are aligned with previous experiments in English, where domain-specific models outperform generic models (Lee et al., 2019; Alsentzer et al., 2019; Li et al., 2019; Pyysalo et al., 2013). BioBERTpt trained on clinical narratives had overall better performance when compared with the model trained only on biomedical texts, reaching higher results for entities with more clinical-domain-specific vocabulary, such as *Laboratory*, *Pharmacologic Substance* and *Chemical and Drugs*. The better performance of BioBERTpt(clin) over BioBERTpt(bio) was expected, since the NER evaluation set only contains clinical narratives. Although we evaluated both schemes, IOBES and IOB2, we report only IOB2 as there was no significant difference between them.

The F1-score performance of the *Chemical and Drugs* entities was the most assertive for all models, reaching 0.911 with BioBERTpt(clin). Due to specific characteristics of each entity, such as granularity, specificity and different vocabulary across institutions, some entities achieved low performance, like *Laboratory*, which reached only 0.453 as its highest F1-score with BioBERTpt(clin). The use of imbalanced data can also affect the results, since the entities with lower frequency have fewer and

Table 3: F1-score values for three SemClinBr group of entities, for comparison with baseline. In bold, the highest values.

| Entity / Model | Disorder | Proced.[a] | Drug |
| --- | --- | --- | --- |
| CRF [b] | 0.65 | 0.60 | 0.42 |
| BioBERTpt(bio) | **0.79** | 0.69 | 0.89 |
| BioBERTpt(clin) | 0.78 | 0.69 | **0.91** |
| BioBERTpt(all) | **0.79** | **0.70** | 0.90 |

[a]Procedure
[b]Baseline from previous work (de Souza et al., 2019)

selected vocabulary, leading the models to achieve lower results or overfit the vocabulary vectors.

By evaluating BioBERTpt, we found that the domain can influence the performance of BERT-based models, particularly for domains with unique characteristics such as medical. Our in-domain models achieved higher results for the average metrics. As shown in the statistical tests, the results were significant in relation to the BERT uncased model and the Portuguese BERT versions.

## 4.2 Effect of the contextualized language model

By providing a contextualized word representation and taking advantage of the transformer architecture, BERT-based language models have become a new paradigm for NLP tasks (Liu et al., 2020). The use of BERT-base models in our work had a positive impact on the results when compared to previous works with traditional machine learning algorithms and word embeddings for NER in Portuguese clinical text (de Souza et al., 2019; Lopes et al., 2019). For examples, de Souza et al. (2019) evaluated three groups of entities from the SemClinBr corpus using CRF, without any word embedding. AS shown in Table 3, they obtained for *Disorder* 0.65 of F1-score, compared to our 0.79; for *Procedure*, they achieved 0.60 compared to our 0.70 and for *Drug*, they achieved 0.42 compared to our 0.91. In the work of Lopes et al. (2019), where the authors used BiLSTM-CRF plus fastText on the CLINpt corpus, they achieved 0.759 with their in-domain model for micro F1-score, compared with 0.926 with BioBERTpt(clin), as we can see in Table 2. In general, all BERT-based models performed better in both corpora compared to the results of previous works. Indeed, the generic BERT models performed reasonably well on clinical NER tasks, probably because they were trained with a considerable amount of data, which embraced most of the semantics and syntax of the medical context.

## 4.3 Effect of language

Although the in-domain models performed better than out-of-domain models, the generic Portuguese BERT models (Souza et al., 2019) were outperformed by the BERT multilingual versions. The statistical analyses showed that the Portuguese BERT large version was significantly outperformed not only by the in-domain models, but also by the BERT multilingual uncased. This may be due to a local minima problem or the catastrophic forgetting. As shown by Xu *et al.*, catastrophic forgetting can happen during fine-tuning step, by overwriting previous knowledge of the model with new distinct knowledge, leading to a loss of information on lower layers (Xu et al., 2019). This may have occurred since the linguistic characteristics of clinical texts are very different from the Portuguese corpus used during pre-training phase of Portuguese BERT. As they were trained from a Web Corpus, collected using a search engine with random pairs of content words from 120,000 different Brazilian websites, maybe the new data in the fine-tuning process did not adequately represented the knowledge included in the original training data. The catastrophic forgetting probably occurred because the pre-trained model had to learn new input patterns, or needed to be adapted to a very distinct environment. On the other hand, for the multilingual model, this effect is less noticeable due to the larger and more generic corpus used for training.

## 4.4 Clinical relevance

The World Health Organization (WHO) recently released a list of 13 urgent health challenges the world will face over next decade, which highlights a range of issues, including health care equity and topping infectious diseases (WHO). To face these challenges, access to quality health information is essential, specially considering the information provided only in EHR's clinical narratives.

The BERT-based models proposed in this study and publicly released will support clinical NLP tasks for Portuguese, a language with relative lower resources, in particular in the health domain. Extracting structured information from a large amount of available clinical documents can provide health care assistance and help in the clinical decision-making process, supporting other biomedical tasks and contributing to the urgent health challenges for the next decade [4].

## 5 Conclusions and future work

We proposed a new publicly available Portuguese BERT-based model to support clinical and biomedical NLP tasks. Our NER experiments showed that, compared to out-of-domain contextual word embeddings, BioBERTpt reaches the state-of-the-art on the CLINpt corpus. Additionally, it has better performance for most entities analyzed on the Sem-ClinBR corpus. Our preliminary results are aligned with previous results in other languages, evidencing that domain transfer learning can benefit clinical tasks, in a statistically significant way. In the future, we would like to explore larger transformers-based models in the clinical Portuguese domain and evaluate our model in different clinical NLP tasks, such as negation detection, summarization and de-identification.

## Acknowledgments

This work is related to a project supported by the Leading House for the Latin American Region - Seed Money Grant (No.1922) - of the Centro Latinoamericano-Suizo de la Universidad de San Gallen CLS-HSG. The authors also would like to thank Fundação Araucária, CAPES (Brazilian Coordination for the Improvement of Higher Education Personnel) and CNPq (Brazilian National Council of Scientific and Technologic Development) for their support in this research.

## References

Alan Akbik, Duncan Blythe, and Roland Vollgraf. 2018. Contextual string embeddings for sequence labeling. In *Proceedings of the 27th International Conference on Computational Linguistics*, pages 1638–1649, Santa Fe, New Mexico, USA. Association for Computational Linguistics.

Emily Alsentzer, John Murphy, William Boag, Wei-Hung Weng, Di Jindi, Tristan Naumann, and Matthew McDermott. 2019. Publicly available clinical BERT embeddings. In *Proceedings of the 2nd Clinical Natural Language Processing Workshop*, pages 72–78, Minneapolis, Minnesota, USA. Association for Computational Linguistics.

Jules Berman. 2002. Confidentiality issues for medical data miners. *Artificial intelligence in medicine*, 26:25–36.

Piotr Bojanowski, Edouard Grave, Armand Joulin, and Tomas Mikolov. 2016. Enriching word vectors with subword information. *Transactions of the Association for Computational Linguistics*, 5.

Ondřej Bojar, Rajen Chatterjee, Christian Federmann, Yvette Graham, Barry Haddow, Matthias Huck, Antonio Jimeno Yepes, Philipp Koehn, Varvara Logacheva, Christof Monz, Matteo Negri, Aurélie Névéol, Mariana Neves, Martin Popel, Matt Post, Raphael Rubino, Carolina Scarton, Lucia Specia, Marco Turchi, Karin Verspoor, and Marcos Zampieri. 2016. Findings of the 2016 conference on machine translation. In *Proceedings of the First Conference on Machine Translation: Volume 2, Shared Task Papers*, pages 131–198, Berlin, Germany. Association for Computational Linguistics.

Jacob Devlin, Ming-Wei Chang, Kenton Lee, and Kristina Toutanova. 2018. Bert: Pre-training of deep bidirectional transformers for language understanding.

Tome Eftimov, Barbara Koroušić Seljak, and Peter Korošec. 2017. A rule-based named-entity recognition method for knowledge extraction of evidence-based dietary recommendations. *PLOS ONE*, 12(6):1–32.

Jeremy Howard and Sebastian Ruder. 2018. Universal language model fine-tuning for text classification. pages 328–339.

Lindsey Knake, Monika Ahuja, Erin McDonald, Kelli Ryckman, Nancy Weathers, Todd Burstain, John Dagle, Jeffrey Murray, and Prakash Nadkarni. 2016. Quality of ehr data extractions for studies of preterm birth in a tertiary care center: Guidelines for obtaining reliable data. *BMC Pediatrics*, 16.

John Lafferty, Andrew Mccallum, and Fernando Pereira. 2001. Conditional random fields: Probabilistic models for segmenting and labeling sequence data. pages 282–289.

Guillaume Lample, Miguel Ballesteros, Sandeep Subramanian, Kazuya Kawakami, and Chris Dyer. 2016. Neural architectures for named entity recognition. pages 260–270.

Jinhyuk Lee, Wonjin Yoon, Sungdong Kim, Donghyeon Kim, Sunkyu Kim, Chan Ho So, and Jaewoo Kang. 2019. BioBERT: a pre-trained biomedical language representation model for biomedical text mining. *Bioinformatics*, 36(4):1234–1240.

Fei Li, Yonghao Jin, Weisong Liu, Bhanu Pratap Singh Rawat, Pengshan Cai, and Hong Yu. 2019. Fine-tuning bidirectional encoder representations from transformers (bert)–based models on large-scale electronic health record notes: An empirical study. *JMIR Medical Informatics*, 7.

---

[4]https://www.who.int/news-room/photo-story/photo-story-detail/urgent-health-challenges-for-the-next-decade

Qi Liu, Matt J. Kusner, and Phil Blunsom. 2020. A survey on contextual embeddings. *ArXiv*, abs/2003.07278.

Fábio Lopes, César Teixeira, and Hugo Gonçalo Oliveira. 2019. Contributions to clinical named entity recognition in Portuguese. In *Proceedings of the 18th BioNLP Workshop and Shared Task*, pages 223–233, Florence, Italy. Association for Computational Linguistics.

Tomas Mikolov, Kai Chen, G.s Corrado, and Jeffrey Dean. 2013. Efficient estimation of word representations in vector space. *Proceedings of Workshop at ICLR*, 2013.

Lucas Oliveira, Yohan Gumiel, Lilian Cintho, Sadid Hasan, Deborah Carvalho, Claudia Moro, and Arnon Santos. 2019. Learning portuguese clinical word embeddings: a multi-specialty and multi-institutional corpus of clinical narratives supporting a downstream biomedical task.

Lucas Oliveira, Ana Peters, Adalniza Silva, Caroline Gebeluca, Yohan Gumiel, Lilian Cintho, Deborah Carvalho, Sadid Hasan, and Claudia Moro. 2020. Semclinbr – a multi institutional and multi specialty semantically annotated corpus for portuguese clinical nlp tasks.

Yifan Peng, Shankai Yan, and Zhiyong Lu. 2019. Transfer learning in biomedical natural language processing: An evaluation of bert and elmo on ten benchmarking datasets. In *Proceedings of the 2019 Workshop on Biomedical Natural Language Processing (BioNLP 2019)*.

Jeffrey Pennington, Richard Socher, and Christoper Manning. 2014. Glove: Global vectors for word representation. volume 14, pages 1532–1543.

Matthew Peters, Mark Neumann, Mohit Iyyer, Matt Gardner, Christopher Clark, Kenton Lee, and Luke Zettlemoyer. 2018. Deep contextualized word representations.

Sampo Pyysalo, F Ginter, Hans Moen, T Salakoski, and Sophia Ananiadou. 2013. Distributional semantics resources for biomedical text processing. *Proceedings of Languages in Biology and Medicine*.

Daniel Ranti, Katie Hanss, Shan Zhao, Varun Arvind, Joseph Titano, Anthony Costa, and Eric Oermann. 2020. The utility of general domain transfer learning for medical language tasks.

Mohammad S. Sorower. 2010. A literature survey on algorithms for multi-label learning.

Fábio Souza, Rodrigo Nogueira, and Roberto Lotufo. 2019. Portuguese named entity recognition using bert-crf.

João Vitor de Souza, Yohan Gumiel, Lucas Emanuel Oliveira, and Claudia Maria Moro. 2019. Named entity recognition for clinical portuguese corpus with conditional random fields and semantic groups. In *Anais Principais do XIX Simpósio Brasileiro de Computação Aplicada à Saúde*, pages 318–323, Porto Alegre, RS, Brasil. SBC.

Ashish Vaswani, Noam Shazeer, Niki Parmar, Jakob Uszkoreit, Llion Jones, Aidan Gomez, Lukasz Kaiser, and Illia Polosukhin. 2017. Attention is all you need.

Yuxuan Wang, Yutai Hou, Wanxiang Che, and Ting Liu. 2020. From static to dynamic word representations: a survey. *International Journal of Machine Learning and Cybernetics*.

WHO. World health organization.

Y. Xu, X. Zhong, A. Yepes, and J. Lau. 2019. Forget me not: Reducing catastrophic forgetting for domain adaptation in reading comprehension.

# Dilated Convolutional Attention Network for Medical Code Assignment from Clinical Text

**Shaoxiong Ji[†], Erik Cambria[‡] and Pekka Marttinen[†]**
[†] Department of Computer Science, Aalto University, Finland
{shaoxiong.ji; pekka.marttinen}@aalto.fi
[‡] School of Computer Science and Engineering,
Nanyang Technological University, Singapore
cambria@ntu.edu.sg

## Abstract

Medical code assignment, which predicts medical codes from clinical texts, is a fundamental task of intelligent medical information systems. The emergence of deep models in natural language processing has boosted the development of automatic assignment methods. However, recent advanced neural architectures with flat convolutions or multi-channel feature concatenation ignore the sequential causal constraint within a text sequence and may not learn meaningful clinical text representations, especially for lengthy clinical notes with long-term sequential dependency. This paper proposes a Dilated Convolutional Attention Network (DCAN), integrating dilated convolutions, residual connections, and label attention, for medical code assignment. It adopts dilated convolutions to capture complex medical patterns with a receptive field which increases exponentially with dilation size. Experiments on a real-world clinical dataset empirically show that our model improves the state of the art.

## 1 Introduction

Medical code assignment categorizes clinical documents with sets of codes to facilitate hospital management and improve health record searching (Hsia et al., 1988; Farkas and Szarvas, 2008). These clinical texts comprise physiological signals, laboratory tests, and physician notes, where the International Classification of Diseases (ICD) coding system is widely used for annotation. Most hospitals rely on manual coding by human coders to assign standard diagnosis codes to the discharge summaries for billing purposes. However, this work is and error-prone (Hsia et al., 1988; Farzandipour et al., 2010). Incorrect coding can cause billing mistakes and mislead other general practitioners when patients are readmitted. Intelligent automated coding systems could act as a recommendation system to help coders to allocate correct medical codes to clinical notes.

Automatic medical code assignment has been intensively researched during the past decades (Crammer et al., 2007; Stanfill et al., 2010). Recent advances in natural language processing (NLP) with deep learning techniques have inspired many methods for automatic medical code assignment (Shi et al., 2017; Mullenbach et al., 2018; Li and Yu, 2020). Zhang et al. (2020) incorporated structured knowledge into medical text representations by preserving translational property of concept embeddings. However, several challenges remain in medical text understanding. Diagnosis notes contain complex diagnosis information, which includes a large number of professional medical vocabulary and noisy information such as non-standard synonyms and misspellings. Free text clinical notes are lengthy documents, usually from hundreds to thousands of tokens. Thus, medical text understanding requires effective feature representation learning and complex cognitive process to enable multiple diagnosis code assignment.

Previous neural methods for medical text encoding generally fall into two categories. Medical text modeling is commonly regarded as a synonym of recurrent neural networks (RNNs) that capture the sequential dependency. Such works include AttentiveLSTM (Shi et al., 2017), Bi-GRU (Mullenbach et al., 2018) and HA-GRU (Baumel et al., 2018). The other category uses convolutional neural networks (CNNs) such as CAML (Mullenbach et al., 2018) and MultiResCNN (Li and Yu, 2020). These methods only capture locality but have achieved the optimal predictive performance on medical code assignment.

Inspired by the generic temporal convolutional network (TCN) architecture (Bai et al., 2018), we consider medical text modeling with causal con-



*Proceedings of the 3rd Clinical Natural Language Processing Workshop*, pages 73–78
November 19, 2020. ©2020 Association for Computational Linguistics

straints, where the encoding of the current token only depends on previous tokens, using the dilated convolutional network. We combine it with the label attention network for fine-grained information aggregation.

**Distinction of Our Model**  The MultiResNet is currently the state-of-the-art model. It applies multi-channel CNN with different filters to learn features and further concatenates these features to produce a final prediction. In contrast, our model extends the TCN to sequence modeling that uses a single filter and the dilation operation to control the receptive field. In addition, instead of weight tying used in the TCN, we customize it with label attention pooling to extract relevant rich features.

**Our Contributions**  We contribute to the literature in three ways. (1) We consider medical text modeling from the perspective of imposing the sequential causal constraint in medical code assignment using dilated convolutions, which effectively captures long sequential dependencies and learns contextual representations in the long clinical notes. (2) We propose a dilated convolutional attention network (DCAN), coupling residual dilated convolution, and label attention network for more effective and efficient medical text modeling. (3) Experiments in real-world medical data show improvement over the state of the art. Compared with multi-channel CNN and RNN models, our model also offers a smaller computational cost.

## 2  Proposed Model

This section describes the proposed model - Dilated Convolutional Attention Network (DCAN). It includes three main components, i.e., dilated convolution for learning features from word embeddings of clinical notes, residual connection for stacking a deep neural architecture, and label attention module for prioritizing relevant representation for different labels. The architecture of our proposed model is illustrated in Fig. 1.

Our model benefits from the effective integration of these three neural modules. Dilated convolutions are widely used in audio signal modeling (Oord et al., 2016) and semantic segmentation (Yu and Koltun, 2015). Yu and Koltun (2015) proposed dilated convolutions with an exponentially large receptive filed. Bai et al. (2018) utilized causal convolutions with dilation and tied weighting for sequence modeling. Following their works, we

integrated dilated convolution with label attention network for better medical text encoding to predict diagnosis codes. The dilated convolution follows the causal constraint of sequence modeling. By stacking dilated convolutions with residual connection (He et al., 2016), our DCAN model can be built as a very deep neural network to learn different levels of features. And the final label attention module further extracts the most relevant information to the label space.

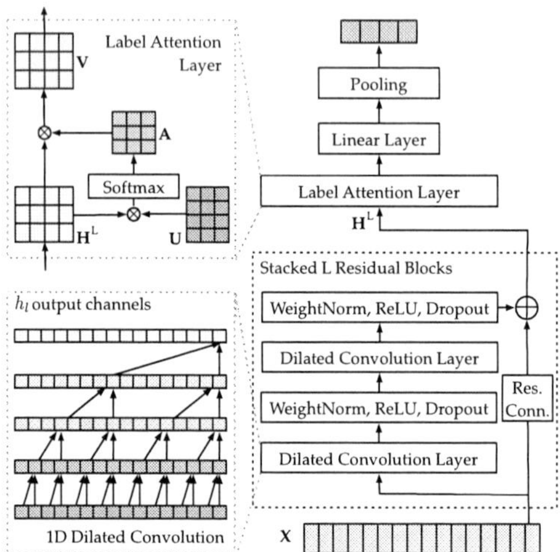


Figure 1: Model architecture of dilated convolutional attention network

### 2.1  Dilated Convolution Layers

A clinical note with $n$ words is denoted as $\{x_0, \ldots, x_n\}$. We use word2vec (Mikolov et al., 2013) to train word embeddings from raw tokens. Word embedding matrix of a clinical note is denoted as $[\mathbf{w}_1, \ldots, \mathbf{w}_n]^T \in \mathbb{R}^{n \times d_e}$, where $d_e$ is the dimension of word vectors. The word embeddings are then inputted into the dilated convolution layers, which are also called convolutions with dilated filters. Specifically, we use a 1D convolution operator to each dimension (i.e. channel) of the word vectors. Given a sequence of one-dimensional elements $\mathbf{x} \in \mathbb{R}^n$ and a convolutional filter $f : \{0, \ldots, k-1\} \to \mathbb{R}$, the one-dimensional dilated convolution $\mathcal{F}_d$ is denoted as

$$\mathcal{F}_d(s) = (\mathbf{x} *_d f)(s) = \sum_{i=0}^{k-1} f(i) \cdot \mathbf{x}_{s-d \cdot i}, \quad (1)$$

where $d$ is the dilation size of the spacing between kernel elements, $s$ is the element of input sequence,

$k$ is the convolving kernel (aka, the filter) size, and $s - d \cdot i$ refers to past time steps. The 1D dilated convolution has $h_l$ output channels, i.e., for each of the $d_e$ input channels $h_l$ features are learned and summed over the input channels. The dilated convolution is followed by a weight normalization, an activation function, and a dropout operation. Two dilated convolution layers ared stacked to a dilated convolution block. It outputs a hidden representation $\mathbf{H}^l \in \mathbb{R}^{n \times h_l}$ of the $l$-th layer, where the dimension $d_h$ of the hidden representation is the number of output channels in the last dilated convolution layer. To expand the receptive field, the dilation size is exponentially increased, i.e., $d_i \in \{2^i\}$ for $i = 0, 1, \ldots, l - 2$.

## 2.2 Residual Connections

Residual connections (He et al., 2016) of $l$ residual blocks are built upon the dilated convolution layers to create deep neural networks. Given the input encoding vector $\mathbf{x}$, the output of residual connection is denoted as $o = \sigma(\mathbf{x} + \mathcal{G}(\mathbf{x}))$, where $\mathcal{G}$ represents neural layers and $\sigma$ is a non-linear activation function. We use residual mechanism between two stacked dilated convolution layers, which is formalized as:

$$\mathbf{H}^{l+1} = \sigma(\mathbf{H}^l + \mathcal{G}(\mathbf{H}^l)). \qquad (2)$$

## 2.3 Label Attention Layer

We apply the label attention layer to prioritize important information in the hidden representation relevant to ICD codes. Specifically, the dot product attention is used to calculate the attention score $\mathbf{A} \in \mathbb{R}^{n \times m}$ as:

$$\mathbf{A} = \mathrm{Softmax}(\mathbf{H}^L \mathbf{U}), \qquad (3)$$

where $\mathbf{H}^L$ (the superscript represents the ordinal of the layer $\mathbf{H}$ and not the power) is the hidden encoding of the $L$-th layer, $\mathbf{U} \in \mathbb{R}^{h_L \times m}$ is the parameter matrix of the label attention layer (also known as the query), and $m$ is the number of ICD codes. The attention matrix $\mathbf{A}$ captures the importance of ICD code and hidden word representation pair. The output of the attention layer is then calculated by multiplying attention $\mathbf{A}$ with the hidden representation from residual dilated convolution layers. The attentive representation $\mathbf{V} \in \mathbb{R}^{m \times h_L}$ is formalized as

$$\mathbf{V} = \mathbf{A}^\mathrm{T} \mathbf{H}^L. \qquad (4)$$

With features representing sequential dependency and label awareness, the final representation is further used for medical code classification.

## 2.4 Classification Layer

The classification layer is a linear fully-connected layer. The $i$-th projected representation $\mathbf{Y}_i \in \mathbb{R}^k$ is calculated as:

$$\mathbf{Y}_i = \mathbf{V}_i \mathbf{W}^\mathrm{T} + \mathbf{b}, \qquad (5)$$

where $\mathbf{W} \in \mathbb{R}^{k \times h_L}$ is the linear weight, $\mathbf{b} \in \mathbb{R}^{1 \times k}$ is the bias, and $\mathbf{Y}_i$ and $\mathbf{V}_i$ are the $i$-th row of $\mathbf{Y}$ and $\mathbf{V}$ for $i \in \{1, \ldots, m\}$. The predicted logits $\hat{\mathbf{y}} \in \mathbb{R}^m$ between 0 and 1 are produced by a pooling operation over the linearly projected matrix $\mathbf{Y}$ and passed into the Sigmoid activation function, denoted as:

$$\hat{\mathbf{y}} = \mathrm{Sigmoid}(\mathrm{Pooling}(\mathbf{Y})). \qquad (6)$$

## 2.5 Training

ICD code assignment is a typical multi-label multi-class classification problem. We adopt the binary cross entropy loss denoted as:

$$\mathcal{L} = \sum_{i=1}^{m} \left[ -y_i \log(\hat{y}_i) - (1 - y_i) \log(1 - \hat{y}_i) \right], \qquad (7)$$

where $y_i \in \{0, 1\}$ is the ground-truth label, $\hat{y}_i$ is the sigmoid score for prediction, and $m$ is the number of ICD codes. To mitigate the effect of noisy labels, we apply label smoothing over ground-truth labels $y$ penalizing model from over-confident predictions. The modified targets $\tilde{y}$ are calculated as:

$$\tilde{y}_i = y_i(1 - \alpha) + \alpha/m, \qquad (8)$$

where $\alpha$ is the smoothing coefficient. We use Adam optimizer (Kingma and Ba, 2014) to train the model with backpropagation.

## 3 Experiments

This section introduces the experimental analysis of real-world clinical datasets. Our proposed models are compared with several recent strong baselines. The code is publicly available at `https://agit.ai/jsx/DCAN`.

## 3.1 Dataset and Settings

This paper focuses on textual discharge summaries from a hospital stay. Following Shi et al. (2017)

Table 1: Results on MIMIC-III dataset with top-50 ICD codes. "-" indicates no results reported in the original paper.

| Model | AUC-ROC | | F1 | | |
| --- | --- | --- | --- | --- | --- |
| | Macro | Micro | Macro | Micro | P@5 |
| CNN (Kim, 2014) | 87.6 | 90.7 | 57.6 | 62.5 | 62.0 |
| C-MemNN (Prakash et al., 2017) | 83.3 | - | - | - | 42.0 |
| Attentive LSTM (Shi et al., 2017) | - | 90.0 | - | 53.2 | - |
| Bi-GRU (Mullenbach et al., 2018) | 82.8 | 86.8 | 48.4 | 54.9 | 59.1 |
| CAML (Mullenbach et al., 2018) | 87.5 | 90.9 | 53.2 | 61.4 | 60.9 |
| DR-CAML (Mullenbach et al., 2018) | 88.4 | 91.6 | 57.6 | 63.3 | 61.8 |
| LEAM (Wang et al., 2018) | 88.1 | 91.2 | 54.0 | 61.9 | 61.2 |
| MultiResCNN (Li and Yu, 2020) | 89.9±0.4 | 92.8±0.2 | 60.6±1.1 | 67.0±0.3 | 64.1±0.1 |
| DCAN (Ours) | **90.2±0.6** | **93.1±0.1** | **61.5±0.7** | **67.1±0.1** | **64.2±0.2** |

and Mullenbach et al. (2018), additional experiment on the subset of MIMIC-III (Johnson et al., 2016) with the top 50 frequent labels is conducted. Free-text discharge summaries are extracted, including raw notes, ICD diagnoses, and procedures for patients. Textual notes related to the same admission are concatenated to a single document to be used as input to our model. Each document is labeled with a set of ICD-9 diagnosis and procedure codes, which are the prediction targets. We use the standard train-test partition. The MIMIC-III dataset with top-50 codes contains 8,066 training, 1,573 development, and 1,729 test instances.

**Settings** We preprocess the textual documents following the preprocessing procedures developed by Mullenbach et al. (2018) and Li and Yu (2020). The NLTK package is utilized for tokenization and all tokens are converted into lowercase. Alphabetic characters such as numbers and punctuations are removed. All documents are truncated at the length of 2500 tokens. We choose some common settings from prior publications. For example, the word embedding dimension is 100, the dropout rate is 0.2. The Adam optimizer Kingma and Ba (2014) is used to optimize our model parameters. The rest choices of hyper-parameters are configured via random search.

## 3.2 Baselines

Baselines models include memory network based C-MemNN (Prakash et al., 2017), the joint embedding model (LEAM) (Wang et al., 2018), RNN-based models like Attentive LSTM (Shi et al., 2017) and Bi-GRU (Mullenbach et al., 2018), and CNN-based models such as vanilla CNN (Kim, 2014), CAML (Mullenbach et al., 2018) and MultiResCNN (Li and Yu, 2020).

## 3.3 Results

We evaluate the F1-score and area under the receiver operating characteristic curve (AUC-ROC) with both micro and macro averaging, and the precision at $k$ codes with $k = 5$ (P@5). The results are shown in Table 1. Our model outperforms the state-of-the-art in all the metrics. To compare with the MultiResCNN model, we follow its setting and run our model for three times. We average the predictive scores and calculate their standard deviation. Our model has a clear improvement in the macro F1-score when the macro score calculates the label-wise average by treating all codes equally. For the other metrics, our model still has a marginal improvement with a lower or comparable standard deviation. We also try the pre-trained Bidirectional Encoder Representations from Transformers(BERT) model (Devlin et al., 2019) for sequence classification. However, the BERT model does not work well in this task. This conclusion is also reported by Li and Yu (2020).

Table 2: Computational cost comparison

| Model | # params. | training time | training ep. |
| --- | --- | --- | --- |
| CAML | 6.2M | 673 s/ep | 85 epochs |
| MultiResCNN | 11.9M | 1161 s/ep | 26 epochs |
| DCAN (Ours) | 8.7M | 951 s/ep | 23 epochs |

**Computational efficiency** We compared the computational efficiency from two perspectives, i.e., number of parameters and convergence epochs, results are shown in Table 2. Not relying on concatenated multi-channel features, our model has fewer trainable parameters and takes less training time than the state-of-the-art MultiResCNN. Moreover, our model converges faster.

## 4 Conclusion

Recent years extensively studies the automatic medical code assignment. Neural clinical text encoding models use CNNs to extract local features and RNNs to preserve sequential dependency. This paper combines both by using dilated convolution. The dilated convolutional attention network (DCAN) consists of dilated convolution layers, residual connections, and the label attention layer. The DCAN model obeys the causal constraint of sequence encoding and learns rich representations to capture label-aware importance. Through experiments on the MIMIC-III dataset, our model shows better predictive performance than the state-of-the-art methods.

## Acknowledgments

We thank Academy of Finland (grants no. 286607 and 294015 to PM) and Finnish Center for Artificial Intelligence for support of this research. We acknowledge the computational resources provided by the Aalto Science-IT project. The authors wish to acknowledge CSC - IT Center for Science, Finland, for computational resources.

## References

Shaojie Bai, J Zico Kolter, and Vladlen Koltun. 2018. An Empirical Evaluation of Generic Convolutional and Recurrent Networks for Sequence Modeling. *arXiv preprint arXiv:1803.01271*.

Tal Baumel, Jumana Nassour-Kassis, Raphael Cohen, Michael Elhadad, and Noemie Elhadad. 2018. Multi-label Classification of Patient Notes: Case Study on ICD Code Assignment. In *Workshops at the Thirty-Second AAAI Conference on Artificial Intelligence*.

Koby Crammer, Mark Dredze, Kuzman Ganchev, Partha Talukdar, and Steven Carroll. 2007. Automatic Code Assignment to Medical Text. In *Biological, Translational, and Clinical language processing*, pages 129–136.

Jacob Devlin, Ming-Wei Chang, Kenton Lee, and Kristina Toutanova. 2019. BERT: Pre-training of Deep Bidirectional Transformers for Language Understanding. In *NAACL-HLT*.

Richárd Farkas and György Szarvas. 2008. Automatic Construction of Rule-based ICD-9-CM Coding Systems. In *BMC Bioinformatics*, volume 9(Suppl 3), pages 1–9. Springer.

Mehrdad Farzandipour, Abbas Sheikhtaheri, and Farahnaz Sadoughi. 2010. Effective Factors on Accuracy of Principal Diagnosis Coding based on International Classification of Diseases, the 10th Revision (ICD-10). *International Journal of Information Management*, 30(1):78–84.

Kaiming He, Xiangyu Zhang, Shaoqing Ren, and Jian Sun. 2016. Deep Residual Learning for Image Recognition. In *Proceedings of the IEEE conference on computer vision and pattern recognition*, pages 770–778.

David C Hsia, W Mark Krushat, Ann B Fagan, Jane A Tebbutt, and Richard P Kusserow. 1988. Accuracy of Diagnostic Coding for Medicare Patients under the Prospective-payment System. *New England Journal of Medicine*, 318(6):352–355.

Alistair EW Johnson, Tom J Pollard, Lu Shen, H Lehman Li-wei, Mengling Feng, Mohammad Ghassemi, Benjamin Moody, Peter Szolovits, Leo Anthony Celi, and Roger G Mark. 2016. MIMIC-III, a Freely Accessible Critical Care Database. *Scientific Data*, 3:160035.

Yoon Kim. 2014. Convolutional Ceural Networks for Sentence Classification. *arXiv preprint arXiv:1408.5882*.

Diederik P Kingma and Jimmy Ba. 2014. Adam: A Method for Stochastic Optimization. *arXiv preprint arXiv:1412.6980*.

Fei Li and Hong Yu. 2020. ICD Coding from Clinical Text Using Multi-Filter Residual Convolutional Neural Network. In *Proceedings of the Thirty-Fourth AAAI Conference on Artificial Intelligence*.

Tomas Mikolov, Ilya Sutskever, Kai Chen, Greg S Corrado, and Jeff Dean. 2013. Distributed Representations of Words and Phrases and their Compositionality. In *Advances in neural information processing systems*, pages 3111–3119.

James Mullenbach, Sarah Wiegreffe, Jon Duke, Jimeng Sun, and Jacob Eisenstein. 2018. Explainable Prediction of Medical Codes from Clinical Text. In *Proceedings of NAACL-HLT*, pages 1101–1111.

Aaron van den Oord, Sander Dieleman, Heiga Zen, Karen Simonyan, Oriol Vinyals, Alex Graves, Nal Kalchbrenner, Andrew Senior, and Koray Kavukcuoglu. 2016. WaveNet: A Generative Model for Raw Audio. *arXiv preprint arXiv:1609.03499*.

Aaditya Prakash, Siyuan Zhao, Sadid A Hasan, Vivek Datla, Kathy Lee, Ashequl Qadir, Joey Liu, and Oladimeji Farri. 2017. Condensed Memory Networks for Clinical Diagnostic Inferencing. In *Thirty-First AAAI Conference on Artificial Intelligence*.

Haoran Shi, Pengtao Xie, Zhiting Hu, Ming Zhang, and Eric P Xing. 2017. Towards Automated ICD Coding Using Deep Learning. *arXiv preprint arXiv:1711.04075*.

Mary H Stanfill, Margaret Williams, Susan H Fenton, Robert A Jenders, and William R Hersh. 2010. A Systematic Literature Review of Automated Clinical Coding and Classification systems. *Journal of the American Medical Informatics Association*, 17(6):646–651.

Guoyin Wang, Chunyuan Li, Wenlin Wang, Yizhe Zhang, Dinghan Shen, Xinyuan Zhang, Ricardo Henao, and Lawrence Carin. 2018. Joint Embedding of Words and Labels for Text Classification. In *Proceedings of the 56th Annual Meeting of the Association for Computational Linguistics (Volume 1: Long Papers)*, pages 2321–2331.

Fisher Yu and Vladlen Koltun. 2015. Multi-scale Context Aggregation by Dilated Convolutions. *arXiv preprint arXiv:1511.07122*.

Xiao Zhang, Dejing Dou, and Ji Wu. 2020. Learning Conceptual-Contexual Embeddings for Medical Text. *AAAI Conference on Artificial Intelligence*.

# Classification of Syncope Cases in Norwegian Medical Records

**Ildikó Pilán[*,†], Pål H. Brekke[‡], Fredrik A. Dahl[‡‡], Tore Gundersen[**], Haldor Husby[**],**
**Øystein Nytrø[††], Lilja Øvrelid[*]**
[*]Dept. of Informatics, University of Oslo, [†]Norwegian Computing Center,
[‡]Dept. of Cardiology, Oslo University Hospital Rikshospitalet,
[‡‡]Dept. of Health Services Research, Akershus University Hospital,
[**]Analysis Dept., Akershus University Hospital,
[††]Dept. of Computer Science, Norwegian University of Science and Technology
`pilan@nr.no`, `paul.brekke@gmail.com`
`{Fredrik.A.Dahl,Tore.Gundersen,haldor.husby}@ahus.no,`
`nytroe@ntnu.no, liljao@ifi.uio.no`



## Abstract

Loss of consciousness, so-called *syncope*, is a commonly occurring symptom associated with worse prognosis for a number of heart-related diseases. We present a comparison of methods for a diagnosis classification task in Norwegian clinical notes, targeting syncope, i.e. fainting cases. We find that an often neglected baseline with keyword matching constitutes a rather strong basis, but more advanced methods do offer some improvement in classification performance, especially a convolutional neural network model. The developed pipeline is planned to be used for quantifying unregistered syncope cases in Norway.


## 1 Introduction

Neural methods have revolutionized the field of NLP, including the clinical domain in recent years. The amount of performance gain, however, may not always be proportional to the increased complexity and decreased transparency that their use might entail, especially in data-sparse domains and target languages. The limited availability of data and its linguistic characteristics, i.e. a high density of terminology, repetitions, abbreviations and misspellings (Allvin et al., 2011), are aspects that influence greatly the efficiency of the NLP methods applied. These have been compared to some extent in previous work (Baumel et al., 2018; Mascio et al., 2020; Karimi et al., 2017), however, they are often evaluated on the same (and often limited) openly available datasets (Pestian et al., 2007; Johnson et al., 2016). The real-world utility of various approaches in clinical text processing, especially for languages other than English, however, remains still to be investigated (Ching et al., 2018). Moreover, comparison to a simple rule-based baseline is

often missing, leaving some uncertainty around the advantage of more advanced methods.

Starting from a close collaboration with Akershus University Hospital, we re-examine the question of the optimal methodological choice in the context of diagnosis coding in Norwegian clinical notes. Diagnosis codes are standard alpha-numeric codes representing a disease, a widely adopted scheme being ICD-10 (World Health Organization et al., 2004). ICD-10 codes are used for a variety of purposes, including hospital billing and reimbursement, population health statistics, and clinical research. Additionally, the re-use of structured health data in clinical decision support and risk assessment has also been suggested. ICD-10 coding is used as a most relevant classification of the reason for contact, underlying conditions or procedures related to the stay. A host of signs, events and observations are not coded. Syncope, or similar signs, may be regarded as secondary or irrelevant for a certain patient, and thus only mentioned but not coded. Clearly, accurate coding is important, but as a human process prone to error and biases, the quality of ICD-10 codes has been questioned. This is the case for *syncope* - a transient loss of conciousness typically due to insufficient blood flow to the brain - which was chosen as the use case for our study. A large study of Danish medical records (Ruwald et al., 2012) found that around a third of actual syncope records did not have the appropriate ICD-10 code. Since syncope can be an important sign of heart disease and a marker of elevated risk of death in certain conditions such as hypertrophic cardiomyopathy (Elliott et al., 2015), being able to retrieve information about patient's syncope events even when an ICD-10 code is not present, is crucial for better risk assessment. Also, this work constitutes a first step in the direction of an automatic




*Proceedings of the 3rd Clinical Natural Language Processing Workshop*, pages 79–84
November 19, 2020. ©2020 Association for Computational Linguistics

diagnosis coding system for Norwegian, which is currently not available. The research questions we investigate in this context are: (i) How do linear and neural models compare to a simple keyword matching baseline for binary automatic diagnosis code classification?; and (ii) How useful are pre-trained embeddings for this task? In what follows, we first describe our health record data and our pre-processing steps. We then compare three types of methods for syncope classification: a rule-based one relying on keyword matching, linear machine learning models and neural models. Besides estimating the amount of unregistered syncope cases in Norway, our processing and classification pipeline can also easily be re-used to train more generic diagnosis code classifiers.

## 2  Background

Since medical language is rather terminology-heavy, rule-based methods can often go a long way in clinical NLP tasks and are, therefore, still rather wide-spread (Koleck et al., 2019). Statistical approaches handle better linguistic phenomena such as synonyms, code-switching and negation, however, they are computationally more expensive, require resources and, in particular neural ones, are often less interpretable (Linzen et al., 2019). Moreover, neural methods substantially alleviate the burden of feature-engineering, but are considerably more challenging in terms of hyper-parameter tuning. Incorporating such models into clinical data processing pipelines is thus an advantage only if they can demonstrate a clear advantage over their simpler counterparts.

Dipaola et al. (2019) developed linear classifiers with manually and automatically selected n-grams as features for classifying syncope in Italian medical records. A frequent target of investigations has been the 2007 Computational Medicine Challenge (CMC) dataset, focusing on automatic ICD coding in radiology reports. Both rule-based (Farkas and Szarvas, 2008) and statistical methods (Crammer et al., 2007) including neural ones (Karimi et al., 2017), have been tested and sometimes compared on this data. Karimi et al. (2017) reported that the performance of a Support Vector Machine (SVM) with term frequency–inverse document frequency (TF-IDF) bag-of-words (BoW) features remained considerably below the results of a Convolutional Neural Network (CNN) with dynamic in-domain pre-trained Word2Vec embeddings with F1 scores

of .65 and .81 respectively. A direct comparison across these works, however, is difficult given differences in the evaluation and data subset used.

More recently, using another dataset, MIMIC-III (Johnson et al., 2016), experiments presented by Baumel et al. (2018) indicated that neural methods outperform linear models for the same type of multi-class classification of ICD codes, although not always by a large margin. Mascio et al. (2020) also described a comparison between linear and neural models, but for different clinical binary classification tasks (e.g. status and negation prediction) and showed that recurrent neural networks tuned for their task performed on par with the more recent, transformer models (Devlin et al., 2019). Rule-based baselines were often not included in these recent studies (Karimi et al., 2017; Baumel et al., 2018; Mascio et al., 2020), the practical advantage of different approaches therefore remains somewhat unclear compared to methods based on heuristics.

## 3  Dataset

Our data consisted of de-identified discharge summaries from Akershus University Hospital Hospital. Half of the notes were diagnosed syncope cases (SYN), the other half were notes with a variety of diagnosis codes for patients with no recorded and coded history of syncope (NONS). The documents were authored between 2005–2016.[1] While patients in SYN were from a variety of departments, all NONS patients were from the Cardiology Department. Moreover, only patients who were $\geq 18$ years old at the time of discharge were included. Table 1 provides an overview of the number of documents and their average length in number of tokens used in our dataset.

|  | SYN | NONS | ALL |
|---|---|---|---|
| **# texts** | 501 | 500 | 1,001 |
| **Avg # tokens** | 667.51 | 546.52 | 607.02 |

Table 1: Overview of the dataset.

The notes contained free text where some structuring is present in the form of titled sections with information about e.g. diagnosis, family history and current status. There were, however, inconsistencies in the section titles as well as in the presence

---

[1] Data from the years 2017-2018 were reserved for evaluating the proportion of syncope cases with no diagnosis code.

and order of these sections. A previous study (Røst et al., 2020) using EHRs from Akershus University Hospital in a text classification task has also identified a need for improving interoperability when exporting such unstructured data.

## 4   Experimental Setup

The first pre-processing step consisted of tokenization with UDPipe (Straka et al., 2016). Diagnosis information reflecting the labels used for classification (SYN vs. NONS) was then removed from the documents using: (i) lexical matching for section title identification; and (ii) UDPipe paragraph information for determining section boundaries. We divided our data into three stratified splits: 70% of it reserved for training, 15% used as validation data for hyper-parameter tuning and the remaining 15% was set aside for testing. We compared a keyword matching baseline to two linear classifiers, a Logistic Regression (LR) classifier and an SVM, and to neural models, namely CNNs. These learning algorithms have been commonly and successfully used in previous NLP studies, including the clinical domain (Dipaola et al., 2019; Karimi et al., 2017).

**Baseline with lexical matching**  (LEXM) We computed a baseline consisting of a simple lexical matching applied to the pre-processed documents using the term *synkope* 'syncope', which would find both its baseform and other derived forms without additional lemmatization. Whenever a document contained this term at least once, it was classified as belonging to the SYN class, and otherwise as NONS.

**Linear models**  For training the linear models, we use scikit-learn (Pedregosa et al., 2011), and we employ Keras with Tensorflow (Abadi et al., 2016) as backend for the neural models. For both SVM and LR, we use BOW features extracted with a TF-IDF vectorizer. We perform a grid search for finding the optimal hyper-parameters on the validation data.

**Neural models**  For the CNN, Word2Vec (Mikolov et al., 2013) embeddings were used as input representation to capture contextual similarity between words. We adopted a common CNN architecture (Kim, 2014) consisting of an input layer of 100 dimensions, a convolutional layer concatenating 100 filters of sizes 3 to 5, with rectified linear units, max pooling and a dropout of 0.5, followed by a fully connected softmax layer. We used binary cross-entropy loss, the Adam Optimizer, a learning rate of 0.001 and a batch size of 32. We trained for 10 epochs with early stopping based on validation accuracy and a patience of 2 epochs.

We experimented with different embedding initializations, inspired by Kim (2014): a randomly initialized one (W2V-R) and two where weights were based on pre-trained embeddings. In one case, weights were not trainable during the learning process (*static*) and in the other, we continued training these weights (*dynamic*). This type of transfer learning consisting of fine-tuning pre-trained embeddings for a specific task is often beneficial when the size of the available training data is small (Kim, 2014).

**Pre-trained embeddings**  In the absence of pre-trained clinical embeddings for Norwegian, we compared two other types of pre-trained embeddings, both 100 dimensional Word2Vec skip-gram models trained with Gensim (Řehůřek and Sojka, 2010): (i) general language embeddings W2V-G trained on OCR-ed books, news and web corpora, namely model nr. 100 from the NLPL repository[2] (Fares et al., 2017); and (ii) domain-related embeddings W2V-M, which we trained on data from the *Norsk legemiddelhåndbok*[3] 'Norwegian drug manual'. The medical vocabulary of these disease and drug descriptions was closely connected to the clinical domain. We used default parameters for training W2V-M, but lowered minimum word count to 1 given the small data size.

## 5   Model Comparison and Error Analysis

In Table 2, we present the classification results for the approaches tested, where R-SENS represents *sensitivity*, i.e. recall for the positive class, SYN, and R-AVG is average recall for both classes. For the CNN models, an average of three runs (and standard deviation) is reported.

Lexical matching provided a rather high baseline, namely .80 accuracy, which suggests that similar terminology matching methods are worth testing and comparing to in terminology-rich domains such as the clinical one. Although we started from a strong baseline, we found that, with increasing computational complexity, performance improved somewhat. LR proved to be the best linear model (.86 accuracy) with L1 penalty, $C = 10$ with a

---

[2] http://vectors.nlpl.eu/repository/
[3] https://www.legemiddelhandboka.no/

| Method | Features | Init | ACC | F1 | PREC | R-SENS | R-AVG |
|--------|----------|------|-----|-----|------|--------|-------|
| LEXM | N/A | N/A | .80 | .80 | .80 | .79 | .80 |
| SVM | BOW | N/A | .85 | .85 | .85 | .87 | .85 |
| LR | BOW | N/A | **.86** | **.86** | **.86** | **.89** | **.86** |
| CNN | w2v-R | Random | **.92** (±.01) | **.92** (±.01) | **.91** (±.01) | **.93** (±.01) | **.92** (±.01) |
| | w2v-G | Static | .87 (±.01) | .87 (±.01) | .87 (±.01) | .85 (±.03) | .87 (±.01) |
| | | Dynamic | .89 (±.00) | .89 (±.01) | .89 (±.01) | .88 (±.01) | .89 (±.01) |
| | w2v-M | Static | .68 (±.04) | .67 (±.05) | .70 (±.02) | .80 (±.07) | .68 (±.04) |
| | | Dynamic | .77 (±.02) | .77 (±.02) | .78 (±.02) | .78 (±.03) | .77 (±.02) |

Table 2: Binary classification results on the test set.

liblinear solver as optimal hyper-parameters based on our grid search. The best neural model w2v-R, achieved .92 accuracy and a sensitivity of .93. To put these results into perspective, Dipaola et al. (2019) reported a sensitivity of .92 for an SVM-based syncope classification model for Italian.

For neural models, initializing embeddings randomly worked best. The number of in-embedding words was rather low in fact for both w2v-G and w2v-M, namely 51% and 27.5% respectively. In addition, w2v-G results might be influenced by a difference in domains. Models with w2v-M produced not only lower scores, but also more instability as standard deviation shows, likely due to the small vocabulary size (50K) and few in-embedding words. Dynamic embeddings showed improvements over static ones, especially for w2v-M, in line with previous findings (Kim, 2014).

We compared our methods also with McNemar's test (McNemar, 1962)[4] and found statistically significant difference in the misclassifications at $\alpha = 0.05$ only between the baseline and CNN-w2v-R ($p = 0.003$), but not between the other two model pairs, namely LR vs. baseline ($p = 0.163$) and LR vs. CNN-w2v-R ($p = 0.077$). Figure 1 shows the receiver-operating characteristic (ROC) curve for LR and CNN-w2v-R on the test set, which also shows a rather similar performance.

To gain a better understanding into what the best performing linear and neural models, LR and CNN-w2v-R respectively have learned, we inspected the 30 words which received the highest weights after training. These included for both models near-synonyms such as *svimmel* 'dizziness' and *bevis-sthetstap* 'unconsciousness' and even the English

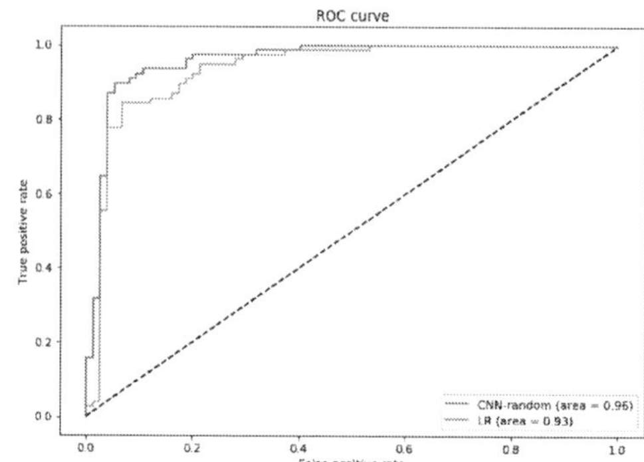

Figure 1: ROC curve for LR and CNN-w2v-R.

translation of the term (*syncope*). Yet another group of informative features described typical circumstances of syncope (e.g. *gulvet* 'floor'). LR also captured inflectional variants like *synkopert*, 'syncopated'. Both models' decisions relied thus on factors relevant to the target medical phenomenon.

Our error analysis revealed that around half of the NONS instances missclassified by both LR and CNN-w2v-R as SYN did contain mentions of 'syncope', but sometimes either as part of a patient's previous history of illnesses or with negation (*aldri synkopert* 'never syncoped'). Slightly more (60%) of misclassifications occurred for NONS texts, however, 23% (LR) and 38% (CNN-w2v-R) of these appeared to be unregistered syncope cases. Manually re-diagnosed data might therefore improve performance.

## 6 Conclusions

We described a set of experiments using keyword-matching as well as machine learning methods for the classification of syncope cases in Norwe-

---

[4]With binomial distribution given the small sample size.

gian clinical notes. Our results indicate that neural methods provide some advantage over a keyword baseline, but the latter performs surprisingly well, which indicates that terminological cues can be easily leveraged for such binary clinical text classification tasks in the absence of access to training data. This type of baseline constitutes thus a valuable starting and reference point for comparison to more advanced methods.

Future work includes hyper-parameter tuning of the neural models and comparing the generalizability of our models to new data, including different note types. We plan to use the developed models for quantifying the amount of unregistered syncope cases in Norway and to extend them to classify a variety of diagnostic codes. Embeddings trained on large Norwegian clinical data would be valuable to boost performance for both this and other tasks.

This work showcases a fruitful collaboration between an NLP research environment and a hospital. Aligning clinical data processing interests and needs is particularly important for smaller languages without publicly available data for both moving the clinical NLP research front forward and to bring findings closer to the clinical practice.

## Ethics

According to Norwegian law, the project has been approved by the hospital's internal Privacy Ombudsman, ref. 2019_15.

## Acknowledgments

This work was funded by the Norwegian Research Council and more specifically by BigMed, an IKT-PLUSS Lighthouse project.

## References

Martín Abadi, Paul Barham, Jianmin Chen, Zhifeng Chen, Andy Davis, Jeffrey Dean, Matthieu Devin, Sanjay Ghemawat, Geoffrey Irving, Michael Isard, Manjunath Kudlur, Josh Levenberg, Rajat Monga, Sherry Moore, Derek G. Murray, Benoit Steiner, Paul Tucker, Vijay Vasudevan, Pete Warden, Martin Wicke, Yuan Yu, and Xiaoqiang Zheng. 2016. Tensorflow: A system for large-scale machine learning. In *Proceedings of the 12th USENIX Conference on Operating Systems Design and Implementation*, OSDI'16, page 265–283, USA. USENIX Association.

Helen Allvin, Elin Carlsson, Hercules Dalianis, Riitta Danielsson-Ojala, Vidas Daudaravičius, Martin Hassel, Dimitrios Kokkinakis, Heljä Lundgrén-Laine, Gunnar H Nilsson, Øystein Nytrø, et al. 2011. Characteristics of Finnish and Swedish intensive care nursing narratives: a comparative analysis to support the development of clinical language technologies. *Journal of Biomedical Semantics*, 2:1–11.

Tal Baumel, Jumana Nassour-Kassis, Raphael Cohen, Michael Elhadad, and Noemie Elhadad. 2018. Multi-label classification of patient notes: case study on ICD code assignment. In *Workshops at the Thirty-Second AAAI Conference on Artificial Intelligence*, pages 409–416.

Travers Ching, Daniel S Himmelstein, Brett K Beaulieu-Jones, Alexandr A Kalinin, Brian T Do, Gregory P Way, Enrico Ferrero, Paul-Michael Agapow, Michael Zietz, Michael M Hoffman, et al. 2018. Opportunities and obstacles for deep learning in biology and medicine. *Journal of The Royal Society Interface*, 15(141):20170387.

Koby Crammer, Mark Dredze, Kuzman Ganchev, Partha Pratim Talukdar, and Steven Carroll. 2007. Automatic code assignment to medical text. In *Biological, translational, and clinical language processing*, pages 129–136, Prague, Czech Republic. Association for Computational Linguistics.

Jacob Devlin, Ming-Wei Chang, Kenton Lee, and Kristina Toutanova. 2019. BERT: Pre-training of deep bidirectional transformers for language understanding. In *Proceedings of the 2019 Conference of the North American Chapter of the Association for Computational Linguistics: Human Language Technologies, Volume 1 (Long and Short Papers)*, pages 4171–4186, Minneapolis, Minnesota. Association for Computational Linguistics.

Franca Dipaola, Mauro Gatti, Veronica Pacetti, Anna Giulia Bottaccioli, Dana Shiffer, Maura Minonzio, Roberto Menè, Alessandro Giaj Levra, Monica Solbiati, Giorgio Costantino, et al. 2019. Artificial intelligence algorithms and natural language processing for the recognition of syncope patients on emergency department medical records. *Journal of Clinical Medicine*, 8(10):1677.

Perry M Elliott, Aris Anastasakis, Michael A Borger, Martin Borggrefe, Franco Cecchi, Philippe Charron, Albert Alain Hagege, Antoine Lafont, Giuseppe Limongelli, Heiko Mahrholdt, et al. 2015. 2014 ESC guidelines on diagnosis and management of hypertrophic cardiomyopathy. *Revista espanola de cardiologia*, 68(1):63.

Murhaf Fares, Andrey Kutuzov, Stephan Oepen, and Erik Velldal. 2017. Word vectors, reuse, and replicability: Towards a community repository of large-text resources. In *Proceedings of the 21st Nordic Conference on Computational Linguistics*, pages 271–276, Gothenburg, Sweden. Association for Computational Linguistics.

Richárd Farkas and György Szarvas. 2008. Automatic construction of rule-base ICD-9-CM coding systems. *BMC Bioinformatics*, 9(S3):S10.

Alistair EW Johnson, Tom J Pollard, Lu Shen, H Lehman Li-Wei, Mengling Feng, Mohammad Ghassemi, Benjamin Moody, Peter Szolovits, Leo Anthony Celi, and Roger G Mark. 2016. MIMIC-III, a freely accessible critical care database. *Scientific data*, 3(1):1–9.

Sarvnaz Karimi, Xiang Dai, Hamed Hassanzadeh, and Anthony Nguyen. 2017. Automatic diagnosis coding of radiology reports: A comparison of deep learning and conventional classification methods. In *BioNLP 2017*, pages 328–332, Vancouver, Canada,. Association for Computational Linguistics.

Yoon Kim. 2014. Convolutional neural networks for sentence classification. In *Proceedings of the 2014 Conference on Empirical Methods in Natural Language Processing (EMNLP)*, pages 1746–1751, Doha, Qatar. Association for Computational Linguistics.

Theresa A Koleck, Caitlin Dreisbach, Philip E Bourne, and Suzanne Bakken. 2019. Natural language processing of symptoms documented in free-text narratives of electronic health records: a systematic review. *Journal of the American Medical Informatics Association*, 26(4):364–379.

Tal Linzen, Grzegorz Chrupała, Yonatan Belinkov, and Dieuwke Hupkes. 2019. *Proceedings of the 2019 ACL Workshop BlackboxNLP: Analyzing and Interpreting Neural Networks for NLP*. Association for Computational Linguistics.

Aurelie Mascio, Zeljko Kraljevic, Daniel Bean, Richard Dobson, Robert Stewart, Rebecca Bendayan, and Angus Roberts. 2020. Comparative analysis of text classification approaches in electronic health records. In *Proceedings of the 19th SIGBioMed Workshop on Biomedical Language Processing*, pages 86–94, Online. Association for Computational Linguistics.

Quinn McNemar. 1962. *Psychological statistics*, volume 3. Wiley New York.

Tomas Mikolov, Kai Chen, Greg Corrado, and Jeffrey Dean. 2013. Efficient estimation of word representations in vector space. In *Proceedings of International Conference on Learning Representations*.

Fabian Pedregosa, Gaël Varoquaux, Alexandre Gramfort, Vincent Michel, Bertrand Thirion, Olivier Grisel, Mathieu Blondel, Peter Prettenhofer, Ron Weiss, Vincent Dubourg, et al. 2011. Scikit-learn: Machine learning in Python. *Journal of Machine Learning Research*, 12(Oct):2825–2830.

John P. Pestian, Chris Brew, Pawel Matykiewicz, DJ Hovermale, Neil Johnson, K. Bretonnel Cohen, and Wlodzislaw Duch. 2007. A shared task involving multi-label classification of clinical free text. In *Biological, translational, and clinical language processing*, pages 97–104, Prague, Czech Republic. Association for Computational Linguistics.

Radim Řehůřek and Petr Sojka. 2010. Software Framework for Topic Modelling with Large Corpora. In *Proceedings of the LREC 2010 Workshop on New Challenges for NLP Frameworks*, pages 45–50. ELRA.

Thomas Brox Røst, Christine Raaen Tvedt, Haldor Husby, Ingrid Andås Berg, and Øystein Nytrø. 2020. Identifying catheter-related events through sentence classification. *International Journal of Data Mining and Bioinformatics*, 23(3):213–233.

Martin Huth Ruwald, Morten Lock Hansen, Morten Lamberts, Søren Lund Kristensen, Mads Wissenberg, Anne-Marie Schjerning Olsen, Stefan Bisgaard Christensen, Michael Vinther, Lars Køber, Christian Torp-Pedersen, et al. 2012. Accuracy of the ICD-10 discharge diagnosis for syncope. *Europace*, 15(4):595–600.

Milan Straka, Jan Hajič, and Jana Straková. 2016. UDPipe: Trainable pipeline for processing CoNLL-U files performing tokenization, morphological analysis, POS tagging and parsing. In *Proceedings of the Tenth International Conference on Language Resources and Evaluation (LREC'16)*, pages 4290–4297, Portorož, Slovenia. European Language Resources Association (ELRA).

World Health Organization et al. 2004. *ICD-10: International Statistical Classification of Diseases and Related Health Problems: Tenth Revision*.

# Comparison of Machine Learning Methods for Multi-label Classification of Nursing Education and Licensure Exam Questions

**John T. Langton**      **Krishna Srihasam**      **Junlin Jiang**

Wolters Kluwer Health, 230 3rd Avenue, Waltham, MA 02451

{john.langto, krishna.srihasam, junlin.jiang} @wolterskluwer.com

## Abstract

In this paper, we evaluate several machine learning methods for multi-label classification of text questions. Every nursing student in the United States must pass the National Council Licensure Examination (NCLEX) to begin professional practice. NCLEX defines a number of competencies on which students are evaluated. By labeling test questions with NCLEX competencies, we can score students according to their performance in each competency. This information helps instructors measure how prepared students are for the NCLEX, as well as which competencies they may need help with. A key challenge is that questions may be related to more than one competency. Labeling questions with NCLEX competencies, therefore, equates to a multi-label, text classification problem where each competency is a label. Here we present an evaluation of several methods to support this use case along with a proposed approach. While our work is grounded in the nursing education domain, the methods described here can be used for any multi-label, text classification use case.

## 1   Introduction

All nurses within the United States must pass the National Council Licensure Examination (NCLEX®) to begin professional practice. A nursing curriculum will typically cover a wide range of topics related to the theory and practice of nursing. However, the NCLEX measures students against a specific set of competencies comprising the activities that entry-level nurses are most commonly expected to perform. These activities are identified by the National Council of State Boards of Nursing (NCSBN) through analysis of nursing practice.

Figure 1 shows a subset of NCLEX competencies called "activity statements" with descriptions. Activity statements are grouped into primary topics and sub-topics, as shown in the image. Nursing education content may be related to one or more competency; they are not mutually exclusive.

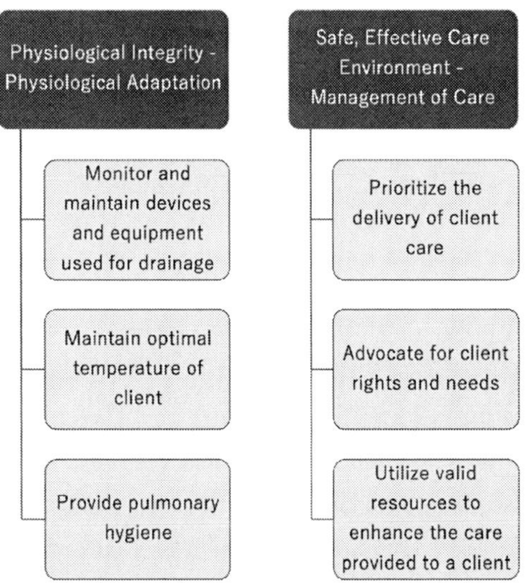


Figure 1: Sample of NCLEX competencies or activity statements.

Passage of the NCLEX has significance not only for students but also for learning institutions. Nursing school accreditation is partially based on how well their student body performs on the NCLEX. If their performance drops below a certain threshold for too many consecutive years, the school risks losing its accreditation. It is, therefore, paramount for instructors to gauge student preparedness for the NCLEX and course correct where necessary. One way to do this is by repeatedly testing students with simulated exams. This approach may reveal that gaps exist, however, it does not necessarily identify what competencies are deficient or what content may address those deficiencies. By labeling both questions and educational content with the competencies that they relate to, instructors can



*Proceedings of the 3rd Clinical Natural Language Processing Workshop*, pages 85–93
November 19, 2020. ©2020 Association for Computational Linguistics

more precisely identify where students are struggling and what content may help with remediation. This approach enables coursework to be tailored for individual students based on their performance in a manner that maximizes likelihood of passing the NCLEX. For instance, if a student incorrectly answers questions related to "Provide pulmonary hygiene" (activity statement shown in Figure 1), the instructor may assign the student additional content (e.g., simulations and practice problems) related to that competency. This general approach is called formative testing.

PrepU is a Wolters Kluwer product for nursing education that features several types of content including books, simulations, videos, audio, and quizzes. To support formative testing in PrepU, quiz questions are tagged with the NCLEX competency related to them. When students take quizzes, their scores can be aggregated according to NCLEX competency. Figure 2 shows an example of the interface displaying this information. The image shows the student achieves a score of 66.7% for the competency "Prioritize the delivery of client care". This is calculated based on the student answering 4 out of 6 questions correctly that were labeled with that competency. There is also a tab that shows class performance so that instructors can see if there is a pattern of multiple students struggling with a particular competency. Instructors can use this information to make changes to the curriculum to address problem areas. Corrective actions may include assigning students additional content or practice materials related to the competencies they are struggling with.

| Activity Statements | No. of Questions Answered Correctly | % of Questions Answered Correctly |
|---|---|---|
| Monitor and maintain devices and equipment used for drainage | 1 of 1 | 100% |
| Obtain specimens other than blood for diagnostic testing | 1 of 1 | 100% |
| Provide care and education for the newborn less than 1 month old through the infant or toddler client through 2 years | 1 of 1 | 100% |
| Apply principles of infection control | 1 of 1 | 100% |
| Facilitate appropriate and safe use of equipment | 1 of 1 | 100% |
| Assess client in coping with life changes and provide support | 2 of 3 | 66.7% |
| Provide information about health promotion and maintenance recommendations | 2 of 3 | 66.7% |
| Prioritize the delivery of client care | 4 of 6 | 66.7% |
| Evaluate client response to medication | 1 of 2 | 50% |
| Follow security plan and procedures | 1 of 2 | 50% |

Figure 2: PrepU screenshot showing quiz results broken down according to NCLEX competencies.

Figure 3: Editorial platform where editors manually tag questions with associated NCLEX competencies.

To aggregate scores according to NCLEX competencies as shown in Figure 2, each question needs to be labeled according to which competencies it relates to. Prior to our work, editors would manually label questions using the editorial platform shown in Figure 3. A drop-down menu shows a selection of NCLEX competencies. The editor must scroll through this list, identify which are appropriate, and select them to add them to the question. This process was costly and time-consuming. One challenge is that each question can belong to more than one competency. Further, different editors may have differing opinions as to which competencies a question relates to. Reconciling these differences and maintaining consistency across editors and content is a huge challenge.

To streamline the labeling of nursing education questions, we integrated a machine learning model for automated tagging into the current workflow. As editors review each question, the model makes suggestions about which NCLEX competencies are related to that question. Rather than scrolling through a long list of options, editors can rapidly click to accept or reject suggestions (though they still have the ability to scroll through all possibilities if they believe none of the suggestions are applicable). This approach has greatly streamlined the process of labeling questions and added additional consistency in the application of labels. The following sections detail the data involved, the modeling techniques evaluated, and the chosen solution.

## 2   The Data

In this paper, we focus on NCLEX competencies related to what are called "activity statements". Activity statements are presented in a hierarchical structure with two levels as shown in Figure 1. We consider only leaf nodes to simplify the problem. Given this consideration, there are 138 activity statements or labels in total.

41125 questions were manually labeled with one or more of the 138 possible activity statements related to them. This data was used for both training and testing of our machine learning models. The distribution of questions across activity statements was non-uniform and presented a class imbalance challenge. The majority of activity statements were assigned to 5 or fewer questions. However, there was a small set of activity statements that were commonly used, and two that were associated with nearly 3000 questions. The distribution of questions to activity statements is shown in Figure 4. Each bar corresponds to one of the 138 activity statements and its height represents the number of questions assigned to it.

Less than 100 questions that were assigned more than one activity statement label. However, there was a desire to accommodate multiple activity statements per question for future labeling efforts. Therefore, we maintained an approach using multi-label classification techniques.

## 3   Related Research

The task of tagging questions with relevant activity statements can be considered a multi-label document classification task where each question is a document. There are several well-known methods for this type of task. Many of them represent a document as a vector of numbers. We can use similarity and/or distance metrics between document vectors to perform several operations such as clustering and classification. A key set of decisions is how to represent documents as vectors, and what distance metrics to use for comparing them. The following sections describe a number of approaches for document vectorization as well as methods for multi-label classification.

### 3.1   Text Vectorization and Classification

Bag of words approaches for document vectorization are quite common and have been used with a number of different algorithms (Mccallum and Nigam, 2001). These approaches use word frequency to determine vector representations for documents and may employ a number of feature selection and normalization techniques (Xu et al., 2009). One dominant technique is called *Term Frequency – Inverse Document Frequency* (TF-IDF).

While bag of words methods have proven quite effective, they suffer a number of weaknesses. When paired with algorithms such as naïve Bayes classifiers, there is no consideration of word order, proximity, or co-occurrence within a document. This can be somewhat mitigated using n-gram techniques (i.e. considering n consecutive words as one element in document vectors). Synonyms can also confound bag of word approaches since two or more words may appear as unique elements in a document vector despite being semantically equivalent. For instance, "water" and "H2O" may show up as distinct vocabulary terms in a TF-IDF vector. When computing the cosine similarity between the vector for a document that discusses "water" and one that discusses "H2O", the result would inaccurately indicate they were dissimilar.

Word embeddings using neural networks are a more recent and popular method for vectorizing text (Kim, 2014). Long Short Term Memory (LSTM) and Gated Recurrent Unit (GRU) are recurrent neural network (RNN) models that leverage connections between adjacent nodes in a single layer to better address word order and context. Huang, Xu, and Yu (Huang et al., 2015) compare several ensembles of bidirectional LSTMs and Conditional Random Fields (CRF) for sentence classification. Neural network models have specifically been used for multi-label document classification (Baumel et al., 2017) (Lenc and Král, 2017).

One of the most recent advances in natural language processing with neural networks is the use of pretrained, deep transformer models such as BERT (Devlin et al., 2018). BERT has outperformed many competing methods in standard language understanding tasks and has been used specifically for document classification (Adhikari et al., 2019). There is a great deal of research combining these different approaches for multiple use cases.

### 3.2   Multi-label Classification

Multi-label classification refers to a classification problem where each item being classified can belong to more than one class (or label) at the same time. This contrasts with standard classification

Figure 4: Sample distributions of number of questions per NCLEX activity statement.

where each item is assigned to only one class. A trivial example would be classifying geometric shapes where a square could be both a square and a rectangle.

There are a few standard techniques for dealing with multi-label classification. Many transform the problem into a standard classification task. One approach is to train a binary classifier for every label independently. Each classifier is then executed on the same input to predict whether its associated label should be applied (Read et al., 2015). In this scenario, each classifier only has the knowledge of one label and only makes predictions for membership or non-membership in that label group or class. This strategy is similar to "one-versus-rest" approaches, however, it often employs techniques more analogous to one class classification or anomaly detection. An extension to this method is to chain multiple binary classifiers together in a sequence. The predictions from one classifier is passed as a feature to the next classifier until a final set of predictions is output. Probabilistic methods can be used to optimize the order of classifiers.

Another common approach for multi-label classification is to take the power set of label permutations and treat each as an independent class. This approach transforms the problem into a standard multi-class classification task. Newton et. al. compare a number of methods for such problem transformations (SpolaôR et al., 2013). For instance, we can transform a set of 3 labels, $(A, B, C)$, into a power set of classes: $\{(A), (B)(C), (A, B), (A, C), (B, C)\}$.

## 4 Evaluating Vectorization Methods and Similarity Metrics for Clustering and Classification

We began our analysis by evaluating how different vectorization techniques and similarity metrics

perform at differentiating questions related to one label (i.e., activity statement) from another. The ability to differentiate questions in this manner directly affects the performance of classification and clustering algorithms. The results helped establish a baseline of how much overlap there was between questions in different label groups. It also informed decisions on which vectorization methods and similarity metrics to use with what algorithms for evaluation.

To perform this analysis, we leveraged techniques often used in clustering. The nursing education questions were grouped into clusters based on the activity statements they were associated with. This resulted in 138 clusters, one for each of the activity statements. Questions associated with more than one activity statement were included in the groups for each. We experimented with several vectorization methods (techniques for transforming the questions into numeric vectors) as well as similarity metrics for comparing vectors. We converged on using cosine similarity to compare vectors because of its ability to deal with both sparse and dense vectors when normalized. The vectorizations evaluated included the following:

- term frequency – inverse document frequency (TF-IDF)

- word embeddings pretrained on google news [(Mikolov et al., 2013)]

- word embeddings pretrained on PubMed [(Pyysalo et al., 2013)]

- word embeddings pretrained on PubMed and updated on text content from Wolters Kluwer nursing education

For each vectorization method, we computed the silhouette score across our manually constructed clusters. The silhouette score measures the similarity of questions within a cluster (cohesion) versus the dissimilarity of questions in one cluster as compared to those in other clusters (separation). Higher silhouette scores indicate better cohesion within clusters and separation between clusters. In clustering, this measure can help inform the number of clusters to use. For our analysis, we were more interested in what vectorization methods achieved better separation of questions assigned to different NCLEX labels. The vectorizations achieving the best silhouette scores could be expected to perform better in classification tasks. We therefore controlled the number of clusters to the number of activity statements, i.e. 138.

Table 1 shows the different vectorization methods evaluated along with their respective silhouette scores. We also include metrics based on the cohesion component of the silhouette score. Specifically, the binary relevance scores measure the distance between question vectors that are all tagged with the same label. The table reports the mean, minimum, maximum, and standard deviation of binary relevance scores across all 138 label clusters.

Figure 5 shows the silhouette scores for every pair of activity statement clusters using TF-IDF vectorization of questions. TF-IDF resulted in the highest silhouette score of -.02. However, the scores for all vectorization methods were relatively low. This result indicated two things 1) there is a great degree of similarity between questions assigned to different activity statement labels, and 2) no vectorization method performed much better than the others. This result indicated that algorithms may need further grouping and sampling of questions to better differentiate them during classification.

We hypothesized that ignoring the current labels and clustering questions may achieve better separation for classification algorithms. To evaluate this hypothesis, we performed a standard clustering of questions using the various vectorization methods. Normally we would optimize the number of clusters based on the silhouette score or other related metrics. However, in the interest of time, we used a fixed number of 512 clusters. This number was estimated from the number of questions and their distribution across activity statements. The resulting silhouette scores improved by .02 on average but did not reflect a significant change. On average, each cluster contained questions from five different

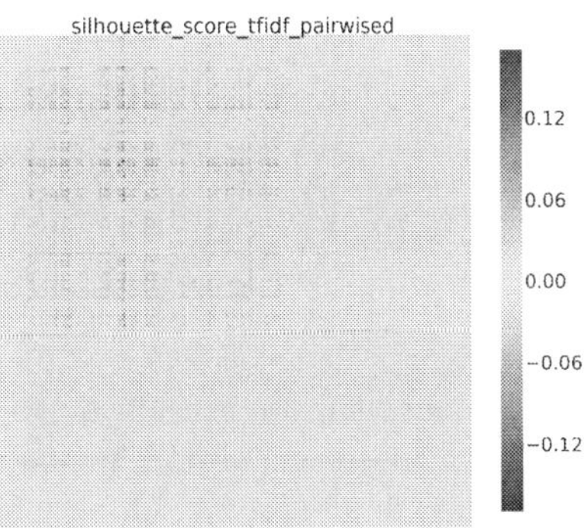

Figure 5: Distribution of pairwise silhouette scores across activity statements.

activity statement label groups. This result motivated some of the modeling experiments described in the following section.

## 5   Modeling

We use micro-averaged area under the receiver operating characteristic (AUC-ROC) to compare multiple algorithms for the described use case. This metric is able to address class imbalance and is used canonically for benchmarking models (Harutyunyan et al., 2019). Note that the metrics reported here only reference the AUC score of first label predicted. In production, the top five labels with the highest confidence values are shown to users and results in an accuracy of 95% in predicting all relevant labels. This is discussed further in Section 5.6. Nonetheless, the initial AUC score of the first prediction was a good benchmark for comparing models. The following sections provide details on each algorithm evaluated.

### 5.1   One versus Rest Support Vector Machines (SVM) with TF-IDF Vectorization

The first model employed a variant of TF-IDF vectorization referred to as Term Frequency – Inverse Label Frequency (TF-ILF). The primary difference is in what is regarded as a "document". Instead of individual questions being treated as a document, questions are grouped according to their labels and then the group is treated as a document.

| Vectorization Method | Silhouette Score | Mean Binary Relevance | Max Binary Relevance | Min Binary Relevance | Std Dev Binary Relevance |
| --- | --- | --- | --- | --- | --- |
| TF-IDF | -0.02 | 0.0 | 0.01 | -0.003 | 0.0001 |
| Google | -0.21 | -0.02 | 0.09 | -0.14 | 0.04 |
| PMC | -0.22 | -0.02 | 0.17 | -0,13 | 0.05 |
| PrepU | -0.91 | -0.07 | 0.3 | -0.27 | 0.08 |

Table 1: Silhouette scores for different vectorization Methods

This document specification results in a slight difference in how document vectors are normalized. The vocabulary for the vectorization included the use of bi-grams and tri-grams (i.e., 2 and 3 word sequences). After eliminating stop words (e.g., "a", "and", "the"), stemming, and performing synonym replacement, the total vocabulary was constrained to 30,000 features. Specifically, we kept only the 30,000 features with the highest TF-ILF values.

All questions were first vectorized. Each vector was then labeled according to the manually assigned labels using the LabelEncoder python class from the SciKit Learn package (Pedregosa et al., 2011). To address the multi-label issue (each question could have more than one activity statement label), we employed a one-versus-rest approach using support vector machines. A binary classifier was trained for each activity statement label with SciKit Learn's LinearSVC algorithm. This approach resulted in 138 models. The hyperparameters for the algorithm included an L2 penalty and ran with 1000 maximum iterations. Models were evaluated using cross-validation with the CalibratedClassifierCV python class. Cross-validation provides a more robust evaluation and can reveal variability between multiple executions of the algorithm.

Given a question as input, each classifier would predict whether a single activity statement label should be assigned to the question, without regard to any other labels. We computed confidence thresholds for each classifier as to whether to accept its prediction or not. Thresholds were established using evaluation metrics such as recall and precision. Questions were then fed into each classifier and any label predictions that met the required thresholds were assigned. In this manner, questions could be assigned more than one label provided more than one model prediction met the required threshold.

**The micro-averaged AUC-ROC of the SVM model was .968.**

## 5.2 Convolutional Neural Network

A convolutional neural network (CNN) model was trained using a Keras tokenizer and word embeddings pretrained on articles from PubMed [(Pyysalo et al., 2013)]. LabelEncoder was used again to encode question labels. The model used a softmax activation function and categorical cross-entropy for the loss function. The output of the model was structured as per-label probabilities between 0 and 1. The softmax output enabled more than one label to have a non-zero probability for a given question input therefore addressed the multi-label problem. Details of the network architecture are shown in Figure 6.

**The micro-averaged AUC-ROC of the CNN model was .972.**

## 5.3 Bidirectional LSTM

A bidirectional LSTM was trained using many of the same parameters as the CNN including a softmax activation function, categorical cross-entropy loss function, and word embeddings pretrained on PubMed. The important difference in this neural network is that layer nodes were connected in a sequential manner, both forward and backwards. Attention was also used to bias more important weights in the network architecture. Details of the network architecture are shown in Figure 7.

**The micro-averaged AUC-ROC of the bidirectional LSTM model was .940.**

## 5.4 Random Forrest Ensemble of SVM, CNN, and LSTM Models

All models had similar AUC metrics. We hypothesized that different models may perform well on different subsets of labels. If this were true, it would be possible to combine the models in an ensemble to increase overall performance across all labels. We trained an ensemble classifier to evaluate this hypothesis.

```
Layer (type)                   Output Shape        Param #   Connected to
==================================================================================
main_input (InputLayer)        (None, 100)         0
embedding_layer (Embedding)    (None, 100, 200)    6795600   main_input[0][0]
Conv1D_128_2 (Conv1D)          (None, 99, 128)     51328     embedding_layer[0][0]
Conv1D_128_4 (Conv1D)          (None, 97, 128)     102528    embedding_layer[0][0]
Conv1D_128_8 (Conv1D)          (None, 93, 128)     204928    embedding_layer[0][0]
Conv1D_128_16 (Conv1D)         (None, 85, 128)     409728    embedding_layer[0][0]
Pool_99 (MaxPooling1D)         (None, 1, 128)      0         Conv1D_128_2[0][0]
Pool_97 (MaxPooling1D)         (None, 1, 128)      0         Conv1D_128_4[0][0]
Pool_93 (MaxPooling1D)         (None, 1, 128)      0         Conv1D_128_8[0][0]
Pool_85 (MaxPooling1D)         (None, 1, 128)      0         Conv1D_128_16[0][0]
Flatten_2 (Flatten)            (None, 128)         0         Pool_99[0][0]
Flatten_4 (Flatten)            (None, 128)         0         Pool_97[0][0]
Flatten_8 (Flatten)            (None, 128)         0         Pool_93[0][0]
Flatten_16 (Flatten)           (None, 128)         0         Pool_85[0][0]
document_vector (Concatenate)  (None, 512)         0         Flatten_2[0][0]
                                                             Flatten_4[0][0]
                                                             Flatten_8[0][0]
                                                             Flatten_16[0][0]
dropout_1 (Dropout)            (None, 512)         0         document_vector[0][0]
dense_1 (Dense)                (None, 138)         70794     dropout_1[0][0]
==================================================================================
Total params: 6,634,906
Trainable params: 6,634,906
Non-trainable params: 0
```

Figure 6: Architecture of convolutional neural network for multi-label text classification.

```
Layer (type)                         Output Shape                      Param #
==================================================================================
main_input (InputLayer)              (None, 100)                       0
embedding_layer (Embedding)          (None, 100, 200)                  7284800
LSTM_128 (Bidirectional)             (None, 100, 256)                  336896
attention_weighted_average_1 [(None, 256), (None, 100)                 256
dropout_1 (Dropout)                  (None, 256)                       0
dense_1 (Dense)                      (None, 138)                       35466
==================================================================================
Total params: 7,657,418
Trainable params: 7,657,418
Non-trainable params: 0
```

Figure 7: Architecture of LSTM recurrent neural network for multi-label text classification.

A random forest model was trained on the outputs of the previously described models to weight the predictions of each and make a final prediction. Questions were first vectorized and input to each component model (i.e., the SVMs, CNN, and LSTM). The output probabilities of each model was then fed into the random forest. Specifically, the inputs of the random forest were 414 values between 0 and 1 consisting of:

- a probability from each of 138 binary SVMs

- a probability for each of 138 output nodes of the CNN

- a probability for each of 138 output nodes of the LSTM

The output of the random forest was a binary vector of 138 elements. Each element corresponded to an activity statement label. A value of 1 indicated the input question should have that label and a value of 0 indicated that it should not.

| Modeling Method | AUC-ROC (micro-avg) |
|---|---|
| TF-ILF+SVM | 0.968 |
| CNN | 0.972 |
| LSTM | 0.940 |
| Ensemble | 0.937 |

Table 2: AUC of different methods

**The micro-averaged AUC-ROC of the random forest ensemble combining the output of the other models was .937.**

## 5.5 Model Comparison and Discussion

Table 2 shows the micro-averaged AUC-ROC of the models evaluated. The best performing model was the CNN. However, none of the algorithms performed dramatically different from one another. We believe that several confounding factors in the data were equally challenging for the various methods.

Class imbalance likely complicated classification attempts and may also indicate other issues with the manual labeling process. Editors, pressed for time, may choose labels that are higher in the drop-down list of the editorial platform. They may also choose labels that are less precise but more general and, therefore, likely to be acceptable. These behaviors could explain why a small set of activity statements labels were associated with thousands of questions whereas the rest of the labels were only associated with a few questions each.

We also found that editors sometimes disagree about question labels. To address this issue, there is a manual process for label reconciliation. Senior editors can be consulted to make final decisions where necessary. Editors also pointed out that questions could be assigned far more activity statements than is currently the case. To optimize the adaptive quizzing experience for users, editors limit labeling to one or two labels that best fit the question.

## 5.6 Final Model Evaluation

The best performing model was the CNN though there was not a significant difference between the methods evaluated. While we limited the time spent on hyper-parameter tuning of the ensemble approach, it was interesting that it fared the worst in our evaluation. The AUC-ROC score enabled us to compare modeling approaches but does not reflect the performance in production. When de-

| Number of Tags Shown | Accuracy |
| --- | --- |
| Top 5 labels | 0.95 |
| Top 3 labels | 0.76 |
| Top 1 labels | 0.47 |

Table 3: TF-ILF+SVM Model Accuracy

ployed, the model shows users the top five label predictions. Users can pick any subset of those labels to apply them to the question being reviewed. To get a sense of accuracy in production, we log how many times we cover all relevant labels in the top N predictions as shown in Table 3.

## 6 Impact Analysis

We are currently logging editor activity and calculating metrics to perform a thorough impact analysis. Initial estimates show that time spent on labeling questions with NCLEX tags went from a few minutes pre-machine learning to less than one minute after our solution was deployed. There are tens of thousands of questions in Wolters Kluwer products like PrepU and CoursePoint and more content being generated every year. This impact is therefore significant, measuring several hours and potentially up to $100,000 or more savings annually.

Editors have responded very positively and regularly use machine learning label suggestions in their current workflow. That said, it will take some time for them to accept a completely automated process. Perhaps more importantly, subject matter experts have assessed that the consistency and quality of labels assigned to questions increase with the model suggestions. Nursing content editors often apply labels based on their personal understanding of content, which is sometimes subjective. There may also be biases in selecting "convenient" labels when having to choose from a lengthy list in a complicated workflow. The predictive model provides consistent label suggestions which in turn results in more consistent labels being assigned.

## 7 Future Work

The class imbalance of this task motivates the potential use of *active machine learning*. Some labels have only been assigned to a handful of questions. For these labels, we may work with editors to find more exemplar questions or create new ones. These new questions can then be merged with training data and the model retrained to ameliorate ef-

fects of class imbalance. In active learning, this process is typically repeated in an iterative process to target problem areas for a model. By selectively labeling new questions and down sampling over represented labels, we can fine tune data for retraining models to improve overall accuracy. Active machine learning has specifically been used for multi-label text classification problems (Yang et al., 2009).

Another area for further study is the evaluation of more recent, deep, transformer models. Because there is a great deal of semantic similarity between questions, these models may not fare better than more traditional vectorization and classification techniques. We intend to evaluate this hypothesis in future work.

There are many different tag sets and taxonomies that can be used to label nursing education content. Tagging both content and questions supports more advanced features such as dynamic remediation and adaptive learning. For instance, when a student answers a question incorrectly, learning software can automatically provide links to learning materials that are related to that topics addressed in that question. We are actively investigating how tagging and organizing content can support various use cases for adaptive learning.

## References


Ashutosh Adhikari, Achyudh Ram, Raphael Tang, and Jimmy Lin. 2019. DocBERT: BERT for Document Classification. *arXiv e-prints*, page arXiv:1904.08398.

Tal Baumel, Jumana Nassour-Kassis, Michael Elhadad, and Noémie Elhadad. 2017. Multi-label classification of patient notes a case study on ICD code assignment. *CoRR*, abs/1709.09587.

Jacob Devlin, Ming-Wei Chang, Kenton Lee, and Kristina Toutanova. 2018. BERT: pre-training of deep bidirectional transformers for language understanding. *CoRR*, abs/1810.04805.

Hrayr Harutyunyan, Hrant Khachatrian, David C. Kale, Greg Ver Steeg, and Aram Galstyan. 2019. Multitask learning and benchmarking with clinical time series data. *Scientific Data*, 6(1).

Zhiheng Huang, Wei Xu, and Kai Yu. 2015. Bidirectional LSTM-CRF models for sequence tagging. *CoRR*, abs/1508.01991.

Yoon Kim. 2014. Convolutional neural networks for sentence classification. In *Proceedings of the 2014 Conference on Empirical Methods in Natural Language Processing (EMNLP)*, pages 1746–1751,

Doha, Qatar. Association for Computational Linguistics.

Ladislav Lenc and Pavel Král. 2017. Word embeddings for multi-label document classification. In *Proceedings of the International Conference Recent Advances in Natural Language Processing, RANLP 2017*, pages 431–437, Varna, Bulgaria. INCOMA Ltd.

Andrew Mccallum and Kamal Nigam. 2001. A comparison of event models for naive bayes text classification. *Work Learn Text Categ*, 752.

Tomas Mikolov, Wen tau Yih, and Geoffrey Zweig. 2013. Linguistic regularities in continuous space word representations. In *HLT-NAACL*, pages 746–751. The Association for Computational Linguistics.

F. Pedregosa, G. Varoquaux, A. Gramfort, V. Michel, B. Thirion, O. Grisel, M. Blondel, P. Prettenhofer, R. Weiss, V. Dubourg, J. Vanderplas, A. Passos, D. Cournapeau, M. Brucher, M. Perrot, and E. Duchesnay. 2011. Scikit-learn: Machine learning in Python. *Journal of Machine Learning Research*, 12:2825–2830.

Sampo Pyysalo, F Ginter, Hans Moen, T Salakoski, and Sophia Ananiadou. 2013. Distributional semantics resources for biomedical text processing. *Proceedings of Languages in Biology and Medicine*.

Jesse Read, Luca Martino, Pablo M. Olmos, and David Luengo. 2015. Scalable multi-output label prediction: From classifier chains to classifier trellises. *Pattern Recognition*, 48(6):2096 – 2109.

Newton SpolaôR, Everton Alvares Cherman, Maria Carolina Monard, and Huei Diana Lee. 2013. A comparison of multi-label feature selection methods using the problem transformation approach. *Electron. Notes Theor. Comput. Sci.*, 292:135–151.

Jinzhong Xu, Jie Liu, and Xiaoming Liu. 2009. Research on topic relevancy of sentences based on hownet semantic computation. In *9th International Conference on Hybrid Intelligent Systems (HIS 2009), August 12-14, 2009, Shenyang, China*, pages 195–198. IEEE Computer Society.

Bishan Yang, Jian-Tao Sun, Tengjiao Wang, and Zheng Chen. 2009. Effective multi-label active learning for text classification. In *Proceedings of the ACM SIGKDD International Conference on Knowledge Discovery and Data Mining*, pages 917–926.

# Clinical XLNet: Modeling Sequential Clinical Notes and Predicting Prolonged Mechanical Ventilation


**Kexin Huang**[*1]**, Abhishek Singh**[*2]**, Sitong Chen**[*1]**, Edward T. Moseley**[3]**,**
**Chih-Ying Deng**[3]**, Naomi George**[4]**, Charlotta Lindvall**[34]

[1]Harvard, [2]MIT, [3]Dana Farber Cancer Institute, [4]Brigham and Women's Hospital

kexinhuang@hsph.harvard.edu, abhi24@mit.edu,
sitong_chen@hms.harvard.edu, nrgeorge@bwh.harvard.edu,
{edward_moseley,chih-ying_deng}@dfci.harvard.edu,
charlotta_lindvall@dfci.harvard.edu



## Abstract

Clinical notes contain rich information, which is relatively unexploited in predictive modeling compared to structured data. In this work, we developed a new clinical text representation Clinical XLNet that leverages the temporal information of the sequence of the notes. We evaluated our models on prolonged mechanical ventilation prediction problem and our experiments demonstrated that Clinical XLNet outperforms the best baselines consistently. The models and scripts are made publicly available.


## 1 Introduction

Unstructured clinical notes within Electronic Health Records (EHR) contain valuable information to support clinical decisions (Murdoch and Detsky, 2013). However, most prognostic models used in medical practice currently rely on scoring systems that only incorporate structured data (Gall et al., 1986; Gall, 1993; Vincent et al., 1996; Rapsang and Shyam, 2014).

A major challenge to utilize unstructured clinical data is in representing notes in ways that allow effective mining of clinically meaningful knowledge. There are many recent advances in the standard Natural Language Processing domain, such as BERT (Devlin et al., 2019), XLNet (Yang et al., 2019). However, clinical notes are far different from the general domain text (Wikipedia, Book-Corpus, etc). For example, clinical notes contain jargon and abbreviations, different grammar and syntax. It is notoriously difficult to obtain an effective note representation. Recently, ClinicalBERT, which adapts the BERT model from the standard NLP domain to model clinical notes (Huang et al., 2019; Alsentzer et al., 2019) achieved superior performance in clinical text prediction. However, previous works still have the following limitations:

- **Notes representation could be improved.** In the standard NLP domain, BERT ignores the discrepancy of masked positions between the pretraining and finetuning stage. An autoregressive pretraining method named XLNet was recently developed and empirically outperforms BERT on many NLP tasks (Yang et al., 2019).

- **Failure to incorporate the temporal dimension of clinical notes.** Clinical notes have a temporal dimension where the order of information in sequential notes can provide additional predictive signals. Most previous models (Huang et al., 2019; Alsentzer et al., 2019) only aggregate individual risk scores from each note which ignore the temporal information charted in EHR.

In this paper, we present Clinical XLNet, which processes a patient's notes and predicts clinical outcomes. In particular, this model mitigates the aforementioned limitations via the following technical contributions:

- **Improved clinical notes representation.** We apply the permutation language modeling method proposed in XLNet on a corpus of clinical notes to generate better clinical embeddings, as demonstrated in Section. 4.

- **Inclusion of temporal information.** We maintain the temporal order of the note embeddings generated from Clinical XLNet and feed them into a bidirectional LSTM layer (Hochreiter and Schmidhuber, 1997), which leverages information along the temporal dimension (Fig. 1).

We examined Clinical XLNet's performance on a new but important clinical NLP task: predicting




*Proceedings of the 3rd Clinical Natural Language Processing Workshop*, pages 94–100
November 19, 2020. ©2020 Association for Computational Linguistics

Table 1: Cohort Statistics. For continuous variable, it reports mean with the standard deviation. For categorical variable, the count is given with percentage.

| Statistics | All | MV $\geq$ 7d | MV < 7d | Survive < 90d | Survive $\geq$ 90d |
|---|---|---|---|---|---|
| Stays/Admissions | 7,287 | 3,412 | 3,875 | 2,680 | 4,607 |
| Age | 64.3 (16.7) | 63.8 (16.6) | 64.8 (16.9) | 69.3 (15.4) | 61.4 (16.8) |
| Male | 4,072 (55.8) | 1,936 (56.7) | 2,136 (55.1) | 1,474 (55.0) | 2598 (56.4) |
| Ethnicity | | | | | |
| White | 5,159 (70.8) | 2,431 (71.2) | 2,728 (70.4) | 1,844 (68.8) | 3,315 (72.0) |
| Black | 590 (8.1) | 259 (7.6) | 331 (8.5) | 202 (7.5) | 388 (8.4) |
| Hispanic/Latino | 215 (2.9) | 89 (2.6) | 126 (3.3) | 51 (1.9) | 164 (3.6) |
| Asian | 150 (2.1) | 65 (1.9) | 85 (2.2) | 54 (2.0) | 96 (2.1) |
| Others | 1,173 (16.1) | 568 (16.6) | 902 (23.3) | 529 (19.7) | 644 (14.0) |
| Notes | | | | | |
| Word Count | 1774 (1645) | 1745 (1610) | 1799 (1674) | 1811 (1730) | 1753 (1593) |
| Note Count | 9.78 (4.70) | 9.54 (4.51) | 10.0 (4.86) | 9.72 (4.70) | 9.82 (4.70) |

prolonged mechanical ventilation (PMV). Mechanical ventilation is to use an artificial breathing machine to assist or replace patient's breath. PMV stands for longer than normal period of mechanical ventilation. PMV consumes substantial healthcare resources, results in financial and emotional burdens for patients and their families, and is associated with high one-year mortality around 50-60% (Mcgee, 2010; Nelson et al., 2015; Unroe, 2010). It is projected that over 600,000 patients in the United States will require PMV by 2020 (Zilberberg et al., 2008).

Patients with PMV can have a surgical procedure called tracheostomy to establish better airway access for long-term mechanical ventilation (Cox et al., 2004). Tracheostomy is associated with improved patient comfort, decreased duration of ICU and hospital stay, and reduced mortality (Mallick and Bodenham, 2010). However, the decision to place a tracheostomy is challenging for two main reasons: (1) tracheostomy may not be necessary if a patient's condition improves without requiring PMV, and (2) tracheostomy may not be helpful if the patient is at high risk of short-term mortality. Thus, an *early* and *correct* decision of tracheostomy is critical and depends on the likelihood of PMV and short-term mortality. Accurately predicting these factors using patients' clinical notes could support clinical decision making.

We compared Clinical XLNet with several state-of-the-art baselines including BERT (Devlin et al., 2019), XLNet (Yang et al., 2019), and Clinical-BERT (Huang et al., 2019) on both PMV and mortality predictions. We performed meticulous cohort curation in MIMIC-III dataset (Johnson et al., 2016) to set up an actionable prediction task ac-cording to the real clinical setting. Clinical notes used in this prediction task were strictly within the 48-hour time window starting from the initial mechanical ventilation event. Experimental results showed that Clinical XLNet outperformed the best baselines consistently (Section. 4).

## 2   Data

We use the Multiparameter Intelligent Monitoring in Intensive Care III (MIMIC-III) dataset (Johnson et al., 2016) hosted on PhysioNet (Goldberger et al., 2000) for our model development and experiment. It consists of 61,532 ICU stays out of 58,976 hospital admissions from 46,476 patients in the intensive care unit of the Beth Israel Deaconess Medical Center (BIDMC) between 2001 and 2012 and it has 2,083,180 clinical note events.

**Cohort Selection.** Comprehensive inclusion and exclusion criteria were applied to the MIMIC-III dataset to generate our patient cohort who were above 18 years old, and were on mechanical ventilation for at least 2 days with more than 6 hours each day. We excluded patients who were organ donors or transferred patients from other hospitals. As certain diseases always lead to PMV, to alleviate confounding, we further removed patients with neuromuscular disease, head and neck cancer, and extensive burns (Oakden-Rayner et al., 2020). For each hospital admission, we used the first ICU stay. For clinical notes, we included nursing and respiratory notes within 48 hours from the start of the first ventilation event. The reason for only selecting nursing related notes was to expand the cohort as MIMIC-III is missing physician notes from 2001 to 2008. Additional criteria that are applied in our data curation process are in Fig. 2 in the appendix.

In the end, we obtained a cohort of 7,287 unique patients and their corresponding 73,224 clinical notes. Table. 1 shows the cohort demographics.

**Cohort Labels.** Our cohort was labeled with PMV and 90-day mortality as a binary outcome. PMV was defined as being on mechanical ventilation for more than 7 days with at least 6 hours each day (Boles JM, 2007). Short-term mortality was defined as death occurring within 90 days of the first ICU admission. We use 90 days in contrast to 30 days because recent studies showed that 30 days mortality may underestimate the evaluation (Mise et al., 2015; Hirji et al., 2020).

## 3   Methods

This section presents our Clinical XLNet framework (Fig. 1). Clinical XLNet is an extension of XLNet (Yang et al., 2019) on the clinical text domain. It first generates a deep latent representation for clinical notes and then by applying a bidirectional LSTM (Bi-LSTM) layer, it also leverages the sequential order of notes.

**Problem Settings.** Our target task aims to leverage a patient's clinical notes to predict variables such as PMV and mortality. We denote a patient as P, and each patient P is associated with an ordered sequence of notes $\{N_1, \cdots, N_i\}$, where i is the total number of notes.

To predict mortality $L_M$ and PMV $L_P$, we aim to learn two mappings $\mathcal{M} : \{N_1, \cdots, N_i\} \longrightarrow [0, 1]$ and $\mathcal{P} : \{N_1, \cdots, N_i\} \longrightarrow [0, 1]$ where $[0, 1]$ is a probability that measures the likelihood of having mortality and PMV respectively.

**Pretraining Clinical XLNet.** The XLNet is pretrained on common language corpora such as Book-Corpus, Wikipedia, Common Crawl and etc. However, these corpora are different from clinical notes which are filled with jargon, abbreviations and difficult syntax and grammar. Hence, to learn an effective representation of clinical notes, we further pre-trained the XLNet using nursing, nursing/others, and respiratory therapy notes available in the MIMIC-III dataset. The clinical notes used in pre-training were NOT in the holdout test set to avoid biased results.

XLNet is a stack of Transformer-XL encoder (Dai et al., 2019). For pre-training, it uses Permutation Language Modeling (PLM) to tackle the challenge of [MASK] token information gap between pre-training and finetuning in BERT (Devlin et al., 2019). For each sequence, it is appended with a [CLS] classification token at the beginning of the sequence for downstream task usage. For a more detailed description, we refer the readers to the original paper (Yang et al., 2019).

A patient is associated with many notes, and each notes length varies. Since XLNet can only take 512 maximum tokens, we follow (Huang et al., 2019) to first concatenate all the notes and partition them into snippets $N_i$. Then, we use the last encoder layer hidden representation $E_i$ of the [CLS] token to represent the note snippet. As we train with a supervised signal in the downstream task, [CLS] token would gather useful information in the entire note sequence due to the Transformer-XL's self-attention mechanism. Now, given a temporally ordered sequence of note snippets associated with a patient, we obtain a temporally-ordered sequence of notes representations $\{E_1, \cdots, E_i\}$.

**Finetuning Clinical XLNet.** To leverage the temporal information among the note snippets, we feed $\{E_1, \cdots, E_i\}$ into a sequential modeling layer. Specifically, we use Bi-LSTM model (Graves and Schmidhuber, 2005; Hochreiter and Schmidhuber, 1997). We use bidirectional model because not only the latter notes depend on the previous notes as patients develop their symptoms in a temporal order but also the latter notes may contain useful clinical knowledge to help enrich the representation of previous notes. The output of the Bi-LSTM layer $H_N$ is then fed into a predictor neural network, which at last, generates a probability p that measures the likelihood of downstream target variable, PMV, and mortality. The network is then tuned using binary classification loss.

**Pre-Finetuning.** As each patient is associated with many notes snippets and each snippet corresponds to a large model, it is computationally infeasible to train the model end-to-end. In order to alleviate the memory cost of end-to-end training for every clinical note, we propose to approximate the task-specific note representation through an additional pre-finetuning stage. We assume that any part of the notes associated with a patient is correlated to the label. Thus, during pre-finetuning, we use one piece of note as input, and further train the pre-trained Clinical XLNet through the downstream task label signal from the corresponding patient. The pre-finetuned network can then generate

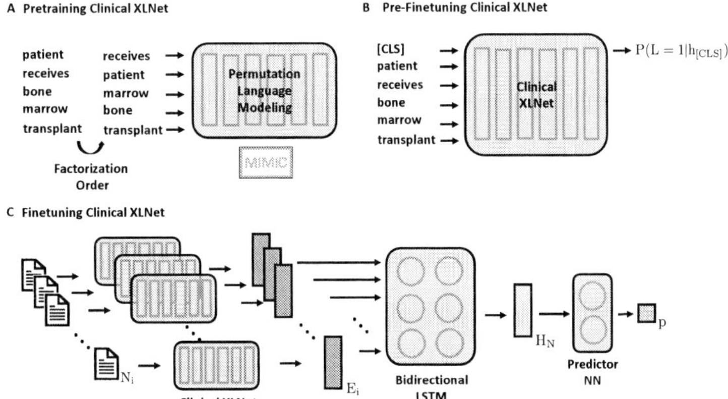


Figure 1: Clinical XLNet framework. A. We first pre-trained the XLNet embedding with MIMIC-III clinical notes dataset using Permutation Language Modeling. After pre-training, given a clinical note, the model outputs a numerical vector to be used as a note representation. B. To alleviate the computation burden from training end-to-end, the pre-finetuning stage uses the supervised signal to further tune the pre-trained network with input consisting of individual note $N_i$. The pre finetuned stage then generates a static task-specific note representation. C. Given a sequence of a patient's notes $\{N_1, \cdots, N_i\}$, the pre-finetuned Clinical XLNet network generates a sequence of representation of notes $\{E_1, \cdots, E_i\}$. The ordered representation sequence is then fed into a bidirectional LSTM layer, which then outputs a fixed size latent vector $H_N$, representing the entire sequence. $H_N$ is finally fed into a predictor neural network to generate a probability $p$ measuring the likelihood of the target variable.

a task specific note representation. Then, during the finetuning stage, we freeze the note representation module, and use a static fixed note representation from the pre-finetuned Clinical XLNet to feed into the Bi-LSTM layer.

## 4    Experiments

To evaluate our model, we examined the prediction performance under a realistic setup. We used the first 48 hours of clinical notes starting from the initial mechanical ventilation event to predict two variables: mechanical ventilation longer than 7 days and 90-days mortality. [1]

**Hyperparameters.**    For the data split, we first obtain a 10% holdout test set. Then we generate different 8:1 train:validation splits using different random seeds for model performance robustness examination. For the pre-training, we further pre-train the XLNet embedding for another 200K steps using 16 batch size. For the pre-finetuning, we use 32 batch size with learning rate 1e-5 for four epochs with early stopping on the area under the receiver operating characteristic curve (AUROC) score of validation. For finetuning, we used a two layers Bi-LSTM module with batch size 128 and learning rate 1e-4. The pre-training and pre-finetuning pro-

---

[1]Code and models are available at `https://github.com/lindvalllab/clinicalXLNet`.

Table 2: AUROC result with three independent data splits mean and standard deviation.

| Method | PMV | Mortality |
|---|---|---|
| LSTM | $0.613 \pm 0.006$ | $0.590 \pm 0.034$ |
| LSTM + Attention | $0.604 \pm 0.009$ | $0.743 \pm 0.007$ |
| HAN | $0.606 \pm 0.007$ | $0.715 \pm 0.013$ |
| RCNN | $0.620 \pm 0.003$ | $0.744 \pm 0.010$ |
| BERT | $0.616 \pm 0.022$ | $0.734 \pm 0.047$ |
| XLNet | $0.611 \pm 0.007$ | $0.664 \pm 0.017$ |
| ClinicalBERT | $0.648 \pm 0.011$ | $0.774 \pm 0.006$ |
| **Clinical XLNet** | $\mathbf{0.663 \pm 0.011}$ | $\mathbf{0.779 \pm 0.006}$ |
| Clinical XLNet- mean | $0.656 \pm 0.003$ | $0.773 \pm 0.003$ |

ccss was conducted on a server with 2 Intel Xeon E5-2670v2 2.5GHZ CPUs, 128GB RAM, and 2 NVIDIA Tesla P40 GPUs.

**Baselines.**    We conducted a thorough set of experiments with several popular baselines:

- **LSTM** (Hochreiter and Schmidhuber, 1997) is the classic language modeling method that uses long term document memory.

- **LSTM + Attention** adds an attention layer on top of the sequence output of LSTM hidden layers.

- **Hierarchical    Attention    Networks (HAN)** (Hochreiter and Schmidhuber, 1997) is a hierarchical LSTM designed specifically for document level text classification.

- **Recurrent Convolutional Neural Network (RCNN)** (Yang et al., 2016) uses a recurrent structure on the classic CNN network to capture contextual information as far as possible.

- **BERT** (Devlin et al., 2019) uses transformer encoder with the same pre-train and finetune procedure as Clinical XLNet.

- **XLNet** (Yang et al., 2019) is Clinical XLNet without pre-training on clinical text.

- **ClinicalBERT** (Huang et al., 2019; Alsentzer et al., 2019) further pre-trains on BERT using MIMIC-III notes dataset.

- **Clinical XLNet-mean** is an ablation study that uses the average of the prediction scores from each note, instead of the bidirectional LSTM layers.

Note that for BERT, XLNet, and ClinicalBERT, we all attach a bidirectional-LSTM layer on top of them to leverage the sequential dimension of notes. And for ClinicalBERT, we pre-train using the same corpus as the Clinical XLNet. These steps ensure a fair comparison between note representation power. Note that it is computationally infeasible to test the ablation of pre-finetuning.

**Results.** Table. 2 reports the result for our prolonged mechanical ventilation and 90-days mortality tasks. Clinical XLNet achieves the best results with AUROC score of 0.663 ($\pm$ 0.011) and 0.779 ($\pm$ 0.006) for PMV and 90-days mortality respectively. From the difference between clinically pre-trained embedding Clinical XLNet & Clinical BERT and no pre-trained model BERT & XLNet, we demonstrate the necessity of pre-training on domain-specific corpus. From the difference between Clinical BERT and Clinical XLNet, we show our Clinical XLNet has better note representation. From the difference between Clinical XLNet and Clinical XLNet-mean, we see the usage of sequential modeling of the temporal dimension of notes.

## 5 Discussion

In this work, we propose a method for predicting prognosis based on only contextual information available from clinician notes. The proposed method is based on the recent advancements in the field of NLP. Therefore we compare it with other recently proposed methods in NLP for a fair comparison. We perform one ablation study to show the relevance of the proposed sequential modeling of the notes embedding in the time domain and we compare against several state of the art baselines which have been used extensively in the natural language domain as well as in the clinical context.

**Clinical Relevance.** Our work provides timely aid in clinical decision making. For a patient under the ICU observation, the clinical team could start the evaluation to consider a tracheotomy procedure as soon as 48 hours after mechanical ventilation. The time period of 48 hours was chosen in consultation with a team of clinicians. Furthermore, a predictive analytics on the prolonged mechanical ventilation for seven days or more is important for clinicians in deciding the tracheotomy decision. Besides, the doctors could reduce the risk of a burdensome procedure and treatment by considering the patient's 90-days mortality prediction. This approach assist patients and their families by providing more time to process and make a major decision.

**Model Efficiency.** The proposed method uses XLNet (Yang et al., 2019) which uses TransformerXL (Dai et al., 2019) as the base architecture to extract embedding from the notes. Since every set of notes require their individual embeddings, we run the base architecture for multiple runs where the number of runs is proportional to the number of notes. Therefore, obtaining the embedding for the whole sequence of notes is computationally expensive both during the training as well as inference. However, there is a recent line of work (Lan et al., 2019) which can allow executing the transformer based models at a much lesser computational cost.

**Limitations and Future Work.** Our proposed method only mines task relevant information from clinical notes from nurses and respiratory therapists. However, one can utilize other sources of data as well such as structured notes. While structured data are commonly used in prognostic models, our preliminary study showed that they did not improve the performance by any significant factor. One future direction could be to explore a novel architecture design that could utilize both sources of information to improve the performance further. Another future direction would be to explore ways of combining multiple sources of clinical notes such as physician notes, admission notes, and dsischarge notes.

## Acknowledgement

The project was conceived, designed and conducted during the 2019 fall course HST.953 Collaborative Data Science in Medicine at the Harvard-MIT Division of Health Science and Technology. We express our thanks to all HST faculty for support and guidance during this project.

## References

Emily Alsentzer, John R. Murphy, Willie Boag, Wei-Hung Weng, Di Jin, Tristan Naumann, and Matthew B. A. McDermott. 2019. Publicly available clinical BERT embeddings. *NAACL Clinical NLP Workshop*.

Connors A Herridge M Marsh B Melot C et al Boles JM, Bion J. 2007. Weaning from mechanical ventilation. *Eur Respir J.*, 29:1033–10563.

Christopher E. Cox, Shannon S. Carson, George M. Holmes, Ann Howard, and Timothy S. Carey. 2004. Increase in tracheostomy for prolonged mechanical ventilation in north carolina, 1993–2002. *Critical Care Medicine*, 32(11):2219–2226.

Zihang Dai, Zhilin Yang, Yiming Yang, Jaime G. Carbonell, Quoc V. Le, and Ruslan Salakhutdinov. 2019. Transformer-xl: Attentive language models beyond a fixed-length context. In *ACL*.

Jacob Devlin, Ming-Wei Chang, Kenton Lee, and Kristina Toutanova. 2019. Bert: Pre-training of deep bidirectional transformers for language understanding. In *NAACL-HLT*.

J. R. Le Gall. 1993. A new simplified acute physiology score (saps ii) based on a european/north american multicenter study. *JAMA: The Journal of the American Medical Association*, 270(24):2957–2963.

Jean-Roger Le Gall, P. Loirat, and Λ. Alpcrovitch. 1986. Apache ii-a severity of disease classification system. *Critical Care Medicine*, 14(8):754.

Ary L Goldberger, Luis AN Amaral, Leon Glass, Jeffrey M Hausdorff, Plamen Ch Ivanov, Roger G Mark, Joseph E Mietus, George B Moody, Chung-Kang Peng, and H Eugene Stanley. 2000. Physiobank, physiotoolkit, and physionet: components of a new research resource for complex physiologic signals. *Circulation*, 101(23):e215–e220.

Alex Graves and Jürgen Schmidhuber. 2005. Framewise phoneme classification with bidirectional lstm and other neural network architectures. *Neural networks : the official journal of the International Neural Network Society*, 18 5-6:602–10.

Sameer Hirji, Siobhan McGurk, Spencer Kiehm, Julius Ejiofor, Fernando Ramirez-Del Val, Ahmed A Kolkailah, Natalia Berry, Piotr Sobieszczyk, Marc Pelletier, Pinak Shah, et al. 2020. Utility of 90-day mortality vs 30-day mortality as a quality metric for transcatheter and surgical aortic valve replacement outcomes. *JAMA cardiology*, 5(2):156–165.

Sepp Hochreiter and Jürgen Schmidhuber. 1997. Long short-term memory. *Neural Computation*, 9:1735–1780.

Kexin Huang, Jaan Altosaar, and Rajesh Ranganath. 2019. Clinicalbert: Modeling clinical notes and predicting hospital readmission. *CoRR*.

Alistair EW Johnson, Tom J Pollard, Lu Shen, H Lehman Li-wei, Mengling Feng, Mohammad Ghassemi, Benjamin Moody, Peter Szolovits, Leo Anthony Celi, and Roger G Mark. 2016. Mimic-iii, a freely accessible critical care database. *Scientific data*, 3:160035.

Zhenzhong Lan, Mingda Chen, Sebastian Goodman, Kevin Gimpel, Piyush Sharma, and Radu Soricut. 2019. Albert: A lite bert for self-supervised learning of language representations. *arXiv preprint arXiv:1909.11942*.

Abhiram Mallick and Andrew R Bodenham. 2010. Tracheostomy in critically ill patients. *European Journal of Anaesthesiology*, page 1.

William T. Mcgee. 2010. Expectations and outcomes of prolonged mechanical ventilation. *Critical Care Medicine*, 38(5):1393–1394.

Yoshihiro Mise, Jean-Nicolas Vauthey, Giuseppe Zimmitti, Nathan H Parker, Claudius Conrad, Thomas A Aloia, Jeffery E Lee, Jason B Fleming, and Matthew HG Katz. 2015. 90-day postoperative mortality is a legitimate measure of hepatopancreatobiliary surgical quality. *Annals of surgery*, 262(6):1071.

Travis B. Murdoch and Allan S. Detsky. 2013. The inevitable application of big data to health care. *Jama*, 309(13):1351.

Judith Nelson, Shannon Carson, and Thomas Bice. 2015. To trach or not to trach: Uncertainty in the care of the chronically critically ill. *Seminars in Respiratory and Critical Care Medicine*, 36(06):851–858.

Luke Oakden-Rayner, Jared Dunnmon, Gustavo Carneiro, and Christopher Ré. 2020. Hidden stratification causes clinically meaningful failures in machine learning for medical imaging. In *Proceedings of the ACM Conference on Health, Inference, and Learning*, pages 151–159.

Amy Rapsang and Devajit C. Shyam. 2014. Scoring systems in the intensive care unit: A compendium. *Indian Journal of Critical Care Medicine*, 18(4):220–228.

Mark Unroe. 2010. One-year trajectories of care and resource utilization for recipients of prolonged mechanical ventilation. *Annals of Internal Medicine*, 153(3):167.

J. L. Vincent, R. Moreno, J. Takala, S. Willatts, A. De Mendonça, H. Bruining, C. K. Reinhart, P. M. Suter, and L. G. Thijs. 1996. The sofa (sepsis-related organ failure assessment) score to describe organ dysfunction/failure. *Intensive Care Medicine*, 22(7):707–710.

Zhilin Yang, Zihang Dai, Yiming Yang, Jaime G. Carbonell, Ruslan Salakhutdinov, and Quoc V. Le. 2019. Xlnet: Generalized autoregressive pretraining for language understanding. *NeurIPS*.

Zichao Yang, Diyi Yang, Chris Dyer, Xiaodong He, Alex Smola, and Eduard Hovy. 2016. Hierarchical attention networks for document classification. In *Proceedings of the 2016 conference of the North American chapter of the association for computational linguistics: human language technologies*, pages 1480–1489.

Marya D. Zilberberg, Rose S. Luippold, Sandra Sulsky, and Andrew F. Shorr. 2008. Prolonged acute mechanical ventilation, hospital resource utilization, and mortality in the united states. *Critical Care Medicine*, 36(3):724–730.

# Automatic recognition of abdominal lymph nodes from clinical text


Yifan Peng[1,3,*], Sungwon Lee[2,*], Daniel Elton[2], Tommy Shen[2], Yu-xing Tang[2],
Qingyu Chen[1], Shuai Wang[2], Yingying Zhu[2,4], Ronald M. Summers[2,†], Zhiyong Lu[1,†]

[1]National Center for Biotechnology Information (NCBI), National Library of
Medicine (NLM), National Institutes of Health (NIH), Bethesda, MD 20894; [2]Imaging
Biomarkers and Computer-Aided Diagnosis Laboratory, Radiology and Imaging
Sciences Department, NIH Clinical Center, Bethesda, MD 20892; [3]Department of
Population Health Sciences, Weill Cornell Medicine, New York, NY 10065;
[4]Department of Computer Science and Engineering, University of Texas at Arlington,
Arlington, TX 76019


## Abstract


Lymph node status plays a pivotal role in
the treatment of cancer. The extraction of
lymph nodes from radiology text reports enables large-scale training of lymph node detection on MRI. In this work, we first propose an ontology of 41 types of abdominal lymph nodes with a hierarchical relationship. We then introduce an end-to-end approach based on the combination of rules and
transformer-based methods to detect these abdominal lymph node mentions and classify
their types from the MRI radiology reports.
We demonstrate the superior performance of
a model fine-tuned on MRI reports using
BlueBERT, called MriBERT. We find that
MriBERT outperforms the rule-based labeler
(0.957 vs 0.644 in micro weighted F1-score)
as well as other BERT-based variations (0.913
- 0.928). We make the code and MriBERT
publicly available at https://github.com/
ncbi-nlp/bluebert, with the hope that this
method can facilitate the development of medical report annotators to produce labels from
scratch at scale.


## 1 Introduction

Lymph nodes are organs of the lymphatic system
that are present throughout the body. Their status
plays a pivotal role in the staging and treatment of
cancer (Amin et al., 2017). The development of
deep learning (DL) for computer vision has led to
increasing interest in applying DL-based AI to identify and segment lymph nodes and detect lymph
nodes and detecting lymph node metastasis in imaging studies, such as Magnetic Resonance Imaging
(MRI). Applications of machine learning to MRI
not only contribute to improving diagnostic accuracy but also reduce the workload of radiologists

and enable them to spend additional time on high-
level decision-making tasks. However, DL algorithms need to be sufficiently trained and evaluated
using large-scale data before clinical adoption. Unlike general computer vision tasks, medical image
analysis currently does not have enough annotated
data (comparable to ImageNet and MS COCO),
which is mainly because the conventional methods for harvesting labels cannot be applied in the
clinical domain, as it requires extensive clinical expertise and because of security and privacy issues.
Therefore, there is an unmet need to construct a
large-scale annotated dataset of lymph nodes to
increase the generalizability and robustness of the
DL algorithms.

Radiologists report any abnormal lymph node
detected in computed tomography (CT) and MRI
exams by describing the regional name (type) of
the lymph node. Example MRI scans and annotations are shown in Figure 1, where the radiologist describes the lymph node with the sentence
"Abdominal/pelvic lymph nodes: There is intraperitoneal and retroperitoneal lymphadenopathy, for example, enlarged mesenteric/peripancreatic lymph
node measuring **Bookmark1**[[(2.8 cm x 1.3 cm)
(series 6, image 24)]], periportal lymph node measuring **Bookmark2**[[(2.8 cm x 1.7 cm) (series 6,
image 19)]], retroperitoneal left paraaortic lymph
node conglomerate measuring **Bookmark3**[[(3.8
cm x 3.1 cm) (series 6, image 22)]], and retroperitoneal aortocaval lymph node measuring **Book-
mark4**[[(2.0 cm x 1.3 cm) (series 6, image 25)]]".
The radiologist places a hyperlink (hereafter "bookmark") in the context to refer to the specified lymph
node annotation in the image. Therefore, clinical
reports provide a detailed and personalized account
of assessments, offering a better context for clinical
decision making and follow up.

Natural language processing (NLP) has been explored recently to unlock evidence buried in clin-

---


* These authors contributed equally to this work.
† Co-corresponding.





*Proceedings of the 3rd Clinical Natural Language Processing Workshop*, pages 101–110
November 19, 2020. ©2020 Association for Computational Linguistics

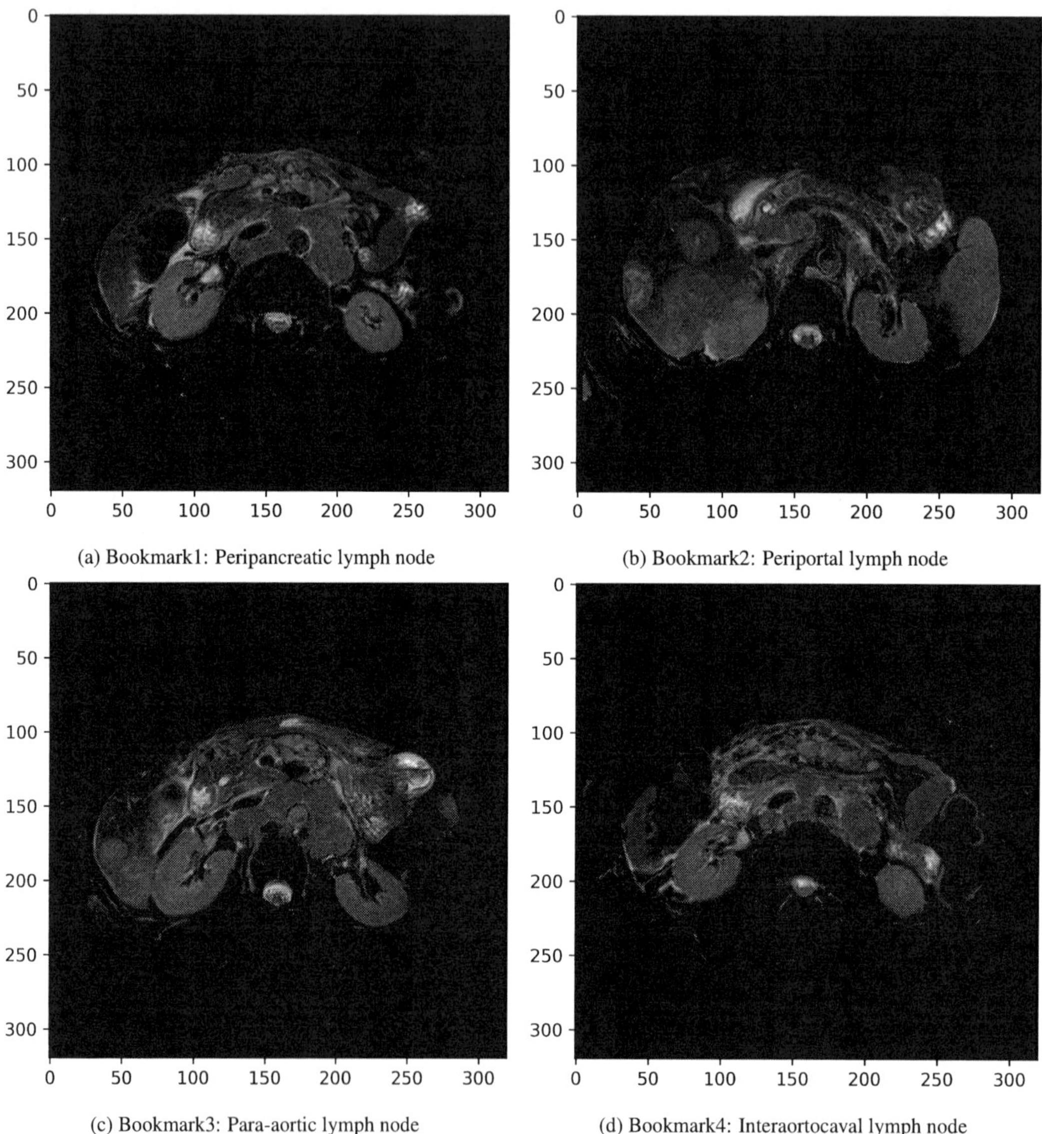

(a) Bookmark1: Peripancreatic lymph node      (b) Bookmark2: Periportal lymph node

(c) Bookmark3: Para-aortic lymph node      (d) Bookmark4: Interaortocaval lymph node

Figure 1: Sample sentence with lymph node bookmarks: "Abdominal/pelvic lymph nodes: There is intraperitoneal and retroperitoneal lymphadenopathy, for example enlarged mesenteric/peripancreatic lymph node measuring Bookmark1[[(2.8 cm x 1.3 cm) (series 6, image 24)]], periportal lymph node measuring Bookmark2[[(2.8 cm x 1.7 cm) (series 6, image 19)]], retroperitoneal left paraaortic lymph node conglomerate measuring Bookmark3[[(3.8 cm x 3.1 cm) (series 6, image 22)]], and retroperitoneal aortocaval lymph node measuring Bookmark4[[(2.0 cm x 1.3 cm) (series 6, image 25)]]. "

ical narratives, making it available for large-scale analysis. In the clinical domain, NLP has been applied to identify positive, negative, and uncertain findings from radiology reports (Peng et al., 2018; Irvin et al., 2019; Yan et al., 2018). For MRI reports, NLP has been used to identify breast imaging lexicons for breast cancer (Sippo et al., 2013; Liu et al., 2019). However, most of these systems are rule-based, and few studies have investigated NLP in MRI reports of the lymph nodes.

To tackle these obstacles and challenges, this paper outlines a framework based on deep learning to harvest lymph node annotations and construct an annotated dataset of lymph nodes by automatically extracting lymph nodes from clinical reports. The contributions of this study are threefold: (1) We construct an ontology of 41 types of abdominal lymph nodes with a hierarchical relationship. (2) We develop a transformer-based deep learning module to extract and classify the abdominal lymph node types (or a non-abdominal lymph node or not a lymph node) for each bookmark mentioned in the sentence. (3) We make codes and pre-trained models publicly available.

The rest of the paper is organized as follows. We first present related work in Section 2. Then, we describe the method to construct the ontology and dataset in Section 3, followed by our experimental setup, results, and discussion in Section 4. We conclude with future work in the last section.

## 2 Related work

In recent years, there has been considerable interest in harvesting information and knowledge from free-text on electronic health records (EHRs) (Jensen et al., 2017). However, manually annotating a large dataset to fulfill the needs of deep learning models downstream is time-consuming and expensive. Therefore, researchers have applied NLP systems to identify structured labels from radiology reports (Irvin et al., 2019; Johnson et al., 2019; Wang et al., 2017; Smit et al., 2020).

Previous efforts in this area have focused mostly on two directions. One is the rule-based methods. NegEx, in combination with the Unified Medical Language System (UMLS), is a widely used algorithm that utilizes regular expressions to determine the negative concepts in the clinical narratives (Chapman et al., 2013; Aronson and Lang, 2010; Chapman et al., 2011). NegBio extended NegEx by utilizing universal dependencies and sub-

graph matching to detect both negative and uncertain lung diseases in chest X-rays and was used to generate labels for the NIH Chest X-ray and MIMIC-III-CXR datasets (Johnson et al., 2019; Wang et al., 2017; Peng et al., 2018). The CheXpert labeler further extended NegBio by increasing the rule sets and improving the NLP pipeline to construct report-level disease annotations (Irvin et al., 2019). CheXpert++ trained a hybrid rule- and BERT- based labeler on the radiograph domain but offers additional commentary on the utility of active-learning strategies to inform the interplay between the hybrid and rule-based labeler (McDermott et al., 2020).

The other direction is to apply machine learning methods to construct labels (Huang and Lowe, 2007; Clark et al., 2011; Xue et al., 2019; Peng et al., 2019a). Huang et al. described a hybrid approach to automatically detect negations in clinical radiology reports (Huang and Lowe, 2007). Clark et al. combine machine learning (conditional random field and maximum entropy) and rules to determine the assertion status of medical problems mentioned in clinical reports (Clark et al., 2011). Recently, deep learning approaches have also been studied intensively. Chen et al. applied CNNs to classify pulmonary embolism in chest CT reports (Chen et al., 2018). Drozdov et al. compared thirteen supervised classifiers and demonstrate that bidirectional long short-term memory (BiLSTM) networks with attention mechanisms effectively identify labels in CXR reports (Drozdov et al., 2020). Wood et al. present a transformer-based network for brain magnetic resonance imaging (MRI) radiology report classification, which automates this task by assigning image labels based on free-text expert radiology reports (Wood et al., 2020). Smit et al. introduced a BERT-based approach to medical image report labeling that exploits both the scale of available rule-based systems and the quality of expert annotations (Smit et al., 2020).

## 3 Methods

In this section, we first describe the process of constructing the abdominal lymph node ontology and gold-standard labels from the MRI reports associated with lymph nodes on MRI images. Then we demonstrate the development of the transformer-based method to detect lymph nodes from the reports.

## 3.1 Abdominal lymph node ontology construction

The labeling task in this study is to extract the presence of abdominal lymph nodes from radiology reports. Therefore, the first step is to construct the lymph node ontology. The challenge here is that the nomenclature of abdominal lymph nodes is complicated. Most of them are named after the anatomical organs their lymphatics are draining from, but some are named after an adjacent structure, and some are named for an anatomical compartment space. This makes them have confusing synonyms or sometimes overlapping areas, giving them a hierarchy. To make a standardized version of the abdominal lymph node ontology, we used three widely used guidelines (Amin et al., 2017) and textbooks (Harisinghani, 2013; Richter and Feyerabend, 2012) to establish the hierarchical relationship, representative synonyms, and relationships with overlapping areas.

## 3.2 MRI dataset

For model development and validation, we collected large-scale MRI studies from NIH Clinical Center, performed between Jan 2015 to Sept 2019, along with their associated radiology reports. (Figure 2). The majority (63%) of the MRI studies were from the oncology department. The initial search from the Picture Archiving and Communication System (PACS) database at the NIH Clinical Center returns 21,786 studies with 9,343 patients. We excluded non-abdomen studies and studies with missing reports. The final dataset consists of a total of 2,099 lymph node bookmarks from 1,379 studies of 917 unique patients, and their corresponding text reports retrospectively from the Picture Archiving and Communication System (PACS) database at the NIH Clinical Center. These lymph node labels were reviewed by a radiologist with 12 years of post-graduate experience. The study was a retrospective study and was approved by the Institutional Review Board with a waiver of informed consent. This data set comprised the reference (gold) standard for our evaluation and comparative analysis.

## 3.3 Framework

We developed a hybrid system to extract abdominal lymph nodes from the MRI reports. It consists of two modules: (1) a rule-based lymph node detection, and (2) a transformer-based lymph node

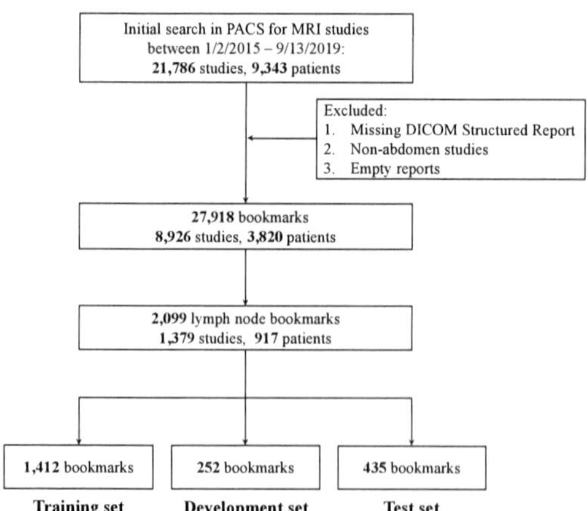


Figure 2: The training, development, and test sets for classification of lymph node types from MRI reports.

classification (Figure 3).

### 3.3.1 Sentence extraction with potential lymph node bookmarks

In the reports of our institute, radiologists describe the lymph nodes and insert hyperlinks, size measurements, or slice numbers in the sentence to refer to the imaging findings of interest (called a bookmark). A bookmark thus is a hyperlink connection between the annotation in the image and the written description in the report. From the reports, we selected the full sentences that included the hyperlink, presuming that they had information most relevant to the connected image annotation.

In this step, we extract sentences with bookmarks that potentially link to lymph nodes. We first split the reports into sections. For our reports, the text is often organized into five sections: Clinical Indication, Technique, Comparison, Findings, and Impression. Among others, the "Findings" section lists the normal, abnormal, or potentially abnormal observations the radiologist saw in each area of the abdomen or pelvis in the exam. Hence, this section is often organized by organs such as the liver and kidney, blood vessels, and lymph nodes.

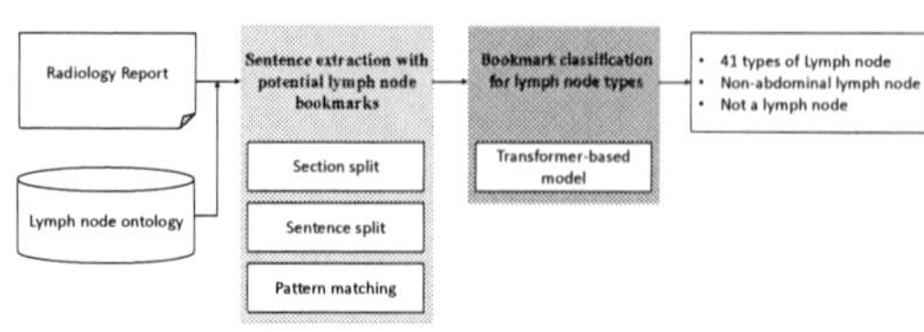


Figure 3: The architecture of the framework.

Table 1: The number of bookmarks in one sentence.

| # bookmarks per sentence | n | (%) |
| --- | --- | --- |
| 1 | 1,457 | 69.4 |
| 2 | 409 | 19.5 |
| 3 | 149 | 7.1 |
| 4 | 63 | 3.0 |
| 5 | 15 | 0.7 |
| 6 | 6 | 0.3 |

Each section/subsection begins with a heading and ends with one or more empty lines. If available, the section headings were phrases from the beginning of a new line to a colon (e.g., "Liver and Gallbladder:"). We, therefore, use this information to split the reports into sections. Second, we tokenized the sentences using NLTK (Bird, 2006).

If a report contains the "Lymph node" subsection, we extracted sentences with lymph nodes from this subsection; otherwise, we extracted sentences with "lymph node" mentioned in the "Finding section" using regular expressions. We skipped the reports if it is not sectioned (0.3%). In our study, 85% of lymph node bookmarks are from the "Lymph node" subsection, and the remaining 16% are from reports with the "Lymph node" subsection but "Finding section" sections.

### 3.3.2 Bookmark classification for the abdominal lymph node type

After obtained candidate bookmarks that may link to lymph nodes, the next step is to classify bookmarks for the lymph node types. Here, we use the full sentences that included the bookmark, presuming that they had information most relevant to the connected image annotation. However, the bookmarked sentences often contain a complex mixture of information describing not only various bookmarked lymph nodes but also other bookmarked abnormalities. A sample sentence is shown in Figure 1. There are four bookmarks in a sentence, each of which has a different lymph node type. Table 1 shows that more than 30% of sentences have at least two bookmarks.

To solve this problem, we developed a transformer-based deep learning module with 43 labels (41 abdominal lymph node types, non-abdominal lymph node, and not a lymph node). Specifically, we treat the lymph node recognition task as a sentence classification by replacing the bookmark of interest in the sentence with a prede-

fined tag \$BMK\$. Suppose that $h_0$ is the output embedding of the token [CLS], the probability that a bookmark labeled as class c is predicted by a fully connected layer and a logistic regression with softmax: $P(c|X) = softmax(ah_0 + b)$. We fine-tune the model on the training set using the categorical cross-entropy loss, $-\sum_c \delta(y_c = \hat{y})logP(c|X)$ where $\delta(y_c = \hat{y}) = 1$ if the classification $\hat{y}$ of $X$ is the correct ground-truth for the class $c \in C$; otherwise $\delta(y_c = \hat{y}) = 0$.

BERT is a contextualized word representation model that is pretrained based on a masked language modeling using bidirectional transformers (Devlin et al., 2019). In this paper, we fine-tuned the model using the BlueBERT base model (Peng et al., 2019b). The BlueBERT was pre-trained on the combination of PubMed and MIMIC-III clinical notes. We also compared the performance of our method using other BERT variants.

## 4 Results

### 4.1 Abdominal lymph node ontology

We construct an ontology of 41 abdominal lymph nodes relevant to MRI (Figure 4). Because of the nature of lymph node nomenclature, the labels had to have a hierarchical structure and some labels overlapped with others (Harisinghani, 2013; Richter and Feyerabend, 2012; Amin et al., 2017). Those subgroups include coarse, high-level lymph nodes such as "mediastinal lymph node", "retroperitoneal lymph node", and "pelvic lymph node", as well as fine-grained lymph nodes such as "perigastric lymph node along greater curvature" and "pericecal lymph node". Table 2 shows the distribution of lymph nodes in the dataset, which is imbalanced. The majority of abdominal lymph nodes in the dataset are periportal and para-aortic lymph nodes.

### 4.2 Results of the lymph node classification

We trained the model on one NVIDIA® V100 GPU using the TensorFlow framework26. We used the Adamax optimizer (Kingma and Ba, 2015) with a learning rate of $10^{-5}$ and a batch size of 32. We used the BlueBERT base model as the domain-specific language model. As a result, all the tokenized texts using wordpieces (Wu et al., 2016) were chopped to spans no longer than 128 tokens. We set the maximum number of epochs to 30.

To evaluate the performance of the framework, we use 70% for training, 10% for development, and

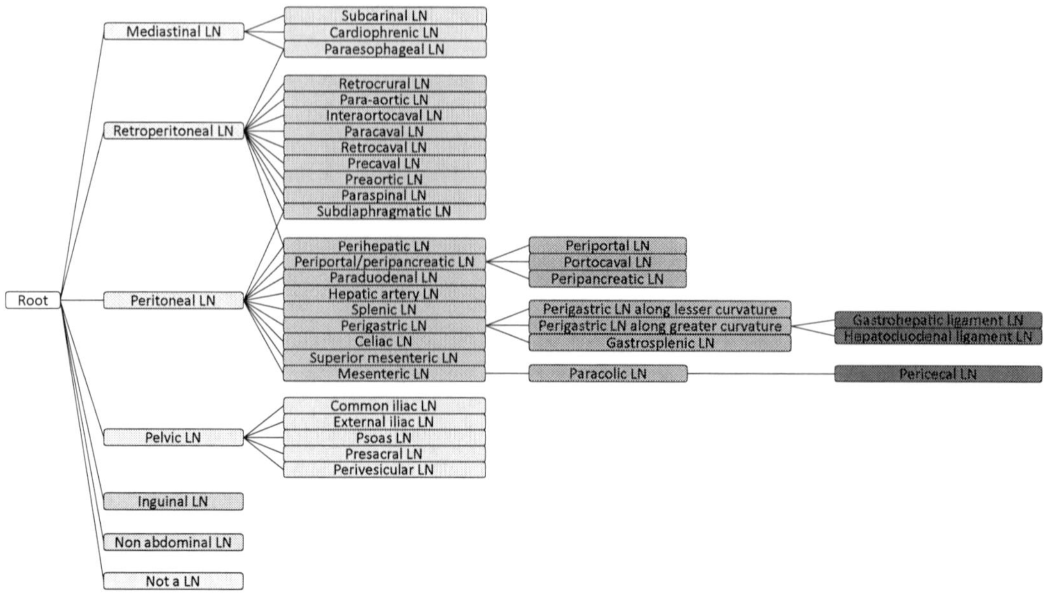


Figure 4: The abdominal lymph node (LN) ontology.

Table 2: The distribution of lymph node in the dataset.

| Lymph node | n | (%) | Lymph node | n | (%) |
|---|---|---|---|---|---|
| Periportal | 300 | 14.30 | Paraduodenal | 11 | 0.50 |
| Para-aortic | 278 | 13.20 | Subcarinal | 9 | 0.40 |
| Retroperitoneal | 257 | 12.20 | Superior mesenteric | 9 | 0.40 |
| Mesenteric | 186 | 8.90 | Paraesophageal | 8 | 0.40 |
| Portocaval | 125 | 6.00 | Peritoneal | 7 | 0.30 |
| Peripancreatic | 120 | 5.70 | Paraspinal | 7 | 0.30 |
| Interaortocaval | 95 | 4.50 | Paracolic | 7 | 0.30 |
| Gastrohepatic ligament | 73 | 3.50 | Pericecal | 7 | 0.30 |
| Retrocrural | 44 | 2.10 | External iliac | 6 | 0.30 |
| Paracaval | 39 | 1.90 | Pelvic | 6 | 0.30 |
| Retrocaval | 32 | 1.50 | Inguinal | 6 | 0.30 |
| Mediastinal | 26 | 1.20 | Perigastric LN along GC | 5 | 0.20 |
| Periportal/peripancreatic | 24 | 1.10 | Perigastric | 4 | 0.20 |
| Common iliac | 21 | 1.00 | Hepatoduodenal ligament | 4 | 0.20 |
| Cardiophrenic | 20 | 1.00 | Hepatic artery | 3 | 0.10 |
| Precaval | 19 | 0.90 | Splenic | 2 | 0.10 |
| Psoas | 18 | 0.90 | Presacral | 1 | 0.00 |
| Celiac | 17 | 0.80 | Perigastric LN along LC | 1 | 0.00 |
| Perihepatic | 14 | 0.70 | Non-abdominal LN | 238 | 11.30 |
| Subdiaphragmatic | 12 | 0.60 | Not a LN | 26 | 1.20 |
| Preaortic | 12 | 0.60 | | | |

GC - greater curvature. LC - lesser curvature

20% for testing. Table 3 shows the performance of our systems on the classification of 5 coarse-grained lymph node types by (P)recision, (R)ecall, and (F)1-score. The micro metrics count the total true positives, false negatives, and false positives across all lymph node types. The macro metrics calculate precision, recall, and F1 for each lymph node type and find their unweighted mean. The

Table 3: Test results on the classification of 5 coarse-grained lymph node types.

| Lymph nodes | P | R | F |
| --- | --- | --- | --- |
| Mediastinal LN | 0.778 | 1.000 | 0.875 |
| Retroperitoneal LN | 0.975 | 0.994 | 0.985 |
| Peritoneal LN | 0.959 | 0.989 | 0.974 |
| Pelvic LN | 1.000 | 0.923 | 0.960 |
| Inguinal LN | 1.000 | 1.000 | 1.000 |
| Non-abdominal LN | 0.952 | 0.784 | 0.860 |
| Not a LN | 1.000 | 0.500 | 0.667 |
| *micro* | 0.959 | 0.959 | 0.959 |
| *macro* | 0.952 | 0.884 | 0.903 |
| *micro weighted* | 0.960 | 0.959 | 0.957 |

weighted metrics calculate precision, recall, and F1 for each lymph node type and find their average weighted by the number of true instances for each type. Our system achieved an overall precision of 0.960, recall of 0.959, and F1-score of 0.957. We achieved F1-score $\geq$ 0.850 on all coarse-grained lymph node types. On the other hand, we observed that on "negative" cases (not a lymph node), the recall is 0.5. This is because the dataset has fewer negative instances (26) in total, which may not be sufficient to train and test the model. In the future, more negative cases shall be manually included to handle the imbalanced dataset. However, we consider it not a major issue in our framework since the first step utilizes rigid extraction patterns and achieves high precision.

Table 4 shows the performance on the classification of all fine-grained lymph node types. Our system achieved an overall precision of 0.925, recall of 0.913, and F1-score of 0.912. We achieved F1-score 1.00 on 8 types, $\geq$ 0.90 on 17 types, and $\geq$ 0.80 on 23 types.

We also compare our model on BERT variants: ClinicalBERT (Alsentzer et al., 2019), BioBERT (Lee et al., 2020), and BlueBERT. The Clinical-BERT was pretrained on MIMIC-III generic clinical text. The BioBERT was pretrained on PubMed. For reference, we include a rule-based system where the type of lymph node is selected based on the nearest keyword (e.g., cardiophrenic, inguinal, etc.) from the bookmark in the sentence. Table 5 shows that deep-learning based methods can successfully classify the type of each lymph node mentioned in the sentences. The system using BlueBERT (MriBERT) outperforms that using

BioBERT. This observation shows the impact of using clinical notes during the pre-training process. On the other hand, the system using ClinicalBERT achieved lower performance. It may suggest that the MIMIC-III clinical text alone may not be large enough to sufficiently pre-train the BERT model.

## 5 Conclusion

In this study, we introduced an ontology of 41 types of abdominal lymph nodes with a hierarchical relationship. We then proposed an end-to-end framework for combining rules and deep learning for accurate bookmark classification for lymph node types from MRI reports. In this framework, the rule-based method is first used to extract sentences with potential lymph node bookmarks. Then a BERT-based model pretrained on MRI reports was used to classify each bookmark into one of 41 types of abdominal lymph node, non-abdominal lymph nodes, or not a lymph node. We evaluated our framework on 2,099 bookmarks manually annotated by a radiological expert. We also compared our framework with a rule-based system and other BERT-based models. We find that our framework achieved 0.912 in F1-score, which outperforms the rule-based system and other BERT variations.

Our study has several limitations. First, our model is limited to the 41 abdominal lymph nodes. While we believe the list is comprehensive, we may miss some lymph node types due to training corpus bias. Second, our evaluation is performed on a single corpus. Cross-institutional experiments need to be performed in the future to evaluate the generalizability of the model.

While our work only scratches the surface of using text mining techniques and deep learning to extract the lymph node from radiology reports, we hope it will shed light on the development of generalizable NLP models that can extract highly accurate labels.

## Acknowledgment

This work was supported by the Intramural Research Programs of the NIH National Library of Medicine and NIH Clinical Center. This work was also supported by the National Library of Medicine of the NIH under award number 4R00LM013001. This work utilized the computational resources of the NIH HPC Biowulf cluster (http://hpc.nih.gov).

Table 4: Test results on the classification of fine-grained lymph node types.

| Lymph nodes | P | R | F | Lymph nodes | P | R | F |
|---|---|---|---|---|---|---|---|
| Periportal | 0.903 | 0.933 | 0.918 | Subdiaphragmatic | 1.000 | 0.667 | 0.800 |
| Para-aortic | 0.902 | 0.982 | 0.940 | Preaortic | 0.500 | 0.333 | 0.400 |
| Retroperitoneal | 0.980 | 0.962 | 0.971 | Paraduodenal | 1.000 | 0.667 | 0.800 |
| Mesenteric | 0.900 | 0.947 | 0.923 | Subcarinal | 0.667 | 1.000 | 0.800 |
| Portocaval | 0.889 | 0.960 | 0.923 | Superior mesenteric | 1.000 | 0.500 | 0.667 |
| Peripancreatic | 0.923 | 1.000 | 0.960 | Paraesophageal | 1.000 | 1.000 | 1.000 |
| Interaortocaval | 1.000 | 1.000 | 1.000 | Peritoneal | 1.000 | 1.000 | 1.000 |
| Gastrohepatic ligament | 0.938 | 1.000 | 0.968 | Paraspinal | 1.000 | 1.000 | 1.000 |
| Retrocrural | 1.000 | 1.000 | 1.000 | Paracolic | 1.000 | 0.500 | 0.667 |
| Paracaval | 0.667 | 0.500 | 0.571 | Pericecal | 0.500 | 1.000 | 0.667 |
| Retrocaval | 0.667 | 0.857 | 0.750 | External iliac | 1.000 | 1.000 | 1.000 |
| Mediastinal | 0.625 | 0.833 | 0.714 | Pelvic | 1.000 | 1.000 | 1.000 |
| Periportal/peripancreatic | 0.833 | 1.000 | 0.909 | Inguinal | 0.667 | 1.000 | 0.800 |
| Common iliac | 1.000 | 1.000 | 1.000 | Perigastric LN along LC | 0.500 | 1.000 | 0.667 |
| Cardiophrenic | 0.750 | 0.750 | 0.750 | Non-abdominal LN | 0.975 | 0.765 | 0.857 |
| Precaval | 0.750 | 0.750 | 0.750 | Not a LN | 1.000 | 0.333 | 0.500 |
| Psoas | 1.000 | 1.000 | 1.000 | *micro* | 0.913 | 0.913 | 0.913 |
| Celiac | 1.000 | 1.000 | 1.000 | *macro* | 0.861 | 0.859 | 0.839 |
| Perihepatic | 1.000 | 0.667 | 0.800 | *micro weighted* | 0.925 | 0.913 | 0.912 |

GC - greater curvature. LC - lesser curvature

Table 5: Test results of various methods on lymph node classification.

| Models | Coarse-grained LN types | | | Fine-grained LN types | | |
|---|---|---|---|---|---|---|
| | P | R | F | P | R | F |
| Rule-based | 0.827 | 0.579 | 0.644 | 0.699 | 0.453 | 0.533 |
| ClinicalBERT | 0.914 | 0.915 | 0.913 | 0.878 | 0.878 | 0.874 |
| BioBERT | 0.932 | 0.931 | 0.928 | 0.896 | 0.887 | 0.885 |
| BlueBERT (MriBERT) | **0.960** | **0.959** | **0.957** | **0.925** | **0.913** | **0.912** |

## References

Emily Alsentzer, John Murphy, William Boag, Wei-Hung Weng, Di Jindi, Tristan Naumann, and Matthew McDermott. 2019. Publicly available clinical BERT embeddings. In *Proceedings of the 2nd Clinical Natural Language Processing Workshop*, pages 72–78, Minneapolis, Minnesota, USA. Association for Computational Linguistics.

Mahul B. Amin, American Joint Committee on Cancer, and American Cancer Society, editors. 2017. *AJCC Cancer Staging Manual*, eight edition / editor-in-chief, mahul b. amin, md, fcap ; editors, stephen b. edge, md, facs [and 16 others] ; donna m. gress, rhit, ctr - technical editor ; laura r. meyer, capm - managing editor edition. American Joint Committee on Cancer, Springer, Chicago IL.

Alan R Aronson and François-Michel Lang. 2010. An overview of MetaMap: Historical perspective and recent advances. *Journal of the American Medical Informatics Association : JAMIA*, 17(3):229–236.

Steven Bird. 2006. NLTK: The natural language toolkit. In *Proceedings of the COLING/ACL on Interactive Presentation Sessions*, pages 69–72. Association for Computational Linguistics.

Brian E. Chapman, Sean Lee, Hyunseok Peter Kang, and Wendy W. Chapman. 2011. Document-level classification of CT pulmonary angiography reports based on an extension of the ConText algorithm. *Journal of Biomedical Informatics*, 44(5):728–737.

Wendy W Chapman, Dieter Hillert, Sumithra Velupillai, Maria Kvist, Maria Skeppstedt, Brian E Chapman, Mike Conway, Melissa Tharp, Danielle L Mowery, and Louise Deleger. 2013. Extending the NegEx lexicon for multiple languages. *Studies in health technology and informatics*, 192:677–681.

Matthew C. Chen, Robyn L. Ball, Lingyao Yang, Nathaniel Moradzadeh, Brian E. Chapman, David B. Larson, Curtis P. Langlotz, Timothy J. Amrhein, and Matthew P. Lungren. 2018. Deep Learning to Classify Radiology Free-Text Reports. *Radiology*, 286(3):845–852.

Cheryl Clark, John Aberdeen, Matt Coarr, David Tresner-Kirsch, Ben Wellner, Alexander Yeh, and Lynette Hirschman. 2011. MITRE system for clinical assertion status classification. *Journal of the American Medical Informatics Association : JAMIA*, 18(5):563–567.

Jacob Devlin, Ming-Wei Chang, Kenton Lee, and Kristina Toutanova. 2019. BERT: Pre-training of Deep Bidirectional Transformers for Language Understanding. In *Proceedings of the 2019 Conference of the North American Chapter of the Association for Computational Linguistics: Human Language Technologies, Volume 1 (Long and Short Papers)*, pages 4171–4186, Minneapolis, Minnesota. Association for Computational Linguistics.

Ignat Drozdov, Daniel Forbes, Benjamin Szubert, Mark Hall, Chris Carlin, and David J. Lowe. 2020. Supervised and unsupervised language modelling in Chest X-Ray radiological reports. *PLOS ONE*, 15(3):e0229963.

Mukesh G. Harisinghani, editor. 2013. *Atlas of Lymph Node Anatomy*. Springer, New York.

Yang Huang and Henry J. Lowe. 2007. A novel hybrid approach to automated negation detection in clinical radiology reports. *Journal of the American Medical Informatics Association*, 14(3):304–311.

Jeremy Irvin, Pranav Rajpurkar, Michael Ko, Yifan Yu, Silviana Ciurea-Ilcus, Chris Chute, and Henrik Marklund. 2019. Chexpert: A large chest radiograph dataset with uncertainty labels and expert comparison. In *Proceedings of the AAAI Conference on Artificial Intelligence*, volume 33, pages 590–597.

Kasper Jensen, Cristina Soguero-Ruiz, Karl Oyvind Mikalsen, Rolv-Ole Lindsetmo, Irene Kouskoumvekaki, Mark Girolami, Stein Olav Skrovseth, and Knut Magne Augestad. 2017. Analysis of free text in electronic health records for identification of cancer patient trajectories. *Scientific Reports*, 7(1):46226.

Alistair E. W. Johnson, Tom J. Pollard, Nathaniel R. Greenbaum, Matthew P. Lungren, Chih-ying Deng, Yifan Peng, Zhiyong Lu, Roger G. Mark, Seth J. Berkowitz, and Steven Horng. 2019. MIMIC-CXR-JPG, a large publicly available database of labeled chest radiographs. *arXiv preprint*.

Diederik P. Kingma and Jimmy Ba. 2015. Adam: A method for stochastic optimization. In *International Conference on Learning Representations (ICLR)*, pages 1–15.

Jinhyuk Lee, Wonjin Yoon, Sungdong Kim, Donghyeon Kim, Sunkyu Kim, Chan Ho So, and Jaewoo Kang. 2020. BioBERT: A pre-trained biomedical language representation model for biomedical text mining. *Bioinformatics (Oxford, England)*, 36(4):1234–1240.

Yi Liu, Li-Na Zhu, Qing Liu, Chao Han, Xiao-Dong Zhang, and Xiao-Ying Wang. 2019. Automatic extraction of imaging observation and assessment categories from breast magnetic resonance imaging reports with natural language processing. *Chinese Medical Journal*, 132(14):1673–1680.

Matthew B. A. McDermott, Tzu Ming Harry Hsu, Wei-Hung Weng, Marzyeh Ghassemi, and Peter Szolovits. 2020. CheXpert++: approximating the chexpert labeler for speed,differentiability, and probabilistic output. *arXiv:2006.15229 [cs, stat]*.

Yifan Peng, Xiaosong Wang, Le Lu, Mohammadhadi Bagheri, Ronald Summers, and Zhiyong Lu. 2018. NegBio: A high-performance tool for negation and uncertainty detection in radiology reports. In *AMIA Joint Summits on Translational Science Proceedings*.

*AMIA Joint Summits on Translational Science*, volume 2017, pages 188–196.

Yifan Peng, Ke Yan, Veit Sandfort, Ronald M. Summers, and Zhiyong Lu. 2019a. A self-attention based deep learning method for lesion attribute detection from CT reports. In *2019 IEEE International Conference on Healthcare Informatics (ICHI)*. IEEE.

Yifan Peng, Shankai Yan, and Zhiyong Lu. 2019b. Transfer learning in biomedical natural language processing: An evaluation of BERT and ELMo on ten benchmarking datasets. In *Proceedings of the Workshop on Biomedical Natural Language Processing (BioNLP)*, pages 58–65.

E Richter and Thomas Feyerabend. 2012. *Normal Lymph Node Topography: CT Atlas.* Springer Berlin Heidelberg, Berlin.

Dorothy A. Sippo, Graham I. Warden, Katherine P. Andriole, Ronilda Lacson, Ichiro Ikuta, Robyn L. Birdwell, and Ramin Khorasani. 2013. Automated extraction of BI-RADS final assessment categories from radiology reports with natural language processing. *Journal of Digital Imaging*, 26(5):989–994.

Akshay Smit, Saahil Jain, Pranav Rajpurkar, Anuj Pareek, Andrew Y. Ng, and Matthew P. Lungren. 2020. CheXbert: Combining Automatic Labelers and Expert Annotations for Accurate Radiology Report Labeling Using BERT. *arXiv:2004.09167 [cs]*.

Xiaosong Wang, Yifan Peng, Le Lu, Zhiyong Lu, Mohammadhadi Bagheri, and Ronald M Summers. 2017. Chestx-ray8: Hospital-scale chest x-ray database and benchmarks on weakly-supervised classification and localization of common thorax diseases. In *2017 IEEE Conference on Computer Vision and Pattern Recognition (CVPR)*, pages 3462–3471. IEEE.

David A. Wood, Jeremy Lynch, Sina Kafiabadi, Emily Guilhem, Aisha Al Busaidi, Antanas Montvila, Thomas Varsavsky, Juveria Siddiqui, Naveen Gadapa, Matthew Townend, Martin Kiik, Keena Patel, Gareth Barker, Sebastian Ourselin, James H. Cole, and Thomas C. Booth. 2020. Automated Labelling using an Attention model for Radiology reports of MRI scans (ALARM). *arXiv:2002.06588 [cs]*.

Yonghui Wu, Mike Schuster, Zhifeng Chen, Quoc V Le, Mohammad Norouzi, Wolfgang Macherey, Maxim Krikun, Yuan Cao, Qin Gao, Klaus Macherey, et al. 2016. Google's neural machine translation system: Bridging the gap between human and machine translation. *arXiv preprint arXiv:1609.08144*.

Kui Xue, Yangming Zhou, Zhiyuan Ma, Tong Ruan, Huanhuan Zhang, and Ping He. 2019. Fine-tuning BERT for joint entity and relation extraction in Chinese medical text. In *2019 IEEE International Conference on Bioinformatics and Biomedicine (BIBM)*, pages 892–897. IEEE.

Ke Yan, Xiaosong Wang, Le Lu, and Ronald M. Summers. 2018. DeepLesion: Automated mining of large-scale lesion annotations and universal lesion detection with deep learning. *Journal of medical imaging (Bellingham, Wash.)*, 5(3):036501.

# How You Ask Matters: The Effect of Paraphrastic Questions to BERT Performance on a Clinical SQuAD Dataset


**Sungrim Moon[1], Jungwei Fan[1,2]**
[1]Division of Digital Health Sciences
[2]Center for the Science of Health Care Delivery
Mayo Clinic
200 1st Street SW, Rochester, MN 55905
moon.sungrim@mayo.edu
fan.jung-wei@mayo.edu



## Abstract

Reading comprehension style question-answering (QA) based on patient-specific documents represents a growing area in clinical NLP with plentiful applications. Bidirectional Encoder Representations from Transformers (BERT) and its derivatives lead the state-of-the-art accuracy on the task, but most evaluation has treated the data as a pre-mixture without systematically looking into the potential effect of imperfect train/test questions. The current study seeks to address this gap by experimenting with full versus partial train/test data consisting of paraphrastic questions. Our key findings include 1) training with all pooled question variants yielded best accuracy, 2) the accuracy varied widely, from 0.74 to 0.80, when trained with each single question variant, and 3) questions of similar lexical/syntactic structure tended to induce identical answers. The results suggest that how you ask questions matters in BERT-based QA, especially at the training stage.


## 1 Introduction

In clinical NLP, there has been vital interest in developing question-answering (QA) systems, e.g., AskHERMES (Cao et al., 2011), MiPACQ (Cairns et al., 2011), and MEANS (Abacha and Zweigenbaum, 2015). One specific type of clinical QA targets on locating any suitable answer within a given document (a.k.a. reading comprehension), which is helpful for answering patient-specific questions based on information mentioned in clinical notes. Recently, BERT (Devlin et al., 2018) and its derivatives have struck impressive success in this task for general English, represented by SQuAD (Rajpurkar et al., 2018), and for clinical text with promising results (Wen et al., 2020; Soni and Roberts, 2020).

However, an under-explored area in performing BERT-assisted QA is: how the system would behave if the input question is asked in a different (paraphrastic) way? Most existing experiments have assumed that the train and test data belong to a closed space with pre-assembled syntactic and lexical diversity (i.e., paraphrastic questions) representing what the users could ever ask, and faithfully evaluate the both diverse train/test sets in a symmetric manner. In practice, there are at least two possible scenarios concerning the potential effect from a differently-asked test question: 1) the system is trained with, or has seen, the question construct, 2) the system has never seen the question construct during training. Here by "construct" we refer to paraphrases like: "why is the patient prescribed medication-X?" versus "why does the patient take medication-X?". More examples are in Table 1.

Ideally, a BERT QA model is supposed to provide a consistent answer as long as the user asked a semantically-equivalent (paraphrastic) question. This is important in a production system because a user should not be required to ask only questions conforming to "template" constructs. Therefore, in this study we set to understand how such paraphrastic perturbation in asking would affect a BERT-based QA model. We used a dataset that contained finite question constructs, but purposefully injected experiments with using




*Proceedings of the 3rd Clinical Natural Language Processing Workshop*, pages 111–116
November 19, 2020. ©2020 Association for Computational Linguistics

limited constructs in the training and/or testing to simulate the asymmetric perturbations of interest. For example, training on only one question construct and testing on the other different constructs (i.e., unseen ways of asking).

Our major findings can be summarized as follows:

1. Models trained with all pooled constructs still gave the best accuracy.
2. When training was limited to each single construct, certain constructs gave overall higher accuracy across all test constructs. Accuracy also varied depending on the test construct, but the effect was not strong as the choice of the training construct.
3. Certain test question constructs tended to induce identical answers, as revealed via a clustering analysis.

## 2 Related work

Pampari et al. (2018) created the emrQA corpus by template-based semantic extraction from the i2b2 NLP challenge datasets (i2b2 2019). The emrQA includes more than 400,000 QA pairs and has served as a valuable resource in clinical QA research (Wen et al., 2020; Soni and Roberts, 2020). Most of the previous studies reported strong performance by BERT, especially when it was pre-trained with domain-specific text, e.g., the Clinical BERT (Alsentzer et al., 2019) was trained with about 2 million clinical notes from the MIMIC-III database (Johnson et al., 2016). For compatibility with using BERT-based reading comprehension QA, the SQuAD format is commonly adopted. Task-wise, the SQuAD 2.0 (Rajpurkar et al., 2018) also introduced unanswerable questions that require QA systems to know when not to answer if no suitable evidence is present in the text.

Besides the relevant backgrounds above, there have been NLP studies that reported the effect of paraphrastic questions in QA system performance. Buck et al. (2017) and Dong et al. (2017) developed approaches to paraphrasing questions for optimal answer accuracy in retrieval-based QA, where candidate answers were searched and ranked from a large set of documents. The closest work for reading comprehension QA we identified was by Gan and Ng (2019), which investigated the effect of question variants on a general English SQuAD dataset. They demonstrated that unseen paraphrastic test questions hurt the accuracy of deep learning QA models, and proposed a countermeasure by pre-augmenting the training data with machine-generated paraphrastic questions.

## 3 Methods

### 3.1 Research questions

We designed our experiments around the following three research questions:

- How does the accuracy change by training the model with a pool of multiple question constructs versus training by only each construct?
- How does the accuracy vary across different training question constructs and across different test question constructs?
- Do some of the test question constructs tend to elicit similar answers out of a trained model?

### 3.2 Dataset

We used the emrQA as the base dataset and selected only those "why"-questions in this study due to our application research interest. Within the why-QA subset, we further considered three levels of QAs, from broad to specific:

*All* – all the why-QAs (see Appendix A).

*Med* – why-QAs about medication.

*Q0~Q8* – the 9 individual question constructs in the *Med* set, as elaborated in Table 1.

| Label | Question construct |
|-------|--------------------|
| *Q0* | Why was [medication] prescribed? |
| *Q1* | Why was [medication] originally prescribed? |
| *Q2* | Why was the patient prescribed [medication]? |
| *Q3* | Why is the patient prescribed [medication]? |
| *Q4* | Why has the patient been prescribed [medication]? |
| *Q5* | Why was the patient on [medication]? |
| *Q6* | Why is the patient on [medication]? |
| *Q7* | Why does the patient take [medication]? |
| *Q8* | Why is the patient taking [medication]? |

Table 1: The 9 different question constructs in the medication why-QAs.

| Corpus | | *All* | *Med* | *Qi* |
|---|---|---|---|---|
| Train | HasAns | 8,835 | 3,807 | 423 |
| | NoAns | 7,985 | 3,726 | 414 |
| Dev | HasAns | 3,024 | 1,260 | 140 |
| | NoAns | 2,725 | 1,242 | 138 |
| Test | HasAns | 9,232 | 4,572 | 508 |
| | NoAns | 8,204 | 4,428 | 492 |

Table 2: Number of the train/dev/test QAs in the three cascaded levels. *Qi* represents each of *Q0-Q8*.

All the QAs were prepared into the SQuAD 2.0 format. The train/dev/test splits are detailed in Table 2, which also breaks down with showing the answerable (HasAns) versus unanswerable (NoAns) QA counts. The dev partition was for setting the optimal threshold of "do not answer" before processing the final held out test partition. Note that the numbers in column *Qi* were made identical across *Q0-Q8* respectively, so there should not be any bias in inflating any of them.

### 3.3 Training and evaluation

All of the models started from the pre-trained Clinical BERT, followed by a modest fine-tuning with 1,833 general English why-QAs from the SQuAD 2.0 corpus. On top of that, the experiments involved three parts (Table 2 for denotations):

A. Fine-tune/calibrate on *All* train/dev (one model), test on each *Qi* test set.

B. Fine-tune/calibrate on *Med* train/dev (one model), test on each *Qi* test set.

C. Fine-tune/calibrate on *Qi* train/dev (nine models), test on each *Qi* test set. This is basically crossover between *Q0-Q8*.

Each fine-tuning (or simply referred as "training") was done with 10 epochs, batch_train_size=32, learning_rate=3e-5, and max_seq_length=128. The jobs were run on a Tesla V100 with compute capability 7.0 and 18 GB of memory.

The official SQuAD 2.0 evaluation script was used, and we reported primarily the accuracy as F1-weighted overlaps between the gold and the system answers. As a semi-qualitative assessment of question similarity (in terms of the triggered model behavior), we computed the number of agreed (case-insensitive and remove articles) answers between each pair of *Qi* test sets in experiment B above and performed hierarchical clustering to group the 9 question constructs.

## 4 Results

### 4.1 Pooled training made stronger model

The model accuracies are reported in Figure 1, where Figure 1b is specifically to show precision (positive predictive value, or PPV) on those HasAns QAs that were indeed answered by each model. It can be seen that the *All* model (blue line at the top) outperformed the *Med* model (orange line) and every individual *Qi* model, suggesting that training with additional non-medication why-QA entries still benefited the accuracy. The benefit is more apparent in PPV (Figure 1b) and fluctuates mildly across the test constructs *Q0~Q8* (X-axis). In comparison to the individual *Qi* models, the pooled *Med* model also exhibits clear advantage but with varying margins (elaborated in 4.2).

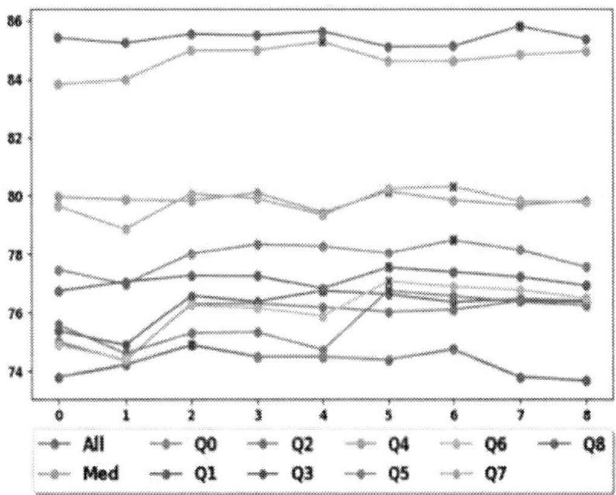

Figure 1a: Accuracies of the different models. X-axis: test question construct, Y-axis: accuracy.

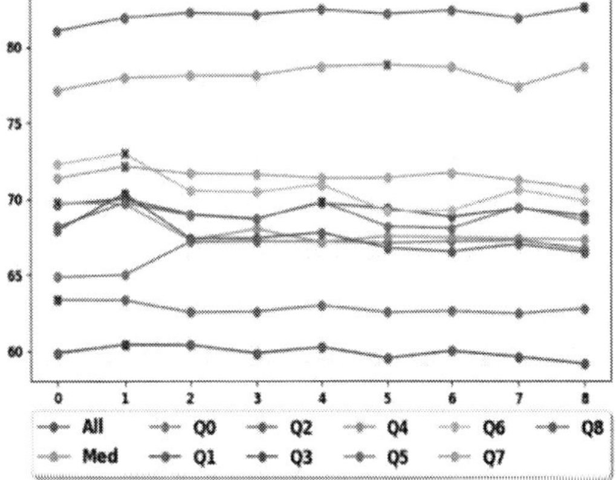

Figure 1b: Accuracies of the different models, on the answerable and indeed answered subset.

## 4.2  Accuracy varied depending on the question construct

The accuracy appears to be strongly affected by which specific question construct was used for training. For example, *Q7* (cyan line in Figure 1) exhibits about 4% drop compared to *Med* (orange), while *Q1* (red) has 10% or wider gap below *Med*. Manual inspection of 569 disagreements between *Q1* and *Q7* did show the *Q1* model frequently refrained from answering (141/569=25%) or gave irrelevant answers (286/569=50%). In addition, such question-dependent behavior changes again when we look at PPV specifically. For example, in Figure 1a the *Q4* model (pink) performs comparably well as the *Q7* model, but in Figure 1b its relative rank drops to the middle tier indicating that *Q4* gave many incorrect answers.

Within each line (a trained model), the variance of accuracy across different test questions does not appear as drastic (up to ~2%) compared to that observed across models. However, one puzzling observation is that the peak accuracy within each line of *Q0~Q8* is usually not at where the train and test question align. (e.g., train on *Q0*, test on *Q0*)

## 4.3  Some questions were more likely to obtain same answers

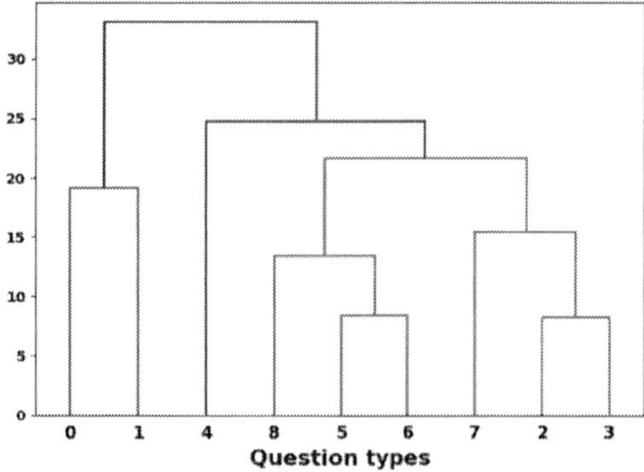


Figure 2: Question similarity clustering based on answer agreement. X-axis: test questions *Q0~Q8*. Y-axis: # of agreed answers by the model *Med*.

The hierarchical dendrogram for clustering the question constructs is shown in Figure 2. When trained on the pooled of *Med* constructs (i.e., the orange line in Figure 1a), some of the test question constructs turned out to yield closer answers than others. Specifically, *Q0* and *Q1* form a cluster (green in Figure 2), *Q4* sort of stands alone, and the others form another subtree (red) enclosing further sub-clusters. Some intuitive explanations could be derived by inspecting the lexical/syntactic contents of the questions: For example, between *Q0* and *Q1* the only difference is an additional "originally" in *Q1*. Likewise, a single switch of tense between "was" and "is" appears to account for the two tight clusters (*Q2* and *Q3*) as well as (*Q5* and *Q6*).

# 5  Discussion

## 5.1  Recap the rationale

Many would think it a trivial fact that different questions surely contribute to varying answers. However, we believe it is worth a break-down analysis beyond the monolithic thinking of just "the more the better". No matter how well planned, one can always legitimately ask "what if" the training questions were not exhaustive and some real user threw in unexpected questions. Therefore, this study was meant to expose such behavior out of a BERT-based QA model by putting it under the stress of partial train/test questions.

## 5.2  Featured findings, raised questions

Our findings did validate some trivial knowledge such as the more robust models gained by pooling diverse training data and that similar questions tended to elicit similar answers. On the other hand, we have findings to highlight: 1) a model's accuracy is determined strongly by what questions it is trained on and not as much by what test questions it is asked to answer, 2) there appear to be "better ways to ask" especially in training that would yield generally higher accuracy. That said, our findings somewhat circle back to corroborating the common strategy that focuses on enriching the training diversity to achieve robust performance – plus, the "good" questions need adequate presence.

The micro-level, quality-oriented observations could not be revealed without diving into those question-specific comparisons. For fundamental computational linguistics research, our findings pointed an interesting direction to explore: why certain question constructs (e.g., *Q7* "Why does the patient take [medication]?") appear to be more transferrable (at least accuracy-wise) after being learned by BERT? Methods for inspecting the attention mechanism under the hood might help, but we suspect that new approaches of even better interpretability likely need to be designed. Specifically, one phenomenon that puzzled us was the peak accuracy did not always happen at the point when a single-question model was tested on questions of the same training construct.

## 5.3 Limitations

Our experiments on why-QAs and the focus on medication-related questions could limit the generalizability. The diversity of those question variants was bound to what emrQA had offered, and we did not know how that compared to the natural distribution of variants asked by humans. Besides, the emrQA corpus might have embedded noise and quality issues (Yue et al., 2020) that affected the results. Lastly, we still do not have explanation to many findings, and it is unclear if BERT can represent other QA models especially in terms of the question-specific behaviors.

## 5.4 Future work

The current study looked mainly into syntactic variants of the questions, and we will further research the independent or interactive effect of lexico-syntactic variants of concepts (e.g., medication) mentioned in both the question and answer document. Based on our findings, we plan to experiment optimizing the QA accuracy through ensemble approaches such as voting - the hypothesis is the chance of achieving a convergent (correct) answer should be increased by asking the same question in different ways.

## 6 Conclusion

We found that how you ask matters in a BERT-based clinical QA task, especially at the training stage. By controlling the train and test questions to individual lexical/syntactic constructs, our crossover evaluation showed that certain question constructs consistently yielded higher accuracy. Accordingly, it suggests that the most effective way to secure robust performance is still by training with diverse, sizable questions. Our results also brought up a somewhat nuanced inquiry: how come some question constructs seem to act "linguistically superior" to others, and whether it is a universal or BERT-dependent phenomenon?

## Acknowledgments

Deidentified clinical records used in this research were provided by the i2b2 National Center for Biomedical Computing funded by U54LM008748 and were originally prepared for the Shared Tasks for Challenges in NLP for Clinical Data organized by Dr. Ozlem Uzuner, i2b2 and SUNY. We thank the anonymous reviewers for their constructive feedback.

## References


Asma B. Abacha and Pierre Zweigenbaum. 2015. MEANS: A medical question-answering system combining NLP techniques and semantic Web technologies. *Information processing & management* 51, no. 5:570-594. https://www.sciencedirect.com/science/article/pii/S0306457315000515

Emily Alsentzer, John R. Murphy, Willie Boag, Wei-Hung Weng, Di Jin, Tristan Naumann, and Matthew B.A. McDermott. 2019. Publicly available clinical bert embeddings. *ClinicalNLP workshop at NAACL.* https://arxiv.org/pdf/1904.03323.pdf

Christian Buck, Jannis Bulian, Massimiliano Ciaramita, Wojciech Gajewski, Andrea Gesmundo, Neil Houlsby, and Wei Wang. "Ask the right questions: Active question reformulation with reinforcement learning." arXiv preprint arXiv:1705.07830 (2017). https://arxiv.org/abs/1705.07830

Brian L. Cairns, Rodney D. Nielsen, James J. Masanz, James H. Martin, Martha S. Palmer, Wayne H. Ward, and Guergana K. Savova. 2011. The MiPACQ clinical question answering system. *In AMIA annual symposium proceedings*, vol. 2011, p. 171. American Medical Informatics Association. https://www.ncbi.nlm.nih.gov/pmc/articles/PMC3243235

YongGang Cao, Feifan Liu, Pippa Simpson, Lamont Antieau, Andrew Bennett, James J. Cimino, John Ely, and Hong Yu. 2011, AskHERMES: An online question answering system for complex clinical questions. *Journal of biomedical informatics* 44, no. 2:277-288. https://www.ncbi.nlm.nih.gov/pmc/articles/PMC3433744/pdf/nihms400508.pdf

Jacob Devlin, Ming-Wei Chang, Kenton Lee, and Kristina Toutanova. 2018. BERT: Pre-training of Deep Bidirectional Transformers for Language Understanding. *Computing Research Repository*, https://arxiv.org/abs/1810.04805

Li Dong, Jonathan Mallinson, Siva Reddy, and Mirella Lapata. "Learning to paraphrase for question answering." arXiv preprint arXiv:1708.06022 (2017). https://arxiv.org/abs/1708.06022

Wee Chung Gan and Hwee Tou Ng. 2019. Improving the Robustness of Question Answering Systems to Question Paraphrasing. *In Proceedings of the 57th Annual Meeting of the Association for Computational Linguistics*, pages 6065–6075, Florence, Italy. Association for Computational Linguistics. https://www.aclweb.org/anthology/P19-1610.pdf

Alistair E.W. Johnson, Tom J. Pollard, Lu Shen, Liwei H. Lehman, Mengling Feng, Mohammad Ghassemi, Benjamin Moody, Peter Szolovits, Leo A. Celi, and Roger G. Mark. 2016. MIMIC-III, a freely accessible critical care database. *Scientific Data*, 3, https://www.nature.com/articles/sdata201635.pdf

Olga Kovaleva, Alexey Romanov, Anna Rogers, and Anna Rumshisky. 2019. Revealing the Dark Secrets of BERT. *In Proceedings of the 2019 Conference on Empirical Methods in Natural Language Processing and the 9th International Joint Conference on Natural Language Processing (EMNLP-IJCNLP)*, pages 4356–4365, Hong Kong, China. Association for Computational Linguistics. https://www.aclweb.org/anthology/D19-1445/

Anusri Pampari, Preethi Raghavan, Jennifer Liang, and Jian Peng. 2018. emrqa: A large corpus for question answering on electronic medical records. arXiv preprint arXiv:1809.00732

Pranav Rajpurkar, Robin Jia, and Percy Liang. 2018. Know what you don't know: Unanswerable questions for squad. *In Proceedings of the Association for Computational Linguistics.* https://arxiv.org/abs/1806.03822

Pranav Rajpurkar, Jian Zhang, Konstantin Lopyrev, and Percy Liang. 2016. SQuAD: 100,000+ questions for machine comprehension of text. arXiv preprint arXiv:1606.05250.

Sarvesh Soni and Kirk Roberts. 2020. Evaluation of Dataset Selection for Pre-Training and Fine-Tuning Transformer Language Models for Clinical Question Answering. *In Proceedings of the LREC*, p5534–5540. https://www.aclweb.org/anthology/2020.lrec-1.679.pdf

The i2b2 2019 NLP Research Data Sets. Secondary The i2b2 NLP Research Data Sets. https://www.i2b2.org/NLP/DataSets/Main.php (accessed August, 2020)

Andrew Wen, Mohamed Y. Elwazir, Sungrim Moon, and Jungwei Fan. 2020. Adapting and evaluating a deep learning language model for clinical why-question answering, *JAMIA Open*, 3(1):16-20. https://academic.oup.com/jamiaopen/article/3/1/16/5722318

Xiang Yue, Bernal J. Gutierrez, and Huan Sun. "Clinical Reading Comprehension: A Thorough Analysis of the emrQA Dataset." arXiv preprint arXiv:2005.00574 (2020). https://arxiv.org/abs/2005.00574

## Appendix A. All the why-question types

Why does the patient take |medication|
Why has the patient been prescribed |medication|
Why is the patient on |medication|
Why is the patient prescribed |medication|
Why is the patient taking |medication|
Why was |medication| originally prescribed
Why was |medication| prescribed
Why was the patient on |medication|
Why was the patient prescribed |medication|
Why did the patient have |test|
Why did they patient get |test|
Why was |test| done on this patient
Why was |test| performed
Why did the patient have |treatment|
Why did the patient need |treatment|
Why is the patient on |treatment|
Why was the patient on |treatment|

# Relative and Incomplete Time Expression Anchoring for Clinical Text


**Louise Dupuis**
IoPPN, King's College London
Université Paris-Saclay, CentraleSupélec
louise.dupuis@kcl.ac.uk

**Nicol Bergou**
IoPPN, King's College London
nicol.2.bergou@kcl.ac.uk

**Hegler Tissot**
IHI, University College London
h.tissot@ucl.ac.uk

**Sumithra Velupillai**
IoPPN, King's College London
sumithra.velupillai@kcl.ac.uk



## Abstract

Extracting and modeling temporal information in clinical text is an important element for developing timelines and disease trajectories. Time information in written text varies in preciseness and explicitness, posing challenges for NLP approaches that aim to accurately anchor temporal information on a timeline. Relative and incomplete time expressions (RI-Timexes) are expressions that require additional information for their temporal anchor to be resolved, but few studies have addressed this challenge specifically. In this study, we aimed to reproduce and verify a classification approach for identifying anchor dates and relations in clinical text, and propose a novel relation classification approach for this task.


## 1 Introduction

Temporal information is a crucial aspect of the analysis of clinical texts in electronic health records in order to improve understanding of disease trajectories. Being able to extract and model time information, such as dates and durations of events, leads to knowledge about the temporal context of clinically important information like symptoms or treatments, and can be used e.g. to reconstruct a patient's timeline. With such timelines, a wide range of applications can be developed, such as population-based observational retrospective studies on temporal patterns in diseases and treatments, or individualised patient summaries.

Several solutions have been proposed and developed to extract and normalize temporal information from text both in the general and clinical NLP domains (Leeuwenberg and Moens, 2019; Derczynski, 2017; Tissot et al., 2019). The most widely used model for annotating temporal information and cues for NLP applications is the TimeML model (Pustejovsky et al., 2010), where *time expressions* (timexes) are a core element. These are typically annotated into types (e.g. dates, durations) and normalized to a temporal value that can be used for further temporal reasoning.

However, accurate normalization of relative and incomplete temporal expressions is still an understudied area. Relative and incomplete time expressions (RI-Timexes), as defined in (Sun et al., 2015) are time expressions that require another timex for their value to be resolved. For example, in the following sentences *"He arrived on 09/18/2002. Three days later, he was transferred to the Medical Intensive Care Unit."*, the normalized temporal value of the date timex *"09/18/2002"* does not depend on any context. Such expressions are called *absolute timexes*. *RI-Timexes*, on the other hand, require additional contextual information. For example, to assign and compute the normalized temporal value of the RI-Timex *"Three days later"*, we need information about what this expression refers to in the narrative – in this case, the previous date timex *"09/18/2002"*. The temporal expression that the relative timex refers to is called the *anchor*. An anchor relation, which specifies the link between the two expressions, can also be defined. With these two pieces of information, it becomes feasible to compute a normalized value for the RI-Timex (09/21/2002 in this case).

In the clinical domain, two of the most widely used temporal extraction and normalization tools are the java-based libraries HeidelTime (Strötgen and Gertz, 2010) and SUTime (Chang and Manning, 2012). Their approach to normalize relative time expressions is to define one main anchor date for the whole document (Document Creation Time,




*Proceedings of the 3rd Clinical Natural Language Processing Workshop*, pages 117–129
November 19, 2020. ©2020 Association for Computational Linguistics

DCT), and all timexes in the document are resolved relatively to this. This method might work well on e.g. short texts that refer to a single event, but is not necessarily appropriate for longer narrative notes, for example clinical assessments relating to a patient's history.

Adaptations and variations of these systems were used by several teams in the 2012 i2b2 NLP Challenge on Temporal Relations in Clinical Data (Sun et al., 2013a), and the best performing system on timex normalization yielded value accuracy of 0.73 (Sun et al., 2013b). In the analysis of these results, it was found that relative time expressions were a major source of submitted system's errors. In the proposed solutions, the main approaches relied on either defining a single anchor date (the DCT) for the whole text, or creating a set of rules that anchors expressions based on specific signal words, such as *"operation"*, or *"birth"* (Sun et al., 2015). According to Leeuwenberg and Moens (2019), almost all current state-of-the-art NLP systems use handcrafted rules based on lexical patterns to solve timex normalization. However, such rules have limitations, and not many deal with anchoring RI-Timexes in clinical notes.

One study specifically addresses the problem of anchoring RI-Timexes (Sun et al., 2015). They propose two simplification hypotheses, for identifying and classifying the anchor date and anchor relation respectively: they restrict the anchor date possibilities to four different temporal expressions (admission date, discharge date, previous timex, and previous absolute timex), and the anchor relation to three possibilities (before, after, and equal/during). This allows them to approach the problem as a multi-class classification problem. They manually annotated three corpora following these hypotheses, and proposed a supervised machine-learning approach, along with a rule-based approach for the final relative value normalization.

To our knowledge, there have been no further studies on alternative approaches for identifying and classifying anchor dates and relations for RI-Timexes in clinical text. Our long-term goal is to develop approaches for modelling time information that can be used for clinical timeline reconstruction, for which novel approaches for identifying, anchoring and normalizing RI-Timexes are needed. Our contribution in this study is a) we aimed to reproduce the findings published in Sun et al. (2015), allowing to verify the viability of their hypothesis, and to define a baseline against which we could compare new approaches; b) we propose an alternative annotation model for anchoring RI-Timexes, and developed and applied a new, adapted, annotation model; and c) we propose a new computational approach and model the problem as a relation classification problem, using a BERT transformer model (Devlin et al., 2019) trained on clinical data (Alsentzer et al., 2019).[1]

## 2 Materials and Methods

### 2.1 Data

We used the 2012 i2b2 NLP temporal challenge dataset (Sun et al., 2013a). This data is a subset of the MIMIC III database (Johnson et al., 2016), which contains de-identified electronic health record data associated with over 40K patients admitted to the Beth Israel Deaconess Medical Center in Boston, Massachusetts between 2001 and 2012, available under a data use agreement.

### 2.1.1 2012 TIMEX i2b2

The 2012 i2b2 data set contains 310 discharge summaries, annotated with time expressions, events, and temporal links in the TimeML format (Pustejovsky et al., 2003). They contain an 'Admission' section, which usually presents the clinical history of the patient and the reason for their hospitalisation, and a 'Discharge' section, which summarizes the course of the hospital stay (annotated as SECTIME). The annotation guidelines are presented in (Sun et al., 2013a). For our study, we only used the timex annotations, of which there are 4185 in total, out of which 2,992 are dates and times. The dataset is divided into a training set of 190 documents and a test set of 120 documents.

### 2.1.2 2015 RI-TIMEX i2b2 subset

We also had access to RI-Timex annotations from Sun et al. (2015), for a subset of the 2012 i2b2 data set (henceforth called 2015 RI-Timex i2b2 subset). These annotations specify anchor dates and anchor relations for 484 relative and incomplete temporal expressions, for 104 documents from the 2012 i2b2 data set (all of which are part of the 2012 i2b2 test set). The data was annotated based on the following assumptions:

1. The anchor date for a RI-Timex is either one of the section times (i.e. the 'Admission Date'

---

[1]Annotation guidelines and code are available at https://github.com/KCL-Health-NLP/NeuralTime

or the 'Discharge Date'), the previous timex or the previous absolute timex. Here, "previous" is to be understood as "when going backward in the text" – the "previous timex" is the temporal expression that comes directly before the RI-Timex in the text, the previous absolute timex is the first of the previous expressions to be an absolute timex. Note that these four possibilities are not mutually exclusive, as the previous timex can be the previous absolute timex as well.

2. Anchor relations are restricted to three possibilities: 'Before', 'Equal' or 'After' the anchor date.

The annotations were generated through the following process: a) to isolate the RI-Timexes, they applied a pattern-based filter on all timexes annotated with the types 'date' and 'time' to identify absolute timexes; b) the remaining timexes were manually reviewed to identify RI-Timexes; c) each identified RI-Timex was then assigned an anchor date that could be 'Admission', 'Dicharge', 'Previous Timex', or 'Previous Absolute Timex', and an anchor relation 'Before', 'Equal' or 'After'; d) an 'Other' category exists for cases where none of the four possibilities works. In particular, they chose the anchor date and relation using a limited context window containing the neighboring sentences. Tables 1 and 2 show the distribution of the anchor date types and anchor relation categories. For our study, we randomly divided these 484 annotations into a training set and a test set, respectively covering 411 and 73 examples. Note that sometimes, the discharge, previous timex and previous absolute timex could refer to the same actual timex, which is why the numbers of anchor relations in the table add up to more than the total of RI-Timexes.

|          | A   | D  | PT  | PAT | Other | $\sum$ |
|----------|-----|----|-----|-----|-------|--------|
| Training | 246 | 81 | 143 | 118 | 6     | 594    |
| Test     | 43  | 14 | 27  | 21  | 1     | 106    |
| Total    | 289 | 95 | 170 | 139 | 7     | 700    |

Table 1: Anchor date type distribution: 2015 RI-Timex i2b2 data. A: Admission Date: D: Discharge Date: PT: Previous Timex; PAT: Previous Absolute Timex

## 2.2  2020 RI-TIMEX i2b2: Corpus development

To generate a new gold standard with RI-Timex anchor date type and relation annotations on the entire

|          | Before | Equal | After | None | $\sum$ |
|----------|--------|-------|-------|------|--------|
| Training | 51     | 169   | 185   | 6    | 411    |
| Test     | 8      | 28    | 36    | 1    | 73     |
| Total    | 59     | 197   | 221   | 7    | 484    |

Table 2: Anchor relation annotation distribution: 2015 RI-Timex i2b2 data.

2012 i2b2 data set, we defined a new annotation model to represent these concepts, which allowed us to not limit ourselves to only the four anchor date possibilities defined by Sun et al. (2015).

### 2.2.1  Absolute timex filtering

To identify potential RI-Timexes, we started by reproducing the method of filtering out the most common absolute timexes. Following Sun et al. (2015)'s methodology, we applied this filtering only to the timexes of type 'Date' and 'Time'. The total number of 'Date' and 'Time' timexes in the 2012 i2b2 dataset is 2,992, and 586 SECTIMEs (3.578 in total). The format we defined as representative of absolute timexes to filter out are, with "x" as a digit includes:
   a) xx/xx/xx
   b) xx/xx/xxxx
   c) xx/xx
   d) x/xx
   e) the four previous format with '-' instead of '/'
   f) all other expressions similar to x:xx

After this first filtering step, we obtained 1668 absolute timexes filtered and 1324 relative timexes.

### 2.2.2  Annotation guidelines

The goal of this annotation task is to differentiate absolute from RI-Timexes, and to link the latter to anchor dates. In our annotation guidelines, we define the following concepts:

Absolute time expression: an expression which contains all the information needed to normalize it to a standard date, e.g. "12/05/2020";

Relative time expression: an expression whose temporal meaning is stated as a relative value against another time expression, e.g. "two days" in "two days before the admission";

Incomplete time expression:  an expression which holds only partial information : the context is needed to determine the calendar date, e.g. "in December";

Anchor date: the reference point which can be used to infer the normalized value of a relative or incomplete temporal expression;

Anchor relation: the nature of the temporal link between a relative or incomplete expression and their anchor date.

We kept the anchor relation restricted to the three possibilities: 'Before', 'Equal' or 'After'. The main difference between our annotation model and the one from Sun et al. (2015) is that we did not restrict the options for the anchor date, which could be any of the date and time timexes in the text.

We used the annotation tool that was developed for the i2b2 challenge (MAE). We generated annotation tags for RI-Timexes, and for the absolute timexes. Examples of relative and absolute time expressions as XML tags are shown in Figure 1. The annotators were given the following instructions:

a) for every absolute timex, decide whether it is truly an absolute timex or a RI-Timex that was mislabelled in the filtering, which is done by modifying the "absolute" attribute;

b) for every RI-Timex instance, decide whether it is truly a RI-Timex;

c) for every true RI-Timex, chose an anchor, i.e. another date – this is done by creating an ANCHORLINK, which is a link entity between a RI-Timex and another time expression, the anchor date; the anchorlink has a 'relation' attribute which the annotator needs to complete with either 'before', 'equal' or 'after'.

Three annotators worked on the annotations: two computer scientists, and researcher in life sciences. We divided the annotation process into three phases. Phase 1: we had three annotators, and each pair of annotators double-annotated a set of ten documents, for which inter-annotator agreement (IAA) was calculated, and we analysed disagreements to refine the guidelines. Phase 2: two annotators double-annotated a new set independently using the updated guidelines, after which IAA was again calculated. In the final phase, the remaining set was split in two and annotated separately.

## 2.3 Experimental setup

### 2.3.1 Baseline: Binary classification

We reproduced the methodology of Sun et al. (2015). To predict the anchor date for a given RI-Timex, four binary classifiers were trained, to discern if the RI-Timex is anchored to one of the four possible anchor dates. Similarly, for anchor relations, three binary classifiers were trained.

Sun et al. (2015) used SVM classifiers from the LibSVM implementation. These types of classi-fiers are especially adapted to text classification, as they can handle high dimensional inputs such as those created by one-hot encoded word vectors. We used the SVM algorithms of the sklearn library. As the hyperparameters were not specified in Sun et al. (2015), we performed hyperparameter optimization using 10-fold cross validation on the training set of both data sets. The optimized hyperparameters are included in the appendix.

The following set of features are used in Sun et al. (2015):

* The bag-of-word representation of a window of 8 tokens before and after the timex, as well as the timex itself. All numbers are normalized to a uniform token

* The bag-of-word of the previous timex

* The TimeML type of the previous timex (Date, Duration, Frequency, or Time)

We developed our binary-classification models with a mostly equivalent but slightly modified set of features:

* The numbers written in all letters were not normalized

* We did not include the type of the previous timex, as we only considered Date and Time types

In the original paper, the expression "previous timex" was ambiguous as it was not clear whether or not it included the previous absolute time expression. We chose to use bag of word representation of both the previous timex and the previous absolute timex.

### 2.3.2 Relation classification approach

A common way to model the resolution of temporal relations in text is to classify pairs of temporal entities. We define our problem as a relation classification problem where, given two temporal expressions $r$ and $p$, with $r$ being a RI-Timex and $p$ a potential anchor date, the task is to decide whether or not $r$ is anchored to $p$, and the nature of the anchor relation: 'Before', 'Equal' or 'After'.

**Model Choice:** recent literature has shown some attempts to use neural models to classify temporal relations in text (Lin et al., 2019). We propose to use the BERT transformer model, to solve our anchor date relation problem. Transformer models such as BERT are trained on large corpora to generate a contextual language model, and can be fine-tuned to specific NLP tasks. This enables transfer learning and allows state-of-the-art performances

```
<RTIMEX3 id="T7" start="815" end="841" text="one day prior to admission" type="DATE" relative="TRUE" val="1999-03-29"/>
```

```
<ATIMEX3 id="T18" start="3646" end="3652" text="4/2/99" type="DATE" absolute="TRUE" val="1999-04-02"/>
```

Figure 1: Examples: RI-Timex and Absolute Time Expression annotations in XML tag format.

using relatively small task-specific data sets, without having to retrain the model from scratch. We use a version of BERT that was pre-trained on the whole MIMIC corpus (Alsentzer et al., 2019), making it especially adapted to the i2b2 dataset.

**Input Definition:** While not constrained within a sentence by previous models (Lin et al., 2019), BERT was not designed to solve problems of long-distance relations within a text. There is a limitation on the size of the input text sequences it can accept (512 tokens). As our problem might require longer text sequences, we defined an adapted input representation. For example, the method used by Lin et al. (2019) was to pass as input to BERT a single sequence of tokens with the relevant timexes tagged. For this method to work, both of the expressions from the candidate relation have to be part of a 512 token window in the text. We performed data analysis to quantify how many of our annotated relations were long-distance relations, and in particular, how many of the linked expressions were more than 512 tokens apart. We observed that the percentage of timexes where the number of tokens between the RI-Timex and its anchor date is greater that 512 is 33%.

We solved this problem by using the sequence pair classification feature of BERT: we transformed the inputs into a window of about 200 tokens around the two expressions. 7.6% of the anchor dates are located *after* the RI-TIMEX in the text, which means that the window of tokens had to cover both sides of each expression to be able to capture the relationship between them.

**Data Augmentation:** To create our candidate relation pairs, we generated all *(RI- timex, potential anchor)* pairs, where the potential anchors were all timexes from the Date or Time annotations. There are 17 786 examples of such pairs in total. 93% (16 638) pairs are not an anchor pair; 6.5% (1148)

pairs are. To improve class representation, we used two techniques:

- Oversampling, which means augmenting the number of cases for the underrepresented class. There was a natural way of increasing the number of anchor dates, using the normalized value of the absolute timexes. In particular, for each RI-timex, we used every absolute timex that had the same normalized value as the original anchor date, as additional anchors. This method doubled the number of training examples that were actually anchor/timex pairs.

- Undersampling, which is the process of reducing the number of examples from the dominant class. We report results obtained when keeping only 50% of the training examples that were not an anchor/timex pair.

After oversampling and undersampling, we obtained 5316 training examples, out of which 1304 (24%) are anchor dates. 20% of the train set was used as a validation set to assess the performance of the model during training. We did not apply either oversampling nor undersampling on the blind test set. Table 3 reports the label distribution. We used the implementation of ClinicalBert from the huggingface transformers library (Alsentzer et al., 2019). We fine-tuned the model using an NVIDIA GPU. Technical details and hyper-parameters are reported in the appendix.

| | Is ⚓ | B | E | A | $\sum$ |
|---|---|---|---|---|---|
| Training | 1086 | 138 | 459 | 452 | 4222 |
| Validation | 255 | 36 | 111 | 108 | 1094 |
| Test | 501 | 76 | 199 | 226 | 8474 |

Table 3: Label distribution on the 2020 RI-Timex data for the BERT inputs

**Output definition:** Our goal is for the model to predict if the first expression is anchored to the second one and, if it is, what is the nature of the relation between them (Before, Equal or After). We cast this as a multi-label classification problem, where the model outputs a vector of four probabilities: the probability that the relation is an anchor ("Is ⚓") relation, and the probabilities that this relation is of the type Equal, Before or After. This way, if the model is sure that the first timex is anchored to the second, but unsure about the nature of their relation, it has the possibility to output different levels of probability for these two elements.

## 2.4 Evaluation approach and metrics

### 2.4.1 Inter-Annotator Agreement Evaluation

We evaluate the anchor date annotations as either strict or relaxed. The relaxed version takes into account that there are often several valid options as anchor dates: two links are considered equivalent if their anchor dates have the same normalized value.

### 2.4.2 Classification Evaluation

An important part of our work is to compare our results with those obtained by Sun et al. (2015). Direct comparison is impossible as we did not have access to their full annotated data. However, to the best of our knowledge, we did the maximum to reproduce their precise methodology. The authors only report results on 10-fold cross validation on the training set. Furthermore, they only report accuracy. We report precision, recall and f-score on both the 10-fold CV and the test sets, as well as accuracy on the test set.

## 3 Results

We report results for our annotation process: the inter-annotator agreements, and a comparison between our annotations and the annotations from Sun et al. (2015). We also report results for our classification experiments: the two attempts to reproduce Sun et al. (2015)'s methodology with distinct datasets and our anchor date predictions with a fine-tuned BERT model.

### 3.1 2020 RI-TIMEX i2b2 Annotation

Our annotation guidelines and resulting annotations are similar to the model used by Sun et al. (2015). The main difference is that we allow the anchor date to be *any* timex within the document, whereas they restrict the possibilities to four cases: one of the section times (Admission and Discharge date), the previous timex or the previous absolute

timex. Results on the inter-annotator agreement on a subset of the corpus are presented in Table 4.

|  | Phase 1 | | | Phase 2 |
|---|---|---|---|---|
|  | **B1 P1** | **B2 P2** | **B3 P3** | **B4 P1** |
| A: Strict | 78 | 83 | 43 | 60 |
| A: Relaxed | 80 | 100 | 49 | 76 |

Table 4: Annotation agreement results on a subset 10 docs in each batch (B), and annotator pair (P) in two phases for guideline refinement. Adjudication was done by one of the annotators after consensus discussions with all annotators. A: Anchoring annotations of each identified RI-Timex.

Tables 5 and 6 show the resulting distributions of anchor date types and anchor relations, respectively. Note that as the anchor date categories are not mutually exclusive, the percentages do not add up to 100%. The 'Other' category for the anchor date types represents anchors that did not fall into the four categories used in Sun et al. (2015). They represent 7% of cases, thus indicating a substantial number of cases that were not naturally anchored to the four previously used categories.

|  | **A** | **D** | **PAT** | **PRT** | **O** | **N** | $\sum$ |
|---|---|---|---|---|---|---|---|
| $n$ | 523 | 191 | 281 | 177 | 83 | 18 | 1273 |
| $\%$ | 45.0 | 16.4 | 24.2 | 15.2 | 7.1 | 1.5 | - |

Table 5: Distribution of annotation labels on the 2020 RI-Timex corpus: anchor date types. A: Admission; D: Discharge; PAT: Previous Absolute Timex; PRT: Previous Timex; O: Other; N: None

|  | **Before** | **Equal** | **After** | **None** | **Total** |
|---|---|---|---|---|---|
| $n$ | 161 | 476 | 512 | 18 | 1167 |
| $\%$ | 13.7 | 40.8 | 43.8 | 1.5 | 100 |

Table 6: Distribution of annotation labels on the 2020 RI-Timex corpus: anchor relations.

## 3.2 Classification

### 3.2.1 Baseline: Binary classification

We reproduced Sun et al. (2015)'s methodology on the 2015 RI-Timex subset and the 2020 RI-Timex data: bag-of-word representation of the time expression, the previous timex, and previous absolute timex with an SVM model.

Results on the 2015 RI-Timex subset and the 2020 RI-Timex data are presented in Table 7(a) and (b), respectively. For comparison, Table 8 shows the classification results reported by Sun et al. (2015) on the feature set that we used. Note that they only reported accuracy for this task.

| Scores | Anchor dates | | | | | | | | Anchor relations | | | | | |
|---|---|---|---|---|---|---|---|---|---|---|---|---|---|---|
| | A | | D | | PT | | PAT | | Before | | Equal | | After | |
| Phase → | CV | T | CV | T | CV | T | CV | T | CV | T | CV | T | CV | T |
| Precision | 76.7 | 80.4 | 82.2 | 63.6 | 71.5 | 75.0 | 69.5 | 74.3 | 90.5 | 100 | 78.1 | 82.8 | 85.5 | 86.5 |
| Recall | 82.6 | 86.0 | 60.6 | 50.0 | 70.8 | 55.3 | 70.5 | 78.8 | 66.7 | 50 | 72.6 | 87.7 | 83.7 | 88.9 |
| F-score | 79.4 | 83.1 | 68.8 | 56.0 | 70.8 | 63.6 | 69.4 | 76.5 | 76.0 | 66.7 | 74.3 | 84.2 | 84.1 | 87.7 |
| Accuracy | - | 79.5 | - | 84.9 | - | 67.1 | - | 78.1 | - | 94.5 | - | 87.7 | - | 87.7 |

(a) 2015 RI-Timex data

| Scores | A | | D | | PT | | PAT | | Before | | Equal | | After | |
|---|---|---|---|---|---|---|---|---|---|---|---|---|---|---|
| Precision | 77.7 | 81.1 | 75.3 | 81.6 | 93.8 | 84.2 | 82.7 | 77.2 | 87.9 | 86.0 | 82.4 | 74.7 | 84.3 | 84.7 |
| Recall | 73.7 | 79.2 | 64.8 | 44.4 | 80.0 | 82.5 | 76.6 | 83.6 | 63.6 | 56.5 | 78.4 | 80.4 | 84.1 | 78.4 |
| F-score | 74.5 | 80.1 | 68.2 | 57.5 | 86.2 | 83.3 | 78.7 | 80.3 | 72.3 | 69.2 | 80.0 | 77.4 | 84.0 | 81.4 |
| Accuracy | - | 80.4 | - | 88.4 | - | 90.0 | - | 85.3 | - | 92.1 | - | 81.8 | - | 84.1 |

(b) 2020 RI-Timex data

Table 7: Results on the 2015 RI-Timex data (a) and 2020 RI-Timex data (b), anchor dates and relations. A: Admission; D: Discharge; PT: Previous Timex; PAT: Previous Absolute Timex. Each row presents results for the two evaluation phases: 10-fold cross validation (CV) and test set (T).

| A | D | PT | PAT | Before | Equal | After |
|---|---|---|---|---|---|---|
| 77.56 | 92.47 | 68.91 | 75.16 | 93.4 | 81.4 | 92.1 |

Table 8: Accuracy for the 10-fold Cross validation on the training set reported by (Sun et al., 2015). A: Admission; D: Discharge; PT: Previous Timex; PAT: Previous Absolute Timex.

| | | Is ⚓ | B | E | A | Avg |
|---|---|---|---|---|---|---|
| Valid. | P | 85.2 | 85.0 | 86.5 | 83.0 | 85.5 |
| | R | 88.2 | 94.4 | 81.0 | 86.1 | 86.7 |
| | F | 86.7 | 89.4 | 83.7 | 84.5 | 85.8 |
| Test | P | 34.0 | 35.4 | 29.4 | 29.4 | 32.2 |
| | R | 76.2 | 60.5 | 57.2 | 72.1 | 70.3 |
| | F | 47.0 | 44.6 | 39.2 | 41.8 | 44.1 |

Table 9: Results of the anchor relation classification by BERT on the validation and test sets. Is ⚓: Is an anchor: B: Before; E: Equal; A: After. P: Precision; R: Recall; F: F-score.

### 3.2.2 Relation classification

Table 9 shows the results on the validation set after 15 epochs of fine-tuning the Clinical BERT model on our relation classification task, and on the final model applied on the test set. The results on the validation set range between 81-91% precision and 85-91% recall, yielding an average overall F-score of 87.6%. Results drop on the blind test sets, with an average of 70% recall and 32% precision. For comparison purposes, we also computed results on the test set where we performed oversampling. When the number of positive anchor relations went from 501 to 1086 (for 8474 total testing examples), the precision rose to 62-70%, and the average f-score is 67.2. Detailed results on this oversampled test set are presented in the appendix.

## 4 Discussion and Conclusion

We present a study on identifying and classifying anchor dates and relations specifically for RI-Timexes in clinical text. We attempted to reproduce the findings by Sun et al. (2015), in order to produce a baseline against which we could compare new approaches. Because the full dataset used in that study was not available, we developed new guidelines and produced a new reference standard of annotations with anchor date types and relations (2020 RI-TIMEX i2b2 data). We applied the methodology presented in Sun et al. (2015) on the 2015 RI-Timex subset, and our 2020 RI-Timex i2b2 data, reaching comparable results. We also propose to approach this problem as a relation classification task. To this end, we re-train the Clinical BERT model on our data. Results on the validation set were promising, but dropped on the test set.

### 4.1 Annotations and Corpus development

The additional guidelines that were defined after the first phase to solve ambiguous cases are presented in the appendix. One example concerns expressions relating to post-operation timelines – it was decided that all post-operative expressions should be anchored to the operation date, the exception to that rule being if there was another time expression which can serve as anchor for the post-operative expression with the relation 'EQUAL'.

An analysis of the annotation disagreements on the second round revealed that the main disagreements were due to longer, more complicated cases. For instance, in one case, there were two operation dates in the same document, in another there were two admission dates. Other examples included cases where events were unclear. *"Day of transfer"*, for example, could refer to a transfer between services or to the admission date.

Our annotation model allowed us to select more possibilities for anchor date types, while still being able to map our data to the 2015 RI-Timex subset. We observed that 7% of the RI-Timexes were anchored to dates located later in the text, indicating that the four categories proposed by Sun et al. (2015) had limitations.

Multi-anchor dates are still a challenge. For every RI-Timex, there are often more than one timex that can be an appropriate anchor date. This can be problematic if a machine learning model tries to mimic manual annotation labels. Not only does it need to learn what constitutes an acceptable anchor date, but also how to discriminate between potential alternative anchor dates. A solution for this problem could be to modify the guidelines and annotate as many anchor relations as possible.

### 4.2 Classification approaches

Sun et al. (2015) only report classification accuracy, and comparison with our results show that this distorts results to be more advantageous. For instance, the "Before" category and the "Discharge date" category are under-represented in the two datasets that we used. We can see that there is a sharp difference between the accuracy and f-score on these categories. In both cases, the accuracy is high but does not represent the actual performance of the model. It is notable that the results we have using our annotations are better than the one we obtained using their data subset. This is probably linked to the total number of samples. Another explanation would be that our annotations better capture the natural anchoring of RI-Timexes and are thus easier to predict for the model.

There could be several explanations to the difference in results between the validation set (around 90% f-score on average) and the test set (45%) on our BERT-based relation classification approach. One is that the model's hyperparameters were chosen to maximise results on the validation set, thus leading to a form of overfitting on the validation set, even though the model was never trained on this data. However, we repeated the experiment with the same hyperparameters and a different random validation set, and the results were similar. Further-

more, this would not explain the difference between the precision (about 30%) and recall (70%).

The likelier explanation lies in the oversampling process that we applied to the validation set but not to the test set. We have seen that to ensure inter-annotator agreement on which anchor date to pick, we had to define very precise, unambiguous guidelines which favored some solutions over others. These guidelines might be very difficult for the model to capture. Furthermore, the nature of the input means that the model only has access to the RI-Timex and the potential anchor date, but does not have any information about a competing anchor date that could have been preferred by a human annotator. By generating more instances of coherent anchor date/timex tuples, we decrease the complexity of the problem and allow it to generalise better. The fact that when we oversample the test set the results change dramatically supports this hypothesis. The results would probably improve even more if we could generate all anchoring relations accurately.

Another issue is the way input is processed in these types of transformer models. In our work, the model only had access to a small part of the context (200 token window of text on each side of the expression). To be able to reach the performance of a human, the model would need to be able to access and analyse the whole text, just as annotators did. One very interesting solution is the use of a context-aware neural network, as presented in Meng and Rumshisky (2018). The neural network reads the text linearly while using an external memory to store relations, and can then use the global context to classify them. Other alternatives could be to still leverage the power of pre-trained transformer models, by using solutions to pass entire, long texts to the model instead (Pappagari et al., 2019). A deep learning approach is potentially not the most appropriate to represent complex temporal relations, for example Li et al. (2020) recently reported good results using an ontology.

### 4.3 Conclusion

Our results on reproducing previous findings were promising. Our newly developed corpus results in comparable results using the same classification approach, but highlights limitations in the previous approach. Casting the problem as a relation classification task shows promise, but might require further considerations.

**References**

Emily Alsentzer, John R Murphy, Willie Boag, Wei-Hung Weng, Di Jin, Tristan Naumann, and Matthew McDermott. 2019. Publicly available clinical bert embeddings. *arXiv preprint arXiv:1904.03323*.

Angel X. Chang and Christopher Manning. 2012. SU-Time: A library for recognizing and normalizing time expressions. In *Proceedings of the Eighth International Conference on Language Resources and Evaluation (LREC-2012)*, pages 3735–3740, Istanbul, Turkey. European Languages Resources Association (ELRA).

Leon R. A. Derczynski. 2017. *Automatically Ordering Events and Times in Text*. Studies in Computational Intelligence. Springer International Publishing.

Jacob Devlin, Ming-Wei Chang, Kenton Lee, and Kristina Toutanova. 2019. BERT: Pre-training of deep bidirectional transformers for language understanding. In *Proceedings of the 2019 Conference of the North American Chapter of the Association for Computational Linguistics: Human Language Technologies, Volume 1 (Long and Short Papers)*, pages 4171–4186, Minneapolis, Minnesota. Association for Computational Linguistics.

Alistair EW Johnson, Tom J Pollard, Lu Shen, H Lehman Li-Wei, Mengling Feng, Mohammad Ghassemi, Benjamin Moody, Peter Szolovits, Leo Anthony Celi, and Roger G Mark. 2016. Mimic-iii, a freely accessible critical care database. *Scientific data*, 3(1):1–9.

Artuur Leeuwenberg and Marie-Francine Moens. 2019. A survey on temporal reasoning for temporal information extraction from text. *Journal of Artificial Intelligence Research*, 66:341–380.

Fang Li, Jingcheng Du, Yongqun He, Hsing-Yi Song, Mohcine Madkour, Guozheng Rao, Yang Xiang, Yi Luo, Henry W Chen, Sijia Liu, et al. 2020. Time event ontology (teo): to support semantic representation and reasoning of complex temporal relations of clinical events. *Journal of the American Medical Informatics Association*, 27(7):1046–1056.

Chen Lin, Timothy Miller, Dmitriy Dligach, Steven Bethard, and Guergana Savova. 2019. A bert-based universal model for both within-and cross-sentence clinical temporal relation extraction. In *Proceedings of the 2nd Clinical Natural Language Processing Workshop*, pages 65–71.

Yuanliang Meng and Anna Rumshisky. 2018. Context-aware neural model for temporal information extraction. In *Proceedings of the 56th Annual Meeting of the Association for Computational Linguistics (Volume 1: Long Papers)*, pages 527–536.

Raghavendra Pappagari, Piotr Zelasko, Jesús Villalba, Yishay Carmiel, and Najim Dehak. 2019. Hierarchical transformers for long document classification. In *2019 IEEE Automatic Speech Recognition and Understanding Workshop (ASRU)*, pages 838–844. IEEE.

James Pustejovsky, José M Castano, Robert Ingria, Roser Sauri, Robert J Gaizauskas, Andrea Setzer, Graham Katz, and Dragomir R Radev. 2003. Timeml: Robust specification of event and temporal expressions in text. *New directions in question answering*, 3:28–34.

James Pustejovsky, Kiyong Lee, Harry Bunt, and Laurent Romary. 2010. Iso-timeml: An international standard for semantic annotation. In *LREC*.

Jannik Strötgen and Michael Gertz. 2010. Heideltime: High quality rule-based extraction and normalization of temporal expressions. In *Proceedings of the 5th International Workshop on Semantic Evaluation*, SemEval '10, page 321–324, USA. Association for Computational Linguistics.

Weiyi Sun, Anna Rumshisky, and Ozlem Uzuner. 2013a. Annotating temporal information in clinical narratives. *Journal of biomedical informatics*, 46:S5–S12.

Weiyi Sun, Anna Rumshisky, and Ozlem Uzuner. 2013b. Evaluating temporal relations in clinical text: 2012 i2b2 challenge. *Journal of the American Medical Informatics Association*, 20(5):806–813.

Weiyi Sun, Anna Rumshisky, and Ozlem Uzuner. 2015. Normalization of relative and incomplete temporal expressions in clinical narratives. *Journal of the American Medical Informatics Association*, 22(5):1001–1008.

Hegler Tissot, Marcos Didonet Del Fabro, Leon Derczynski, and Angus Roberts. 2019. Normalisation of imprecise temporal expressions extracted from text. *Knowledge and Information Systems*, 61(3):1361–1394.

## Appendix

### Annotation Instructions and Guidelines

The goal of this annotation task is to differentiate absolute from relative or incomplete time expressions, and to link the latter to anchor dates.

- Absolute time expression : an expression which contains all the information needed to normalize it to a standard date. Eg : "12/05/2020"

- Relative time expression : an expression whose temporal meanings is stated as a relative value against another time expression. Eg " two days before the admission"

- Incomplete time expression : an expression which holds only partial information : the context is needed to determine the calendar date. Eg : "in December"

- Anchor date : The reference point which can be used to infer the normalized value of a relative or incomplete temporal expression.

Instructions

1. Load the data in the annotation tool

   Once loaded, the following tabs should appear :

   - - RTIMEX3 : these are the relative time expressions, the main focus of the annotation process
   - - ATIMEX3 : the absolute time expressions, here to provide anchorage for the RTIMEX3
   - - SECTIME : These are special annotations for the admission and discharge date
   - - ANCHORLINK : These links will be created by the annotator to join a RTIMEX3 to an anchor date (an ATIMEX3 or SECTIME).

2. The text should appear along with the annotations outlined in different colors. The RTIMEX3 are in blue, the ATIMEX3 in red, the discharge and admission date are usually double annotated as both absolute time expressions and SECTIME so they are underlinded. The ANCHORLINKs are empty as they will be created during the annotation process 6. The process is as follows : The focus should be on each RTIMEX3 annotations until they are all annotated

   - First, the "relative" column must be filled : with "TRUE" if the expression is indeed a relative time expression, "FALSE" if it is an absolute timex3 which was not correctly filtered. Common example would be : "May 1997", "On Christmas of 2002", "April 2nd 2015"
   - If "relative" is TRUE, an ANCHORLINK has to be created This is done by holding down the ctrl key (or the command key, if you are on a Mac) and left click each of the entities that will be included in the link, with the RTIMEX3 first and the Anchor Date second. For precise instructions on how to select the appropriate anchor date, see the "Guidelines" section. A link window will pop up and ask you to confirm the two dates and the link type. Special case - if the anchor date is the admission or discharge date : because these are double annotated as ATIMEX3 and SECTIME, the program will let you choose between the two instances. They have the same value so it does not matter too much but the SECTIME should be preferred.
   - Once the ANCHORLINK is created, the "relation" attribute has to be filled with either BEFORE, EQUAL or AFTER

3. Check the ATIMEXEs : sometimes, an expression marked as an absolute time expression is in fact a relative one. For this, the "absolute" attribute of the A-TIMEXes as to be filled with True or False. If the expression is in fact a relative one, it has to be anchored.

4. Output the file Once all the RI-TIMEXES are filtered and anchored, choose the "Export as XML" option in the File menu, and save the file with its original name in a separate folder.

5. Upload the data

Guidelines for Ambiguous Cases :

- SELECTING THE ANCHOR DATE When selecting the anchor date, the first potential anchor dates to study are : the previous absolute timex, the previous timex, the admission date and the discharge date. One should prioritize absolute anchor dates over relative ones, and if there is still an ambiguity, "EQUAL" relations over "BEFORE" and "AFTER". These four possibilities are to be prioritised, but other anchor dates are valid as well.

- POSTOPERATIVE DAYS As a general rule, expressions relating to the "post-operation" concept should be anchored to the day of the operation. The exception to that rule is if there is another time expression which can serve as anchor for the POD with the relation "EQUAL"

- AGE RELATED EXPRESSIONS : Some time expressions annotated as dates age in fact age expressions. If this case arises, one has to change the type of the expression to "AGE_RELATED".

- INCOMPLETE EXPRESSIONS Some expressions are not relative but rather incomplete: their normalized value depends on one or more missing information, such as the year. ex "Labor Day" In this case, they should still be annotated as RI-TIMEXs, and if they cannot be anchored, it is possible to change the "mod" attribute of the expressions to "EXT", to signify that there is a need for external information.

- NON-ANNOTATED EXPRESSIONS Sometimes, expression which should be annotated as either RI-TIMEXs or A-TIMEX are not annotated at all : this is likely an error coming from i2b2's gold standard, and we should let them as is. No annotation should be added to the documents.

- INCOMPLETE TIMES Eg "2.30 pm" They are to be anchored to the day they belong to. Usually they are wrongly annotated as absolute time expressions.

- SECTION TIMES Usually, imprecise expressions found at the beginning of a document relate to the Admission date, and those found at the end to the Discharge date.

## SVM Classification : Optimized Hyperparameters

Here we report the optimized hyperparameters for each binary classification category:

- Admission Date : 'C': 1000, 'gamma': 0.0001, 'kernel': 'rbf'

- Discharge Date : 'C': 100, 'gamma': 0.001, 'kernel': 'rbf'

- Previous Timex : 'C': 100, 'gamma': 0.001, 'kernel': 'rbf'

- Previous Absolute Timex = 'C': 100, 'gamma': 0.001, 'kernel': 'rbf'

- Before = 'C': 1000, 'gamma': 0.0001, 'kernel': 'rbf'

- Equal = 'C': 100, 'gamma': 0.001, 'kernel': 'rbf'

- After = 'C': 1000, 'gamma': 0.0001, 'kernel': 'rbf'

## BERT Relation Classification : Model Specification

The BERT model was trained for 15 epochs on a NVIDIA GPU with the following characteristics :

NVIDIA-SMI 415.18 — Driver Version· 415.18 — CUDA Version: 10.0

The hyperparameters were :
Length of input : 512

Learning rate : 2e-5
Number of training epochs : 15
Gradient accumulation steps : 0.9
Batch size : 5
fp16 : False

**Additional Results**

**Detailed results and distribution of BERT Relation classification**

|  |  | Is ⚓ | B | E | A | Avg |
|---|---|---|---|---|---|---|
| Valid. | P | 85.2 | 85.0 | 86.5 | 83.0 | 85.5 |
|  | R | 88.2 | 94.4 | 81.0 | 86.1 | 86.7 |
|  | F | 86.7 | 89.4 | 83.7 | 84.5 | 85.8 |
| Test | P | 34.0 | 35.4 | 29.4 | 29.4 | 32.2 |
|  | R | 76.2 | 60.5 | 57.2 | 72.1 | 70.3 |
|  | F | 47.0 | 44.6 | 39.2 | 41.8 | 44.1 |
| O. Test | P | 70.6 | 70.0 | 62.1 | 62.3 | 67.0 |
|  | R | 73.0 | 49.1 | 56.8 | 71.5 | 67.5 |
|  | F | 71.7 | 57.7 | 59.4 | 66.6 | 67.2 |

Table 10: Results of the anchor relation classification by BERT on the validation and test sets. O. Test : Oversampled Test Set; Is ⚓: Is an anchor: B: Before; E: Equal; A: After. P: Precision; R: Recall; F: F-score.

|  | Is ⚓ | B | E | A | Total |
|---|---|---|---|---|---|
| Train. | 1049 | 138 | 459 | 452 | 4222 |
| Valid. | 255 | 36 | 111 | 108 | 1094 |
| Test | 501 | 76 | 199 | 226 | 8474 |
| O. Test | 1086 | 185 | 419 | 482 | 8474 |

Table 11: Distributions of examples in the anchor relation classification dataset .O.Test : Oversampled Test Set; Is ⚓: Is an anchor: B: Before; E: Equal; A: After. P: Precision; R: Recall; F: F-score.

**Package Versions**

**Package versions on the local system**

Python version : 3.7.6
  gensim==3.8.1
  h5py==2.10.0
  matplotlib==3.2.1
  nltk==3.4.5
  numpy==1.18.1
  pandas==1.0.3
  scikit-learn==0.22.2.post1
  scipy==1.4.1
  sklearn==0.0
  spacy==2.2.3
  torch==1.5.0+cpu
  torchvision==0.6.0+cpu
  tqdm==4.43.0
  transformers==2.11.0

**Package Versions on the GPU server (BERT model training)**

Python version : 3.7.6
    torch==1.5.1+cu92
    torchvision==0.6.1+cu92

# MeDAL: Medical Abbreviation Disambiguation Dataset for Natural Language Understanding Pretraining


**Zhi Wen[1], Xing Han Lu[1], Siva Reddy[1,2,3]**

[1]McGill University
[2]Facebook CIFAR AI Chair
[3]Mila – Quebec Artificial Intelligence Institute
{zhi.wen,xing.han.lu}@mail.mcgill.ca
siva@cs.mcgill.ca



## Abstract

One of the biggest challenges that prohibit the use of many current NLP methods in clinical settings is the availability of public datasets. In this work, we present MeDAL, a large medical text dataset curated for abbreviation disambiguation, designed for natural language understanding pre-training in the medical domain. We pre-trained several models of common architectures on this dataset and empirically showed that such pre-training leads to improved performance and convergence speed when fine-tuning on downstream medical tasks.


## 1 Introduction

Recent work in mining medical texts focus on building deep learning models for different medical tasks, such as mortality prediction (Grnarova et al., 2016) and diagnosis prediction (Li et al., 2020). However, because of the private nature of medical records, there are few large-scale, publicly available medical text datasets that are suitable for pre-training models, and real-world, private datasets are often small-scale and imbalanced. As a result, one of the biggest challenge in building deep learning-based NLP systems for biomedical corpora is the availability of public datasets (Wang et al., 2018).

To tackle this problem, we present **Me**dical **D**ataset for **A**bbreviation Disambiguation for Natural **L**anguage Understanding (MeDAL)[1], a large dataset of medical texts curated for the task of medical abbreviation disambiguation, which can be used for pre-training natural language understanding models. Figure 1 shows an example of sample in the dataset, where the true meaning of the abbreviation 'DHF' is inferred from its context, and Figure 2 shows the pretraining framework. Although this dataset can be used for building abbreviation-expansion systems, its main purpose is to enable

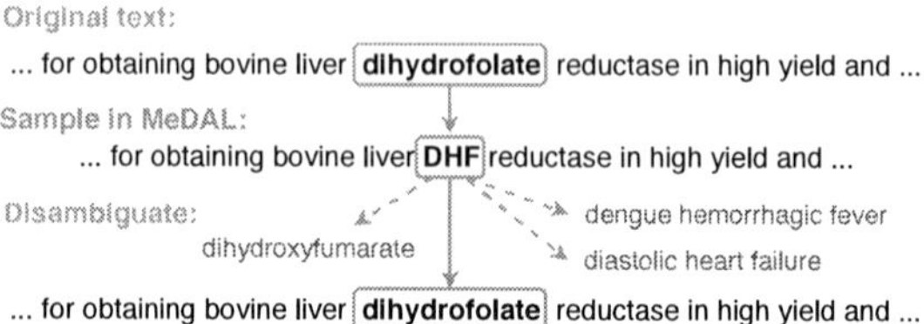


Figure 1: A sample in the MeDAL dataset.

effective pre-training and improve performance on downstream tasks during fine-tuning.

The motivation behind using abbreviation disambiguation as the pre-training task is two-fold. First, abbreviations are widely used in medical records by healthcare professionals and can often be ambiguous (Xu et al., 2007; Islamaj Dogan et al., 2009).[2] The ubiquitousness of abbreviations poses a restriction on building deep learning models for medical tasks, such as mortality prediction (Grnarova et al., 2016) and diagnosis prediction (Li et al., 2020).

Second, we believe that understanding natural language in a knowledge-rich domain such as medicine requires understanding of domain knowledge at some level, similar to how humans can understand medical text only after receiving medical training. The abbreviation disambiguation task enables models to use domain knowledge to understand the global and local context, as well as the possible meanings of the abbreviation in the medical domain.

Medical abbreviation disambiguation has long been studied (Skreta et al., 2019; Li et al., 2019; Finley et al., 2016; Liu et al., 2018; Joopudi et al., 2018; Jin et al., 2019) and our work builds upon many of them. In particular, our data generation process is inspired by the reverse substitution tech-

---

[1]https://github.com/BruceWen120/medal

[2]For example, 'MR' is a commonly used abbreviation which has a number of possible meanings, including 'morphinone reductase', 'magnetoresistance' and 'menstrual regulation', depending on the context.




*Proceedings of the 3rd Clinical Natural Language Processing Workshop*, pages 130–135
November 19, 2020. ©2020 Association for Computational Linguistics

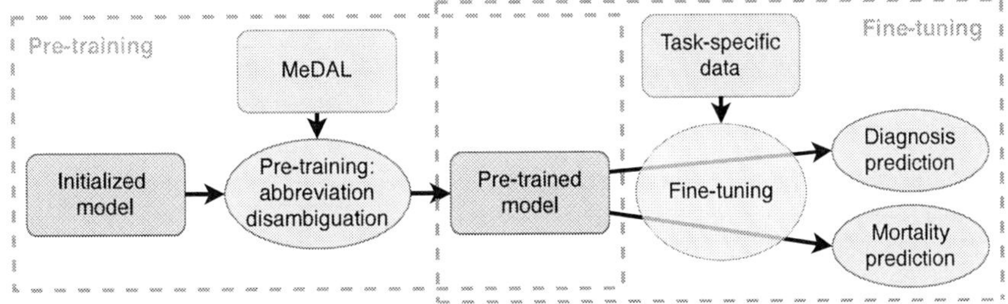

Figure 2: Diagram of using MeDAL for pre-training NLU models in medical domain.

nique (Skreta et al., 2019; Finley et al., 2016).

Our work differs from them in mainly two aspects. First, instead of trying to improve performance on abbreviation disambiguation itself, we propose to use it as a pre-training task for transfer learning on other clinical tasks. Second, existing datasets for medical abbreviation disambiguation, for instance CASI (Moon et al., 2014), are small compared to datasets used for general language model pre-training, and as noted by Li et al. (2019) some are erroneous. Thus, we chose to construct a new dataset large enough for effective pre-training.

Our main contributions are: a) we present a large dataset for pre-training on the task of medical abbreviation disambiguation. b) we provide empirical evidence of the benefit of abbreviation pre-training for a wide range of deep learning architectures.

## 2 Abbreviation Disambiguation

### 2.1 Dataset Summary

The MeDAL dataset consists of 14,393,619 articles and on average 3 abbreviations per article. The statistics of MeDAL are summarized in Table 1.

The distribution of number of words and the distribution of number of abbreviations are shown in Figure 3a and Figure 3b, respectively.

### 2.2 Dataset Creation

The MeDAL dataset is created from PubMed abstracts which are released in the 2019 annual baseline.[3] PubMed is a search engine that indexes scientific publications in biomedical domain. The PubMed corpus contains 18,374,626 valid abstracts with 80 words in each abstract on average.

We use reverse substitution (Skreta et al., 2019) to generate samples without human labeling. We identify full terms in text that have known abbreviations and replace them with their abbreviations.

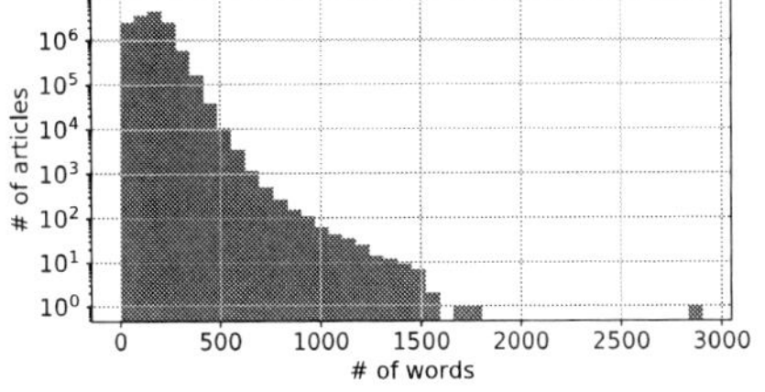

(a) Word count distribution

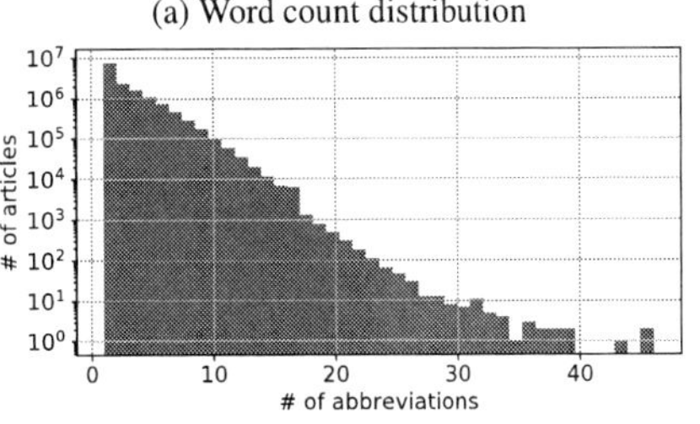

(b) Abbreviation count distribution

Figure 3: Distributions of number of words and number of abbreviations.

For reverse substitution, mappings of abbreviations to expansions established by Zhou et al. (2006) are used. Mappings where the abbreviation maps to only one expansion or the expansion maps to multiple abbreviations are discarded, resulting in 24,005 valid pairs of mappings. Among the valid mappings are 5,886 abbreviations, which means each abbreviation maps to about 4 expansions on average.

To avoid completely removing all expansions and making them unseen to models, the expansions are substituted with a pre-defined probability. For our study, expansions are substituted with a probability of 0.3, although our processing scripts allow for other values for future use.

### 2.3 Pretraining

The task of abbreviation disambiguation is treated as a classification problem, where the classes are all possible expansions.

---

[3]https://www.nlm.nih.gov/databases/download/pubmed_medline.html

Considering the huge size of the dataset and the associated computational cost, a subset of 5 million data points are sampled from the complete corpus, which are split into 3 million training samples, 1 million validation samples and 1 million test samples. This subset is used throughout this study.

When creating this subset, because the distribution of true expansions is highly imbalanced, a sampling strategy is adopted which essentially removes classes in increasing order of frequency in an iterative manner. The sampling strategy works in the following way: from each class label, $N_C = min(F_C, T)$ samples that have this label are randomly selected, where $F_C$ is the frequency of that class in the unsampled dataset, and $T$ is a threshold that is computed using Algorithm 1 such that each class can have at most $T$ samples, and $\sum_C N_C$ is equal to the total number of samples $N$.

The strategy iteratively removes classes, and at every iteration decreases $N'$ (which corresponds to the number of remaining samples) and $L$ (which corresponds to the number of labels remaining). Then, the rate $r$ is calculated based on how many classes $L$ can fit in the remaining $N'$ if each remaining $L$ has exactly $r$ samples. In this way, it is ensured that the moment the current class frequency $f_C$ being iterated is greater than the desired rate $r$, the sampling stops.

---

**Algorithm 1** Compute threshold $T$

---

**Require:** array of class frequency $f$, $N > 0$
  Sort $f$ in increasing order
  $L \leftarrow length(f)$
  $N' \leftarrow N$
  **for** each $f_C \in f$ **do**
    $N' \leftarrow N' - f_C$
    $L \leftarrow L - 1$
    $r = round(N'/L)$
    **if** $f_C \geq r$ **then**
      **return** $r + 1$
    **end if**
  **end for**

---

## 3  Evaluation Tasks

**Mortality Prediction**   As a downstream task to evaluate models' performance in clinical settings, mortality prediction aims at predicting the mortality of a patient at the end of a hospital admission, using ICU patient notes. The mortality prediction dataset is generated from MIMIC-III (Johnson

| total # of articles | 14,393,619 |
|---|---|
| median # of words | 150 |
| mean # of words | 152.47 |
| median # of abbreviations | 2 |
| mean # of abbreviations | 3.04 |

Table 1: Statistics of the MeDAL dataset

et al., 2016). Medical notes in this MIMIC-III comprise of free-form text documents written by nurses, doctors, and many types of specialists, and are written throughout the patient's stay. Only notes written by physicians and nurses at least twenty-four hours before the end of the discharge time are used, for the goal is to accurately predict whether a patient is at risk of dying by the end of the admission. In order to balance positive and negative samples (roughly 10% of patients expire at the end of an admission) while keeping as much text diversity as possible, we sample at most four notes from each surviving patient.

The dataset generated has a total of 137,607 negative samples and 138,864 positively-labelled notes. Then, using stratified random splitting, we selected 75%/10%/15% of the patients to be included in the training/validation/test splits. As an example of the ubiquitousness of abbreviations, 'MR' appears 1,612 times in 1,366 samples in the test set alone.

**Diagnosis Prediction**   Similar to mortality prediction, diagnosis prediction aims to predict the diagnoses associated with a hospital admission from medical notes written during the admission. The same MIMIC-III medical notes and the same splits from mortality prediction are used, with seven training samples that have no diagnosis recorded removed. In MIMIC-III, diagnoses are recorded with International Classification of Diseases (ICD) codes, which are standardized codes designed for billing purposes. We discard minor distinctions of ICD codes under the same category by taking the first three digits (for codes that start with 'E' or 'V' the first four digits) of ICD codes.[4] After grouping, there are 1,204 unique diagnosis codes.

Top-k recall is used for evaluation of models based on the similarities to real-life medical decision making (Choi et al., 2015), which is defined as the number of diagnosis codes in that admission that are present in the top k predictions of the

---

[4]For example, codes 4800 to 4809 represent viral pneumonia of different causes, and they are grouped into one ICD code 480.

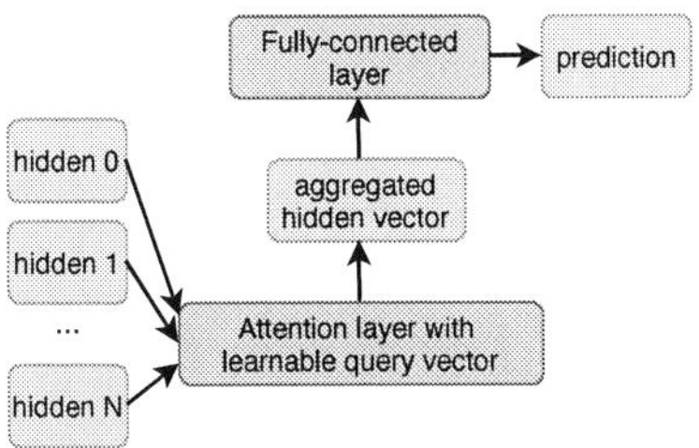

Figure 4: Attention output layer for mortality and diagnosis prediction.

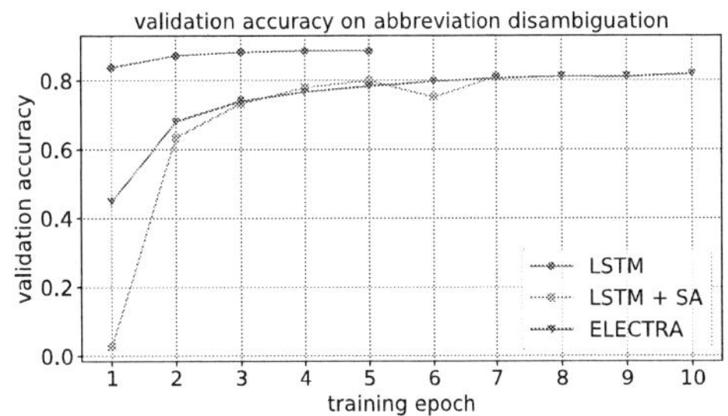

Figure 5: Validation accuracy on abbreviation disambiguation. 'SA' stands for self attention layer.

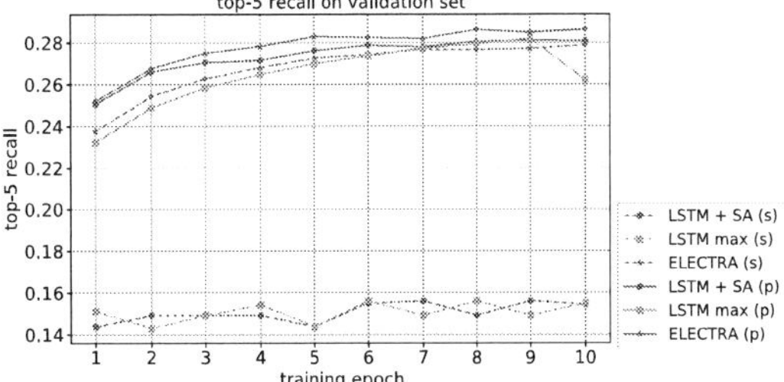

Figure 6: Top-5 recall on diagnosis prediction validation set. 'SA' stands for self attention layer. 'max' represents max-pooling output layer. '(s)' and '(p)' indicates whether the model is trained from scratch or pretrained, respectively.

model, divided by the number of diagnosis codes in that admission in total. Note that since most admissions have multiple diagnoses, a small k would result in a top-k recall less than 100% even if all of the top k predictions are correct.[5] On our dataset, the highest possible top-5, top-10 and top-30 recalls are 50.17%, 79.48% and 99.88% on validation set, and 49.75%, 79.23% and 99.79% on test set.

## 4  Models

The models are first pre-trained on the MeDAL dataset, then pre-trained weights are used to initialize models for training on the downstream tasks. We compared this training strategy with training respective models from scratch to validate the benefit of pre-training.

**LSTM**  BiLSTM is used as a baseline model. Specifically, the BiLSTM consists of three layers with hidden size of 512. Pre-trained Fasttext model is used for word embeddings (Bojanowski et al., 2017).

**LSTM + Self Attention**  To allow for leveraging information extracted by LSTM in a flexible manner, soft attention layers are added on top of LSTM. The attention layer is largely based on the soft attention by Bahdanau et al. (2014). Its detailed formulation is included in Appendix A.

**Transformers**  We used the pre-trained ELECTRA-small discriminator (Clark et al., 2020) as an example of Transformer-based (Vaswani et al., 2017) model and, since it was not pre-trained on medical text, we compared its performance with or without pre-training on abbreviation disambiguation.

---

[5]For instance, if an admission has 10 diagnoses codes, the highest possible top-5 recall for it would be $5/10 = 50\%$ which is when all of the top 5 predictions are correct.

**Task-specific Output Layer**  Depending on the task, the output layer can take various forms. For abbreviation disambiguation, the output layer is a fully-connected layer, whose input is the hidden vector at the location of the abbreviation from the previous layers and output space is all possible expansions. For mortality or diagnosis prediction which are not associated with any specific token, hidden vectors from the previous layers need to be first aggregated into one vector. This can be achieved by either a pooling layer or an additional attention layer with a learnable query vector. Then the output layer is a fully connected layer that takes the aggregated vector as input. The attention output layer is illustrated in Figure 4. In preliminary experiments we found attention output layer generally improves models' performance compared to max-pooling output layer, and therefore it is used throughout the rest of the study unless otherwise noted.

## 5  Results

Models' performance on the pre-training task, abbreviation disambiguation, is shown in Figure 5. As the goal is not to optimize performance on this

| Model | Validation accuracy | |
| --- | --- | --- |
| | Pretrained | From scratch |
| LSTM | **82.67%** | 82.17% |
| LSTM+SA | **82.46%** | 80.29% |
| ELECTRA | **84.19%** | 83.92% |
| | Test accuracy | |
| LSTM | **82.80%** | 82.61% |
| LSTM+SA | **82.98%** | 79.96% |
| ELECTRA | **84.43%** | 83.25% |

Table 2: Results on mortality prediction. Bold font indicates the training strategy (pre-trained or from scratch) that has higher accuracy.

task, Figure 5 serves to confirm the models are properly pre-trained.

After pre-training, models are fine-tuned on the two downstream tasks to evaluate the benefit of pre-training. On the mortality prediction task, all three models that are pre-trained perform better than their from-scratch counterparts, shown in Table 2.

The benefit of pre-training is more significant on diagnosis prediction, shown in Figure 6. Both LSTM and LSTM + self attention perform considerably better if they pre-trained. In fact, the two models' performance increase by more than 70% relatively. While for ELECTRA the gain is not as significant, pre-training leads to faster convergence during fine-tuning.

On the two downstream tasks, experiment results show that pre-training improves ELECTRA's performance even when the model is already fully pre-trained on non-medical texts and is among the state-of-the-art, and bring the other models' performance close to ELECTRA's. This shows that pre-training on the MeDAL dataset can generally improves models capabilities of understanding language in medical domain. The complete results can be found in Appendix C.

## 6  Conclusion and Discussion

In this work, we present MeDAL, a large dataset on abbreviation disambiguation, designed for pre-training natural language understanding models in the medical domain. We pre-trained a variety of models using common architectures and empirically showed that such pre-training leads to improvement in performance as well as faster convergence when fine-tuning on two downstream clinical tasks.

## References

Dzmitry Bahdanau, Kyunghyun Cho, and Yoshua Bengio. 2014. Neural Machine Translation by Jointly Learning to Align and Translate.

Piotr Bojanowski, Edouard Grave, Armand Joulin, and Tomas Mikolov. 2017. Enriching Word Vectors with Subword Information. *Transactions of the Association for Computational Linguistics*, 5:135–146.

Edward Choi, Mohammad Taha Bahadori, Andy Schuetz, Walter F. Stewart, and Jimeng Sun. 2015. Doctor AI: Predicting Clinical Events via Recurrent Neural Networks.

Kevin Clark, Minh-Thang Luong, Quoc V. Le, and Christopher D. Manning. 2020. ELECTRA: Pretraining Text Encoders as Discriminators Rather Than Generators. In *International Conference on Learning Representations*.

Gregory P. Finley, Serguei V.S. Pakhomov, Reed McEwan, and Genevieve B. Melton. 2016. Towards Comprehensive Clinical Abbreviation Disambiguation Using Machine-Labeled Training Data. *AMIA ... Annual Symposium proceedings. AMIA Symposium*, 2016:560–569.

Paulina Grnarova, Florian Schmidt, Stephanie L. Hyland, and Carsten Eickhoff. 2016. Neural Document Embeddings for Intensive Care Patient Mortality Prediction.

R. Islamaj Dogan, G. C. Murray, A. Neveol, and Z. Lu. 2009. Understanding PubMed(R) user search behavior through log analysis. *Database*, 2009(0):bap018–bap018.

Qiao Jin, Jinling Liu, and Xinghua Lu. 2019. Deep Contextualized Biomedical Abbreviation Expansion. In *BioNLP 2019*, pages 88–96. Association for Computational Linguistics (ACL).

Alistair E.W. Johnson, Tom J. Pollard, Lu Shen, Li Wei H. Lehman, Mengling Feng, Mohammad Ghassemi, Benjamin Moody, Peter Szolovits, Leo Anthony Celi, and Roger G. Mark. 2016. MIMIC-III, a freely accessible critical care database. *Scientific Data*, 3(1):1–9.

Venkata Joopudi, Bharath Dandala, and Murthy Devarakonda. 2018. A convolutional route to abbreviation disambiguation in clinical text. *Journal of Biomedical Informatics*, 86:71–78.

Diederik P. Kingma and Jimmy Ba. 2014. Adam: A Method for Stochastic Optimization.

Irene Li, Michihiro Yasunaga, Muhammed Yavuz Nuzumlalı, Cesar Caraballo, Shiwani Mahajan, Harlan Krumholz, and Dragomir Radev. 2019. A Neural Topic-Attention Model for Medical Term Abbreviation Disambiguation.

Yue Li, Pratheeksha Nair, Xing Han Lu, Zhi Wen, Yuening Wang, Amir Ardalan Kalantari Dehaghi, Yan Miao, Weiqi Liu, Tamas Ordog, Joanna M. Biernacka, Euijung Ryu, Janet E. Olson, Mark A. Frye, Aihua Liu, Liming Guo, Ariane Marelli, Yuri Ahuja, Jose Davila-Velderrain, and Manolis Kellis. 2020. Inferring multimodal latent topics from electronic health records. *Nature communications*, 11(1):2536.

Yue Liu, Tao Ge, Kusum S. Mathews, Heng Ji, and Deborah L. McGuinness. 2018. Exploiting Task-Oriented Resources to Learn Word Embeddings for Clinical Abbreviation Expansion. In *BioNLP 2015*.

Sungrim Moon, Serguei Pakhomov, Nathan Liu, James O Ryan, and Genevieve B Melton. 2014. A sense inventory for clinical abbreviations and acronyms created using clinical notes and medical dictionary resources. *Journal of the American Medical Informatics Association*, 21(2):299–307.

Marta Skreta, Aryan Arbabi, Jixuan Wang, and Michael Brudno. 2019. Training without training data: Improving the generalizability of automated medical abbreviation disambiguation.

Ashish Vaswani, Noam Shazeer, Niki Parmar, Jakob Uszkoreit, Llion Jones, Aidan N. Gomez, Lukasz Kaiser, and Illia Polosukhin. 2017. Attention Is All You Need.

Yanshan Wang, Liwei Wang, Majid Rastegar-Mojarad, Sungrim Moon, Feichen Shen, Naveed Afzal, Sijia Liu, Yuqun Zeng, Saeed Mehrabi, Sunghwan Sohn, and Hongfang Liu. 2018. Clinical information extraction applications: A literature review.

Hua Xu, Peter D. Stetson, and Carol Friedman. 2007. A study of abbreviations in clinical notes. *AMIA ... Annual Symposium proceedings / AMIA Symposium. AMIA Symposium*, 2007:821–825.

W. Zhou, V. I. Torvik, and N. R. Smalheiser. 2006. ADAM: another database of abbreviations in MEDLINE. *Bioinformatics*, 22(22):2813–2818.

# Knowledge Grounded Conversational Symptom Detection
## with Graph Memory Networks


Hongyin Luo[1]  Shang-Wen Li[2]  James Glass[1]
[1]MIT CSAIL
[2]Amazon AI
hyluo@mit.edu, shangwel@amazon.com, glass@mit.edu



## Abstract

In this work, we propose a novel goal-oriented dialog task, automatic symptom detection. We build a system that can interact with patients through dialog to detect and collect clinical symptoms automatically, which can save a doctor's time interviewing the patient. Given a set of explicit symptoms provided by the patient to initiate a dialog for diagnosing, the system is trained to collect implicit symptoms by asking questions, in order to collect more information for making an accurate diagnosis. After getting the reply from the patient for each question, the system also decides whether current information is enough for a human doctor to make a diagnosis. To achieve this goal, we propose two neural models and a training pipeline for the multi-step reasoning task. We also build a knowledge graph as additional inputs to further improve model performance. Experiments show that our model significantly outperforms the baseline by 4%, discovering 67% of implicit symptoms on average with a limited number of questions.


## 1 Introduction

In a typical clinical conversation between a patient and a doctor, the patient initiates the dialog by providing a number of explicit symptoms as a self-report. Based on this information, the doctor asks about other possible symptoms, in order to make an accurate diagnosis and suggest treatments. This is a multi-step reasoning process. At each step, the doctor choose a symptom to ask or concludes the diagnosis by considering the dialog history and possible diseases.

With recent advances in deep reinforcement learning (Mnih et al., 2013) and task-oriented dialog systems (Bordes et al., 2016; Wen et al., 2016), recent studies have proposed human-computer dialog systems for automatic diagnosis (Wei et al., 2018). The automatic diagnosis system applied a deep Q network (DQN) to decide whether to continue the dialog by asking about a symptom or conclude the diagnosis by predicting a disease. Xu et al. (2019) proposed a knowledge-routed DQN that improves this process by considering relations among diseases and symptoms. The systems described above can achieve around 70% accuracy in making a diagnosis among 4 common diseases and detects a few implicit symptoms.

However, the automatic diagnosis systems is far from being ready for clinical diagnosis, since there is still a gap in accuracy between the system and human doctors. Furthermore, he current legislation system has to be amended such that liability can be clarified when the system mis-diagnoses. As a result, current machines are not ready to replace human doctors, but they can still detect symptoms automatically to assist doctors making decision more efficiently.

In this work, we propose a system that automatically detects clinical symptoms of a patient through dialog, instead of diagnosing. With such symptom information collected, a doctor can be more knowledgeable before interviewing the patient. Only those symptoms not covered by the dialog system should be asked during the interview. Thus both the time and cost of the clinical interviews can be reduced. Meanwhile, the diagnosis is still made by the doctor, which guarantees the accuracy and responsibility.

Table 1 shows two example conversations generated by a dialog agent for automatic diagnosis (AD) and a dialog agent for automatic symptom detection (ASD). AD and ASD agents conclude the conversations differently. The goal of the AD system is making the correct diagnosis, so it concludes the conversation with a prediction of the possible disease. The ASD system aims at discovering as many implicit symptoms as possible, thus it stops the conversation when after deciding that current




*Proceedings of the 3rd Clinical Natural Language Processing Workshop*, pages 136–145
November 19, 2020. ©2020 Association for Computational Linguistics

| **I. Automatic Diagnosis (AD)** |
| --- |

| | |
| --- | --- |
| **User:** | The baby has a Runny Nose. |
| **Agent:** | Does the baby cough? |
| **User:** | Yes, the baby is coughing. |
| **Agent:** | Does the baby have a fever? |
| **User:** | I am not sure. |
| **Agent:** | It is upper respiratory infection |

| **II. Automatic Symptom Detection (ASD)** |
| --- |

| | |
| --- | --- |
| **User:** | The baby has a Runny Nose. |
| **Agent:** | Does the baby cough? |
| **User:** | Yes, the baby is coughing. |
| **Agent:** | Does the baby sneeze? |
| **User:** | Yes, the baby is sneezing. |
| **Agent:** | Does the baby have a fever? |
| **User:** | I am not sure. |
| **Agent:** | Does the baby have a headache? |
| **User:** | Yes, the baby has a headache. |
| **Agent:** | Does the baby have Phlegm? |
| **User:** | Yes, the baby has Phlegm. |
| **Agent:** | Thank you for the information! A report has been sent to your doctor. |

Table 1: Two examples of dialog between different systems and a user. Conversation I is generated by an automatic diagnosis system, and conversation II is generated by an automatic symptom detection system. The explicit symptom is highlighted in blue, the implicit symptoms are highlighted in red, and unrelated symptoms are marked in green.

information is enough for a doctor to make diagnosis. As shown in Table 1, the number of turns of the ASD system is possibly more than an AD system, and it covers more implicit symptoms that are not mentioned in the patient's self-report.

In this work, we focus on the conversational ASD task. We propose a system that predicts implicit symptoms and whether to conclude the conversation with neural networks. To train the neural networks, we borrow the idea of the masked language model (Devlin et al., 2018) and simulate both training and test datasets. To improve the performance of the system, we annotate a medical knowledge graph based on an online medical dictionary. Then we propose a graph memory network (GMemNN) architecture to utilize the external knowledge graph. We also propose two metrics: symptom hit rate and unrelate rate to evaluate the performance of the system.

We make following contributions in this paper,

- We propose the conversational symptom detection task and evaluation metrics.
- We annotate a knowledge graph in the medical domain to enrich the current corpus.
- We propose a graph memory network (GMemNN) architecture to build the dialog agent, which produces the state-of-the-art performance.

## 2 Related Work

### 2.1 Task-Oriented Dialog Systems

Task-oriented dialog systems aim at completing a specific task by interacting with users through natural language, and the main challenge is learning a dialog policy manager (Papineni et al., 2001). Typical applications include flight booking (Seneff and Polifroni, 2000), movie recommendation (Dodge et al., 2015; Fazel-Zarandi et al., 2017), restaurant reservation (Bordes et al., 2016), and vision grounding (Chattopadhyay et al., 2017). Recently, such systems have been applied in automatic diagnosis (Wei et al., 2018; Xu et al., 2019; Luo et al., 2020). The authors of De Vries et al. (2017) proposed the GuessWhat game, which requires computers to guess a visual object given a natural language description by asking a series of questions. The GuessWhat game is similar with our task in the medical domain.

### 2.2 Knowledge and Graph Processing

Many tasks require processing knowledge in different formats. Sukhbaatar et al. (2015) proposed memory networks (MemNNs) for question answering. The context of the question, or knowledge, is stored in an external memory bank and the model reads information from the memory with an attention mechanism. The MemNN model is also applied in question answering in the movie domain (Miller et al., 2016), video question answering (Luo et al., 2019), and stance detection (Mohtarami et al., 2018). The neural Turing machine (Graves et al., 2014) and the neural computer (Graves et al., 2016) also applied external memory banks, and enable the models to write into and read from the external memory cells dynamically.

In many tasks, knowledge can be organized as graphs. Recent studies have proposed different neural models for processing graph-structured data. The graph neural networks (GNNs) (Scarselli et al., 2008) uses neural networks to perform message propagation on graphs. The graph convolutional networks (GCNs) (Kipf and Welling, 2016) employed a multi-layer architecture to learn node embeddings by integrating the information of the nodes and their neighbors. The graph attention networks (Veličković et al., 2017) integrates node embeddings with an attention mechanism. Shang et al. (2019) proposed a graph augmented memory network (GAMENet) model for medication recommendation. A similar idea that combines graphs and memory networks is proposed in Pham et al. (2018) for molecular activity prediction. In this work, we also propose a memory network architecture that processes graph-structured knowledge, but focus on bipartite graphs.

## 3 Data and Task Definition

In this section, we formally define the automatic symptom detection task and describe the corpus used to train and evaluate the model. We first introduce the Muzhi corpus (Wei et al., 2018), then describe the task based on the corpus. Lastly, we describe the medical knowledge graph we annotated and the annotation method.

### 3.1 Muzhi Corpus

We train and evaluate our models using the Muzhi corpus. The corpus was collected from a online medical forum[1], including 4 common diseases and 66 symptoms. The corpus contains 710 dialog sessions represented as 710 user goals. Each user goal includes a set of explicit symptoms as the user's self report, and a set of implicit symptoms queried by doctors. An example of a user goal is shown in Table 2.

In the example, 1 means that the patient confirms a symptom, while 0 means that the patient is confident that the symptom does not exist. Other symptoms not listed in the user goal are considered either unrelated to the diagnosis, or the patient is not sure about their existence. In the Muzhi corpus, each user goal contains 2.35 explicit symptoms and 3.26 implicit symptoms on average.

### 3.2 Automatic Conversational Symptom detection Task

The goal of the automatic conversational symptoms detection (ASD) task is detecting as many implicit symptoms as possible through dialogs with the patients, limiting the number of dialog turns. The initial input of a dialog agent is the set of explicit

| Disease_tag | Bronchiolitis | |
|---|---|---|
| **Exp Sym** | Runny Nose: 1 | Cough: 1 |
| **Imp Sym** | Sore Throat: 1 | Emesis: 0 |
| | Harsh Breath: 1 | Fever: 0 |

Table 2: An example of a user goal in the Muzhi corpus, containing explicit symptoms and implicit symptoms. 1 means a symptom is confirmed by the patient, while 0 means that a symptom is denied by the patient.

symptoms. Based on the query and user response of each step, the system decides a new symptom to ask, or stop the dialog.

All implicit symptoms, including the positive and negative ones, are considered as the target of the system. The user goals are collected from real doctor-patient conversation, so we consider every queried symptom a necessary step of making an accurate diagnosis. The systems are evaluated with two metrics. We say model A outperforms model B if model A discovers more implicit symptoms, and queries less unrelated symptoms.

### 3.3 Medical Knowledge Graph

We annotate a medical knowledge graph to provide information about the relations among symptoms and diseases based on the symptoms included in the Muzhi corpus. As described above, we have 66 symptoms in total. We regard each symptom and disease as a node in the graph and annotate symptom-symptom and symptom-disease edges based on the A-Hospital[2] website, which contains webpages for both symptoms and diseases.

We propose a novel annotation method to build the medical knowledge graph considering complications. The symptom pages in A-Hospital describes a series of diseases that can cause a symptom. Meanwhile, it also listed most possible symptoms to appear if the target symptom is caused by a certain disease. We regard these symptoms as complications and make use of this information. In practice, we annotate the knowledge graph with the following method,

1. For each symptom $s$ and its related disease $d$, add edge $(s, d)$.
2. For each symptom $s$, its related disease $d$, and complication $c$, add edge $(s, c)$.

An example of the annotated knowledge is shown in Figure 1, and Table 3 summaries the

---

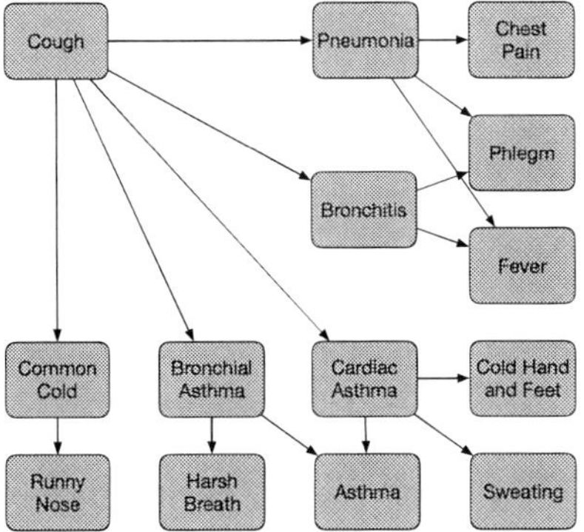

Figure 1: An example of an annotated symptom in the knowledge graph. Red blocks represent symptoms and blue blocks stands for disease. "Cough" is the target symptom and other symptoms are complications.

| Items | Statistics |
| --- | --- |
| Num. Sym. | 66 |
| Num. Dise. | 28 |
| Num. Edge | 1094 |
| Num. S-D Edge | 284 |
| Num. S-C Edge | 810 |

Table 3: A statistics of the annotated knowledge graph of symptoms, diseases, and complications. Note that both symptom-disease and symptom-complication edges exist.

knowledge graph we annotated. In the table, S-D edge stands for symptom-disease edge and S-C edge stands for symptom-disease-symptom edge. The number of S-C edge is lower than multiplying the number of symptoms per disease and diseases per symptom is that only a subset of symptoms caused by a disease are regarded as significant complications of a given symptom.

## 4 Methods

In this section, we introduce the structure and pipeline of the proposed automatic symptom detection system, including dialog state representation, the neural models for predicting symptoms and dialog actions, the training strategy, and the evaluation metrics.

### 4.1 Dialog State Representation

Automatic symptom detection is a multi-step reasoning task handled by action and symptom predictions. Both tasks are accomplished with neural networks based on the current dialog state.

The first step of building such a system is representing dialog states with vectors that can be processed by the neural networks. Following the method applied in Wei et al. (2018) for vectorizing the dialog states, each dialog state consists of 4 parts:

**I. UserAction**: The user action of the previous dialog turn. Possible actions are:

- **SelfReport**: A user sends a self-report containing a set of explicit symptoms.
- **Confirm**: A user confirms that a queried symptom exists.
- **Deny**: A user indicates that a queried symptom does not exist.
- **NotSure**: A user replies "not sure" when an unrelated symptom is queried.

**II. AgentAction**: The previous action of the dialog agent. Possible actions are:

- **Initiate**: The system initiate the dialog and ask the user to send the self-rport.
- **Request**: The system query about the existence of a symtom.

**III. Slots**: Contains all symptoms appeared in the dialog history and their status. Each symptom has 4 possible status,

- **Confirmed**: Confirmed by the user.
- **Denied**: Denied by the user.
- **Unrelated**: The symptom is not necessary for the doctor to make an accurate diagnosis.
- **NotQueried**: A symptom has not been queried by the agent.

**IV. NumTurns**: Indicates the length of the dialog history, in other words, current number of turns.

In each step, only one value is selected for UserAction, AgentAction, and NumTurns, and we represent them with one-hot vectors $a^u$, $a^r$, and $n$ respectively. We use a 66-dimension vector $s$ to represent the Slots, where each dimension indicates the status of a symptom. If a symptom is confirmed, the corresponding dimension is set to 1. If a symptom is denied, the corresponding dimension is set to $-1$. If a symptom is unrelated to the diagnosis process, and the dimension is set to $-2$. All other dimensions are set to 0. The final input of the neural networks at the $t$-th step is represented as

$$x_t = [a_t^u, a_t^r, n_t, s_t] \qquad (1)$$

which is genereted by concatenating all the vectors decribed above

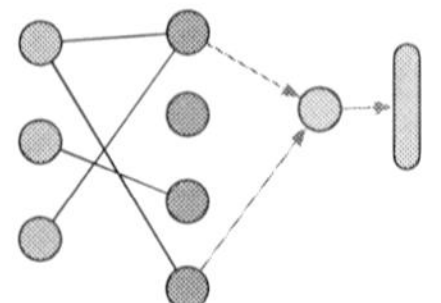 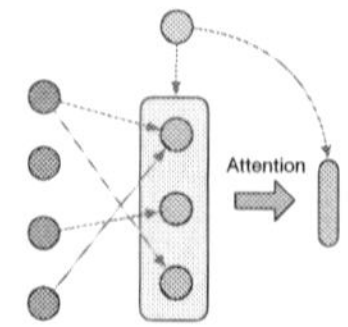 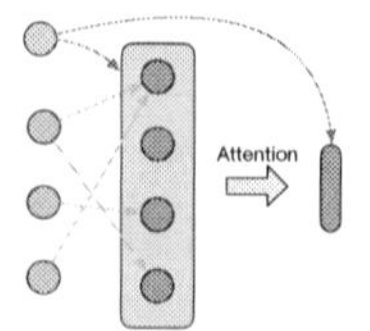 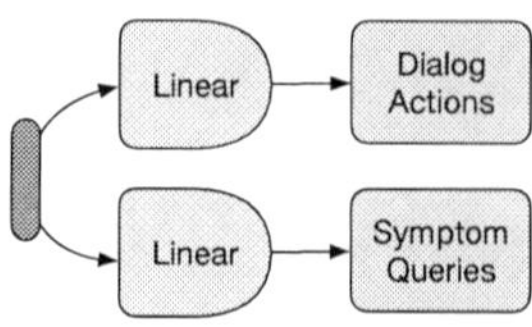



(a) Initiate patient embedding with edges with input slots.

(b) Integrate disease information with attention.

(c) Integrate symptom information with attention.

(d) Predict action and symptom with linear transformations.

Figure 2: The 4 steps for processing an input dialog state with a graph memory network (GMemNN). The gray nodes stand for patient, the red nodes represent symptoms, and the blue nodes represent diseases. The edges with arrows, which are labeled with same color as their source nodes, indicate the direction of message propagation.

## 4.2 Models

### 4.2.1 Multi-Layer Perceptrons

The first neural model we apply in this work is a multi-layer perceptron (MLP) with 1 hidden layer. The same neural network is applied in Wei et al. (2018) and Xu et al. (2019) for the automatic diagnosis task. With input $x$, the feed forward process of the MLP is shown as follows,

$$
\begin{aligned}
h &= ReLU(W_1 \cdot x + b_1) \\
y &= Softmax(W_2 \cdot h + b_2)
\end{aligned}
\tag{2}
$$

where Softmax calculates probabilistic distribution by

$$
Softmax(a_i) = \frac{e^{a_i}}{\sum_j e^{a_j}}
\tag{3}
$$

The MLP is used for both implicit symptom and dialog action predictions. Note that the MLP model only uses the dialogs in the training set, and does not use the knowledge graph we annotated.

### 4.2.2 Graph Memory Networks

Limited by the structure, MLPs cannot directly utilize the knowledge graph, which contains necessary medical knowledge for clinical diagnosis. Inspired by previous studies on processing knowledge and graphs (Sukhbaatar et al., 2015; Veličković et al., 2017), we propose graph memory networks (GMemNN) that utilizes the medical knowledge graph to improve the performance of the automatic symptom detection system.

The knowledge graph is stored in an external memory bank. In each step, we regard a patient as a node connected with the known symptoms in the graph. Our purpose is to learn the embedding of the patient node and predict dialog actions and symptoms based on it. The prediction using GMemNN contains 4 steps: 1. encoding dialog states, 2. integrating potential disease information, 3. integrating complication symptoms, and 4. predicting action/symptom. The 4 steps are illuminated in Figure 2.

**Dialog State Encoding** The GMemNN encodes the input dialog states with a lookup matrix, or a linear transformation. Given an input dialog state representation $x$, the network encodes the dialog state with

$$
u^0 = W_x \cdot x + b_x
\tag{4}
$$

Note that no non-linear activation is applied on $u$ at this step, and $u$ is considered as the initial embedding of the patient node in the graph.

**Integrating Disease Information** After encoding the dialog state, we update the patient embedding using the embeddings of possible diseases. We calculate an embedding to summarize potential diseases using the attention mechanism for reading from the memory bank applied in the memory networks (Sukhbaatar et al., 2015).

Similar with the method applied in the MemNN, we first calculate two sets of embeddings for the diseases based on their neighbors, or related symptoms, in the knowledge graph. In this paper, we use $W_m^s$ to denote the symptom embedding matrices for calculating attentions on memory, and $W_c^s$ to denote the symptom embeddings for calculating outputs. The related symptoms are summarized with the adjacency matrix $A_d$ between symptoms and diseases.

$$
\begin{aligned}
d_{i,m}^1 &= d_{i,m}^0 + A_d^i W_m^s D_{d,i}^{-1} \\
d_{i,c}^1 &= d_{i,c}^0 + A_d^i W_c^s D_{d,i}^{-1}
\end{aligned}
\tag{5}
$$

where $d_{i,\cdot}^1$ represents the updated embedding of disease $i$, $d_{i,\cdot}^0$ is the initial disease embedding, $W^s$ stands for the symptom embedding matrix for updating disease embeddings. $A_d^i$ is the $i$-th row of $A_d$, and $D_{d,i}$ is the disease node degree for normalization. This is a variant of the normalization method proposed in Kipf and Welling (2016).

Then we summarize potential diseases using $d_{m}^{1}$, $d_{c}^{1}$, and the initial input embedding $u^{0}$.

$$e^{d} = \sum_{i} \alpha_{i}^{d} \cdot d_{i,c}^{1}$$
$$\alpha_{i}^{d} = Softmax(u^{0} \cdot d_{i,m}^{1}) \tag{6}$$

Then we update the initial patient embedding $u^{0}$ by integrating disease embeddings.

$$u^{d} = ReLU(u^{0} + e^{d}) \tag{7}$$

**Integrating Symptom Information** After integrating the information of possible diseases, the model continues integrating the complication symptom information to produce the final patient embedding. For symptom $i$, given the initial symptom embeddings $s_{i,\cdot}^{0}$, the adjacency matrix $A_{s}$ between symptom and symptom, we calculate symptom embeddings with

$$s_{i,m}^{1} = s_{i,m}^{0} + A_{s}^{i}W_{m}^{s}D_{s,i}^{-1} + A_{d}^{\cdot,i}W_{m}^{d}D_{d,\cdot,i}^{-1}$$
$$s_{i,c}^{1} = s_{i,c}^{0} + A_{s}^{i}W_{c}^{s}D_{s,i}^{-1} + A_{d}^{\cdot,i}W_{c}^{d}D_{d,\cdot,i}^{-1} \tag{8}$$

where $W_{\cdot}^{s}$ is the complication symptom embedding matrix, $W_{\cdot}^{d}$ is the disease embedding matrix. $D_{s,i}$ is the number of neighbor symptoms of symptom $i$, and $D_{d,i}$ is the number of neighbor diseases of symptom $i$.

Similarly, we summarize the complication symptoms by

$$e^{s} = \sum_{i} \alpha_{i}^{s} \cdot s_{i,c}^{1}$$
$$\alpha_{i}^{s} = Softmax(u^{d} \cdot s_{i,m}^{1}) \tag{9}$$

Then we get the final patient embedding by integrating $u^{d}$ with the complication symptoms embedding

$$u^{d,s} = ReLU(u^{d} + e^{s}) \tag{10}$$

$u^{d,s}$ stands for a patient embedding that has integrated both disease and symptom information.

**Action/Sympotom Prediction** The GMemNN model predicts both dialog actions and symptoms with linear transformations based on the same patient embedding $u^{d,s}$.

$$y^{act} = W^{act} \cdot u^{d,s} + b_{act}$$
$$y^{sym} = W^{sym} \cdot u^{d,s} + b_{sym} \tag{11}$$

The action and symptom distributions are calculated with $y^{act}$ and $y^{sym}$ with the Softmax function. The available dialog actions are Conclude and Query, and the prediction space of the symptom prediction network is the 66 symptoms except the known symptoms.

### 4.2.3 Training

The Muzhi dataset does not contain any dialog history to mimic. Inspired by the masked language model training pipeline proposed by Devlin et al. (2018), we construct our own training set by randomly masking and sampling symptoms.

**Symptom Prediction** We build the training set by simulating dialog states from user goals in the original training set of the Muzhi corpus. We consider user goal $g_{i}$ with explicit symptom set $S_{e}$ and implicit symptom set $S_{i}$ as an example, where $|S_{e}| = n_{e}$ and $|S_{i}| = n_{i}$. We simulate $t$ dialog states based on $g_{i}$ with the following steps.

- Select the entire explicit symptom set $S_{e}$.
- Randomly select $n_{i}' \in [0, n_{i})$ and sample $n_{i}'$ implicit symptoms to construct $S_{i}' \subset S_{i}$
- Randomly select $n_{u} \in [0, T_{max} - n_{i}')$ and sample $n_{u}$ unrelated symptoms to construct set $S_{u}$. $T_{max}$ stands for the maximum number of symptoms can be queried.
- Set the number of turns with $t = n_{i}' + n_{u}$.
- If $n_{i}' = n_{u} = 0$, set AgentAction to "Initiate". Else set the AgentAction to "Request".
- Randomly select a symptom $s \in S_{i} \cup S_{u}$. If $s \in S_{u}$, set UserAction to "NotSure", else set it to "Confirm" or "Deny" based on $g_{i}$.
- Set current slot to $S_{e} \cup S_{i}' \cup S_{u}$.
- Randomly select a implicit symptom $s_{l} \in S_{i} - S_{i}'$ as the prediction label.

**Action Prediction** We simulate dialog states for the dialog action prediction task with the same procedure as described above, except that we can involve all implicit symptoms. If all implicit symptoms are included, the training label will set to "Conclude", otherwise the label will be "Query".

We train MLPs and GMemNNs on both tasks after the training sets are generated. The models are trained with the simulated dialog states and labels with the stochastic gradient descent (SGD) algorithm.

## 5 Experiments

We train and evaluate our models on the Muzhi corpus. The symptom predictor and the dialog action predictor are trained separately. Using the same strategy of simulating the training set, we also generated test sets for symptom prediction and action prediction respectively using the test user goals with the same method. The generated test sets are used for evaluating the performances of our models on both unit tasks.

| Unit Task | Model | Acc (%) | Stdv (%) |
|---|---|---|---|
| Action | MLP | 94.14 | 0.27 |
| Prediction | GMemNN | 94.50 | 0.42 |
| Symptom | MLP | 45.10 | 0.62 |
| Prediction | GMemNN | 47.88 | 1.18 |

Table 4: Unit task evaluation results of the action and symptom prediction tasks. Acc stands for average accuracy, and Stdv stands for the standard deviation of the accuracies. The statistics are obtained by running 10 experiments for each model on each task.

After evaluating the models in with the unit tasks, we conduct conversational evaluations using the trained models and a user simulator. We evaluate the performance of the models by accounting the number of implicit and unrelated symptoms queried in the conversations.

## 5.1 Action Prediction

For action prediction, we simulate 20 dialog states for each user goal in both training and test sets. All simulated states contain the entire explicit symptom sets. 10 of the 20 states also contain the complete implicit symptom sets, thus they are labeled with "1", meaning that the dialog system should conclude the dialog given these states in a dialog. The other states only contains a proper subset of implicit symptoms. These states are labeled with "0", meaning that the agent should continue querying symptoms. We have 11,360 training states and 2,840 test states.

We train an MLP and a GMemNN model on the simulated training sets. The MLP model has one hidden layer with 128 neurons, while the size of the hidden layers of GMemNN is set to 64. The models are trained with stochastic gradient descent (SGD) algorithm. The learning rate for training the MLP is 0.025, and is set to 0.035 for training the GMemNN. A weight decay rate of 0.001 is applied for training both models. Both models are trained for 40 epochs.

The experimental results are shown in Table 4. All experimental results are obtained by running 5 independent experiments for each model from data simulation. The GMemNN model outperformed the MLP model with a small margin. The experimental results indicated that action prediction is not a hard classification task that external knowledge and complex neural networks do not help much.

## 5.2 Implicit Symptom Prediction

For implicit symptom prediction, we simulate 10 dialog states for each user goal in both training and test sets. All dialog states contains the complete explicit symptom set and a proper subset of implicit symptoms. A random number of unrelated symptoms are also included. The label for training set is randomly sampled from implicit symptoms that are not included in the dialog state.

We train the neural networks for the implicit symptom prediction task with SGD. The architectures of MLP and GMemNN are the same as the models applied for action prediction respectively. We also apply the same hyper-parameter settings for training as the previous task.

The experimental results of symptom prediction are shown in Table 4, which are also collected by runing 5 independent experiments from data simulation. The GMemNN model significantly outperformed the basic MLP model by 2.7% on average and the performance is more stable. Comparing with the action prediction task, symptom prediction is much more difficult. As a result, domain specific knowledge can improve the performance more significantly.

## 5.3 Conversational Evaluation

We also evaluate our model by conducting dialogs using the original test split of user goals in the Muzhi corpus. For each test user goal, we generate a conversation using the dialog action predictor, the implicit symptom predictor, and a rule-based user simulator.

The user simulator initiates a dialog by providing a set of explicit symptoms as the initiate state. In each dialog step, the action predictor decides if the current state is informative enough to conclude the dialog. If a conclusion action is predicted, the system stops the conversation. Otherwise, the system queries the user simulator with a symptom selected by the symptom predictor. If the selected symptom is positive in the implicit symptom set, the user simulator confirms the query. If it is negative in the implicit symptom set, the user simulator denies the query. If the selected symptom is not in the implicit, the user simulator responses "NotSure". The dialog continues until the "Conclusion" action is selected, or the maximum limit of dialog turns is reached.

For each test user goal, we calculate the number of unrelated symptoms queried $N_u$, the number of

| Model | **Hit** (%) | **UnRel** (%) | **F1** (%) |
|---|---|---|---|
| MLP-AD | 9.62 | 83.37 | 18.75 |
| MLP-ASD | 63.26 | 81.88 | 31.35 |
| GMemNN | **67.30** | **81.05** | **32.59** |

Table 5: The experimental results of the conversational evaluation. MLP-AD stands for the pretrained state-of-the-art MLP model for automatic diagnosis (AD) provided by the authors of Xu et al. (2019). MLP-ASD stands for the MLP model for automatic symptom detection (ASD) in this work. Hit stands for average hit rate $R_h$, UnRel stands for average unrelated rate $R_u$.

dialog turns $N$, and the ratio of detected implicit $R_d$. Given the number of all implicit symptoms $N_i$ and the number of the detected implicit symptoms $N_i'$, we calculate the hit rate $R_h$, unrelated rate $R_u$, and the F1 score by

$$R_h = \frac{N_i'}{N_i},\ R_u = \frac{N_u}{N},\ F_1 = \frac{2R_h(1 - R_u)}{R_h + 1 - R_u} \quad (12)$$

We evaluate the models by calculating and comparing $R_d$, $R_u$, and F1 score averaged by the number of conversations. The experimental results are shown in Table 5.

The experiments are conducted by setting the tolerate rate (TolR) to 10, meaning allowing the agent to query up to 10 symptoms. The experimental results showed that the MLP-ASD and GMemNN models detected significantly more implicit symptoms than the MLP-AD model (Xu et al., 2019), which makes diagnosis by querying only 9.62% of implicit symptoms that a human doctor would ask about. Comparing the MLP-AD and GMemNN models, the GMemNN model significantly outperformed the MLP model by 4.04% hit rate with 0.83% lower unrelated rate. The improvement on F1 score is 1.24%.

We use tolerate rate (TolR) to limit the number of dialog turns. If the symptom predictor is completely random and the TolR equals to the number of symptoms, the hit rate $R_h$ will be 100%. However, querying all symptoms costs too much time for the patient. Since the average number of symptoms per user goal is 3.26, the average unrelate rate $R_u$ of such a system will be $(66 - 3.26)/66 = 95.06\%$ and the F1 score will be as low as 9.45%.

To understand the effect of the tolerate rate, we visualized the relation between $R_h$, $R_u$, and TolR in Figure 3. The plot indicates that increasing TolR

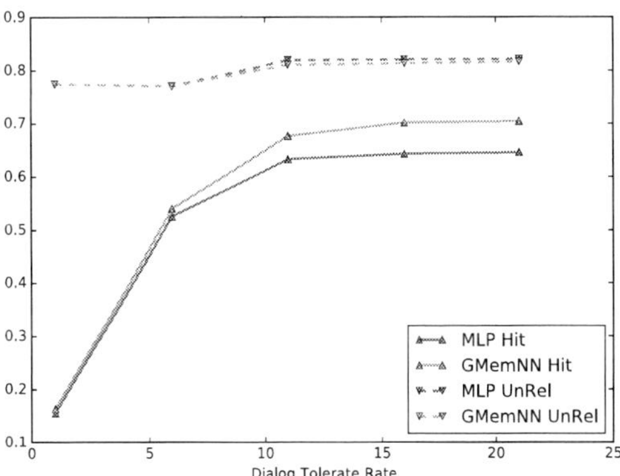


Figure 3: The effect of tolerate rate on hit rate and un-relate rate for the MLP and the GMemNN models.

from 1 to 10 can significantly improve the hit rates. However, the improvement vanishes after the 15th query because having too many queried symptoms makes the dialog states noisy. When the TolR is less than 10, the performance gap between The MLP and GMemNN model is not as large as the cases where TolR is larger than 10. There are two reasons for this phenomenon. I. some symptoms are queried by human doctors very frequently and they are equally easy for both models to predict; II. The GMemNN has better ability to model and process noisy inputs.

## 6 Conclusion

In this work, we propose a new task: detecting implicit symptoms of patient with an automatic dialog system. We construct the system with a dialog action prediction module and a symptom query module. We first implement and evaluate a baseline system based on multi-layer perceptrons (MLPs). To improve the performance of the system, we annotate a medical-domain knowledge graph and propose the graph memory network (GMemNN) model. We systematically evaluate and compare both models with unit tasks and conversations. We also studied how the number of dialog turns effects the performance of the systems. Experiments showed that both models can detect more than 60% implicit symptoms using limited turns of dialogs, which significantly outperformed the state-of-the-art automatic diagnosis system. In future work, we will expand the knowledge graph and aim to assist human doctors by making the clinical interview process more efficient.

## References

Antoine Bordes, Y-Lan Boureau, and Jason Weston. 2016. Learning end-to-end goal-oriented dialog. *arXiv preprint arXiv:1605.07683*.

Prithvijit Chattopadhyay, Deshraj Yadav, Viraj Prabhu, Arjun Chandrasekaran, Abhishek Das, Stefan Lee, Dhruv Batra, and Devi Parikh. 2017. Evaluating visual conversational agents via cooperative human-ai games. In *Fifth AAAI Conference on Human Computation and Crowdsourcing*.

Harm De Vries, Florian Strub, Sarath Chandar, Olivier Pietquin, Hugo Larochelle, and Aaron Courville. 2017. Guesswhat?! visual object discovery through multi-modal dialogue. In *Proceedings of the IEEE Conference on Computer Vision and Pattern Recognition*, pages 5503–5512.

Jacob Devlin, Ming-Wei Chang, Kenton Lee, and Kristina Toutanova. 2018. Bert: Pre-training of deep bidirectional transformers for language understanding. *arXiv preprint arXiv:1810.04805*.

Jesse Dodge, Andreea Gane, Xiang Zhang, Antoine Bordes, Sumit Chopra, Alexander Miller, Arthur Szlam, and Jason Weston. 2015. Evaluating prerequisite qualities for learning end-to-end dialog systems. *arXiv preprint arXiv:1511.06931*.

Maryam Fazel-Zarandi, Shang-Wen Li, Jin Cao, Jared Casale, Peter Henderson, David Whitney, and Alborz Geramifard. 2017. Learning robust dialog policies in noisy environments.

Alex Graves, Greg Wayne, and Ivo Danihelka. 2014. Neural turing machines. *arXiv preprint arXiv:1410.5401*.

Alex Graves, Greg Wayne, Malcolm Reynolds, Tim Harley, Ivo Danihelka, Agnieszka Grabska-Barwińska, Sergio Gómez Colmenarejo, Edward Grefenstette, Tiago Ramalho, John Agapiou, et al. 2016. Hybrid computing using a neural network with dynamic external memory. *Nature*, 538(7626):471.

Thomas N Kipf and Max Welling. 2016. Semi-supervised classification with graph convolutional networks. *arXiv preprint arXiv:1609.02907*.

Hongyin Luo, Shang-Wen Li, and James Glass. 2020. Prototypical q networks for automatic conversational diagnosis and few-shot new disease adaption. *arXiv preprint arXiv:2005.11153*.

Hongyin Luo, Mitra Mohtarami, James Glass, Karthik Krishnamurthy, and Brigitte Richardson. 2019. Integrating video retrieval and moment detection in a unified corpus for video question answering. *Proc. Interspeech 2019*, pages 599–603.

Alexander Miller, Adam Fisch, Jesse Dodge, Amir-Hossein Karimi, Antoine Bordes, and Jason Weston. 2016. Key-value memory networks for directly reading documents. *arXiv preprint arXiv:1606.03126*.

Volodymyr Mnih, Koray Kavukcuoglu, David Silver, Alex Graves, Ioannis Antonoglou, Daan Wierstra, and Martin Riedmiller. 2013. Playing atari with deep reinforcement learning. *arXiv preprint arXiv:1312.5602*.

Mitra Mohtarami, Ramy Baly, James Glass, Preslav Nakov, Lluís Màrquez, and Alessandro Moschitti. 2018. Automatic stance detection using end-to-end memory networks. *arXiv preprint arXiv:1804.07581*.

Kishore A Papineni, Salim Roukos, and Robert T Ward. 2001. Natural language task-oriented dialog manager and method. US Patent 6,246,981.

Trang Pham, Truyen Tran, and Svetha Venkatesh. 2018. Graph memory networks for molecular activity prediction. In *2018 24th International Conference on Pattern Recognition (ICPR)*, pages 639–644. IEEE.

Franco Scarselli, Marco Gori, Ah Chung Tsoi, Markus Hagenbuchner, and Gabriele Monfardini. 2008. The graph neural network model. *IEEE Transactions on Neural Networks*, 20(1):61–80.

Stephanie Seneff and Joseph Polifroni. 2000. Dialogue management in the mercury flight reservation system. In *Proceedings of the 2000 ANLP/NAACL Workshop on Conversational systems-Volume 3*, pages 11–16. Association for Computational Linguistics.

Junyuan Shang, Cao Xiao, Tengfei Ma, Hongyan Li, and Jimeng Sun. 2019. Gamenet: Graph augmented memory networks for recommending medication combination. In *Proceedings of the AAAI Conference on Artificial Intelligence*, volume 33, pages 1126–1133.

Sainbayar Sukhbaatar, Jason Weston, Rob Fergus, et al. 2015. End-to-end memory networks. In *Advances in neural information processing systems*, pages 2440–2448.

Petar Veličković, Guillem Cucurull, Arantxa Casanova, Adriana Romero, Pietro Lio, and Yoshua Bengio. 2017. Graph attention networks. *arXiv preprint arXiv:1710.10903*.

Zhongyu Wei, Qianlong Liu, Baolin Peng, Huaixiao Tou, Ting Chen, Xuanjing Huang, Kam-Fai Wong, and Xiangying Dai. 2018. Task-oriented dialogue system for automatic diagnosis. In *Proceedings of the 56th Annual Meeting of the Association for Computational Linguistics (Volume 2: Short Papers)*, pages 201–207.

Tsung-Hsien Wen, David Vandyke, Nikola Mrksic, Milica Gasic, Lina M Rojas-Barahona, Pei-Hao Su, Stefan Ultes, and Steve Young. 2016. A network-based end-to-end trainable task-oriented dialogue system. *arXiv preprint arXiv:1604.04562*.

Lin Xu, Qixian Zhou, Ke Gong, Xiaodan Liang, Jianheng Tang, and Liang Lin. 2019. End-to-end knowledge-routed relational dialogue system for automatic diagnosis. *arXiv preprint arXiv:1901.10623*.

# Pretrained Language Models for Biomedical and Clinical Tasks: Understanding and Extending the State-of-the-Art


**Patrick Lewis[†‡], Myle Ott[†], Jingfei Du[†], Veslin Stoyanov[†]**

[†]Facebook AI Research; [‡]University College London
{plewis,myleott,jingfeidu,ves}@fb.com



## Abstract

A large array of pretrained models are available to the biomedical NLP (BioNLP) community. Finding the best model for a particular task can be difficult and time-consuming. For many applications in the biomedical and clinical domains, it is crucial that models can be built quickly and are highly accurate. We present a large-scale study across 18 established biomedical and clinical NLP tasks to determine which of several popular open-source biomedical and clinical NLP models work well in different settings. Furthermore, we apply recent advances in pretraining to train new biomedical language models, and carefully investigate the effect of various design choices on downstream performance. Our best models perform well in all of our benchmarks, and set new State-of-the-Art in 9 tasks. We release these models in the hope that they can help the community to speed up and increase the accuracy of BioNLP and text mining applications.


## 1 Introduction

The pretrain-and-finetune approach has become the dominant paradigm for NLP applications in the last few years (Peters et al., 2018; Devlin et al., 2019; Yang et al., 2019; Conneau et al., 2020, inter alia.), bringing significant performance gains in many areas of NLP. Models trained on Wikipedia and WebText (Radford et al., 2019) generally perform well on a variety of target domains, but various works have noted that pretraining on in-domain text is an effective method for boosting downstream performance further (Peters et al., 2018; Beltagy et al., 2019; Li et al., 2019; Gururangan et al., 2020). Several pretrained models are available specifically in the domain of biomedical and clinical NLP driving forward the state of the art including BioBERT (Lee et al., 2019), SciBERT (Beltagy et al., 2019), ClinicalBERT (Alsentzer et al., 2019) and BioMedRoBERTa (Gururangan et al., 2020).

While it is great to have multiple options, it can be difficult to make sense of what model to use in what case — different models are often compared on different tasks. To further complicate matters, more powerful general-purpose models are being released continuously. It is unclear whether it is better to use a more powerful general-purpose model like RoBERTa, or a domain-specific model derived from an earlier model such as BioBERT. And given the opportunity to pretrain a new model, it is unclear what are the best practices to do that efficiently.

Our goal is to understand better the landscape of pretrained biomedical and clinical NLP models. To that effect, we perform a large-scale study across 18 established biomedical and clinical NLP tasks. We evaluate four popular bioNLP models using the same experimental setup. We compare them to general purpose RoBERTa checkpoints. We find that BioBERT performs best overall on biomedical tasks, but the general-purpose RoBERTA-large model performs best on clinical tasks. We then take advantage of recent advances in pretraining by adapting RoBERTa (Liu et al., 2019) to biomedical and clinical text. We investigate what choices are important in pretraining for strong downstream bioNLP performance, including model size, vocabulary/tokenization choices and training corpora. Our best models perform well across all of the tasks, establishing a new state of the art on 9 tasks. Finally, we apply knowledge distillation to train a smaller model that outperforms all other models with similar computational requirements. We will release our pretrained models and the code used to run our experiments.[1]

---

[1]Models and code are available at https://github.com/facebookresearch/bio-lm




*Proceedings of the 3rd Clinical Natural Language Processing Workshop*, pages 146–157
November 19, 2020. ©2020 Association for Computational Linguistics

## 2 Tasks and Datasets

We select a broad range of datasets to cover both scientific and clinical textual domains, and common modelling tasks – namely i) Sequence labelling tasks, covering Named Entity Recognition (NER) and de-identification (De-id) and ii) Classification tasks, covering relation extraction, multi-class and multi-label classification and Natural Language Inference (NLI)-style tasks. These tasks were also selected to optimize overlap with previous work in the space, drawing tasks from the BLUE benchmark (Peng et al., 2019), BioBERT (Lee et al., 2019), SciBERT (Beltagy et al., 2019) and ClinicalBERT (Alsentzer et al., 2019). The tasks are summarized in Table 1 and described in the following subsections.

### 2.1 Sequence Labelling Tasks

**BC5-CDR** (Li et al., 2016) is an NER task requiring the identification of Chemical and Disease concepts from 1,500 PubMed articles. There are 5,203 and 4,182 training instances for chemicals and diseases respectively.

**JNLPBA** (Collier and Kim, 2004) is an NER task requiring the identification of entities of interest in micro-biology, with 2,000 training PubMed abstracts.

**NCBI-Disease** (Doğan et al., 2014) requires identification of disease mentions in PubMed abstracts. There are 6,892 annotations from 793 abstracts.

**BC4CHEMD** (Krallinger et al., 2015) requires the identification of chemical and drug mentions from PubMed abstracts. There are 84,310 annotations from 10,000 abstracts.

**BC2GM** (Smith et al., 2008) requires the identification of 24,583 protein and gene mentions from 20,000 sentences from PubMed.

**LINNAEUS** (Gerner et al., 2010) is a collection of 4,077 species annotations from 153 PubMed articles.

**Species-800** (Pafilis et al., 2013) is a collection 3,708 species annotations in 800 PubMed abstracts.

**I2B2-2010/VA** (Uzuner et al., 2011) is made up of 871 de-identified clinical reports. The task requires labelling a variety of medical concepts in clinical text.

**I2B2-2012** (Sun et al., 2013b,a) is made up of 310 de-identified clinical discharge summaries. The task requires the identification of temporal events within these summaries.

**I2B2-2014** (Stubbs and Uzuner, 2015; Stubbs et al., 2015) is made up of 1,304 de-identified longitudinal medical records. The task requires the labelling of spans of text of private health information.

### 2.2 Classification Tasks

**HOC** (Baker et al., 2016) is a multi-label classification task requiring the classification of cancer concepts for PubMed Articles. We follow (Peng et al., 2019) and report abstract-level F1 score.

**MedNLI** (Romanov and Shivade, 2018) is a 3-class NLI dataset built from 14K pairs of sentences in the clinical domain.

**ChemProt** (Krallinger et al., 2017) requires classifying chemical-protein interactions from 1,820 PubMed articles. We follow the standard practice of evaluating over the 5 most common classes.

**GAD** (Bravo et al., 2015) is a binary relation extraction task for 5330 annotated gene-disease interactions from PubMed. We use the cross-validation splits from Lee et al. (2019).

**EU-ADR** (van Mulligen et al., 2012) is a small data binary relation extraction task with 355 annotated gene-disease interactions from PubMed. We use the cross-validation splits from Lee et al. (2019).

**DDI-2013** (Herrero-Zazo et al., 2013) is a relation extraction task requiring recognition of drug-drug interactions. There are 4 classes to extract from 4920 sentences from PubMed, as well as many sentences which do not contain relations.

**I2B2-2010-RE** (Uzuner et al., 2011) in this setting of I2B2-2010, we focus on the relation extraction task to detect 8 clinical events.

## 3 Pretraining Corpora

There is a wide range of text corpora in the biomedical and clinical domains. We limit our options to data that is freely available to the public so that models can be open-sourced.

| Task Name | Domain | Task | Metric | Task Name | Domain | Task | Metric |
|---|---|---|---|---|---|---|---|
| BC5-CDR-Chemical | PubMed | N.E.R. | F1 | I2B2-2012 | Clinical | N.E.R. | F1 |
| BC5-CDR-Disease | PubMed | N.E.R. | F1 | I2B2-2014 | Clinical | De-ID | F1 |
| JNLPBA | PubMed | N.E.R. | F1 | HOC | PubMed | Multi-label classif. | Macro-F1 |
| NCBI-D | PubMed | N.E.R. | F1 | ChemProt | PubMed | Rel. extract. | Macro-F1 |
| BC4CHEMD | PubMed | N.E.R. | F1 | GAD | PubMed | Binary Rel. Extract. | F1 |
| BC2GM | PubMed | N.E.R. | F1 | EU-ADR | PubMed | Binary Rel. Extract. | F1 |
| LINNEAEUS | PubMed | N.E.R. | F1 | DDI-2013 | PubMed | Rel. Extract. | Micro-F1 |
| Species-800 | PubMed | N.E.R. | F1 | I2B2-2010-RE | Clinical | Rel. extract. | F1 |
| I2B2-2010 | Clinical | N.E.R. | F1 | MedNLI | Clinical | NLI | Acc |

Table 1: Summary of our considered tasks

**PubMed abstracts** PubMed[2] is a free resource containing over 30 million citations and abstracts of biomedical literature. PubMed abstracts are a popular choice for pretraining biomedical language models (Lee et al., 2019; Peng et al., 2020) because of the collection's large size and broad coverage. Following past work, we obtained all PubMed abstracts published as of March 2020. After removing empty abstracts we retained 27GB of text from 22 million abstracts, consisting of approximately 4.2 billion words.

**PubMed Central full-text** PubMed Central[3] (PMC) is an open access collection of over 5 million full-text articles from biomedical and life science research, which has been used in past scientific language modeling work (Beltagy et al., 2019). Following past work, we obtained all PubMed Central full-text articles published as of March 2020. We use the `pubmed_parser` package[4] to extract plain text from each article. After removing empty paragraphs and articles with parsing failures we retained 60GB of text from 3.4 million articles, consisting of approximately 9.6 billion words.

**MIMIC-III** The Medical Information Mart for Intensive Care, third update (MIMIC-III) consists of deidentified clinical data from approximately 60k intensive care unit admissions. Following related work (Zhu et al., 2018; Peng et al., 2019), we extract all physician notes resulting in 3.3GB of text and approximately 0.5 billion words.

**Other corpora** Other authors have used subsets of papers on Semantic Scholar (Gururangan et al., 2020; Ammar et al., 2018), but these corpora are not generally publicly available. The CORD-19 dataset (Wang et al., 2020) is a publicly-available corpus of articles focusing on COVID-19, but is largely subsumed by PMC, so we do not directly include it in our work.

## 4 Pretrained Models

We compare five publicly-available language models which together form a representative picture of the state-of-the-art in biomedical and clinical NLP. We use the HuggingFace Transformers library to access the model checkpoints (Wolf et al., 2019).

**SciBERT** (Beltagy et al., 2019) is a masked language model (MLM) pretrained from scratch on a corpus of 1.14M papers from Semantic Scholar (Ammar et al., 2018), of which 82% are in the biomedical domain. SciBERT uses a specialized vocabulary built using Sentence-Piece (Sennrich et al., 2016; Kudo, 2018)[5] on their pretraining corpus. We use the uncased SciBERT variant.

**BioBERT** (Lee et al., 2019) is based on the BERT-base model (Devlin et al., 2019), with additional pretraining in the biomedical domain. We use BioBERT-v1.1. This model was was trained for 200K steps on PubMed and PMC for 270K steps, followed by an additional 1M steps of training on PubMed, using the same hyperparameter settings as BERT-base.

**ClinicalBERT** (Alsentzer et al., 2019) is also based on BERT-base, but with a focus on clinical tasks. We use the "Bio+Clinical BERT" checkpoint, which is initialized from BioBERT, and then trained using texts from MIMIC-III for 150K steps using a batch size of 32.

**RoBERTa** (Liu et al., 2019) is a state-of-the-art general purpose model. We experiment with RoBERTa-base and RoBERTa-large to understand

[2] https://pubmed.ncbi.nlm.nih.gov
[3] https://www.ncbi.nlm.nih.gov/pmc
[4] https://github.com/titipata/pubmed_parser

[5] https://github.com/google/sentencepiece

how general domain models perform on biomedical tasks. Both models are pretrained with much larger batch sizes than BERT, and use dynamic masking strategies to prevent the model from over-memorization of the training corpus. RoBERTa outperforms BERT on general-domain tasks (Liu et al., 2019).

**BioMed-RoBERTa** (Gururangan et al., 2020) is a recent model based on RoBERTa-base. BioMed-RoBERTa is initialized from RoBERTa-base, with an additional pretraining of 12.5K steps with a batch size of 2048, using a corpus of 2.7M scientific papers from Semantic Scholar (Ammar et al., 2018).

### 4.1 Pretraining New Models

In addition to these publicly available models, we also pretrain new models on the corpora in Section 3 and examine which design criteria are important for strong downstream performance on Bio-NLP tasks. We have three criteria we are interested in studying: i) The effect of model size on downstream performance; ii) the effect of pretraining corpus on downstream performance; and, iii) whether tokenizing with a domain-specific vocabulary has a strong effect on downstream performance.

We pretrain a variety of models based on the RoBERTa-base and RoBERTa-large architectures, with detailed ablations discussed in section 6.1. We use the PubMed data, and optionally include MIMIC-III. We initialize our models with the RoBERTa checkpoints, except when we use a domain-specific vocabulary, then we retrain the model from a random initialization. Our domain-specific vocabulary is a byte-level byte-pair encoding (BPE) dictionary learned over our PubMed pretraining corpus (Radford et al., 2019; Sennrich et al., 2016). Both the general-purpose (RoBERTa) and domain-specific vocabularies contain 50k subword units. Our best performing models use PubMed abstracts, PMC and MIMIC-III pretraining and a domain-specific vocabulary, and are referred to as "ours-base" and "ours-large" in the following sections.

## 5 Experimental Setup

### 5.1 Pretraining

We largely follow the pretraining methodology of Liu et al. (2019). We pretrain models using FAIRSEQ (Ott et al., 2019) on input sequences of 512 tokens, of which 15% are masked and later predicted.[6] We pretrain with batches of 8,192 sequences and use the AdamW optimizer (Loshchilov and Hutter, 2019) with $\beta_1 = 0.9, \beta_2 = 0.98, \epsilon = 1e - 6$. We regularize the model with dropout ($p = 0.1$) and weight decay ($\lambda = 0.01$). We pretrain all models for 500k steps using mixed precision on V100 GPUs. We linearly warmup the learning for the first 5% of steps and linearly decay the learning rate to 0 over the remaining steps. We use a learning rate of 6e-4 for base models and 4e-4 for large models.

### 5.2 Fine-tuning

We fine-tune models using 5 different seeds and report the median result on the test sets.

For sequence labelling tasks, we use learning rate of 1e-5 and a batch size of 32. For all sequence labelling tasks, we train for 20 epochs in total and choose the best checkpoint based on validation set performance (evaluating every 500 optimization steps). We fine-tuned the models with 5 seeds and report the median test results across these seeds.

For classification tasks, we use a learning rate of 0.002 and a batch size of 16. For HOC, ChemProt, MedNLI and I2B2-2010-RE, we run for a maximum of 10 epochs, and perform early stopping, evaluating performance on validation data every 200 optimization steps. As GAD and EU-ADR are split into 10 train/test cross-validation partitions, we choose early-stopping hyperparameters using one fold, and report the median test results on the other 9 folds.

## 6 Results

Table 2 shows our main results. The first columns show results for the general-purpose RoBERTa-base checkpoint, the next four show results for the specialized models mentioned in Section 4. The Roberta-large column shows results for the general-purpose RoBERTa-large checkpoint. The "ours-base" and "ours-large" columns refers to our proposed RoBERTa-base and RoBERTa-large sized models respectively, which were trained using PubMed and MIMIC-III data and a domain-specific vocabulary. We observe the following: i) RoBERTa-large outperforms RoBERTa-base consistently, despite having access to the same training

---

[6]Following Devlin et al. (2019) and Liu et al. (2019), with 10% probability we randomly unmask a masked token or replace it with a random token.

| Task Name | RoBERTa-base | SciBERT | BioBERT | Clinical-BERT | BioMed-RoBERTa | Ours-base | RoBERTa-large | Ours-large |
|---|---|---|---|---|---|---|---|---|
| **BC5CDR-C.** | 87.3 | 91.9 | 91.9 | 90.6 | 90.3 | 92.9 | 90.8 | **93.7** |
| **BC5CDR-D.** | 77.6 | 83.6 | 83.3 | 81.3 | 80.6 | 83.8 | 82.3 | **85.2** |
| **JNLPBA** | 79.5 | 80.3 | 80.4 | 79.3 | 80.2 | 80.6 | 80.1 | **81.0** |
| **NCBI-disease** | 84.7 | 86.9 | 87.6 | 86.1 | 86.1 | 87.7 | 87.1 | **89.0** |
| **BC4CHEMD** | 88.6 | 91.8 | 92.2 | 90.3 | 89.7 | 92.7 | 90.6 | **93.7** |
| **BC2GM** | 82.7 | 85.7 | 85.6 | 83.9 | 84.2 | 87.0 | 85.3 | **88.0** |
| **LINNEAEUS** | 79.8 | 84.1 | 86.2 | 84.8 | 84.2 | 85.3 | 87.8 | **88.4** |
| **Species-800** | 75.8 | 77.8 | 79.2 | 77.4 | 77.3 | 79.6 | 78.3 | **81.1** |
| **I2B2-2010** | 83.5 | 86.3 | 86.0 | 86.3 | 85.0 | 88.1 | 87.3 | **89.7** |
| **I2B2-2012** | 74.9 | 77.6 | 77.6 | 78.0 | 76.4 | 79.5 | 78.3 | **80.8** |
| **I2B2-2014** | 95.6 | 95.2 | 94.7 | 94.6 | 95.2 | 95.5 | 95.8 | **96.3** |
| **HOC** | 86.0 | 84.7 | 86.6 | 86.2 | **86.7** | 86.5 | 85.2 | 86.6 |
| **ChemProt** | 69.6 | 69.7 | 73.9 | 68.5 | 75.7 | 75.4 | 71.7 | **76.2** |
| **GAD** | 79.4 | 78.7 | 81.2 | 79.2 | 81.6 | **82.2** | 73.4 | 81.1 |
| **EU-ADR** | 85.0 | **85.5** | 85.0 | 85.1 | 85.0 | 85.0 | 85.0 | 85.0 |
| **DDI-2013** | 79.0 | 79.1 | 79.9 | 77.3 | 80.7 | 81.0 | 80.5 | **82.1** |
| **I2B2-2010-RE** | 72.4 | 69.8 | 74.4 | 74.0 | 75.0 | 75.0 | 75.2 | **78.6** |
| **MedNLI** | 81.4 | 79.7 | 82.5 | 81.8 | 85.1 | 87.1 | 83.3 | **88.5** |
| **Mean (Seq. Lab.)** | 82.7 | 85.6 | 85.9 | 84.8 | 84.5 | 86.6 | 85.8 | **87.9** |
| **Mean (Classif.)** | 79.0 | 78.2 | 80.5 | 78.9 | 81.4 | 81.7 | 79.2 | **82.6** |
| **Mean (PubMed)** | 81.1 | 83.1 | 84.1 | 82.3 | 83.3 | 84.6 | 82.9 | **85.5** |
| **Mean (Clinical)** | 81.6 | 81.7 | 83.0 | 82.9 | 83.3 | 85.1 | 84.0 | **86.8** |
| **Mean (all)** | 81.3 | 82.7 | 83.8 | 82.5 | 83.3 | 84.7 | 83.2 | **85.8** |

Table 2: Test results on all tasks for our RoBERTa baselines, publicly available models and our best Large and Base-sized models. All results are the median of 5 runs with different seeds

corpora; ii) We find that BioBERT performs best from the publicly available models that we experiment with; and iii) our newly introduced models perform well, achieving the best results for 17 out of the 18 tasks in our experiments, often by a large margin. The exception is EU-ADR, which has a small test set where all models achieve essentially the same classification accuracy.

Digging deeper, we note that standard RoBERTa-large is competitive with the four specialized models on sequence labelling tasks (85.8 vs 85.9) and outperforms them on clinical tasks (84.0 vs 83.3), despite having no specialized biomedical or clinical pretraining. This suggests that larger, more powerful general-purpose models could be a good default choice compared to smaller, less powerful domain-specific models.

Nevertheless, applying domain-specific training to otherwise-comparable models results in significant performance gains in our experiments, as shown by comparing ours-base and ours-large to RoBERTa-base and RoBERTa-large in Table 2, (+3.5% and +2.6% mean improvement), consistent with findings from previous work (Gururangan et al., 2020).

## 6.1 Ablations

The "ours-base" and "ours-large" models shown in Table 2 refer to the best language models that we trained in our experiments described in Section 4.1. These models use the RoBERTa architectures, are initialized with random weights, use a BPE vocabulary learnt from PubMed, and are pretrained on both our PubMed and MIMIC-III corpora. We performed a detailed ablation study to arrive at these models, and in what follows, we analyse the design decisions in detail. A summary of these results are shown in Table 3, a description of task groupings in Table 4, and full results can be found in Appendix A.2.

### 6.1.1 Effect of vocabulary

The effect of learning a dedicated biomedical vocabulary for base and large models can be analysed by comparing row 2 to row 3, row 4 to 5, and row 7 to 8 in Table 3. A dedicated vocabulary consistently improves sequence labelling tasks, improving results for base models by 0.7% and our large model by 0.6% on average. The difference is less consistent for classification tasks, improving the large model by 0.5%, but reducing performance on the small model by 0.7%. A specialized domain-specific vocabulary was also shown to be

| Model | Mean Clin-ical | Pub-Med | Seq. Lab. | Classif. | All |
|---|---|---|---|---|---|
| (1) RoBERTa-base | 81.6 | 81.1 | 82.7 | 79.0 | 81.3 |
| (2) +PM | 83.5 | 84.1 | 85.7 | 81.1 | 83.9 |
| (3) +PM+Voc. | 83.4 | 84.4 | 86.5 | 80.4 | 84.1 |
| (4) +PM+M3 | 85.0 | 84.0 | 85.9 | 81.6 | 84.2 |
| (5) +PM+M3+Voc. | <u>85.1</u> | <u>84.6</u> | <u>86.6</u> | <u>81.8</u> | <u>84.7</u> |
| (6) RoBERTa-large | 84.0 | 82.9 | 85.8 | 79.2 | 83.2 |
| (7) +PM+M3 | 85.7 | 85.1 | 87.3 | 82.1 | 85.3 |
| (8) +PM+M3+Voc. | **86.8** | **85.5** | **87.9** | **82.6** | **85.8** |

Table 3: Ablation test set results. Rows 5 and 8 correspond to "ours-base'" and "ours-large" in Table 2 respectively. **Bold** indicates the best model overall, <u>Underlined</u> indicates the best base model. "PM" indicates training with PubMed and PMC corpora and "M3" refers to the MIMIC-III corpus. "Voc" indicates using a dedicated biomedical vocabulary. Details of the tasks incuded in each column are given in Table 4

| Task group | Tasks in group |
|---|---|
| Clinical | I2B2-2010, I2B2-2012, I2B2-2014, I2B2-2010-RE, MedNLI |
| PubMed | BC5CDR-C, BC5CDR-D, JNLPBA, NCBI-D, BC4CHEMD, BC2GM, Linneaus, Species-800, HOC, ChemProt, GAD, EU-ADR, DDI-2013 |
| Seq. Lab. | BC5CDR-C, BC5CDR-D, JNLPBA, NCBI-D, BC4CHEMD, BC2GM, Linneaus, Species-800, I2B2-2010, I2B2-2012, I2B2-2014 |
| Classif. | HOC, ChemProt, GAD, EU-ADR, DDI-2013, I2B2-2010-RE, MedNLI |

Table 4: High-level task groupings. "Clinical" indicates clinical tasks, "PubMed" indicates tasks based on PubMed, "Seq. Lab." refers to sequence labelling, i.e. N.E.R. and De-ID. "Classif." refers to classification, i.e. relation extraction, multi-label classification and NLI.

useful in Beltagy et al. (2019). Since our specialized vocabulary models are trained from scratch only on biomedical data, we see that Wikipedia and WebText (Radford et al., 2019) pretraining is not necessary for strong performance.

### 6.1.2 Effect of training corpora

Table 3 also shows the results of text corpora. Rows 1 and 2 show that, unsurprisingly, including PubMed pretraining improves results over a RoBERTa-only model, by 2.6%. Comparing row 2 to row 4 and row 3 to 5 shows that including MIMIC-III in pretraining results in a large improvement on clinical tasks over PubMed-only models (+1.5% and +1.7%) but has little effect on PubMed-based tasks (-0.1% and +0.1%).

### 6.1.3 Effect of model size

Consistent with findings from the recent literature (Devlin et al., 2019; Liu et al., 2019; Radford et al., 2019; Brown et al., 2020), we find that large models perform consistently better than comparable smaller ones. Comparing row 1 to row 6, row 4 to 7, and row 5 to 8 in Table 3 shows average improvements of 2%, 1.6% and 0.9% respectively. These improvements are mostly driven by improved sequence labelling performance for large models.

### 6.2 Comparisons to the state-of-the-art

The focus of this paper was not to set the state-of-the-art on specific downstream tasks, but rather to evaluate which models consistently perform well. As such, we prioritized consistent hyperparameter search and did not consider task-specific tuning. Nevertheless, the models that we trained compare favorably to the state-of-the-art. Table 5 shows the best results obtained for each task in our experiments. In some cases, models used in our experiments have been reported with higher results in the literature. We attribute such difference to variance in test performance, small differences in pre-processing and differing levels of hyperparameter optimization and tuning. We control for test-set variance by running each model 5 times with different random seeds and reporting median results. We also use standard hyperparameter settings as reported in the literature. Table 5 compares our results to numbers reported in the literature. The best model in our experiments sets a new State-of-the-Art in 9 out of 18 tasks, and comes within 0.1% of the best reported result in another 3 tasks.

## 7 Distillation

In Section 6.1.3, we noted that larger models result in better accuracy. However, they also require more computational resources to run, limiting their applicability. Recent work addresses this issue by distilling larger models into smaller ones while retaining performance. Next, we investigate whether distillation works well in the BioNLP space.

### 7.1 Distillation Technique

Knowledge distillation (Hinton et al., 2015) aims to transfer the performance from a more accurate and computationally expensive *teacher model* into a more efficient *student model*. Typically, the student network is trained to mimic the output distribution

| Task Name | State-of-the-Art | | Our | Task Name | State-of-the-Art | | Our |
| | Method | Score | best | | Method | Score | best |
| --- | --- | --- | --- | --- | --- | --- | --- |
| BC5CDR-C. | Lee et al. (2019) | 93.5 | **93.7** | I2B2-2012 | Si et al. (2019) | **80.9** | 80.8 |
| BC5CDR-D. | Lee et al. (2019) | **87.2** | 85.2 | I2B2-2014 | Lee et al. (2019) | 93.0 | **96.3** |
| JNLPBA | Yoon et al. (2019) | 78.6 | **81.0** | HOC | Peng et al. (2019) | **87.3** | 87.2* |
| NCBI-disease | Lee et al. (2019) | **89.4** | 89.0 | ChemProt | Lee et al. (2019) | **76.5** | 76.4* |
| BC4CHEMD | Lee et al. (2019) | 92.4 | **93.7** | GAD | Bhasuran et al. (2018) | **83.9** | 82.2‡ |
| BC2GM | Lee et al. (2019) | 84.7 | **88.0** | EU-ADR | Lee et al. (2019) | **86.5** | 85.5† |
| LINNEAEUS | Giorgi and Bader (2018) | **93.5** | 88.4 | DDI-2013 | Peng et al. (2020) | 81.0 | **82.1‡** |
| Species-800 | Lee et al. (2019) | 75.3 | **81.1** | I2B2-2010-RE | Peng et al. (2019) | 76.4 | **78.6** |
| I2B2-2010 | Si et al. (2019) | **90.3** | 89.7 | MedNLI | Peng et al. (2020) | 84.2 | **88.5** |

Table 5: Our best models compared to best reported results in the literature. The best model in our experiments unless otherwise stated is RoBERTa-large with PubMed, MIMIC-III and specialized vocabulary ("ours-large" in Table 2). Other models are indicated by: (*) RoBERTa-large + PubMed + MIMIC-III; (†) SciBERT; (‡) RoBERTa-base + PubMed + MIMIC-III + vocab.

or internal activations of the teacher network, while keeping the teacher network's weights fixed.

In NLP, prior work has exploring distilling larger BERT-like models into smaller ones. Most of this work trains the student network to mimic a teacher that has already been finetuned for a specific task, i.e., *task-specific distillation* (Tsai et al., 2019; Turc et al., 2019; Sun et al., 2020). Recently, Sanh et al. (2020) showed that it is also possible to distill BERT-like models in a task-agnostic way by training the student to mimic the teacher's outputs and activations on the pretraining objective, i.e., masked language modeling (MLM). Task-agnostic distillation is appealing because it enables the distilled student model to be applied to a variety of downstream tasks. Accordingly, we primarily explore *task-agnostic distillation* in this work.

Recent work has also shown the importance of student network initialization. For example, Sanh et al. (2020) find that initializing the student network with a subset of layers from the teacher network outperforms random initialization; unfortunately this approach constrains the student network to the same embedding and hidden dimension as the teacher. Turc et al. (2019) instead advocate initializing the student model via standard MLM pretraining, finding that it outperforms the layer subset approach. Unfortunately, they only consider task-specific distillation, where the teacher network has already been finetuned to the end task, reducing the generality of the resulting student network.

We combine the approaches from Sanh et al. (2020) and Turc et al. (2019) by initializing the student network via standard MLM pretraining and then performing task-agnostic distillation by training the student to mimic a pretrained teacher on the MLM objective. We use our pretrained base model as the student network and large model as the teacher network. We also experiment with aligning the hidden states of the teacher's and student's last layer via a cosine embedding loss (Sanh et al., 2020). Since our student and teacher networks have different hidden state sizes, we learn a linear projection from the student's hidden states to the dimension of the teacher's hidden states prior to computing this loss.

We distill each student for 50k steps. Similar to pretraining (Section 5.1), we distill with a batch size of 8,192 and linearly warmup the learning rate for the first 5% of steps. We use a learning rate of 5e-4 and largely follow the distillation hyperparameter choices of Sanh et al. (2020). In particular, our loss function is a weighted combination of the original MLM cross entropy loss (with a weight $\alpha_{MLM} = 5.0$), a KL divergence loss term encouraging the student to match the teacher's outputs (with a weight $\alpha_{KL} = 2.0$) and optionally a cosine embedding loss term to align the student's and teacher's last layer hidden states (with a weight $\alpha_{cos} = 1.0$). For the KL loss we additionally employ a temperature of 2.0 to smooth the teacher's output distribution, following Sanh et al. (2020) and originally advocated by Hinton et al. (2015).

## 7.2 Distillation Results

Results for distillation are shown in Table 6. Since distillation trains the student for an additional 50k steps, we also include a baseline that just trains the student (base) model for longer without any distillation loss terms ("ours-base + train longer").

We find that distillation only slightly outperforms the original base model (+0.2% on average) and the original base model trained longer (+0.1% on average). Aligning the student and teacher hid-

| Model | Mean | Clin-ical | Pub Med | Seq. Lab. | Classif. | All |
|---|---|---|---|---|---|---|
| ours-base | | 85.1 | 84.6 | 86.6 | 81.8 | 84.7 |
| + train longer | | 85.0 | 84.7 | 86.6 | 81.8 | 84.8 |
| ours-large | | 86.8 | 85.5 | 87.9 | 82.6 | 85.8 |
| *Distillation results (teacher = large; student = base)* | | | | | | |
| distill | | 85.1 | 84.8 | 86.8 | 81.9 | 84.9 |
| distill + align | | 85.2 | 84.9 | 86.9 | 81.9 | 85.0 |

Table 6: Distillation results in context with our base and large models. Distillation outperforms both the original base model and the base model trained longer. Aligning the student and teacher's hidden states further improves performance, but the best student underperforms the large (teacher) model.

den states via a cosine embedding loss brings additional albeit slight gains (+0.1% on average relative to the "distill" model). This result is consistent with findings from Turc et al. (2019) showing that pretrained student models are a competitive baseline. The best student ("distill + align") improves upon the base model (+0.3% on average) but underperforms the large teacher (-0.8% on average).

## 8 Related Work

Pretrained word representations have been used in NLP modelling for many years (Mikolov et al., 2013; Pennington et al., 2014; Bojanowski et al., 2016), and have been specialised for BioNLP applications (Chiu et al., 2016; Wang et al., 2018b; Zhang et al., 2019). More recently, contextual embeddings have led to robust improvements across most NLP tasks, notably, ELMo (Peters et al., 2018) and BERT (Devlin et al., 2019), followed more recently by models such as XLNet (Yang et al., 2019), RoBERTa (Liu et al., 2019), XLM and XLM-RoBERTa (Lample and Conneau, 2019; Conneau et al., 2020) amongst others.

Several works adapt such models to scientific and biomedical domains. Four such models – SciBERT (Beltagy et al., 2019), BioBERT (Lee et al., 2019), ClinicalBERT (Alsentzer et al., 2019) and BioMed-RoBERTA (Gururangan et al., 2020) – are extensively covered in Section 4. Others include BlueBERT (Peng et al., 2019), which continues to pretrain BERT with data from PubMed and MIMIC-III. Zhu et al. (2018) and Si et al. (2019) train ELMo and BERT models on clinical data. In concurrent work, Gu et al. (2020) train models for PubMed-like text, but do not consider clinical text.

Methods for training or finetuning models on downstream tasks is also an active area of research.

We focus on well-established single-task finetuning techniques for BERT-like models using standard hyperparameter settings. Si et al. (2019) use complex task-specific models to yield strong results on clinical tasks, and Peng et al. (2020) investigate STILTS methods (Phang et al., 2019) on a suite of BioNLP tasks, achieving gains over baselines.

In this work, we build a suite of 18 tasks to evaluate our models. Aggregated benchmarks have become a common tool in NLP research, popularized by the GLUE benchmark (Wang et al., 2018a) for language understanding and its successor Super-GLUE (Wang et al., 2019). Evaluating on a suite of tasks is common in BioNLP too. Lee et al. (2019) evaluate on a set of 15 tasks, Peng et al. (2019) evaluate on 10 tasks referred to as "BLUE", Beltagy et al. (2019) and Gururangan et al. (2020) evaluate on 7 and 2 biomedical tasks respectively. Unfortunately, often there is little overlap between efforts, and different metrics and dataset splits are often used, making cross-model comparisons challenging, hence our efforts to evaluate all models on a single testbed. In concurrent work, Gu et al. (2020) also note this problem, and release a similar suite of tasks, referred to as BLURB, but do not include clinical tasks. We plan to evaluate our models on the "BLURB" benchmarks in future work.

## 9 Conclusion

We have thoroughly evaluated 6 open-source language models on 18 biomedical and clinical tasks. Of these models, we found that BioBERT was the best on biomedical tasks, but general-purpose RoBERTa-large performed best on clinical tasks. We then pretrained 6 of our own large-scale specialized biomedical and clinical language models. We determined that the most effective models were larger, used a dedicated biomedical vocabulary and included both biomedical and clinical pretraining. These models outperform all the other models in our experiments. Finally, we demonstrate that our base model can be further improved by knowledge distillation from our large model, although there remains a gap between the distillation-improved base model and our large model.

## Acknowledgments

The authors would like to thank Jinhyuk Lee, Kyle Lo, Yannis Papanikolaou, Andrea Pierleoni, Daniel O'Donovan and Sampo Pyysalo for their feedback and comments.

# References

Emily Alsentzer, John Murphy, William Boag, Wei-Hung Weng, Di Jindi, Tristan Naumann, and Matthew McDermott. 2019. Publicly Available Clinical BERT Embeddings. In *Proceedings of the 2nd Clinical Natural Language Processing Workshop*, pages 72–78, Minneapolis, Minnesota, USA. Association for Computational Linguistics.

Waleed Ammar, Dirk Groeneveld, Chandra Bhagavatula, Iz Beltagy, Miles Crawford, Doug Downey, Jason Dunkelberger, Ahmed Elgohary, Sergey Feldman, Vu Ha, Rodney Kinney, Sebastian Kohlmeier, Kyle Lo, Tyler Murray, Hsu-Han Ooi, Matthew Peters, Joanna Power, Sam Skjonsberg, Lucy Wang, Chris Wilhelm, Zheng Yuan, Madeleine van Zuylen, and Oren Etzioni. 2018. Construction of the Literature Graph in Semantic Scholar. In *Proceedings of the 2018 Conference of the North American Chapter of the Association for Computational Linguistics: Human Language Technologies, Volume 3 (Industry Papers)*, pages 84–91, New Orleans - Louisiana. Association for Computational Linguistics.

Simon Baker, Ilona Silins, Yufan Guo, Imran Ali, Johan Högberg, Ulla Stenius, and Anna Korhonen. 2016. Automatic semantic classification of scientific literature according to the hallmarks of cancer. *Bioinformatics*, 32(3):432–440. Publisher: Oxford Academic.

Iz Beltagy, Kyle Lo, and Arman Cohan. 2019. SciBERT: A Pretrained Language Model for Scientific Text. In *Proceedings of the 2019 Conference on Empirical Methods in Natural Language Processing and the 9th International Joint Conference on Natural Language Processing (EMNLP-IJCNLP)*, pages 3615–3620, Hong Kong, China. Association for Computational Linguistics.

Balu Bhasuran, Jeyakumar Natarajan, and . . 2018. Automatic extraction of gene-disease associations from literature using joint ensemble learning. *PloS One*, 13(7):e0200699.

Piotr Bojanowski, Edouard Grave, Armand Joulin, and Tomas Mikolov. 2016. Enriching Word Vectors with Subword Information. *arXiv:1607.04606 [cs]*. ArXiv: 1607.04606.

Àlex Bravo, Janet Piñero, Núria Queralt-Rosinach, Michael Rautschka, and Laura I. Furlong. 2015. Extraction of relations between genes and diseases from text and large-scale data analysis: implications for translational research. *BMC bioinformatics*, 16:55.

Tom B. Brown, Benjamin Pickman Mann, Nick Ryder, Melanie Subbiah, Jean Kaplan, Prafulla Dhariwal, Arvind Neelakantan, Pranav Shyam, Girish Sastry, Amanda Askell, Sandhini Agarwal, Ariel Herbert-Voss, G. Krüger, Tom Henighan, Rewon Child, Aditya Ramesh, Daniel M. Ziegler, Jeffrey Wu, Clemens Winter, Christopher Hesse, Mark Chen, Eric J Sigler, Mateusz Litwin, Scott Gray, Benjamin Chess, Jack Clark, Christopher Berner, Sam McCandlish, Alec Radford, Ilya Sutskever, and Dario Amodei. 2020. Language models are few-shot learners.

Billy Chiu, Gamal Crichton, Anna Korhonen, and Sampo Pyysalo. 2016. How to Train good Word Embeddings for Biomedical NLP. In *Proceedings of the 15th Workshop on Biomedical Natural Language Processing*, pages 166–174, Berlin, Germany. Association for Computational Linguistics.

Nigel Collier and Jin-Dong Kim. 2004. Introduction to the Bio-entity Recognition Task at JNLPBA. In *Proceedings of the International Joint Workshop on Natural Language Processing in Biomedicine and its Applications (NLPBA/BioNLP)*, pages 73–78, Geneva, Switzerland. COLING.

Alexis Conneau, Kartikay Khandelwal, Naman Goyal, Vishrav Chaudhary, Guillaume Wenzek, Francisco Guzmán, Edouard Grave, Myle Ott, Luke Zettlemoyer, and Veselin Stoyanov. 2020. Unsupervised cross-lingual representation learning at scale. In *Proceedings of the 58th Annual Meeting of the Association for Computational Linguistics*. Association for Computational Linguistics.

Jacob Devlin, Ming-Wei Chang, Kenton Lee, and Kristina Toutanova. 2019. BERT: Pre-training of Deep Bidirectional Transformers for Language Understanding. In *Proceedings of the 2019 Conference of the North American Chapter of the Association for Computational Linguistics: Human Language Technologies, Volume 1 (Long and Short Papers)*, pages 4171–4186, Minneapolis, Minnesota. Association for Computational Linguistics.

Rezarta Islamaj Doğan, Robert Leaman, and Zhiyong Lu. 2014. NCBI Disease Corpus: A Resource for Disease Name Recognition and Concept Normalization. *Journal of biomedical informatics*, 47:1–10.

Martin Gerner, Goran Nenadic, and Casey M. Bergman. 2010. LINNAEUS: a species name identification system for biomedical literature. *BMC bioinformatics*, 11:85.

John M. Giorgi and Gary D. Bader. 2018. Transfer learning for biomedical named entity recognition with neural networks. *Bioinformatics (Oxford, England)*, 34(23):4087–4094.

Yu Gu, Robert Tinn, Hao Cheng, Michael Lucas, Naoto Usuyama, Xiaodong Liu, Tristan Naumann, Jianfeng Gao, and Hoifung Poon. 2020. Domain-Specific Language Model Pretraining for Biomedical Natural Language Processing. *arXiv:2007.15779 [cs]*. ArXiv: 2007.15779.

Suchin Gururangan, Ana Marasović, Swabha Swayamdipta, Kyle Lo, Iz Beltagy, Doug Downey, and Noah A. Smith. 2020. Don't Stop Pretraining: Adapt Language Models to Domains and Tasks. *arXiv:2004.10964 [cs]*. ArXiv: 2004.10964.

María Herrero-Zazo, Isabel Segura-Bedmar, Paloma Martínez, and Thierry Declerck. 2013. The DDI corpus: An annotated corpus with pharmacological substances and drug–drug interactions. *Journal of Biomedical Informatics*, 46(5):914–920.

Geoffrey Hinton, Oriol Vinyals, and Jeffrey Dean. 2015. Distilling the knowledge in a neural network. In *NIPS Deep Learning and Representation Learning Workshop*.

Martin Krallinger, Obdulia Rabal, Saber Ahmad Akhondi, Martín Pérez Pérez, Jésús López Santamaría, Gael Pérez Rodríguez, Georgios Tsatsaronis, Ander Intxaurrondo, José Antonio Baso López, Umesh Nandal, Erin M. van Buel, A. Poorna Chandrasekhar, Marleen Rodenburg, Astrid Lægreid, Marius A. Doornenbal, Julen Oyarzábal, Anália Lourenço, and Alfonso Valencia. 2017. Overview of the BioCreative VI chemical-protein interaction Track.

Martin Krallinger, Obdulia Rabal, Florian Leitner, Miguel Vazquez, David Salgado, Zhiyong Lu, Robert Leaman, Yanan Lu, Donghong Ji, Daniel M. Lowe, Roger A. Sayle, Riza Theresa Batista-Navarro, Rafal Rak, Torsten Huber, Tim Rocktäschel, Sérgio Matos, David Campos, Buzhou Tang, Hua Xu, Tsendsuren Munkhdalai, Keun Ho Ryu, SV Ramanan, Senthil Nathan, Slavko Žitnik, Marko Bajec, Lutz Weber, Matthias Irmer, Saber A. Akhondi, Jan A. Kors, Shuo Xu, Xin An, Utpal Kumar Sikdar, Asif Ekbal, Masaharu Yoshioka, Thaer M. Dieb, Miji Choi, Karin Verspoor, Madian Khabsa, C. Lee Giles, Hongfang Liu, Komandur Elayavilli Ravikumar, Andre Lamurias, Francisco M. Couto, Hong-Jie Dai, Richard Tzong-Han Tsai, Caglar Ata, Tolga Can, Anabel Usié, Rui Alves, Isabel Segura-Bedmar, Paloma Martínez, Julen Oyarzabal, and Alfonso Valencia. 2015. The CHEMDNER corpus of chemicals and drugs and its annotation principles. *Journal of Cheminformatics*, 7(1):S2.

Taku Kudo. 2018. Subword Regularization: Improving Neural Network Translation Models with Multiple Subword Candidates. *arXiv:1804.10959 [cs]*. ArXiv: 1804.10959.

Guillaume Lample and Alexis Conneau. 2019. Cross-lingual Language Model Pretraining. *arXiv:1901.07291 [cs]*. ArXiv: 1901.07291.

Jinhyuk Lee, Wonjin Yoon, Sungdong Kim, Donghyeon Kim, Sunkyu Kim, Chan Ho So, and Jaewoo Kang. 2019. BioBERT: a pre-trained biomedical language representation model for biomedical text mining. *Bioinformatics*, 36(4):1234–1240. _eprint: https://academic.oup.com/bioinformatics/article-pdf/36/4/1234/32527770/btz682.pdf.

Jiao Li, Yueping Sun, Robin J. Johnson, Daniela Sciaky, Chih-Hsuan Wei, Robert Leaman, Allan Peter Davis, Carolyn J. Mattingly, Thomas C. Wiegers, and Zhiyong Lu. 2016. BioCreative V CDR task corpus: a resource for chemical disease relation extraction. *Database: The Journal of Biological Databases and Curation*, 2016.

Margaret Li, Stephen Roller, Ilia Kulikov, Sean Welleck, Y.-Lan Boureau, Kyunghyun Cho, and Jason Weston. 2019. Don't Say That! Making Inconsistent Dialogue Unlikely with Unlikelihood Training. *arXiv:1911.03860 [cs]*. ArXiv: 1911.03860.

Yinhan Liu, Myle Ott, Naman Goyal, Jingfei Du, Mandar Joshi, Danqi Chen, Omer Levy, Mike Lewis, Luke Zettlemoyer, and Veselin Stoyanov. 2019. Roberta: A robustly optimized BERT pretraining approach. *arXiv preprint arXiv:1907.11692*.

Ilya Loshchilov and Frank Hutter. 2019. Decoupled weight decay regularization. In *International Conference on Learning Representations*.

Tomas Mikolov, Ilya Sutskever, Kai Chen, Greg Corrado, and Jeffrey Dean. 2013. Distributed Representations of Words and Phrases and Their Compositionality. In *Proceedings of the 26th International Conference on Neural Information Processing Systems - Volume 2*, NIPS'13, pages 3111–3119, USA. Curran Associates Inc. Event-place: Lake Tahoe, Nevada.

Erik M. van Mulligen, Annie Fourrier-Reglat, David Gurwitz, Mariam Molokhia, Ainhoa Nieto, Gianluca Trifiro, Jan A. Kors, and Laura I. Furlong. 2012. The EU-ADR corpus: annotated drugs, diseases, targets, and their relationships. *Journal of Biomedical Informatics*, 45(5):879–884.

Myle Ott, Sergey Edunov, Alexei Baevski, Angela Fan, Sam Gross, Nathan Ng, David Grangier, and Michael Auli. 2019. fairseq: A fast, extensible toolkit for sequence modeling. In *Proceedings of NAACL-HLT 2019: Demonstrations*.

Evangelos Pafilis, Sune P. Frankild, Lucia Fanini, Sarah Faulwetter, Christina Pavloudi, Aikaterini Vasileiadou, Christos Arvanitidis, and Lars Juhl Jensen. 2013. The SPECIES and ORGANISMS Resources for Fast and Accurate Identification of Taxonomic Names in Text. *PloS One*, 8(6):e65390.

Yifan Peng, Qingyu Chen, and Zhiyong Lu. 2020. An Empirical Study of Multi-Task Learning on BERT for Biomedical Text Mining. *arXiv:2005.02799 [cs]*. ArXiv: 2005.02799.

Yifan Peng, Shankai Yan, and Zhiyong Lu. 2019. Transfer Learning in Biomedical Natural Language Processing: An Evaluation of BERT and ELMo on Ten Benchmarking Datasets. In *Proceedings of the 18th BioNLP Workshop and Shared Task*, pages 58–65, Florence, Italy. Association for Computational Linguistics.

Jeffrey Pennington, Richard Socher, and Christopher Manning. 2014. Glove: Global Vectors for Word

Representation. In *Proceedings of the 2014 Conference on Empirical Methods in Natural Language Processing (EMNLP)*, pages 1532–1543, Doha, Qatar. Association for Computational Linguistics.

Matthew E. Peters, Mark Neumann, Mohit Iyyer, Matt Gardner, Christopher Clark, Kenton Lee, and Luke Zettlemoyer. 2018. Deep contextualized word representations. *arXiv:1802.05365 [cs]*. ArXiv: 1802.05365.

Jason Phang, Thibault Févry, and Samuel R. Bowman. 2019. Sentence Encoders on STILTs: Supplementary Training on Intermediate Labeled-data Tasks. *arXiv:1811.01088 [cs]*. ArXiv: 1811.01088.

Alec Radford, Jeff Wu, Rewon Child, David Luan, Dario Amodei, and Ilya Sutskever. 2019. Language models are unsupervised multitask learners.

Alexey Romanov and Chaitanya Shivade. 2018. Lessons from Natural Language Inference in the Clinical Domain. In *Proceedings of the 2018 Conference on Empirical Methods in Natural Language Processing*, pages 1586–1596, Brussels, Belgium. Association for Computational Linguistics.

Victor Sanh, Lysandre Debut, Julien Chaumond, and Thomas Wolf. 2020. DistilBERT, a distilled version of BERT: smaller, faster, cheaper and lighter. *arXiv:1910.01108 [cs]*. ArXiv: 1910.01108.

Rico Sennrich, Barry Haddow, and Alexandra Birch. 2016. Neural Machine Translation of Rare Words with Subword Units. In *Proceedings of the 54th Annual Meeting of the Association for Computational Linguistics (Volume 1: Long Papers)*, pages 1715–1725, Berlin, Germany. Association for Computational Linguistics.

Yuqi Si, Jingqi Wang, Hua Xu, and Kirk Roberts. 2019. Enhancing Clinical Concept Extraction with Contextual Embeddings. *Journal of the American Medical Informatics Association*, 26(11):1297–1304. ArXiv: 1902.08691.

Larry Smith, Lorraine K. Tanabe, Rie Johnson nee Ando, Cheng-Ju Kuo, I.-Fang Chung, Chun-Nan Hsu, Yu-Shi Lin, Roman Klinger, Christoph M. Friedrich, Kuzman Ganchev, Manabu Torii, Hongfang Liu, Barry Haddow, Craig A. Struble, Richard J. Povinelli, Andreas Vlachos, William A. Baumgartner, Lawrence Hunter, Bob Carpenter, Richard Tzong-Han Tsai, Hong-Jie Dai, Feng Liu, Yifei Chen, Chengjie Sun, Sophia Katrenko, Pieter Adriaans, Christian Blaschke, Rafael Torres, Mariana Neves, Preslav Nakov, Anna Divoli, Manuel Maña-López, Jacinto Mata, and W. John Wilbur. 2008. Overview of BioCreative II gene mention recognition. *Genome Biology*, 9 Suppl 2:S2.

Amber Stubbs, Christopher Kotfila, and Ozlem Uzuner. 2015. Automated systems for the de-identification of longitudinal clinical narratives: Overview of 2014 i2b2/UTHealth shared task Track 1. *Journal of biomedical informatics*, 58(Suppl):S11–S19.

Amber Stubbs and Ozlem Uzuner. 2015. Annotating longitudinal clinical narratives for de-identification: the 2014 i2b2/UTHealth Corpus. *Journal of biomedical informatics*, 58(Suppl):S20–S29.

Weiyi Sun, Anna Rumshisky, and Ozlem Uzuner. 2013a. Annotating temporal information in clinical narratives. *Journal of Biomedical Informatics*, 46 Suppl:S5–12.

Weiyi Sun, Anna Rumshisky, and Ozlem Uzuner. 2013b. Evaluating temporal relations in clinical text: 2012 i2b2 Challenge. *Journal of the American Medical Informatics Association : JAMIA*, 20(5):806–813.

Zhiqing Sun, Hongkun Yu, Xiaodan Song, Renjie Liu, Yiming Yang, and Denny Zhou. 2020. MobileBERT: a compact task-agnostic BERT for resource-limited devices. In *Proceedings of the 58th Annual Meeting of the Association for Computational Linguistics*, pages 2158–2170, Online. Association for Computational Linguistics.

Henry Tsai, Jason Riesa, Melvin Johnson, Naveen Arivazhagan, Xin Li, and Amelia Archer. 2019. Small and practical BERT models for sequence labeling. In *Proceedings of the 2019 Conference on Empirical Methods in Natural Language Processing and the 9th International Joint Conference on Natural Language Processing (EMNLP-IJCNLP)*, pages 3632–3636, Hong Kong, China. Association for Computational Linguistics.

Iulia Turc, Ming-Wei Chang, Kenton Lee, and Kristina Toutanova. 2019. Well-Read Students Learn Better: On the Importance of Pre-training Compact Models. *arXiv:1908.08962 [cs]*. ArXiv: 1908.08962.

Özlem Uzuner, Brett R South, Shuying Shen, and Scott L DuVall. 2011. 2010 i2b2/VA challenge on concepts, assertions, and relations in clinical text. *Journal of the American Medical Informatics Association : JAMIA*, 18(5):552–556.

Alex Wang, Yada Pruksachatkun, Nikita Nangia, Amanpreet Singh, Julian Michael, Felix Hill, Omer Levy, and Samuel Bowman. 2019. SuperGLUE: A Stickier Benchmark for General-Purpose Language Understanding Systems. In H. Wallach, H. Larochelle, A. Beygelzimer, F. d\textquotesingle Alché-Buc, E. Fox, and R. Garnett, editors, *Advances in Neural Information Processing Systems 32*, pages 3261–3275. Curran Associates, Inc.

Alex Wang, Amanpreet Singh, Julian Michael, Felix Hill, Omer Levy, and Samuel Bowman. 2018a. GLUE: A Multi-Task Benchmark and Analysis Platform for Natural Language Understanding. In *Proceedings of the 2018 EMNLP Workshop BlackboxNLP: Analyzing and Interpreting Neural Networks for NLP*, pages 353–355, Brussels, Belgium. Association for Computational Linguistics.

Lucy Lu Wang, Kyle Lo, Yoganand Chandrasekhar, Russell Reas, Jiangjiang Yang, Doug Burdick, Darrin Eide, Kathryn Funk, Yannis Katsis, Rodney Kinney, Yunyao Li, Ziyang Liu, William Merrill, Paul Mooney, Dewey Murdick, Devvret Rishi, Jerry Sheehan, Zhihong Shen, Brandon Stilson, Alex Wade, Kuansan Wang, Nancy Xin Ru Wang, Chris Wilhelm, Boya Xie, Douglas Raymond, Daniel S. Weld, Oren Etzioni, and Sebastian Kohlmeier. 2020. CORD-19: The COVID-19 Open Research Dataset. *arXiv:2004.10706 [cs]*. ArXiv: 2004.10706.

Yanshan Wang, Sijia Liu, Naveed Afzal, Majid Rastegar-Mojarad, Liwei Wang, Feichen Shen, Paul Kingsbury, and Hongfang Liu. 2018b. A comparison of word embeddings for the biomedical natural language processing. *Journal of Biomedical Informatics*, 87:12–20.

Thomas Wolf, Lysandre Debut, Victor Sanh, Julien Chaumond, Clement Delangue, Anthony Moi, Pierric Cistac, Tim Rault, R'emi Louf, Morgan Funtowicz, and Jamie Brew. 2019. Huggingface's transformers: State-of-the-art natural language processing. *ArXiv*, abs/1910.03771.

Zhilin Yang, Zihang Dai, Yiming Yang, Jaime Carbonell, Russ R Salakhutdinov, and Quoc V Le. 2019. Xlnet: Generalized autoregressive pretraining for language understanding. In *Advances in neural information processing systems*, pages 5754–5764.

Wonjin Yoon, Chan Ho So, Jinhyuk Lee, and Jaewoo Kang. 2019. CollaboNet: collaboration of deep neural networks for biomedical named entity recognition. *BMC Bioinformatics*, 20(10):249.

Yijia Zhang, Qingyu Chen, Zhihao Yang, Hongfei Lin, and Zhiyong Lu. 2019. BioWordVec, improving biomedical word embeddings with subword information and MeSH. *Scientific Data*, 6(1):52. Number: 1 Publisher: Nature Publishing Group.

Henghui Zhu, Ioannis Ch Paschalidis, and Amir Tahmasebi. 2018. Clinical Concept Extraction with Contextual Word Embedding. *arXiv:1810.10566 [cs]*. ArXiv: 1810.10566.

# Assessment of DistilBERT performance on Named Entity Recognition task for the detection of Protected Health Information and medical concepts

**Macarious Abadeer**
School of Computer Science
Carleton University
Ottawa, Canada
`macarious.abadeer@carleton.ca`

## Abstract

Bidirectional Encoder Representations from Transformers (BERT) models achieve state-of-the-art performance on a number of Natural Language Processing tasks. However, their model size on disk often exceeds 1 GB and the process of fine-tuning them and using them to run inference consumes significant hardware resources and runtime. This makes them hard to deploy to production environments. This paper fine-tunes DistilBERT, a lightweight deep learning model, on medical text for the named entity recognition task of Protected Health Information (PHI) and medical concepts. This work provides a full assessment of the performance of DistilBERT in comparison with BERT models that were pre-trained on medical text. For Named Entity Recognition task of PHI, DistilBERT achieved almost the same results as medical versions of BERT in terms of $F1$ score at almost half the runtime and consuming approximately half the disk space. On the other hand, for the detection of medical concepts, DistilBERT's $F1$ score was lower by 4 points on average than medical BERT variants.

## 1 Introduction

Clinical records play an important role in the discovery of disease treatment and the advancement of medical research (Jagannatha and Yu, 2016). The clinical text corpora used for research includes doctor's notes, clinical study reports and medical articles. There are several regulations that control the use and transfer of personal information such as General Data Protection Regulation (GDPR) in Europe, Personal Information Protection and Electronic Documents Act (PIPEDA) in Canada and Health Insurance Portability and Accountability Act (HIPAA) in the US. HIPAA Safe Harbor for example lists 18 attributes that can potentially identify an individual and dictates that all of them

need to be de-identified before a dataset can be shared for secondary use such as research (HIPAA, 2015). One possible approach is the manual annotation and de-identification of clinical text. This approach is simply not feasible due to the high cost of experts manually annotating clinical documents (Friedrich et al., 2019). Due to the advancement of Natural Language Processing research, the de-identification of PHI was framed as a Named Entity Recognition (NER) problem that can be solved by deep learning techniques. This work fine-tuned a deep learning model on a medical corpus and assessed its quality in detecting PHI and medical concepts in comparison with models whose embeddings were generated from a medical corpus.

The paper is organized as follows: in the next section we review the state-of-the-art for solving NER tasks used in the detection of PHI. In Section 3 and 4 we define the problem and detail our methodology. In Section 5 we present our results and we finally conclude in Section 6.

## 2 Related Work

In a major breakthrough in NLP research, a simpler neural network architecture was introduced by Vaswani et al. (2017) called Transformers which is an attention-based mechanism. Its main premise was to do away with recurrence and convolution in neural networks. Self attention generates a representation by connecting different positions of a given sequence. Self attention is easier to parallelize and enables better understanding of long-range dependencies. Transformers enabled the introduction of Bidirectional Encoder Representations from Transformers (BERT) by Devlin et al. (2019). BERT allows the generation of representations utilizing context from both directions of a sequence. It consists of two steps: pre-training and fine-tuning. Pre-training is the unsupervised learn-



*Proceedings of the 3rd Clinical Natural Language Processing Workshop*, pages 158–167
November 19, 2020. ©2020 Association for Computational Linguistics

ing step to generate the representations. BERT was pre-trained on Wikipedia and BookCorpus. The pre-training step consists of two tasks: Masked Language Model (MLM) which masks a certain percentage of the input sequence and attempts to predict those missing tokens. The second pre-training task is Next Sentence Prediction (NSP) which was specifically added to help with tasks involving relationship between a pair of sentences such as Question Answering. The fine-tuning is the supervised learning portion where BERT is trained on custom datasets by the user for their respective tasks with little to no feature engineering required for a specific NLP downstream task. Further attempts have been made to improve on the original BERT such as RoBERTa introduced by Liu et al. (2019) which assessed the impact of different hyperparameters and concluded that training over longer sequences and removing NSP achieves better results. Other BERT variations were also pre-trained on medical domain corpora such as BioBERT (Lee et al., 2019), BlueBERT (Peng et al., 2019) and ClinicalBERT (Alsentzer et al., 2019) that were pre-trained on PubMed which contains biomedical research articles and MIMIC-III which contains doctors' notes from the intensive care unit admissions. The medical versions of BERT proposed higher $F1$ score performance when evaluated on biomedical tasks including NER.

BERT and its variations, however, require extensive computational resources to deploy in production environments. To address these limitations, DistilBERT was introduced by Sanh et al. (2019). The authors applied the concept of knowledge distillation to produce a lighter version of BERT that is 40% smaller, 60% faster and achieves 97% of the original BERT $F1$ score when measured on Question Answering task. It can also be deployed on lower power computing chips such as mobile devices to run predictions. Further studies were published to assess the performance of DistilBERT compared to other state-of-the-art models. In a study by Büyüköz et al. (2020), it compared DistilBERT's performance against ELMo on two text classification tasks. The first was a binary classification task of protest and non-protest news from English articles from local newspapers in India and China. The second task was a sentence classification task of movie reviews on Rotten Tomatoes. The authors concluded that DistilBERT generalizes better than ELMo while having similar $F1$ score.

Wang et al. (2020) also used DistilBERT for a machine translation task to generate synthetic data to diagnose language impairment in children. DistilBERT achieved 5% and 15% higher $F1$ scores when compared with ELMo and Word2Vec respectively.

## 3   Problem Statement

Although BERT achieved state-of-the-art for a wide variety of NLP tasks, they are hard to train and deploy in a production environment as they require excessive computational power. For example, the original BERT took 4 days to pre-train on 4 TPUs. Furthermore, there are few limitations of using a non-medical corpus to train a model for medical tasks (Patel et al., 2017). There are medical-specific terms that do not usually exist in general corpora such as news or Wikipedia. There are other terms that mean something else in a medical context. The idea of training on domain-specific corpora was explored by Cengiz et al. (2019) where the authors pre-trained BERT on specific domains such as telephone conversations, travel guides, government records and fiction novels. This achieved higher performance for related tasks than the generic version of BERT.

While versions of BERT pre-trained on medical text are publicly available as pointed out in Section 2, these models share the same computational power limitations of the original BERT. For example, the pre-training of ClinicalBERT took 18 days on a single GPU.

There are no studies we could find as of date that fine-tuned and assessed the performance of DistilBERT on medical tasks such as NER of PHI in medical records. Although in the context of de-identification predictions performance is more critical than runtime, the resource limitations may pose a challenge for healthcare organizations to comply with privacy regulations. Especially if they need to generate pre-trained embeddings or incrementally fine-tune their models on new data frequently.

The question we attempt to answer through this paper is how DistilBERT performs when fine-tuned on medical corpora compared to medical pre-trained versions of BERT. Is it possible to achieve a comparable result to medical pre-trained BERT variations such as ClinicalBERT with a much lighter version such as DistilBERT?

## 4   Method

DistilBERT is based on the concept of knowledge distillation introduced by Hinton et al. (2015). The main characteristic of a machine learning model evaluation is how it performs on unseen data. While high-confidence predictions are picked during inference, there are useful information in low-confidence predictions that can help explain how well a model can generalize. Knowledge distillation is a compression algorithm that involves the transfer of such information from the main model, called the teacher, to a smaller distilled version, called the student. Further details on knowledge distillation are in the paper by Hinton et al. (2015). DistilBERT consists of the same two steps as the original BERT: pre-training, which in this case creates the student model and fine-tuning which uses the pre-trained student model to train on a custom dataset for a specific task. DistilBERT was pre-trained on the same datasets as the original BERT: BookCorpus and Wikipedia. The assessment approach was to use the pre-trained DistilBERT and fine-tune it on i2b2 2010 and i2b2 2014 datasets for NER and compare the results with ClinicalBERT (Alsentzer et al., 2019) and BlueBERT (Peng et al., 2019) that were both pre-trained on medical text. The comparison was done in terms of runtime and $F1$ score.

The `transformers` package developed by Hugging Face Co[1] was used for all the experiments in this work. Its developers are also the creators of DistilBERT and it hosts a wide variety of pre-trained BERT models including the ones mentioned in Section 2. The package is implemented in `python` and this work was implemented in PyTorch.

Throughout this paper, by 'training' we are referring to the supervised learning step that BERT and its variants call 'fine-tuning' in order to avoid confusion with hyperparameter tuning. By 'pre-training' we are referring to the unsupervised step that generates the embeddings.

### 4.1   Datasets

**i2b2 2014 - PHI:**   A dataset compiled by the National Center for Biomedical Computing (NCBC) also known as i2b2: Informatics for Integrating Biology and the Bedside. It contains doctors' notes provided by Partners HealthCare System in Boston.

The 2014 version has an annotated text of PHI labels. The raw data is an XML file with positions of the PHI labels.

In total, there are 23 different labels with the top 3 accounting to 69% of all label instances (DATE, DOCTOR, HOSPITAL) and the bottom 7 having insignificant counts accounting to near-zero percentages. Since it was shown by Sokolova (2011) that using granular entities for PHI achieves better de-identification results than binary classification of whether an entity is a PHI, we chose to use all the labels for NER classification instead of binary PHI/non-PHI classification.

**i2b2 2010 - Concepts:**   This dataset is also compiled by NCBC. It is another NER task that is focused on the extraction of medical concepts from patient reports. Specifically, it extracts medical problems, treatments, and tests. This dataset was included to validate whether models pre-trained on general domain corpora perform poorly on detecting medical terms and if yes, how poorly. Furthermore, medical history contains rich information about patients that HIPAA (2015) advised can individually identify a person.

Access to both datasets was requested through the Department of Biomedical Informatics[2] at Harvard Medical School which is provided for free to researchers and students.

The BERT model and its variations including DistilBERT expect NER datasets to be in CONLL-2003 format introduced by Tjong Kim Sang and De Meulder (2003). It was designed for NER tasks. Every line contains the word, a space, and the label of the entity in BIO format: B indicates the beginning token of a label, I for inside a multi-token label, and O for a token outside the entities to predict. Sequences are separated by two empty lines.

In order to produce the training, development and testing datasets in CONLL format from the raw files, we used the same scripts[3] used by ClinicalBERT authors (Alsentzer et al., 2019).

BERT variants including DistilBERT have a hard limit on sequence length set to 512 tokens. Some sequences in the raw datasets exceeded that limit. Those longer sequences had to be further split to fit the different sequence length experiments. The script referred to in the `transformers` pack-

---

[1] `https://github.com/huggingface/`
`transformers`

[2] `https://portal.dbmi.hms.harvard.edu`
[3] `https://github.com/EmilyAlsentzer/`
`clinicalBERT`

age's documentation[4] was used for splitting longer sequences. Table 1 shows token and sequence count after pre-processing.

|       | i2b2 2010 | | i2b2 2014 | |
|-------|-----------|--------|-----------|--------|
|       | tokens    | seq.   | tokens    | seq.   |
| train | 126,111   | 14,511 | 425,566   | 45,641 |
| dev   | 7,612     | 1,804  | 58,053    | 5,241  |
| test  | 229,992   | 27,626 | 306,441   | 32,587 |

Table 1: Tokens and Sequence Count for i2b2 2010 and i2b2 2014 after pre-processing

The train/test split for both i2b2 2010 and 2014 was already done by i2b2. In order to compare with other papers that used the same datasets as baseline, the train/test split was not modified even though i2b2 2010's training dataset has fewer tokens than its testing dataset.

### 4.2 Training

The NER examples provided by the `transformers` package was used as a starting point for training and evaluation. The full list of parameters used is discussed in Section 4.4. Adam optimizer (Kingma and Ba, 2014), a replacement to the generic stochastic gradient descent, was used for computing the loss function. The optimizer is initialized with learning rate, weight decay as well as the Adam $\varepsilon$ constant set to $10^{-8}$ to avoid division by zero in the Adam calculation when the gradient approaches zero. A learning schedule was setup to dynamically modify the learning rate during training. The learning rate linearly increases during a phase of "warmup" steps, then linearly decreases after the warmup period. This is done because early on during training the model is far from convergence therefore updating the weights does not need to happen frequently. For every epoch in training, the loss is calculated, optimizer and scheduler steps incremented, model evaluated on the development set, and checkpoint is saved to disk.

### 4.3 Evaluation

The evaluation uses `seqeval.metrics` package to calculate precision, recall and $F1$ score. A classification report was also produced to display the scores for every label as well as the micro and macro average across labels for all 3 metrics. The classification report calculates the individual label scores using instances of the labels. For example, it does not calculate the scores for `B-DATE` and `I-DATE` individually but for the whole `DATE` label.

We ranked the best run based on micro average $F1$ score followed by recall if there's a tie in $F1$. In the context of de-identification, high recall is more critical since incorrectly annotating a non-PHI as a PHI token is less damaging than the opposite; or "leaking" personal information.

### 4.4 Experiments

The experiments were run on a GeForce GTX 1080 Ti, with 6 virtual cores, 64 GB of memory, 126 GB in hard drive storage and running Ubuntu 18.04.

The following are the different models that were experimented with:

**distilbert-base-cased:** DistilBERT English language model distilled from the cased version of Toronto BookCorpus and English Wikipedia.

**distilbert-base-uncased:** DistilBERT English language model distilled from the lowercase corpus version of distilbert-base-cased.

For the comparison with BERT variants pre-trained on medical corpus we used the following models:

**BlueBERT** Formerly known as NCBI BERT. A pre-trained version of BERT on uncased PubMed abstracts and MIMIC-III notes (Peng et al., 2019).

**BioClinicalBERT:** Also known as Clinical-BERT (Alsentzer et al., 2019). Another implementation of PubMed+MIMIC-III BERT which also included a hospital discharge summary corpus but pre-trained on cased text.

Both the cased and uncased versions of Distil-BERT models are listed since they produced significantly different results. This is also required for a direct comparison since ClinicalBERT used a cased corpus while BlueBERT used an uncased one. Therefore, when comparing with Clinical-BERT, the cased version of DistilBERT was used. While when comparing with BlueBERT, the uncased version was used.

In total, 40 experiments were run to choose best-performing training parameters based on the highest micro average $F1$. For maximum sequence lengths, experiments ranged from using 128 to maximum allowed of 512. In terms of batch sizes,

---



[4] `https://github.com/stefan-it/fine-tuned-berts-seq`

16 and 32 were experimented with. Using a high maximum sequence length with a high batch size, however, resulted in out of memory issues. Therefore, 32 batch size was only used with maximum sequence length up to 256 while a batch size of 16 was used for higher maximum sequence lengths. All the experiments ran for 3 training epochs except one experiment ran for 2 epochs on the i2b2 2014 dataset to match the parameters reported by Alsentzer et al. (2019) for ClinicalBERT. The full range of parameters used in the experiments are shown in Table 2. The rest are all the defaults built-in the `transformers` package.

| Parameter | Values |
| --- | --- |
| max. seq. length | $\{128, 150, 256, 300, 512\}$ |
| batch size | $\{16, 32\}$ |
| learning rate | $5 \times 10^{-5}$ |
| training epochs | $\{2, 3\}$ |
| lowercase corpus | $\{True, False\}$ |

Table 2: Parameters experimented with

## 5 Results

We can draw the following insights from the results presented in Table 3. In terms of micro average $F1$ score, the performance gap between DistilBERT and its medical variants were dataset-specific. For the detection of PHI using i2b2 2014, DistilBERT scored within 0.5% of its clinical variants. It scored 0.56% higher than BlueBERT but 0.45% lower than ClinicalBERT. While for the detection of medical terms using i2b2 2010, the medical variants of BERT achieved 5% higher $F1$ score on average than DistilBERT. These results show that for the context of de-identification, using DistilBERT does not suffer in performance. This can be attributed to the generic nature of PHI labels such as dates, names and addresses that exist in general-domain corpus such as Wikipedia. While in the context of detecting medical terms, using a compressed model such as DistilBERT can result in significantly lower score than medically pre-trained models. Overall, the cased version of the models achieved $F1$ score of 6.82% higher on average than the uncased versions regardless of the dataset. This performance gap can be attributed to the importance of case information to the NER task according to BERT documentation[5].

<hr>

[5] `https://github.com/google-research/bert`

Another aspect of the results we were interested in was runtime. As mentioned in Section 3, the original BERT is heavy to use requiring significant computing resources. DistilBERT runtime was 43% faster on average than the medical variants of BERT. It also produced a model that was consistently 60% smaller in size than BlueBERT and ClinicalBERT.

The per-label performance for all models and both datasets is shown in Appendix A. We can draw the following insights from the per-label comparison. As shown by support numbers column, the testing dataset for i2b2 2014 did not have significant counts for entities such as FAX, DEVICE and EMAIL therefore producing unpredictable $F1$ scores. This subsequently drove the average $F1$ lower. However, of the top 4 frequent labels (DATE, DOCTOR, PATIENT and HOSPITAL), DATE had the highest $F1$ score. On the other hand, HOSPITAL had the lowest $F1$ with significant support number (877 instances) achieving 48 $F1$ score which contributed to a lower micro $F1$ average for DistilBERT Uncased. On the other hand, DistilBERT cased model performed significantly better for the HOSPITAL label achieving 88 $F1$ score. As discussed earlier, casing features are important in the context of NER tasks. For English nouns, casing is particularly important. For example, hospital names are written with a capital first letter.

For i2b2 2010, since labels are all medical concepts, DistilBERT had trouble recognizing all 3 entities of treatment, problem and test achieving an $F1$ ranging from 78 to 82. For comparison, BlueBERT achieved 84-85 for all 3 entities and ClinicalBERT achieved 87.

The parameters that yielded the best performance out of all 40 runs are shown in Table 4. The parameters were dataset-specific but the same across all models.

In terms of relative performance, DistilBERT model's $F1$ score was, on average, 95% that of medically pre-trained BERT score for i2b2 2010 containing medical terms but on par for i2b2 2014 dataset. This result is 2 points lower than reported by Sanh et al. (2019) for question answering task. The performance degradation of using a distilled model is therefore task- as well as data-specific.

## 6 Conclusion

In this work the main contribution was a full performance assessment of DistilBERT in terms of

|  | Cased | | | | Uncased | | | |
| --- | --- | --- | --- | --- | --- | --- | --- | --- |
|  | DistilBERT | | ClinicalBERT | | DistilBERT | | BlueBERT | |
|  | 2010 | 2014 | 2010 | 2014 | 2010 | 2014 | 2010 | 2014 |
| F1 | 83.48 | 94.85 | 87.51 | 95.38 | 79.56 | 86.44 | 84.05 | 86.05 |
| Min. | 19 | 60 | 34 | 102 | 18 | 31 | 34 | 50 |

Table 3: DistilBERT vs BERT Variants Results on i2b2 2010 & 2014 in terms of micro average $F1$ and runtime

|  | i2b2 2014 | i2b2 2010 |
| --- | --- | --- |
| seq length | 150 | 300 |
| batch | 32 | 16 |
| epochs | 3 | |
| learning rate | $5 \times 10^{-5}$ | |

Table 4: Parameters for best performing runs on i2b2 2010 and i2b2 2014

runtime and $F1$ score for the detection of medical concepts and PHI labels in medical records. Distil-BERT was trained on a medical corpus using i2b2 2014 and i2b2 2010 datasets and compared the results with ClinicalBERT and BlueBERT; both are BERT variants that were pre-trained on medical corpora. For NER task of detecting PHI labels in medical records, DistilBERT achieved comparable results with twice the speed at approximately half the runtime. Its uncased version also performed slightly better in terms of $F1$ than BlueBERT. However, for detecting medical concepts such as problems, treatments and tests, DistilBERT's $F1$ score was lower by 5% on average than models such as BlueBERT and ClinicalBERT whose embeddings were generated from pre-training on medical corpus. Therefore, in the context of de-identification, using a distilled version of BERT such as Distil-BERT produces very similar performance results at approximately 43% of the runtime compared to medically-trained BERT versions even when PHI labels are extracted from medical documents. Results shown here can guide the decision of adopting DistilBERT at healthcare organizations that need to frequently fine-tune their models on new medical data and use it for the detection of PHI labels. The reduced model size can also simplify the deployment process without performance degradation.

## 7 Future Work

Since DistilBERT achieved the same performance as medically-trained versions of BERT when detecting PHI labels even in medical context but suffered performance degradation when detecting medical concepts, future research can investigate and assess how DistilBERT performs on medical concepts if the student model was generated from a medical pre-trained teacher such as BlueBERT or Clinical-BERT. This involves pre-training DistilBERT using the same corpora as ClinicalBERT or BlueBERT in an unsupervised fashion to generate the embeddings. These embeddings can then be used for the fine-tuning step.

## References

Emily Alsentzer, John Murphy, William Boag, Wei-Hung Weng, Di Jindi, Tristan Naumann, and Matthew McDermott. 2019. Publicly available clinical BERT embeddings. In *Proceedings of the 2nd Clinical Natural Language Processing Workshop*, pages 72–78, Minneapolis, Minnesota, USA. Association for Computational Linguistics.

Berfu Büyüköz, Ali Hürriyetoğlu, and Arzucan Özgür. 2020. Analyzing ELMo and DistilBERT on socio-political news classification. In *Proceedings of the Workshop on Automated Extraction of Socio-political Events from News 2020*, pages 9–18, Marseille, France. European Language Resources Association (ELRA).

Cemil Cengiz, Ulaş Sert, and Deniz Yuret. 2019. KU_ai at MEDIQA 2019: Domain-specific pre-training and transfer learning for medical NLI. In *Proceedings of the 18th BioNLP Workshop and Shared Task*, pages 427–436, Florence, Italy. Association for Computational Linguistics.

Jacob Devlin, Ming-Wei Chang, Kenton Lee, and Kristina Toutanova. 2019. BERT: Pre-training of deep bidirectional transformers for language understanding. In *Proceedings of the 2019 Conference of the North American Chapter of the Association for Computational Linguistics: Human Language Technologies, Volume 1 (Long and Short Papers)*, pages 4171–4186, Minneapolis, Minnesota. Association for Computational Linguistics.

Max Friedrich, Arne Köhn, Gregor Wiedemann, and Chris Biemann. 2019. Adversarial learning of privacy-preserving text representations for de-identification of medical records. In *Proceedings of* the 57th Annual Meeting of the Association for Computational Linguistics*, pages 5829–5839, Florence, Italy. Association for Computational Linguistics.

Geoffrey Hinton, Oriol Vinyals, and Jeff Dean. 2015. Distilling the knowledge in a neural network. *stat*, 1050:9.

HIPAA. 2015. Guidance regarding methods for de-identification of protected health information in accordance with the health insurance portability and accountability act (hipaa) privacy rule. Accessed: April 11, 2020.

Abhyuday N Jagannatha and Hong Yu. 2016. Bidirectional RNN for medical event detection in electronic health records. In *Proceedings of the 2016 Conference of the North American Chapter of the Association for Computational Linguistics: Human Language Technologies*, pages 473–482, San Diego, California. Association for Computational Linguistics.

Diederik P. Kingma and Jimmy Ba. 2014. Adam: A method for stochastic optimization.

Jinhyuk Lee, Wonjin Yoon, Sungdong Kim, Donghyeon Kim, Sunkyu Kim, Chan Ho So, and Jaewoo Kang. 2019. BioBERT: a pretrained biomedical language representation model for biomedical text mining. *Bioinformatics*, 36(4):1234–1240.

Yinhan Liu, Myle Ott, Naman Goyal, Jingfei Du, Mandar Joshi, Danqi Chen, Omer Levy, Mike Lewis, Luke Zettlemoyer, and Veselin Stoyanov. 2019. Roberta: A robustly optimized bert pretraining approach. *arXiv preprint arXiv:1907.11692*.

Kevin Patel, Divya Patel, Mansi Golakiya, Pushpak Bhattacharyya, and Nilesh Birari. 2017. Adapting pre-trained word embeddings for use in medical coding. In *BioNLP 2017*, pages 302–306, Vancouver, Canada,. Association for Computational Linguistics.

Yifan Peng, Shankai Yan, and Zhiyong Lu. 2019. Transfer learning in biomedical natural language processing: An evaluation of bert and elmo on ten benchmarking datasets. In *Proceedings of the 2019 Workshop on Biomedical Natural Language Processing (BioNLP 2019)*, pages 58–65.

Victor Sanh, Lysandre Debut, Julien Chaumond, and Thomas Wolf. 2019. Distilbert, a distilled version of bert: smaller, faster, cheaper and lighter. *arXiv preprint arXiv:1910.01108*.

Marina Sokolova. 2011. Evaluation measures for detection of personal health information. In *Proceedings of the Second Workshop on Biomedical Natural Language Processing*, pages 19–26, Hissar, Bulgaria. Association for Computational Linguistics.

Erik F. Tjong Kim Sang and Fien De Meulder. 2003. Introduction to the CoNLL-2003 shared task: Language-independent named entity recognition. In *Proceedings of the Seventh Conference on Natural Language Learning at HLT-NAACL 2003*, pages 142–147.

Ashish Vaswani, Noam Shazeer, Niki Parmar, Jakob Uszkoreit, Llion Jones, Aidan N Gomez, Łukasz Kaiser, and Illia Polosukhin. 2017. Attention is all you need. In *Advances in neural information processing systems*, pages 5998–6008.

Yiyi Wang, Emily Prud'hommeaux, Meysam Asgari, and Jill Dolata. 2020. Automated scoring of clinical expressive language evaluation tasks. In *Proceedings of the Fifteenth Workshop on Innovative Use of NLP for Building Educational Applications*, pages 177–185, Seattle, WA, USA â†' Online. Association for Computational Linguistics.

# A  Per-label Performance

## A.1  i2b2 2014

|  | precision | recall | f1 | support |
|---|---|---|---|---|
| DATE | 0.97 | 0.96 | 0.96 | 4988 |
| DOCTOR | 0.82 | 0.78 | 0.8 | 1915 |
| PATIENT | 0.79 | 0.75 | 0.77 | 881 |
| HOSPITAL | 0.56 | 0.41 | 0.48 | 877 |
| AGE | 0.98 | 0.98 | 0.98 | 764 |
| MEDICALRECORD | 0.96 | 0.96 | 0.96 | 422 |
| CITY | 0.76 | 0.74 | 0.75 | 260 |
| PHONE | 0.89 | 0.94 | 0.92 | 215 |
| IDNUM | 0.85 | 0.81 | 0.83 | 195 |
| STATE | 0.71 | 0.79 | 0.75 | 190 |
| PROFESSION | 0.75 | 0.7 | 0.72 | 179 |
| ZIP | 0.97 | 0.96 | 0.97 | 140 |
| STREET | 0.87 | 0.89 | 0.88 | 136 |
| COUNTRY | 0.6 | 0.24 | 0.34 | 117 |
| USERNAME | 0.99 | 0.96 | 0.97 | 92 |
| ORGANIZATION | 0.57 | 0.41 | 0.48 | 82 |
| OTHER | 0 | 0 | 0 | 13 |
| DEVICE | 0 | 0 | 0 | 8 |
| FAX | 0 | 0 | 0 | 2 |
| EMAIL | 0 | 0 | 0 | 1 |

Table 5: DistilBERT Uncased

|  | precision | recall | f1 | support |
|---|---|---|---|---|
| DATE | 0.99 | 0.99 | 0.99 | 4987 |
| DOCTOR | 0.95 | 0.95 | 0.95 | 1915 |
| PATIENT | 0.91 | 0.92 | 0.92 | 881 |
| HOSPITAL | 0.9 | 0.87 | 0.88 | 875 |
| AGE | 0.98 | 0.98 | 0.98 | 764 |
| MEDICALRECORD | 0.97 | 0.99 | 0.98 | 422 |
| CITY | 0.78 | 0.9 | 0.84 | 260 |
| PHONE | 0.93 | 0.97 | 0.95 | 215 |
| IDNUM | 0.8 | 0.88 | 0.84 | 195 |
| STATE | 0.88 | 0.8 | 0.84 | 190 |
| PROFESSION | 0.86 | 0.84 | 0.85 | 180 |
| ZIP | 1 | 0.96 | 0.98 | 140 |
| STREET | 0.95 | 0.97 | 0.96 | 136 |
| COUNTRY | 0.77 | 0.62 | 0.69 | 117 |
| USERNAME | 0.96 | 0.96 | 0.96 | 92 |
| ORGANIZATION | 0.7 | 0.55 | 0.62 | 82 |
| OTHER | 0 | 0 | 0 | 13 |
| DEVICE | 0 | 0 | 0 | 8 |
| FAX | 0 | 0 | 0 | 2 |
| EMAIL | 1 | 1 | 1 | 1 |

Table 6: DistilBERT Cased

|  | precision | recall | f1 | support |
|---|---|---|---|---|
| DATE | 0.97 | 0.96 | 0.97 | 4988 |
| DOCTOR | 0.82 | 0.75 | 0.79 | 1915 |
| PATIENT | 0.76 | 0.78 | 0.77 | 881 |
| HOSPITAL | 0.55 | 0.4 | 0.46 | 877 |
| AGE | 0.98 | 0.97 | 0.98 | 764 |
| MEDICALRECORD | 0.96 | 0.98 | 0.97 | 422 |
| CITY | 0.76 | 0.69 | 0.72 | 260 |
| PHONE | 0.9 | 0.95 | 0.93 | 215 |
| IDNUM | 0.87 | 0.77 | 0.82 | 195 |
| STATE | 0.67 | 0.77 | 0.72 | 190 |
| PROFESSION | 0.69 | 0.7 | 0.69 | 179 |
| ZIP | 0.96 | 0.96 | 0.96 | 140 |
| STREET | 0.88 | 0.9 | 0.89 | 136 |
| COUNTRY | 0.63 | 0.15 | 0.24 | 117 |
| USERNAME | 0.94 | 0.96 | 0.95 | 92 |
| ORGANIZATION | 0.53 | 0.44 | 0.48 | 82 |
| OTHER | 0 | 0 | 0 | 13 |
| DEVICE | 0 | 0 | 0 | 8 |
| FAX | 0 | 0 | 0 | 2 |
| EMAIL | 0 | 0 | 0 | 1 |

Table 7: BlueBERT

|  | precision | recall | f1 | support |
|---|---|---|---|---|
| DATE | 0.99 | 0.99 | 0.99 | 4987 |
| DOCTOR | 0.94 | 0.95 | 0.94 | 1915 |
| PATIENT | 0.93 | 0.93 | 0.93 | 881 |
| HOSPITAL | 0.88 | 0.86 | 0.87 | 875 |
| AGE | 0.98 | 0.98 | 0.98 | 764 |
| MEDICALRECORD | 0.97 | 0.99 | 0.98 | 422 |
| CITY | 0.76 | 0.85 | 0.8 | 260 |
| PHONE | 0.94 | 0.98 | 0.96 | 215 |
| IDNUM | 0.82 | 0.86 | 0.84 | 195 |
| STATE | 0.86 | 0.78 | 0.82 | 190 |
| PROFESSION | 0.8 | 0.87 | 0.83 | 180 |
| ZIP | 0.99 | 0.97 | 0.98 | 140 |
| STREET | 0.98 | 0.98 | 0.98 | 136 |
| COUNTRY | 0.68 | 0.48 | 0.56 | 117 |
| USERNAME | 0.94 | 0.96 | 0.95 | 92 |
| ORGANIZATION | 0.42 | 0.41 | 0.42 | 82 |
| OTHER | 0 | 0 | 0 | 13 |
| DEVICE | 0 | 0 | 0 | 8 |
| FAX | 0 | 0 | 0 | 2 |
| EMAIL | 0 | 0 | 0 | 1 |

Table 8: ClinicalBERT

## A.2   i2b2 2010

|           | precision | recall | f1   | support |
|-----------|-----------|--------|------|---------|
| problem   | 0.77      | 0.79   | 0.78 | 12592   |
| treatment | 0.79      | 0.79   | 0.79 | 9346    |
| test      | 0.81      | 0.82   | 0.82 | 9226    |

Table 9: DistilBERT Uncased

|           | precision | recall | f1   | support |
|-----------|-----------|--------|------|---------|
| problem   | 0.82      | 0.85   | 0.83 | 12593   |
| treatment | 0.82      | 0.84   | 0.83 | 9345    |
| test      | 0.84      | 0.84   | 0.84 | 9226    |

Table 10: DistilBERT Cased

|           | precision | recall | f1   | support |
|-----------|-----------|--------|------|---------|
| problem   | 0.83      | 0.84   | 0.84 | 12592   |
| treatment | 0.84      | 0.83   | 0.84 | 9346    |
| test      | 0.84      | 0.86   | 0.85 | 9226    |

Table 11: BlueBERT

|           | precision | recall | f1   | support |
|-----------|-----------|--------|------|---------|
| problem   | 0.86      | 0.88   | 0.87 | 12593   |
| treatment | 0.86      | 0.88   | 0.87 | 9345    |
| test      | 0.86      | 0.87   | 0.87 | 9226    |

Table 12: ClinicalBERT

# Distinguishing between Dementia with Lewy Bodies (DLB) and Alzheimer's Disease (AD) using Mental Health Records: a Classification Approach

Zixu Wang[1], Julia Ive[2], Sinéad Moylett[3], Christoph Mueller[1,5],
Rudolf N. Cardinal[3,4], Sumithra Velupillai[1], John O'Brien[3,4], and Robert Stewart[1,5]

[1]Institute of Psychiatry, Psychology & Neuroscience, King's College London, UK
[2]Department of Computing, Imperial College London, UK
[3]Department of Psychiatry, University of Cambridge, UK
[4]Cambridgeshire & Peterborough NHS Foundation Trust, UK
[5]South London and Maudsley NHS Foundation Trust, UK

{zixu.wang,christoph.mueller,sumithra.velupillai,robert.stewart}@kcl.ac.uk
j.ive@imperial.ac.uk, rnc1001@cam.ac.uk
{smm212,john.obrien}@medschl.cam.ac.uk

## Abstract

While dementia with Lewy bodies (DLB) is the second most common type of neurodegenerative dementia following Alzheimer's disease (AD), it is difficult to distinguish from AD. We propose a method for DLB detection by using mental health record (MHR) documents from a (3-month) period before a patient has been diagnosed with DLB or AD. Our objective is to develop a model that could be clinically useful to differentiate between DLB and AD across various datasets from different healthcare institutions. We cast this as a classification task using convolutional neural network (CNN), an efficient neural model for text classification. We experiment with different representation models, and explore the features that contribute to model performances. In addition, we apply temperature scaling, a simple but efficient model calibration method, to produce more reliable predictions. We believe the proposed method has important potential for clinical applications using routine healthcare records, and for generalising to other relevant clinical record datasets. To the best of our knowledge, this is the first attempt to distinguish DLB from AD using mental health records, and to improve the reliability of DLB predictions.

## 1 Introduction

Alzheimer's disease (AD) is the most prevalent type of dementia, characterised by progressive cognitive impairment such as memory loss. Dementia with Lewy bodies (DLB), also known as Lewy body dementia, is the second most common type of neurodegenerative dementia following Alzheimer's

disease (AD), with the defining features of fluctuating cognition, recurrent visual hallucinations, rapid eye movement (REM) sleep behaviour disorder, and Parkinsonian motor symptoms in addition to dementia (Walker et al., 2015). Particularly in the early stages, prior to diagnosis, DLB and AD are difficult to distinguish, hence the detection rates of DLB are sub-optimal, with a large proportion of cases missed or misdiagnosed as AD (Kane et al., 2018). Detection of DLB is, however, crucial as compared to AD and other forms of dementia (*e.g.* Parkinson's disease dementia (PDD)[1]). DLB has a worse prognosis across key outcomes such as mortality, hospitalisation, move into residential care, quality of life, and healthcare costs (Mueller et al., 2017). Moreover, not only is early diagnosis paramount, different types of treatments can have different impacts on these patient groups, *e.g.* antipsychotics, which adds to the importance of accurate and timely diagnoses.

Due to the challenges in recognising DLB clinically, it has been difficult to recruit large research cohorts of representative patients with DLB, and the increasing use of routinely collected healthcare data has been suggested as a potential solution to this shortage. Applying classical methods of symptom ascertainment using natural language processing (NLP) in routinely collected data is however difficult in patients with DLB, as clinicians tend to record the defining features only if they have also

---

[1]The distinction between DLB and PDD is largely around the degree of cognitive impairment and timing of motor symptoms, and they are on a continuum, hence the distinction is less clinically important in this case. Thus, we do not focus on this distinction here.



*Proceedings of the 3rd Clinical Natural Language Processing Workshop*, pages 168–177
November 19, 2020. ©2020 Association for Computational Linguistics

made the correct DLB diagnosis (Mueller et al., 2018). Therefore, we applied novel neural models of NLP to test whether these can be clinically useful to distinguish DLB and AD, and to provide assistance to mitigate expensive outcomes from misdiagnoses of DLB.

This task is challenging because DLB and AD share certain clinical and biological similarities that make them particularly difficult to differentiate. Motivated by the emergence of neural models and NLP methods applied to the biomedical domain, we cast this as a binary text classification task, where we use convolutional neural networks (CNNs) (LeCun et al., 1998; Krizhevsky et al., 2012; Kim, 2014) to address it. Additionally, the generalisation of well-trained models is notably more difficult, since different formats and grammatical patterns emerge in MHRs across different healthcare institutions. In order to test the efficiency of our proposed methodology, we use three datasets from two different MHR (clinical documentation) systems and healthcare institutions, with the aim of comparing the model's performances on similar datasets containing relevant data, but with different contextual structures.

To assist the analysis of our experimental results, and to bridge the gap between model accuracy and confidence, we also study an approach where the model confidence estimates are calibrated. Confidence calibration is important for classification models. Classification networks must not only be accurate, but should also indicate when they are likely to be incorrect; a well-calibrated network matches its confidence to its accuracy so that it is confident when it is accurate, and uncertain when it is not. We use the calibration method named temperature scaling, where expected calibration error (ECE), the expectation of the differences between confidence and accuracy, is used as the primary empirical metric to measure calibration (Guo et al., 2017).

In this paper, we present our preliminary work towards automatically distinguishing individuals diagnosed with DLB or AD using neural network models and MHR texts. This methodology can provide an efficient technique for detecting and intervening DLB. Our contributions are threefold: 1) we introduce a CNN approach for the classification on DLB and AD using MHRs; 2) we investigate the performance of the proposed model on two MHR datasets from two different healthcare institutions

with different formats and patterns; 3) we also apply a neural model calibration method to help in understanding when the model predictions tend to be brittle, so that the model can output confidence scores with higher reliability.

## 2 Related Work

With the success of neural models for many NLP tasks, deep learning methods, as well as word embeddings, have started to be applied to the biomedical and/or clinical domains (Cohen and Demner-Fushman, 2014; Wang et al., 2018; Kormilitzin et al., 2020) including mental health, such as automatic detection and classification of cognitive impairment.

For example, three neural models (CNNs-, LSTM-RNNs-, and CNN-LSTM-based) were applied to distinguish AD and Control patients from DementiaBank (Karlekar et al., 2018; Becker et al., 1994). CNN-LSTM model achieves state-of-the-art performance on the AD classification task. Since neural models are usually black-boxes and it is hard to interpret the reasoning for final classification decisions, various visualisation techniques have been proposed for neural networks (Mahendran and Vedaldi, 2015; Samek et al., 2016; Li et al., 2016; Kádár et al., 2017). Karlekar et al. (2018) illustrated two visualisation methods for interpretation, based on activation clustering and first-derivative saliency methods, to assist the analysis and consolidation of distinctive grammatical patterns of contextual information from AD patients.

Early detection plays a crucial part in the study of dementia. Pan et al. (2019) proposes a hierarchical model that encompasses both the hierarchical and sequential structures of picture description with attention mechanism, and detecting signs of cognitive decline at both the word and sentence levels, by using the DementiaBank and an in-house database of Cookie Theft picture descriptions (Mirheidari et al., 2017). Pan et al. (2019) shows both the proposed hierarchical structure and the attention mechanism contribute to the improvement in AD detection.

Most NLP studies addressing dementia use language transcripts from clinical cohorts, such as the DementiaBank (Becker et al., 1994). To our knowledge, very few studies have used MHR documents and NLP for modelling detection of dementia types, and we are not aware of any studies using NLP and MHRs for detection of DLB. McCoy Jr.

et al. (2020) presents a study using electronic health record (EHR) data for stratifying risk for dementia onset, using a bespoke NLP approach for scoring symptoms in the clinical texts. This NLP approach, however, relies on pre-defined terms, and addresses a slightly different clinical problem.

When applying neural networks to real-world decision-making systems, classification networks must not only be accurate, but also should indicate when they are likely to be incorrect. A network should provide a calibrated confidence measure in addition to its prediction. Calibrated confidence estimates are also important for model interpretability. Guo et al. (2017) identify methods, which can alleviate miscalibrated problems in neural networks, and offer insight and intuition into network training and architectural trends that may cause miscalibration. Good confidence estimates can provide valuable extra information to establish trustworthiness in early detection of cognitive impairment.

## 3  Methodology

Our proposed approach uses a CNN model to distinguish DLB and AD patients. We compare the performance of using an embedding layer (`Emb-layer`) and pre-trained embeddings (`BioWord2Vec`) on our classification task, and finally apply a post-processing method (temperature scaling) for model calibration.

### 3.1  Input representation: word embeddings

We compare two approaches for the input, using high-dimensional word vectors (Mikolov et al., 2013): 1) a randomly initialised embedding layer and trained with the neural network, and 2) pre-trained biomedical word embeddings.

For the pre-trained embeddings, we use `BioWord2Vec`, distributed word representations proposed in Zhang et al. (2019).[2] The biomedical word embeddings are learnt based on medical subject heading (MeSH) terms and text sequences, employing the fastText (Bojanowski et al., 2017) subword embedding model.

`BioWord2Vec` outperforms the current state-of-the-art non-contextualised word embeddings in most BioNLP and/or ClinicalNLP tasks, suggesting that the sub-word information and domain knowledge are indeed able to improve the quality of biomedical word representations and better capture their semantics.

### 3.2  Convolutional Neural Network

We apply the convolutional neural network (CNN) model (Kim, 2014) on our DLB and AD classification task. The input to the model are all documents of each patient concatenated and represented as a matrix using each of the embedding configurations. We use filters that slide over full rows of the matrix. The height of the filters may vary, but sliding windows over 3-5 words at a time are typical. Next, we max-pool (a sample-based discretisation process) the result of the convolutional layer into a long feature vector, add dropout regularisation, and the result is then passed to a softmax layer that outputs probabilities over two classes.

We use a logistic regression (`LR`) model as a baseline. Documents are pre-processed by tokenising and lowercasing. We compare two different text representations: bag-of-words (`BoW`) and term frequency-inverse document frequency (`TF-IDF`) counts. For `TF-IDF` counts, we selected a minimum document frequency of 5 and a maximum of 5,000 features.

### 3.3  Temperature Scaling

Temperature scaling is a post-processing technique which can almost perfectly restore network calibration (Guo et al., 2017), and can be easily added to any models. For classification problems, the neural network model outputs a vector known as the logits. The logits vector is passed through a softmax function to get class probabilities. Temperature scaling simply divides the logits vector by a learnt scalar parameter, *i.e.*

$$P(\hat{\mathbf{y}}) = \frac{\exp(\mathbf{z}/T)}{\sum_j \exp(z_j/T)} \qquad (1)$$

where $\hat{\mathbf{y}}$ is the prediction, $\mathbf{z}$ is the logit, and $T$ is the learnt parameter. $T$ is learnt on the validation set, where $T$ is chosen to minimise negative log-likelihood (NLL). Intuitively, temperature scaling simply softens the neural network outputs. This makes the network slightly less confident, which in turn makes the confidence scores reflect true probabilities.

---

[2]These non-contextualised embedding have performed the best in our setting. We have also conducted the experiments using the contextualised BioBERT (Lee et al., 2019) embeddings available at that time but it has a comparative worse performance due to its specifics of the subword tokenisation and larger clinical document lengths, as compared to the standard configurations in the BioBERT pre-training framework. During the preparation of this paper, more work on advanced pre-trained word embeddings emerged and we applied `BioWord2Vec`, one that was most relevant to our datasets.

This post-processing calibration method is applied on our DLB and AD classification task, to narrow the gap between model confidence and accuracy. The calibrated confidence provides further assistance when deciding whether the individual prediction might be reliable or incorrect.

A scalar summary statistic for calibration can be useful to compare two distributions: accuracy and confidence. The difference between accuracy and confidence is defined as:

$$\mathbb{E}_{\hat{P}}\left[\left|P(\hat{Y} = y | \hat{P} = p) - p\right|\right] \quad (2)$$

where $\hat{Y}$ is a class prediction, and $\hat{P}$ is its associated confidence, *i.e.* the probability of correctness.

In practice, the model predictions are grouped into $M$ interval bins (each of size $\frac{1}{M}$). Expected calibration error (ECE) is computed as the weighted average of the bins' accuracy/confidence differences:

$$\text{ECE} = \sum_{m=1}^{M} \frac{|B_m|}{N} |\text{acc}(B_m) - \text{conf}(B_m)| \quad (3)$$

where $B_m$ is a set of indices where the prediction confidence of samples falls into the interval $\left(\frac{m-1}{M}, \frac{m}{M}\right]$, and $n$ is the total number of samples across all bins. Perfect calibration is achieved when $\text{ECE} = 0$, that is $\text{acc}(B_m) = \text{conf}(B_m)$ $\forall$ bins $m$.

## 4 Materials and Experimental Setup

By applying two types of word embeddings (`Emb-layer` and `BioWord2Vec`) for word representations, convolutional neural network (CNN) for model training, and temperature scaling for model calibration, we investigated and evaluated the efficiency of our proposed methodology on three datasets from two healthcare institutions.

### 4.1 Datasets

We use de-identified mental health records (MHRs) from (1) the Clinical Record Interactive Search (**CRIS** [3]) database at the South London and Maudsley (*SLaM* (Perera et al., 2016)) NHS Trust; and (2) the Clinical Records Anonymisation and Text Extraction (**CRATE** [4]) database at the Cambridgeshire & Peterborough NHS Foundation Trust

| Dataset / # patients | DLB | AD |
|---|---|---|
| CRIS | 90 | 750 |
| CRIS[†] | 90 | 90 |
| CRATE | 98 | 80 |

Table 1: Dataset Statistics - number of DLB and AD patients in each dataset. The ground truth for CRIS is extracted without human annotation.

(*CPFT*). From each MHR database, we extract documents for patients diagnosed either with DLB or AD.

Acquisition of ground truth differed for the two datasets. For CRIS, the MHRs are identified using an information extraction technique that matched any text strings associated with a diagnosis statement of Lewy body dementia or disease. The performance of this automatic extraction was verified by DLB experts as described in Mueller et al. (2018). For CRATE, two experienced clinicians with knowledge of DLB diagnostic criteria and symptom presentation have determined ground truth DLB cases in a set of records pre-selected by an information extraction procedure. Cases were identified as ground truth DLB if a diagnosis had been given by a clinician within the healthcare institution and was the most recent recorded diagnosis within the MHR (see Price et al. (2017) for more details on data collection for CRATE). To have a more comparable dataset to CRATE, we also created CRIS[†], in which we randomly selected AD cases from CRIS to obtain a more balanced distribution, while the DLB cases remain identical to CRIS.

Within each dataset, we have information about the `Patient_ID` and the `Diagnosis_Date` of DLB and AD patients respectively. For each patient with any of these diagnoses, we use only the text written *upon the first consultation until the date 3 months before the diagnosis* (concatenated into one document). The intuition is that we would like to remove MHRs closer to the date of diagnosis that could be more informative of the two diseases, and hence making the differentiation using NLP trivial. There is a total of 90 DLB patients and 750 AD patients in CRIS[5], and 98 DLB patients and 80 AD patients in CRATE[6] (see Table 1). In CRIS[†], the

---

[3]The de-identified CRIS database has received ethical approval for secondary analysis: Oxford REC C, reference 18/SC/0372.

[4]The de-identified CRATE database has received ethical approval - NHS Research Ethics 17/EE/0442.

[5]The distribution of DLB and AD patients from CRIS is close to the real distribution because diagnosed DLB is currently about 5% of all dementias and there is evidence that DLB should be around 10%, AD is around 70% (Mueller et al., 2017).

[6]The more balanced distribution of CRATE is an outcome

| Datasets | Max | Min | Median |
|---|---|---|---|
| CRIS | 206,228 | 319 | 4,406 |
| CRIS$^\dagger$ | 187,438 | 463 | 4,243 |
| CRATE | 733,388 | 28 | 2,710 |

Table 2: Statistics of document length, where **Max**, **Min**, and **Median** refer to the number of words of the document.

| Datasets | Vocabulary size | Overlap |
|---|---|---|
| CRIS | 186,002 | 47,360 (25.5%) |
| CRIS$^\dagger$ | 65,444 | 31,343 (47.9%) |
| CRATE | 66,785 | 20,220 (29.9%) |

Table 3: Statistics of vocabulary (`BioWord2Vec` contains 2,324,849 distinct words in total where 2,309,172 words come from the PubMed and 15,677 from MeSH.). The reason that there is a larger overlap in CRIS$^\dagger$ might be from higher contextual consistency between CRIS$^\dagger$ and `BioWord2Vec`.

AD cases were extracted randomly from CRIS with the aim of making the results more comparable by equalising the number of DLB and AD patients (closer to the distribution in CRATE).

The length of each document varies in the datasets, ranging from tens of words to hundreds of thousands (see Table 2). On average, documents are longer in CRIS and CRIS$^\dagger$. Since the standard CNN model used for text classification takes the maximum length of samples as the uniform length, we considered normalising the length to its median for optimised usage of computational resources [7] (as shown in Table 2) to pad/cut documents to the same length, and use the latest diagnosis records as the training samples if the document exceeds the median.

## 4.2 Experimental Setup

In our binary classification task we consider DLB cases as positive and AD cases as negative. We pre-process the datasets by lowercasing and tokenising using regular expression operations. We use 5-fold cross-validation (CV) to segment the training datasets and ensure that particular subgroups have no deterministic effect on final model performance. All our models use an Adam optimizer (Kingma and Ba, 2014), with a learning rate of 0.001. We

used a 2-D CNN. Filter sizes of $[3, 4, 5]$ were used with 128 filters per filter size. Batch size was set to 32. To avoid overfitting, we apply dropout to the output of all the functional layers (Srivastava et al., 2014), with the dropout rate set to 0.5. The final criteria are calculated by averaging the 5-fold cross-validation results.

In the ablation study, we remove important words from the training data and to trace changes in model performance. These important words are either the most informative of DLB and AD (*e.g.* Model B where a list of terms, expressions, and abbreviations related to the diagnoses of DLB and AD; and was composed manually), or obtained from our baseline model which contribute the most to the `LR` predictions (Model C). We believe these words are also indicative to neural models. Four models are designed and compared:

- **Model A:** The training data are the raw text for all the datasets.
- **Model B:** "lewy", "body", "bodies", "dlb", "ad", "lbd", "dementia" are removed from original text.
- **Model C:** "parkinson", "hallucinations", "visual", "symptoms" are removed from original text.
- **Model D:** Words mentioned in **Model B** and **Model C** are all removed from original text.

We use the temperature scaling calibration method, which does not affect the model's accuracy. We would want the confidence estimates (output probabilities) to be calibrated. For example, given 100 predictions, each with confidence of 0.8, we expect that 80 should be correctly classified. A perfect calibration should be an identity function between accuracy and confidence. We decide to measure calibration by using expected calibration error (ECE).

## 4.3 Evaluation

In order to test the efficiency of our model, we report the performances based on precision, recall, and F1-score. All the reported results are the average of 5-fold cross-validation (CV). We also report F1-scores for each fold. In addition, to better understand the underlying data, we extract the top-20 words contributing the most to the DLB classification in the `LR` model with both the `BoW` and `TF-IDF` counts representations.

---

of the manual extraction.

[7]For the CNN model, we use the sequence length 4,406 for CRIS and 2,710 for CRATE; for CRIS$^\dagger$, we applied the same median length (2,710) as CRATE, in order to make the results more comparable.

| Datasets | Model | Word Representation | Precision | Recall | F1-score |
|---|---|---|---|---|---|
| CRIS | LR | BoW | 0.76 | 0.63 | 0.66 (0.48, 0.72, 0.73, 0.67, 0.70) |
| | | TF-IDF | 0.91 | 0.52 | 0.49 (0.51, 0.44, 0.50, 0.67, 0.34) |
| | CNN | Emb-layer | **0.92** | **0.85** | **0.87 (0.91, 0.87, 0.82, 0.87, 0.88)** |
| | | BioWord2Vec | 0.75 | 0.55 | 0.63 (0.11, 0.78, 0.58, 0.91, 0.80) |
| CRIS[†] | LR | BoW | 0.71 | 0.67 | 0.68 (0.69, 0.72, 0.80, 0.54, 0.65) |
| | | TF-IDF | 0.75 | 0.75 | 0.75 (0.72, 0.75, 0.72, 0.80, 0.75) |
| | CNN | Emb-layer | **0.87** | 0.81 | 0.73 (0.63, 0.78, 0.76, 0.77, 0.74) |
| | | BioWord2Vec | 0.76 | **0.85** | **0.78 (0.81, 0.68, 0.83, 0.80, 0.82)** |
| CRATE | LR | BoW | 0.75 | 0.65 | 0.69 (0.78, 0.75, 0.52, 0.59, 0.81) |
| | | TF-IDF | 0.71 | **0.85** | **0.77 (0.75, 0.69, 0.79, 0.84, 0.78)** |
| | CNN | Emb-layer | **0.88** | 0.59 | 0.70 (0.68, 0.67, 0.71, 0.73, 0.73) |
| | | BioWord2Vec | 0.63 | 0.82 | 0.71 (0.71, 0.71, 0.71, 0.69, 0.73) |

Table 4: DLB classification results (CRIS, CRIS[†], and CRATE), using a logistic regression (LR) model with bag-of-words (BoW) or TF-IDF counts representation, and using CNN with embeddings from the training data (Emb-layer) or pre-trained embeddings (BioWord2Vec): precision, recall, and F1-score, average from 5-fold cross-validation (F1-scores for each fold are shown in brackets).

| Dataset | LR | F1-score | Features (words) |
|---|---|---|---|
| CRIS | BoW | 0.66 | **hallucinations**, [person name], today, night, [person name], currently, [person name], body, **symptoms**, [person name], **parkinson**, score, continues, review |
| | TF-IDF | 0.49 | **hallucinations**, rivastigmine, **parkinson**, formcheckbox, lithium, quetiapine, [person name], reg, **visual**, [person name], [person name], night |
| CRATE | BoW | 0.69 | [person name], **hallucinations**, mr, place, change, opmh, allowance, [person name], [person name], note, stanground, [person name], time, [person name], mental |
| | TF-IDF | 0.77 | mr, **hallucinations**, **parkinson**, [person name], care, ext, liaison, transfer, mood, able, risk, review, **visual**, carers, **symptoms**, admission, lodge, [person name] |

Table 5: Top-20 words contributing the most to the DLB detection using logistic regression (LR) with BoW and TF-IDF counts representation (a minimum document frequency of 5 and a maximum of 5,000 features).

## 5 Results

Overall classification results are reported in Table 4. Two kinds of word representations are used with the LR model: BoW and TF-IDF. Using BoW features resulted in higher F1-score (0.66) as compared to TF-IDF features (0.49) for CRIS; while the opposite is observed for CRATE (0.69 for BoW and 0.77 with TF-IDF features). In general, CNN achieves better results compared to the baseline LR (0.87 for CNN with Emb-layer on CRIS), and lower deviation for each fold in 5-fold cross-validation. On CRATE, the LR model with TF-IDF features performs best (0.77).

Comparing the performances of random initialised word embeddings (Emb-layer) and pre-trained BioWord2Vec, the result using Emb-layer achieves higher F1-score (0.87) than BioWord2Vec (0.63) for CRIS. Results on CRATE using Emb-layer and BioWord2Vec are, on the other hand, quite close considering F1-scores and their stabilities for 5-fold CV.

However, for CRIS[†], using pre-trained embeddings BioWord2Vec (0.78) performs better than Emb-layer (0.73), with more comparable data sizes of DLB and AD. Our proposed model CNN with BioWord2Vec achieves the highest F1-score (0.78) among four models (LR with BoW and TF-IDF, CNN with Emb-layer and BioWord2Vec). With the same settings, the F1-score is also higher than that of CRIS (0.63) with lower deviation, which might be the outcome of a more balanced dataset. In comparison to CRATE (0.71), although the F1-score on CRIS[†]

| Datasets | CNN | A | B | C | D |
|---|---|---|---|---|---|
| CRIS | `Emb-layer` | 0.879 | 0.490 | 0.810 | 0.321 |
|  | `BioWord2Vec` | 0.636 | 0.633 | 0.543 | 0.500 |
| CRIS$^\dagger$ | `Emb-layer` | 0.738 | 0.652 | 0.730 | 0.733 |
|  | `BioWord2Vec` | 0.784 | 0.785 | 0.637 | 0.700 |
| CRATE | `Emb-layer` | 0.703 | 0.649 | 0.692 | 0.667 |
|  | `BioWord2Vec` | 0.712 | 0.702 | 0.690 | 0.640 |

Table 6: Comparison of models (F1-scores) with different input texts.

(0.77) is slightly higher, the CRATE has a comparatively lower deviation. This result might be inherited from the fact that there is a significant increase in the overlap between CRIS$^\dagger$ and CRATE datasets (see Table 3).

We also report the top-20 most important features contributing to the prediction in the `LR` model using `BoW` and `TF-IDF` counts representations (see Table 5). It is obvious that "hallucinations", "parkinson", "visual", "symptoms" are ranked highly in both CRIS and CRATE.

Inspired by the important features from `LR`, our baseline method, we removed the top-ranked important words from the pilot training data. We observed that after removing the core dementia-related words we still obtain similar F1-scores for CRATE using both types of embeddings (see Table 6: models B-D compared to A). These words, however, seem to contribute more to the predictions of CRIS patients and as informative as DLB symptoms in this case. Results for CRIS$^\dagger$ indicate the efficiency of a more balanced dataset and higher vocabulary overlap with `BioWord2Vec`, where we obtained less performance decrease when removing informative words. This would imply the remainder sets of words could also contribute to the model predictions.

Using **Model A** as the base model for model calibration, where raw text serves input to our CNN model with the `BioWord2Vec` word representation, we obtain well-calibrated model for all CRIS, CRIS$^\dagger$, and CRATE (see Table 7).

It is worth noting that models trained on three datasets experience some degrees of miscalibration. (1) The confidences of two models (before and after calibration) decrease from over-confident to a reliable level after temperature scaling. The difference between two confidence scores indicates the performance of calibration and the model's stability. If the confidence level drops significantly (for instance, CRATE), this means there is more uncertainty in the calibrated model estimates, but

less gap between accuracy and confidence. (2) According to Guo et al. (2017), the ECE is typically between 4% to 10% on benchmark datasets. In our experiment, we expected the scores of ECE to be higher, as MHRs are much more free-formed and noisy. Through the comparison of ECE before and after calibration, we can observe that temperature scaling does calibrate on the datasets, which is also supported by the reduction in confidence and NLL. (3) The NLL is often used to define how well a neural network classifies data. A high NLL means the classification is inaccurate. A low NLL otherwise indicates the prediction matches that of the expected value. The NLL decrease in our models on the datasets means that the calibration produces more reliable prediction outputs.

## 6 Discussion

To our knowledge, this is the first study on automatically distinguishing dementia with Lewy bodies (DLB) from Alzheimer's disease (AD) using MHRs. We investigated the performance of CNN models using different embedding representations on MHRs from two different healthcare institutions, and incorporating the method of model calibration into DLB classification to obtain reliable predictions.

To be able to apply NLP models to real-world biomedical tasks, we need first to embrace the challenges of the datasets. In our case, we face a range of such challenges: small data size, hence reduced reliability of predictions; class imbalance; noisy data; and contextual differences between datasets. These might be the reasoning behind higher deviation and instability of F1-scores observed in some predictions (see Table 4).

We attempted to mitigate these challenges by using a set of fairly standard techniques. We use 5-fold CV to ensure that every example appears during both training and testing. Using 5-fold CV, important information is more likely to be learnt, and consequently obtaining better approximations and enhancing robustness, whereas with larger datasets there is more chance to have a proper distribution of information for both training and testing.

Since most MHRs are written with different formats and grammatical patterns, we considered using pre-trained biomedical word embeddings (`BioWord2Vec`) to get a unified word representation across different datasets. Those embeddings helped our models to rely less on explicit indica-

| Datasets | Confidence | ECE (%) | NLL |
|---|---|---|---|
| CRIS | $0.97 \rightarrow 0.87\ (\Delta = 0.10)$ | $8.234 \rightarrow 4.701$ | $7.335 \rightarrow 3.027$ |
| CRIS$^\dagger$ | $0.88 \rightarrow 0.81\ (\Delta = 0.07)$ | $11.627 \rightarrow 9.525$ | $2.853 \rightarrow 1.531$ |
| CRATE | $0.88 \rightarrow 0.65\ (\Delta = 0.23)$ | $15.745 \rightarrow 8.351$ | $1.089 \rightarrow 0.633$ |

Table 7: Model Calibration on CNN/BioWord2Vec combination (Before Calibration $\rightarrow$ After Calibration).

tors of diagnoses (*e.g.* direct mentions of a diagnosis) while producing predictions and stabilised performance over cross-validation splits. However, using those embeddings might be hindered by excessive noise (concatenation of words and punctuation, misspellings) in data and hence poor vocabulary overlap. Better performance in this case can naturally be achieved if more in-domain data is available and embeddings are trained from scratch.

Finally, to improve the reliability of model predictions, temperature scaling, a simple but efficient calibration method, is used to narrow the gap between accuracy and confidence. The ECE scores from both before and after calibrations are used as the primary measures of model calibration. The well-calibrated model decreases in confidence. This can reflect the true probability of model predictions, and can provide a good assistance and reference when evaluating the model outputs.

Our proposed model and calibration method could prove useful clinically. Currently in clinical care there is a high level of under-diagnosis as well as lack of confidence in making a DLB diagnosis. Moreover, appropriate treatment is crucial, *e.g.* it is important to avoid antipsychotic prescribing for this patient group. Although the F1-scores and calibration results are not always perfect, they indicate that using routine healthcare data could be valuable for predictive model development even in cases where it is hard to obtain large datasets.

## 7 Conclusion

In this paper, we propose to use a CNN approach for the task of detecting DLB patients by distinguishing them from AD patients. Our well-calibrated models are relatively robust after using temperature scaling, where calibrated probabilities are more informative of good probability estimates and true predictions. The proposed model is investigated on two MHR datasets from two different healthcare institutions, and achieves competitive results using two types of embeddings (Emb-layer and BioWord2Vec). The pre-trained biomedical word embeddings (BioWord2Vec) are effi-

cient for all three datasets whilst CRIS relies much more on in-domain word distributions. In particular, BioWord2Vec can achieve lower deviations on model performance in ablation study.

Future work will be focused on the effectiveness of contextualised embeddings for a more general methodology where the detection of DLB can be realised across healthcare institutions. We would also like to investigate more effective pre-processing techniques to purify and clean the raw texts before feeding into advanced models, and to mitigate the noise commonly existed in health records. The code is available at `https://github.com/zixuwang1996/dlb_ad_classification`.

## Acknowledgments

The work was funded by an Alzheimer's Society Biomedical Grant and the UK National Institute of Health Research (NIHR) Cambridge Biomedical Research Centre. RS is part-funded by: i) the National Institute for Health Research (NIHR) Biomedical Research Centre at the South London and Maudsley NHS Foundation Trust and King's College London; ii) a Medical Research Council (MRC) Mental Health Data Pathfinder Award to King's College London; iii) an NIHR Senior Investigator Award; iv) the National Institute for Health Research (NIHR) Applied Research Collaboration South London (NIHR ARC South London) at King's College Hospital NHS Foundation Trust. RNC's research is supported by the UK Medical Research Council (grant MC_PC_17213 to RNC). The *CPFT* Research Database is supported by the UK National Institute of Health Research (NIHR) Cambridge Biomedical Research Centre. We thank Cambridgeshire and Peterborough NHS Foundation Trust (*CPFT*) for supports in using the Clinical Records Anonymisation and Text Extraction (CRATE) system.

We would like to thank all anonymous reviewers for their helpful comments. The views expressed are those of the author(s) and not necessarily those of the NHS, the NIHR, nor the Department of Health and Social Care.

## References

James T. Becker, François Boiler, Oscar L. Lopez, Judith Saxton, and Karen L. McGonigle. 1994. The Natural History of Alzheimer's Disease: Description of Study Cohort and Accuracy of Diagnosis. *Archives of Neurology*, 51(6):585–594.

Piotr Bojanowski, Edouard Grave, Armand Joulin, and Tomas Mikolov. 2017. Enriching word vectors with subword information. *Transactions of the Association for Computational Linguistics*, 5:135–146.

Kevin Bretonnel Cohen and Dina Demner-Fushman. 2014. *Biomedical natural language processing*, volume 11. John Benjamins Publishing Company.

Chuan Guo, Geoff Pleiss, Yu Sun, and Kilian Q. Weinberger. 2017. On calibration of modern neural networks. In *Proceedings of the 34th International Conference on Machine Learning*, volume 70 of *Proceedings of Machine Learning Research*, pages 1321–1330, International Convention Centre, Sydney, Australia. PMLR.

Ákos Kádár, Grzegorz Chrupała, and Afra Alishahi. 2017. Representation of linguistic form and function in recurrent neural networks. *Computational Linguistics*, 43(4):761–780.

Joseph PM Kane, Ajenthan Surendranathan, Allison Bentley, Sally AH Barker, John-Paul Taylor, Alan J Thomas, Louise M Allan, Richard J McNally, Peter W James, Ian G McKeith, et al. 2018. Clinical prevalence of lewy body dementia. *Alzheimer's research & therapy*, 10(1):19.

Sweta Karlekar, Tong Niu, and Mohit Bansal. 2018. Detecting linguistic characteristics of Alzheimer's dementia by interpreting neural models. In *Proceedings of the 2018 Conference of the North American Chapter of the Association for Computational Linguistics: Human Language Technologies, Volume 2 (Short Papers)*, pages 701–707, New Orleans, Louisiana. Association for Computational Linguistics.

Yoon Kim. 2014. Convolutional neural networks for sentence classification. In *Proceedings of the 2014 Conference on Empirical Methods in Natural Language Processing (EMNLP)*, pages 1746–1751, Doha, Qatar. Association for Computational Linguistics.

Diederik P. Kingma and Jimmy Ba. 2014. Adam: A method for stochastic optimization. Cite arxiv:1412.6980Comment: Published as a conference paper at the 3rd International Conference for Learning Representations, San Diego, 2015.

Andrey Kormilitzin, Nemanja Vaci, Qiang Liu, and Alejo Nevado-Holgado. 2020. Med7: a transferable clinical natural language processing model for electronic health records. *arXiv preprint arXiv:2003.01271*.

Alex Krizhevsky, Ilya Sutskever, and Geoffrey E Hinton. 2012. Imagenet classification with deep convolutional neural networks. In F. Pereira, C. J. C. Burges, L. Bottou, and K. Q. Weinberger, editors, *Advances in Neural Information Processing Systems 25*, pages 1097–1105. Curran Associates, Inc.

Yann LeCun, Léon Bottou, Yoshua Bengio, and Patrick Haffner. 1998. Gradient-based learning applied to document recognition. *Proceedings of the IEEE*, 86(11):2278–2324.

Jinhyuk Lee, Wonjin Yoon, Sungdong Kim, Donghyeon Kim, Sunkyu Kim, Chan Ho So, and Jaewoo Kang. 2019. BioBERT: a pre-trained biomedical language representation model for biomedical text mining. *Bioinformatics*.

Jiwei Li, Xinlei Chen, Eduard Hovy, and Dan Jurafsky. 2016. Visualizing and understanding neural models in NLP. In *Proceedings of the 2016 Conference of the North American Chapter of the Association for Computational Linguistics: Human Language Technologies*, pages 681–691, San Diego, California. Association for Computational Linguistics.

Aravindh Mahendran and Andrea Vedaldi. 2015. Understanding deep image representations by inverting them. In *IEEE Conference on Computer Vision and Pattern Recognition*.

Thomas H. McCoy Jr., Larry Han, Amelia M. Pellegrini, Rudolph E. Tanzi, Sabina Berretta, and Roy H. Perlis. 2020. Stratifying risk for dementia onset using large-scale electronic health record data: A retrospective cohort study. *Alzheimer's & Dementia*, n/a(n/a). Publisher: John Wiley & Sons, Ltd.

Tomas Mikolov, Ilya Sutskever, Kai Chen, Greg S Corrado, and Jeff Dean. 2013. Distributed representations of words and phrases and their compositionality. In C. J. C. Burges, L. Bottou, M. Welling, Z. Ghahramani, and K. Q. Weinberger, editors, *Advances in Neural Information Processing Systems 26*, pages 3111–3119. Curran Associates, Inc.

Bahman Mirheidari, DJ Blackburn, Kirsty Harkness, Traci Walker, Annalena Venneri, Markus Reuber, and Heidi Christensen. 2017. An avatar-based system for identifying individuals likely to develop dementia. In *Interspeech 2017*, pages 3147–3151. ISCA.

Christoph Mueller, Clive Ballard, Anne Corbett, and Dag Aarsland. 2017. The prognosis of dementia with lewy bodies. *The Lancet Neurology*, 16(5):390–398.

Christoph Mueller, Gayan Perera, Anto P Rajkumar, Manorama Bhattarai, Annabel Price, John T O'Brien, Clive Ballard, Robert Stewart, and Dag Aarsland. 2018. Hospitalization in people with dementia with lewy bodies: Frequency, duration, and cost implications. *Alzheimer's & Dementia: Diagnosis, Assessment & Disease Monitoring*, 10:143–152.

Yilin Pan, Bahman Mirheidari, Markus Reuber, Annalena Venneri, Daniel Blackburn, and Heidi Christensen. 2019. Automatic hierarchical attention neural network for detecting ad.

Gayan Perera, Matthew Broadbent, Felicity Callard, Chin-Kuo Chang, Johnny Downs, Rina Dutta, Andrea Fernandes, Richard D Hayes, Max Henderson, Richard Jackson, Amelia Jewell, Giouliana Kadra, Ryan Little, Megan Pritchard, Hitesh Shetty, Alex Tulloch, and Robert Stewart. 2016. Cohort profile of the South London and Maudsley NHS Foundation Trust Biomedical Research Centre (SLaM BRC) Case Register: current status and recent enhancement of an Electronic Mental Health Record-derived data resource. *BMJ Open*, (3).

Annabel Price, Redwan Farooq, Jin-Min Yuan, Vandana B Menon, Rudolf N Cardinal, and John T O'Brien. 2017. Mortality in dementia with lewy bodies compared with alzheimer's dementia: a retrospective naturalistic cohort study. *BMJ Open*, 7(11).

Wojciech Samek, Alexander Binder, Gregoire Montavon, Sebastian Lapuschkin, and Klaus Muller. 2016. Evaluating the visualization of what a deep neural network has learned. *IEEE Transactions on Neural Networks and Learning Systems*.

Nitish Srivastava, Geoffrey Hinton, Alex Krizhevsky, Ilya Sutskever, and Ruslan Salakhutdinov. 2014. Dropout: A simple way to prevent neural networks from overfitting. *Journal of Machine Learning Research*, 15:1929–1958.

Zuzana Walker, Katherine L Possin, Bradley F Boeve, and Dag Aarsland. 2015. Lewy body dementias. *The Lancet*, 386(10004):1683–1697.

Yanshan Wang, Sijia Liu, Naveed Afzal, Majid Rastegar-Mojarad, Liwei Wang, Feichen Shen, Paul Kingsbury, and Hongfang Liu. 2018. A comparison of word embeddings for the biomedical natural language processing. *Journal of biomedical informatics*, 87:12–20.

Yijia Zhang, Qingyu Chen, Zhihao Yang, Hongfei Lin, and Zhiyong Lu. 2019. Biowordvec, improving biomedical word embeddings with subword information and mesh. *Scientific data*, 6(1):1–9.

# Weakly Supervised Medication Regimen Extraction from Medical Conversations


**Dhruvesh Patel***
College of Information and Computer Sciences
University of Massachusetts Amherst
dhruveshpate@cs.umass.edu

**Sandeep Konam**
Abridge AI Inc.
san@abridge.com

**Sai P. Selvaraj**
Abridge AI Inc.
prabhakarsai@abridge.com



## Abstract

Automated Medication Regimen (MR) extraction from medical conversations can not only improve recall and help patients follow through with their care plan, but also reduce the documentation burden for doctors. In this paper, we focus on extracting spans for *frequency*, *route* and *change*, corresponding to medications discussed in the conversation. We first describe a unique dataset of annotated doctor-patient conversations and then present a weakly supervised model architecture that can perform span extraction using noisy classification data. The model utilizes an attention bottleneck inside a classification model to perform the extraction. We experiment with several variants of attention scoring and projection functions and propose a novel transformer-based attention scoring function (TAScore). The proposed combination of TAScore and Fusedmax projection achieves a 10 point increase in Longest Common Substring F1 compared to the baseline of additive scoring plus softmax projection.


## 1 Introduction

Patients forget 40-80% of the medical information provided by healthcare practitioners immediately (Mcguire, 1996) and misconstrue 48% of what they think they remembered (Anderson et al., 1979), and this adversely affects patient adherence. Automatically extracting information from doctor-patient conversations can help patients correctly recall doctor's instructions and improve compliance with the care plan (Tsulukidze et al., 2014). On the other hand, clinicians spend up to 49.2% of their overall time on EHR and desk work, and only 27.0% of their total time on direct clinical face time with

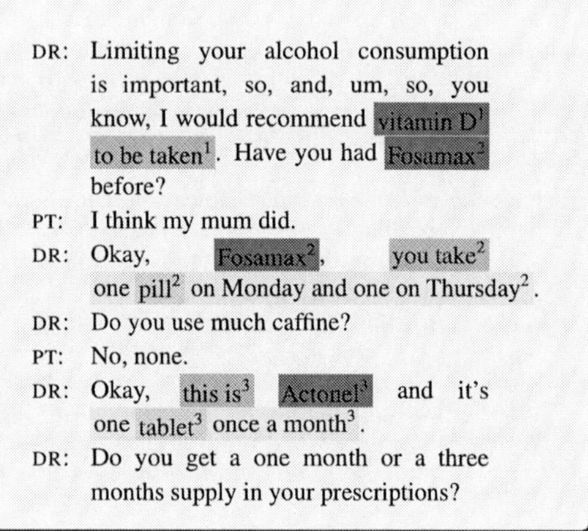

Figure 1: An example excerpt from a doctor-patient conversation transcript. Here, there are three medications mentioned indicated by the superscript. The extracted attributes, change, route and frequency, for each medications are also shown.

patients (Sinsky et al., 2016). Increased data management work is also correlated with increased doctor burnout (Kumar, 2016). Information extracted from medical conversations can also aid doctors in their documentation work (Rajkomar et al., 2019; Schloss and Konam, 2020), allow them to spend more face time with the patients, and build better relationships.

In this work, we focus on extracting Medication Regimen (MR) information (Du et al., 2019; Selvaraj and Konam, 2019) from the doctor-patient conversations. Specifically, we extract three attributes, i.e., *frequency*, *route* and *change*, corresponding to medications discussed in the conversation (Figure 1). Medication Regimen information can help doctors with medication orders cum renewals, medication reconciliation, verification of

---

*Work done as an intern at Abridge AI Inc.




*Proceedings of the 3rd Clinical Natural Language Processing Workshop*, pages 178–193
November 19, 2020. ©2020 Association for Computational Linguistics

reconciliations for errors, and other medication-centered EHR documentation tasks. It can also improve patient engagement, transparency and better compliance with the care plan (Tsulukidze et al., 2014; Grande et al., 2017).

MR attribute information present in a conversation can be obtained as spans in text (Figure 1) or can be categorized into classification labels (Table 2). While the classification labels are easy to obtain at scale in an automated manner – for instance, by pairing conversations with billing codes or medication orders – they can be noisy and can result in a prohibitively large number of classes. Classification labels go through normalization and disambiguation, often resulting in label names which are very different from the phrases used in the conversation. This process leads to a loss of granular information present in the text (see, for example, row 2 in Table 2). Span extraction, on the other hand, alleviates this issue as the outputs are actual spans in the conversation. However, span extraction annotations are relatively hard to come by and are time-consuming to annotate manually. Hence, in this work, we look at the task of MR attribute span extraction from doctor-patient conversation using weak supervision provided by the noisy classification labels.

The main contributions of this work are as follows. We present a way of setting up an MR attribute extraction task from noisy classification data (Section 2). We propose a weakly supervised model architecture which utilizes attention bottleneck inside a classification model to perform span extraction (Section 3 & 4). In order to favor sparse and contiguous extractions, we experiment with two variants of attention projection functions (Section 3.1.2), namely, softmax and Fusedmax (Niculae and Blondel, 2017). Further, we propose a novel transformer-based attention scoring function TAScore (Section 3.1.1). The combination of TAScore and Fusedmax achieves significant improvements in extraction performance over a phrase-based (22 LCSF1 points) and additive softmax attention (10 LCSF1 points) baselines.

## 2 Medication Regimen (MR) using Weak Supervision

Medication Regimen (MR) consists of information about a prescribed medication akin to attributes of an entity. In this work, we specifically focus on *frequency*, *route* of the medication and any *change* in

| Attribute | Normalized Classes |
|---|---|
| *frequency* | Daily \| Every morning \| At Bedtime \| Twice a day \| Three times a day \| Every six hours \| Every week \| Twice a week \| Three times a week \| Every month \| Other \| None |
| *route* | Pill \| Injection \| Topical cream \| Nasal spray \| Medicated patch \| Ophthalmic solution \| Inhaler \| Oral solution \| Other \| None |
| *change* | Take \| Stop \| Increase \| Decrease \| None \| Other |

Table 1: The normalized labels in the classification data.

the medication's *dosage* or *frequency* as shown in Figure 1. For example, given the conversation excerpt and the medication "Fosamax" as shown in Figure 1, the model needs to extract the spans "one pill on Monday and one on Thursday", "pill" and "you take" for attributes *frequency*, *route* and *change*, respectively. The major challenge, however, is to perform the attribute span extraction using noisy classification labels with very few or no span-level labels. The rest of this section describes the dataset used for this task.

### 2.1 Data

The data used in this paper comes from a collection of human transcriptions of 63000 fully-consented and de-identified doctor-patient conversations. A total of 57000 conversations were randomly selected to construct the training (and dev) conversation pool and the remaining 6000 conversations were reserved as the test pool.

**The classification dataset:** All the conversations are annotated with MR tags by expert human annotators. Each set of MR tags consists of the *medication* name and its corresponding attributes *frequency*, *route* and *change*, which are normalized free-form instructions in natural language phrases corresponding to each of the three attributes (see Table 8 in A.4). Each set of MR tags is grounded to a contiguous window of utterances' *text*,[1] around a medication mention as evidence for that set. Hence, each set of grounded MR tags can be written as *<medication, text, frequency, route, change>*, where the last three entries correspond to the three MR attributes.

The free-form instructions for each attribute in the MR tags are normalized and categorized into manageable number of classification labels to avoid long tail and overlapping classes. This process re-

---

[1] The *text* includes both the spoken words and the speaker information.

| *text* | *medication* | Classification labels | | |
|---|---|---|---|---|
| | | *frequency* | *route* | *change* |
| . . . I would recommend vitamin D to be taken. Have you had Fosamax before?. . . | vitamin D | none | none | take |
| . . . I think my mum did. Okay, Fosamax, you take one pill on Monday and one on Thursday. Do you have much caffine? No, none. . . | Fosamax | Twice a week | pill | take |
| Do you have much caffine? No, none. Okay, this is Actonel and it's, one tablet once a month.. . . | Actonel | Once a month | pill | take |

Table 2: Classification examples resulting from the conversation shown in Figure 1.

sults in classes shown in Table 1.[2] As an illustration, this annotation process when applied to the conversation piece shown in Figure 1 would result in the three data points shown in Table 2. Using this procedure on both the training and test conversation pools, we obtain 45,059 training, 11,212 validation and 5,458 test classification data points.[3]

**The extraction dataset:** Since the goal is to extract spans related to MR attributes, we would ideally need a dataset with span annotations to perform this task in a fully supervised manner. However, span annotation is laborious and expensive. Hence, we re-purpose the classification dataset (along with its classification labels) to perform the task of span extraction using weak supervision. We also manually annotate a small fraction of the train, validation and test sets (150, 150 and 500 data-points respectively) for attribute spans to see the effect of supplying a small number of strongly supervised instances on the performance of the model. In order to have a good representation of all the classes in the test set, we increase the sampling weight of data-points which have rare classes. Hence, our test set is relatively more difficult compared to a random sample of 500 data-points. All the results are reported on our test set of 500 difficult data-points annotated for attribute spans.

For annotating attribute spans, the annotators were given instructions to mark spans which provide minimally sufficient and natural evidence for the already annotated attribute class as described below.

**Sufficiency:** Given only the annotated span for a particular attribute, one should be able to predict the correct classification label. This aims to encourage the attribute spans to cover all distinguishing information for that attribute.

**Minimality:** Peripheral words which can be replaced with other words without changing the attribute's classification label should not be included in the extracted span. This aims to discourage marking entire utterances as attribute spans.

**Naturalness:** The marked span(s) if presented to a human should sound like complete English phrases (if it has multiple tokens) or a meaningful word if it has only a single token. In essence, this means that the extractions should not drop stop words from within phrases. This requirement aims to reduce the cognitive load on the human who uses the model's extraction output.

### 2.2 Challenges

Using medical conversations for information extraction is more challenging compared to written doctor notes because the spontaneity of conversation gives rise to a variety of speech patterns with disfluencies and interruptions. Moreover, the vocabulary can range from colloquial to medical jargon.

In addition, we also have noise in our classification dataset with its main source being annotators' use of information outside the grounded *text* window to produce the free-form tags. This happens in two ways. First, when the free-form MR instructions are written using evidence that was discussed elsewhere in the conversation but is not present in the grounded *text* window. Second, when the annotator uses their domain knowledge instead of using just the information in the grounded *text* window – for instance, when the *route* of a *medication* is not explicitly mentioned, the annotator might use the *medication*'s common *route* in their free-form instructions. Using manual analysis of the 800 data-points across the train, dev and test sets, we find that 22% of *frequency*, 36% of *route* and 15% of *change* classification labels, have this noise.

In this work, our approach to extraction depends

---

[2]The detailed explanation for each of the classes can be found in Table 7 in Appendix A.1.

[3]The dataset statistics are given in Appendix A.1.

on the size of the auxiliary task's (classification) dataset to overcome above mentioned challenges.

## 3 Background

There have been several successful attempts to use neural attention (Bahdanau et al., 2015) to extract information from text in an unsupervised manner (He et al., 2017; Lin et al., 2016; Yu et al., 2019). Attention scores provide a good proxy for importance of a particular token in a model. However, when there are multiple layers of attention, or if the encoder is too complex and trainable, the model no longer provides a way to produce reliable and faithful importance scores (Jain and Wallace, 2019).

We argue that, in order to bring in the faithfulness, we need to create an attention bottleneck in our classification + extraction model. The attention bottleneck is achieved by employing an attention function which generates a set of attention weights over the encoded input tokens. Attention bottleneck forces the classifier *to only see* the portions of input that pass through it, thereby enabling us to trade the classification performance for extraction performance and getting span extraction with weak supervision from classification labels.

In the rest of this section, we provide general background on neural attention and present its variants employed in this work. This is followed by the presentation of our complete model architecture in the subsequent sections.

### 3.1 Neural Attention

Given a query $\mathbf{q} \in \mathbb{R}^m$ and keys $\mathbf{K} \in \mathbb{R}^{l \times n}$, the attention function $\alpha \colon \mathbb{R}^m \times \mathbb{R}^{l \times n} \to \Delta^l$ is composed of two functions: a scoring function $S \colon \mathbb{R}^m \times \mathbb{R}^{l \times n} \to \mathbb{R}^l$ which produces unnormalized importance scores, and a projection function $\Pi \colon \mathbb{R}^l \to \Delta^l$ which normalizes these scores by projecting them to an $(l-1)$-dimensional probability simplex.[4]

#### 3.1.1 Scoring Function

The purpose of the scoring function is to produce importance scores for each entry in the key $\mathbf{K}$ w.r.t the query $\mathbf{q}$ for the task at hand, which in our case is classification. We experiment with two scoring functions: additive and transformer-based.

**Additive:** This is same as the scoring function used in Bahdanau et al. (2015), where the scores

---

[4]Throughout this work $l$ represents the sequence length dimension and $\Delta^l = \{\mathbf{x} \in \mathbb{R}^l \mid \mathbf{x} > 0, \|\mathbf{x}\|_1 = 1\}$ represents a probability simplex.

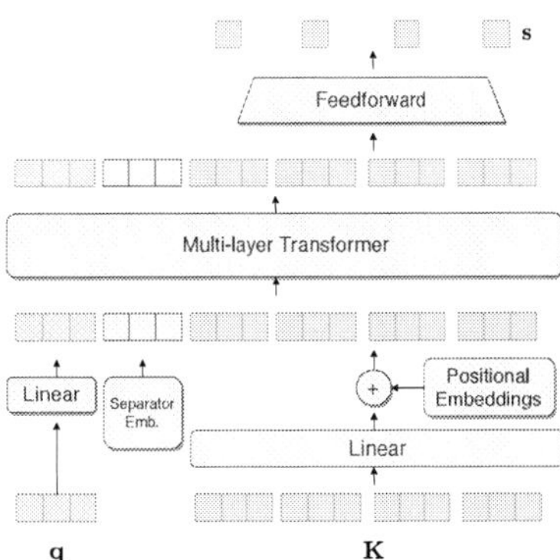


Figure 2: Architecture of TAScore. $\mathbf{q}$ and $\mathbf{K}$ are input query and keys, respectively, and $\mathbf{s}$ are the output scores.

are produced as follows:

$$s_j = \mathbf{v}^T \tanh(\mathbf{W}_q\, \mathbf{q} + \mathbf{W}_k\, \mathbf{k}_j)\,,$$

where, $\mathbf{v} \in \mathbb{R}^m$, $\mathbf{W}_q \in \mathbb{R}^{m \times m}$ and $\mathbf{W}_k \in \mathbb{R}^{m \times n}$ are trainable weights.

**Transformer-based Attention Score (TAScore):** While the additive scoring function is simple and easy to train, it suffers from one major drawback in our setting: since we freeze the weights of our embedder and do not use multiple layers of trainable attention (Section 4.4), the additive attention can struggle to resolve references – finding the correct attribute when there are multiple entities of interest, especially when there are multiple distinct medications (Section 6.4). For this reason, we propose a novel multi-layer transformer-based attention scoring function (TAScore) which can perform this reference resolution while also preserving the *attention bottleneck*. Figure 2 shows the architecture of TAScore. The query and key vectors are projected to the same space using two separate linear layers while also adding sinusoidal positional embeddings to the key vectors. A special trainable separator vector is added between the query and key vectors and the entire sequence is passed through a multi-layer transformer (Vaswani et al., 2017). Finally, scalar scores (one corresponding to each vector in the key) are produced from the outputs of the transformer by passing them through a feed-forward layer with dropout.

### 3.1.2 Projection Function

A projection function $\Pi \colon \mathbb{R}^l \to \Delta^l$ in the context of attention distribution, normalizes the real valued importance scores by projecting them to an $(l -$

1)-dimensional probability simplex $\Delta^l$. Niculae and Blondel (2017) provide a unified view of the projection function as follows:

$$\Pi_\Omega(\mathbf{s}) = \arg\max_{\mathbf{a}\in\Delta^l} \mathbf{a}^T\mathbf{s} - \gamma\Omega(\mathbf{a}) \,.$$

Here, $\mathbf{a} \in \Delta^l$, $\gamma$ is a hyperparameter and $\Omega$ is a regularization penalty which allows us to introduce problem specific inductive bias into our attention distribution. When $\Omega$ is strongly convex, we have a closed form solution to the projection operation as well as its gradient (Niculae and Blondel, 2017; Blondel et al., 2020). Since we use the attention distribution to perform extraction, we experiment with the following instances of projection functions in this work.

**Softmax:** $\Omega(\mathbf{a}) = \sum_{i=1}^{l} a_i \log a_i$

Using the negative entropy as the regularizer, results in the usual softmax projection operator $\Pi_\Omega(\mathbf{s}) = \frac{\exp(\mathbf{s}/\gamma)}{\sum_{i=1}^{l} \exp(s_i/\gamma)}$ .

**Fusedmax:** $\Omega(\mathbf{a}) = \frac{1}{2}\|\mathbf{a}\|_2^2 + \sum_{i=1}^{l} |a_{i+1} - a_i|$

Using squared loss with fused-lasso penalty (Niculae and Blondel, 2017), results in a projection operator which produces sparse as well as contiguous attention weights[5]. The fusedmax projection operator can be written as $\Pi_\Omega(\mathbf{s}) = P_{\Delta^l}(P_{TV}(s))$, where

$$P_{TV}(\mathbf{s}) = \arg\min_{\mathbf{y}\in\mathbb{R}^l} \|\mathbf{y} - \mathbf{s}\|_2^2 + \sum_{d=1}^{l-1} |y_{d+1} - y_d|$$

is the proximal operator for 1d Total Variation Denoising problem, and $P_{\Delta^l}$ is the euclidean projection operator. Both these operators can be computed non-iteratively as described in Condat (2013) and Duchi et al. (2008), respectively. The gradient of Fusedmax operator can be efficiently computed as described in Niculae and Blondel (2017).[6]

**Fusedmax*:** We observe that while softmax learns to focus on the right region of text, it tends to assign very low attention weights to some tokens of phrases resulting in multiple discontinuous spans per attribute, while Fusedmax on the other hand, almost always generates contiguous attention weights. However, Fusedmax makes more mistakes in identifying the overall region that contains

---

[5]Some example outputs of softmax and fusedmax on random inputs are shown in Appendix A.3

[6]The pytorch implementation to compute fusedmax used in this work is available at https://github.com/dhruvdcoder/sparse-structured-attention.

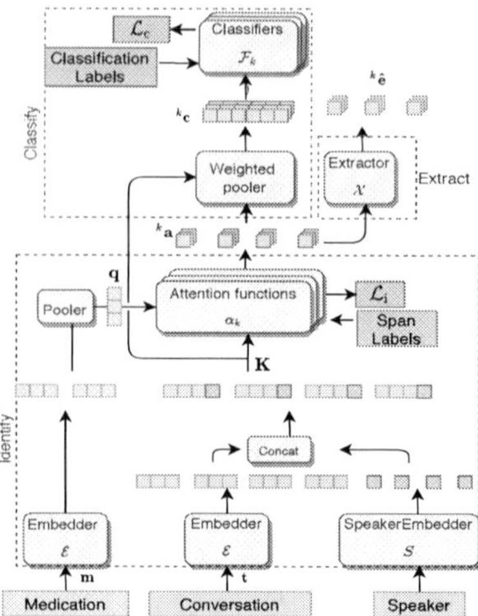

Figure 3: Complete model for weakly supervised MR attribute extraction.

the target span (Section 6.3). In order to combine the advantages of softmax and Fusedmax, we first train a model using softmax as the projector and then swap the softmax with Fusedmax in the final few epochs. We call this approach Fusedmax*.

## 4 Model

Our classification + extraction model uses MR attributes classification labels to extract MR attributes. The model can be divided into three phases: identify, classify and extract (Figure 3). The identify phases encodes the input text and medication name and uses the attention bottleneck to produce attention over the text. Classify phase computes the context vector using the attention from the identify phases and classifies the context vectors. Finally, the extract phase uses the attention from the identify phase to extract spans corresponding to MR attributes.

**Notation:** Let the dataset $\mathcal{D}$ be $\{(\mathbf{x}^{(1)}, \mathbf{y}^{(1)}), \ldots (\mathbf{x}^{(N)}, \mathbf{y}^{(N)})\}$. Each $\mathbf{x}$ consists of a medication $m$ and conversation text $\mathbf{t}$, and each $\mathbf{y}$ consists of classification labels for *frequency*, *route* and *change*, i.e, $\mathbf{y} = ({}^f y, {}^r y, {}^c y)$, respectively. The number of classes for each attribute is denoted by ${}^{(\cdot)}n$. As seen from Table 1, ${}^f n = 12$, ${}^r n = 10$ and ${}^c n = 8$. The length of a text excerpt is denoted by $l$. The extracted span for attribute $k \in \{f, r, c\}$ is denoted by a binary vector ${}^k\mathbf{e}$ of length $l$, such that ${}^k e_j = 1$, if $j^{\text{th}}$ token is in the extracted span for attribute $k$.

### 4.1 Identify

As shown in the Figure 3, the *identify* phase finds the most relevant parts of the text w.r.t each of the three attributes. For this, we first encode the text as well as the given medication using a contextualized token embedder $\mathcal{E}$. In our case, this is 1024 dimensional BERT (Devlin et al., 2019)[7]. Since BERT uses WordPiece representations (Wu et al., 2016), we average these wordpiece representations to form the word embeddings. In order to supply the speaker information, we concatenate a 2-dimensional fixed vocabulary speaker embedding to every token embedding in the text to obtain speaker-aware word representations.

We then perform average pooling of the medication representations to get a single vector representation for the medication[8]. Finally, with the given medication representation as the query and the speaker-aware token representations as the key, we use three separate attention functions (attention bottleneck), one for each attribute (no weight sharing), to produce three sets of normalized attention distributions $^f\hat{\mathbf{a}}$, $^r\hat{\mathbf{a}}$ and $^c\hat{\mathbf{a}}$ over the tokens of the text. The *identify* phase can be succinctly described as follows:

$$^k\mathbf{a} = {}^k\alpha(\mathcal{E}(m), \mathcal{E}(t)) \ , \quad \text{where } k \in \{f, r, c\}$$

Here, each $^k\hat{\mathbf{a}}$ is an element of the probability simplex $\Delta^l$ and is used to perform attribute extraction (Section 4.3).

### 4.2 Classify

We obtain the attribute-wise context vectors $^k\mathbf{c}$, as the weighted sum of the encoded tokens ($\mathbf{K}$ in Figure 3) where the weights are given by the attribute-wise attention distributions $^k\mathbf{a}$. To perform the classification for each attribute, the attribute-wise context vectors are used as input to feed-forward neural networks $\mathcal{F}_k$ (one per attribute), as shown below:[9]

$$^k\mathbf{p} = \text{softmax}\left(\mathcal{F}_k(^k\mathbf{c})\right)$$

$$^k\hat{y} = \underset{j \in \{1,2,\dots,{}^kn\}}{\arg\max} \ {}^kp_j \ , \quad \text{where } k \in \{f, r, c\}.$$

---

[7]The pre-trained weight for BERT is from the HuggingFace library(Wolf et al., 2019)

[8]Most medication names are single word, however a few medicines have names which are upto 4-5 words.

[9]Complete set of hyperparameters used is given in Appendix A.2

### 4.3 Extract

The spans are extracted from the attention distribution using a fixed extraction function $\mathcal{X} \colon \Delta^l \to \{0, 1\}^l$, defined as:

$$^k\hat{e}_j = \mathcal{X}_k(^k\mathbf{a})_j = \begin{cases} 1 & \text{if } {}^ka_j > {}^k\gamma \\ 0 & \text{if } {}^ka_j \leq {}^k\gamma \ , \end{cases}$$

where $^k\gamma$ is the extraction threshold for attribute $k$. For softmax projection function, it is important to tune the attribute-wise extraction thresholds $\gamma$. We tune these using extraction performance on the extraction validation set. For fusedmax projection function which produces spare weights, the thresholds need not be tuned, and hence are set to 0.

### 4.4 Training

We train the model end-to-end using gradient descent, except the *extract* module (Figure 3), which does not have any trainable weights, and the embedder $\mathcal{E}$. Freezing the embedder is vital for the performance, since not doing so results in excessive dispersion of token information to other nearby tokens, resulting in poor extractions.

The total loss for the training is divided into two parts as described below.
**(1) Classification Loss $\mathcal{L}_c$:** In order to perform classification with highly class imbalanced data (see Table 1), we use weighted cross-entropy:

$$\mathcal{L}_c = \sum_{k \in \{f,r,c\}} -\,{}^kw_{k_y} \ \log\left(^kp_{k_y}\right) \ ,$$

where the class weights $^kw_{k_y}$ are obtained by inverting each class' relative proportion.

**(2) Identification Loss $\mathcal{L}_i$:** If span labels e are present for some subset $\mathcal{A}$ of training examples, we first normalize these into ground truth attention probabilities $\mathbf{a}$:

$$^ka_j = \frac{^ke_j}{\sum_{j=1}^l {}^ke_j} \quad \text{for } k \in \{f, r, c\}$$

We then use KL-Divergence between the ground truth attention probabilities and the ones generated by the model ($\hat{\mathbf{a}}$) to compute identification loss $\mathcal{L}_i = \sum_{k \in \{f,r,c\}} \text{KL}\left(^k\mathbf{a}\middle\|^k\hat{\mathbf{a}}\right)$ Note that $\mathcal{L}_i$ is zero for data-points that do not have span labels. Using these two loss functions, the overall loss $\mathcal{L} = \mathcal{L}_c + \lambda\mathcal{L}_i$.

| Model | | | Span labels | Token-wise extraction F1 | | | | LCSF1 | | | | Classification F1 | | | |
|---|---|---|---|---|---|---|---|---|---|---|---|---|---|---|---|
| Encoder | Scorer | Projector | | freq. | route | change | Avg. | freq. | route | change | Avg. | freq. | route | change | Avg. |
| *Phrase-based baseline* | | | - | 41.03 | 48.57 | 10.75 | 33.45 | 36.26 | 50.41 | 11.54 | 32.73 | - | - | - | - |
| BERT | Additive | Softmax | 0 | 51.22 | 46.27 | 22.81 | 40.10 | 39.87 | 46.40 | 18.92 | 35.06 | 51.51 | 54.06 | 51.65 | 52.40 |
| BERT | Additive | Fusedmax | 0 | 47.55 | 51.31 | 5.10 | 34.65 | 46.39 | 59.10 | 4.82 | 36.77 | 43.54 | 42.91 | 9.19 | 31.88 |
| BERT | TAScore | Softmax | 0 | 66.53 | 48.96 | 27.61 | 47.70 | 61.49 | 47.34 | 22.49 | 43.77 | 44.93 | 51.34 | 46.49 | 47.58 |
| BERT | TAScore | Fusedmax | 0 | 56.35 | 44.04 | 22.07 | 40.82 | 61.96 | 50.27 | 25.25 | 45.82 | 51.95 | 48.37 | 43.00 | 47.77 |
| BERT | Additive | Softmax | 150 | 61.56 | 45.08 | 33.54 | 46.73 | 57.90 | 48.14 | 28.28 | 44.77 | 55.62 | 52.42 | 50.40 | 52.81 |
| BERT | Additive | Fusedmax | 150 | 47.05 | 52.49 | 27.69 | 42.41 | 42.37 | 57.50 | 30.63 | 43.50 | 54.04 | 48.40 | 52.28 | 51.57 |
| BERT | Additive | Fusedmax* | 150 | 65.90 | 47.30 | 34.77 | 49.32 | 67.15 | 51.12 | 36.04 | 51.30 | 56.46 | 42.63 | 50.68 | 49.93 |
| BERT | TAScore | Softmax | 150 | 66.53 | 54.35 | 34.27 | **51.72** | 62.90 | 53.05 | 28.33 | 48.09 | 50.13 | 45.86 | 47.16 | 47.72 |
| BERT | TAScore | Fusedmax | 150 | 58.24 | 58.09 | 25.09 | 47.32 | 57.93 | 64.05 | 26.70 | 49.56 | 51.61 | 53.95 | 43.51 | 49.69 |
| BERT | TAScore | Fusedmax* | 150 | 66.90 | 54.85 | 33.28 | 51.67 | 70.10 | 60.05 | 35.92 | **55.36** | 64.26 | 44.50 | 51.21 | **53.32** |

Table 3: Attribute extraction performance for various combinations of scoring and projection functions. The avg. columns represent the macro average of the corresponding metric across the attributes.

| Training Type | Model | Tokenwise Extraction F1 | | | | Classification F1 | | | |
|---|---|---|---|---|---|---|---|---|---|
| | | freq. | route | change | avg. | freq. | route | change | avg. |
| Classification only | BERT Classifiers | - | - | - | - | 74.72 | 40.82 | 55.76 | 58.48 |
| Classification only | BERT+TAScore+Fusedmax* | 58.55 | 45.00 | 24.43 | 42.66 | 52.45 | 46.37 | 43.00 | 47.27 |
| Extraction only | BERT+TAScore+Fusedmax* | 53.79 | 44.44 | 14.32 | 37.18 | - | - | - | - |
| Classification +Extraction | BERT+TAScore+Fusedmax* | 66.90 | 54.85 | 33.28 | 51.67 | 64.26 | 44.50 | 51.21 | 53.32 |

Table 4: Effect of performing extraction+classification jointly in our proposed model. While the *Extraction Only* training only uses the 150 examples which are explicitly annotated with span labels, the *Classification only* training uses the complete training dataset with classification labels.

## 5 Metrics

**Token-wise F1 (TF1)**: Each token in text is either part of the extracted span (positive class) for an attribute or not (negative class). Token-wise F1 score is the F1 score of the positive class obtained by considering all the tokens in the dataset as separate binary classification data points. TF1 is calculated separately for each attribute.

**Longest Common Substring F1 (LCSF1)**: LCSF1 measures if the extracted spans, along with being part of the gold spans, are contiguous or not. Longest Common Substring (LCS) is the longest overlapping contiguous span of tokens between the predicted and gold spans. LCSF1 is defined as the harmonic mean of LCS-Recall and LCS-Precision which are defined per extraction as:

$$\text{LCS-Recall} = \frac{\#\text{tokens in LCS}}{\#\text{tokens in gold span}}$$

$$\text{LCS-Precision} = \frac{\#\text{tokens in LCS}}{\#\text{tokens in predicted span}}$$

## 6 Results and Analysis

Table 3 shows the results obtained by various combinations of attention scoring and projection functions on the task of MR attribute extraction in terms of the metrics defined in Section 5. It also shows the classification F1 score to emphasize how the attention bottleneck affects classification performance. The first row shows how a simple phrase based extraction system would perform on the task.[10]

### 6.1 Effect of Span labels

In order to see if having a small number of extraction training data-points (containing explicit span labels) helps the extraction performance, we annotate 150 (see Section 2 for how we sampled the datapoints) of the training data-points with span labels. As seen from Table 3, even a small number of examples with span labels ($\approx 0.3\%$) help a lot with the extraction performance for all models. We think this trend might continue if we add more training span labels. We leave the finding of the right balance between annotation effort and extraction performance as a future direction to explore.

### 6.2 Effect of classification labels

In order to quantify the effect of performing the auxiliary task of classification along with the main task of extraction, we train the proposed model in three different settings. (1) The *Classification*

---

[10]The details about the phrase based baseline are presented in Appendix A.4

*Only* uses the complete dataset (~45k) but only with the classification labels. (2) The *Extraction Only* setting only uses the 150 training examples that have span labels. (3) Finally, the *Classification+Extraction* setting uses the 45k examples with classification labels along with the 150 examples with the span labels to train the model. Table 4 (rows 2, 3 and 4) shows the effect of having classification labels and performing extraction and classification jointly using the proposed model. The model structure and the volume of the classification data (~45k examples) makes the auxiliary task of classification extremely helpful for the main task of extraction, even with the presence of label noise.

It is worth noting that the classification performance of the proposed method is also improved by explicit supervision to the extraction portion of the model (row 2 vs 4, Table 4). In order to set a reference for classification performance, we train strong classification only models, one for each attribute, using pretrained BERT. These *BERT Classifiers*, are implemented as described in Devlin et al. (2019) with input consisting of the text and medication name separated by a [SEP] token (row 1). Based on the improvements achieved in the classification performance using span annotations, we believe that having more span labels can further close the gap between the classification performance of the proposed model and the BERT Classifiers. However, this work focuses on extraction performance, hence improving the classification performance is left to future work.

## 6.3 Effect of projection function

While softmax with post-hoc threshold tuning achieves consistently higher TF1 compared to fusedmax (which does not require threshold tuning), the later achieves better LCSF1. We observe that while the attention function using softmax projection focuses on the correct portion of the text, it drops intermediate words, resulting in multiple discontinuous spans. Fusedmax on the other hand almost always produces contiguous spans. Figure 4 further illustrates this point using a test example. The training trick which we call fusedmax* swaps the softmax projection function with fusedmax during the final few epochs to combine the strengths of both softmax and fusedmax. This achieves high LCSF1 as well as TF1.



(a) BERT+TAScore+Fusedmax*



(b) BERT+TAScore+Softmax

Figure 4: Difference in extracted spans for MR attributes with models that uses Fusedmax* and Softmax, for the medication Actonel. Blue: *change*, green: *route* and yellow: *frequency*. Refer Figure 1 for ground-truth annotations.

## 6.4 Effect of scoring function

Table 5 shows the percent change in the extraction F1 if we use TAScore instead of additive scoring (everything else being the same). As seen, there is a significant improvement irrespective of the projection function being used.

| Scorer | TF1 (Δ%) | | | LCSF1 (Δ%) | | |
|---|---|---|---|---|---|---|
| | MM (77.3) | SM (22.7) | All (100) | MM (77.3) | SM (22.7) | All (100) |
| softmax | +11.1 | +10.6 | +10.6 | +6.5 | +6.6 | +6.3 |
| fusedmax | +12.1 | +8.3 | +11.5 | +16.4 | +15.5 | +13.9 |
| fusedmax* | +5.4 | +1.9 | +4.7 | +9.25 | +1.1 | +7.9 |

Table 5: MR extraction improvement (%) brought by TAScore over additive scorer in the full test set (All=100%), and test subset with single medication (SM=22.7%) and multiple medications (MM=77.3%) in the *text*.

The need for TAScore stems from the difficulty of the additive scoring function to resolve references between spans when there are multiple medications present. In order to measure the efficacy of TAScore for this problem, we divide the test set into two subsets: data-points which have multiple distinct medications in their text (MM) and data-points that have single medication only. As seen from the first two columns for both the metrics in Table 5, using TAScore instead of additive results in more improvement in the MM subset compared to the SM-subset, showing that using transformer scorer does help with resolving references when multiple medications are present in the text.

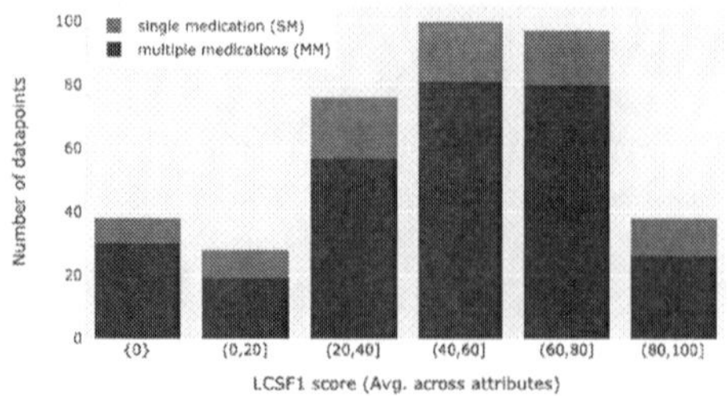

Figure 5: Distribution of the Avg. LCSF1 for the best performing model (BERT+TAScore+Fusedmax*). A significant number ($\approx 10\%$) of datapoints with multiple medication in their *text* get LCSF1 of zero (1st bar).

Figure 5 shows the distribution of Avg. LCSF1 (average across all three attributes). It can be seen that there are a significant number of datapoints in the MM subset which get LCSF1 of zero, showing that even when the transformer scorer achieves improvement on MM subset, it gets quite a lot of these data-points completely wrong. This shows that the there is still room for improvement.

## 6.5 Discussion

In summary, our analysis reveals that Fusedmax/Fusedmax* favors contiguous extraction spans which is a necessity for our task. Irrespective of the projection function used, the proposed scoring function TAScore improves the extraction performance when compared to the popular additive scoring function. The proposed model architecture is able to establish a synergy between the classification and span extraction tasks where one improves the performance of the other. Overall, the proposed combination of TAScore and Fusedmax* achieves a 22 LCSF1 points improvement over the phrase-based baseline and 10 LCSF1 points improvement over the naive additive and softmax combination.

## 7 Related Work

Existing literature directly related to our work can be bucketed into two categories – related methods and related tasks.

**Methods:** The recent work on generating rationales/explanations for deep neural network based classification models (Lei et al., 2016; Bastings et al., 2020; Paranjape et al., 2020) is closely related to ours in terms of the methods used. Most of these works use binary latent variables to perform extraction as an intermediate step before classification. Our work is closely related to (Jain et al., 2020; Zhong et al., 2019), who use attention scores to generate rationales for classification models. These works, however, focus on generating *faithful* and *plausible* explanation for classification as opposed to extracting the spans for attributes of an entity, which is the focus of our work. Moreover, our method can be generalized to any number of attributes while all these methods would require a separate model for each attribute.

**Tasks:** Understanding doctor-patient conversations is starting to receive attention recently (Rajkomar et al., 2019; Schloss and Konam, 2020). Selvaraj and Konam (2019) performs MR extraction by framing the problem as a generative question answering task. This approach is not efficient at inference time – it requires one forward pass for each attribute. Moreover, unlike a span extraction model, the generative model might produce hallucinated facts. Du et al. (2019) obtain MR attributes as spans in text; however, they use a fully supervised approach which requires a large dataset with span-level labels.

## 8 Conclusion and Future work

We provide a framework to perform MR attribute extraction from medical conversations with weak supervision using noisy classification labels. This is done by creating an attention bottleneck in the classification model and performing extraction using the attention weights. After experimenting with several variants of attention scoring and projection functions, we show that the combination of our transformer-based attention scoring function (TAScore) combined with Fusedmax* achieves significantly higher extraction performance compared to the other attention variants and a phrase-based baseline.

While our proposed method achieves good performance, there is still room for improvement, especially for text with multiple medications. Data augmentation by swapping or masking medication names is worth exploring. An alternate direction of future work involves improving the naturalness of extracted spans. Auxiliary supervision using a language modeling objective would be a promising approach for this.

## Acknowledgments

We thank University of Pittsburgh Medical Center (UPMC) and Abridge AI Inc. for providing access to the de-identified data corpus.

## References

J. L. Anderson, Sally Dodman, M. Kopelman, and A. Fleming. 1979. Patient Information Recall in a Rheumatology Clinic. *Rheumatology*, 18:18–22.

Dzmitry Bahdanau, Kyunghyun Cho, and Yoshua Bengio. 2015. Neural machine translation by jointly learning to align and translate. *CoRR*, abs/1409.0473.

Joost Bastings, Wilker Aziz, and Ivan Titov. 2020. Interpretable neural predictions with differentiable binary variables. In *ACL 2019 - 57th Annual Meeting of the Association for Computational Linguistics, Proceedings of the Conference*, pages 2963–2977. Association for Computational Linguistics.

Lukas Biewald. 2020. Experiment tracking with weights and biases. Software available from wandb.com.

Mathieu Blondel, Andre F.T. Martins, and Vlad Niculae. 2020. Learning with fenchel-young losses. *Journal of Machine Learning Research*, 21(35):1–69.

Laurent Condat. 2013. A direct algorithm for 1-D total variation denoising. *IEEE Signal Processing Letters*, 20(11):1054–1057.

Jacob Devlin, Ming-Wei Chang, Kenton Lee, and Kristina Toutanova. 2019. BERT: Pre-training of deep bidirectional transformers for language understanding. In *Proceedings of the 2019 Conference of the North American Chapter of the Association for Computational Linguistics: Human Language Technologies, Volume 1 (Long and Short Papers)*, pages 4171–4186, Minneapolis, Minnesota. Association for Computational Linguistics.

Nan Du, Mingqiu Wang, Linh Tran, Gang Li, and Izhak Shafran. 2019. Learning to infer entities, properties and their relations from clinical conversations. *arXiv preprint arXiv:1908.11536*.

John Duchi, Shai Shalev-Shwartz, Yoram Singer, and Tushar Chandra. 2008. Efficient projections onto the l1-ball for learning in high dimensions. In *Proceedings of the 25th International Conference on Machine Learning*, ICML '08, page 272–279, New York, NY, USA. Association for Computing Machinery.

Matt Gardner, Joel Grus, Mark Neumann, Oyvind Tafjord, Pradeep Dasigi, Nelson F. Liu, Matthew Peters, Michael Schmitz, and Luke S. Zettlemoyer. 2017. Allennlp: A deep semantic natural language processing platform.

Stuart W Grande, Mary Ganger Castaldo, Elizabeth Carpenter-Song, Ida Griesemer, and Glyn Elwyn. 2017. A digital advocate? reactions of rural people who experience homelessness to the idea of recording clinical encounters. *Health Expectations*, 20(4):618–625.

Ruidan He, Wee Sun Lee, Hwee Tou Ng, and Daniel Dahlmeier. 2017. An unsupervised neural attention model for aspect extraction. In *Proceedings of the 55th Annual Meeting of the Association for Computational Linguistics (Volume 1: Long Papers)*, pages 388–397, Vancouver, Canada. Association for Computational Linguistics.

Sarthak Jain and Byron C. Wallace. 2019. Attention is not explanation. In *NAACL-HLT*.

Sarthak Jain, Sarah Wiegreffe, Yuval Pinter, and Byron C Wallace. 2020. Learning to Faithfully Rationalize by Construction.

Shailesh Kumar. 2016. Burnout and doctors: prevalence, prevention and intervention. In *Healthcare*, volume 4, page 37. Multidisciplinary Digital Publishing Institute.

Tao Lei, Regina Barzilay, and Tommi Jaakkola. 2016. Rationalizing neural predictions. In *EMNLP 2016 - Conference on Empirical Methods in Natural Language Processing, Proceedings*, pages 107–117.

Yankai Lin, Shiqi Shen, Zhiyuan Liu, Huanbo Luan, and Maosong Sun. 2016. Neural relation extraction with selective attention over instances. In *Proceedings of the 54th Annual Meeting of the Association for Computational Linguistics (Volume 1: Long Papers)*, pages 2124–2133, Berlin, Germany. Association for Computational Linguistics.

Lisa C. Mcguire. 1996. Remembering what the doctor said: Organization and adults' memory for medical information. *Experimental Aging Research*, 22:403–428.

Vlad Niculae and Mathieu Blondel. 2017. A regularized framework for sparse and structured neural attention. In *Advances in neural information processing systems*, pages 3338–3348.

Bhargavi Paranjape, Mandar Joshi, John Thickstun, Hannaneh Hajishirzi, and Luke Zettlemoyer. 2020. An Information Bottleneck Approach for Controlling Conciseness in Rationale Extraction. Technical report.

Alvin Rajkomar, Anjuli Kannan, Kai Chen, Laura Vardoulakis, Katherine Chou, Claire Cui, and Jeffrey Dean. 2019. Automatically charting symptoms from patient-physician conversations using machine learning. *JAMA internal medicine*, 179(6):836–838.

Benjamin Schloss and Sandeep Konam. 2020. Towards an automated soap note: Classifying utterances from medical conversations. *Machine Learning for Health Care, 2020*, arXiv:2007.08749. Version 3.

Sai P Selvaraj and Sandeep Konam. 2019. Medication regimen extraction from clinical conversations. *arXiv preprint arXiv:1912.04961*.

Christine Sinsky, Lacey Colligan, Ling Li, Mirela Prgomet, Sam Reynolds, Lindsey Goeders, Johanna Westbrook, Michael Tutty, and George Blike. 2016. Allocation of physician time in ambulatory practice: a time and motion study in 4 specialties. *Annals of internal medicine*, 165(11):753–760.

Maka Tsulukidze, Marie-Anne Durand, Paul J Barr, Thomas Mead, and Glyn Elwyn. 2014. Providing recording of clinical consultation to patients– a highly valued but underutilized intervention: a scoping review. *Patient Education and Counseling*, 95(3):297–304.

Ashish Vaswani, Noam Shazeer, Niki Parmar, Jakob Uszkoreit, Llion Jones, Aidan N Gomez, Ł ukasz Kaiser, and Illia Polosukhin. 2017. Attention is all you need. In I. Guyon, U. V. Luxburg, S. Bengio, H. Wallach, R. Fergus, S. Vishwanathan, and R. Garnett, editors, *Advances in Neural Information Processing Systems 30*, pages 5998–6008. Curran Associates, Inc.

Thomas Wolf, Lysandre Debut, Victor Sanh, Julien Chaumond, Clement Delangue, Anthony Moi, Pierric Cistac, Tim Rault, R'emi Louf, Morgan Funtowicz, and Jamie Brew. 2019. Huggingface's transformers: State-of-the-art natural language processing. *ArXiv*, abs/1910.03771.

Yonghui Wu, Mike Schuster, Zhifeng Chen, Quoc V. Le, Mohammad Norouzi, Wolfgang Macherey, Maxim Krikun, Yuan Cao, Qin Gao, Klaus Macherey, Jeff Klingner, Apurva Shah, Melvin Johnson, Xiaobing Liu, Łukasz Kaiser, Stephan Gouws, Yoshikiyo Kato, Taku Kudo, Hideto Kazawa, Keith Stevens, George Kurian, Nishant Patil, Wei Wang, Cliff Young, Jason Smith, Jason Riesa, Alex Rudnick, Oriol Vinyals, Greg Corrado, Macduff Hughes, and Jeffrey Dean. 2016. Google's neural machine translation system: Bridging the gap between human and machine translation.

Bowen Yu, Zhenyu Zhang, Tingwen Liu, Bin Wang, Sujian Li, and Quangang Li. 2019. Beyond word attention: Using segment attention in neural relation extraction. In *IJCAI*, pages 5401–5407.

Ruiqi Zhong, Steven Shao, and Kathleen McKeown. 2019. Fine-grained sentiment analysis with faithful attention.

# A  Appendices

## A.1  Data

The complete set of *normalized* classification labels for all three medication attributes and their meaning is shown in Table 7.

Average statistics about the dataset are shown in Table 6.

|                          | min | max | mean | $\sigma$ |
|--------------------------|-----|-----|------|----------|
| #utterances in *text*    | 3   | 20  | 7.8  | 2.3      |
| #words in *text*         | 12  | 565 | 80.8 | 41.0     |
| #words in *freq* span    | 1   | 21  | 4.4  | 2.6      |
| #words in *route* span   | 1   | 9   | 1.5  | 1.0      |
| #words in *change* span  | 1   | 34  | 6.8  | 4.9      |

Table 6: Statistics of extraction labels (#words) and the corresponding *text*

## A.2  Hyperparameters

We use AllenNLP (Gardner et al., 2017) to implement our models and Weights&Biases (Biewald, 2020) to manage our experiments. Following is the list of hyperparameters used in our experiments:

1. **Contextualized Token Embedder:** We use 1024-dimensional 24-layer `bert-large-cased` obtained as a pre-trained model from HuggingFace[11]. We freeze the weights of the embedder in our training. The max sequence length is set to 256.

2. **Speaker embedding:** 2-dimensional trainable embedding with vocabulary size of 4 as we only have 4 unique speakers in our dataset: doctor, patient, caregiver and nurse.

3. **Softmax and Fusedmax:** The temperatures of softmax and fusedmax are set to a default value of 1. The sparsity weight of fusedmax is also set to its default value of 1 for all attributes.

4. **TAScore:** The transformer used in TAScore is a 2-layer transformer encoder where each layer is implemented as in Vaswani et al. (2017). Both the hidden dimensions inside the transformer (self-attention and feedforward) are set to 32 and all the dropout probabilities are set to 0.2. The linear layer for the query has input and output dimensions of 1024 and 32, respectively. Due to the concatenation of speaker embedding, the linear layer for keys has input and output dimensions of 1026 and 32, respectively. The feedforward layer (which generates scalar scores for each token) on top of the transformer is 2-layered with relu activations and hidden sizes (16, 1).

5. **Classifiers:** The final classifier for each attribute is a 2-layer feedforward network with hidden sizes (512, "number of classes for the attribute") and dropout probability of 0.2.

## A.3  Examples: Projection Functions

Figures 6 and 7 show examples of outputs of projection functions softmax and fusedmax on random input scores.

## A.4  Phrase based extraction baseline

We implement a phrase based extraction system to provide a baseline for the extraction task. A lexicon of relevant phrases is created for each class for each attribute as shown in Table 8. We then look for string matches within these phrases and the text for the data-point. If there are matches then the longest match is considered as an extraction span for that attribute.

[11]`https://huggingface.co/`
`bert-large-cased`

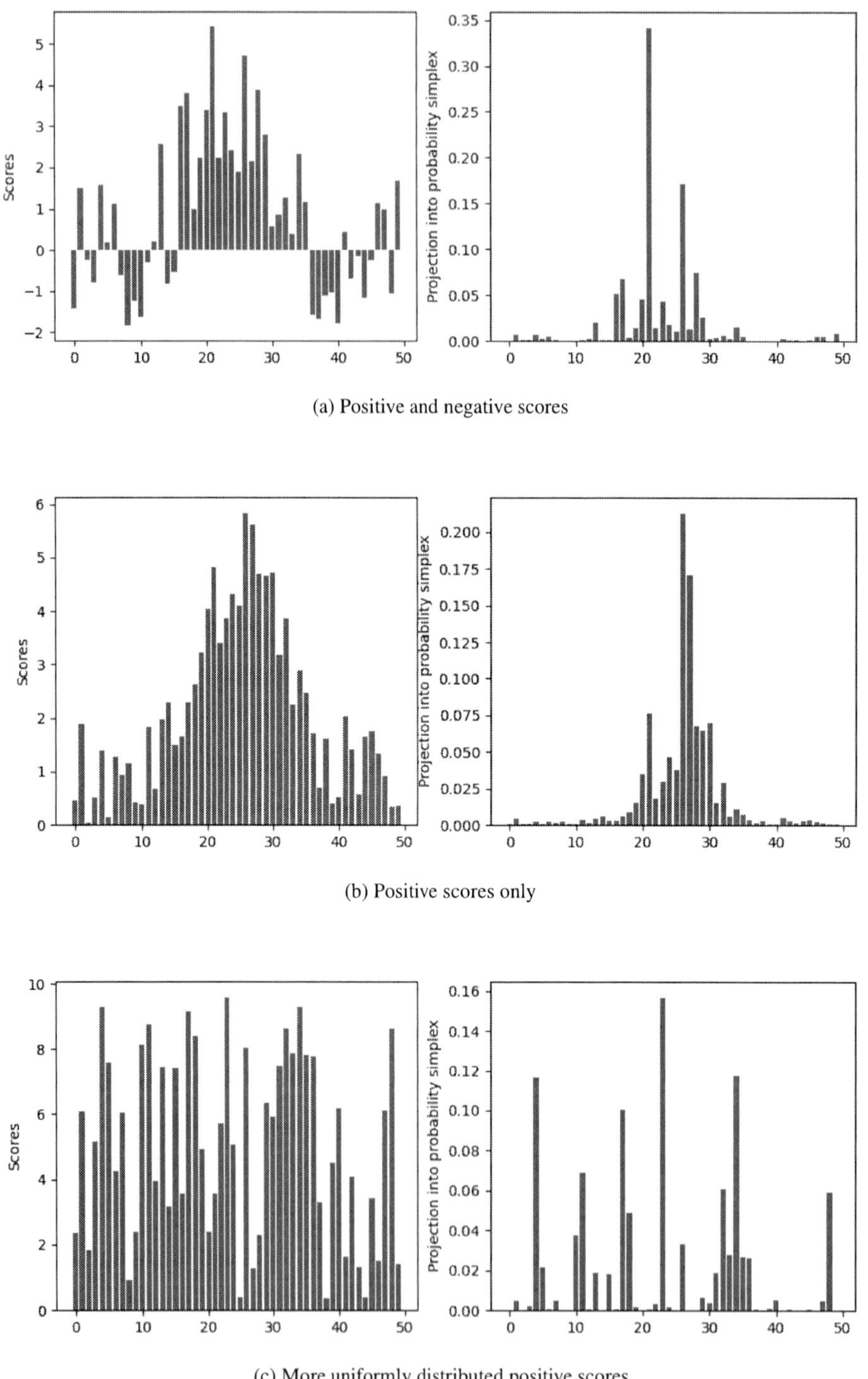

(a) Positive and negative scores

(b) Positive scores only

(c) More uniformly distributed positive scores

Figure 6: Sample outputs (right column) of softmax function on random input scores (left column).

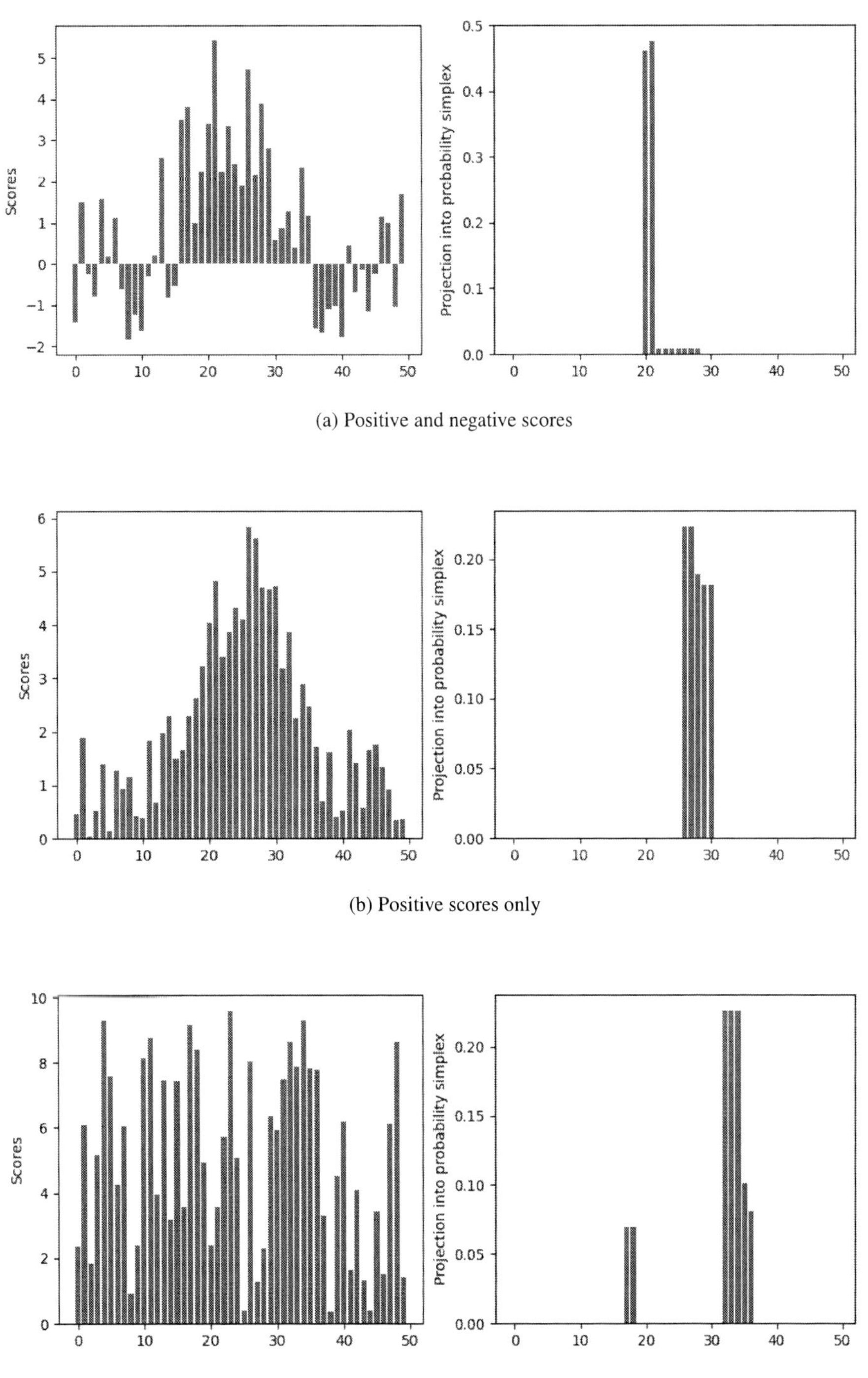

(a) Positive and negative scores

(b) Positive scores only

(c) More uniformly distributed positive scores

Figure 7: Sample outputs (right column) of fusedmax function on random input scores (left column).

| Attribute | class | Meaning | class proportion |
|---|---|---|---|
| *frequency* | Daily | Take the medication once a day (specific time not mentioned). | 8.0 |
| | Every morning | Take the medication once every morning. | 0.9 |
| | At Bedtime | At Bedtime | 1.7 |
| | Twice a day | Twice a day | 6.5 |
| | Three times a day | Three times a day | 1.6 |
| | Every six hours | Every six hours | 0.2 |
| | Every week | Every week | 0.9 |
| | Twice a week | Twice a week | 0.2 |
| | Three times a week | Three times a week | 0.3 |
| | Every month | Every month | 0.3 |
| | Other | Other | 1.5 |
| | None | None | 77.9 |
| *route* | Pill | Pill | 6.8 |
| | Injection | Injection | 3.5 |
| | Topical cream | Topical cream | 1.0 |
| | Nasal spray | Nasal spray | 0.5 |
| | Medicated patch | Medicated patch | 0.2 |
| | Ophthalmic solution | Ophthalmic solution | 0.2 |
| | Inhaler | Inhaler | 0.2 |
| | Oral solution | Oral solution | 0.1 |
| | Other | Other | 2.1 |
| | None | None | 85.5 |
| *change* | Take | Take | 83.1 |
| | Stop | Stop | 6.5 |
| | Increase | Increase | 5.2 |
| | Decrease | Decrease | 2.0 |
| | None | None | 1.6 |
| | Other | Other | 1.4 |

Table 7: Complete set of normalized classification labels for all three medication attributes and their explanation

| Attribute | Class | Phrases |
| --- | --- | --- |
| freq | Every Morning | everyday in the morning \| every morning \| morning |
| | At Bedtime | everyday before sleeping \| everyday after dinner \| every night \| after dinner \| at bedtime \| before sleeping |
| | Twice a day | twice a day \| 2 times a day \| two times a day \| 2 times per day \| two times per day |
| | Three times a day | 3 times a day \| 3 times per day \| 3 times every day |
| | Every six hours | every 6 hours \| every six hours |
| | Every week | every week \| weekly \| once a week |
| | Twice a week | twice a week \| two times a week \| 2 times a week \| twice per week \| two times per week \| 2 times per week |
| | Three times a week | 3 times a week \| 3 times per week |
| | Every month | every month \| monthly \| once a month |
| | Other | |
| | None | |
| route | Pill | tablet \| pill \| capsule \| mg |
| | Injection | pen \| shot \| injector \| injection \| inject |
| | Topical cream | cream \| gel \| ointment \| lotion |
| | Nasal spray | spray \| nasal conversation transcript. |
| | Medicated patch | patch |
| | Ophthalmic solution | ophthalmic \| drops \| drop |
| | Oral solution | oral solution |
| | Other | |
| | None | |
| change | Take | take \| start \| put you on \| continue |
| | Stop | stop \| off |
| | Increase | increase |
| | Decrease | reduce \| decrease |
| | Other | |
| | None | |

Table 8: Phrases used in the phrase based baseline. These are also the most frequently occurring phrases in the free-form annotations.

# Extracting Relations between Radiotherapy Treatment Details


**Danielle S. Bitterman[1,2,3], Timothy A. Miller[3], David Harris[3], Chen Lin[3],**
**Sean Finan[3], Jeremy L. Warner[4,5], Raymond H. Mak[2], Guergana K. Savova[3]**

[1]Harvard Radiation Oncology Program, Boston, MA
[2]Department of Radiation Oncology, Brigham and Women's Hospital/Dana-Farber Cancer
Institute, Boston MA
[3]Boston Children's Hospital Informatics Program, and Harvard Medical School, Boston,
MA
[4]Division of Hematology/Oncology, Vanderbilt University, Nashville, TN
5Department of Biomedical Informatics, Vanderbilt University, Nashville, TN



## Abstract

We present work on extraction of radiotherapy treatment information from the clinical narrative in the electronic medical records. Radiotherapy is a central component of the treatment of most solid cancers. Its details are described in non-standardized fashions using jargon not found in other medical specialties, complicating the already difficult task of manual data extraction. We examine the performance of several state-of-the-art neural methods for relation extraction of radiotherapy treatment details, with a goal of automating detailed information extraction. The neural systems perform at 0.82-0.88 macro-average F1, which approximates or in some cases exceeds the inter-annotator agreement. To the best of our knowledge, this is the first effort to develop models for radiotherapy relation extraction and one of the few efforts for relation extraction to describe cancer treatment in general.


## 1 Introduction

Radiotherapy is the use of ionizing radiation, which is radiation with enough energy to remove electrons from atoms and molecules, to treat disease (Gunderson and Tepper, 2020). The predominant indication for radiotherapy is the treatment of cancer, where it exerts its antineoplastic effect via DNA damage, which preferentially kills cancer cells over health tissue cells (McDermott and Orton, 2010). Radiotherapy plays a central role in the curative and palliative treatment of many cancers. It is estimated that up to 30% of cancer patients receive radiotherapy as a part of their first-line treatment, and approximately 50% of all cancer patients receive radiotherapy during the course of their cancer care (Delaney et al., 2005; Smith et al., JCO 2010).

Despite its importance in cancer treatment, radiotherapy is included in cancer registries in only high-level, often cursory detail, if at all. For example, radiotherapy details are only available by custom request in the publicly available Surveillance, Epidemiology, and End Results Program (SEER) cancer registry, acknowledging incompleteness and errors in this manually extracted data (Surveillance, Epidemiology, and End Results Program). The reason for this is multifold. First, radiotherapy is a highly technical field not extensively taught in medical school, and uses its own jargon not found in other medical texts. Additionally, radiation treatment details are frequently not entered into the electronic medical records (EMR) as structured data. Instead, radiotherapy is described in clinical free text using descriptive and very non-standardized language. Radiotherapy treatment descriptions are more similar to the documentation of operative procedures than to documentation of medication regimens. Because radiation is personalized to each patient's disease and anatomy, it cannot be described with standard reporting of the type of radiation, dose, and frequency. Additionally, radiotherapy is often delivered in multiple phases, each treating a different anatomical site to different doses and with different types of radiation, yielding complex descriptions of treatment courses. These features, in concert with a lack of widely used standardized nomenclatures (Mir et al., 2020; Phillips et al., 2020; Traverso et al., 2018), limit manual data extraction, hindering the potential of




*Proceedings of the 3rd Clinical Natural Language Processing Workshop*, pages 194–200
November 19, 2020. ©2020 Association for Computational Linguistics

big data to improve cancer research and clinical care.

While algorithms for named entity recognition have previously been reported for radiotherapy details (Bitterman et al., 2020) and other cancer therapies (Yin et al., 2018; Wang et al., 2019; Yim et al, 2016; Savova et al., 2019), relation extraction remains a relatively underexplored task in clinical NLP (Sheikhalishahi et al., 2019). There are few examples of relation extraction models for cancer characteristics in general (Bozkurt et al., 2016; Savova et al., 2017; Sheikhalishahi et al., 2019), and to the best of our knowledge none for cancer treatment, including radiotherapy. Identifying treatment entities in isolation and not linking them to a specific treatment instance is insufficient to coherently describe cancer therapies, especially because concurrent and serial treatments are often described together in the same note. For example, extracting frequency without linking it to a specific treatment is not informative by itself. Relation extraction is a critical component of information extraction for radiotherapy as this treatment is often given in multiple sequential or nested phases. Linking relevant treatment entities with the same phase is necessary to summarize how and why a treatment was delivered, necessary components to understanding treatment outcomes and quality. However, this is a very challenging task even for expert human annotators, as demonstrated by the challenges in accurate extraction of such data for SEER. Therefore, there is a need for more reliable relation extraction methods for radiotherapy.

Relations can be modeled in various ways in neural networks, including inserting special tokens around the arguments of interest and using this augmented text as input into the model (Dligach et al., 2017), and using token position embeddings to encode the relative distance of words to the arguments (Zeng et al., 2014; Nguyen and

Grishman et al., 2015; Shi and Lin et al., 2019; Wang et al., 2019). Using the former approach, we aimed to investigate several approaches for relation extraction from clinical texts describing radiotherapy, with a goal of augmenting reporting of cancer treatment details for research and clinical purposes.

The contributions of the work described in the paper are (1) the definition of the task of radiotherapy information extraction from the EMR clinical narrative, (2) the creation of resources for the task (annotation guidelines and corpus), (3) the exploration of state-of-the-art neural methods to this highly impactful clinical task, and (4) establishing a baseline for the task.

## 2   Data

Data for this work consisted of texts describing radiotherapy from three complementary sources. First, we included 270 clinical descriptions of radiotherapy regimens from HemOnc.org, which is a publicly available wiki of cancer and blood disorder treatment regimens and interventions. Second, we included 73 radiotherapy descriptions from a state cancer registry. These are abstractions from patients' EMR, often copied and pasted from clinician notes, describing details of cancer treatment for use by cancer registrars within a patient-level XML. We used the entire text of the XML categories that contained radiotherapy details as model input. Third, 79 completed breast and colorectal cancer clinician notes that contained radiotherapy details from the THYME corpus from Clinical TempEval (Bethard et al., 2015) and an internal corpus with breast cancer notes.

Annotation guidelines for radiotherapy properties and treatment instances were developed (Bitterman et al., 2020).[1] If an overall radiotherapy treatment course was delivered in more than one

<hr>

*Dose-Treatment Site relationship is represented as:*

…She presented after a screening mammogram showed a nodule in the *left breast upper outer quadrant*. After lumpectomy, she was treated with radiation to a dose of 50 Gy in 25 fractions to the *left breast*, followed by a boost of RT_DosageStart **10 Gy** RTDosage_End in 5 fractions to the TxSiteStart **tumor bed** TxSiteEnd…

Figure 1: Mock text segment describing radiotherapy with start and stop tokens, illustrating the Dose-Treatment Site relationship between the two bolded entities: 10 Gy (Dose) and tumor bed (Treatment Site). The zigzag and dashed lines indicate adjacent spans describing two different radiotherapy instances, and italicized entities are non-related anatomical/treatment sites close to the anchor dose mention. Both of these

<hr>

[1]https://github.com/RTParse/RTAnnot

| Relation | IAA |
|---|---|
| Dose-Dose | 0.94 |
| Dose-Treatment Site | 0.90 |
| Dose-Frequency | 1.00 |
| Dose-Fraction Number | 0.98 |
| Dose-Boost | 0.67 |
| None | 0.74 |

Table 1: Inter-Annotator Agreement (IAA) for the six relation categories.

phase, as described above, each phase was considered a separate radiotherapy instance (Figure 1). Gold annotations for relations between the following key properties were created: Dose, Fraction Number, Fraction Frequency, Treatment Site, and Boost. Radiotherapy is most often delivered in many small doses, or fractions, over a given period of time. Dose is any description of radiation dosage in the text, either the total dose or fractional doses, generally described using the unit Gray (Gy). Fraction Number is any mention of the number of fractions delivered, and Fraction Frequency is the frequency of fraction delivery. Treatment site is the actual or relative anatomical site that is targeted with radiotherapy. Boost is a mention that conveys the treatment instance is a second phase of radiotherapy that brings a smaller treatment site to a higher dose. Properties that described the same treatment instance were linked together as a relation.

Two expert human annotators completed gold annotations for 47 radiotherapy instances containing 310 relation instances to calculate inter-annotator agreement, after which a single human annotator completed the gold annotations. As most radiotherapy instances included Dose, we chose to classify the relations between each Dose mention and every other property mentioned in the radiation instance. Thus, Dose mentions served as the anchor for the relations within a radiotherapy instance and were labeled as Dose-Mention. Of note, Dose-Dose refers to a relation of two different Dose mentions in the same radiotherapy instance. In our dataset, there were on average 1.4 radiation instances per document. Documents were split into train, development, and test sets. The gold annotated HemOnc.org corpus will be made publicly available for research purposes.

## 3   Methods

We explored two state-of-the-art neural network methods for this task. First, we used Flair (Akbik et al., 2018), which is a pre-trained character language model trained on one billion words of text (Chelba et al., 2013) to train a multi-layer Long Short-Term Memory (LSTM) (Hochreiter and Schmidhuber, 1997) to generate contextual embeddings. Text is then passed into this model, put into an LSTM to obtain a text representation, and this is passed into a final linear layer for classification. We were motivated to explore this approach as we hypothesized that the contextual character embedding may be better at handling the rare and misspelled words in cancer texts, as well as numbers and short abbreviations common in radiation descriptions. Models had a hidden state of 128 and a dropout of 0.15-0.24, and were trained for 100 epochs using a mini-batch size of 8 and learning rate starting at 0.2 with an anneal factor of 0.5, using an SGD optimizer (Robbins and Monro, 1951; Kiefer and Wolfowitz, 1952; Bottou et al., 2016). Second, we assessed the performance of bidirectional encoder representations from transformers (BERT) base uncased model, fine-tuned on this relation task using a recurrent neural network to predict the class label (Devlin et al.; 2019). We chose to explore this method given the excellent relation classification performance of attention-based models in biomedical texts (Verga et al., 2018; Wei et al., 2019; Lee et al., 2020). These models had a hidden size of 128 and dropout of 0.5, and were trained for 30 epochs using a mini-batch size of 8 and learning rate starting at 0.00003 with an anneal factor of 0.5, using an Adam optimizer (Kingma and Ba, 2014). For all, the model that performed best on the development set was evaluated on the held-out test set. Rule-based methods were considered, but as there are often more than one radiotherapy instance mentioned in a clinical text, frequently in close proximity and described in nested fashion, we did not feel there was a straightforward approach (Figure 1).

To generate candidate relations, we extracted text windows encompassing two different token lengths on each side of the gold annotated Dose mention anchor: 46 tokens and 90 tokens (95th and 99th percentile of token span lengths between Dose-Mentions in the same gold radiotherapy instances in the train and development sets, respectively). Every Dose-Mention pair in the text window was considered a candidate relation. For each relation candidate, start and stop tokens were inserted around the Dose and candidate property (Figure 1). The text segment was labeled with a

| Flair/BERT Models | Precision | | Recall | | F1 | |
|---|---|---|---|---|---|---|
| | 92 Token Windows | 180 Token Windows | 92 Token Windows | 180 Token Windows | 92 Token Windows | 180 Token Windows |
| Dose-Dose | 0.77/0.88 | 0.79/0.68 | 0.75/0.82 | 0.83/0.81 | 0.76/0.85 | 0.81/0.74 |
| Dose-Treatment Site | 0.84/0.79 | 0.61/0.76 | 0.86/0.88 | 0.92/0.89 | 0.85/0.83 | 0.73/0.82 |
| Dose-Fraction Frequency | 0.79/0.78 | 0.84/0.88 | 0.95/0.90 | 1.00/1.00 | 0.86/0.84 | 0.91/0.93 |
| Dose-Fraction Number | 0.95/0.94 | 0.90/0.87 | 0.93/0.96 | 0.92/0.95 | 0.94/0.95 | 0.91/0.91 |
| Dose-Boost | 1.00/0.85 | 0.56/0.60 | 0.69/0.85 | 0.69/0.92 | 0.82/0.85 | 0.62/0.73 |
| None | 0.95/0.95 | 0.98/0.98 | 0.95/0.94 | 0.94/0.95 | 0.95/0.95 | 0.96/0.96 |
| Average | 0.88/0.87 | 0.78/0.80 | 0.86/0.89 | 0.88/0.92 | 0.86/0.88 | 0.82/0.85 |

Table 2: Results of the two Flair and two BERT relation classification models, developed using two different text windows around the anchor Dose entity. The first result is from Flair, the second – from BERT (Flair/BERT)

positive Dose-Property relation if the Dose and candidate property were in the same radiotherapy instance.

The precision (True Positives/Predictions), recall (True Positives/Gold Positives), and F1 score ((2*Precision*Recall)/(precision+recall)) are reported for each model. Error analysis via manual inspection was carried out to better understand how and where the models performed poorly.

## 4    Evaluation

Table 1 shows the IAA for each of the relation categories. IAA was $\geq 0.9$ for all categories except for Dose-Boost (0.67) and None (0.74). Of note, there were only 6 total Boost mentions in the pilot dataset, limiting interpretation of this IAA.

Table 2 shows the performance of the Flair and BERT relation classification models. Overall, the best performing model was the BERT model fine-tuned on the 92 token text windows (macro-average F1: 0.88), followed by the Flair model fine-tuned on the 92 token text windows (macro-average F1: 0.86). Precision for the Flair model with this window was on average slightly higher than that for the BERT model. The models fine-tuned on the 180 text windows had slightly worse performance (BERT model macro-F1: 0.85, Flair model macro-F1: 0.82).

Qualitative error analysis of each model revealed five main categories of failure: 1) human errors in gold labeling, 2) false positives due to two mentions being in close proximity despite relating to different treatment instances, 3) false negatives

| Error Type | Text | Gold Label | Predicted Label |
|---|---|---|---|
| Human error in gold labeling | "…2 Gy fractions **once per day** x 15 fractions (total dose: **30 Gy**)…" | None | Dose-Frequency |
| False positive due to two mentions in close proximity | "…Synchronously, PTV1 and PTV2 received **45** and **50.4 Gy**, respectively..." | None | Dose-Dose |
| False negative due to distant related mentions | "…**1.5 Gy** fractions x 16 fractions, given twice per day (4 to 6 hour interval between treatments) on days 1 to 5, 8 to 10. Total dose during consolidation is **24 Gy**..." | Dose-Dose | None |
| Incorrect label in texts with atypical treatment description | "...additional treatment up to a total of **55.8 Gy** was administered to original bony tumors and the postinduction chemotherapy soft tissue volumes plus a **2 cm margin**..." | Dose-Treatment Site | None |

Table 3: Examples of error types identified in qualitative error analysis. The mentions being classified are bolded in the text.

because related mentions were distant and/or crossing sentence boundaries 4) incorrect labeling in texts with very atypical descriptions of treatment, 5) incorrect labeling in tabular text, and 6) other/unknown. Examples of errors are shown in Table 3. All models suffered from similar methods of failure, and texts describing radiotherapy courses with several phases appeared to be particularly challenging. Interestingly, the BERT model fine-tuned on the 180 token text windows was better able to correctly label relations in tables than the other models, although there were only rare examples of tables in these corpora.

Additionally, in the Flair models using the 92 and 180 token window texts, there were 3 and 8 true positive relations, respectively, that were labeled with an incorrect label other than "None". All incorrect labels in the BERT models were either a "None" label assigned to a true relation, or a false positive relation assigned to a true "None" relation.

## 5    Discussion and Conclusion

The neural models had very good performance on the radiotherapy relations explored in these experiments, often approaching or exceeding IAA. The performance of the BERT and Flair models were overall comparable, with the best BERT model outperforming the best Flair model. Interestingly, the size of the text windows used for fine-tuning appeared to have a larger impact on performance than the type of model itself, with shorter texts yielding better results. This may be due to the frequent repetition of similar but unrelated entities and treatments in clinical texts, and optimizing this parameter should be explored when developing models for clinical relation extraction.

These findings suggest that neural methods may be a good avenue for clinical relation extraction for complex, highly specialized treatments such as radiotherapy. Future work will develop models to extract relations between Dose and additional relevant entities, and will investigate end-to-end entity and relation extraction systems for robust information extraction pipelines.

## Acknowledgements

The work was supported by funding from the United States National Institutes of Health -- UG3CA243120 from the National Cancer Institute. The content is solely the responsibility of the authors and does not necessarily represent the official views of the National Institutes of Health.

## References

Alan Akbik, Duncan Blythe, and Roland Vollgraf. 2018. Contextual string embeddings for sequence labeling. *In Proceedings of the 27th International Conference on Computational Linguistics*, pages 1638–1649. Retrieved from https://www.aclweb.org/anthology/C18-1139/

Danielle Bitterman, Timothy Miller, David Harris, Chen Lin, Sean Finan, Jeremy Warner, Ray Mak, Guergana Savova. 2020. Extracting radiotherapy treatment details using neural network-based natural language processing. *Presented at the Poster to be presented at the 62nd Annual Meeting of the American Society for Radiation Oncology.*

Steven Bethard, Leon Derczynski, Guergana Savova, James Pustejovsky, and Marc Verhagen. 2015. Semeval-2015 task 6: Clinical tempeval. *In Proceedings of the 9th international workshop on semantic evaluation (SemEval 2015)*, pages 806–814. Retrieved from https://www.aclweb.org/anthology/S15-2136.pdf

Léon Bottou, Frank E. Curtis, and Jorge Nocedal. 2016. Optimization Methods for Large-Scale Machine Learning. June. *arXiv [stat.ML].* Retrieved from arXiv.

Selen Bozkurt, Jafi A. Lipson, Utku Senol, and Daniel L. Rubin. 2015. Automatic abstraction of imaging observations with their characteristics from mammography reports. *Journal of the American Medical Informatics Association: JAMIA*, 22(e1):e81–92, April. Retrieved from http://dx.doi.org/10.1136/amiajnl-2014-003009

Ciprian Chelba, Tomas Mikolov, Mike Schuster, Qi Ge, Thorsten Brants, Phillipp Koehn, and Tony Robinson. 2013. One Billion Word Benchmark for Measuring Progress in Statistical Language Modeling. December. *arXiv [cs.CL].* Retrieved from arXiv.

Geoff Delaney, Susannah Jacob, Carolyn Featherstone, and Michael Barton. 2005. The role of radiotherapy in cancer treatment: estimating optimal utilization from a review of evidence-based clinical guidelines. *Cancer,*

104(6):1129–1137, September. Retrieved from http://dx.doi.org/10.1002/cncr.21324

Jacob Devlin, Ming-Wei Chang, Kenton Lee, and Kristina Toutanova. 2018. BERT: Pre-training of Deep Bidirectional Transformers for Language Understanding. October. *arXiv [cs.CL]*. Retrieved from arXiv.

Dmitriy Dligach, Timothy Miller, Chen Lin, Steven Bethard, and Guergana Savova. 2017. Neural temporal relation extraction. *In Proceedings of the 15th Conference of the European Chapter of the Association for Computational Linguistics: Volume 2, Short Papers*, pages 746–751. Retrieved from https://www.aclweb.org/anthology/E17-2118.pdf

Leonard Gunderson MD MS and Joel E. Tepper. 2015. *Clinical Radiation Oncology*. Elsevier Health Sciences, August. Retrieved from https://play.google.com/store/books/details?id=NmFyCgAAQBAJ

HemOnc.org - A Hematology Oncology Wiki. Retrieved June 18, 2020, from http://hemonc.org

Sepp Hochreiter and Jürgen Schmidhuber. 1997. Long Short-Term Memory. *Neural Computation*. Retrieved from http://dx.doi.org/10.1162/neco.1997.9.8.1735

J. Kiefer and J. Wolfowitz. 1952. Stochastic Estimation of the Maximum of a Regression Function. *Annals of Mathematical Statistics*, 23(3):462–466, September. Retrieved August 10, 2020, from https://projecteuclid.org/euclid.aoms/1177729392

Diederik P. Kingma and Jimmy Ba. 2014. Adam: A Method for Stochastic Optimization. December. *arXiv [cs.LG]*. Retrieved from arXiv.

Jinhyuk Lee, Wonjin Yoon, Sungdong Kim, Donghyeon Kim, Sunkyu Kim, Chan Ho So, and Jaewoo Kang. 2020. BioBERT: a pre-trained biomedical language representation model for biomedical text mining. *Bioinformatics*, 36(4):1234–1240, February. Retrieved from https://doi.org/10.1093/bioinformatics/btz682

THYME. Retrieved August 9, 2020, from http://thyme.healthnlp.org

Patrick N. McDermott and Colin G. Orton. 2010. *The physics & technology of radiation therapy.* Medical Physics Publishing.

Romaana Mir, Sarah M. Kelly, Ying Xiao, Alisha Moore, Catharine H. Clark, Enrico Clementel, Coreen Corning, Martin Ebert, Peter Hoskin, Coen W. Hurkmans, Satoshi Ishikura, Ingrid Kristensen, Stephen F. Kry, Joerg Lehmann, Jeff M. Michalski, Angelo F. Monti, Mitsuhiro Nakamura, Kenton Thompson, Huiqi Yang, et al. 2020. Organ at risk delineation for radiation therapy clinical trials: Global Harmonization Group consensus guidelines. *Radiotherapy and oncology: journal of the European Society for Therapeutic Radiology and Oncology*, June. http://dx.doi.org/10.1016/j.radonc.2020.05.038

Thien Huu Nguyen and Ralph Grishman. 2015. Relation extraction: Perspective from convolutional neural networks. *In Proceedings of the 1st Workshop on Vector Space Modeling for Natural Language Processing*, pages 39–48. Retrieved from https://www.aclweb.org/anthology/W15-1506.pdf

Mark H. Phillips, Lucas M. Serra, Andre Dekker, Preetam Ghosh, Samuel M. H. Luk, Alan Kalet, and Charles Mayo. 2020. Ontologies in radiation oncology. *Physica medica: PM: an international journal devoted to the applications of physics to medicine and biology: official journal of the Italian Association of Biomedical Physics* , 72:103–113, April. Retrieved from http://dx.doi.org/10.1016/j.ejmp.2020.03.017

Herbert Robbins and Sutton Monro. 1951. A Stochastic Approximation Method. *Annals of Mathematical Statistics*, 22(3):400–407, September. Retrieved August 10, 2020, from http://projecteuclid.org/euclid.aoms/1177729586

Marta Recasens, Christian Danescu-Niculescu-Mizil, and Dan Jurafsky. 2013. Linguistic Models for Analyzing and Detecting Biased Language. *In Proceedings of the 51st Annual Meeting of the Association for Computational Linguistics*, pages 1650–1659, Sofia, Bulgaria.

Guergana K. Savova, Eugene Tseytlin, Sean Finan, Melissa Castine, Timothy Miller, Olga Medvedeva, David Harris, Harry Hochheiser, Chen Lin, Girish Chavan, and Rebecca S. Jacobson. 2017. DeepPhe: A Natural Language

Processing System for Extracting Cancer Phenotypes from Clinical Records. *Cancer research*, 77(21):e115–e118, November. Retrieved from http://dx.doi.org/10.1158/0008-5472.CAN-19-0579

Seyedmostafa Sheikhalishahi, Riccardo Miotto, Joel T. Dudley, Alberto Lavelli, Fabio Rinaldi, and Venet Osmani. 2019. Natural Language Processing of Clinical Notes on Chronic Diseases: Systematic Review. *JMIR medical informatics*, 7(2):e12239, April. Retrieved from http://dx.doi.org/10.2196/12239

Peng Shi and Jimmy Lin. 2019. Simple BERT Models for Relation Extraction and Semantic Role Labeling. April. *arXiv [cs.CL]*. Retrieved from arXiv.

Benjamin D. Smith, Bruce G. Haffty, Lynn D. Wilson, Grace L. Smith, Akshar N. Patel, and Thomas A. Buchholz. 2010. The future of radiation oncology in the United States from 2010 to 2020: will supply keep pace with demand? *Journal of clinical oncology: official journal of the American Society of Clinical Oncology*, 28(35):5160–5165, December. Retrieved from http://dx.doi.org/10.1200/JCO.2010.31.2520

Surveillance, Epidemiology, and End Results Program. (n.d.). . Retrieved August 9, 2020, from https://seer.cancer.gov/

Khajamoinuddin Syed, William Sleeman Iv, Kevin Ivey, Michael Hagan, Jatinder Palta, Rishabh Kapoor, and Preetam Ghosh. 2020. Integrated Natural Language Processing and Machine Learning Models for Standardizing Radiotherapy Structure Names. *Healthcare (Basel, Switzerland)*, 8(2), April. Retrieved from http://dx.doi.org/10.3390/healthcare8020120

Alberto Traverso, Johan van Soest, Leonard Wee, and Andre Dekker. 2018. The radiation oncology ontology (ROO): Publishing linked data in radiation oncology using semantic web and ontology techniques. *Medical physics*, 45(10):e854–e862, October. Retrieved from http://dx.doi.org/10.1002/mp.12879

Patrick Verga, Emma Strubell, and Andrew McCallum. 2018. Simultaneously Self-Attending to All Mentions for Full-Abstract Biological Relation Extraction. February. *arXiv [cs.CL]*. Retrieved from arXiv.

Gary Walker, Ergin Soysal, and Hua Xu. 2019. Development of a Natural Language Processing Tool to Extract Radiation Treatment Sites. *Cureus*, 11(10):e6010, October. Retrieved from http://dx.doi.org/10.7759/cureus.6010

Haoyu Wang, Ming Tan, Mo Yu, Shiyu Chang, Dakuo Wang, Kun Xu, Xiaoxiao Guo, and Saloni Potdar. 2019. Extracting Multiple-Relations in One-Pass with Pre-Trained Transformers. February. *arXiv [cs.CL]*. Retrieved from arXiv.

Liwei Wang, Lei Luo, Yanshan Wang, Jason Wampfler, Ping Yang, and Hongfang Liu. 2019. Natural language processing for populating lung cancer clinical research data. *BMC medical informatics and decision making*, 19(Suppl 5):239, December. Retrieved from http://dx.doi.org/10.1186/s12911-019-0931-8

Qiang Wei, Zongcheng Ji, Yuqi Si, Jingcheng Du, Jingqi Wang, Firat Tiryaki, Stephen Wu, Cui Tao, Kirk Roberts, and Hua Xu. 2019. Relation Extraction from Clinical Narratives Using Pre-trained Language Models. *AMIA ... Annual Symposium proceedings / AMIA Symposium. AMIA Symposium*, 2019:1236–1245.

Wen-Wai Yim, Meliha Yetisgen, William P. Harris, and Sharon W. Kwan. 2016. Natural Language Processing in Oncology: A Review. *JAMA oncology*, 2(6):797–804, June. Retrieved from http://dx.doi.org/10.1001/jamaoncol.2016.0213

Zhijun Yin, Morgan Harrell, Jeremy L. Warner, Qingxia Chen, Daniel Fabbri, and Bradley A. Malin. 2018. The therapy is making me sick: how online portal communications between breast cancer patients and physicians indicate medication discontinuation. *Journal of the American Medical Informatics Association: JAMIA*, 25(11):1444–1451, November. Retrieved from http://dx.doi.org/10.1093/jamia/ocy118

Daojian Zeng, Kang Liu, Siwei Lai, Guangyou Zhou, and Jun Zhao. 2014. Relation classification via convolutional deep neural network. *In Proceedings of COLING 2014, the 25th International Conference on Computational Linguistics: Technical Papers*, pages 2335–2344. Retrieved from https://www.aclweb.org/anthology/C14-1220.pdf

# Cancer Registry Information Extraction via Transfer Learning

You-Chen Zhang[1], Ti-Hao Wang[2], Yi-Hsin Yang[3],
Yan-Jie Lin[4], Chung-Yang Wu[1], Yu-Cheng Chang[1], Pin-Jou Lu[1],
Chih-Jen Huang[5], Yu-Tsang Wang[6], Sheau-Fang Yang[7]
Kuan-Chung Hsiao[3], Ko-Jiunn Liu[3], Li-Tzong Chen[3], Tsang-Wu Liu[3*]
I-Shou Chang[3*], Kun-San Clifford Chao[8*], Hong-Jie Dai[1,3,9*]

[1]Intelligent System Lab, College of Electrical Engineering and Computer Science,
Department of Electrical Engineering, National Kaohsiung University of Science and
Technology, Kaohsiung, Taiwan R.O.C.
[2]Department of Radiation Oncology, China Medical University Hospital, China Medical
University, Taichung, Taiwan, R.O.C.
[3]National Institute of Cancer Research, National Health Research Institutes, Tainan,
Taiwan, R.O.C.
[4]Institute of Population Health Sciences, National Health Research Institutes, Miaoli,
Taiwan R.O.C.
[5]Cancer Center, Kaohsiung Medical University Hospital, Kaohsiung Medical University,
Taiwan R.O.C.
[6]Division of Medical Statistics and Bioinformatics, Department of Medical Research,
Kaohsiung Medical University Hospital, Kaohsiung Medical University, Taiwan R.O.C.
[7]Department of Pathology, Kaohsiung Medical University Hospital, Kaohsiung Medical
University, Taiwan R.O.C.
[7]Department of Public Health, Kaohsiung Medical University, Taiwan R.O.C.
[8] Cancer Center, China Medical University Hospital, China Medical University, Taichung,
Taiwan, R.O.C.
[9]School of Post-Baccalaureate Medicine, Kaohsiung Medical University, Kaohsiung,
Taiwan R.O.C.

## Abstract

A cancer registry is a critical and massive database for which various types of domain knowledge are needed and whose maintenance requires labor-intensive data curation. In order to facilitate the curation process for building a high-quality and integrated cancer registry database, we compiled a cross-hospital corpus and applied neural network methods to develop a natural language processing system for extracting cancer registry variables buried in unstructured pathology reports. The performance of the developed networks was compared with various baselines using standard micro-precision, recall and F-measure. Furthermore, we conducted experiments to study the feasibility of applying transfer learning to rapidly develop a well-performing system for processing reports from different sources that might be presented in different writing styles and formats. The results demonstrate that the transfer learning method enables us to develop a satisfactory system for a new hospital with only a few annotations and suggest more opportunities to reduce the burden of cancer registry curation.

## 1   Introduction

Cancer is a main cause of mortality worldwide and has been the leading cause of death over several decades in our country. A cancer registry system has been established by Taiwan Society of Cancer Registry and supported by Ministry of Health and Welfare (MOHW) over 40 years. How to extract massive data concisely and maintain high quality

---

* Corresponding authors



*Proceedings of the 3rd Clinical Natural Language Processing Workshop*, pages 201–208
November 19, 2020. ©2020 Association for Computational Linguistics

continuously are critical issues and burdens of healthcare system. However, the maintenance of an individual cancer registry from patient healthcare trajectories needs different types of domain knowledge which is pronouncedly both labor-intensive and time-consuming. In addition, how to validate and integrate between different hospitals or between local healthcare resource and national database are crucial topics.

To facilitate the integration of models for a specific cancer, applying information technology tools to improve acquisition and classification of patients' healthcare trajectories can enable more accurate phenotyping of cancer information. Nevertheless, addressing the issues needs more cooperation both on information technology and medical expertise. In order to assist integration among the institutes, a national project was established under the Cancer Center Support Grant Program (CCSG) supported by MOHW. As the coordinator of this project, we conducted research studies and cooperated with several hospitals to establish a platform to work out a model system based on existing cancer data.

One major goal of this project is to apply natural language processing (NLP) techniques to automatically analyze unstructured data including surgical reports, pathology reports, oncology clinical notes, and laboratory findings that may not be easy to acquire or share across hospitals for specific cancers. Pathology reports are usually abundant and contain operative findings, general tumor information, pathological assessment, cancer staging, and end-results which need to be extracted and classified clearly. In the pilot study, we focus on tasks including the collection and de-identification of pathology reports, data annotation for developing and evaluating deep learning-based NLP systems to extract cancer registry variables from different hospital sites.

To standardize the annotation of pathology material for developing our NLP system, the variables and their definitions were defined by the

Table 1: Datasets collected from two medical centers for this study.

| Source | CMUH | KMUH |
| --- | --- | --- |
| # of Reports | 393 | 1615 |
| Training Set | 293 | 1515 |
| Test set | 100 | 100 |
| Period | 2007~2013 | 2009~2015 |

consensus from expertise committee composed of hospital investigators and annotators. Furthermore, we applied transfer learning and conducted experiments to examine the performance of the developed neural networks on the cross-hospital pathology materials to gain insights on how effective and concise transfer learning can be. The results not only enable us to understand which layers of the developed network convey the most important parameters for transfer but also let us know how many annotations are needed for training a system for a new hospital to achieve reasonable performance.

## 2    Method

### 2.1    Datasets

In the presented study, we primarily focused on the colorectal cancer, which is the third leading cause of cancer-specific death in Taiwan. We cooperated with two medical centers, namely China Medical University Hospital (CMUH) and Kaohsiung Medical University Chung-Ho Memorial Hospital (KMUH), to collect colorectal pathology reports and the data were excluded non-tumor reports as well as the reports without cancer registration data for compiling our corpora. Table 1 shows the grouping and the number of the collected datasets.

### 2.2    Corpus Construction

In order to produce high quality annotations for developing our system, we established a NLP working group focusing on the construction of high-quality corpora. For our purpose, the annotation process was conducted by eight annotators based on an annotation guideline developed by consulting the committee composed of hospital investigators and cancer registrars. According to the standard of American Joint Committee on Cancer, nine cancer registry variables were defined for extraction in order to achieving a better understanding and unified effects on pathological materials. Table 2 summarizes the nine variables defined for the colorectal cancer including stage classification (SC), pathological TNM classifications (TNM), the number of examined nodes (NE) and positive nodes (PN), tumor size (TS), histology types (H), and grades (G). The entire annotation process is elaborated as follows.

A preliminary consistency test was conducted by asking the annotators to individually annotate

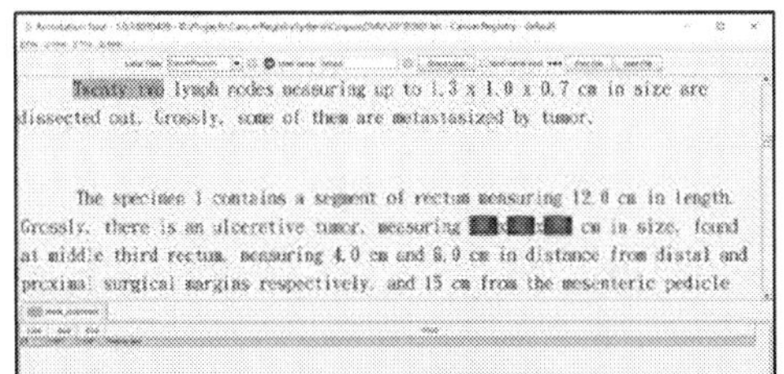

Figure 1: An example pathology report and the annotation tool used for annotation.

Afterwards a labeling meeting was organized to discuss issues and concerns encountered during the annotation process and the annotation guideline was adjusted according to the conclusion of the meeting. The above process was conducted iterative until they achieved an agreement above substantial. Finally, the remaining unlabeled datasets were evenly distributed to all annotators for labeling. The same annotation process was applied individually for the data collected from the two hospitals.

The aforementioned 100 annotation data generated by all annotators individually on the same reports were collected as the test set for evaluating the performance of the developed systems. They were combined by voting; only those annotations that were annotated by more than four annotators at the same time were kept. The other reports evenly annotated by annotators were collected as the training sets.

an identical set of 100 reports randomly selected from the collected datasets. All of them used the annotation tool (Figure 1) developed by our collaborator to conduct their annotations. We then measured their inter-annotation agreement by Kappa statistic (Viera & Garrett, 2005).

## 2.3 Cancer Registry Information Extraction with Different Approaches

For a given pathology report, our clinical toolkit (Dai, Syed-Abdul, Chen, & Wu, 2015) was employed to segment sentences and generate tokens based on MedPost (Smith, Rindflesch, & Wilbur, 2004). The numerical normalization method proposed by Tsai et al. (2006) was employed to reduce variations in numerical parts of each token. We then formulated the problem as a sequential labeling task and applied the IOB-2 tag scheme to encode the span information generated by annotators. All sequences including those that did not contain any annotations were included in the training set to train a neural sequence labeling network model whose architecture is briefly described as follows.

The input of the network is the pre-processed sequence of tokens in a pathology report and the output being the sequence of labels for each token. The input tokens was represented as a vector by concatenating the pre-trained word representations obtained by using GloVe (Pennington, Socher, & Manning, 2014) and RoBERTa (Liu et al., 2019). The parameters of the concatenated vectors were kept fixed during the training process.

Table 2: The nine cancer registry variables defined for this study.

| Type | Description | Example |
| --- | --- | --- |
| SC | Stage classifications including clinical, pathological, post-therapy/neoadjuvant therapy, retreatment/recurrence and autopsy | p., yp., rp., a., c. |
| T | Size or contiguous extension of the primary tumor | Primary tumor (T): Tx, T0, Tis, T1, T1, T2, T3, T4a, T4b |
| N | The absence, or presence and extent of cancer in the regional draining lymph nodes | Regional lymph nodes (N): Nx, N0, N1a, N1b, N1c, N2, N2a, N2b |
| M | The absence or presence of distant spread or metastases | Distant Metastasis (M): M0, M1, M1a, M1b |
| NE | Regional lymph nodes examined | Any numeric values |
| PN | Regional lymph nodes positive | Any numeric values |
| TS | Size of tumor | Any numeric values |
| H | Histology | Adenocarcinoma |
| G | Tumor grade; a measure of how abnormal the cancer cells look under the microscope. | Description likes: well differentiated, and undifferentiated |

The concatenated representation was then feed to a fully connected layer (denoted as FC1) along with a variational dropout before passing the embeddings into the bidirectional long-short term memory (BiLSTM) network with one layer consisting of 256 hidden nodes. The output of the BiLSTM layer goes through another fully connected layer (denoted as FC2) to generate an output of a size equal to the number of the classes, which becomes the input of the inference layer in which a conditional random field (CRF) layer was used to model the dependencies between labels in neighborhoods with the Viterbi loss to jointly decode the best chain of labels for the given sequence.

In addition to the aforementioned architecture, we implemented the following baselines for comparison:

- Dictionary-based approach: For a given token, output the most frequent assigned tag estimated on the training sets.

- Support vector machine (SVM): Formulate the task as a token-based classification task and apply SVM with a polylinear kernel to learn a classification model.

- CRF: The normalized word features with a context window of three along with transition features were used for training a CRF model.

- BiLSTM: Similar to the aforementioned network architecture, but a linear layer was used instead of the CRF layer as the output layer.

All of the above neural networks were implemented by using PyTorch trained on NVidia Tesla P-100 GPUs. CRF was implemented by using CRF++[1] and scikit-learn[2] were used for the remaining implementations.

## 2.4 Transfer Learning for Extracting Information between Different Hospitals

Transfer learning (Pan & Yang, 2009) aims to learn a better model on a target domain by leveraging the knowledge previously learned from a source domain. In this study, the transductive transfer learning technology was applied by transferring the parameters in different layers of the BiLSTM-CRF model trained on the dataset of the source hospital to the target hospital by retraining the model with transferred parameters on the target hospital's dataset via fine-tuning. In our experiments, we didn't freeze any layers but fine-tuned all transferred parameters in different layers.

## 2.5 Experiment Configurations

We conducted three experiments to study the characteristics of the compiled corpora and the effectiveness of the developed models on the compiled corpora. The first compared the proposed model with the aforementioned baseline methods. The second examined the effectiveness of transfer learning and the last checked the robustness of the developed models under the evaluation of cross-corpus. The standard micro-precision (P), recall (R) and F-measure (F) were used to evaluate the models' outputs against the gold annotations.

For training the neural networks in all of our experiments, we randomly kept 50 reports in the training sets as the validation sets to determine the best performed models during the training process. The validation sets were not used in training. The mini-batch gradient descent along with the stochastic gradient descent algorithm (with a learning rate of 0.1, a momentum of 0.9 and a weight decay of $10^{-5}$) was used for optimizing the parameters. Unless specifically described, the batch size and epoch were set to 2,048 and 150 respectively in the following experiments. The training process was early stopped if the learning rate was lower than $10^{-5}$. For consistency, we used the same set of hyper-parameters and a fixed random seed across all experiments.

## 3 Results

### 3.1 Corpus Statistics

A total of 2,008 reports collected from the two hospitals were annotated. The final Kappa values estimated for CMUH and KMUH are 0.802 (substantial) and 0.914 (almost perfect) respectively. Table 3 shows the detail statistics of the compiled corpora. As one can see that the size of KMUH is much larger than that of CMUH. Although the size of the KMUH corpus is much larger than that of CMUH, the annotations for pathological M is much less in KMUH. It's because that pathological M stage need the other

---

[1] https://taku910.github.io/crfpp/

[2] https://scikit-learn.org/

Table 3: Corpus statistics for the compiled corpora used in this work.

| | CMUH | | | KMUH | | |
|---|---|---|---|---|---|---|
| **Type** | **Training** | **Test** | **Total** | **Training** | **Test** | **Total** |
| Histology | 558 | 136 | 694 | 4,517 | 273 | 4,790 |
| Grade | 519 | 140 | 659 | 4,410 | 265 | 4,675 |
| Numbers of examined nodes | 623 | 189 | 812 | 2,021 | 153 | 2,174 |
| Numbers of positive nodes | 554 | 177 | 731 | 2,021 | 153 | 2,175 |
| Staging classification | 670 | 161 | 831 | 1,441 | 99 | 1,540 |
| Pathological T | 400 | 122 | 522 | 1,440 | 99 | 1,539 |
| Pathological N | 380 | 122 | 502 | 898 | 61 | 959 |
| Pathological M | 373 | 124 | 497 | 6 | 0 | 6 |
| Tumor size | 1,112 | 383 | 1,495 | 1,606 | 115 | 1,721 |
| Numbers of reports | 293 | 100 | 393 | 1,515 | 100 | 1,615 |
| Numbers of sentences | 21,229 | 5,699 | 26,928 | 63,887 | 3,966 | 67,853 |
| Numbers of sentences with annotations | 2,348 | 596 | 2,944 | 9,007 | 578 | 9,585 |
| Numbers of annotations | 5,189 | 1,554 | 6,743 | 18,360 | 1,218 | 19,578 |

reports (*e.g.*, image reports from other examination division) to conclude the outcome, the pathological M stage was shown inconclusive results on the current pathological data frequently in KMUH.

## 3.2 Performance Comparison with Different Methods

In the first experiment, we trained the developed models on the two training sets separately and evaluated their performance on the test sets of the two hospitals. The results were illustrated in Table 4.

In general, the developed models performed better on the KMUH test set which may be owing to the larger numbers of training samples. The CRF model achieved a comparable F-score on the KMUH test set but its F-score is lower than that of BiLSTM-CRF by 0.214 on the CMUH test set. Table 5 shows the detail results for the nine annotation types of the BiLSTM-CRF model on the two test sets. Overall, the developed networks demonstrated promising F-scores for all items.

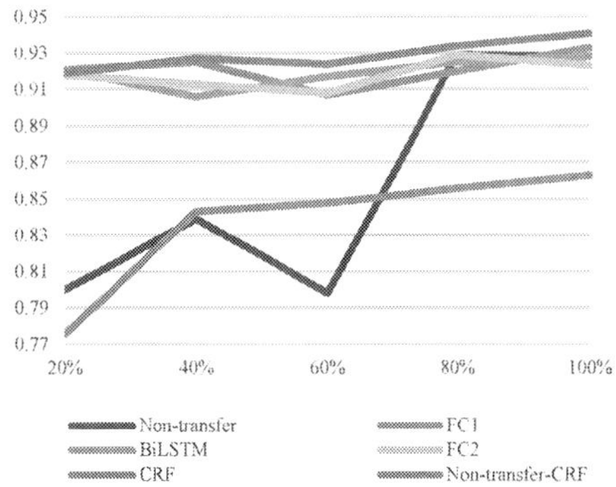


Figure 2: Impact of F-score by fine-tuning the models with the parameters up to each layer pre-trained on KMU on the varied sizes of the CMU training set.

## 3.3 The Effect of Transfer Learning

In this experiment, we would like to gain insights on what extent transfer learning improves the performance on the cross-hospital datasets. We used KMUH as the source dataset since its size is

Table 4: Performance comparison among different approaches.

| | CMUH | | | KMUH | | |
|---|---|---|---|---|---|---|
| **Type** | **P** | **R** | **F** | **P** | **R** | **F** |
| Dictionary-based | 0.71 | 0.51 | 0.59 | 0.61 | 0.48 | 0.54 |
| SVM | 0.69 | 0.42 | 0.53 | 0.8 | 0.55 | 0.65 |
| CRF | 0.950 | 0.790 | 0.863 | 0.967 | 0.983 | 0.975 |
| BiLSTM | 0.823 | 0.638 | 0.719 | 0.975 | 0.975 | 0.975 |
| BiLSTM-CRF | 0.943 | 0.908 | 0.925 | 0.977 | 0.975 | 0.976 |

Table 5: Detail precision, recall and F-score for each cancer registry item of the BiLSTM-CRF model.

| Type | CMUH | | |
|------|------|------|------|
| | P | R | F |
| G | 0.843 | 0.879 | 0.860 |
| H | 0.810 | 0.875 | 0.841 |
| NE | 0.973 | 0.968 | 0.971 |
| PN | 0.994 | 0.938 | 0.965 |
| SC | 0.946 | 0.988 | 0.967 |
| TS | 0.969 | 0.812 | 0.884 |
| T | 1.000 | 0.992 | 0.996 |
| N | 0.918 | 0.918 | 0.918 |
| M | 1.000 | 0.944 | 0.971 |
| **Type** | **KMUH** | | |
| G | 0.996 | 0.996 | 0.996 |
| H | 0.968 | 0.985 | 0.976 |
| NE | 1.000 | 0.961 | 0.980 |
| PN | 0.981 | 1.000 | 0.990 |
| SC | 0.970 | 0.990 | 0.980 |
| TS | 0.991 | 0.913 | 0.950 |
| T | 0.921 | 0.939 | 0.930 |
| N | 0.952 | 0.967 | 0.959 |
| M | n/a | n/a | n/a |

larger than that of CMUH. We conducted experiments to examine the effect of transfer knowledge learned from KMUH to CMUH by 1) analyzing the importance of each layer of the developed neural networks, and 2) quantifying the performance gain by varying the sizes (20%~100%) of the CMUH training set when we fine-tuned the model pre-trained on KMUH. Note that because the size of the 20% CMUH dataset is quite small, we reduced the batch size to 512 for this case.

Figure 2 shows the results. Here "Non-transfer" refers to that we only used the reduced sizes of the CMUH training set to develop the BiLSTM-CRF models without relying on any pre-trained parameters. "FC1" initialized the learned parameters of the FC1 layer of the BiLSTM-CRF model by adopting the pre-trained parameters on the KMUH corpus, "BiLSTM" further included the learned parameters of the BiLSTM layer of the source model and so on. Consider the comparable results achieved by CRF models, we also include the configuration "Non-transfer-CRF" in which we trained several CRF models by using the corresponding reduced CMUH datasets.

In Figure 2, we can observe that with more numbers of the training samples used, the performance can be apparently improved for the 'Non-transfer' models. However, the improvement for the CRF models is relatively flat comparing with that of the neural networks. On the other hand, even with only 20% of the CMUH training set, the models learned with transferred parameters achieved satisfactory F-scores, which outperformed the 'Non-transfer' models trained on more training samples (being equal or less than 60%) of the full CMUH training set. The above results give us an insight that we can exploit the parameters of the neural networks learned from source hospitals to rapidly develop a reliable system relying on a small annotated dataset to boost the annotation process in the new hospital for creating and evaluating a customized system.

The results shown in Figure 2 also reveal the importance of parameters of each layer of the developed model in the manner of transfer learning. We can observe that transferring parameters of all layers in general leading to slightly better F-scores, but transferring the parameters of the first layer only is almost as efficient as transferring all. The result is consistent with the observations of other previous works (Giorgi & Bader, 2018, 2020; Lee, Dernoncourt, & Szolovits, 2018) and the hypothesis that the lower layers of a neural network learn generic features and the higher layers learn task-specific (or we can say that hospital-specific) features.

### 3.4 Cross-corpus Evaluations

To assess the performance of the developed model in a more realistic setup, we conducted cross-

Table 6: Cross-corpus evaluation among different approaches.

| | CMUH | | | KMUH | | |
|------|------|------|------|------|------|------|
| Method | P | R | F | P | R | F |
| CRF | 0.737 | 0.242 | 0.364 | 0.663 | 0.314 | 0.426 |
| BiLSTM-CRF | 0.631 | 0.376 | 0.472 | 0.925 | 0.483 | 0.634 |
| Transferred BiLSTM-CRF | 0.944 | 0.938 | 0.941 | 0.932 | 0.644 | 0.762 |

datasets experiments. For this purpose, we used the dataset from one hospital for training, and the dataset from another for testing. The experiments provide an estimate of the cross-hospital generalization ability of the developed models.

Table 6 shows the results. Given that both corpora were annotated by the same annotators under the same annotation guideline, we can still see the generality of the developed models is not well; a larger drop in performance can be found on both datasets. The results exhibited that the format and the writing styles of the descriptive pathology in surgical biopsy reports across hospitals are heterogeneous in real-world scenarios.

We also estimated the performance of the transferred model on its source dataset in Table 6. The result illustrates an apparent drop of F-score from 0.976 to 0.762 on the KMUH test set. The results demonstrated that the developed systems suffered the catastrophic forgetting problem (French, 1999) which is now known to be a challenge for artificial neural networks when the network is trained sequentially on multiple tasks because the weights in the network that are important for the original task are now changed to meet the objectives of the new task.

## 4   Conclusions

In this work, we investigated the feasibility of applying transfer learning via neural networks on the task of extraction cancer registry information from cross-hospital pathology reports. Because the writing styles and formats of the pathology reports is different in each hospital, to estimate the requirements of the number of annotated datasets when we migrate from one hospital to the others and iteratively improve the effectiveness of the developed systems, we conducted experiments to quantify the impact of transfer learning on the datasets collected from two hospitals. From the evaluations of the results, we confirmed that when transfer learning is adopted, the model pre-trained on a source hospital can be trained with fewer annotations of the target hospital and achieve satisfactory performance as when the full training set of the target hospital is used. The results suggest us to apply the transfer learning techniques for developing a customized system for a new hospital with only a few annotations. We will develop method to estimate the required numbers of annotations based on the language properties of the narrative reports and the characteristics of the developed neural networks. Furthermore, our experiment results also reveal challenges requiring to be addressed including the generalizability and catastrophic forgetting problem, which should be addressed in the future.

## Acknowledgement

This study was supported by the Ministry of Health and Welfare [grand number: MOHW109-TDU-B-212-134026] and the Ministry of Science and Technology of Taiwan [Grant numbers: MOST 109-2221-E-992-074-MY3].

## References

Dai, H.-J., Syed-Abdul, S., Chen, C.-W., & Wu, C.-C. (2015). Recognition and Evaluation of Clinical Section Headings in Clinical Documents Using Token-Based Formulation with Conditional Random Fields. *BioMed Research International, 2015.*

French, R. M. (1999). Catastrophic forgetting in connectionist networks. *Trends in cognitive sciences, 3*(4), 128-135.

Giorgi, J. M., & Bader, G. D. (2018). Transfer learning for biomedical named entity recognition with neural networks. *Bioinformatics, 34*(23), 4087-4094.

Giorgi, J. M., & Bader, G. D. (2020). Towards reliable named entity recognition in the biomedical domain. *Bioinformatics, 36*(1), 280-286.

Lee, J. Y., Dernoncourt, F., & Szolovits, P. (2018). *Transfer Learning for Named-Entity Recognition with Neural Networks.* Paper presented at the Proceedings of the Eleventh International Conference on Language Resources and Evaluation (LREC 2018).

Liu, Y., Ott, M., Goyal, N., Du, J., Joshi, M., Chen, D., . . . Stoyanov, V. (2019). Roberta: A robustly optimized bert pretraining approach. *arXiv preprint arXiv:1907.11692.*

Pan, S. J., & Yang, Q. (2009). A survey on transfer learning. *IEEE Transactions on knowledge and data engineering, 22*(10), 1345-1359.

Pennington, J., Socher, R., & Manning, C. D. (2014). Glove: Global vectors for word representation. *Proceedings of the Empiricial Methods in Natural Language Processing (EMNLP 2014), 12*, 1532-1543.

Smith, L., Rindflesch, T., & Wilbur, W. J. (2004). MedPost: A Part of Speech Tagger for BioMedical Text. *Bioinformatics, 20*(14), 2320-2321. doi:10.1093/bioinformatics/bth227

Tsai, R. T.-H., Sung, C.-L., Dai, H.-J., Hung, H.-C., Sung, T.-Y., & Hsu, W.-L. (2006). NERBio: using selected word conjunctions, term normalization, and global patterns to improve biomedical named entity recognition. *BMC Bioinformatics, 7*(Suppl 5), S11.

Viera, A. J., & Garrett, J. M. (2005). Understanding interobserver agreement: the kappa statistic. *Fam med, 37*(5), 360-363.

# PHICON: Improving Generalization of Clinical Text De-identification Models via Data Augmentation


**Xiang Yue**
The Ohio State University
yue.149@osu.edu

**Shuang Zhou**
The Hong Kong Polytechnic University
shuang.zhou@connect.polyu.hk



## Abstract

De-identification is the task of identifying protected health information (PHI) in the clinical text. Existing neural de-identification models often fail to generalize to a new dataset. We propose a simple yet effective data augmentation method PHICON to alleviate the generalization issue. PHICON consists of **PHI** augmentation and **Con**text augmentation, which creates augmented training corpora by replacing PHI entities with named-entities sampled from external sources, and by changing background context with synonym replacement or random word insertion, respectively. Experimental results on the i2b2 2006 and 2014 de-identification challenge datasets show that PHICON can help three selected de-identification models boost F1-score (by at most 8.6%) on cross-dataset test. We also discuss how much augmentation to use and how each augmentation method influences the performance.[1]


## 1 Introduction

Clinical text in electronic health records (EHRs) often contain sensitive information. In the United States, Health Insurance Portability and Accountability Act (HIPPA)[2] requires that protected health information (PHI) (e.g., name, street address, phone number) must be removed before EHRs are shared for secondary uses such as clinical research (Meystre et al., 2014).

The task of identifying and removing PHI from clinical texts is referred as de-identification. Although many neural de-idenfication models such as LSTM-based (Dernoncourt et al., 2017; Liu et al., 2017; Jiang et al., 2017; Khin et al., 2018) and BERT-based (Alsentzer et al., 2019; Tang et al., 2019) have achieved very promising performance, identifying PHI still remains challenging in the

real-world scenario: even well-trained models often *fail to generalize to a new dataset*. For example, we conduct cross-dataset test on i2b2 2006 and i2b2 2014 de-identification challenge datasets[3] (i.e., train a widely-used de-identification model NeuroNER (Dernoncourt et al., 2017) on one dataset and test it on the other one). The result in Figure 1 shows that model's performance (F1-score) on the new dataset decreases up to 33% compared to the original test set. The poor generalization issue on de-identification is also reported in previous studies (Stubbs et al., 2017; Yang et al., 2019; Johnson et al., 2020; Hartman et al., 2020).

To explore what factors lead to poor generalization, we sample some error examples and find that the model might focus too much on specific entities and does not really learn language patterns well. For example, in Figure 2, given a sentence *"She met Washington in the Ohio Hospital"*, the model tends to recognize the entity *"Washington"* as the "Location" instead of the "Name" if *"Washington"* appears as "Location" in the training many times. Such cases appear more frequently in a new testing set, thus leading to poor generalization.

To prevent the model overfitting on specific cases and encourage it to learn general language patterns, one possible way is to enlarge training data (Yang et al., 2019). However, clinical texts are usually difficult to obtain, not to mention the requirement of tremendous expert effort for annotations (Yue et al., 2020). To solve this, we introduce our data augmentation method PHICON, which consists of **PHI** augmentation and **Con**text augmentation. Specifically, PHI augmentation replaces the original PHI entity in the training set with a same type named-entity sampled from external sources (such as Wikipedia). For example, in Figure 2, *"Ohio Hospital"* is replaced by an randomly-sampled "Hospital" entity *"Alaska Health Center"*. In terms of context aug-

---






*Proceedings of the 3rd Clinical Natural Language Processing Workshop*, pages 209–214
November 19, 2020. ©2020 Association for Computational Linguistics

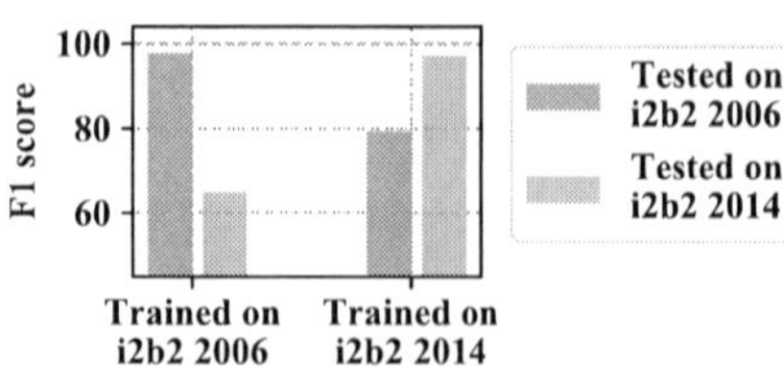

Figure 1: The result of cross-dataset test based on a base model (Dernoncourt et al., 2017). Performance on the new dataset drops up to 33% compared to the original test set, showing the model suffers from generalizability issue.

Figure 2: Toy examples of our PHICON data augmentation. SR: synonym replacement. RI: random insertion.

mentation, we randomly replace or insert some non-stop words (e.g., verb, adverb) in sentences to create new sentences as an example shown in Figure 2. The augmented data does not change the meaning of original sentences but increase the diversity of the data. It can better help the model to learn contextual patterns and prevent the model focusing on specific PHI entities. Data augmentation is widely used in many NLP tasks (Xie et al., 2017; Ratner et al., 2017; Kobayashi, 2018; Yu et al., 2018; Bodapati et al., 2019; Wei and Zou, 2019) to improve model's robustness and generalizability. However, to the best of our knowledge, no work explores its potential in the clinical text de-identification task.

We test two LSTM-based models: NeuroNER (Dernoncourt et al., 2017), DeepAffix (Yadav et al., 2018) and one BERT-based (Devlin et al., 2019) model: ClinicalBERT (Alsentzer et al., 2019) with our PHICON. Cross-dataset evaluations on i2b2 2006 dataset and i2b2 2014 dataset show that PHICON can boost the models' generalization performance up to 8.6% in terms of F1-score. We also discuss how much augmentation we need and conduct the ablation study to explore the effect of PHI augmentation and context augmentation. To summarize, our PHICON is simple yet effective and can be used together with any existing machine learning-based de-identification systems to improve their generalizability on new datasets.

## 2 PHICON

To understand what factors lead to the poor generalization, we check some error examples and find that most of the PHI entities in these error examples do not appear in training set or appear as a different PHI type (e.g., Washington [Name v.s. Location]). We argue that neural models might focus on too much on specific entities (e.g., recognizing "Washington" as "Location") but fail to learn general language patterns (e.g., "met" is not usually followed by a "Location" entity but a "Name" entity instead). Consequently, such unseen or Out-Of-Vocabulary PHI entities might be hard to be identified correctly, thus leading to lower performance. To help models better identify these unseen PHI entities, we may encourage models to learn contextual patterns or linguistic characteristics and prevent models focusing too much on specific PHI tokens.

**PHI Augmentation.** To achieve this goal, we first introduce PHI augmentation: create more training corpora by replacing original PHI entities in the sentence with other named-entities of the same PHI type. For example, in Figure 2, *"Washington"* is replaced by a randomly-sampled Name entity *"William"* and *"Ohio Hospital"* is replaced by an randomly-sampled Hospital entity *"Alaska Health Center"*.

We construct 11 candidate lists for sampling different PHI types. The lists are either obtained by scraping the online web sources (e.g., Wikipedia Lists) or by randomly generating based on predefined regular expressions (the number and the source of each candidate list is shown in Table 1).

**Context Augmentation.** To further help models focus on contextual patterns and reduce overfitting, inspired by previous work (Wei and Zou, 2019), we leverage two text editing techniques: synonym replacement (SR) and random insertion (RI) to modify background context for data augmentation (examples are shown in Figure 2). Specifically, SR is implemented by finding four types of non-stopping words (adjectives, verbs, adverbs and nouns) in sentences, and then replacing them with synonyms from WordNet (Fellbaum and Miller, 1998). RI is implemented by inserting random adverbs in front of verbs and adjectives in sentences, as well as inserting random adjectives in front of nouns in sentences.

| Scraped from the Web | | |
|---|---|---|
| **PHI Type** | **Number** | **Source** |
| Organization | 1,300 | https://en.wikipedia.org/wiki/Category:Lists_of_organizations |
| Hospital | 5,400 | https://en.wikipedia.org/wiki/Lists_of_hospitals_in_the_United_States<br>https://www.hospitalsafetygrade.org/all-hospitals |
| Location | 27,500 | https://en.wikipedia.org/wiki/List_of_Main_Street_Programs_in_the_United_States<br>https://en.wikipedia.org/wiki/List_of_United_States_cities_by_area<br>https://en.wikipedia.org/wiki/List_of_United_States_cities_by_population |
| Patient | 14,900 | https://en.wikipedia.org/wiki/List_of_most_popular_given_names |
| Doctor | 18,000 | https://en.wikipedia.org/wiki/List_of_most_common_surnames_in_North_America |
| **Randomly Generated by Python scripts based on Regular Expressions** | | | | | |
| ID | 20,000 | Username | 3,000 | Zip | 4,000 |
| Date | 32,900 | Phone | 21,000 | Medical Record | 4,900 |

Table 1: The named-entity lists used for PHI augmentation, which are scraped from the Web or randomly generated.

| | | i2b2 2006 | i2b2 2014 | # PHI of each type | i2b2 2006 | | | i2b2 2014 | | |
|---|---|---|---|---|---|---|---|---|---|---|
| | | | | | **Train** | **Dev** | **Test** | **Train** | **Dev** | **Test** |
| #notes | **Train** | 622 | 912 | CONTACT | 159 | 32 | 41 | 394 | 31 | 96 |
| | **Dev** | 90 | 132 | DATE | 4887 | 649 | 1562 | 9102 | 974 | 2268 |
| | **Test** | 177 | 260 | ID | 3399 | 527 | 883 | 1000 | 166 | 312 |
| | **Total** | 889 | 1304 | LOCATION | 1761 | 252 | 648 | 3161 | 433 | 919 |
| **#avg tokens / note** | | 631.7 | 810.8 | NAME | 3163 | 452 | 1064 | 5156 | 745 | 1439 |
| **#avg PHI / note** | | 21.9 | 20.1 | Total | 13369 | 1912 | 4198 | 18813 | 2349 | 5034 |

Table 2: Statistics of the i2b2 2006 and 2014 datasets.

For each sentence containing PHI entities in the corpus, we can apply both PHI augmentation and Context augmentation to obtain the augmented data $D_{aug}$. We can run $\alpha$ times (by setting different random seeds) to obtain different sizes of augmented data (e.g., $\alpha = 2$ means augmenting the original dataset twice). Though with the $\alpha$ increases, we can obtain larger augmented training corpora, it may also bring much noise. We recommend a small value for $\alpha$ (See more discussions in Section 4.2). Then we merge the $D_{aug}$ with the original dataset $D$ to form the final dataset $D_{new}$ for training: $D_{new} = D \cup \alpha\, D_{aug}$.

In summary, PHICON can significantly increase the diversity of training data without involving more labeling efforts. The augmented data can increase data diversity and enrich contextual patterns, which could prevent the model focusing too much on specific PHI entities and encourage it to learn general language patterns.

## 3 Experimental Setup

### 3.1 Datasets

We adopt two widely-used de-identification datasets: i2b2 2006 dataset and i2b2 2014 dataset,

and split them into training, validation and testing set with proportion of 7:1:2, based on notes number. We remove low frequency (occur less than 20 times) PHI types from the datasets. To avoid PHI inconsistency between the two datasets, we map and merge some fine-grained level PHI types into a coarse-grained level type, and finally preserve five PHI categories: Name (Doctor, Patient, Username), Location (Hospital, Location, Zip, Organization), Date, ID (ID, Medical Record), Contact (Phone). The statistics of the datasets are shown in Table 2.

### 3.2 Setup

**Base Models.** We select two LSTM-based models: NeuroNER (Dernoncourt et al., 2017)[4], DeepAffix (Yadav et al., 2018)[5] and one BERT model: ClinicalBERT (Alsentzer et al., 2019)[6]. All hyperparameters are kept the same as the original papers.
**Evaluation.** To evaluate models' generalizability, we use the cross-dataset test on the two i2b2 challenge datasets: (1) Train the model on i2b2 2006 training set, and test on the whole i2b2 2014 dataset (Train + Dev + Test) (abbreviated

---

[4]https://github.com/Franck-Dernoncourt/NeuroNER
[5]https://github.com/vikas95/Pref_Suff_Span_NN
[6]https://github.com/EmilyAlsentzer/clinicalBERT

as "2006→2014") (2) Train the model on i2b2 2014 training set, and test on the whole i2b2 2006 dataset (Train + Dev + Test) (abbreviated as "2014→2006"). For all experiments, we average results from five runs. We follow Dernoncourt et al. (2017) and report the micro-F1 score on binary token level.

## 4 Results

### 4.1 Does PHICON improve generalization?

In our preliminary experiments, we find that poor generalization tends to be more severe when the training set size is small. Thus, we consider the following training set fractions (%): $\{20, 40, 60, 80, 100\}$ and we set the augmentation factor $\alpha = 2$ considering both effectiveness and time-efficiency (See the influence of $\alpha$ in Section 4.2). Table 3 shows the overall results, and interesting findings include:

(1) PHICON improves the generalizability of each de-identification model under different training sizes consistently. The results are not surprising as both PHI augmentation and context augmentation increase linguistic richness and enable models to focus more on language patterns, so as to help to train more generalized models.

(2) In general, the performance boost is large when the training data size is relatively small. This is because PHICON plays larger role at the low-resource case as it can significantly increase data diversity, language patterns, and linguistic richness.

(3) The performance boost on the BERT-based model is less obvious than that on LSTM-based models. Since ClinicalBERT has already been pre-trained on large-scale corpus: MIMIC-III clinical notes (Johnson et al., 2016). It is reasonable that the augmented data does not lead to large boost on ClinicalBERT. But there is still significant boost when training data size is relatively small.

(4) The boost on the setting "2006→2014" is larger than that in the setting "2014→2006". Because i2b2 2014 dataset has more data and more comprehensive PHI patterns than i2b2 2006 dataset. Data augmentation is usually more effective when the training set size is smaller (Wei and Zou, 2019).

**Improvement for each PHI category**. To further understand PHICON, we show the performance ( "2014→2006") of the base model NeuroNER and NeuroNER + PHICON on each category of PHI in Figure 3. Firstly, we can see that when the training data is relatively small (e.g., 20%), the

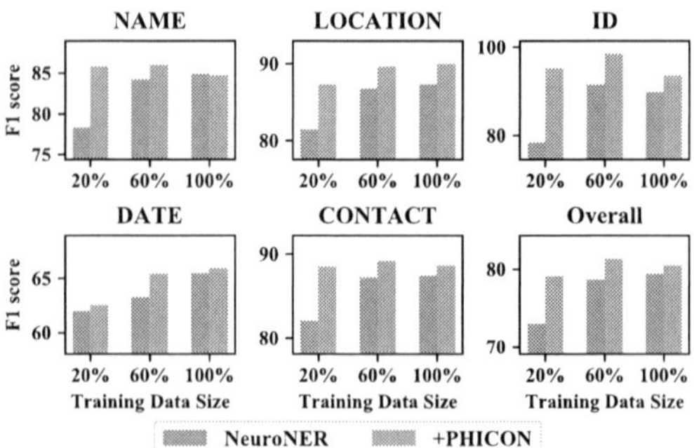



Figure 3: Performance of NeuroNER w/o and w/ PH-ICON on each PHI type (setting: 2014→2006)

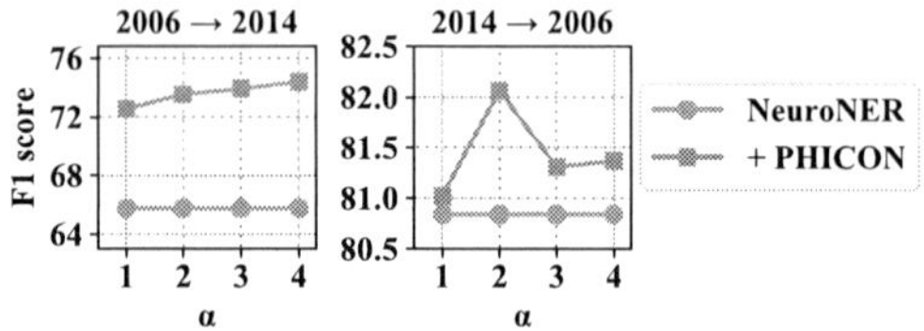



Figure 4: Data augmentation under different augmentation factors can boost model generalization. The left picture indicates that the model is trained on i2b2 2006 dataset and evaluated on i2b2 2014 validation set.

improvement on each PHI category is generally significant. With the training set size increases, the contribution of the augmented data becomes small. However, for the PHI categories that have less training data in the dataset (e.g., Location and ID; See Table 2), PHICON still contributes much improvement. Thus, we conclude that PHICON may be more helpful in the low-resource training data case.

### 4.2 How much augmentation?

In this section, we discuss the influence of the augmentation factor, $\alpha$, on the cross-dataset test performance. In Figure 4, we report the performance on dev set based on the model NeuroNER for $\alpha = \{1, 2, 3, 4\}$. In the first setting ("2006→2014"), we can see the performance is steadily boosted with the increase of the factor $\alpha$; while in the second setting ("2014→2006"), the performance first goes up and then drops down. This difference might be caused by the data size of the two datasets (2014 dataset is larger). When the corpus is large, enlarging the augmentation factor might not lead to better performance, as the real data may have already covered very diverse language patterns. In addition, more augmented data might bring some

**Trained on i2b2 2006, Tested on i2b2 2014**

| Model | Training Data Size | | | | |
|---|---|---|---|---|---|
| | 20% | 40% | 60% | 80% | 100% |
| NeuroNER (Dernoncourt et al., 2017) | 0.5990 | 0.6021 | 0.6364 | 0.6436 | 0.6482 |
| + PHICON | **0.6670** | **0.6979** | **0.7025** | **0.7063** | **0.7166** |
| DeepAffix (Yadav et al., 2018) | 0.5590 | 0.5875 | 0.6069 | 0.5976 | 0.6118 |
| + PHICON | **0.6699** | **0.6543** | **0.6905** | **0.7170** | **0.6982** |
| ClinicalBERT (Alsentzer et al., 2019) | 0.7055 | 0.7149 | 0.7351 | 0.7454 | 0.7519 |
| + PHICON | **0.7310** | **0.7412** | **0.7500** | **0.7586** | **0.7569** |

**Trained on i2b2 2014, Tested on i2b2 2006**

| Model | Training Data Size | | | | |
|---|---|---|---|---|---|
| | 20% | 40% | 60% | 80% | 100% |
| NeuroNER (Dernoncourt et al., 2017) | 0.7303 | 0.7513 | 0.7864 | 0.7891 | 0.7936 |
| + PHICON | **0.7911** | **0.7944** | **0.8135** | **0.8175** | **0.8051** |
| DeepAffix (Yadav et al., 2018) | 0.6950 | 0.7467 | 0.7852 | 0.7774 | 0.7736 |
| + PHICON | **0.7523** | **0.7706** | **0.7919** | **0.7827** | **0.8085** |
| ClinicalBERT (Alsentzer et al., 2019) | 0.8989 | 0.9043 | 0.9030 | 0.9069 | 0.9123 |
| + PHICON | **0.9004** | **0.9076** | **0.9059** | **0.9078** | **0.9145** |

Table 3: Cross-dataset test performance (micro-F1 score on binary token level) on two experiment settings for models with and without PHICON on different training set sizes. All the numbers are the average from 5 runs.

| Model | 2006 → 2014 | 2014 → 2006 |
|---|---|---|
| NeuroNER | 0.648 | 0.794 |
| + PHI Aug | 0.670 | 0.804 |
| + Context Aug | 0.659 | 0.803 |
| + PHICON | **0.717** | **0.805** |

Table 4: Ablation study on PHICON. PHI augmentation and context augmentation contribute to the overall generalization boost.

noise, which could decrease the performance. In terms of time efficiency, when $\alpha$ is increased by 1, the training time would roughly double if we set the same epoch number. So considering effectiveness, efficiency and data size, we recommend to set $\alpha$ a relative small value (e.g., 2) in the real application.

## 4.3 Ablation Study

In this section, we perform an ablation study on PHICON based on NeuroNER to explore the effect of each component: PHI augmentation and context augmentation. Table 4 shows that the two components of PHICON both contribute to boosting model generalization. Performance boost from PHI augmentation is obvious than context augmentation, i.e., PHI augmentation plays a major role. When combining both, PHICON results in larger boost than each of them.

## 5 Conclusion

In this paper, we explore the generalization issue on clinical text de-identification task. We propose a data augmentation method named PHICON that augments both PHI and context to boost model generalization. The augmented data can increase data diversity and enrich contextual patterns in training data, which may prevent the model overfitting on specific PHI entities and encourage it to focus more on language patterns. Experimental results demonstrate that our PHICON can help improve models' generalizability, especially in the low-resource training case (i.e., the size of the original training set is small). We also discuss how much augmentation to use and how each augmentation method influences the performance. In the future research, we will explore more advanced data augmentation techniques for improving the de-identification models' generalization performance.

## Acknowledgments

We thank Prof. Kwong-Sak LEUNG and Sunny Lai in The Chinese University of Hong Kong as well as anonymous reviewers for their helpful comments.

## References

Emily Alsentzer, John Murphy, William Boag, Wei-Hung Weng, Di Jin, Tristan Naumann, and Matthew McDermott. 2019. Publicly available clinical BERT embeddings. In *Proceedings of the 2nd Clinical Natural Language Processing Workshop*, pages 72–78, Minneapolis, Minnesota, USA. Association for Computational Linguistics.

Sravan Babu Bodapati, Hyokun Yun, and Yaser Al-Onaizan. 2019. Robustness to capitalization errors in named entity recognition. In *Proceedings of the 5th Workshop on Noisy User-generated Text, W-NUT@EMNLP 2019, Hong Kong, China, November 4, 2019*, pages 237–242. Association for Computational Linguistics.

Franck Dernoncourt, Ji Young Lee, Özlem Uzuner, and Peter Szolovits. 2017. De-identification of patient notes with recurrent neural networks. *JAMIA*, 24:596–606.

J. Devlin, Ming-Wei Chang, Kenton Lee, and Kristina Toutanova. 2019. Bert: Pre-training of deep bidirectional transformers for language understanding. In *NAACL-HLT*.

C Fellbaum and G Miller. 1998. *WordNet : an electronic lexical database*. MIT Press.

Tzvika Hartman, Michael D. Howell, Jeff Dean, Shlomo Hoory, and Yossi Matias. 2020. Customization scenarios for de-identification of clinical notes. *BMC Medical Informatics and Decision Making*, 20(1).

Zhipeng Jiang, Chao Zhao, Bin He, Yi Guan, and Jingchi Jiang. 2017. De-identification of medical records using conditional random fields and long short-term memory networks. *JBI*, 75S:S43–S53.

Alistair E. W. Johnson, Lucas Bulgarelli, and Tom J. Pollard. 2020. Deidentification of free-text medical records using pre-trained bidirectional transformers. In *ACM CHIL '20: ACM Conference on Health, Inference, and Learning, Toronto, Ontario, Canada, April 2-4, 2020 [delayed]*, pages 214–221. ACM.

Alistair E. W. Johnson, Tom J. Pollard, Lu Shen, Li wei H. Lehman, Mengling Feng, Mohammad M. Ghassemi, Benjamin Moody, Peter Szolovits, Leo Anthony Celi, and Roger G. Mark. 2016. Mimic-iii, a freely accessible critical care database. *Scientific Data*, 3.

Kaung Khin, Philipp Burckhardt, and Rema Padman. 2018. A deep learning architecture for de-identification of patient notes: Implementation and evaluation. *ArXiv*, abs/1810.01570.

Sosuke Kobayashi. 2018. Contextual augmentation: Data augmentation by words with paradigmatic relations. In *NAACL'18*, pages 452–457.

Zengjian Liu, Buzhou Tang, Xiaolong Wang, and Qingcai Chen. 2017. De-identification of clinical notes via recurrent neural network and conditional random field. *JBI*, 75S:S34–S42.

Stéphane M Meystre, Óscar Ferrández, F Jeffrey Friedlin, Brett R South, Shuying Shen, and Matthew H Samore. 2014. Text de-identification for privacy protection: a study of its impact on clinical text information content. *JBI*, 50:142–150.

Alexander J Ratner, Henry Ehrenberg, Zeshan Hussain, Jared Dunnmon, and Christopher Ré. 2017. Learning to compose domain-specific transformations for data augmentation. In *NeurIPS*, pages 3236–3246.

Amber Stubbs, Michele Filannino, and Özlem Uzuner. 2017. De-identification of psychiatric intake records: Overview of 2016 cegs n-grid shared tasks track 1. *JBI*, 75S:S4–S18.

Buzhou Tang, Dehuan Jiang, Qing cai Chen, Xiaolong Wang, Jun Yan, and Ying Shen. 2019. De-identification of clinical text via bi-lstm-crf with neural language models. *AMIA ... Annual Symposium proceedings. AMIA Symposium*, 2019:857–863.

Jason W. Wei and Kai Zou. 2019. EDA: easy data augmentation techniques for boosting performance on text classification tasks. In *EMNLP-IJCNLP'19*, pages 6381–6387. Association for Computational Linguistics.

Ziang Xie, Sida I Wang, Jiwei Li, Daniel Lévy, Aiming Nie, Dan Jurafsky, and Andrew Y Ng. 2017. Data noising as smoothing in neural network language models. *ICLR'17*.

Vikas Yadav, Rebecca Sharp, and Steven Bethard. 2018. Deep affix features improve neural named entity recognizers. In *Proceedings of the Seventh Joint Conference on Lexical and Computational Semantics*, pages 167–172, New Orleans, Louisiana. Association for Computational Linguistics.

Xi Yang, Tianchen Lyu, Qian Li, Chih-Yin Lee, and Yonghui Wu. 2019. A study of deep learning methods for de-identification of clinical notes in cross-institute settings. *BMC Medical Informatics and Decision Making*, 19(Suppl 5):232.

Adams Wei Yu, David Dohan, Minh-Thang Luong, Rui Zhao, Kai Chen, Mohammad Norouzi, and Quoc V Le. 2018. Qanet: Combining local convolution with global self-attention for reading comprehension. In *ICLR'18*.

Xiang Yue, Bernal Jimenez Gutierrez, and Huan Sun. 2020. Clinical reading comprehension: A thorough analysis of the emrQA dataset. In *ACL'20*, pages 4474–4486, Online. Association for Computational Linguistics.

# Where's the Question? A Multi-channel Deep Convolutional Neural Network for Question Identification in Textual Data

George Michalopoulos, Helen Chen, Alexander Wong
University of Waterloo,
Waterloo, Canada
{gmichalo, helen.chen, alexander.wong}@uwaterloo.ca

## Abstract

In most clinical practice settings, there is no rigorous reviewing of the clinical documentation, resulting in inaccurate information captured in the patient medical records. The gold standard in clinical data capturing is achieved via "expert-review", where clinicians can have a dialogue with a domain expert (reviewers) and ask them questions about data entry rules. Automatically identifying "real questions" in these dialogues could uncover ambiguities or common problems in data capturing in a given clinical setting.

In this study, we proposed a novel multi-channel deep convolutional neural network architecture, namely Quest-CNN, for the purpose of separating real questions that expect an answer (information or help) about an issue from sentences that are not questions, as well as from questions referring to an issue mentioned in a nearby sentence (e.g., *can you clarify this?*), which we will refer as *"c-questions"*. We conducted a comprehensive performance comparison analysis of the proposed multi-channel deep convolutional neural network against other deep neural networks. Furthermore, we evaluated the performance of traditional rule-based and learning-based methods for detecting question sentences. The proposed Quest-CNN achieved the best F1 score both on a dataset of data entry-review dialogue in a dialysis care setting, and on a general domain dataset.

## 1 Introduction

In healthcare, real-world data (RWD) refers to patient data routinely collected during clinic visits, hospitalization, as well as patient-reported results. In recent years, RWD's volume has become enormous, and invaluable insights and real-world evidence can be generated from these datasets using the latest data processing and analytical techniques. However, RWD's quality remains one of the main challenges that prevent novel machine learning methods from being readily adopted in healthcare. Therefore, creating data quality tools is of great importance in health care and health data sciences. Erroneous data in healthcare systems could jeopardize a patient's clinical outcomes and affect the care provider's ability to optimize its performance.

Common data quality issues include missing critical information about medical history, wrong coding of a condition, and inconsistency in documentation across different care sites. Manual review by domain experts is the gold standard for achieving the highest data quality but is unattainable in regular care practices. Recent developments in the field of Natural Language Processing (NLP) has attracted great interest in the healthcare community since algorithms for identifying variables of interest and classification algorithm for diseases have been recently developed (Jiang et al., 2017).

In this paper, we presented a novel model for the extraction of queries (questions) in a corpus of dialogue between data entry clinicians and expert reviewers in a multi-site dialysis environment. The main contributions of this work are: (i) To the best of our knowledge, we are the first to benchmark the performance of different rule and learning-based methods for the extraction of question sentences from logs of real-world (medical) systems by providing specific misclassification cases that emphasize the limitation of each technique. (ii) We proposed a new deep neural network architecture, namely Quest-CNN which unifies syntactic, semantic and statistical features and is capable of identifying real questions that expect an answer, questions referring to an issue mentioned in a nearby sentence (*c-questions*) and sentences that are not questions. (iii) We examined the importance of the above mentioned features and we experimented extensively with different state of



*Proceedings of the 3rd Clinical Natural Language Processing Workshop*, pages 215–226
November 19, 2020. ©2020 Association for Computational Linguistics

the art deep learning models in order to determine the best architecture for this particular task. (iv) We investigated the effect of incorporating domain knowledge on the performance of a model by examining whether word embeddings and semantic features (that will be described in section 4.1) which are pre-trained in a domain-specific dataset rather than in a general dataset are more beneficial for the model. Finally, in addition to evaluating our model's performance in a medical context, we also experimented in section 5 with a general-domain dataset (questions in the Twitter social platform) to show our model's generalizability.

The rest of the paper is organized as follows. Related work is presented in section 2. The different question detection methods that will be examined, are described in section 3. Section 4 details the characteristics of the proposed multi-channel CNN model. Finally, the results of the experiments are reported in section 5 and a conclusion and a plan for future work are given in section 6.

## 2 Related Work

Different question-detection methods have mainly been focused on the extraction of questions in social online settings (e.g. emails, Twitter) (Li et al., 2011; Zhao and Mei, 2013). These methods can be classified into two categories: (i) Rule based methods that make use of rules like 5W1H words (What, Who, Where, When, Why, How) or question marks (QM) to identify questions (ii) Learning-based methods, which train a classifier based on the patterns of sentences.

Recently, different deep-neural networks have achieved a state-of-the-art results in text classification. In the **KIM-CNN** model(Kim, 2014) $t$ filters are applied to the concatenated word embeddings of each document in order to produce $t$ feature maps, which are fed to a max pooling layer, in order to create a $t$-dimensional representation of the document. In addition, in (Liu et al., 2017) the **XML-CNN** network was introduced, where a dynamic max-pooling scheme and a hidden bottleneck layer were used to achieve a better representation of documents. Another state-of-the art deep model is **Seq-CNN** (Johnson and Zhang, 2015) where each word is represented as a $\|V\|$-dimensional one-hot vector where $V$ is the vocabulary of the dataset and the concatenation of the word vectors are passed through a convolutional layer, followed by a special dynamic pooling layer. Furthermore, in **FastText**

(Joulin et al., 2017) the embedding of the words that appear in a document were averaged to create a document representation. Finally, a comprehensive analysis of clinical-domain embedding methods is presented in (Khattak et al., 2019).

## 3 Question detection

As mentioned above, the task of identifying sentences that contain questions and *c-questions* can be broken into two sub-problems: (i) Detecting question sentences from unstructured data (logs) (ii) Correctly identifying the *c-questions* and the real questions that require an answer.

In order to create the corpus of candidate questions, we explored both rule and learning based approaches. We also compared the performance of each method on the task of identifying questions on (medical) unstructured text and analyzed the most common misclassification cases.

**Rule-based Approach:** In particular, we employed the following rules: (i) The last character of a sentence is a question mark (ii) The rules that were introduced in (Efron and Winget, 2010) (e.g I* [try*,like, need] to [find, know]) (iii) The sentence contains a 5W1H word (iv) The refined 5W1H rules from (Li et al., 2011): The sentence contains a 5W1H word at its beginning or it contains auxiliary words (e.g. "what is" instead of what or "how does" instead of how)

**Learning-based Approach:** These approaches learn specific patterns that can be used to identify sentences that are questions. In this study, we evaluated the following methods: (i) A Naive Bayes Classifier which was trained on the NPS Chat Corpus that consists of over 10,000 posts from instant messaging sessions (Bird et al., 2009). As these posts have been labeled with dialogue act types, such as *"Statement"*,*"ynQuestion"*, we used the classifier without any further training. (ii) The syntactic parser from the Stanford CoreNLP Natural Language Processing Toolkit (Manning et al., 2014) which provides a full syntactic analysis of an input sentence. The question-sentences were identified, by examining the syntactic structure of each sentence in the dataset.

## 4 Quest-CNN Architecture

In this section, we describe our proposed model which has as input all the sentences that the above question extraction method identified as questions and it distinguished between the sentences that are

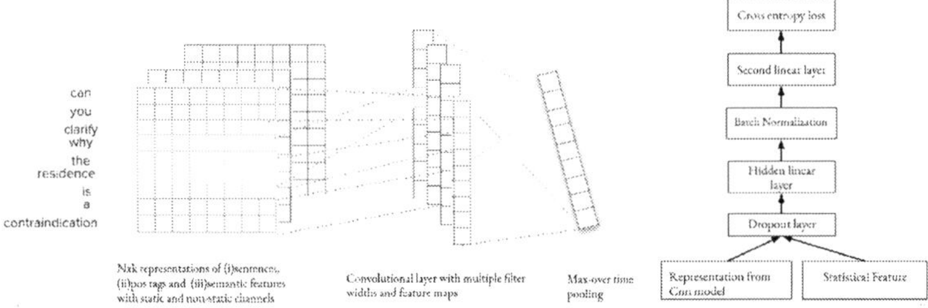



Figure 1: Proposed architecture of Quest-CNN with the (three) feature channels for an example sentence

actual questions and *c-questions*.

The architecture of our model is depicted in Figure 1. The key characteristic of our model is its capability of unifying the syntactic properties of questions, the semantic features of words by incorporating domain knowledge and statistical features (section 4.1) in a multi-channel CNN scenario.

Let $x_i \in \mathbb{R}^k$ be the $k$-dimensional word vector corresponding to the $i$-word of each sentence. Each sentence can be presented as the concatenation of the word embeddings of its words. By using multiple $t$ convolutional filters the model can capture multiple features for each sentence, as each filter $u \in \mathbb{R}^{hk}$ will create one feature $c_i$ for each word region $x_{i:i+h-1}$ (of size $h$):

$$c_i = f(u^T \cdot x_{i:i+h-1} + b)$$

where $b \in \mathbb{R}$ is a bias term and $f$ is a nonlinear activation function such as the rectified linear unit (ReLU). By padding the end of the sentence, the model can produce a feature map $c_u = [c_1, c_2, ..., c_{n-h+1}]$ that is associated to a filter $u$,

where $n$ is the number of words of the largest sentence. In addition, by using $t$ filters (with different window sizes) the model can create $t$ feature maps that are passed through a max pooling operation in order to obtain one value $c_{max}$ for each filter. The output of the pooling layer is then concatenated with the vector of the statistical features of each sentence thus creating a richer representation of each sentence. Finally, the representation of the sentences are passed through two fully connected layers and a softmax layer that outputs the probability distribution over the labels of the sentences.

Finally, our model consists of multiple channels that represent different features. Each filter $i$ is applied to all the channels and the feature map $c_i$ is calculated by adding the results in each channel. In the ablation study (section 5.2.3), we presented the performance of different variations of the model which consist of one to three channels and use (or not) the information of the statistical features.

## 4.1 Feature description

Since the classification of the sentences is challenging due to their short length, we tried to utilize not only lexical features but also syntactical features, statistical features and semantic features using domain knowledge. In particular, we investigated the influence of the above mentioned features by creating multiple feature-channels for each sentence.

**Word representation:** The first channel consists of the $k$-dimensional word embeddings of the words of a sentence where $x_i \in R^k$ corresponds to the $i$-th word in the current sentence. For the initialization of the word embeddings, we examine multiple options. We can either randomly initialize the vectors and then allow their modification during training or use pre-trained word embeddings that were trained in a much bigger corpus.

In the second case, we also investigated the effect of two popular pre-trained word embedding datasets. The first one is a general domain dataset, the Google News dataset that contains **300**-dimension word2vec embeddings that were trained on 100 billions words (Mikolov et al., 2013). The second one is the Multiparameter Intelligent Monitoring in Intensive Care (MIMIC) III dataset which is a publicly available ICU dataset (Johnson et al., 2016) that consists of medical data (e.g. laboratory tests, medical notes) collected between 2001 and 2012. Since a training course is mandatory in order to access it, there are no available word embeddings. Thus we trained our own embedding model that produced **300**-dimension word2vec embeddings based on the **NOTEEVENTS** table which consists of 2,083,180 rows of patients notes. We believed that the comparison of the effectiveness of our model when it is provided with a large general domain dataset or a smaller specific domain dataset can be a useful guide not only to our work-case but for other NLP problems as well. Words that do not appear in the pre-trained vocabulary are randomly initialize using a uniform distribution in the range $[-\sqrt{\frac{3}{dim}}, +\sqrt{\frac{3}{dim}}]$ (where $dim$ is the dimension of word vector)(Aguilar et al., 2017).

**POS-tagging word representation:** Questions usually have specific syntactic structures and by including this channel we hoped to capture these meaningful syntactic features. By obtaining the POS tags of the words in each sentence, we produced embeddings of each POS tag which has the same dimension as the word embeddings. The vectors of POS tags in the model can either be initialized randomly using a uniform distribution in the range $[-\sqrt{\frac{3}{dim}}, +\sqrt{\frac{3}{dim}}]$ and allow their modification during training or they can be created as one-hot vectors (vectors with all 0s and one 1 which indicates the existence of a specific POS tag word). By comparing these two representations we aimed to understand whether a richer representation of POS-tagging word can significantly improve the performance of the model.

**Semantic Features:** Semantic features were also introduced in order to boost the model's performance by connecting different words that share a semantic meaning. In order to extract relevant clinical entities, we used the UMLS Metathesaurus, a large biomedical thesaurus, which organizes words by (medical) groups and links similar words (Humphreys et al., 1998). The identification of the medical words and their UMLS groups was accomplished using the open-source Apache clinical Text Analysis and Knowledge Extraction System (cTakes)(Savova et al., 2010). We examined two different strategies for incorporating semantic features: (i) Replacing the words that appear in the database with their respective medical group name or (ii) Creating a new channel where, for each group, a new vector is created which was initialized either randomly or by using the pre-trained word2vec vectors as described above.

As our final goal for the model is to work in any domain, in the experiment section, we also presented our model's accuracy by extracting concepts from WordNet, which is an extensive lexical database where words are grouped into sets of synonyms (synsets).

Finally, four statistical features were included in the model namely the length of the sentence, the number of words, the number of capitalized words and the coverage of the vocabulary. These features were introduced in (Zhao and Mei, 2013) for the identification of questions in the Twitter platform.

## 4.2 Regularization

For regularization, we used "embedding dropout", an idea that was introduced in language modeling in (Merity et al., 2018), and performed dropout on entire word embeddings, thus removing some words in each training phrase. Although the "embedding dropout" technique was used for the purpose of regularization RNN-based models, we observed that it can work equally well in a CNN-based model as its main purpose is to make a model rely less on a small set of input words.

In addition, we applied dropout on the last two fully connected linear layers. The Dropout mechanism randomly sets a portion of hidden units to zero during training, thus preventing the co-adaptation of neurons (Srivastava et al., 2014).

## 5  Experiments

In this section, we presented the result of an empirical evaluation on the question-detection methods that were described in section 3 and our proposed model in section 4. In particular, we analyzed the performance of the rule and learning based methods and we provided specific examples that highlighted their limitations. We also provided a comparison between different deep learning text classification methods that were described in section 2 in order to show the efficiency of our proposed model. Finally, we conducted an ablation study that demonstrated the importance of the features (channels) for achieving high-accuracy results.

**Datasets.** The main dataset used in this study is a review log consists of the query-answer dialogue in the Dialysis Measurement, Analysis and Reporting System (DMAR®). DMAR® is a web-based application that collects patient-level, clinical data within a renal program (Blake et al., 2013; Oliver et al., 2010) and its review module facilitates the "query-answer" style of communication between the reviewer (Neurologist) and users (renal coordinators) during routine care process. A user would post a question to the reviewer only when she/he was unsure about the correctness of patient data (for example *why the hernia was considered absolute contraindications?'*). Therefore, the questions in this dialogue dataset provided a good indicator of data quality issues. The dataset used in this study was extracted from DMAR® between 2013-2019. [1] This dataset offered a rare (in terms of quantity) opportunity to examine a vast array of different questions types during medical data review processes over a fairly long period of time in a multi-sites real-world clinical setting. The annotations of the sentences were created by manually checking each sentence, as a ground truth was non existent. Unfortunately, due to the sensitive nature of the dataset (contains medical information of patients), we cannot provide a link to a downloadable version of the data without the approval of the research ethics boards.

In addition, in order to test our model in a general setting, we experiment with the Twitter dataset which was created and analyzed in (Zhao and Mei, 2013). This dataset contains 2462 tweets which were annotated by two human annotators as questions (conveying an information need) or non-questions. This dataset was used to evaluate the models in the binary classification task to separate actual questions from sentences that do not require an answer. Table 1 lists the statistics of both datasets.

For the evaluation of the question detection methods, the accuracy, recall and F1 score (the harmonic mean between recall and precision) were reported. For the evaluation of the deep-learning models, we reported the micro-averaged F1 score and the F1 score for the multi-class and binary-class dataset respectively on the testing and the validation set. [2]

|  | DMAR | Twitter |
|---|---|---|
| Comments | 22125 | 2462 |
| Questions-Sentences | 4486 | 2462 |
| Actual questions | 2575 | 1262 |
| C-questions | 136 | - |
| Comments with ? | 2722 | 2462 |
| Comments with 5W1H | 1780 | 836 |
| A.N. of words | 15.0020 | 11.4130 |
| A.N. coverage of words | 0.0006 | 0.0011 |
| A.N. of capitalize words | 2.3148 | 2.1397 |
| A.N. lengths | 85.4490 | 66.3850 |

Table 1: Statistics of the datasets; we use the acronym A.N for average number

---

[1] REB# 18-1604 approved by the Conjoint Health Research Ethics Board (CHREB), University of Calgary.

[2] `https://scikit-learn.org/stable/modules/generated/sklearn.metrics.f1_score.html`

## 5.1 Question Extraction

The performance of different question extraction methods on the DMAR dataset was presented in Table 2. The results showed that simple rules method, i.e. identifying question marks, had a medium performance. The reason for the misclassification cases may be due to the language patterns in casual conversational log, where people sometimes forgot to add a question mark (?) in a question (*what symptoms did the patient present.*) or they used a question mark to show irony (*the procedure has already begun so maybe an update next time?*), or tried to be polite when they encouraged a person to take action (*please see comments?*).

By adding the 5H1W rule, the recall could be boosted but the precision dropped significantly, due to the fact that many sentences could contain 5W1H but are not questions (e.g. *just wait and see what happens*). Furthermore, we observed that by applying the refined rules introduced in (Li et al., 2011), the model could maintain almost the same recall, while achieving a significant improvement in precision. Finally, the results revealed that the rules in (Efron and Winget, 2010) had the overall best (F1) performance. This indicated that even if these rules were made for a different context (twitter), they could be applied to other domains (e.g. medical).

| Methods | Prec. (%) | Recall (%) | F1 (%) |
|---|---|---|---|
| Naive Bayes | 77.2 | 55.8 | 64.8 |
| Parsing algorithm | **93.0** | 38.7 | 54.7 |
| QM | 86.2 | 91.1 | 88.6 |
| QM & 5W1H | 59.3 | **94.9** | 73.0 |
| Rule 1 Li et al.(2011) | 83.9 | 91.6 | 87.6 |
| Rule 2 Li et al.(2011) | 82.6 | 91.6 | 86.9 |
| Rule 1,2 Li et al.(2011) | 86.1 | 91.2 | 88.6 |
| Rule Efron et al.(2010) | 86.2 | 91.8 | **88.9** |

Table 2: Precision, Recall and F1 scores for question identification methods; best results are **bolded**

By investigating the performance of the learning-based approaches, we observed that the parsing algorithm could significantly improve the precision of question-detection but with low recall performance as it missed a large number of questions. This is largely caused by the irregular syntax patterns used in real-life casual conversation (e.g. *he is still sitting in my baseline?*). Finally, the Naive Bayes Classifier identified half of the questions with low precision which indicates that using transfer learning (it is trained on the NPS Chat Corpus) cannot achieve a good performance especially in cases where the conversation is domain-specific, such as in a clinical setting or a electronic medical record system. Thus, methods of this type would need to be trained with domain-specific examples, which are usually resource-intense.

It should be noted that we did not evaluate the different question extraction methods on the Twitter dataset as it was constructed by tweets that were all "potential" questions (they all contain a question mark) and thus it cannot provide a fair comparison of the methods. To evaluate the QUEST-CNN model's ability to identify the actual question and the *c-questions*, we used the Twitter dataset and the dataset that contains all the sentences extracted by all the question extraction methods from the DMAR dataset.

### 5.2  Multichannel-CNN experiments

In this section, we reported the evaluation of our proposed model in identifying questions and *c-questions*. Firstly, we presented a comparison of our model with the other deep-learning models that were described in section 2. In addition, we also tested the performance of a bi-directional LSTM (BI-LSTM) model that used as input all the features that we described in section 4.1 where the last hidden state is fed to a fully-connected softmax layer. Finally, we compared our model to logistic regression (LR) using an one-vs-rest multi-class objective and a support vector machine (SVM) model using a linear kernel. For the last two methods, we used the tf-idf measure of the words as features.

In addition, we conducted an ablation analysis of our model. In summary, the baseline was a **CNN-rand** model where the word embeddings were randomly initialized but could be modified during training. We also provided the performance of our model when the word2vec embeddings were used (Google News or MIMIC) and we examined whether allowing further training of the embeddings (**CNN-non static**) can achieve better results than keeping them static(**CNN-static**). Finally, we examined whether the statistical, the POS-tag and the semantic features were meaningful features and which form of the features (as they were described in section 4.1) could achieve a better performance (**multi-channel** scenario).

All the experiments were performed with Py-

Torch 0.4.1. Scikit-learn 0.22.2 was used to implement the SVM, the LR model and the computation of the tf-idf vectors. All experiments were executed on a Intel(R) Core(TM) i7-8665U CPU @ 1.90GHz with 15 GB RAM running Ubuntu 18.04.3 LTS.

#### 5.2.1  Hyperparameter Tuning

In order to address the concerns of reproducibility of the NLP community (Dodge et al., 2019), we provided the search strategy and the bound for each hyperparameter as follows: the batch size was set between 32 and 64; the dropout embedding and the learning rate were from a uniform distribution on the interval $[0, 0.5]$, $[0, 0.2]$ and $[1e\text{-}6, 1e\text{-}1]$ respectively; the filter sizes of the models were between $(2,3,4)$, $(3,4,5)$ and $(2,4,8)$; the feature map, the dynamic pool, hidden linear layer and the hidden size of the BI-LSTM were from a discrete uniform distribution on the interval $[100, 200]$, $[2, 6]$, $[40, 100]$, $[25, 75]$ respectively; the SEQ-CNN filter size was between the values 2,3,4 and feature map from a discrete uniform distribution on the interval $[800, 1200]$. The best assignment was chosen based on the F1 value achieved on the DMAR validation set after 50 search trials. We did not perform any other dataset-specific tuning. An implementation of all the models is downloadable in our github repository [3].

In the interest of providing a fair comparison we tuned the hyperparameters of each model. To train XML-CNN, we selected a dynamic pooling window of length 3, a learning rate 5e-5, a batch size of 32, feature map 128, hidden linear layer of size 77, filter sizes of $(3,4,5)$ and dropout of 0.338. For Kim-CNN, we used batch size 64, filter sizes of $(2,4,8)$, feature map of 164, learning rate 0.003 and dropout 0.077. For FastText, we used a batch size of 64 with learning rate 0.051. For training the Bi-LSTM, we chose a batch size of 64, learning rate 0.004, dropout of 0.056 and hidden size of 50. For SEQ-CNN, we used a batch size of 32, learning rate 0.084, filter size of 4, feature map 1033 and dropout 0.215. Finally, for the SVM and the LR model, we chose the default hyperpameters of the scikit-learn library.

For the QuestCNN, we used a batch size of 32, a learning rate 0.012, a feature map of 160, filter sizes of $(3,4,5)$, a hidden linear layer of size 96, a dropout rate of 0.164 and an embedding dropout of 0.016. In addition, we applied spatial batch normal-

---

[3]`https://github.com/gmichalo/question_`
`identification_on_medical_logs`

| Model | DMAR | | | | TWITTER | | | |
|---|---|---|---|---|---|---|---|---|
| | Test F1 | Val. F1 | R.T | param. | Test F1 | Val. F1 | R.T | param. |
| | % | % | sec. | | % | % | sec. | |
| LR | 64.3±0.2 | 65.0±0.4 | 0.5 | 4091 | 53.2±0.3 | 57.4±0.5 | 0.3 | 7133 |
| SVM | 76.8±0.4 | 77.2±0.2 | 0.7 | 4091 | 61.2±0.3 | 61.6±0.4 | 0.4 | 7133 |
| KimCNN | 83.9±0.3 | 84.4±0.2 | 536 | 2578371 | 61.7±0.4 | 62.7±0.5 | 180 | 4171778 |
| BILSTM | 82.9±0.2 | 83.3±0.2 | 168 | 1593715 | 58.9±0.4 | 59.3±0.4 | 100 | 5706010 |
| XMLCNN | 85.5+0.2 | 86.0+0.3 | 319 | 2209953 | 61.1+0.5 | 61.6+0.5 | 158 | 3803775 |
| SeqCNN | 84.2±0.1 | 84.4±0.1 | 3191 | 1243735 | 64.7±0.2 | 65.1±0.2 | 3142 | 1242701 |
| FastText | 77.8±0.1 | 79.9±0.1 | **45** | 1200003 | 63.0±0.3 | 63.6±0.4 | **36** | 2793602 |
| QuestCNN | **86.9±0.2** | **87.4±0.3** | 594 | 2988183 | **65.5±0.2** | **66.7±0.3** | 399 | 7100486 |

Table 3: Results of mean ± standard deviation of five runs from each model on the test and the validation test; average running time (R.T.) and number of trainable parameters (param.) are also provided for each model. The number of parameters is different between datasets as we included the embeddings vectors that are fine-tuned for each dataset; all models used the same (MIMIC) embedding; best values are **bolded**

ization to the output of each channel of our model and batch normalization to the output of the hidden linear layer which is a technique for normalizing layer inputs. This technique has been shown to accelerate the training of different deep learning models (Ioffe and Szegedy, 2015). The Adam optimizer (Kingma and Ba, 2015) was chosen, with cross-entropy loss, as our optimization objective. Finally, each model was trained for 30 epochs.

Furthermore, in Figure 2, we provided the validation performance of the models based on the technique in (Dodge et al., 2019) that measures the mean and variance of the performance of a model as a function of the number of hyperparameter trials. Finally, as the datasets do not have a standard dev set, we split the dataset to 80% training, 10% validation and 10% testing. In order to present more robust results, we ran our model on five different seeds and we provided the average scores for the testing and the validation set.

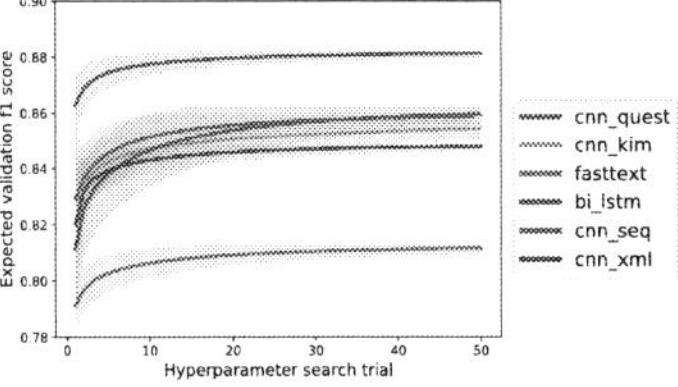

Figure 2: Expected validation performance of all the deep learning models over 50 hyperparameter trials. The standard deviation of the expected performance is represented as the shaded area in the graph

### 5.2.2 Deep Learning Model comparison

The mean and standard deviation (SD) of the scores for our model and the other competing models on the task of identifying questions are reported in Table 3. QUEST-CNN was shown to have achieved the best F1 score for both datasets (86.9% and 65.5%). This is due to the fact that the model utilizes information from all the features (syntactic, semantic, statistical) and uses regularization and normalization techniques. In section 5.2.3, we analyzed in detail the effect of each feature. The FastText model performed the poorest on DMAR (77.8%) as this model didn't consider the word order of the sentence but it required the least amount of running time. In addition, Kim-CNN, XML-CNN and Seq-CNN architectures had similar performances on the DMAR dataset (83.9%, 85.5% 84.2%) but on the twitter dataset Seq-CNN had the second best performance (after Quest-CNN) with 64.2%. However, the running time of the Seq-CNN is the largest by a considerable margin. Furthermore, the Bi-LSTM model which utilized all the features, achieved a non-optimal performance, which confirmed our hypothesis that a CNN-architecture is more suitable for the task of question identification. Also, it should be noted that SVM and LR achieved a decent performance. SVM in particular, achieved a similar performance to the FastText model on the DMAR dataset and even surpassed the BI-LSTM on the Twitter dataset.

### 5.2.3 Ablation Study

The comparison of the performance of different variants of our model is presented in Figure 3. Firstly, even our baseline model (CNN-rand) per-

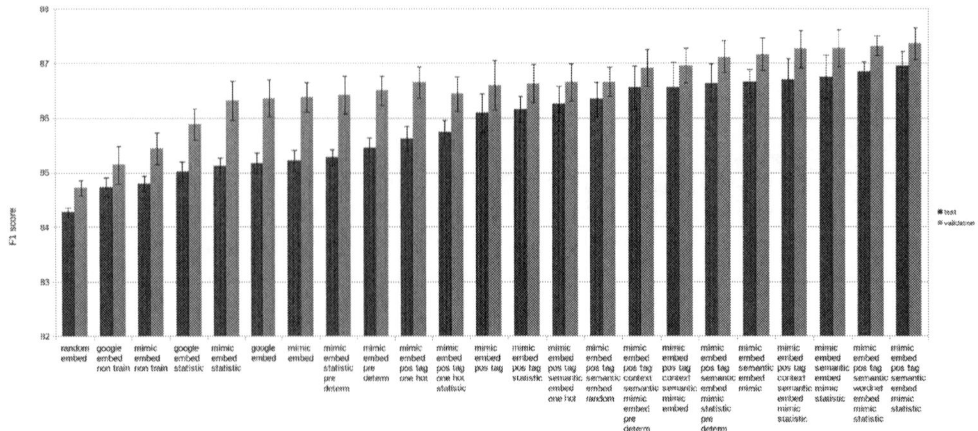

Figure 3: F1 scores of the Ablation study for the Quest-CNN in the DMAR dataset; the word context means that we did not create a new channel but we replaced the words in the sentence with their semantic group name.

formed better than classic machine learning models (LR and SVM). In addition, by using pre-trained vectors a static model could achieve a better performance than CNN-rand. Further fine-tuning of the pre-trained models could improve the performance even more. Finally, the multi-channel model achieved a better performance than the single channel model in every case, as the best performance was achieved by using all the 3 feature types and the statistical features. We observed that the strategy of creating a new channel for the semantic features achieved a better performance than replacing the words with their respective medical group name. This provided evidence that a richer representation of the sentences could help the model to make more accurate evaluations.

### 5.2.4 Using Domain Knowledge

By comparing the behavior of our model when it utilizes pre-trained word embeddings from a general (Google) or a specific (Mimic) domain, (for the word embedding channel and for the semantic feature channel) we observed that the MIMIC III pre-trained embeddings have a more positive effect on the behavior of the model. In addition, we experimented with the creation of the semantic channel by either using medical group names (from UMLS, a medical Metathesaurus) or concepts from WordNet (a general-domain database). For WordNet, as the assignment of words to concepts can be ambiguous, we considered only the first concept. This choice was based on the assumption that WordNet returns a list of concepts where the most common meaning is listed first (Elberrichi

et al., 2008). Similar to the embeddings case, we observed that concepts from a specific domain are more beneficial for the performance of the model (Figure 3). These experiments indicated that when applying a classification model on documents of a specific domain (i.e medical), exploiting domain knowledge from a dataset is more advantageous than using general knowledge from a larger dataset. Finally, our experiments showed that using one-hot representation was generally weaker than a word embedding representation, even if the embeddings were initialized randomly and were allowed to be further updated during the training phase of the model.

### 5.2.5 Using Pre-determined Characteristics

Finally, we examined whether adding information from the question extraction method could improve the performance of the model. Specifically, for each sentence, a $n$-vector was created where $n$ was the number of question extraction methods. For each position $i$ was set to 1 if the $i$ method classified the sentence as a question. Otherwise, it was set to 0. This vector was concatenated with the output of the max-pooling layer of the Quest-CNN model (like the statistical features) and then fed to the last fully connected layers in our model. By comparing the performance of the model when these characteristics were available to it (Figure 3), we could observe that our model was capable of identifying these characteristics on its own, and any external guidance would not further improve the performance of the model.

## 6 Conclusion and Future work

In this paper, we have provided an analysis of the performance of existing methods for question extraction with real-world misclassification examples that showed the weak point of each method. Furthermore, we have proposed a novel approach for the automatic identification of real questions and *c-questions*. We have also shown empirically that the proposed architecture of unifying syntactic, semantic and statistical features achieved a state-of-the-art F1 score for this particular task. Finally, we have presented the relevance of exploiting domain knowledge in the overall performance of a model.

We are in the process of obtaining access to datasets from different application contexts in order to examine the generalizability of our model. As for future work, we plan to extend our work by calculating the similarity of questions in order to create groups of questions that represent the most impactful "problems" of a given application environment. Finally, we plan to compare our model with recent language representation models like the BERT model in (Devlin et al., 2019) both for the task of question identification and for the task of creating the above mentioned "problem" groups.

## References


Gustavo Aguilar, Suraj Maharjan, Adrian Pastor López-Monroy, and Thamar Solorio. 2017. A multi-task approach for named entity recognition in social media data. In *Proceedings of the 3rd Workshop on Noisy User-generated Text*, pages 148–153, Copenhagen, Denmark. Association for Computational Linguistics.

Steven Bird, Ewan Klein, and Edward Loper. 2009. *Natural Language Processing with Python*, 1st edition. O'Reilly Media, Inc.

Peter Blake, Robert Quinn, and Matthew Oliver. 2013. Peritoneal dialysis and the process of modality selection. *Peritoneal dialysis international : journal of the International Society for Peritoneal Dialysis*, 33:233–41.

Jacob Devlin, Ming-Wei Chang, Kenton Lee, and Kristina Toutanova. 2019. BERT: Pre-training of deep bidirectional transformers for language understanding. In *Proceedings of the 2019 Conference of the North American Chapter of the Association for Computational Linguistics: Human Language Technologies, Volume 1 (Long and Short Papers)*, pages 4171–4186, Minneapolis, Minnesota. Association for Computational Linguistics.

Jesse Dodge, Suchin Gururangan, Dallas Card, Roy Schwartz, and Noah A. Smith. 2019. Show your work: Improved reporting of experimental results. In *Proceedings of EMNLP*.

Miles Efron and Megan Winget. 2010. Questions are content: A taxonomy of questions in a microblogging environment. *Proceedings of the American Society for Information Science and Technology*, 47:1 – 10.

Zakaria Elberrichi, Abdellatif Rahmoun, and Mohamed Bentaallah. 2008. Using wordnet for text categorization. *Int. Arab J. Inf. Technol.*, 5:16–24.

Betsy L. Humphreys, Donald A. B. Lindberg, Harold M. Schoolman, and G. Octo Barnett. 1998. The Unified Medical Language System: An Informatics Research Collaboration. *Journal of the American Medical Informatics Association*, 5(1):1–11.

Sergey Ioffe and Christian Szegedy. 2015. Batch normalization: Accelerating deep network training by reducing internal covariate shift. In *Proceedings of the 32nd International Conference on International Conference on Machine Learning - Volume 37*, ICML'15, page 448–456. JMLR.org.

Fei Jiang, Yong Jiang, Hui Zhi, Yi Dong, Hao Li, Sufeng Ma, Yilong Wang, Qiang Dong, Haipeng Shen, and Yongjun Wang. 2017. Artificial intelligence in healthcare: past, present and future. *BMJ*, 2:svn–2017.

Alistair EW Johnson, Tom J Pollard, Lu Shen, H Lehman Li-wei, Mengling Feng, Mohammad Ghassemi, Benjamin Moody, Peter Szolovits, Leo Anthony Celi, and Roger G Mark. 2016. Mimic-iii, a freely accessible critical care database. *Scientific data*, 3:160035.

Rie Johnson and Tong Zhang. 2015. Effective use of word order for text categorization with convolutional neural networks. In *Proceedings of the 2015 Conference of the North American Chapter of the Association for Computational Linguistics: Human Language Technologies*, pages 103–112, Denver, Colorado. Association for Computational Linguistics.

Armand Joulin, Edouard Grave, Piotr Bojanowski, and Tomas Mikolov. 2017. Bag of tricks for efficient text classification. In *Proceedings of the 15th Conference of the European Chapter of the Association for Computational Linguistics: Volume 2, Short Papers*, pages 427–431, Valencia, Spain. Association for Computational Linguistics.

Faiza Khan Khattak, Serena Jeblee, Chloé Pou-Prom, Mohamed Abdalla, Christopher Meaney, and Frank Rudzicz. 2019. A survey of word embeddings for clinical text. *Journal of Biomedical Informatics: X*, 4:100057.

Yoon Kim. 2014. Convolutional neural networks for sentence classification. In *Proceedings of the 2014 Conference on Empirical Methods in Natural Language Processing (EMNLP)*, pages 1746–1751, Doha, Qatar. Association for Computational Linguistics.

Diederik P. Kingma and Jimmy Ba. 2015. Adam: A method for stochastic optimization. In *3rd International Conference on Learning Representations, ICLR 2015, San Diego, CA, USA, May 7-9, 2015, Conference Track Proceedings*.

Baichuan Li, Xiance Si, Michael R. Lyu, Irwin King, and Edward Y. Chang. 2011. Question identification on twitter. In *Proceedings of the 20th ACM International Conference on Information and Knowledge Management*, CIKM '11, page 2477–2480, New York, NY, USA. Association for Computing Machinery.

Jingzhou Liu, Wei-Cheng Chang, Yuexin Wu, and Yiming Yang. 2017. Deep learning for extreme multilabel text classification. In *Proceedings of the 40th International ACM SIGIR Conference on Research and Development in Information Retrieval*, SIGIR '17, page 115–124, New York, NY, USA. Association for Computing Machinery.

Christopher Manning, Mihai Surdeanu, John Bauer, Jenny Finkel, Steven Bethard, and David McClosky. 2014. The Stanford CoreNLP natural language processing toolkit. In *Proceedings of 52nd Annual Meeting of the Association for Computational Linguistics: System Demonstrations*, pages 55–60, Baltimore, Maryland. Association for Computational Linguistics.

Stephen Merity, Shirish Nitish Keskar, and Richard Socher. 2018. Regularizing and optimizing lstm language models. *International conference on learning representations*.

Tomas Mikolov, Ilya Sutskever, Kai Chen, Greg S Corrado, and Jeff Dean. 2013. Distributed representations of words and phrases and their compositionality. In *Advances in neural information processing systems*, pages 3111–3119.

Matthew Oliver, Amit Garg, Peter Blake, John Johnson, Mauro Verrelli, James Zacharias, Sanjay Pandeya, and Robert Quinn. 2010. Impact of contraindications, barriers to self-care and support on incident peritoneal dialysis utilization. *Nephrology, dialysis, transplantation : official publication of the European Dialysis and Transplant Association - European Renal Association*, 25:2737–44.

Guergana K Savova, James J Masanz, Philip V Ogren, Jiaping Zheng, Sunghwan Sohn, Karin C Kipper-Schuler, and Christopher G Chute. 2010. Mayo clinical text analysis and knowledge extraction system (ctakes): architecture, component evaluation and applications. *Journal of the American Medical Informatics Association*, 17(5):507–513.

Nitish Srivastava, Geoffrey Hinton, Alex Krizhevsky, Ilya Sutskever, and Ruslan Salakhutdinov. 2014. Dropout: A simple way to prevent neural networks from overfitting. *J. Mach. Learn. Res.*, 15(1):1929–1958.

Zhe Zhao and Qiaozhu Mei. 2013. Questions about questions: An empirical analysis of information needs on twitter. In *Proceedings of the 22nd International Conference on World Wide Web*, WWW '13, page 1545–1556, New York, NY, USA. Association for Computing Machinery.

# Appendices

## A  UMLS Metathesaurus

As we described in the paper, for the creation of the semantic features of our model, relevant medical group names from the UMLS Metathesaurus were extracted. An example of mapping words to medical group names can be observed in Figure 4 where different words that have a medical significance can be categorized as a medical procedure, a disorder or an anatomy term.

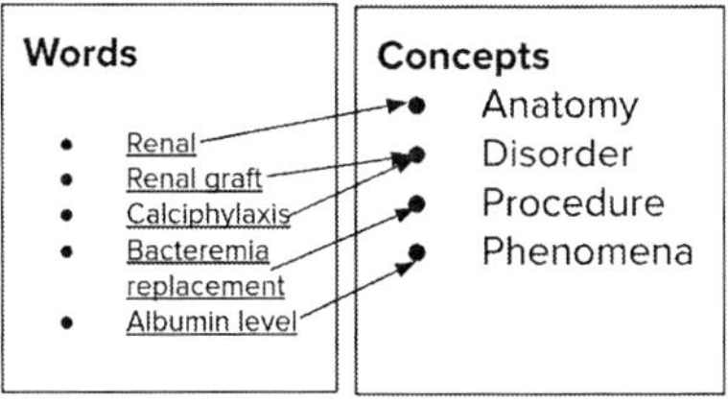


Figure 4: Example of mapping words to medical group

We also provide a complete list of all the Semantic Group Names and Semantic Type Names in Table 4 that our semantic feature model can choose from. In our experiment, we chose to only use the more general Semantic Group Names, since sentences are generally short in length, so we wanted to have a dense connection between different words that are semantically similar as possible. Finally, it should be noted that UMLS also contained additional Semantic groups (like Occupations, Organizations), which we decided to remove from the process of creation of semantic features, as these groups are irrelevant to the domain of the testing dataset. However, these medical groups did not influence the general performance of our model.

## B  C-question Format

In this paper, we introduced the notion of *c-question*, which is a question referring to an issue mentioned in a nearby sentence. The annotations of the sentences were created by manually checking each sentence and we adhered to the following rules:

A sentence can be classified as a *c-question* if:

- It can be classified as a real question i.e it expects an answer (information or help) about an issue.

| Group Name | Semantic Type Name |
| --- | --- |
| Anatomy | Anatomical Structure |
| Anatomy | Body Location or Region |
| Anatomy | Body Part, Organ, or Organ Component |
| Anatomy | Body Space or Junction |
| Anatomy | Body Substance |
| Anatomy | Body System |
| Anatomy | Cell |
| Anatomy | Cell Component |
| Anatomy | Embryonic Structure |
| Anatomy | Fully Formed Anatomical Structure |
| Anatomy | Tissue |
| Disorders | Anatomical Abnormality |
| Disorders | Cell or Molecular Dysfunction |
| Disorders | Congenital Abnormality |
| Disorders | Disease or Syndrome |
| Disorders | Experimental Model of Disease |
| Disorders | Finding |
| Disorders | Injury or Poisoning |
| Disorders | Mental or Behavioral Dysfunction |
| Disorders | Neoplastic Process |
| Disorders | Pathologic Function |
| Disorders | Sign or Symptom |
| Phenomena | Biologic Function |
| Phenomena | Environmental Effect of Humans |
| Phenomena | Human-caused Phenomenon or Process |
| Phenomena | Laboratory or Test Result |
| Phenomena | Natural Phenomenon or Process |
| Phenomena | Phenomenon or Process |
| Procedures | Diagnostic Procedure |
| Procedures | Educational Activity |
| Procedures | Health Care Activity |
| Procedures | Laboratory Procedure |
| Procedures | Molecular Biology Research Technique |
| Procedures | Research Activity |
| Procedures | Therapeutic or Preventive Procedure |

Table 4: The Semantic Group Names and the Semantic Type Names from UMLS library that were used for the semantic features.

- The issue of the question should not be recognizable from the sentence of the question. Usually the question would used a demonstrative pronoun (can you clarify this?).

- The issue of the question should only be identified in a nearby sentence.

|  | question | c-question |
|---|---|---|
| A.N. of coverage | $6.10^{-4}$ | $2.10^{-4}$ |
| A.N. of length | 83.1 | 24.8 |
| A.N. of words | 14.4 | 4.9 |
| A.N. of dem. pronoun | 0.3 | 0.3 |

Table 5: Statistics of questions and c-questions; we use the acronym A.N for average number and dem. for demonstrative pronoun.

Finally, in Table 5, we list the statistics of the sentences that were classified as question-sentences and the *c-questions* in order to make the distinguishment between these categories more understandable. For example, we can observe that even if the average number of words of questions is 2.9 higher than the average number of words in *c-questions*, the average number of demonstrative pronouns is the same for both categories.

# Learning from Unlabelled Data for Clinical Semantic Textual Similarity

**Yuxia Wang**     **Karin Verspoor**     **Timothy Baldwin**
School of Computing and Information Systems
The University of Melbourne
Victoria, Australia
`yuxiaw@student.unimelb.edu.au`
`karin.verspoor@unimelb.edu.au`  `tb@ldwin.net`



## Abstract

Domain pretraining followed by task fine-tuning has become the standard paradigm for NLP tasks, but requires in-domain labelled data for task fine-tuning. To overcome this, we propose to utilise unlabelled domain data by assigning pseudo-labels from a general model. We evaluate the approach on two clinical STS datasets, and achieve $r = 0.80$ on N2C2-STS. Further investigation reveals that if the data distribution of unlabelled sentence pairs is closer to the test data, we can obtain better performance. By leveraging a large general-purpose STS dataset and small-scale in-domain training data, we obtain further improvements to $r = 0.90$, a new SOTA.


## 1 Introduction

Semantic textual similarity (STS) measures the degree of semantic equivalence between two text snippets, based on a graded numerical value, with applications including question answering (Yadav et al., 2020), duplicate detection (Poerner and Schütze, 2019), and entity linking (Zhou et al., 2020).

Modern pretrained language models have achieved impressive results for general STS (Devlin et al., 2019). However in low-resource domains without in-domain labelled data, results are generally lower (Wang et al., 2020b). In the clinical domain in particular, annotation requires medical experts (Wang et al., 2018; Romanov and Shivade, 2018), meaning that labelled datasets are generally small, hampering clinical STS.

We address the question of how to apply pretrained language models to such domain-specific tasks where there is little or no labelled data, focusing specifically on the task of clinical STS.

Employing a general STS model generally yields poor results over technical domains due to covariate shift. To bridge this gap, a standard approach is to pretrain the LM on in-domain text, such as ClinicalBERT (Alsentzer et al., 2019) using MIMIC-III (Johnson et al., 2016). However, existing research has tended to estimate effectiveness under the fine-tuning setting, rather than via inference tasks (Peng et al., 2019; Wang et al., 2020b).

In this paper, we first evaluate domain pretraining approaches for clinical STS, with no labelled data. Based on the assumption that general STS models trained on large-scale STS datasets will perform reasonably well on clinical sentence pairs (Section 4), we then experiment with learning from the pseudo-labelled data (Section 5).

Experimental results show both domain pretraining and pseudo-labelled data fine-tuning improve clinical STS, and the combination of the two achieves the best performance of $r = 0.80$ on N2C2-STS (Section 6.3). Further analysis shows that the score distribution and volume of pseudo-labelled pairs influence the performance of fine-tuning. We also find that training for more iterations leads to minor improvements.

The paper makes three major contributions: (1) we propose a simple pseudo-training method, and show it to perform well on clinical STS; (2) we evaluate several existing approaches to clinical STS in a zero-shot setting, and benchmark against our method; and (3) we achieve state-of-the-art results of $r = 0.90$ for N2C2-STS.

## 2 Related Work

The general approach to domain-specific task modelling is: (1) pretrain a language model (LM) on a large volume of open-domain text (Devlin et al., 2019; Liu et al., 2019); and (2) fine-tune on domain-specific text and task-specific labelled data (Gururangan et al., 2020; Peng et al., 2019). For this approach, however, domain-specific labelled data is required, an assumption that we seek to relax.




*Proceedings of the 3rd Clinical Natural Language Processing Workshop*, pages 227–233
November 19, 2020. ©2020 Association for Computational Linguistics

For STS, in the absence of labelled data, the simplest approach is to calculate the cosine similarity between the CLS-vectors of two sentences or averaged last-layer embeddings, but this tends to perform poorly, even worse than averaged GloVe (Pennington et al., 2014) embeddings. SBERT (Reimers and Gurevych, 2019) proposed to use a Siamese structure based on BERT to learn sentence representations, where they fine-tuned the model over general NLI data, and continued to fine-tune on general STS data (STS-B) (Cer et al., 2017). In this work, we experiment with this approach specifically in the clinical context.

## 3 Datasets and Tasks

We select two available clinical STS benchmark datasets for evaluation: MedSTS (Wang et al., 2018) and N2C2-STS (Wang et al., 2020a). The latter annotated 412 instances as new test bed, and updated train partition by labelling extra 574 instances and merging the former train and test cases (see Table 1). Our aim is to predict a score, given a sentence pair $(S1, S2)$, closing to the gold label — a numerical value ranging from 0 to 5, where 0 refers to completely dissimilar semantics while 5 is completely equivalent in the meaning.

For example,

*S1:* Discussed goals, risks, alternatives, advanced directives, and the necessity of other members of the surgical team participating in the procedure with the **patient**.

*S2:* Discussed risks, goals, alternatives, advance directives, and the necessity of other members of the healthcare team participating in the procedure with the **patient and his mother**.

*Label:* 4, as the two sentences are mostly equivalent and differ only in unimportant details (in bold).

Pearson's correlation ($r$) and Spearman's correlation ($\rho$) between the predicted and gold standard scores are used as evaluation metrics.

## 4 Observations

In modern NLP, large amounts of high-quality training data are a key element in building successful systems (Aharoni and Goldberg, 2020). This is also the case with STS, where additional training data has been shown to improve accuracy (Wang et al., 2020b). However, domain shifts inevitably lead to performance drops (Gururangan et al., 2020). Therefore, we ask: **RQ1** Can large-scale general-domain labelled STS data be transferred to train

| Dataset | Len | Train Size | Test Size |
|---|---|---|---|
| MedSTS | 25.4 | 750 | 318 |
| N2C2-STS | 19.3 | 1642 | 412 |

Table 1: Clinical STS datasets. Train and Test Size = number of text pairs. Len = mean sentence length in tokens.

| Eval set / Model | Data | $r$ | $\rho$ |
|---|---|---|---|
| **STS-B dev:** | | | |
| CLS-BERT | STS-B train | .900 | .896 |
| CLS-BERT | STS-G | .928 | .927 |
| **N2C2-STS test:** | | | |
| HConvBERT | STS-B train + N2C2-STS train | .894 | .830 |
| HConvBERT | STS-G + N2C2-STS train | .902 | .836 |

Table 2: Pearson's $r$ and Spearman's $\rho$ evaluation on STS-B dev (upper half) and N2C2-STS test (bottom half), based on fine-tuning over STS-B train (5,749) and STS-G (28,518), for CLS-BERT and HConvBERT.

clinical STS models? **RQ2** How does low-quality training data impact clinical STS performance, vs. high-quality labelled data or no labelled data?

**Effect of Larger General STS Corpus.** We source general-domain labelled data from: (1) SemEval-STS shared tasks 2012–2017 (Agirre et al., 2012, 2013, 2014, 2015, 2016; Cer et al., 2017); and SICK-R (Marelli et al., 2014). This results in a total of 28,518 labelled sentence pairs, which we refer to as "STS-G".

We adapt a BERT encoder connected to a linear regression layer to fine-tune a general-domain STS model using STS-G, where the CLS-vector is used to represent the sentence pair (CLS-BERT). We compare this with a model trained only on STS-B. We evaluate both models on STS-B dev (same setup as Section 6.1).

For clinical STS, we employ a hierarchical convolution (HConv) model based on BERT (updating parameters of the last four layers), where the model is first fine-tuned with STS-B, then N2C2-STS is augmented by back-translation (Wang et al., 2020b). The model architecture and hyperparameter settings are the same as the original paper, such that we merely replace STS-B with STS-G, and observe that more training data improves clincial STS.

As shown in Table 2, the extra training data in STS-G results in an increase in $r$ of up to .028, in the case of HConvBERT (Wang et al., 2020b), resulting in a new SOTA of $r = .902$.

**Discussion.** Though general-domain data lacks clinical information, the model clearly benefits from the extra out-of-domain training data (answering RQ1). This inspires us to rethink the clinical STS task as a combination of domain-specific text understanding and domain-invariant task learning, leading to the question: can the two aspects be learned separately? That is, can task learning take place via large volumes of general-domain labelled data, and domain-specific characteristics be learned from silver-standard labelled domain data, such as low-quality clinical sentence pairs labelled by a general STS model?

## 5 Method

Next, we investigate the use of pseudo-labelled clinical data based on the general STS model.

### 5.1 Pseudo-Labelled Sentence Pairs

Gururangan et al. (2020) illustrate that if the data distribution of the text used for pretraining is more similar to the task data, the performance will be better. Based on this, we propose a distribution-centric strategy for generating and selecting sentence pairs.

**Generation.** Two data sources — MIMIC-III clinical notes and N2C2-STS training data (ignoring labels) — are used to generate unlabelled sentence pairs. We sample 10,000 discharge summaries from MIMIC-III, which we segment into 27 parts based on section subtitles. Of these, we select five sections we consider to be most related to the N2C2-STS task: *diagnosis*, *medications*, *history of present illness*, *follow-up instructions* and *physical exam*. After sentence segmentation using SpaCy (Honnibal and Montani, 2017), we randomly sample sentence pairs from each section partition.

**Labelling and Sampling.** We take the CLS-BERT model trained on STS-G, and generate a score for all sentence pairs. To balance the data, we group into 5 equal-width bands based on score: $[0.0, 1.0]$, $(1.0, 2.0]$, $(2.0, 3.0]$, $(3.0, 4.0]$ and $(4.0, 5.0]$. We use all pairs whose assigned score is above 3.0, and sample $N$ pairs from the other three intervals.

### 5.2 Iterative Training

We fine-tune the model over the resulting pseudo-labelled data, repeat the process of labelling and sampling, and further fine-tune the model on the second set of pseudo-labelled data.

| Score | $[0.0, 1.0]$ | $(1.0, 2.0]$ | $(2.0, 3.0]$ | $(3.0, 4.0]$ | $(4.0, 5.0]$ |
|---|---|---|---|---|---|
| 500k | 229622 | 211405 | 54517 | 4015 | 441 |
| STS-PL | 4015 | 4015 | 4015 | 4015 | 441 |
| 100k | 45602 | 42479 | 10996 | 839 | 84 |
| STS-PS | 1500 | 1500 | 1500 | 839 | 84 |
| 500k | 399975 | 81282 | 16841 | 1468 | 434 |
| STS-DP | 1468 | 1468 | 1468 | 1468 | 434 |

Table 3: Score distribution of 500k sentence pairs used for STS-PL and 100k pairs used for STS-PS. STS-DP is based on a domain-pretrained model (see Section 6.3).

## 6 Experiments

We first evaluate existing approaches for clinical STS in the zero-shot setting, and compare with our method. Then we analyse the impact of the volume of sampled instances and data distribution on the fine-tuning quality. We experiment with the number of iterations in Section 6.5.

### 6.1 Experimental Setup

We evaluate over MedSTS and N2C2-STS. As gathering naturally occurring pairs of sentences with different degrees of semantic similarity is very challenging (Wang et al., 2018), only 84 instances in $(4.0, 5.0]$ are sampled from a group of 100k unlabelled sentence pairs (see Table 3). To increase the number of instances with high similarity, another group of 500k unlabelled sentence pairs is generated from discharge summaries. Limiting to cases above 3.0, (1) "STS-PS" (Pseudo-labelled Small) = 5,423 pairs, is sampled from 100k based on $N = 1500$; and (2) "STS-PL" (Pseudo-labelled Large) = 16,501 pairs, is sampled from 500k based on $N = 4015$.

Unless otherwise indicated, pseudo labelling is based on CLS-BERT$_{base}$-STS-G (see Section 4). All models are trained with a batch size of 16, learning rate of 2e-5, and 3 epochs with linear scheduler setting warmup proportion of 0.1 of fine-tuning. For all CLS-BERT models, we update all 12 layers, and for HConvBERT we update the last 4 layers.

### 6.2 Results

We perform experiments over three models (SBERT, CLS-BERT, and HConvBERT), two pre-training configurations (general and clinical), and four training datasets (general gold-labelled STS-B and STS-G, clinical pseudo-labelled STS PL and STS-PS).

Results are presented in Tables 4 and 5 for N2C2-STS and MedSTS, resp. Here, the subscripts for

| Model | Data | $r$ | $\rho$ |
|---|---|---|---|
| **Standard labels:** | | | |
| IBM-N2C2 | N2C2-STS train | .901 | — |
| HConvBERT$_{base}$ | N2C2-STS train + STS-G | .902 | .836 |
| **Zero-shot setting:** | | | |
| SBERT$_{base}$ | NLI | .378 | .392 |
| SBERT$_{base}$ | NLI + STS-B | .603 | .604 |
| CLS-BERT$_{base}$ | STS-B | .682 | .689 |
| CLS-BERT$_{clinical}$ | STS-B | .694 | .697 |
| CLS-BERT$_{base}$ | STS-B + STS-PL | .780 | .755 |
| CLS-BERT$_{base}$ | STS-B + STS-PS | .777 | .749 |
| CLS-BERT$_{base}$ | STS-G | .721 | .720 |
| CLS-BERT$_{clinical}$ | STS-G | **.788** | **.768** |
| CLS-BERT$_{base}$ | STS-G + STS-PL | *.781* | *.767* |
| CLS-BERT$_{base}$ | STS-G + STS-PS | .763 | .750 |
| HConvBERT$_{base}$ | STS-B | .728 | .719 |
| HConvBERT$_{clinical}$ | STS-B | .522 | .526 |
| HConvBERT$_{base}$ | STS-B + STS-PL | .760 | .740 |
| HConvBERT$_{base}$ | STS-B + STS-PS | .758 | .733 |
| HConvBERT$_{base}$ | STS-G | .731 | .716 |
| HConvBERT$_{clinical}$ | STS-G | .653 | .653 |
| HConvBERT$_{base}$ | STS-G + STS-PL | .768 | .749 |
| HConvBERT$_{base}$ | STS-G + STS-PS | .752 | .734 |

Table 4: Results on N2C2-STS, based on fine-tuning on STS-B, STS-G, STS-PS and STS-PL.

| Model | Data | $r$ | $\rho$ |
|---|---|---|---|
| **Standard labels:** | | | |
| CLS-BERT$_{P+M}$ | MedSTS train | .848 | — |
| **Zero-shot setting:** | | | |
| Baseline | — | .618 | — |
| SBERT$_{base}$ | NLI | .608 | .594 |
| SBERT$_{base}$ | NLI + STS-B | .731 | .679 |
| CLS-BERT$_{base}$ | STS-B | .786 | .716 |
| CLS-BERT$_{clinical}$ | STS-B | .788 | .693 |
| CLS-BERT$_{base}$ | STS-B + STS-PL | *.808* | .726 |
| CLS-BERT$_{base}$ | STS-B + STS-PS | **.815** | **.739** |
| CLS-BERT$_{base}$ | STS-G | .792 | .694 |
| CLS-BERT$_{clinical}$ | STS-G | .800 | .694 |
| CLS-BERT$_{base}$ | STS-G + STS-PL | .801 | .709 |
| CLS-BERT$_{base}$ | STS-G + STS-PS | .800 | .702 |
| HConvBERT$_{base}$ | STS-B | .776 | .698 |
| HConvBERT$_{clinical}$ | STS-B | .719 | .655 |
| HConvBERT$_{base}$ | STS-B + STS-PL | .798 | .713 |
| HConvBERT$_{base}$ | STS-B + STS-PS | .798 | .716 |
| HConvBERT$_{base}$ | STS-G | .799 | .727 |
| HConvBERT$_{clinical}$ | STS-G | .764 | .690 |
| HConvBERT$_{base}$ | STS-G + STS-PL | .803 | .712 |
| HConvBERT$_{base}$ | STS-G + STS-PS | .806 | .723 |

Table 5: Results on MedSTS, based on fine-tuning on STS-B, STS-G, STS-PS and STS-PL.

model descriptors – "base" and "clinical" – correspond to the two pretraining configurations, general and clinical. The "Data" column indicates the corpus used for fine-tuning, and A+B means that the model is first fine-tuned on A then fine-tuned on B. The model using general ("base") pretraining and fine-tuning only on STS-B or STS-G is referred to as the "general STS model".

Both pretraining using in-domain text ("clinical") and fine-tuning on pseudo-labelled data (+STS-PS/STS-PL) improve performance over the general STS model, with fine-tuning on pseudo-labelled data generally performing better than domain pretraining, in addition to being computationally cheaper.

It may be argued that the performance improvement is gained simply as a result of using an enlarged data set for fine-tuning, instead of learning domain characteristics from clinical pseudo-labelled data. However, for both datasets, and under CLS-BERT$_{base}$ and HConvBERT$_{base}$, comparing results using: (1) STS-B with size of 5,749; (2) STS-B + STS-PS with size of 11,172 (5,749 + 5.423); and (3) STS-G with size of 28,518, we find that both (2) and (3) have higher $r$ and $\rho$ than (1), suggesting that enlarging the data size for fine-tuning is beneficial to improving performance. Simutaneously, (2) always performs much better than (3) though (3) is larger and has more gold la-

bels; this indicates the gains are mainly attributable to learned domain characteristics rather than merely increased data. Moreover, based on the results for CLS-BERT$_{base}$ and HConvBERT$_{base}$ using STS-PL and STS-PS, it would appear that the amount and score distribution of the pseudo-labelled data influences fine-tuning performance, which we return to investigate further in Section 6.4.

## 6.3 Combination of Domain Pretraining (DP) and Fine-tuning

We adapt CLS-BERT$_{clinical}$-STS-G to predict scores for 500,000 pairs, generating STS-DP (6,306) after sampling as shown in Table 3. We continue to fine-tune CLS-BERT$_{clinical}$-STS-G using STS-DP, boosting the performance to $r = .803$ and $\rho = .788$, from $r = .788$ and $\rho = .768$.

## 6.4 Impact of Data Distribution and Amount

In this section, we investigate how data source, score distribution — percentage of instances distributed in five score interval, and the volume of sampled instances influence fine-tuning performance. Based on CLS-BERT$_{base}$ with STS-G, we continue to fine-tune over five different groups of data: (1) N2C2-STS training data without gold-standard labels, where the score distribution of pseudo labels is $0.04, 0.15, 0.25, 0.35, 0.21$; (2) data sampled from STS-PL in the same volume

| Exp. | Source | Amount | Score distribution | $r$ | $\rho$ |
|---|---|---|---|---|---|
| 0 | — | 0 | — | .721 | .720 |
| 1 | N2C2-STS | 1642 | $0.04, 0.15, 0.25, 0.35, 0.21$ | **.788** | **.788** |
| 2 | STS-PL | 1642 | $0.04, 0.15, 0.25, 0.35, 0.21$ | .766 | .738 |
| 3 | STS-PL | 1650 | $0.20, 0.20, 0.20, 0.20, 0.20$ | .761 | .731 |
| 4 | STS-PL | 1648 | $0.24, 0.24, 0.24, 0.24, 0.03$ | .767 | .748 |
| 5 | STS-PL | 16501 | $0.24, 0.24, 0.24, 0.24, 0.03$ | *.781* | *.767* |

Table 6: Results for CLS-BERT$_{\text{base}}$-STS-G on N2C2-STS based on fine-tuning on different datasets. Exp.1 is N2C2-STS train data removing gold-standard labels, Exp.2 is sampled from STS-PL with same score distribution as Exp.1, Exp.3 is uniformly sampled from STS-PL, Exp.4 is proportionally sampled from STS-PL and Exp.5 is full STS-PL.

and with the score distribution as (1); (3) uniformly sampled from STS-PL with 330 pairs in each score interval; (4) proportionally sampled from STS-PL at a ratio of $1/10$ for each score interval; and (5) full STS-PL.

Comparing Experiments 2, 3 and 4 in Table 6, which have same data source and size (1.6k), and differ only in score distribution, we observe only minor performance differences. Experiments 1 and 2 rely on different sources, where Experiment 1 has the same source as the test data, and performs much better than Experiment 2. An aligned data source therefore is the optimal scenario. Looking at Experiments 4 and 5, where the difference is in the amount of sampled data, it is clear that more instances brings further improvements. But *Could performance be improved consistently with increased pseudo-labelled data?*

To answer this question, we proportionally sampled from STS-PL by ratio of 0.1, 0.2, 0.3, 0.4, 0.6, 0.8, 1.0, and also sampled from 500k unlabelled sentence pairs setting $N = 5000, 6000, 7000, 7500, 8000$, resulting in 12 subsets in sizes ranging from 1,648 to 28,456, for fine-tuning based on CLS-BERT$_{\text{base}}$-STS-G. As shown in Figure 1,[1] from 0 to 16,501, both $r$ and $\rho$ gradually increase, and then fluctuate around 0.77 and 0.76 resp. This reveals the trade-off between increasing the number of pseudo-labelled fine-tuning instances and error propagation due to cumulative noise.

## 6.5 Impact of Number of Iterations

Based on CLS-BERT$_{\text{base}}$ with STS-G, we investigate the impact of multiple iterations of fine-tuning

---

[1]Random sampling affects the model performance, particularly when the data size is less than 5000, so we sampled five times for 1648, 3300 and 4948, so these results are averages over multiple samples of the given size.

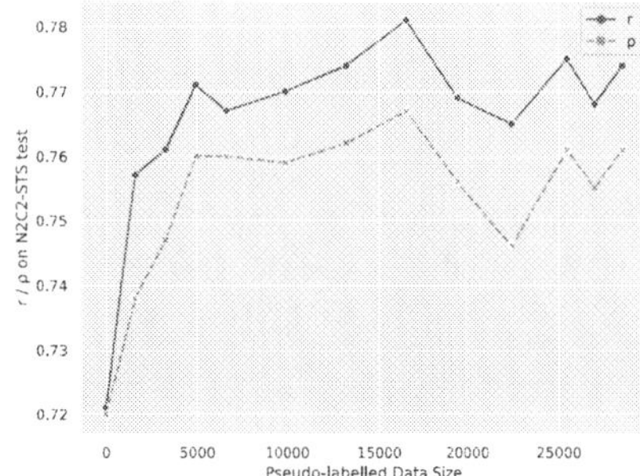

Figure 1: Impact of pseudo-labelled data size on N2C2-STS test.

| Iteration | Amount | Score distribution | $r$ | $\rho$ |
|---|---|---|---|---|
| 1 | 16501 | $0.243, 0.243, 0.243, 0.243, 0.027$ | .781 | .767 |
| 2 | 22205 | $0.245, 0.245, 0.245, 0.245, 0.020$ | .788 | .765 |
| 3 | 27320 | $0.245, 0.245, 0.245, 0.245, 0.020$ | .788 | .759 |

Table 7: Results on N2C2-STS through differing number of iterations of iterative fine-tuning. Amount = number of fine-tuning instances.

in Table 7, as introduced in Section 5.2. The performance boost from additional iterations is modest. Increasing iterations from 2 to 3, the accuracy does not improve, which is consistent with the findings in Figure 1.

## 7 Conclusion

In this paper, we have proposed a simple method of pseudo-labelling in-domain data and iterative training, to improve clinical STS. Evaluation over two clinical STS datasets demonstrates the effectiveness of the approach, and domain pretraining is shown to achieve further improvements. Further investigation indicated that keeping the distribution of pseudo-labelled instances close to that of the in-domain data improves performance. We also observed modest improvements through more iterations of iterative training. Our work provides an alternative approach to employing domain-specific unlabelled data to support clinical STS. As future work, we plan to explore the application of our method to other model structures such as SBERT.

## Acknowledgments

This work was supported in part by China Scholarship Council (CSC). We are grateful to the anonymous reviewers for their insightful comments.

# References


Eneko Agirre, Carmen Banea, Claire Cardie, Daniel Cer, Mona Diab, Aitor Gonzalez-Agirre, Weiwei Guo, Inigo Lopez-Gazpio, Montse Maritxalar, Rada Mihalcea, et al. 2015. Semeval-2015 task 2: Semantic textual similarity, english, spanish and pilot on interpretability. In *Proceedings of the 9th international workshop on semantic evaluation (SemEval 2015)*, pages 252–263.

Eneko Agirre, Carmen Banea, Claire Cardie, Daniel Cer, Mona Diab, Aitor Gonzalez-Agirre, Weiwei Guo, Rada Mihalcea, German Rigau, and Janyce Wiebe. 2014. Semeval-2014 task 10: Multilingual semantic textual similarity. In *Proceedings of the 8th international workshop on semantic evaluation (SemEval 2014)*, pages 81–91.

Eneko Agirre, Carmen Banea, Daniel Cer, Mona Diab, Aitor Gonzalez-Agirre, Rada Mihalcea, German Rigau, and Janyce Wiebe. 2016. Semeval-2016 task 1: Semantic textual similarity, monolingual and cross-lingual evaluation. In *Proceedings of the 10th International Workshop on Semantic Evaluation (SemEval-2016)*, pages 497–511.

Eneko Agirre, Daniel Cer, Mona Diab, Aitor Gonzalez-Agirre, and Weiwei Guo. 2013. * sem 2013 shared task: Semantic textual similarity. In *Second Joint Conference on Lexical and Computational Semantics (* SEM), Volume 1: Proceedings of the Main Conference and the Shared Task: Semantic Textual Similarity*, pages 32–43.

Eneko Agirre, Mona Diab, Daniel Cer, and Aitor Gonzalez-Agirre. 2012. Semeval-2012 task 6: A pilot on semantic textual similarity. In *Proceedings of the First Joint Conference on Lexical and Computational Semantics-Volume 1: Proceedings of the main conference and the shared task, and Volume 2: Proceedings of the Sixth International Workshop on Semantic Evaluation*, pages 385–393. Association for Computational Linguistics.

Roee Aharoni and Yoav Goldberg. 2020. Unsupervised domain clusters in pretrained language models. In *Proceedings of the 58th Annual Meeting of the Association for Computational Linguistics*, pages 7747–7763, Online. Association for Computational Linguistics.

Emily Alsentzer, John Murphy, William Boag, Wei-Hung Weng, Di Jindi, Tristan Naumann, and Matthew McDermott. 2019. Publicly available clinical BERT embeddings. In *Proceedings of the 2nd Clinical Natural Language Processing Workshop*, pages 72–78, Minneapolis, Minnesota, USA.

Daniel Cer, Mona Diab, Eneko Agirre, Iñigo Lopez-Gazpio, and Lucia Specia. 2017. SemEval-2017 task 1: Semantic textual similarity multilingual and crosslingual focused evaluation. In *Proceedings of the 11th International Workshop on Semantic Evaluation (SemEval-2017)*, pages 1–14, Vancouver, Canada.

Jacob Devlin, Ming-Wei Chang, Kenton Lee, and Kristina Toutanova. 2019. BERT: Pre-training of deep bidirectional transformers for language understanding. In *Proceedings of the 2019 Conference of the North American Chapter of the Association for Computational Linguistics: Human Language Technologies, Volume 1 (Long and Short Papers)*, pages 4171–4186, Minneapolis, Minnesota.

Suchin Gururangan, Ana Marasović, Swabha Swayamdipta, Kyle Lo, Iz Beltagy, Doug Downey, and Noah A. Smith. 2020. Don't stop pretraining: Adapt language models to domains and tasks. In *Proceedings of the 58th Annual Meeting of the Association for Computational Linguistics*, pages 8342–8360, Online. Association for Computational Linguistics.

Matthew Honnibal and Ines Montani. 2017. spaCy 2: Natural language understanding with Bloom embeddings, convolutional neural networks and incremental parsing. To appear.

Alistair EW Johnson, Tom J Pollard, Lu Shen, H Lehman Li-Wei, Mengling Feng, Mohammad Ghassemi, Benjamin Moody, Peter Szolovits, Leo Anthony Celi, and Roger G Mark. 2016. Mimic-iii, a freely accessible critical care database. *Scientific data*, 3(1):1–9.

Yinhan Liu, Myle Ott, Naman Goyal, Jingfei Du, Mandar Joshi, Danqi Chen, Omer Levy, Mike Lewis, Luke Zettlemoyer, and Veselin Stoyanov. 2019. Roberta: A robustly optimized bert pretraining approach. *arXiv preprint arXiv:1907.11692*.

Marco Marelli, Luisa Bentivogli, Marco Baroni, Raffaella Bernardi, Stefano Menini, and Roberto Zamparelli. 2014. Semeval-2014 task 1: Evaluation of compositional distributional semantic models on full sentences through semantic relatedness and textual entailment. In *Proceedings of the 8th international workshop on semantic evaluation (SemEval 2014)*, pages 1–8.

Yifan Peng, Shankai Yan, and Zhiyong Lu. 2019. Transfer learning in biomedical natural language processing: An evaluation of BERT and ELMo on ten benchmarking datasets. In *Proceedings of the 18th BioNLP Workshop and Shared Task*, pages 58–65, Florence, Italy. Association for Computational Linguistics.

Jeffrey Pennington, Richard Socher, and Christopher Manning. 2014. Glove: Global vectors for word representation. In *Proceedings of the 2014 conference on empirical methods in natural language processing (EMNLP)*, pages 1532–1543.

Nina Poerner and Hinrich Schütze. 2019. Multi-view domain adapted sentence embeddings for low-resource unsupervised duplicate question detection. In *Proceedings of the 2019 Conference on Empirical Methods in Natural Language Processing and the*

*9th International Joint Conference on Natural Language Processing (EMNLP-IJCNLP)*, pages 1630–1641, Hong Kong, China. Association for Computational Linguistics.

Nils Reimers and Iryna Gurevych. 2019. Sentence-BERT: Sentence embeddings using Siamese BERT-networks. In *Proceedings of the 2019 Conference on Empirical Methods in Natural Language Processing and the 9th International Joint Conference on Natural Language Processing (EMNLP-IJCNLP)*, pages 3982–3992, Hong Kong, China. Association for Computational Linguistics.

Alexey Romanov and Chaitanya Shivade. 2018. Lessons from natural language inference in the clinical domain. In *Proceedings of the 2018 Conference on Empirical Methods in Natural Language Processing*, pages 1586–1596, Brussels, Belgium. Association for Computational Linguistics.

Yanshan Wang, Naveed Afzal, Sunyang Fu, Liwei Wang, Feichen Shen, Majid Rastegar-Mojarad, and Hongfang Liu. 2018. MedSTS: a resource for clinical semantic textual similarity. *Language Resources and Evaluation*, pages 1–16.

Yanshan Wang, Sunyang Fu, and Hongfang Liu. 2020a. Overview of the 2019 n2c2/ohnlp track on clinical semantic textual similarity. Preprint.

Yuxia Wang, Fei Liu, Karin Verspoor, and Timothy Baldwin. 2020b. Evaluating the utility of model configurations and data augmentation on clinical semantic textual similarity. In *Proceedings of the 19th SIGBioMed Workshop on Biomedical Language Processing*, pages 105–111, Online. Association for Computational Linguistics.

Vikas Yadav, Steven Bethard, and Mihai Surdeanu. 2020. Unsupervised alignment-based iterative evidence retrieval for multi-hop question answering. In *Proceedings of the 58th Annual Meeting of the Association for Computational Linguistics*, pages 4514–4525, Online. Association for Computational Linguistics.

Shuyan Zhou, Shruti Rijhwani, John Wieting, Jaime Carbonell, and Graham Neubig. 2020. Improving candidate generation for low-resource cross-lingual entity linking. *Transactions of the Association for Computational Linguistics*, 8:109–124.

# Joint Learning with Pre-trained Transformer on Named Entity Recognition and Relation Extraction Tasks for Clinical Analytics


**Miao Chen**
Covance
`miao.chen`
`@covance.com`

**Ganhui Lan**
Janssen
`ganhuilan`
`@gmail.com`

**Fang Du**
Covance
`fangdu64`
`@gmail.com`

**Victor Lobanov**
Covance
`victor.lobanov`
`@covance.com`



## Abstract

In drug development, protocols define how clinical trials are conducted, and are therefore of paramount importance. They contain key patient-, investigator-, medication-, and study-related information, often elaborated in different sections in the protocol texts. Granular-level parsing on large quantity of existing protocols can accelerate clinical trial design and provide actionable insights into trial optimization. Here, we report our progresses in using deep learning NLP algorithms to enable automated protocol analytics. In particular, we combined a pre-trained BERT transformer model with joint-learning strategies to simultaneously identify clinically relevant entities (i.e. Named Entity Recognition) and extract the syntactic relations between these entities (i.e. Relation Extraction) from the eligibility criteria section in protocol texts. When comparing to standalone NER and RE models, our joint-learning strategy can effectively improve the performance of RE task while retaining similarly high NER performance, likely due to the synergy of optimizing toward both tasks' objectives via shared parameters. The derived NLP model provides an end-to-end solution to convert unstructured protocol texts into structured data source, which will be embedded into a comprehensive clinical analytics workflow for downstream trial design missions such like patient population extraction, patient enrollment rate estimation, and protocol amendment prediction.


## 1 Introduction

Clinical trial protocols, often called "study protocols" or just "protocols", are the foundational documents that specify the detailed plans of conducting clinical trials to validate the safety and/or efficacy of drugs. They contain key information about the targeted disease indications, the eligible patients, the investigated medication, the visit schedules, and the treatment endpoints etc. Across the entire lifecycle of clinical trials starting from study design & planning to data analysis & publication, it is always critical to comprehend this information accurately and unambiguously. However, since protocols are mainly unstructured or semi-structured texts (i.e. natural languages), application of computer-aided information extraction is challenging and thus limited. Current protocol analytic practices are labour- and time-intensive, involving numerous manual resource checking and cross referencing activities. The pressing needs of reducing the costs and boosting the speed of drug development have created an industry-wide demand in developing a more efficient, effective, and scalable mechanism to process text-based protocols.

To address the above demand, we present in this paper our efforts and progresses in developing a deep learning Natural Language Processing (NLP) approach to extract clinically relevant information from protocols. In particular, we targeted two tasks: Named Entity Recognition (NER) and Relation Extraction (RE), and transferred the Bidirectional Encoder Representations from Transformers model (BERT, a pre-trained transformer NLP model) via a joint-learning strategy to extract clinically relevant entities and their syntactic relationships simultaneously by training on our in-house clinical trial protocol corpus.

In alignment with the industry's patient-centric business emphasis, we focused this work on extracting the patient eligibility information from the "Eligibility Criteria" section in the protocols, which unambiguously determines whether a patient could be included in or excluded from the clinical trial. This is particularly important because patient recruitment is an essential and currently rate-limiting step in clinical trials. Accurate parsing of this part of protocols can facilitate quick identification of eligible patients as well as other clinical analytics




*Proceedings of the 3rd Clinical Natural Language Processing Workshop*, pages 234–242
November 19, 2020. ©2020 Association for Computational Linguistics

missions.

Clinical trial protocols are a type of professional documents with rigorous and highly domain-specific terms associated via complex yet precise relations. Like other professionally developed documents, protocols have to pass multiple quality-control checkpoints, and thus require less pre-processing (e.g. text correcting/cleaning) than many other types of documents such as social media posts before submitting to NLP models. On the other hand, the domain-specific nature of protocols requires extra attention when transferring models trained from generic or other professional domains. To elaborate, a protocol contains many clinical and medical terms (e.g. medications and diseases etc.) that are not commonly seen in other domains, but those are exactly the entities that our model needs to recognize; furthermore, it is also challenging that the entities may be connected in dramatically different ways under different domain-specific contexts. For example, in the clinical domain, the word "trial" refers to "clinical trial" that is associated with "patients", "diseases", and "medicines" etc.; whereas in the legal or even generic domains, "trial" commonly means "legal trial" that is frequently connected to "jury", "prosecutor" and "defendant" etc. Therefore, the success of the transfer-learning largely relies on maximizing domain-specific "gradients" for fine-tuning the model parameters.

This presented work is continued from our recent study on clinical protocols, in which we developed standalone BERT-based NLP models for NER and RE tasks for processing the "Eligibility Criteria" section in protocols (Chen et al., 2020).

Based on the observation that different clinically relevant entities are not equally involved in all relations, we hypothesized that by combining the NER and RE tasks in the same BERT network via a joint-learning strategy, the textures of clinical trials may become more visible for training and thus improve the performance of both tasks. As will be shown in the later sections of this paper, our results validated this hypothesis and showed that the joint-learning model can provide significant improvement over standalone models.

This improved model is being embedded into an automated pipeline that aims to accelerate the current manual process of identifying similar clinical trials from the historical protocols, and to streamline the querying process of identifying potentially eligible patients for clinical trials.

## 2 Related Work

NER and RE are two classic NLP tasks that have been studied separately for decades. In its earlier developments, NER, as a sequence labeling task, has mainly employed probabilistic sequence labeling techniques such as conditional random fields (CRF), maximum entropy Markov models, and hidden Markov models (Lafferty et al., 2001; McCallum et al., 2000; Bikel et al., 1998). More recently, researchers have started using deep learning family of algorithms to capture the transitions between hidden states for NER tasks, including recurrent neural networks (RNN), bidirectional long short-term memory (BiLSTM) together with CRF. Lately, pre-trained transformer models, with BERT as a prominent example, have been developed and used to represent contextual embeddings of text and gained great success in NER tasks along with other NLP tasks (Devlin et al., 2018; Lee et al., 2019).

With regard to RE, it is usually treated as a text classification between the interested entity pairs. Many classification algorithms, such as support vector machine, logistic regression, perceptron etc., have been applied to this problem (Bach and Badaskar, 2007; Jurafsky, 2000). Similar to NER, the latest developments in solving RE tasks have also employed deep learning algorithms using neural network models to emulate entity relations with components such as attention, biaffine, and bidirectional tree-structured LSTM-RNNs (Nguyen and Verspoor, 2019; Wang et al., 2019a; Miwa and Bansal, 2016). Pre-trained models were also used to provide contextualized encoding information to the neural network layers for the RE task (Lee et al., 2019; Wang et al., 2019b).

Although they can be tackled independently, NER and RE tasks are in fact synergistically connected: if we knew two entities and their types in a sentence, it would be easier to classify their relations; similarly, if we knew the relation between two phrases, then it would be less challenging to label their entity types. This has naturally motivated efforts in joint or multi-task learning for NER and RE, hoping to achieve better performances in both tasks by simultaneously training the same neural network towards combined objectives. Despite the differences in their details, the practices in NER and RE joint learning usually share a general high-level architecture: they sequentially stack together the word and sequence embedding layers, the NER prediction layer, the NER entity embedding layer, and the relation representation/handling layers. For word and sequence contextualized embedding layers, where many network variations be present, researchers have investigated using BiLSTM, RNN, and BERT pre-trained transformers. (Bekoulis et al., 2018b; Wang et al., 2019a; Giorgi et al., 2019; Huang et al., 2019b; Katiyar and Cardie, 2017). These studies usually emphasized more on evaluating different joint models, leaving the comparison between joint and standalone models to be investigated.

Pre-trained transformer models, e.g. BERT, XL-Net, and GPT, have achieved state-of-the-art performance across a great number of benchmark NLP tasks (Devlin et al., 2018; Yang et al., 2019; Radford et al., 2018). They provide the benefits of representing bidirectional context and encoding text sequence by a series of attention layers. From the transfer learning standpoint, various NLP tasks can be treated as downstream tasks appended to the pre-trained models, and the pre-trained parameters (usually from large scale corpora in a generic domain) together with the NLP task specific parameters are fine-tuned via continued training on a relatively smaller and task-specific training data set. To enhance domain specificity, BERT has also been customized and retrained on specific domains such as the biomedical domain against relevant corpus, examples including BioBERT, ClinicalBERT, and SciBERT (Lee et al., 2019; Alsentzer et al., 2019; Beltagy et al., 2019). Also, there has been a surge in studies applying BERT in specific NLP contexts for fine-tuning tasks such as predicting hospital re-admission, extracting bacteria-biotope relations, biomedical named entity normalization, etc. (Huang et al., 2019a; Jettakul et al., 2019; Li et al., 2019).

We have previously investigated the applications of fine-tuning pre-trained BERT models on a protocol corpus for NER and RE tasks separately. Encouraged by many successful studies on pre-trained transformer and joint models, we continued to explore joint-learning strategies combined with BERT to co-train NER and RE tasks against our in-house clinical protocol corpus. We abstracted a neural architecture from two popular joint models and experimented with a number of variations (Bekoulis et al., 2018b; Giorgi et al., 2019). We believe these continued efforts not only help selecting the best-performing model for our applications, but

also provide a comprehensive understanding of various transfer learning strategies' performance under a real-world setup, shedding light on developing business-oriented AI applications for the healthcare and clinical trial industry.

## 3   Data Set

**Data**. Our data is comprised of the eligibility criteria sections from 470 Covance in-house drug development study protocols (less than 2% of the total number of in-house protocols). The eligibility criteria section in a protocol explicitly and unambiguously defines the rules to include or exclude a patient, thus directly determining the patient population available for the trial. The corpus contains 30,183 criteria sentences in total. We randomly split the sentences into training and test sets with a 2:1 ratio, resulting in 20,122 sentences for training and 10,061 for test.

The sentences were manually annotated by biomedical experts. Clinically relevant entities and the associated entity relations are labelled based on our annotation guideline. We used the BIO tag format to denote the beginning, inside, and outside of the entities (Ramshaw and Marcus, 1999). We focused on 15 types of entities and 7 types of syntactic relations (as shown in Table 1 and Table 2):

Table 1: Train and test data counts for the NER task.

| Entity | Train | Test |
|---|---|---|
| Condition | 12,682 | 8,537 |
| Observation | 7,309 | 5,218 |
| Procedure | 3,406 | 2,234 |
| Device | 221 | 140 |
| Drug | 7,793 | 5,858 |
| Investigational product | 329 | 224 |
| Event | 2,430 | 1,625 |
| Refractory condition | 381 | 278 |
| Demographics | 498 | 381 |
| Measurement | 4,540 | 3,344 |
| Temporal constraints | 6,968 | 4,589 |
| Qualifier/modifier | 7,853 | 5,196 |
| Anatomic location | 427 | 223 |
| Negation cue | 921 | 615 |
| Permission cue | 1,236 | 869 |

## 4   Methodology

### 4.1   Joint Model Overview

After reviewing the previous NER and RE joint models, we established a general network architecture that includes key components for the joint learning while allowing experiment using varia-

Table 2: Train and test data counts for the RE task.

| Relation | Train | Test |
| --- | --- | --- |
| is negated | 703 | 468 |
| is permitted | 1,009 | 673 |
| modified by | 5,715 | 3,810 |
| has value | 3,326 | 2,218 |
| has temporal constraint | 6,169 | 4,112 |
| is located | 215 | 143 |
| specified by | 3,729 | 2,486 |
| *total count* | 20,866 | 13,910 |

tions in local network designs. The main structure of the joint model is shown in Figure 1.

We used BERT pre-trained transformer as the embedding/encoding layer. The NER layer occurs after the BERT layer and uses softmax for NER classification. More specifically, it takes the BERT output vectors as its input and first passes through a fully connected layer and then the output layer where NER labels are classified using softmax function (Goodfellow et al., 2016). The NER classification loss function based on cross-entropy is:

$$loss_{NER} = \sum_{i=1}^{n} -log(\frac{e^{s_{i,l_i}}}{\sum_{j=1}^{k} e^{s_{i,c_j}}}) \qquad (1)$$

where $n$ is the total number of NER tokens, $l_i$ is the actual NER label for the $i^{th}$ token, $k$ is the number of NER label classes, $c_j$ denotes any of the NER label classes, $s_{i,l_i}$ is the linear score for the $i^{th}$ token belonging to its actual class $l_i$, and $s_{i,c_j}$ is the linear score for the $i^{th}$ token belonging to entity class $c_j$.

Following the NER layer, we appended an NER label embedding layer, which is concatenated with the outputs from the previous BERT layer to serve as the input for the subsequent RE task. Because an entity could be paired with other entities before or after it in a sentence, it should be mapped differently in these 2 cases. In our model, the entity vectors are processed in the relation pair handling layer, by 1) mapping them using a fully connected layer to head vectors for representing entities as heads in a pair, and 2) mapping them using a parallel fully connected layer to tail vectors for representing tails in a pair. Then an entity pair, composed of a head and a tail vector, employs a classification function, being either softmax or biaffine function, to produce the RE classification result, i.e., the relation type between the two entities. More details about the RE model variations can be found in section 4.2.1.

The RE loss function is also cross-entropy based:

$$loss_{RE} = \sum_{i=1}^{n} -log(\frac{e^{s_{i,q_i}}}{\sum_{j=1}^{k} e^{s_{i,r_j}}}) \qquad (2)$$

where $n$ is the total number of relations, $q_i$ is the actual relation label for the $i^{th}$ entity pair, $s_{i,q_i}$ is the linear score for the $i^{th}$ relation belonging to its actual class $q_i$, $k$ is the number of relation types, and $s_{i,r_j}$ is the linear score for the $i^{th}$ relation belonging to relation class $r_j$.

The overall joint model loss is derived by summing the NER and RE losses:

$$loss_{joint} = loss_{NER} + loss_{RE} \qquad (3)$$

## 4.2 Model Options

By keeping the NER layers unchanged in this general network architecture, we further experimented with different options for the RE sub-network and evaluated their effects on joint task performance.

### 4.2.1 RE Sub-network Options

For the RE task, we explored methods of representing entities pairs and classifying their relations, which are rendered as the relation handling and the classification layers in Figure 1. We tested two options, denoted as **re_m1** and **re_m2** respectively. Model option **re_m1** is based on (Bekoulis et al., 2018a,b), which passes entity vectors derived from the NER layer through a fully connected layer for obtaining its head entity representation and similarly through another fully connected layer for tail entity representation, and then adds vectors of a pair of entities to serve as the relation vector for the two paired entities (i.e. head and tail entities):

$$h_{i,j} = h_i + h_j \qquad (4)$$

where $h_i$ and $h_j$ are vectors for head and tail entities and $h_{i,j}$ is the resulting vector from summing the two.

We subsequently constructed a fully connected layer to classify the relation vectors. Differing from (Bekoulis et al., 2018a,b), in which the RE classes were assumed to be not mutually exclusive and the RE classification was treated as a multi-label classification task using a sigmoid function, relations in our study are mutually exclusive from each other and henceforth we used a softmax function to classify the relations. Also note that (Bekoulis et al., 2018a,b) used bidirectional LSTM for embedding/encoding and we replaced it with BERT as described in 4.1.

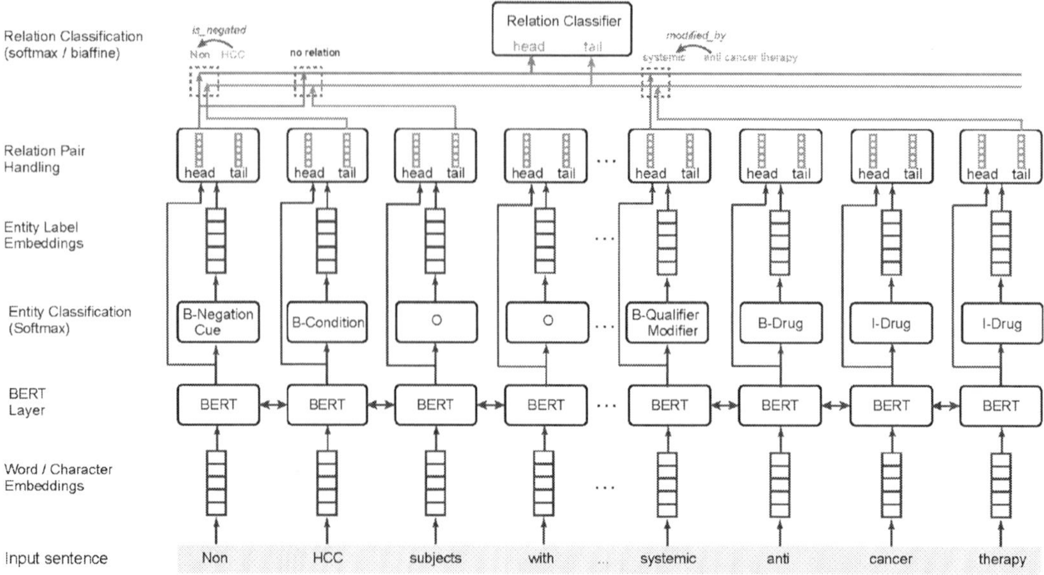



Figure 1: Neural architecture of the joint model for NER and RE tasks.

The other model option, **re_m2**, is similar to the practice in (Giorgi et al., 2019; Nguyen and Verspoor, 2019): we first applied two parallel fully connected layers to derive head and tail entity representation respectively, and then performed biaffine classification using the head and the tail vectors in an entity pair. The biaffine classification function is:

$$biaffine(h_i, h_j) = h_i^T U h_j + W(h_i||h_j) + b \tag{5}$$

where $h_i$ and $h_j$ denotes the head and tail entity vectors respectively, $U$ is a tensor of size of $m \times l \times m$, $W$ is a matrix of size of $l * 2m$, with m being the hidden size of the head/tail vector and $l$ being the number of RE labels, $h_i||h_j$ denotes concatenating the two vectors, and $b$ is a bias vector of size of $l$.

The above biaffine function has a bilinear term $h_i^T U h_j$ and a linear term $W(h_i||h_j)$, along with the bias term. We experimented with either including both the bilinear and linear terms (*bilinear+linear*), or only including the bilinear term (*bilinear only*).

### 4.2.2 RE Negative Sample Construction during Training

A common challenge in RE classification tasks is the overwhelming choices of negative samples. In principle, any entity pair without syntactic relations is a negative sample. To address this challenge, we evaluated two negative sample construction strate-

gies. One strategy is to scan through all the possible entity pairs and mark the pairs without syntactic relations as negative relation samples. Since this option relies on relation information from gold standard data, we denote it as *gs-based*. The other strategy, denoted as *incremental*, incrementally builds negative relation samples based on NER predicted labels, as in (Giorgi et al., 2019; Nguyen and Verspoor, 2019). More specifically, in the *incremental* strategy, an entity pair is included as a negative sample if 1) two entities in this pair are correctly predicted by the NER layer and are without relations, or 2) any of the entities in this pair is incorrectly predicted by the NER. Hence, the former way of constructing negative samples is static as the samples remain unchanged throughout the training, whereas the latter way is dynamic, as whether or not an entity pair is included as a negative sample depends on the NER prediction result during training sessions.

### 4.2.3 Evaluation Options

We evaluated the joint learning model's performance on NER and RE tasks, by reporting micro-level precision, recall, and f1-measure for both tasks. For RE, we evaluated on relations between gold standard entities without considering NER predicted entities (the *gs-based* option), and also evaluated on relations yielded from NER predicted entities (the *end-to-end* option). In other words, the *gs-based* option evaluates RE performance when we know which tokens are actual entities, and the *end-to-end* option evaluates the performance in the scenario when we do not have actual entity information, which is a more realistic scenario when evaluating a RE model's performance in production systems.

### 4.2.4 Standalone Models

To assess the effects of joint learning options, we built NER and RE standalone models from the corresponding sub-networks in the joint learning architecture for NER and RE tasks separately and evaluate their performances.

For the NER standalone model, following the BERT layer, we added a fully connected layer with softmax classification. For the RE standalone model, instead of having an intermediate NER layer, we appended two parallel fully connected layer directly on the BERT output to derive the head and tail entity representations, and then classified entity pair relations using a softmax function. For standalone model evaluations, we employed the same precision/recall/f1-measures as in the joint models by evaluating against the gold standard (the *gs-based* option).

It is worth noting that in real-world practice, we do not know which tokens are entities so we have to use NER prediction as entity input for RE evaluation. Thus, we included a real-world inspired end-to-end metric for RE that evaluates the performance using NER standalone model prediction as inputs, which effectively takes into account the propagated NER prediction errors (the *end-to-end* evaluation option).

### 4.2.5 Pre-trained Models

For pre-trained models, we experimented with BERT base, a smaller version of BERT that comprises 110 million parameters, and BioBERT, a model derived from retraining the original BERT using large-scale biomedical texts (Lee et al., 2019). We chose to use the uncased version of BERT base in which all text is lower cased; and since BioBERT is cased only, we used the model with all original cases preserved in text.

### 4.3 Hyperparameters

We used the same hyperparameter values across all the models as shown in Table 3. For BERT layer hyperparameters we used the same values as in the original BERT model. The models were implemented using the Tensorflow library.

Table 3: Hyperparameter Values.

| Hyperparameters | Value |
|---|---|
| Number of training epochs | 20 |
| Learning rate | $2 \times 10^{-5}$ |
| Training batch size | 32 |
| Maximum sequence length | 128 |
| NER embedding size | 16 |

## 5 Results and Analysis

Our results are summarized in Table 4 and we elaborate our finding below.

**re_m1 vs. re_m2 RE sub-network option**. For the NER task, the four re_m1 models performed similarly to the eight re_m2 models. The highest recall, precision and f1-measure are achieved in re_m2's gs-based negative sampling option (model #12), which performs only marginally better than the other re_m1 and re_m2 models. For the RE task, in the BERT scenario, the re_m2 models greatly outperform the re_m1 models in all three measures (P/R/F). For example, model #5, a re_m2 model using gs-based negative sampling, achieved end-to-end f1-measure of 58.14%, whereas its counterpart, model #1, in the re_m1 model family, has f1-measure of 44.25%, a 13.89% drop from model #5. This result demonstrates that the biaffine classification, the entity pair representation and the classification option used in re_m2, can lead to much better RE performance than softmax classification as used in re_m1. However, for BioBERT pre-trained model, the result is not as decisive: re_m2 does not consistently outperform re_m1. For example, model #15 (re_m2) has better RE performance than model #11 (re_m1) yet model #12 (re_m2) exhibits lower RE performance than model #11 (re_m1).

**Biaffine variations for the re_m2 option**. Within the re_m2 model, we evaluated the strategies to classify relations using both the bilinear and linear parts of the biaffine function (*bilinear + linear*) or using only the bilinear part (*bilinear only*). The results are exhibited as models #3 to #6 (BERT) and #12 to #15 (BioBERT) in Table 4. The two strategies achieved similar results on the NER task for both BERT and BioBERT cases. For RE end-to-end performance, the *bilinear only* strategy combined with BERT and gs-based negative sampling for training (model #5) achieved the best f1-measure and recall; and the *bilinea + lin-*

*ear* strategy together with BioBERT and gs-based negative sampling got the highest precision (model #12). Overall, we observed that the biaffine classification options play a less significant role in model performance comparing to other modeling components such like the negative sampling strategies and pre-trained model options.

**gs-based vs. incremental RE negative sampling**. We tested the two negative sampling strategies on both re_m1 and re_m2 models (models #1 to #6 and #10 to #15 in Table 4). In the case of using pre-trained BERT model, we observed that gs-based negative sampling outperforms the incremental option (models #1 vs. #2, #3 vs. #4, #5 vs. #6) with significant margin. In particular, model #1 exceeded #2 by 4.45% for end-to-end f1-measure, and models #3 and #5 exceeding #4 and #6 by 4.91% and 5.47%, respectively. Interestingly, in contrast, for the BioBERT case, the incremental strategy is superior to the gs-based strategy by an even larger margin, e.g. with model #11 excedding #10 by 19.69%. Therefore the effect of RE negative sampling strategies is jointly determined with the pre-trained model option, and can be significant.

**Joint-learning vs. standalone model**. Our results show that joint-learning models generally improve RE performance over the standalone RE model but do not significantly affect the NER task ( 1% drop in f1-measure). because the incremental strategy requires NER net, the standalone RE can only be evaluated using the gs-based strategy, and we had to use gold standard entity information as RE input. The joint-learning models outperform the standalone RE in most of the scenarios when measured with the gs-based evaluation option. When conducting the end-to-end RE task, the joint-learning models exhibit dramatic performance improvement over the standalone models, e.g. f1-measure of 58.14% for model #5 (joint) vs. 48.15% for #9 (standalone) and 55.37% model #15 (joint) vs. 26.41% for #18 (standalone). Despite of the slightly weaker performance in NER task, the great gain in the end-to-end RE task demonstrates that the joint-learning models a better solution in real-world applications.

**BERT vs. BioBERT**. Comparing between the two pre-trained models, for the NER task, BioBERT yields better result (around 70%) than BERT (around 69%), possibly due to its additional language model pre-trained from biomedical corpus. BERT-based joint-learning models,

when using re_m2 negative sampling strategy, outperforms the re_m1 strategy, but this trend does not hold in the BioBERT-based joint-learning models. BioBERT standalone model performance on the RE task is severely impacted by this configuration (model #18). Although BioBERT-based model achieves reasonable performance in some joint-learning (e.g. model #13) strategies, it fails in others (e.g. model #10). These results indicate that joint-learning with BERT is more robust with more stable performance than BioBERT.

In summary, our results demonstrated that joint-learning is a superior strategy, thanks to its steady and significant performance gain in the end-to-end RE task. However, since no model can achieve the best NER and RE performance simultaneously, it is still necessary to balance the two tasks' performances when choosing the proper joint-learning model to prioritize production needs.

## 6 Conclusion and Future Work

In this reported work, we employed joint-learning models to identify entities and relations in clinical protocols by using pre-trained transformer NLP deep learning models. To the best of our knowledge, this is the first attempt to tackle the NER and RE tasks in a joint and pre-trained deep learning fashion on real-world protocols, which is inherently a corpus of high complexity. Our contribution is three fold: 1) we abstracted a neural network architecture from literature combining pre-trained transformer model with joint learning for NER & RE tasks, 2) we experimented with different model options based on the joint learning network architecture, 3) we examined performance on a complex clinical corpus, which is a less studied but highly impactful domain for such tasks. Our results demonstrated that joint-learning models can greatly improve RE performance over the standalone models despite of a minor decrease in the NER performance. Among all the evaluated joint-learning strategies, the biaffine RE model, gold-standard based negative sampling, together with the BERT pre-trained model, led to generally better performance than other strategies. These results provide evidence on the effectiveness of using joint and deep learning on parsing clinical protocol text, and thus for future work, we will continue exploring more sophisticated joint and multi-task learning network architectures to further enhance the NER and RE parsing performance.

Table 4: NER & RE task performance from joint and standalone models (in percentage).

| No. | Pre-trained model | Method | RE sub-network option | RE negative sampling for training | NER Performance | | | RE Performance | | | | | |
| --- | --- | --- | --- | --- | --- | --- | --- | --- | --- | --- | --- | --- | --- |
| | | | | | | | | gs-based | | | end-to-end | | |
| | | | | | P | R | F | P | R | F | P | R | F |
| 1 | bert | Joint model | re_m1 | gs-based | 66.25 | 72.71 | 69.32 | 70.12 | 51.93 | 59.27 | 47.24 | 43.68 | 44.25 |
| 2 | bert | Joint model | re_m1 | incremental | 66.73 | 73.07 | 69.74 | 69.29 | 34.86 | 43.67 | 52.44 | 34.85 | 39.80 |
| 3 | bert | Joint model | re_m2, bilinear + linear | gs-based | 66.61 | 73.10 | 69.69 | 69.57 | 64.57 | 66.86 | 52.63 | 64.57 | 57.89 |
| 4 | bert | Joint model | re_m2, bilinear + linear | incremental | 66.55 | 72.92 | 69.58 | 70.71 | 51.69 | 59.38 | 54.58 | 51.68 | 52.98 |
| 5 | bert | Joint model | re_m2, bilinear only | gs-based | 66.46 | 73.12 | 69.62 | 70.47 | 64.64 | 67.29 | 52.97 | 64.63 | **58.14** |
| 6 | bert | Joint model | re_m2, bilinear only | incremental | 66.72 | 72.79 | 69.61 | 66.72 | **72.79** | **69.61** | 53.56 | 51.93 | 52.67 |
| 7 | bert | Standalone NER | - | - | 67.79 | 73.19 | 70.37 | - | - | - | - | - | - |
| 8 | bert | Standalone RE | linear | gs-based | - | - | - | 64.37 | 48.85 | 54.89 | - | - | - |
| 9 | bert | Standalone end to end | linear | - | 67.79 | 73.19 | 70.37 | - | - | - | 48.52 | 48.85 | 48.15 |
| 10 | biobert | Joint model | re_m1 | gs-based | 67.93 | 73.49 | 70.58 | 61.84 | 45.81 | 51.53 | 17.35 | 45.79 | 24.59 |
| 11 | biobert | Joint model | re_m1 | incremental | 67.70 | 73.08 | 70.27 | 66.74 | 40.77 | 49.02 | 51.73 | 40.76 | 44.28 |
| 12 | biobert | Joint model | re_m2, bilinear + linear | gs-based | 68.02 | **73.54** | 70.66 | 70.03 | 66.45 | 67.93 | 30.66 | **66.45** | 41.64 |
| 13 | biobert | Joint model | re_m2, bilinear + linear | incremental | 67.71 | 73.33 | 70.38 | 70.44 | 55.21 | 61.50 | 53.48 | 55.21 | 54.22 |
| 14 | biobert | Joint model | re_m2, bilinear only | gs-based | 67.98 | 73.53 | 70.63 | 69.65 | 66.41 | 67.82 | 23.93 | 66.40 | 34.73 |
| 15 | biobert | Joint model | re_m2, bilinear only | incremental | 67.70 | 73.44 | 70.44 | **72.69** | 56.19 | 63.01 | **54.66** | 56.20 | 55.37 |
| 16 | biobert | Standalone NER | - | - | **68.97** | 73.50 | **71.15** | - | - | - | - | - | - |
| 17 | biobert | Standalone RE | linear | gs-based | - | - | - | 63.43 | 52.54 | 57.05 | - | - | - |
| 18 | biobert | Standalone end to end | linear | - | **68.97** | 73.50 | **71.15** | - | - | - | 18.03 | 52.53 | 26.41 |

# References


Emily Alsentzer, John R Murphy, Willie Boag, Wei-Hung Weng, Di Jin, Tristan Naumann, and Matthew McDermott. 2019. Publicly available clinical bert embeddings. *arXiv preprint arXiv:1904.03323*.

Nguyen Bach and Sameer Badaskar. 2007. A review of relation extraction. *Literature review for Language and Statistics II*, 2.

Giannis Bekoulis, Johannes Deleu, Thomas Demeester, and Chris Develder. 2018a. Adversarial training for multi-context joint entity and relation extraction. *arXiv preprint arXiv:1808.06876*.

Giannis Bekoulis, Johannes Deleu, Thomas Demeester, and Chris Develder. 2018b. Joint entity recognition and relation extraction as a multi-head selection problem. *Expert Systems with Applications*, 114:34–45.

Iz Beltagy, Arman Cohan, and Kyle Lo. 2019. Scibert: Pretrained contextualized embeddings for scientific text. *arXiv preprint arXiv:1903.10676*.

Daniel M Bikel, Scott Miller, Richard Schwartz, and Ralph Weischedel. 1998. Nymble: a high-performance learning name finder. *arXiv preprint cmp-lg/9803003*.

Miao Chen, Fang Du, Ganhui Lan, and Victor S Lobanov. 2020. Using pre-trained transformer deep learning models to identify named entities and syntactic relations for clinical protocol analysis. In *AAAI Spring Symposium: Combining Machine Learning with Knowledge Engineering (1)*.

Jacob Devlin, Ming-Wei Chang, Kenton Lee, and Kristina Toutanova. 2018. Bert: Pre-training of deep bidirectional transformers for language understanding. *arXiv preprint arXiv:1810.04805*.

John Giorgi, Xindi Wang, Nicola Sahar, Won Young Shin, Gary D Bader, and Bo Wang. 2019. End-to-end named entity recognition and relation extraction using pre-trained language models. *arXiv preprint arXiv:1912.13415*.

Ian Goodfellow, Yoshua Bengio, and Aaron Courville. 2016. 6.2. 2.3 softmax units for multinoulli output distributions. In *Deep Learning.*, pages 180–184. MIT Press.

Kexin Huang, Jaan Altosaar, and Rajesh Ranganath. 2019a. Clinicalbert: Modeling clinical notes and predicting hospital readmission. *arXiv preprint arXiv:1904.05342*.

Weipeng Huang, Xingyi Cheng, Taifeng Wang, and Wei Chu. 2019b. Bert-based multi-head selection for joint entity-relation extraction. In *CCF International Conference on Natural Language Processing and Chinese Computing*, pages 713–723. Springer.

Amarin Jettakul, Duangdao Wichadakul, and Peerapon Vateekul. 2019. Relation extraction between bacteria and biotopes from biomedical texts with attention mechanisms and domain-specific contextual representations. *BMC bioinformatics*, 20(1):627.

Dan Jurafsky. 2000. *Speech & language processing*. Pearson Education India.

Arzoo Katiyar and Claire Cardie. 2017. Going out on a limb: Joint extraction of entity mentions and relations without dependency trees. In *Proceedings of the 55th Annual Meeting of the Association for Computational Linguistics (Volume 1: Long Papers)*, pages 917–928.

John Lafferty, Andrew McCallum, and Fernando CN Pereira. 2001. Conditional random fields: Probabilistic models for segmenting and labeling sequence data. *ICML proceedings*.

Jinhyuk Lee, Wonjin Yoon, Sungdong Kim, Donghyeon Kim, Sunkyu Kim, Chan Ho So, and Jaewoo Kang. 2019. Biobert: a pre-trained biomedical language representation model for biomedical text mining. *Bioinformatics*.

Fei Li, Yonghao Jin, Weisong Liu, Bhanu Pratap Singh Rawat, Pengshan Cai, and Hong Yu. 2019. Fine-tuning bidirectional encoder representations from transformers (bert)–based models on large-scale electronic health record notes: An empirical study. *JMIR medical informatics*, 7(3):e14830.

Andrew McCallum, Dayne Freitag, and Fernando CN Pereira. 2000. Maximum entropy markov models for information extraction and segmentation. In *ICML*, volume 17, pages 591–598.

Makoto Miwa and Mohit Bansal. 2016. End-to-end relation extraction using lstms on sequences and tree structures. *arXiv preprint arXiv:1601.00770*.

Dat Quoc Nguyen and Karin Verspoor. 2019. End-to-end neural relation extraction using deep biaffine attention. In *European Conference on Information Retrieval*, pages 729–738. Springer.

Alec Radford, Karthik Narasimhan, Tim Salimans, and Ilya Sutskever. 2018. Improving language understanding by generative pre-training.

Lance A Ramshaw and Mitchell P Marcus. 1999. Text chunking using transformation-based learning. In *Natural language processing using very large corpora*, pages 157–176. Springer.

Haoyu Wang, Ming Tan, Mo Yu, Shiyu Chang, Dakuo Wang, Kun Xu, Xiaoxiao Guo, and Saloni Potdar. 2019a. Extracting multiple-relations in one-pass with pre-trained transformers. In *Proceedings of the 57th Annual Meeting of the Association for Computational Linguistics*, pages 1371–1377, Florence, Italy. Association for Computational Linguistics.

Haoyu Wang, Ming Tan, Mo Yu, Shiyu Chang, Dakuo Wang, Kun Xu, Xiaoxiao Guo, and Saloni Potdar. 2019b. Extracting multiple-relations in one-pass with pre-trained transformers. *arXiv preprint arXiv:1902.01030*.

Zhilin Yang, Zihang Dai, Yiming Yang, Jaime Carbonell, Russ R Salakhutdinov, and Quoc V Le. 2019. Xlnet: Generalized autoregressive pretraining for language understanding. In *Advances in neural information processing systems*, pages 5753–5763.

# Extracting Semantic Aspects for Structured Representation of Clinical Trial Eligibility Criteria

[1]*Ishani Mondal,*[2]*Tirthankar Dasgupta , [2]Abir Naskar, [2] Sudeshna Jana, [2]Lipika Dey

[1] Microsoft Research Labs, India [2]TCS Research and Innovation Labs, India

[1]t-imonda@microsoft.com,

[2][dasgupta.tirthankar, abir.naskar, sudeshna.jana, lipika.dey]@tcs.com

## Abstract

Eligibility criteria in the clinical trials specify the characteristics that a patient must or must not possess in order to be treated according to a standard clinical care guideline. As the process of manual eligibility determination is time-consuming, automatic structuring of the eligibility criteria into various semantic categories or aspects is the need of the hour. Existing methods use hand-crafted rules and feature-based statistical machine learning methods to dynamically induce semantic aspects. However, in order to deal with paucity of aspect-annotated clinical trials data, we propose a novel weakly-supervised co-training based method which can exploit a large pool of unlabeled criteria sentences to augment the limited supervised training data, and consequently enhance the performance. Experiments with 0.2M criteria sentences show that the proposed approach outperforms the competitive supervised baselines by 12% in terms of micro-averaged F1 score for all the aspects. Probing deeper into analysis, we observe domain-specific information boosts up the performance by a significant margin.

## 1 Introduction

Clinical trials (CTs) are research studies that are aimed at evaluating a medical, surgical, or behavioral intervention (Embi et al., 2008), (Shivade et al., 2015). Through such trials, researchers aim to find out whether a new treatment, like a new drug or diet or medical device is more effective than the existing treatments for a particular ailment. From an organization's perspective, a successful completion of a trial depends on achieving a significant sample size of patients enrolled for the trial within a limited time period.

---

The first two authors contributed equally*.

Total bilirubin less than or equal to 1.5 mg/dl, except in patients with history of anaemia. Have had their ileostomy or colostomy for at least 3 months. Subjects must be between the age of 18-65 yr old and must not intake alcohol.

Categories of Semantic Aspects are represented using the colors: Health Status ; Lab Test ; Demography ; Life Style ; Treatment Status

However, recruiting enough number of eligible patients to participate in a trial can be a bottleneck. If suitable patients are not found then the trials might get cancelled or delayed significantly. In this case a patient queries the sites like *clinical-trial.gov* to retrieve suitable trials. Due to the complexity of the task which involves repeated reading of the patient's Electronic Health Record (EHR) and the trial criteria for multiple trials, this is not only a labor-intensive and time-consuming task but also prone to human errors. In addition to this, the eligibility criteria often uses complex language structures and medical jargons mentioned in either semi-structured or unstructured way.

Previous works (Koopman and Zuccon, 2016) have formulated the problem of retrieving relevant document collection based on patient query. However, we demonstrate an approach in which the primary eligibility aspects are identified initially for further screening of the patients in terms of inclusion or exclusion strategy, which is the first step towards matching patients with the relevant trials.

In this paper, we propose an effective method which automatically identifies and segregates the clinical trial eligibility criteria into five semantic aspects. Also, the criteria texts speak volume about multiple aspects of the patients that includes *demographic information, health status, treatment history, laboratory test reports* and *life-style*. However, there has been a dearth of annotated crite-



*Proceedings of the 3rd Clinical Natural Language Processing Workshop*, pages 243–248
November 19, 2020. ©2020 Association for Computational Linguistics

ria. Since, prior methods on neural clinical entity recognition models rely on the presence of a large annotated corpora and due to the high cost associated with manual tagging of semantic aspects and limited availability of labeled datasets (Najafabadi et al., 2015), it is difficult to train a deep neural network effectively for such a task. We attempt to combat this difficulty by proposing a novel semi-supervised method based on deep co-training (Blum and Mitchell, 1998) which can harness a large pool of unlabeled clinical trial criteria that are more economical to collect. To the best of our knowledge, we are the first to introduce such a co-training-based method and demonstrate its effectiveness in aspect categorization of clinical trials in comparison to stand-alone sequence-labelling in isolation. The end-product of our experiments is a clinical trial-register that contain details of the different aspects across conditions and interventions.

## 2   Problem Formulation

Given an eligibility criteria sentence in the form of a word sequence $x = (x_1 ...., x_n)$ , where n is the maximum length of the sequence, the task is to predict an output sequence $y = (y_1 , ...., y_n)$ in which each $y_i$ is encoded using standard sequence labeling encoding scheme. Each $y_i$ might take one of the following aspects :

1. **Health Status (Health)**: describes the present medical condition like pregnancy status, disease affected, etc.

2. **Treatment (Trt)**: contains information about the intervention, surgery or therapy related information of the patients.

3. **Lab-Test (Lab)**: It deals with the lab-tests or experimental results.

4. **Demography(Demo)**: This class primarily deals with the age, gender related to the patients undergoing clinical trials.

5. **Life-Style(Life)**: This class primarily deals with the information of the patients regarding their daily habits like diet, exercise etc

6. **Other**: It contains none of the above classes.

Figure 1 illustrates the overview of semantic aspect extraction.

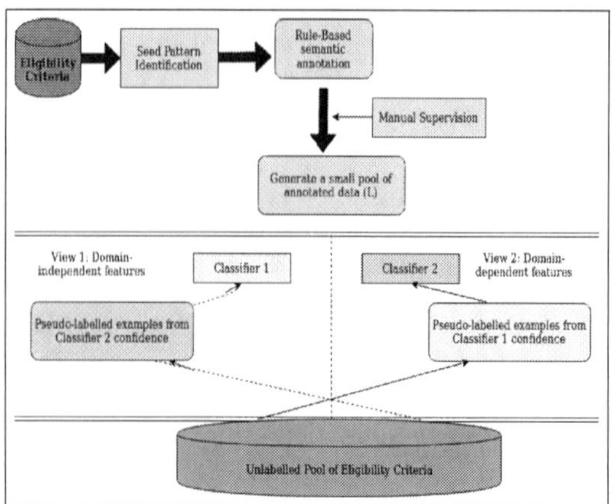


Figure 1: Working Pipeline of Semantic Aspect Extraction from Eligibility Criteria using Co-Training.

|       | Health | Trt | Lab | Life | Demo |
|-------|--------|-----|-----|------|------|
| TS    | 345    | 323 | 456 | 280  | 600  |
| ASL   | 8      | 6   | 9   | 8    | 5    |

Table 1: Statistics of the Manually annotated Dataset. Here, *TS* indicates the total Number of Sequences for each of the different aspects and *ASL* indicates Average length of each Sequence. *Life* indicates Life-Style aspect, *Trt* indicates Treatment aspect, *Lab* indicated Lab-Test Results and *Demo* indicates demography aspect.

## 3   Data Annotation

To induce semantic categorization of aspects in the eligibility criteria, we generate a small pool of annotated data by manually examining some of the most frequently used n-gram patterns such as *history of, upper limit of normal, treated by, Allergy to* as specified in (Luo et al., 2011) in the initial phase. During pre-processing, we filter out the most frequently occurring n-grams (n=2, n=3, n=4, n=5) present in the criteria of the patients. Secondly, the criteria sentences are also tagged with CliNER Tagger (Boag et al., 2015) for extracting out the diseases and drugs. Further details of data are provided in the supplementary material [1]. After these two steps, finally, the false positives are being removed during manual supervision by four independent domain-expert annotators. These include annotations for each of the different categories. The mean Cohen's Kappa (McHugh, 2012) was 0.82, which indicate good inter-annotator agree-

---

[1] https://github.com/Ishani-Mondal/Clinical-Trials-Aspect-Extraction

---

**Algorithm 1** Aspect Extraction using Co-Training Algorithm

---

**Input** U : Large amount of unlabelled criteria sentences, $\tau$ : Co-Training threshold, $V^1$ , $V^2$: Two views of labelled Aspect Annotated Criteria Sentences

**Output** Model Parameters : $\theta_{\text{BiLSTM-CRF}}$, $\theta_{\text{BiGRU-CRF}}$

$\quad T^1, T^2 \leftarrow V^1, V^2$

Initialize the model parameters $\theta_{\text{BiLSTM-CRF}}$, $\theta_{\text{BiGRU-CRF}}$ randomly.

**while** (stopping criteria is not met) **do**

$\quad\quad C^1 \leftarrow$ Train BiLSTM-CRF on $T^1$ (minimize the Aspect Loss)

$\quad\quad C^2 \leftarrow$ Train BiGRU-CRF on $T^2$ (minimize the Aspect Loss)

$\quad\quad$ **for** i=1 to |U| **do**

$\quad\quad\quad$ **if** $C^1$.score($U_i$) $\geq \tau$ **then**

$\quad\quad\quad\quad T^2 \leftarrow T^2 \cup U_i$ , U = U $U_i$

$\quad\quad\quad$ **end if**

$\quad\quad\quad$ **if** $C^2$.score($U_i$) $\geq \tau$ **then**

$\quad\quad\quad\quad T^1 \leftarrow T^1 \cup U_i$ , U = U $U_i$

$\quad\quad\quad$ **end if**

$\quad\quad$ **end for**

**end while**

---

ment. 1500 clinical trial documents from Clinical-Trials.gov[2] are annotated with an average of 16 sentences per document. The manually labelled dataset statistics with the class distributions are specified in the Table 1. While manually inspecting the co-occurence statistics of different aspects in the same criteria sentence of the manually annotated dataset, we observe that around 30% of the eligibility criteria contains more than one aspect, with 65% containing health, life-style, demography aspects, while the remaining 35% contains demography and treatment. For facilitating further research, we will also provide some sample examples of the annotated corpus.

## 4 Methodology

In this work, we experiment with two different methods of aspect extraction. One of the following being the traditional supervised setup of using BiLSTM-CRF/Bi-GRU CRF with input representation optimized using categorical cross-entropy loss (Zhang and Sabuncu, 2018). The second one being the Co-Training (Blum and Mitchell, 1998) method to extract the semantic aspects which has been outlined in Algorithm 1. The later method uses two conditionally independent feature views of the same dataset illustrated below:

1. **Domain-independent**: The contextual pre-trained language models such as, BERT (De-

vlin et al., 2019) (**E1**) (or word2vec (Mikolov et al., 2013) trained on GoogleNews Corpus [3] (**E2**)) embeddings followed by a BiLSTM-CRF ($C^1$) (Huang et al., 2015) feature extractor.

2. **Domain-dependent:** Bio-BERT embeddings (Lee et al., 2020) (**E3**) (or word2vec trained on PubMed [4]) (**E4**) followed by BiGRU-CRF ($C^2$) (Lerner et al., 2020) feature extractor.

At each step of co-training, the classifiers $C^1$ and $C^2$ are trained on respective views of training sets $V^1$ and $V^2$, thereby minimizing the loss function. Each instance from the unlabeled samples (U) is scored using a scoring function computed as follows. First, the current classifier is used to decode the output label distribution for each word in the unlabeled instances. For each word in the output, we choose the output label which has the maximum probability. We compute the score for the sample as the multiplication of the probabilities of each label type for all labeled words in sequence normalized by the total number of words in the sentence. If this confidence score of the sample is greater than some pre-defined threshold $\tau$, the sample has been added to the training set of the other classifier along with its output labels as generated by the classifier. This is the process of generation of weak labels for each sequence. Due to interchange of training data, both classifiers can learn from mistakes of each other and work in synergy.

## 5 Experimental Details

We implement the model using Pytorch 0.3.0. The two classifiers considered for co-training are $C^1$ : Bi-LSTM-CRF and $C^2$ : Bi-GRU-CRF. For both supervised and co-training methods, the training data is divided according to 70-30% train-validation split. The two different views of co-training setup are explained as follows:

**Hyper-parameters for two independent views:**

We run two experiments based on co-training, one using contextual embeddings (C-CTr) and the other using context-independent embeddings (NC-CTr). The hyper-parameter settings for the two views as required by the co-training method are as follows:

---

[2]https://clinicaltrials.gov/

[3]https://github.com/mmihaltz/word2vec-GoogleNews-vectors

[4]http://bio.nlplab.org/

**View 1:** For the first view ($V^1$), we use Bi-LSTM-CRF (Huang et al., 2015) with domain-independent word embeddings. We experiment with both a) (NC-CTr) Word2vec embeddings trained on GoogleNews Corpus with dimension 300 b) (C-CTr) pre-trained *bert-base* (12 layers, 12 attention heads, and 110 million parameters).

**View 2:** For the second view ($V^2$), we use Bi-GRU classifier with domain-dependent word embeddings. We experiment with both a) (NC-CTr) Word2vec embeddings trained on PubMed Corpus with dimension 200 b) (C-CTr) contextualized pre-trained Bio-BERT embeddings.

For both the classifiers, the hidden unit dimensions are set to 300. During training, we use Adam (Kingma and Ba, 2015) optimizer with a learning rate of 0.001 and a batch size of 64. For co-training, $\tau$ has been set to 0.5, epoch size to 200, with early-stopping employed based on the performance of validation set. All the results are reported based on the best hyper-parameter settings after an exhaustive grid search over parameter space.

| Methods | Health | Trt | Lab | Demo | Life |
|---|---|---|---|---|---|
| | F1 | F1 | F1 | F1 | F1 |
| Baseline-1 | 0.78 | 0.73 | 0.72 | 0.70 | 0.80 |
| Baseline-1(1) | 0.73 | 0.64 | 0.68 | 0.65 | 0.76 |
| Baseline-1(2) | 0.75 | 0.60 | 0.68 | 0.61 | 0.73 |
| Baseline-2 | 0.73 | 0.43 | 0.66 | - | - |

Table 2: Macro-F1 score for all the aspects using prior methods with some additional features

| Methods | Health | Trt | Lab | Demo | Life |
|---|---|---|---|---|---|
| | F1 | F1 | F1 | F1 | F1 |
| $C^1$+E1 | 0.72 | 0.70 | 0.65 | 0.80 | 0.70 |
| $C^1$+E2 | 0.68 | 0.61 | 0.62 | 0.75 | 0.67 |
| $C^2$+E3 | **0.73** | **0.70** | **0.66** | **0.81** | **0.72** |
| $C^2$+E4 | 0.70 | 0.64 | 0.63 | 0.77 | 0.67 |

Table 3: Feature ablations on our supervised setup on the train-validation split of our dataset.

## 6   Results and Analysis

In this section, we have provided a detailed analysis of the various results and findings that we have observed during experimentation. There are various criteria on which we have tried to evaluate our semi-supervised approach.

| Methods | Health | Trt | Lab | Demo | Life |
|---|---|---|---|---|---|
| | F1 | F1 | F1 | F1 | F1 |
| w/o CTrain | 0.73 | 0.70 | 0.66 | 0.81 | 0.72 |
| C-CTr(8K) | **0.85** | 0.80 | **0.83** | 0.90 | 0.80 |
| C-CTr(10K) | 0.83 | 0.84 | 0.82 | 0.90 | 0.85 |
| C-CTr(15K) | 0.77 | 0.82 | 0.75 | **0.92** | **0.88** |
| C-CTr (20K) | 0.85 | **0.86** | 0.79 | 0.90 | 0.83 |
| NC-CTr (8K) | 0.76 | 0.77 | 0.74 | 0.74 | 0.75 |
| NC-CTr (10K) | 0.78 | 0.81 | 0.75 | 0.78 | 0.80 |
| NC-CTr (15K) | 0.77 | 0.76 | 0.77 | 0.81 | 0.77 |
| NC-CTr (20K) | 0.78 | 0.77 | 0.77 | 0.82 | 0.79 |

Table 4: Results showing various co-training methodology with different size of unlabelled instances. Trt=Treatment aspect. The scores are reported in the table based on exact match F1-score for all aspects.

**Comparison with the baselines:**
The results of the baseline methods are enumerated in Table 2. We report the results based on exact match of each type of the aspects using F1-score. Following (Luo et al., 2011), we implement the same (**Baseline-2**) on our dataset with UMLS (Bodenreider, 2004) feature representation and "bag-of-words" (BoW) features, and report results for various aspects. Although (Luo et al., 2011) assumes each criteria sentence essentially belongs to a single aspect, we have done an ablation of Baseline-2 without UMLS features (**Baseline-1(1)**) and without BoW (**Baseline-1(2)**). We observe that UMLS feature representation boosts up the performance due to inclusion of domain-specific information. We observed that this work finds resonance with (Chalapathy et al., 2016) in which the corpus uses multiple annotations. Due to availability of their working code, we have experimented with their stand-alone Bi-LSTM-CRF approach, used them as **Baseline-2** and report results for each of the first three annotated aspects.

**Feature ablation on model architecture:**
For the purpose of fair comparison, we experiment with different ablations of feature extractor and types of input representation (in the supervised setup) and present the results of Macro-averaged F1-score in Table 3. It has been observed that Bi-LSTM CRF with domain-specific input representation as Bio-BERT outperforms other ablations.

**Impact of using co-training:**
It is also evident from table 4, when the two independent views consist of contextualized embeddings (C-CTr), the model outperforms the

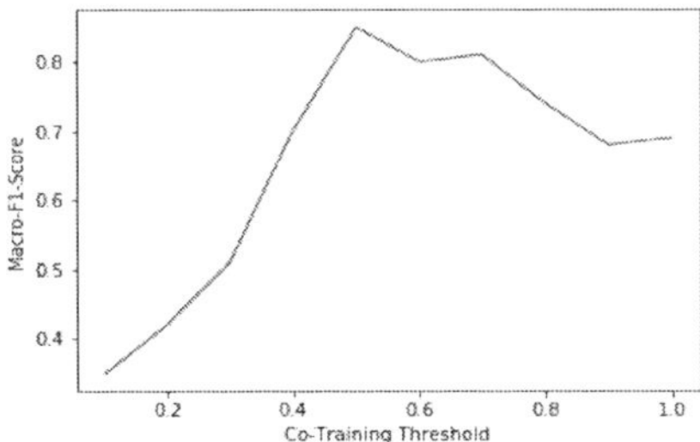



Figure 2: Testing the optimum Co-Training Threshold

non-contextualized features (NC-CTr) by an average margin of 6% F1-Scores. Also, we compare our best architecture for supervised setup with co-training approach. Given that the co-training model trains each classifier separately on different subsets of the training set, it can be sensitive to the choice of $V^1$ and $V^2$. In order to address this issue, we experiment with repeating the same experimnts with various random sampling of the two training subsets. We observe an average F1-score standard deviation (across multiple sampling) of 0.064 for Health class, 0.091 for Treatment class, 0.116 for Lab-Test Results class, 0.055 for Demography class and 0.008 for Life-style class.

### Sensitivity of co-training parameters:

In figure 1, Macro-F1 score (across all aspects) of the co-trained model has been evaluated based on the values of co-training threshold. The values have been chosen from 0 to 1 at an interval of 0.1, in which the optimum value has been observed as 0.5. The sensitivity of co-training parameters has been shown in figure 2.

### Effect of unlabelled data size:

Moreover, the results are fairly constant even when the unlabeled data size varies (enumerated in Table 4) which demonstrates the robustness of our approach. The contextualized representations when augmented with fair amount of semi-automatically annotated samples outperforms the supervised baseline setup.

## 7   Conclusion

In this paper, we have proposed a semi-supervised co-training method to tackle the scarcity of annotated data for the semantic clinical aspect extraction. This method augments a limited pool of annotated data with a large number of unlabeled clinical eligibility criteria outperforming pure supervised

approaches. To the best of our knowledge, we are the first to provide an effective semi-supervised approach to detect the semantic aspects from clinical eligibility criteria which is a promising direction for further research on automatic linking of the patient Electronic Health Records (EHR) to clinical eligibility criteria with promising performance. As a future work, we aim to propose an end-to-end automatic matching system for patient-based clinical trial eligibility with low-cost data annotation.

## Acknowledgments


This work has been done by the first author, Ishani, during her internship with the TCS Research Labs, India. Besides, the authors would like to thank the anonymous reviewers for their valuable feedback.


## References


Avrim Blum and Tom Mitchell. 1998. Combining labeled and unlabeled data with co-training. In *Proceedings of the Eleventh Annual Conference on Computational Learning Theory*, COLT' 98, page 92–100, New York, NY, USA. Association for Computing Machinery.

William Boag, Kevin Wacome, Tristan Naumann, and Anna Rumshisky. 2015. Cliner : A lightweight tool for clinical named entity recognition.

O. Bodenreider. 2004. The unified medical language system (umls): integrating biomedical terminology. *Nucleic acids research*, 32 Database issue:D267–70.

Raghavendra Chalapathy, Ehsan Zare Borzeshi, and Massimo Piccardi. 2016. Bidirectional LSTM-CRF for clinical concept extraction. In *Proceedings of the Clinical Natural Language Processing Workshop (ClinicalNLP)*, pages 7–12, Osaka, Japan. The COLING 2016 Organizing Committee.

Jacob Devlin, Ming-Wei Chang, Kenton Lee, and Kristina Toutanova. 2019. BERT: Pre-training of deep bidirectional transformers for language understanding. In *Proceedings of the 2019 Conference of the North American Chapter of the Association for Computational Linguistics: Human Language Technologies, Volume 1 (Long and Short Papers)*, pages 4171–4186, Minneapolis, Minnesota. Association for Computational Linguistics.

Peter J. Embi, Anil K. Jain, and C. Martin Harris. 2008. Physicians' perceptions of an electronic health record-based clinical trial alert approach to subject recruitment: A survey. *BMC Medical Informatics and Decision Making*, 8:13 – 13

Zhiheng Huang, Wei Xu, and Kai Yu. 2015. Bidirectional lstm-crf models for sequence tagging. *ArXiv*, abs/1508.01991.

Diederik P. Kingma and Jimmy Ba. 2015. Adam: A method for stochastic optimization. *CoRR*, abs/1412.6980.

Bevan Koopman and Guido Zuccon. 2016. A test collection for matching patients to clinical trials. In *Proceedings of the 39th International ACM SIGIR Conference on Research and Development in Information Retrieval*, SIGIR '16, page 669–672, New York, NY, USA. Association for Computing Machinery.

Jinhyuk Lee, Wonjin Yoon, Sungdong Kim, D. Kim, Sunkyu Kim, Chan Ho So, and Jaewoo Kang. 2020. Biobert: a pre-trained biomedical language representation model for biomedical text mining. *Bioinformatics*.

Ivan Lerner, N. Paris, and Xavier Tannier. 2020. Terminologies augmented recurrent neural network model for clinical named entity recognition. *Journal of biomedical informatics*, page 103356.

Zhihui Luo, Meliha Yetisgen-Yildiz, and Chunhua Weng. 2011. Dynamic categorization of clinical research eligibility criteria by hierarchical clustering. *J. of Biomedical Informatics*, 44(6):927–935.

M. McHugh. 2012. Interrater reliability: the kappa statistic. *Biochemia Medica*, 22:276 – 282.

Tomas Mikolov, Ilya Sutskever, Kai Chen, Greg Corrado, and Jeffrey Dean. 2013. Distributed representations of words and phrases and their compositionality. In *Proceedings of the 26th International Conference on Neural Information Processing Systems - Volume 2*, NIPS'13, page 3111–3119, Red Hook, NY, USA. Curran Associates Inc.

Maryam Najafabadi, Flavio Villanustre, Taghi Khoshgoftaar, Naeem Seliya, Randall Wald, and Edin Muharemagic. 2015. Deep learning applications and challenges in big data analytics. *Journal of Big Data*, 2.

Chaitanya Shivade, Courtney Hebert, Marcelo Lopetegui, Marie-Catherine de Marneffe, Eric Fosler-Lussier, and Albert M. Lai. 2015. Textual inference for eligibility criteria resolution in clinical trials. *J. of Biomedical Informatics*, 58(S):S211–S218.

Zhilu Zhang and Mert R. Sabuncu. 2018. Generalized cross entropy loss for training deep neural networks with noisy labels. In *Proceedings of the 32nd International Conference on Neural Information Processing Systems*, NIPS'18, page 8792–8802, Red Hook, NY, USA. Curran Associates Inc.

# An Ensemble Approach for Automatic Structuring of Radiology Reports


**Morteza Pourreza Shahri[1]**
CodaMetrix

**Amir Tahmasebi[1]**
CodaMetrix

**Bingyang Ye[1]**
CodaMetrix

**Henghui Zhu[2]**
Amazon

**Javed Aslam[1]**
CodaMetrix

**Timothy Ferris[3]**
Mass General Physicians
Organization

[1]{morteza,amir,bingyang,jay}@codametrix.com
[2]henghui@amazon.com
[3]ferris.timothy@mgh.harvard.edu



## Abstract

Automatic structuring of electronic medical records is of high demand for clinical workflow solutions to facilitate extraction, storage, and querying of patient care information. However, developing a scalable solution is extremely challenging, specifically for radiology reports, as most healthcare institutes use either no template or department/institute specific templates. Moreover, radiologists' reporting style varies from one to another as sentences are telegraphic and do not follow general English grammar rules. We present an ensemble method that consolidates the predictions of three models, capturing various attributes of textual information for automatic labeling of sentences with section labels. These three models are: 1) Focus Sentence model, capturing context of the target sentence; 2) Surrounding Context model, capturing the neighboring context of the target sentence; and finally, 3) Formatting/Layout model, aimed at learning report formatting cues. We utilize Bidirectional LSTMs, followed by sentence encoders, to acquire the context. Furthermore, we define several features that incorporate the structure of reports. We compare our proposed approach against multiple baselines and state-of-the-art approaches on a proprietary dataset as well as 100 manually annotated radiology notes from the MIMIC-III dataset, which we are making publicly available. Our proposed approach significantly outperforms other approaches by achieving 97.1% accuracy.


## 1 Introduction

Electronic medical records (EMRs), such as radiology reports, contain patient clinical information and are often in the form of "natural language" written or transcribed by providers (Denny et al., 2008). Gathering and disseminating patient information from such notes is required for patient care management. Natural Language Processing (NLP)-driven solutions have been proposed to augment clinical workflows to facilitate such information extraction and structuring processes. Segmentation of medical reports into topically cohesive sections (Cho et al., 2003) is essential for NLP tasks such as relation extraction, Named Entity Recognition (NER), and Question and Answering.

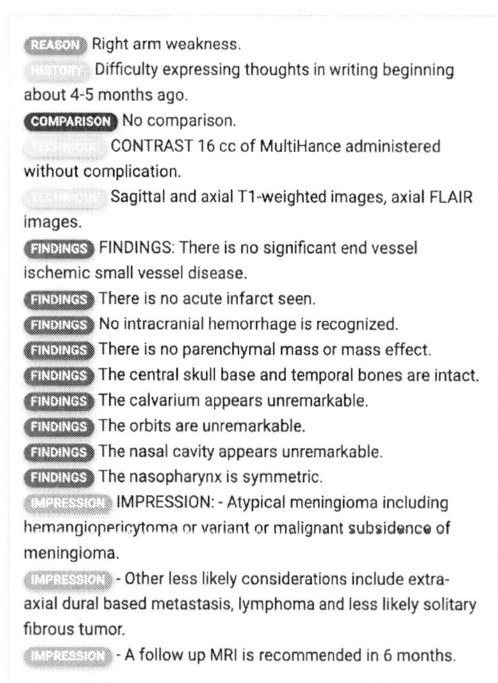


Figure 1: Snapshot of the output of our proposed model on a radiology report. Labels are shown in front of every extracted sentence.

Developing a universal and scalable report segmenting solution is extremely challenging as most healthcare institutes use either no template or institute specific templates. Moreover, providers' style of reporting varies from one to another as sentences are written in a telegraphic format and generally do not follow English grammar rules. Nonethe-




*Proceedings of the 3rd Clinical Natural Language Processing Workshop*, pages 249–258
November 19, 2020. ©2020 Association for Computational Linguistics

less, in the case of radiology reports, the reports are often composed of similar sections, including the reason for the visit, the performed examination, a summary of observations and findings, and finally, the radiologist's impression and recommendation based on the observations.

To extract and structure patient information from notes, most clinical institutes take the approach of developing their specific set of patterns and rules to extract and label the sections within the clinical reports. This requires a substantial amount of effort for defining rules and maintaining them over time. With advancements in machine learning and NLP, researchers have more recently utilized supervised machine learning methods for automatic structuring of radiology reports (Apostolova et al., 2009; Tepper et al., 2012; Haug et al., 2014; Singh et al., 2015; Rosenthal et al., 2019). These machine learning approaches can be divided into three main themes: 1) Methods that solely rely on extracting features from the format of the text and, therefore, are biased on the specific format of the training data (Tepper et al., 2012); 2) More recent efforts that are focused on learning to label based on the context (Rosenthal et al., 2019); and finally, 3) The hybrid approaches that combine formatting and context-driven features (Apostolova et al., 2009). The two latter methods require a reasonably large amount of annotated reports and yet are not scalable solutions as they do not adequately address inter-institute variability unless model training is fine-tuned using annotated data from the target institute.

In this work, we frame the structuring of the radiology reports as a multi-class sentence classification problem. More specifically, this work presents a novel framework to identify various sections in the radiology reports and to label all sentences within the note with their corresponding section category. We propose an ensemble approach that takes advantage of formatting cues as well as context-driven features. We incorporate Recurrent Neural Networks (RNN) and sentence encoders accompanied by a set of engineered features from the reports for the task of section labeling in radiology reports. The proposed approach considers the context of the current text span and the surrounding context that helps make more accurate predictions.

We were motivated by how a non-expert human self-teaches to perform such a task, paying attention to the context while taking formatting cues into account. We hypothesize that each of the three models learns unique and non-overlapping attributes for solving the problem at hand, and therefore, an ensemble approach seems reasonable.

In order to avoid the requirement of access to a large annotated training corpus, we follow a weak learning approach in which we automatically generate the initial training data using generic rules that are implemented using regular expressions and pattern matching.

We consider seven types of section categories and label each sentence with one of these categories. Our approach is not limited to these specific categories and it can be adapted for any template format and writing style. This is thanks to incorporating a broad set of features that are independent of physicians/institutions. Figure 1 depicts a snapshot of the output of our proposed model for automatic labeling of the sentences within a radiology report. The label in front of each line represents the predicted label for the following sentence.

We train and evaluate our proposed approach on a large multi-site radiology report corpus from Mass General Brigham, referred to as MGB. We demonstrate that our proposed solution significantly outperforms common existing methods for automated structuring of radiology reports (Apostolova et al., 2009; Singh et al., 2015) as well as several baseline models. Moreover, we manually annotated 100 reports from the MIMIC-III radiology reports corpus (Johnson et al., 2016), and we report performances on this dataset as well. We also make this dataset publicly available to other researchers[1].

Our main contributions in this study are as follows:

1. Investigating the importance of different types of features, including formatting and layout, as well as semantics and context in section labeling of radiology notes at the sentence level.

2. Achieving state-of-the-art performance for automatic labeling of radiology notes with pre-defined section labels through an ensemble approach incorporating models that are capable of learning context and formatting features.

3. Contributing 100 manually-annotated clinical notes with section labels at sentence-level randomly selected from the MIMIC-III corpus.

[1]https://doi.org/10.5281/zenodo.4074194

The rest of the paper is organized as follows. In section 2, we briefly review current methods for segmenting and structuring clinical reports. Next, we describe our proposed pipeline in section 3. In section 4, we present and discuss our results on independent test sets, and finally, the conclusions and potential future work are presented in section 5.

## 2 Related Work

There have been numerous efforts to address the need for automatic structuring of clinical notes via section labeling, including rule-based methods, machine learning-based methods, and hybrid approaches (Pomares-Quimbaya et al., 2019).

Taira et al. (2001) proposed a rule-based system comprising a structural analyzer, lexical analyzer, parser, and a semantic interpreter to identify sections in radiology reports. Denny et al. (2008) developed a hierarchical section header terminology and a statistical model to extract section labels from sentences. RadBank was introduced by Rubin and Desser, which recognizes the structure of radiology reports and extracts the sections for indexing and search, which falls in rule-based methods (Rubin and Desser, 2008). A known shortcoming of rule-based approaches is that they perform well only on reports that follow a specific template and are written following strict structures. As a result, rule-based systems require updating rules/patterns for each new dataset with new formatting and structure. Furthermore, rule-based approaches perform poorly on reports lacking a coherent structure and/or are not written using a predefined template.

Machine learning-based methods solve this problem by training models that can be applied to other datasets without substantial changes as they learn to rely on features beyond formatting and layout. Singh et al. (2015) presented a system based on the Naïve Bayes classifier to identify sections in radiology reports. (Tepper et al., 2012) employ Maximum Entropy to label various sections in discharged summaries and radiology reports. Cho et al. (2003) proposed a hybrid system to extract and label sentences from medical documents. Their proposed system is composed of a rule-based module that detects the sections with labels and a machine learning classifier that detects the unlabeled sections. Apostolova et al. (2009) employed a set of rules for creating a high-confidence training set and applied Support Vector Machines (SVM) trained

on additional formatting and contextual features to label the sentences from radiology and pathology reports. The main challenge in training such machine learning-based approaches is the need for a relatively large annotated training data.

To the best of our knowledge, the most recent work is proposed by Rosenthal et al. (2019) in which they present a system based on an RNN and a BERT (Devlin et al., 2019) model for predicting sections in EHRs. They use sections from the medical literature (e.g., textbooks, journals, web content) with similar content in EHR sections.

Even though the existing methods address the problems mentioned earlier for the complex task of automatic structuring of radiology reports, an ensemble of several models is shown to yield lower generalization error, as opposed to training individual models (Kotu and Deshpande, 2014).

## 3 Methodology

### 3.1 Approach

In this work, we formulate the task of automated structuring of radiology reports as a supervised multi-class text classification problem. We define the label set as *Reason for Visit, History, Comparison, Technique, Findings, Impression*. Any sentence that cannot be categorized as one of the classes above is labeled as *Others*.

Suppose we have the context $C = s_1s_2...s_n$, where $s_i$ is a sentence in the radiology report. We define a mapping function $f$ that for each sentence $s_i$ from the set of sentences in the report, it maps the sentence to its associated label. The context $C$ can be the entire radiology report or a few sentences from the report. The following sections describe the details of our proposed methodology.

### 3.2 Dataset

Since we do not have access to a publicly-available dataset, we build our own training set using the radiology reports from a multi-institution clinical corpus from Mass General Brigham referred to as the MGB dataset. We randomly selected 856 radiology reports from 12 different clinical sites, i.e., Mass General Brigham. Taking the template and specific formatting/layout of the notes, we develop a weak labeler using regular expressions to detect keywords, including *Findings, Impression, Technique, Comparison, Reason for Visit, History, Indications, Type*, and *Procedure*. Subsequently, we consider all of the sentences between two observed

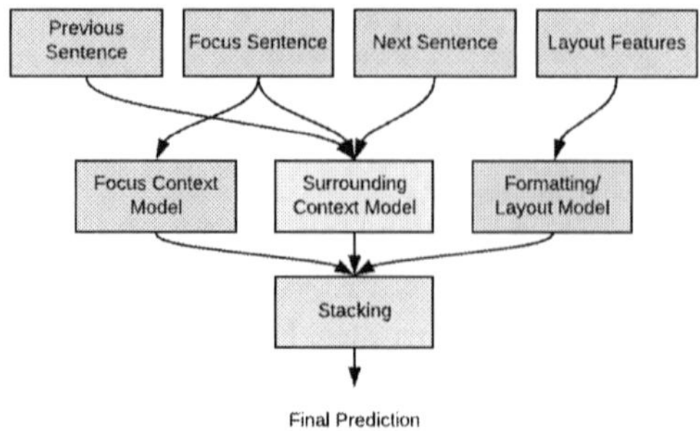



Figure 2: The ensemble model composed of the Focus Context, Surrounding Context, and Formatting/Layout models that combines the three prediction using the *Stacking* method.

keywords as the preceding section. For instance, if the keyword "Findings" appears at position 400 and "Impression" appears at location 700, any sentence in the range of [400, 700) is labeled as *Findings*. One should note that the occurrence of all the keywords in radiology reports is not guaranteed. Therefore, we only pick the sections that appear in the report. Next, we merge *Technique, Procedure*, and *Type* into one category since they convey the same concept. We also combine *History* and *Indications* into one class. Furthermore, we manually correct the automatically assigned labels of sentences using the BRAT annotation tool (Stenetorp et al., 2012). Since only one human annotator corrected the labels, there is no inter-annotator agreement. We split this dataset into three: 686 reports (80%) as the training set, 85 reports (10%) for training the ensemble model, and 85 reports (10%) as the test set.

To comply with data privacy and Health Insurance Portability and Accountability Act (HIPAA), we cannot release this dataset. Nonetheless, we randomly select a separate 100 reports from MIMIC-III corpus with the *CATEGORY* code of Radiology. Subsequently, we manually annotate this dataset, similar to the way we created the MGB dataset, and we employ it as an independent test set. The annotations were performed by two of the co-authors as non-domain experts. No inter-annotator agreement was measured as there was no overlap between labeled reports by two annotators.

### 3.3 Preprocessing

The preprocessing includes removing special characters while keeping lowercase, uppercase, and digits from the text and replacing all other char-

acters with space. We use Simple Sentence Segment[2] for sentence parsing. Subsequently, all of the sentences are tokenized using the SentencePiece tokenizer (Kudo and Richardson, 2018).

We utilize GloVe (Pennington et al., 2014) word embeddings trained in-house on the entire set of radiology reports from multiple-sites (more than two million radiology reports). The pre-trained word embeddings are 300-dimensional. We also repeated our experiments by utilizing the BERT (Devlin et al., 2019) embeddings, trained in-house on the same corpus of radiology reports, as mentioned above. Overall, the GloVe embeddings yield higher performance for the desired task compared to the BERT embeddings. Therefore, for all of the experiments, we report the performance using the GloVe embeddings.

### 3.4 Model

Figure 2 demonstrates the proposed ensemble architecture. As can be seen from the figure, the three models aim to capture and encode formatting information, focus sentence context, as well as the context from the surrounding sentences of the focus sentence.

The intuition for having three models is that relying on one source, either context or format alone, is insufficient to capture all necessary text attributes for the labeling task. For example, a sentence such as "Microlithiasis." may occur in *History*, *Findings* or *Impression* sections and only by taking sentence context, the surrounding context, and the formatting cues altogether, one can determine the most appropriate label.

We combine the individual models' predictions using the *Stacking* method (Wolpert, 1992) to derive the final prediction. The architecture of each model is discussed in detail in the following sections.

### 3.4.1 Focus Context Model

As shown in Figure 3, the proposed architecture for the Focus Context model is composed of a Bi-directional Long Short-Term Memory (LSTM) with 64 units. Subsequently, we encode the sentence using the LSTM's output sequences using max-over-time and mean-over-time pooling and concatenate these two vectors (Blanco et al., 2020). This approach enables us to extract meaningful features from the focus sentence context. The encoded

---

[2] `https://github.com/noc-lab/simple_sentence_segment`

sentence is next passed to a fully-connected layer
with 100 neurons with the *ReLU* activation function and a dropout value of 50%. We stack two
more fully-connected layers with sizes of 30 and
16 with the *ReLU* activation functions and dropout
values of 50% and 30%, respectively. Finally, the
weights are passed to the output layer that employs
a *Softmax* activation function to make the final prediction.

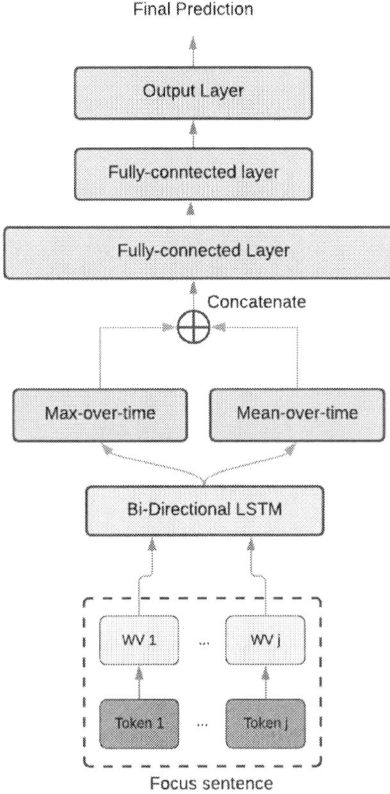


Figure 3: The network architecture of the Focus Context model.

### 3.4.2   Surrounding Context Model

Figure 4 demonstrates the proposed architecture
for the Surrounding Context model. The surrounding context is defined as the sentence immediately
before and the sentence immediately after the focus
sentence. The most efficient size of the surrounding
context can be determined through hyper-parameter
tuning, which is beyond the scope of this work and
is considered for future work. Each sentence is fed
into a Bi-directional LSTM layer. The LSTM layer
for the focus sentence comprises 64 units, whereas
the LSTM layers of surrounding sentences have 16

units. Next, each Bi-LSTM layer's output sequence
is fed into a max-over-time pooling layer to encode
the sequence. The three sentence encoders' outputs
are concatenated and passed into a fully-connected
layer with 50 neurons and *ReLU* activation function. This layer is followed by a Dropout layer with
a value of 50%. The weights are passed to a fully-connected layer with ten neurons and a dropout
value of 30%. Subsequently, the output is fed into
a second fully-connected layer with seven neurons
and the *Softmax* activation function to obtain the
final prediction. In cases where the focus sentence
appears at either the beginning or end of a report,
we use an empty string for the sentence before or
after.

### 3.4.3   Formatting/Layout Model

We propose a third model to learn formatting/layout
related features using neural networks. Motivated
by a prior work (Apostolova et al., 2009), we define
17 features that are described as follows:

1. Number of uppercase, lowercase, and digits
   in the sentence (three features).

2. Normalized relational position of the focus
   sentence to each section headers by searching
   keywords such as reason, history/indications,
   procedure/technique, comparison, findings,
   and impression (six features).

3. If the last character of the previous sentence,
   the current sentence, and the next sentence is
   either period or colon (six features).

4. Normalized position of the current sentence
   in the report (one feature).

5. If the first token in the sentence is uppercase
   or not (one feature).

These features are utilized as input to a neural
network with a stack of three fully-connected layers
with 100, 16, and seven neurons. We add the *ReLU*
activation functions for the first two layers and the
*Softmax* function for the last layer. The first two
layers are followed by dropout layers with values
of 50%.

### 3.4.4   Ensemble: Stacking

As the last step, we train a Logistic Regression
(LR)-based ensemble model using the three models described in the previous sections and using a
holdout stacking set. We start making predictions

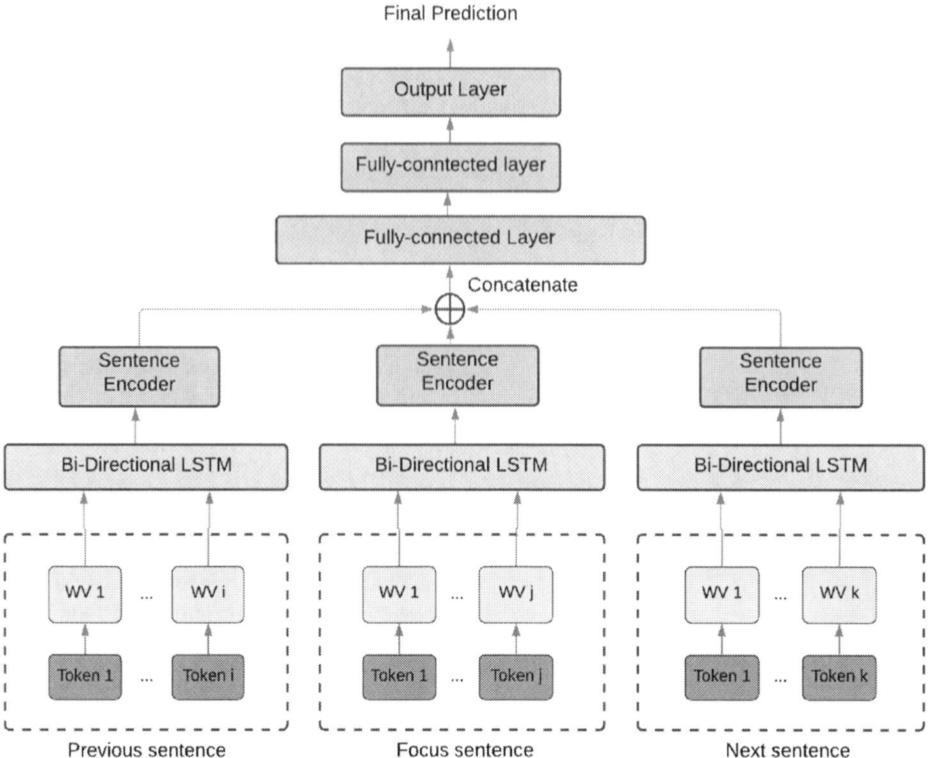



Figure 4: The network architecture of the Surrounding Context model.

using the three models on the holdout set, and we train an LR classifier on their predicted probabilities using Equation 1,

$$p(y = 1) = \sigma(w^T x + b) \tag{1}$$

where $w$ and $b$ are parameters to learn from data, and $\sigma$ is the Sigmoid function. We perform "one-versus-rest" for multi-class classification. The trained classifier can be utilized for making accurate predictions on the test set.

### 3.5 Experimental Setup

We implement four baseline models to compare with our proposed model. The first baseline is a rule-based model using the regular expressions specifically assembled based on the format of radiology reports from the MGB dataset. We refer to this model as the *MGB Rule-based* model. The second baseline is also a rule-based model composed of rules designed specifically for the MIMIC-III dataset. We refer to this model as the *MIMIC Rule-based* model. The third baseline model is a neural network consist of similar architecture to ours, but instead of stacking, we concatenate the outputs and

pass it to a fully-connected layer. We refer to this model as the *Merged* model. We also compare our proposed ensemble model with a Linear SVM model with "balanced" class weights, trained on preprocessed sentences in the form of uni-gram TFIDF vectors.

Most prior approaches utilize specific labeling schema that differ from ours and the corresponding labeled datasets are not publicly available (Cho et al., 2003; Rubin and Desser, 2008; Apostolova et al., 2009; Singh et al., 2015). As a result, we cannot provide a fair comparison of our proposed model with such approaches. Moreover, some studies employ external data sources during training, e.g., journals and textbooks (Rosenthal et al., 2019), which is also not compatible with the radiology report labeling schema, and restricts us from comparing our model with their work. Nevertheless, we implement the two existing methods presented by Apostolova et al. (2009) and Singh et al. (2015), which label sections in radiology reports. Since we did not have access to their code, we tried to replicate their methods to the best of our knowledge and understanding.

|  | MGB-test | | MIMIC-III | |
| Model | Accuracy | m-F1 | Accuracy | m-F1 |
| --- | --- | --- | --- | --- |
| MGB Rule-based | 62.7% | 47.3% | 29.7% | 23.6% |
| MIMIC Rule-based | 57.5% | 31.0% | 33.4% | 30.7% |
| Linear SVM | 89.4% | 82.2% | 66.2% | 63.3% |
| Apostolova et al. (2009) | 90.3% | 84.3% | 72.1% | 69.4% |
| Singh et al. (2015) | 85.9% | 74.7% | 68.8% | 63.6% |
| Formatting/Layout | 92.3% | 75.2% | 42.1% | 40.6% |
| Focus Context | 89.4% | 74.3% | 62.0% | 55.3% |
| Surrounding Context | 93.7% | 88.8% | 71.2% | 67.9% |
| Merged Ensemble | 94.3% | 89.3% | 73.3% | 69.2% |
| **Stacking Ensemble** | **97.1%** | **93.7** | **77.5%** | **74.0%** |

Table 1: Comparison of the results of various models on the MGB-test set and 100 MIMIC-III notes. m-F1 stands for macro F1 score across seven classes.

We implement our proposed model using Keras [3]. We utilize Adam optimizer with a learning rate of 0.001 and Categorical Cross-Entropy loss. We split the training set into two sets: 90% for training and 10% as the validation set. We use early stopping by picking the best validation accuracy value among 30 epochs for the models with the patience value of five. We also set the patience value to 200 among 600 training epochs for the Layout model.

We run our experiments on an *Amazon c5.18xlarge EC2* instance[4]. The average running time for the focus context, surrounding context, Formatting/Layout, and Merged models are roughly 80, 70, 60, and 60 minutes, respectively.

## 4 Results and Discussion

### 4.1 Model Comparison

We compare our proposed Stacking Ensemble model with several prior work as described above. We also report the performance of individual models used in our Stacking Ensemble model to investigate the importance of each model independently. Table 1 summarizes the performance of different approaches in terms of accuracy and macro F1 on the MGB-test set as well as 100 MIMIC-III notes.

It can be observed that, overall, our proposed Stacking Ensemble model outperforms all other approaches on both test sets. By comparing the performance of the three models composing our proposed ensemble model, we observe that the

Surrounding Context model achieves the highest performance among three, emphasizing the importance of the surrounding context in such a labeling task. Furthermore, it can be observed that the Formatting/Layout model performs worse on MIMIC-III set than the MGB-test set. This could be because reports from the MGB set are structured more consistently than MIMIC-III notes. In other words, MIMIC-III notes are not prepared using a specific and consistent template.

Another observation is that the rule-based models, i.e., MGB Rule-based and MIMIC Rule-based, perform poorly compared to machine learning-based approaches even though they are tailored specifically based on the corresponding reports' format and structure. Moreover, we observe that the MIMIC Rule-based model yields lower accuracy than MGB Rule-based model on the MGB-test set and vice versa. This confirms that the performance of rule-based approaches significantly varies across different datasets, and overall, rule-based approaches suffer from generalization and scaling.

Finally, the proposed Stacking Ensemble model yields lower performance on MIMIC-III test set compared to the MGB-test set. This could be because there are significant differences between the two sets of radiology reports in terms of content and format: MGB-test set notes are from inpatient and outpatient care and in general, follow a consistent format; however, MIMIC-III reports are discharge notes from the Emergency Department lacking a consistent structure.

To evaluate the sensitivity of our proposed model to a particular split of the data, we perform 10-

[3] https://keras.io
[4] https://aws.amazon.com/ec2/instance-types

fold cross-validation on the training set (i.e., split between 90% training and 10% validation). The $mean \pm std$ of accuracy and macro F1 across 10-folds are $97.0\% \pm 0.2\%$ and $93.0\% \pm 0.2\%$, respectively.

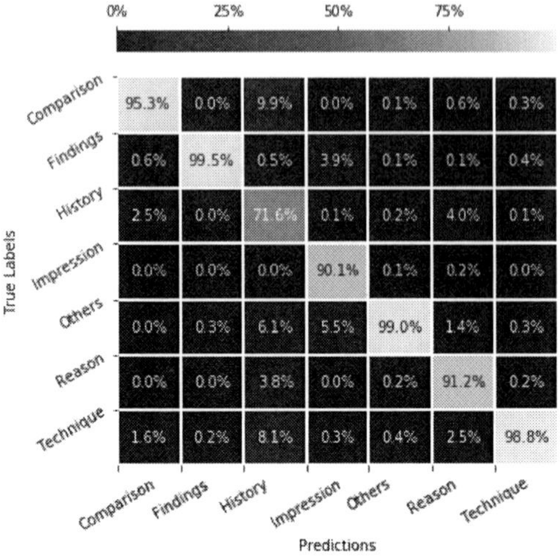

Figure 5: Confusion matrix showing the percentages of true and mislabeled predictions on the MGB-test set.

## 4.2 Error Analysis

We further investigate the performance of the Stacking Ensemble model for each class label separately. Figures 5 and 6 depict the confusion matrices between the predictions and actual labels from each class for MGB-test set and MIMIC-III notes, respectively. It can be observed that among all classes, "History" is the most challenging, and it is occasionally misclassified as "Comparison" in the case of MGB reports, and with "Others" and "Reason" classes in the case of MIMIC-III reports. We consider two possible reasons for this: 1) the similarity of the context between "History" and the other classes as mentioned earlier; and 2) the adjacency of these sections within the radiology reports.

## 4.3 Analysis of Stacking Ensemble Input

To further investigate each type of model's importance in the final ensemble decision, we analyze the weights resulting from the ensemble. We observe the different distribution of weights for different label types. For example, weights are equally distributed among three models for "Finding" and "Impression" sections. On the other hand, we observe unbalanced weight distribution

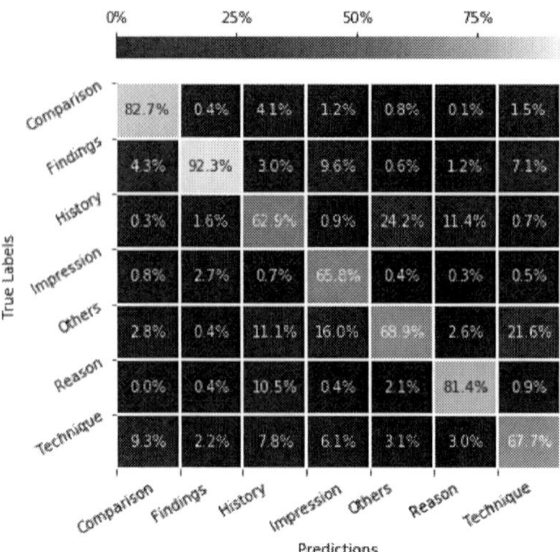

Figure 6: Confusion matrix showing the percentages of correct and incorrect predictions on MIMIC-III set.

for "Technique" and "Comparison" classes. Figure 7 shows the mean of weights for the "Findings" and "Technique" classes on the MGB-test set. It can be seen that all the models are equally important for the "Findings" class, whereas, for the "Technique" class, there is less emphasis on the Formatting/Layout model than the Focus Context and Surrounding Context models.

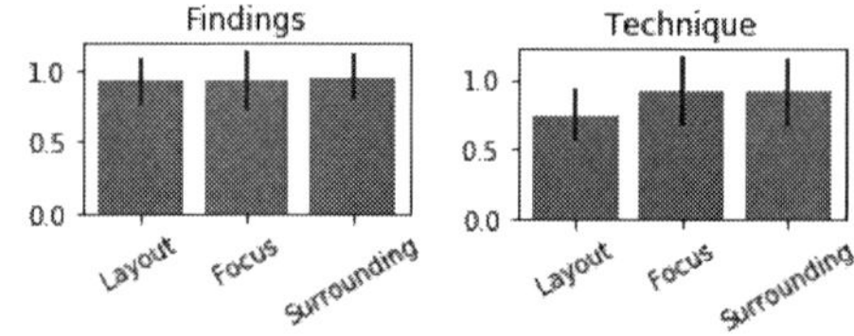

Figure 7: Comparison of the errors of inputs to the Stacking Ensemble model for the Findings and Technique classes on the MGB test set.

## 4.4 Fine-tuning the Stacking Model

As can be seen from Table 1, the proposed ensemble model trained on MGB data does not perform as well on the MIMIC-III set. We try to improve the performance of the proposed ensemble model on the MIMIC-III set by fine-tuning the ensemble part on a MIMIC-III data subset. We split the MIMIC-III data into 20% for fine-tuning and 80% for testing. Table 2 demonstrates the results of running the Stacking Ensemble model on 80% of the MIMIC-III data with and without fine-tuning. As can be seen from the table, we can obtain a 5.5%

increase in accuracy score and a 6.9% increase in macro F1 score. This is achieved by only fine-tuning the ensemble step using a small subset of the MIMIC-III data, while the individual models are still trained on the MGB data.

| Model Type | Accuracy | m-F1 |
|---|---|---|
| Without fine-tuning | 76.3% | 73.9% |
| With fine-tuning | **81.8%** | **80.8%** |

Table 2: Comparison between the performance of Stacking Ensemble model with and without fine-tuning on MIMIC-III data.

To show that the results are not sensitive to any specific split of data, we perform five-fold cross-validation on the MIMIC-III reports by utilizing 20% of reports for training the Logistic Regression classifier, and 80% for testing. We obtain a mean value of 81.5% accuracy with a standard deviation of 0.7% and a mean value of 80.4% macro F1 score with a standard deviation of 0.9%, which shows the insensitivity to the specific split of data.

A known shortcoming of our proposed approach is the sensitivity to the accuracy of the sentence segmentation. Poor sentence parsing results in miss-labeling, specifically, if error in sentence parsing results in combining sentences belonging to two different sections. To address this issue, we are currently working on training a clinical note-specific sentence parsing algorithm.

## 5 Conclusions and Future Work

In this work, we propose an ensemble approach for automatically labeling sentences in radiology reports with section labels. Through the proposed ensemble approach, we achieve the state-of-the-art performance of 97.1% on a relatively sizeable multi-site test set from Mass General Brigham. Our proposed ensemble method is composed of three parallel models that capture various structural and contextual attributes of radiology reports, including formatting/layout, focus context, and the surrounding context. Furthermore, We compared our proposed ensemble model against each of its components and concluded that the combination of all models is more accurate than any individual model.

As future work, we plan to incorporate performance calibration in our ensemble model. It adds the importance of individual models to the ensemble model and enables us to obtain higher performance for unseen data. We also plan to extend this work to other types of reports, i.e., pathology reports and discharge summaries. Another potential future work is to add Conditional Random Field (CRF) to our proposed model.

## References


Emilia Apostolova, David S Channin, Dina Demner-Fushman, Jacob Furst, Steven Lytinen, and Daniela Raicu. 2009. Automatic segmentation of clinical texts. In *2009 Annual International Conference of the IEEE Engineering in Medicine and Biology Society*, pages 5905–5908. IEEE.

Alberto Blanco, Olatz Perez-de Viñaspre, Alicia Pérez, and Arantza Casillas. 2020. Boosting ICD multi-label classification of health records with contextual embeddings and label-granularity. *Computer Methods and Programs in Biomedicine*, 188:105264.

Paul S Cho, Ricky K Taira, and Hooshang Kangarloo. 2003. Automatic section segmentation of medical reports. In *AMIA Annual Symposium Proceedings*, volume 2003, page 155. American Medical Informatics Association.

Joshua C Denny, Randolph A Miller, Kevin B Johnson, and Anderson Spickard III. 2008. Development and evaluation of a clinical note section header terminology. In *AMIA Annual Symposium proceedings*, volume 2008, page 156. American Medical Informatics Association.

Jacob Devlin, Ming-Wei Chang, Kenton Lee, and Kristina Toutanova. 2019. BERT: Pre-training of deep bidirectional transformers for language understanding. In *Proceedings of the 2019 Conference of the North American Chapter of the Association for Computational Linguistics: Human Language Technologies, Volume 1 (Long and Short Papers)*, pages 4171–4186, Minneapolis, Minnesota. Association for Computational Linguistics.

Peter J Haug, Xinzi Wu, Jeffery P Ferraro, Guergana K Savova, Stanley M Huff, and Christopher G Chute. 2014. Developing a section labeler for clinical documents. In *AMIA Annual Symposium Proceedings*, volume 2014, page 636. American Medical Informatics Association.

Alistair EW Johnson, Tom J Pollard, Lu Shen, H Lehman Li-Wei, Mengling Feng, Mohammad Ghassemi, Benjamin Moody, Peter Szolovits, Leo Anthony Celi, and Roger G Mark. 2016. MIMIC-III, a freely accessible critical care database. *Scientific data*, 3(1):1–9.

Vijay Kotu and Bala Deshpande. 2014. *Predictive analytics and data mining: concepts and practice with rapidminer*. Morgan Kaufmann.

Taku Kudo and John Richardson. 2018. SentencePiece: A simple and language independent subword tokenizer and detokenizer for neural text processing. In

*Proceedings of the 2018 Conference on Empirical Methods in Natural Language Processing: System Demonstrations*, pages 66–71, Brussels, Belgium. Association for Computational Linguistics.

Jeffrey Pennington, Richard Socher, and Christopher Manning. 2014. GloVe: Global vectors for word representation. In *Proceedings of the 2014 Conference on Empirical Methods in Natural Language Processing (EMNLP)*, pages 1532–1543, Doha, Qatar. Association for Computational Linguistics.

Alexandra Pomares-Quimbaya, Markus Kreuzthaler, and Stefan Schulz. 2019. Current approaches to identify sections within clinical narratives from electronic health records: a systematic review. *BMC medical research methodology*, 19(1):155.

Sara Rosenthal, Ken Barker, and Zhicheng Liang. 2019. Leveraging medical literature for section prediction in electronic health records. In *Proceedings of the 2019 Conference on Empirical Methods in Natural Language Processing and the 9th International Joint Conference on Natural Language Processing (EMNLP-IJCNLP)*, pages 4864–4873, Hong Kong, China. Association for Computational Linguistics.

Daniel L Rubin and Terry S Desser. 2008. A data warehouse for integrating radiologic and pathologic data. *Journal of the American College of Radiology*, 5(3):210–217.

Mark Singh, Akansh Murthy, and Shridhar Singh. 2015. Prioritization of free-text clinical documents: a novel use of a bayesian classifier. *JMIR medical informatics*, 3(2):e17.

Pontus Stenetorp, Sampo Pyysalo, Goran Topić, Tomoko Ohta, Sophia Ananiadou, and Jun'ichi Tsujii. 2012. BRAT: a web-based tool for NLP-assisted text annotation. In *Proceedings of the Demonstrations at the 13th Conference of the European Chapter of the Association for Computational Linguistics*, pages 102–107.

Ricky K Taira, Stephen G Soderland, and Rex M Jakobovits. 2001. Automatic structuring of radiology free-text reports. *Radiographics*, 21(1):237–245.

Michael Tepper, Daniel Capurro, Fei Xia, Lucy Vanderwende, and Meliha Yetisgen-Yildiz. 2012. Statistical section segmentation in free-text clinical records. In *Lrec*, pages 2001–2008.

David H Wolpert. 1992. Stacked generalization. *Neural networks*, 5(2):241–259.

# Utilizing Multimodal Feature Consistency to Detect Adversarial Examples on Clinical Summaries


**Wenjie Wang**
Emory University
Atlanta, GA, USA
wang.wenjie@emory.edu

**Youngja Park**
IBM Research
Yorktown Heights, NY, USA
young_park@us.ibm.com

**Taesung Lee**
IBM Research
Yorktown Heights, NY, USA
taesung.lee@ibm.com

**Ian Molloy**
IBM Research
Yorktown Heights, NY, USA
molloyim@us.ibm.com

**Pengfei Tang**
Emory University
Atlanta, GA, USA
pengfei.tang@emory.edu

**Li Xiong**
Emory University
Atlanta, GA, USA
lxiong@emory.edu



## Abstract

Recent studies have shown that adversarial examples can be generated by applying small perturbations to the inputs such that the well-trained deep learning models will misclassify. With the increasing number of safety and security-sensitive applications of deep learning models, the robustness of deep learning models has become a crucial topic. The robustness of deep learning models for healthcare applications is especially critical because the unique characteristics and the high financial interests of the medical domain make it more sensitive to adversarial attacks. Among the modalities of medical data, the clinical summaries have higher risks to be attacked because they are generated by third-party companies. As few works studied adversarial threats on clinical summaries, in this work we first apply adversarial attack to clinical summaries of electronic health records (EHR) to show the text-based deep learning systems are vulnerable to adversarial examples. Secondly, benefiting from the multi-modality of the EHR dataset, we propose a novel defense method, *MATCH* (Multimodal feATure Consistency cHeck), which leverages the consistency between multiple modalities in the data to defend against adversarial examples on a single modality. Our experiments demonstrate the effectiveness of *MATCH* on a hospital readmission prediction task comparing with baseline methods.


## 1 Introduction

Deep learning has been shown to be effective in a variety of real-world applications such as computer vision, natural language processing, and speech recognition (Krizhevsky et al., 2012; He et al., 2016; Kim, 2014). It also has shown great potentials in clinical informatics such as medical diagnosis and regulatory decisions (Shickel et al.,

2017), including learning representations of patient records, supporting disease phenotyping, and conducting predictions (Wickramasinghe, 2017; Miotto et al., 2016). However, recent studies show that these models are vulnerable to adversarial examples (Bruna et al., 2013). In image classification, researchers have demonstrated that imperceptible changes in input can mislead the classifier (Goodfellow et al., 2014). In the text domain, synonym substitution or character/word level modification on a few words can also cause the model to misclassify (Liang et al., 2017). These perturbations are mostly imperceptible to human but can easily fool a high-performance deep learning model.

Adversarial examples have received much attention in image and text-domain, yet very few work has been done on Electronic Health Records (EHR). Most existing works on adversarial examples in medical domains have been focused on medical images (Vatian et al., 2019; Ma et al., 2020). A few works have studied adversarial examples in numerical EHR data (Sun et al., 2018; An et al., 2019; Wang et al., 2020). Despite these attempts, there is no work on evaluating the adversarial robustness of clinical natural language processing (NLP) systems, as well as the potential defense techniques.

Although there are some existing defense techniques in the text domain, these methods cannot be directly applied to clinical texts due to the special characteristics of clinical notes. On one hand, for ordinary texts, spelling or syntax checks can easily detect adversarial examples generated by introducing misspelled words. However, there are originally plenty of misspelling words or abbreviations in clinical notes, which places challenges to distinguish whether a misspelled word is under attack. One the other hand, data augmentation is another strategy of some adversarial defense techniques in text domain. For example, Synonyms Encoding Method (SEM) (Wang et al., 2019) is a




*Proceedings of the 3rd Clinical Natural Language Processing Workshop*, pages 259–268
November 19, 2020. ©2020 Association for Computational Linguistics

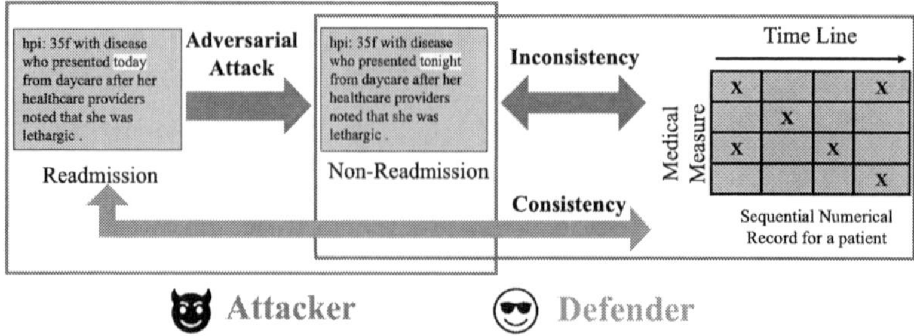


Figure 1: Illustration of *MATCH*: an adversarial attack on the text modal and how *MATCH* detection finds the inconsistency using the numerical features as another modality.

data preprocessing method that inserts a synonym encoder before the input layers to eliminate adversarial perturbations. However, for clinical notes, a large number of words are proper nouns which makes it difficult to generate synonym set thus challenging to apply such defense. Adversarial training (Miyato et al., 2016) has also been applied to increase the generalization ability of textual deep learning models. However, no research has studied the effectiveness of applying adversarial training in the training of text-based clinical deep learning systems.

We note that most existing defense mechanisms have focused on a single modality of the data. However, EHR data always comes in multiple modalities including diagnoses, medications, physician summaries and medical image, which presents both challenges and opportunities for building more robust defense systems. This is because some modalities are particularly susceptible to adversarial attacks and still lack effective defense mechanisms. For example, the clinical summary is often generated by a third-party dictation system and has a higher risk to be attacked. We believe that the correlations between different modalities for the same entity can be exploited to defend against such attacks, as it is not realistic for an adversary to attack all modalities. In this work, we propose a novel defense method, Multimodal feATure Consistency cHeck (*MATCH*), against adversarial attacks by utilizing the multimodal properties in the data. We assume that one modality has been compromised, and the *MATCH* system detects whether an input is adversarial by measuring the consistency between the compromised modality and another uncompromised modality.

To validate our idea, we conduct a case study on predicting the 30-day readmission risk using an EHR dataset. We craft adversarial examples on clinical summary and use the sequential numerical records as another un-attacked modality to detect the adversarial examples. Figure 1 depicts the high-level flow of our system.

The main contributions of this paper include:

- We apply adversarial attack methods to the clinical summaries of electronic health records (EHR) dataset to show the vulnerability of the state-of-the-art clinical deep learning systems.

- We introduce a novel adversarial example detection method, *MATCH*, which automatically validates the consistency between multiple modalities in data. This is the first attempt to leverage multi-modality in adversarial research.

- We conduct experiments to demonstrate the effectiveness of the *MATCH* detection method. The results validate that they outperform existing state-of-the-art defense methods in the medical domain.

## 2    Related Work

There have been many adversarial works on single modality adversarial tasks. Qiu *et al.* (2019) provided a comprehensive summary of the latest progress on adversarial attack and defense technology, categorized by applications including computer vision, natural language processing, cyberspace security, and physical world. Esmaeilpour *et al.* (2019) reviewed the existing adversarial attacks in audio classification. Since our case study focuses on attack and defense of text modality, we mainly review the text-based attacks and defenses in this section.

## 2.1 Attack Methods for Text Data

Kuleshov *et al.* (2018) proposed a Greedy Search Algorithm (GSA), which iteratively changes one word in a sentence and substitute the word with one of the synonymous that improves the objective function the most. Alzantot *et al.* (2018) introduced a Genetic Algorithm (GA) which is a population-based synonym replacement algorithm including processing, sampling and crossover. Gong *et al.* (2018) proposed to search for adversarial examples in the embedding space by applying gradient-based methods on text embedding (*Text-FGM*) and then reconstructed the adversarial texts by the nearest neighbor search. Gao *et al.* (2018) presented the *DeepWordBug* algorithm to generate small perturbations in the character-level. This algorithm does not require the gradient. Ren *et al.* (2019) proposed a new synonym substitution method, Probability Weighted Word Saliency (PWWS), which considered the word saliency as well as the classification probability. Jin *et al.* (2019) proposed TextFooler, an adversarial approach by identifying the important words and then prioritize to replace them with the most semantically similar and grammatically correct words. This is the first attempt to attack the emerging BERT model on text classification. We compare these algorithms from the following aspects:

**Document level vs. Word level.** *Text-FGM* and GA are document level attacks, which apply an attack on the whole text. *DeepWordBug*, GSA, PSWW, and TextFooler are word level attacks that perturb individual words. *DeepWordBug*, PSWW and TextFooler use heuristics to measure the importance of each word and select words to perturb.

**Continuous vs. Discrete.** *Text-FGM* is a continuous attack, because the gradient-based perturbation is applied on the embedding of the words. All other attacks are discrete attacks, which are applied directly on words.

**Semantic vs. Syntactic.** GSA, PSWW, Text-FGM and TextFooler can be categorized as a semantic attack since their strategies are to replace words or text with synonyms, while DeepWordBug is a syntactic attack because it is based on character-level modification. GA can generate both semantically and syntactically similar adversarial examples.

**Back-box vs. White-box.** GSA, GA and *Text-FGM* are white-box attacks, because attackers need to access the model structure and model parameters to calculate the gradient. *DeepWordBug*, TextFooler and PSWW are black-box attacks.

In this paper, we evaluate our detection method against *Text-FGM* and *DeepWordBug*, which represent all the categories mentioned above.

**Text-FGM.** In *Text-FGM*, any gradient based attacks, such as DeepFool (Moosavi-Dezfooli et al., 2016), Fast Gradient Method (FGM) (Goodfellow et al., 2014) (both FGSM and FGVM) can be applied. Applying FGVM on text is defined as follows. Given a classifier $f$ and a word sequence $x = \{x_1, x_2, ...x_n\}$,

$$emb(x)' = emb(x) + \epsilon(\frac{\nabla L}{||\nabla L||_2}) \qquad (1)$$

where $L$ is the loss function and $emb$ denotes the embedding vector. Then, the adversarial example is chosen as $x_{adv} = NNS(emb(x)')$, where $NNS$ represents the nearest neighbor search algorithm which returns the closest word sequence given a perturbed embedding vector.

In the following work, in order to minimize the number of words that need to be perturbed, we iteratively perform perturbation on one word at a time based on the importance score of the words, instead of applying perturbation on the entire sequence. In this way, we can maximize the overall semantic similarity between clean and adversarial sentences.

**DeepWordBug.** *DeepWordBug* first computes the word importance to the target sequence classifier. At each step, it selects the most important word and constructs an adversarial word applying a character level swap, substitution or deletion. It iterates until the label is flipped or the number of words changed is larger than a threshold.

## 2.2 Defense Methods for Text Data

Few works have been done on defending against adversarial examples in the text domain. Existing defense algorithms can be divided into detection and adversarial training.

**Detection.** Most detection methods use spelling check. Gao *et al.* (2018) used Python's Autocorrect 0.3.0 to detect character-level adversarial examples. Li *et al.* (2018) took advantage of a context-aware spelling check service to do the similar work. However, these detections are not effective for word level attacks. Zhou *et al.* (2019) proposed a framework learning to discriminate perturbations (DISP), which learns to discriminate the perturbations and restore the original embeddings.

**Adversarial Training.** Adversarial training has been widely used in the image domain and also been adapted to text domain. Overfitting is the major reason why the adversarial training is sometimes not useful and effective specific to attacks that are used to generate adversarial examples in the training stage. Miyato *et al.* (2016) applied the adversarial training to text domain and achieved the state-of-the-art-performance. Wang *et al.* (2019) proposed Synonyms Encoding Method (SEM), which tried to find a mapping between word and their synonymous neighbors before the input layer. This can be considered as an adversarial training method via data augmentation. Then this mapping works as an encoder applied on classifier. The classifier is forced to be smooth in this way. However, SEM can only work for synonym substitution attacks.

### 2.3 Readmission Prediction

Efforts on building deep learning models for readmission prediction have attracted a growing interest. MIMIC-III (The Multiparameter Intelligent Monitoring in Intensive Care) (Johnson et al., 2016), a publicly available clinical dataset comprising EHR information related to patients admitted to critical care units, has become a common choice for such studies. We demonstrate our framework using a case study on the MIMIC data and adopt the state-of-the-art classification models which are briefly reviewed here.

For numerical records, (Xue et al., 2019) studied the temporal trends of physiological measurements and medications, and used them to improve the performance of ICU readmission risk prediction models. They converted the time series of each variable into trend graphs. Then, they applied frequent subgraph mining to extract important temporal trends. They trained a logistical regression model on grouped temporal trends. (Zebin and Chaussalet, 2019) proposed a heterogeneous bidirectional Long Short Term Memory plus Convolutional neural network (BiLSTM+CNN) model. The combination of them can automate the feature extraction process, by considering both time-series correlation and feature correlation. They outperformed all the benchmark classifiers on most performance measures. At the same time, anothers also proposed a LSTM-CNN based model and achieved

comparable performance (Lin et al., 2019). In this work, we adopt the architecture in (Zebin and Chaussalet, 2019) to conduct readmission prediction on sequential numerical records.

For text data, *Clinical BERT* is recently introduced (Huang et al., 2019; Alsentzer et al., 2019) to model clinical notes by applying the BERT model (?). They outperformed baselines which use both the discharge summaries and the first few days of notes in ICU. In this work, we adopt *Clinical BERT* to predict readmission on text data.

## 3   Method

In this section, we will explain our high-level idea and intuitions behind *MATCH*.

### 3.1   Multi-modality Model Consistency Check

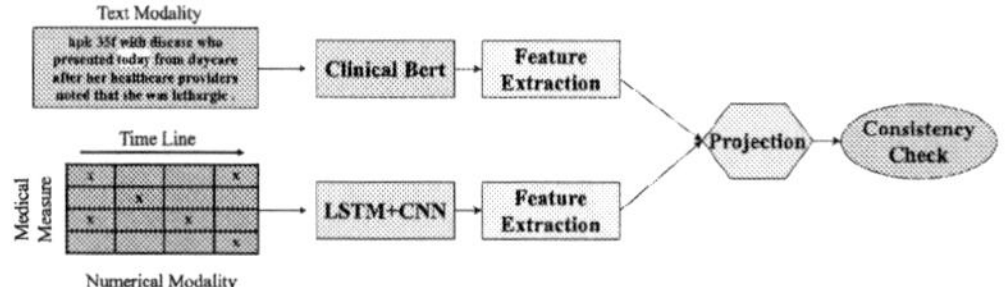


Figure 2: Detection Pipeline

**System Overview.** The main idea of *MATCH* is to reject adversarial examples if the features from one modality are far away from another un-attacked modality's features. In *MATCH*, we assume that there is duplicate information in multiple modalities (e.g., 'gray cat' in an image caption and a gray cat in image) and manipulating information can be harder in one modality than another modality. Thus, it is difficult for an attacker to make coherent perturbations across all modalities. In other words, using the gradient to find the steepest change in the decision surface is a common attack strategy, but such a gradient can be drastically different from modality to modality. Moreover, for a certain modality, even if the adversarial and clean examples are close in the input space, their differences would be amplified in the feature space. Therefore, if another un-attacked modality is introduced, the difference between the two modalities can be a criteria to distinguish adversarial and clean examples. Figure 2 shows our detection pipeline using text and numerical features. Note that, while we use text and numerical modalities for the experiments, our framework works for any modalities.

We first pre-train two models on two modalities separately. These two models are trained only with clean data, and we use the outputs of their last fully-connected layer before logits layer as the extracted features. Note that the extracted features from two modalities are in different feature spaces, which requires a "Projection" step to bring the two feature sets into the same feature space. We train a projection model, a fully-connected layer network, for each modality on the clean examples. The objective function of the projection model is:

$$\min_{\theta_1,\theta_2} MSE(p_{\theta_1}(F_1(m_1)) - p_{\theta_2}(F_2(m_2))) \quad (2)$$

where $m_1$ and $m_2$ represent different modalities. $F_i$ and $p_{\theta_i}$ are the feature extractor and the projector of $m_i$ respectively.

Then, a consistency check model is trained only on clean data by minimizing the consistency level between multi-modal features. The consistency level is defined as the $L_2$ norm of the difference between the projected features from the two modalities. Once all the models are trained, given an input example with two modalities, the system detects it as an adversarial example if the consistency level between two modalities is greater than a threshold $\delta$:

$$||p_{\theta_1}(F_1(m_1)) - p_{\theta_2}(F_2(m_2))||_2 > \delta \quad (3)$$

$\delta$ is decided based on what percentage of clean examples are allowed to pass *MATCH*.

**Predictive Model and Feature Extractor.** For clinical notes, we use pre-trained *Clinical BERT* as our feature extractor. *Clinical BERT* is pre-trained using thr same tasks as (Devlin et al., 2019) and fine-tuned on readmission prediction. *Clinical BERT* also provides a readmission classifier, which is a single layer fully-connected layer. We use this classification representation as the extracted feature.

For sequential numerical records, we adopt the architecture in (Zebin and Chaussalet, 2019) . However, as our data preprocessing steps and selected features are different, we modify the architecture to optimize the performance. Our architecture (Figure 3) employs a stacked-bidirectional-LSTM, followed by a convolutional layer and a fully connected layer. The number of stacks in stacked-bidirectional-LSTM and the number of convolutional layers, as well as the convolution kernel size are tuned during experiments, which arc different from the architecture in (Zebin and Chaussalet, 2019). The output of the final layer is used as the extracted features.

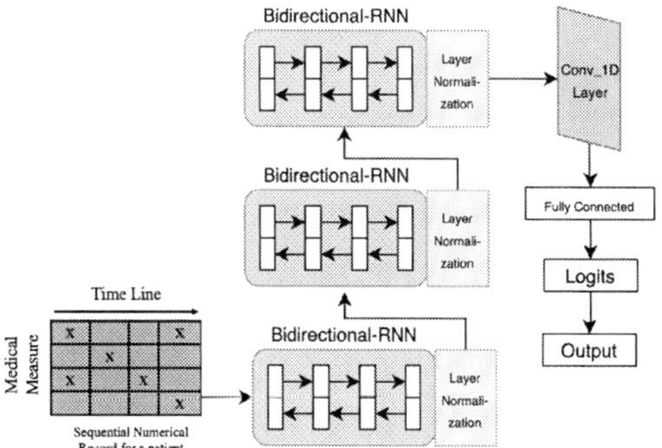

Figure 3: Stacked Bidirectional LSTM+CNN architecture

## 4 Experiments

In this section, we first present the attack performance of two text attack algorithms in order to demonstrate the vulnerability of state-of-the-art clinical deep learning systems. Secondly, we evaluate the effectiveness of the *MATCH* detection method for the readmission classification task using the MIMIC-III data.

### 4.1 Data Preprocessing

**Clinical Summary.** For the clinical summary, which is the target modality the attacker, we directly use the processed data from (Huang et al., 2019). The data contains 34,560 patients with 2,963 positive readmission labels and 48,150 negative labels. In MIMIC-III (Johnson et al., 2016), there are several categories in the clinical notes including ECG summaries, physician notes and discharge summaries. We select the discharge summary as our text modality, as it is most relevant to readmission prediction.

**Numerical Data.** For the other modality which is used to conduct the consistency check, we use the patents' numeric data in their medical records. We use the patient ID from the discharge summary to extract the multivariate time series numerical records consisting of 90 continuous features including vital signs such as heart rate and blood pressure as well as other lab measurements. The features are selected based on the frequency of their appearance in all the patients' records.

Then, we apply a standardization for each feature $x$ across all patients and time steps using the following formula: $x = \frac{x - \bar{x}}{std(x)}$. We pad all the sequences to the same length (120 hours before discharge), because this time window is crucial to predict the readmission rate. We ignore all the previous time steps if a patient stayed more than 120 hours and repeat the last time step if a patient's sequence is shorter than 120 hours. We represent the numerical data as a 3-dimensional tensor: patients $\times$ time step (120) $\times$ features (90).

### 4.2 Predictive Model Performance

For the clinical summary data, we use the pre-trained *Clinical BERT*, whose AUC is 0.768. For the numerical data, the performance of our stacked bi-directional LSTM+CNN model produces AUC 0.65. Although the performance of the numerical data is lower than that of *Clinical BERT*, our experiments indicate that it does not affect *MATCH*'s overall performance. The reason is that we only need this prediction model to learn the feature representation. As long as the two models have a comparable performance with each other, the extracted features from the two modalities have a similar representative ability. *Clinical BERT* is also used as the target classifier under attacked.

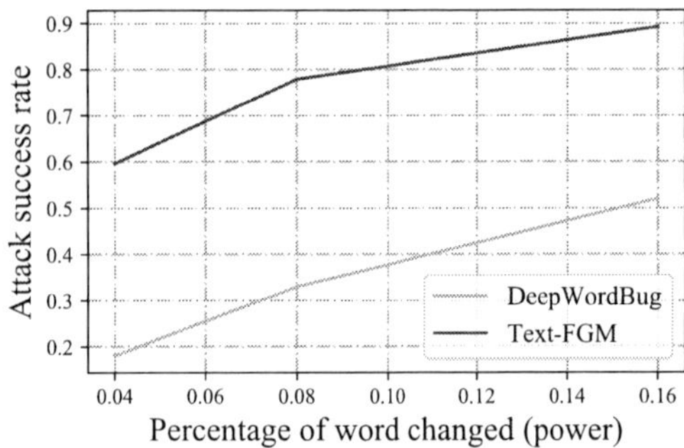

Figure 4: Attack Success Rate Comparison between *Text-FGM* and *DeepWordBug*

| Text-FGM | Clean | DeepWordBug |
|---|---|---|
| he will call you to adjust your coumadin ( also called warfarin ) dose as needed... told by coumadin clinic that you can decrease lab draws , please have result faxed to the coumadin clinic at ... discharge disposition: homes with servants venue: vna discharge diagnosis: primary diagnoses: malignant hypertension ( hypertensive urgency ) acute exacerbation of chronic left brachiocephalic vein occlusion anemia secondary diagnoses... you were confessed and treated for an acute exacerbation of a fungus left brachiocephalic vein ... | he will call you to adjust your coumadin ( also called warfarin ) dose as ... told by coumadin clinic that you can decrease lab draws . please have result faxed to the coumadin clinic at . ... discharge disposition: home with service facility: vna discharge diagnosis: primary diagnoses: malignant hypertension ( hypertensive urgency ) acute exacerbation of chronic left brachiocephalic vein occlusion anemia secondary diagnoses...you were admitted and treated for an acute exacerbation of a chronic left brachiocephalic vein ... | he will call you to adjust your coumadin ( also called warfarin ) dose as needed ... told by coumadin clinic that you can decrease lab draws . please have result faxed to the coumadin clinic at . ... discharge disposition: home with service facility: vna discharge diagonsis: primary diagnoses: malignant hypertension ( hypertensive urgency ) acute exacerbation of chronic left brachiocephalic vein occlusion anemia secondary diagnoses...you were admitted and treated for an acute exacerbation of a chronic left brachiocephalic vein ... |
| hx obtained per ed notes and sister . hpi: 35f with disease who presented tonight from daycare after her healthcare providers noted that she was lethargic . they were initially unable to obtain a blood pressure . the patient was noted to have a very rapidly | hx obtained per ed notes and sister . hpi: 35f with disease who presented today from daycare after her healthcare providers noted that she was lethargic . they were initially unable to obtain a blood pressure . the patient was noted to have a very rapid | hx obtained per ed notes and sister . hpi: 35f with disease who presented today from daycare after her healthcare providers noted that she was lethargic . they were initially unable to obtain a blood pressure . the patient was noted to have a very rapid |

Figure 5: Example of generated adversarial texts with *Text-FGM* and *DeepWordBug*

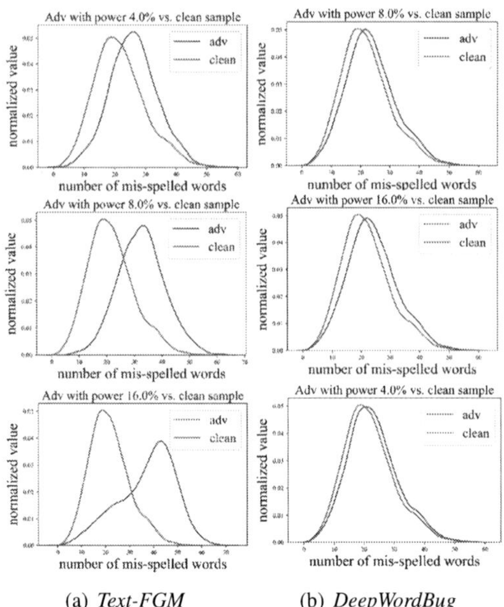


Figure 6: Distribution of misspelled words in adversarial /clean text under different attack power

### 4.3 Attack Results

In this section, we present the attack performance of two text attack algorithms in order to demonstrate the vulnerability of state-of-the-art clinical deep learning systems. We select two attack algorithms that can present all attack categories we mentioned in the related work: *Text-FGM*, a white-box, semantic attack and *DeepWordBug* a black-box, syntactic attack. Besides, these two attack algorithms will also be used to evaluate the performance of our proposed *MATCH*, in order to show that *MATCH* can defense against various kinds of adversarial attacks.

We generate adversarial examples with different attack power levels: 4%, 8%, 16%, which define the maximum percentage of word changes in a text. Then we show the attack success rate under different attack powers, as well as the generated adversarial examples of two attack algorithms. As shown in Figure 4, both *Text-FGM* and *DeepWordBug* can produces high attack success rate on the Clinical Bert model. With higher percentage of word changes, the attack success rate also increased for b0th *Text-FGM* and *DeepWordBug*. This is intuitive because as more perturbations being introduced to the input space, the model is more likely to give a wrong prediction. For *Text-FGM*, it achieves almost 80% attack success rate with only 8% of

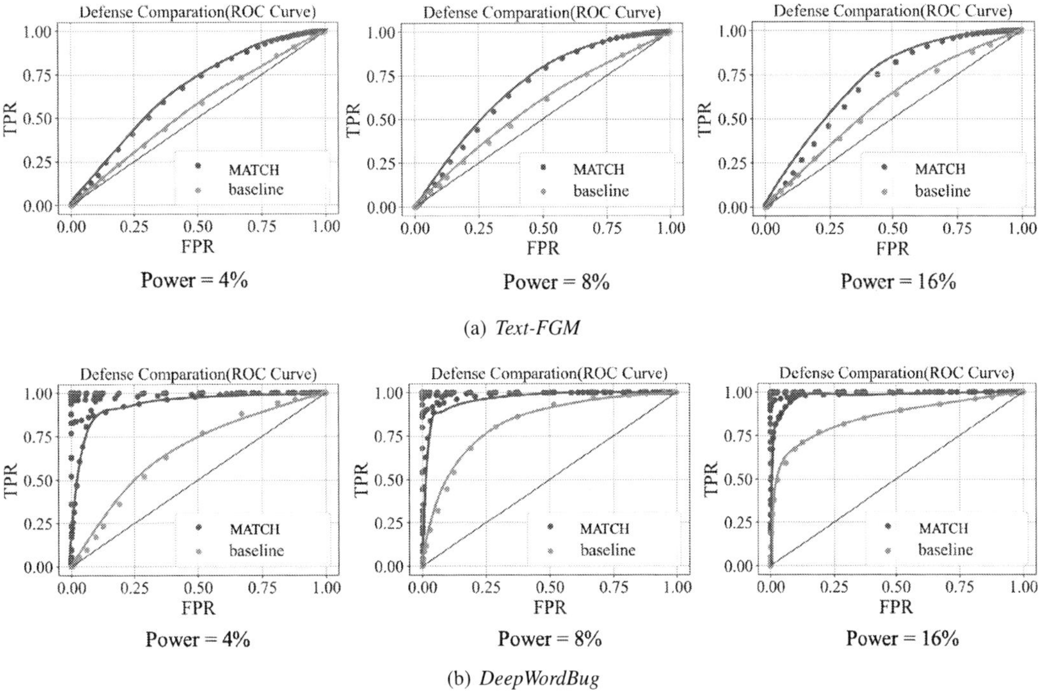



Figure 7: Comparison of the adversarial detection performance between *MATCH* and misspelling check-based defense.

word change, which indicated that the Clinical Bert model are easily fooled and give a wrong prediction. This result indicates the vulnerability of the state-of-the-art text-based medical deep learning systems.

Figure 5 shows several examples of our generated adversarial examples from both attack methods compared to the clean examples. The red words represent the changed words in *Text-FGM*, and green words denote the changed words in *Deep-WordBug*. It is obvious that even the generated adversarial texts are indistinguishable to human knowledge, especially those that generated by *Text-FGM*, but well-trained deep learning models will misclassify.

Besides the attack success rate and the generated adversarial examples, we also present the distribution of the number of misspelled words in the clean and adversarial examples. As shown in Figure 6, the number of misspelled word distributions of the clean and the *Text-FGM* adversarial examples are difficult to separate, while the adversarial examples generated by *DeepWordBug* have a large distribution shift compared to that of the clean examples. Further, as the attack power grows, the distribution shift is more distinguishable. This explains why the

spelling check service is effective to *DeepWordBug* but not useful for the synonym substitution attack.

## 4.4 Defense Result

In this section, we use *Text-FGM* and *DeepWord-Bug*, which represent the two types of attacks, semantic vs. syntactic, to evaluate the performance of *MATCH*

**Comparison with Baseline Detection Methods.** We use mis-spelling check (*pyspellchecker* form python) as a baseline to compare with *MATCH*, which is adopted in (Gao et al., 2018). As shown in Figure 7, we take the attack power (i.e., the percentage of word changes) of 4%, 8% and 16% and use the ROC curve to compare the detection performances between *MATCH* and the mis-spelling check. ROC curve can represent the correlations between True Positive Rate (TPR) and False Positive Rate (FPR). Here, we want to have higher TPR (adversarial examples can be detected) while achieve lower FPR (clean examples can pass the detector). Given the various detection thresholds $\delta$ which allow certain percentage of clean examples to pass detection, these ROC curves illustrate the discriminating ability of *MATCH* on detecting adversarial examples. Similar to *MATCH*, we

Table 1: Comparison of the Adversarial Detection Accuracy

| Attack Levels | Clean | No Defense | *MATCH* | AT |
|---|---|---|---|---|
| 16% | 0.672 | 0.407 | 0.525 | 0.435 |
| 8% | 0.672 | 0.450 | 0.523 | 0.464 |
| 4% | 0.672 | 0.483 | 0.522 | 0.471 |

take the number of misspelled words as a threshold and show the discriminating ability given different thresholds. We can note that *MATCH* significantly outperforms the baseline for both attacks. As mis-spelling check can effectively detect adversarial texts with large misspelling distribution shifts, we take the mis-spelling check as a pre-filter to filter out adversarial examples that are easy to detect. Then, we apply *MATCH* as a secondary detector. We try different combinations of mis-spelling word threshold and feature consistency threshold. The blue lines in the charts show the lower boundary of the ROC curves. For *DeepWordBug*, MATCH can achieve close to 100% TPR and 0% FPR. In addition, both *MATCH* and baseline method works better for *DeepWordBug* because the attack is syntactic, and the examples are easily separable based on the misspelling distribution shifts as observed from Figure 6.

**Comparison with Adversarial Training.** Besides misspelling-check, we also use Adversarial Training (AT) to compare with *MATCH* on *Text-FGM*. As mentioned in the related work, AT is widly applied in image domain to improve the robustness of DNNs. As our prediction is a binary classification, and *MATCH* is a detector, in order to compare with Adversarial Training, we flip the prediction label of examples which are detected as adversarial examples and compare the accuracy with AT. The results in Table 1 show that the accuracy of *MATCH* is much higher than AT and *No Defense*.

**Impact of attack power.** To better illustrate the impact of attack power, we plot the results of varying attack powers in Figure 8. To clarify, for *DeepWordBug* we do not include mis-spelling check as a pre-filter, only showing the performance of *MATCH*. Under *DeepWordBug* with attack power of 16%, *MATCH* can detect more than 60% of the adversarial examples, while misclassifying 30% of the clean examples as adversarial. Under *Text-FGM* with attack power of 16%, *MATCH* can detect more than 60% adversarial examples but only 20% of clean examples are mistaken as adversarial. The ROC curve shows that with a higher attack

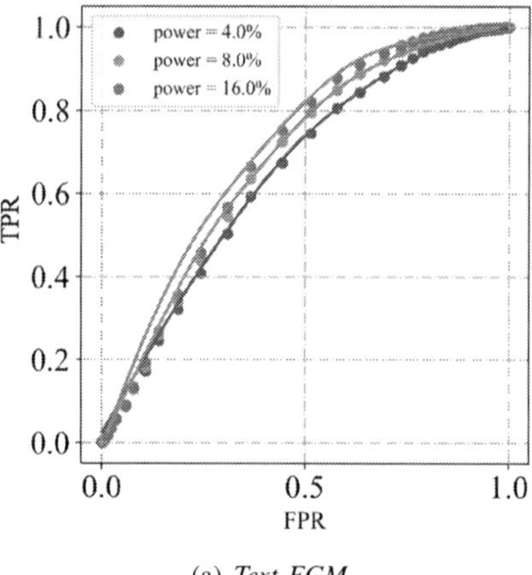


(a) *Text-FGM*

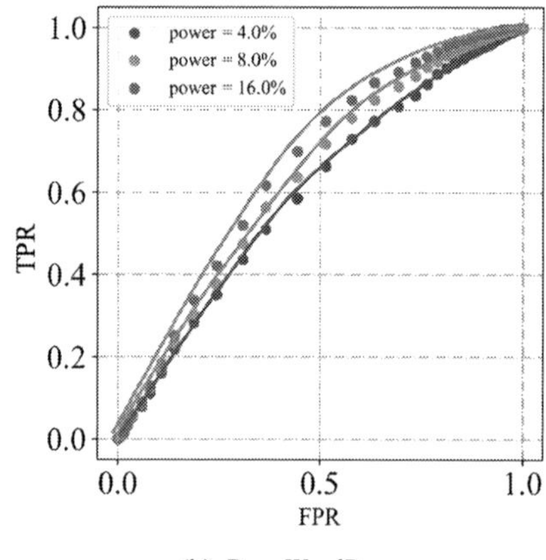


(b) *DeepWordBug*

Figure 8: Detection Result

power, *MATCH* can more easily distinguish adversarial examples from clean examples.

## 5   Conclusion

In this work, we proposed *MATCH*, a novel defense method by taking advantage of another modal's properties to detect adversarial examples on clinical notes. We evaluated our approaches with two different attack strategies: *Text-FGM* and *DeepWordBug*. We conducted experiments on the 30-day readmission prediction task by detecting adversarial examples in text modalities and use numerical modality to do the multi-modal consistency check. Our experiments showed the effectiveness of *MATCH* compared to the baseline methods.

Although we only evaluated *MATCH* on clinical deep learning system and only attack on the clinial text modality, we believe *MATCH* would be a general framework that could work on any multi-modality dataset. In the future, it would be interesting to extending and evaluating the framework for different modalities such as image and audio. Besides, a more complex architecture may be applied to project extracted features.

## References


Emily Alsentzer, John R Murphy, Willie Boag, Wei-Hung Weng, Di Jin, Tristan Naumann, and Matthew McDermott. 2019. Publicly available clinical bert embeddings. *arXiv preprint arXiv:1904.03323*.

Moustafa Alzantot, Yash Sharma, Ahmed Elgohary, Bo-Jhang Ho, Mani Srivastava, and Kai-Wei Chang. 2018. Generating natural language adversarial examples. In *Proceedings of the 2018 Conference on Empirical Methods in Natural Language Processing*, pages 2890–2896.

Sungtae An, Cao Xiao, Walter F. Stewart, and Jimeng Sun. 2019. Longitudinal adversarial attack on electronic health records data. In *The World Wide Web Conference*.

Joan Bruna, Christian Szegedy, Ilya Sutskever, Ian Goodfellow, Wojciech Zaremba, Rob Fergus, and Dumitru Erhan. 2013. Intriguing properties of neural networks.

Jacob Devlin, Ming-Wei Chang, Kenton Lee, and Kristina Toutanova. 2019. Bert: Pre-training of deep bidirectional transformers for language understanding. In *Proceedings of the 2019 Conference of the North American Chapter of the Association for Computational Linguistics: Human Language Technologies, Volume 1 (Long and Short Papers)*, pages 4171–4186.

Mohammad Esmaeilpour, Patrick Cardinal, and Alessandro Lameiras Koerich. 2019. A robust approach for securing audio classification against adversarial attacks. *IEEE Transactions on Information Forensics and Security*.

Ji Gao, Jack Lanchantin, Mary Lou Soffa, and Yanjun Qi. 2018. Black-box generation of adversarial text sequences to evade deep learning classifiers. In *2018 IEEE Security and Privacy Workshops (SPW)*, pages 50–56. IEEE.

Zhitao Gong, Wenlu Wang, Bo Li, Dawn Song, and Wei-Shinn Ku. 2018. Adversarial texts with gradient methods. *arXiv preprint arXiv:1801.07175*.

Ian J Goodfellow, Jonathon Shlens, and Christian Szegedy. 2014. Explaining and harnessing adversarial examples. *arXiv preprint arXiv:1412.6572*.

Kaiming He, Xiangyu Zhang, Shaoqing Ren, and Jian Sun. 2016. Deep residual learning for image recognition. In *Proceedings of the IEEE conference on computer vision and pattern recognition*, pages 770–778.

Kexin Huang, Jaan Altosaar, and Rajesh Ranganath. 2019. Clinicalbert: Modeling clinical notes and predicting hospital readmission. *arXiv preprint arXiv:1904.05342*.

Di Jin, Zhijing Jin, Joey Tianyi Zhou, and Peter Szolovits. 2019. Is bert really robust? natural language attack on text classification and entailment. *arXiv preprint arXiv:1907.11932*.

Alistair EW Johnson, Tom J Pollard, Lu Shen, H Lehman Li-wei, Mengling Feng, Mohammad Ghassemi, Benjamin Moody, Peter Szolovits, Leo Anthony Celi, and Roger G Mark. 2016. Mimic-iii, a freely accessible critical care database. *Scientific data*, 3:160035.

Yoon Kim. 2014. Convolutional neural networks for sentence classification. *arXiv preprint arXiv:1408.5882*.

Alex Krizhevsky, Ilya Sutskever, and Geoffrey E Hinton. 2012. Imagenet classification with deep convolutional neural networks. In *Advances in neural information processing systems*, pages 1097–1105.

Volodymyr Kuleshov, Shantanu Thakoor, Tingfung Lau, and Stefano Ermon. 2018. Adversarial examples for natural language classification problems.

Jinfeng Li, Shouling Ji, Tianyu Du, Bo Li, and Ting Wang. 2018. Textbugger: Generating adversarial text against real-world applications. *arXiv preprint arXiv:1812.05271*.

Bin Liang, Hongcheng Li, Miaoqiang Su, Pan Bian, Xirong Li, and Wenchang Shi. 2017. Deep text classification can be fooled. *CoRR*, abs/1704.08006.

Yu-Wei Lin, Yuqian Zhou, Faraz Faghri, Michael J Shaw, and Roy H Campbell. 2019. Analysis and prediction of unplanned intensive care unit readmission using recurrent neural networks with long short-term memory. *PloS one*, 14(7).

Xingjun Ma, Yuhao Niu, Lin Gu, Yisen Wang, Yitian Zhao, James Bailey, and Feng Lu. 2020. Understanding adversarial attacks on deep learning based medical image analysis systems. *Pattern Recognition*, page 107332.

Riccardo Miotto, Li Li, Brian A Kidd, and Joel T Dudley. 2016. Deep patient: an unsupervised representation to predict the future of patients from the electronic health records. *Scientific reports*, 6:26094.

Takeru Miyato, Andrew M Dai, and Ian Goodfellow. 2016. Adversarial training methods for semi-supervised text classification. *stat*, 1050:7.

Seyed-Mohsen Moosavi-Dezfooli, Alhussein Fawzi, and Pascal Frossard. 2016. Deepfool: a simple and accurate method to fool deep neural networks. In *Proceedings of the IEEE conference on computer vision and pattern recognition*, pages 2574–2582.

Shilin Qiu, Qihe Liu, Shijie Zhou, and Chunjiang Wu.
2019. Review of artificial intelligence adversarial
attack and defense technologies. *Applied Sciences*,
9(5):909.

Shuhuai Ren, Yihe Deng, Kun He, and Wanxiang Che.
2019. Generating natural language adversarial examples through probability weighted word saliency.
In *Proceedings of the 57th Annual Meeting of the
Association for Computational Linguistics*, pages
1085–1097.

Benjamin Shickel, Patrick James Tighe, Azra Bihorac,
and Parisa Rashidi. 2017. Deep ehr: a survey of recent advances in deep learning techniques for electronic health record (ehr) analysis. *IEEE journal
of biomedical and health informatics*, 22(5):1589–
1604.

Mengying Sun, Fengyi Tang, Jinfeng Yi, Fei Wang, and
Jiayu Zhou. 2018. Identify susceptible locations in
medical records via adversarial attacks on deep predictive models. pages 793–801.

Aleksandra Vatian, Natalia Gusarova, Natalia V. Do-
brenko, Sergey Dudorov, Niyaz Nigmatullin, Ana-
toly A. Shalyto, and Artem Lobantsev. 2019. Impact
of adversarial examples on the efficiency of interpretation and use of information from high-tech medical images. *FRUCT*.

Wenjie Wang, Pengfei Tang, Li Xiong, and Xiaoqian
Jiang. 2020. Radar: Recurrent autoencoder based
detector for adversarial examples on temporal ehr.

Xiaosen Wang, Hao Jin, and Kun He. 2019. Natural
language adversarial attacks and defenses in word
level. *arXiv preprint arXiv:1909.06723*.

Nilmini Wickramasinghe. 2017. Deepr: a convolutional net for medical records.

Ye Xue, Diego Klabjan, and Yuan Luo. 2019. Predicting icu readmission using grouped physiological and medication trends. *Artificial intelligence in
medicine*, 95:27–37.

Tahmina Zebin and Thierry J Chaussalet. 2019. Design and implementation of a deep recurrent model
for prediction of readmission in urgent care using
electronic health records. In *2019 IEEE Conference on Computational Intelligence in Bioinformatics and Computational Biology (CIBCB)*, pages 1–5.
IEEE.

Yichao Zhou, Jyun-Yu Jiang, Kai-Wei Chang, and Wei
Wang. 2019. Learning to discriminate perturbations
for blocking adversarial attacks in text classification.
*arXiv preprint arXiv:1909.03084*.

# Advancing Seq2seq with Joint Paraphrase Learning


**So Yeon Min** *
MIT CSAIL
MIT-IBM Watson AI Lab
symin95@alum.mit.edu

**Preethi Raghavan**
IBM Research, Cambridge
MIT-IBM Watson AI Lab
praghav@us.ibm.com

**Peter Szolovits**
MIT CSAIL
MIT-IBM Watson AI Lab
psz@mit.edu



## Abstract

We address the problem of model generalization for sequence to sequence (seq2seq) architectures. We propose going beyond data augmentation via paraphrase-optimized multi-task learning and observe that it is useful in correctly handling unseen sentential paraphrases as inputs. Our models greatly outperform SOTA seq2seq models for semantic parsing on diverse domains (Overnight - up to 3.2% and emrQA - 7%) and Nematus (Sennrich et al., 2017), the winning solution for WMT 2017, for Czech to English translation (CzENG 1.6 - 1.5 BLEU).


## 1 Introduction

Natural language provides a vast number of alternative ways to state something or to ask a question (Bhagat et al., 2009). This poses a daunting challenge to natural language processing methods because there is no possible way to enumerate all these alternatives. As a result, many popular machine learning systems trained on benchmark datasets are surprisingly fragile to such previously unobserved variations of the training input at test time (Jia and Liang, 2017; Belinkov and Bisk, 2017; Goodfellow et al., 2014; Iyyer et al., 2018)[1].

An attempt to ameliorate this is to augment the training data with paraphrases. Regardless of the magnitude of data augmentation, unseen instances may still break the model; data augmentation alone is an insufficient remedy for model brittleness.

We propose to go above and beyond data augmentation in handling model generalization for sequence-to-sequence (seq2seq) architectures and improve model generalization to test sets that entirely consist of unseen paraphrases of the training

---

*Work done while So Yeon Min was a student at MIT.

[1] AllenNLP's competitive BiDAF (Seo et al., 2017) reading comprehension model is not always capable at handling this: https://demo.allennlp.org/reading-comprehension/ODE5ODc2

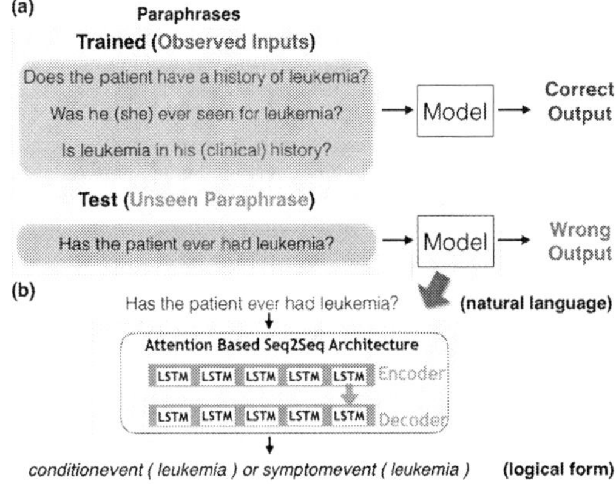



Figure 1: An overview of our work. (a) The objective is to train a seq2seq paraphrase model that is capable of accurately generalizing to unseen sentential paraphrases only observed at test time (red). Phrases highlighted in blue are synonymous when accompanied by a clinical condition, such as leukemia. (b) Example inputs and outputs for semantic parsing with emrQA.

set. Assuming that data augmentation already took place in the training set, either by annotation or off-the-shelf paraphrase generation, we propose new models that actively employ the properties of paraphrase-augmented data as part of the training objective.

We examine sequence models for diverse tasks across diverse domains, consider state of the art models for each of those tasks and incorporate multi-task paraphrase detection and generation learning. We show that our models compare over and above other popular generalization schemes, such as feature-based or fine-tuned word embeddings (Mikolov et al., 2013; Devlin et al., 2018) or paraphrase-based methods such as paraphrase embeddings (Wieting and Gimpel, 2017). The proposed models outperform state-of-the-art models (Pampari et al., 2018; Jia and Liang, 2016; Sennrich et al., 2017) when evaluated across a variety of settings on emrQA (Pampari et al., 2018)




*Proceedings of the 3rd Clinical Natural Language Processing Workshop*, pages 269–279
November 19, 2020. ©2020 Association for Computational Linguistics

and Overnight for semantic parsing and CzENG 1.6 (Bojar et al., 2016) with ParaNMT-50M (Wieting and Gimpel, 2018) for machine translation. Moreover, even when paraphrase augmentation is not available, we demonstrate that the proposed multi-task models improve model generalization with only synthetic, noisy paraphrases from off-the-shelf models.

The main contributions of our work are as follows: (1) We propose novel multi-task learning seq2seq models that significantly improve model generalization to unseen paraphrases at test time, in diverse domains (clinical text, 7 domains of Overnight, English subtitles). (2) Proposed models bring additional major performance boost on top of paraphrase-augmentation, but also work when the training set does not come with paraphrases at all. (3) We introduce new methods of splitting data into train/ test sets that more realistically evaluates model generalization to paraphrases. (4) We present the first competitive baseline for semantic parsing on the emrQA dataset.

## 2   Related Work

Dealing with unseen paraphrastic variants of the input has been a fundamental problem (Mitchell et al., 2018; Ettinger et al., 2017). Recently, multiple works have shown that models easily "break" when evaluated on adversarial examples, which are noisy variants of the training inputs (Goodfellow et al., 2014; Iyyer et al., 2018). However, there is relatively little work that go beyond augmentation and actively optimizes paraphrastic generalization along with learning the main NLP task at hand, in neural settings.

In non-neural settings, the idea that leveraging paraphrases facilitates modeling sentential semantics has been repeatedly verified across various NLP tasks. In semantic parsing, Berant and Liang (2014) deal with understanding the myriad paraphrastic variants in which knowledge base relations can be expressed in human language. They use a paraphrase of the original input utterance as an intermediary, which is used as an ancillary factor in ranking the likelihood of each candidate logical form. In machine translation, Callison-Burch et al. (2006) handles unseen source language phrases by substituting paraphrases of those phrases and then translating the paraphrases.

In neural settings, the most widespread approach is to simply generate paraphrases for data augmen-tation, as used by Fader et al. (2013a) in question answering and Wang et al. (2015) in semantic parsing. There are relatively few approaches that explicitly incorporate pairwise paraphrastic equivalence of inputs as part of the model. In semantic parsing, Dong et al. (2017) applies CNN to learn paraphrase detection in a multi-task manner; Su and Yan (2017) generate the simplest paraphrases for input utterances and use them as intermediaries for mapping input to ouput.

In question answering, several multi-task learning works learn paraphrase detection along with the main task; Bordes et al. (2014) optimizes a multi-task objective (negative cosine similarity) that encourages embeddings of paraphrases to have small angular distance in every other iteration of training. Additionally, Dong et al. (2015) uses an auxiliary multi-task learning objective for paraphrase detection in training multi-column convolutional neural networks for structured question answering. Both of these works leverage the paraphrase clusters of the WIKIANSWERS (Fader et al., 2013b) dataset. However, Dong et al. (2015) found that their multi-task learning method gives almost no advantage. Moreover, both works did not analyze which domains or types of validation inputs benefited from paraphrase learning. Most importantly, these works are fundamentally and methodologically different from ours, in that they leveraged the paraphrases from WIKIANSWERS not as inputs to the main model, but only for learning paraphrase detection. On the other hand, our work uses paraphrase instances for both multi-task paraphrase learning and the main task, which is the driving factor behind the significant performance boost by our models.

Unlike past methods applicable to single tasks, our work shows improvements across several different problems and domains. Also, we introduce the first framework in a neural-sequence-to-sequence setting, unlike past works that apply CNN's or non-neural settings. Furthermore, our approach can be generally applied to any state-of-the-art variants of seq2seq, such as Nematus (Sennrich et al., 2017).

## 3   Paraphrases & Datasets

Paraphrases are sentences or phrases that convey the same meaning using different wording (Bhagat and Hovy, 2013). Methods to construct paraphrases are largely divided into syntactic variation and substitution (Bhagat and Hovy, 2013). *"Does the patient have a history of leukemia?"* and *"Is*

| Para. Types | emrQA |
| --- | --- |
| Syntactic Para's | what medication has the patient used for \|problem\| <br> what medications have been previously used for the treatment of \|problem\| |
| Substitution Para's | is there any mention of \|problem\| in the patients record <br> has been the patient ever been considered for \|problem\| |
| **Para. Types t** | **Overnight** |
| Syntactic Para's | find an additional author to an efron article <br> who is the other author for the article written by efron |
| Substitution Para's | article that at least two article cites <br> articles cited by two or more articles |
| **Para. Types** | **Paraphrase Augmented CzEng 1.6** |
| Syntactic Para's | It was good in spite of the taste <br> Despite the flavor, it felt good |
| Substitution Para's | I took a stool sample from his heart. <br> I took the stool sample after his lungs failed. |

Table 1: Examples of annotated/ synthetically generated paraphrases in diverse domains. Syntactic variation paraphrases and synonymous substitution paraphrases are respective abbreviated as Syntactic Para's and Substitution Para's.

*there leukemia in the patient's history?"* are syntactic paraphrases, with overlapping words reordered. Most paraphrases are not fully syntactic, and involve substitutions with synonymous phrases by matching general semantics to that of a domain sublanguage.

Table 1 shows examples of annotated and synthetic paraphrases that are of syntactic variant/ synonymous substitution types. Some of emrQA and Overnight's paraphrases respectively assume knowledge of clinical ("considered for" ≡ "seen for, diagnosed with" when collocated with a |clinical problem|) and quantitative sublanguage ("at least two" ≡ "one or two"). CzEng 1.6 (Bojar et al., 2016), unlike the two others, do not come with annotated paraphrases. Thus, the paraphrases shown in Table 1 are those generated by ParaNMT-50M (Wieting and Gimpel, 2018). Noticeably, its synthetic paraphrases are quite noisy; "I took a stool sample from his heart" and "I took the stool sample after his lung failed" are not equivalent, but are identified so by the paraphrase generation model.

## 4  Problem Statement

Our setup assumes (1) a paraphrase-augmented dataset, either by annotation or simple off-the-shelf paraphrase generation models, and (2) a baseline seq2seq model (Sutskever et al., 2014) which maps an input sequence to an output sequence. We propose methods to endow additional improvement in model generalization given this setup.

**Naive & Strict Splitting Schemes**  Not all paraphrases are created equal; some paraphrases are much less challenging than others in evaluating model performance. A common yet undesirable scenario in NLP datasets is that the form of input utterances can be repeated across training/ test splits. For example, in Overnight's *recipe* domain, there are several questions in the form of *"how many x are there"* where $x$ is some recipe-related entity, such as *"recipes"*, *"ingredients"*, *"meals"*, etc. With such datasets, the test set often contains too many repeating forms of the training set. Such a train/ test split is an unrealistic evaluation of model generalization. There are numerous ways a user can phrase one's information needs, and all possible forms cannot be seen at training even in the most well-augmented datasets.

We propose a new, more realistic way to split paraphrase-augmented data, with the emrQA dataset as an example (Figure 2). emrQA consists of paraphrase groups of inputs. Within a single group, "templates" are filled with clinical entities to produce actual input instances (Fig 2 purple box). 2(a) shows a naive splitting scheme where the input instances are split at random. On the other hand, 2(b) is a more realistic scenario where *a form that was seen during training **never** appears at test time*. For example, all instances of "Has the pat. ever been exposed to |problem|?" belong to training and never when the model is evaluated. On the other hand, all instances of "Does this patient have a history of |problem|?" never appear during training yet do so at test time; thus, the model is tested whether it can infer the meaning of this form only from its paraphrased forms seen during training (such as "Has the pat. ever been exposed to |problem|?"). While this split is more challenging than the naive one, test instances are still semantically equivalent to some training instance, so the model is expected to catch this and generalize to unseen form. While we used a paraphrase-annotated dataset as an example, 2(b)'s splitting scheme works with non-annotated data, via automatic augmentation with off-the-shelf models.

Thus, given a seq2seq task where we have a training and test set of input-output pairs and several unseen observations in the test set that are paraphrases of the training observations, we want to learn a model that can generalize accurately to these unseen observations, and preferably, even to unseen forms in the strict split of Fig 2(b).

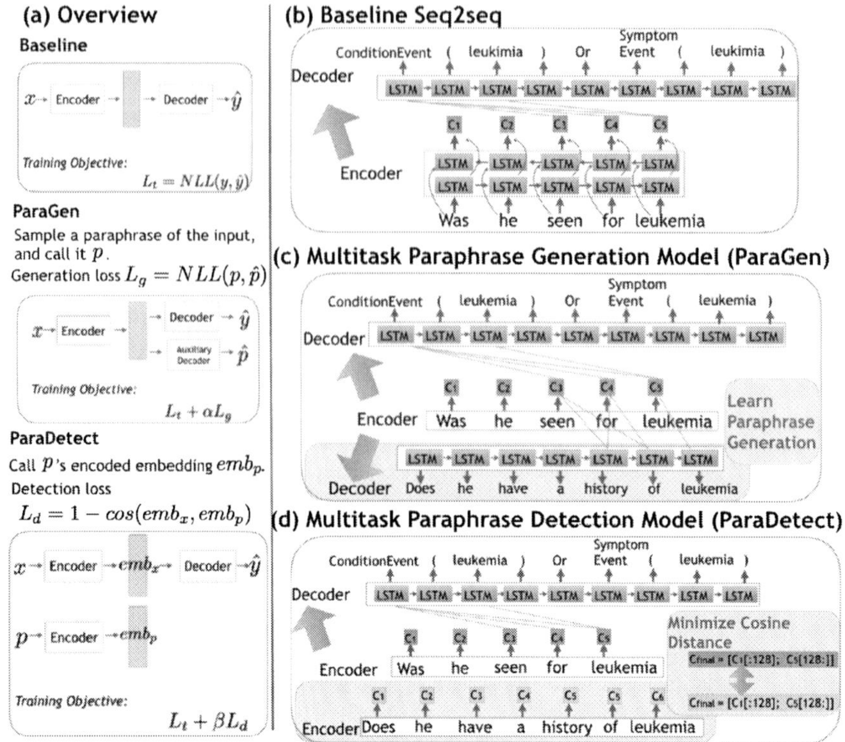



Figure 2: Proposed paraphrase models. (a): Overview of all models; the encoder embeddings of inputs are depicted as gray boxes. (b): Simple Seq2seq (baseline) (c): Multitask Paraphrase Generation Model (d): Multitask Paraphrase Detection Model. Green lines represent attention weights, in (b), (c), (d). Detailed view of the multitask paraphrase generation and detection model is omitted for simplicity.

# 5 Methods: Seq2seq with Joint Paraphrase Learning

We incorporate auxiliary multi-task learning to the main seq2seq task - learning paraphrase generation (*ParaGen*), paraphrase detection (*ParaDetect*), and a combination of both tasks (*ParaGen + ParaDetect*). These methods work with any task whose inputs and outputs are sequences, on paraphrase-augmented data. The goal of our models is to inject paraphrastic inductive bias to the encoder hidden state - so that when it is passed to the decoder, paraphrase inputs have the same end results.

We achieve this by actively employing natural properties that rise from data augmentation as part of the training objective. First, *ParaGen, ParaDetect, ParaGen + ParaDetect* sample a paraphrase of the input and leverage it to reduce intra-class variance of paraphrases in the representation space. The sampled paraphrase is a term inside each model's respective multi-task objective, which affects the encoded input embedding in directions that reward paraphrastic homogeneity when back-propagated. However, paraphrase sampling is only required during training; at test time, the multi-task portion of the model is discarded, and the input is passed through the seq2seq model only. This is a realistic test scenario that does not require paraphrase identification among test inputs; the expectation is that the multi-task training has optimized the backbone seq2seq model's parameters for generalization at test time.

We introduce notations, with semantic parsing on emrQA as a running example (Fig 1). $x$ is an input utterance (e.g., "Does the patient have a history of leukemia") and $p$ is a paraphrase of it sampled from the training set (e.g., "Is leukemia in his clinical history?"). $y$ is the desired output sequence (e.g. "ConditionEvent ( Leukemia ) or SymptomEvent ( Leukemia )"); mapping from $x$ to $y$ is the *main task*, and $L_t$ is the neagtive-log-likelihood (NLL) loss for this main task. $\hat{y}, \hat{p}$ are output sequence and paraphrase generated by the models. Finally, we note that we regard an attention-based (Luong et al., 2015) seq2seq with a bidirectional LSTM encoder and a LSTM decoder, with the dropout

272

probability set to 0.1 (Srivastava et al., 2014), as the backbone baseline model (Figure 3b).

## 5.1 ParaGen: Multitask Paraphrase Generation Model

Given an input utterance $x$, we sample from the training set one of $x$'s paraphrases, $p$, and learn paraphrase generation from $x$ to $p$ along with the main task. More specifically, from a shared encoder that accepts $x$ as an input, we keep two separately parametrized decoders which respectively produce $\hat{y}$ (main task decoder) and $\hat{p}$ (paraphrase generation decoder) as desired outputs (Figure 3c). The resulting objective is a weighted sum of $L_g$, the loss for paraphrase generation, and $L_t$ (main task objective), defined below:

$$L_{total} = L_t + \alpha L_g \tag{1}$$

where $L_g$ is the NLL loss between $p$ and $\hat{p}$, and $\alpha$ is a hyperparameter for the weighted sum.

## 5.2 ParaDetect: Multitask Paraphrase Detection Model

In this model, we again sample a paraphrase $p$ but learn as the auxiliary task, paraphrase detection - to identify whether $x$ and $p$ are paraphrases by looking at their embeddings $emb_x$ and $emb_p$. We keep the same model structure as the baseline, but we pass $p$ into the same encoder used for the input utterance $x$, to generate $emb_p$, a fixed-length vector representation of $p$. Then, we force $emb_x$ and $emb_p$, vector representations of the two paraphrases, to have high cosine similarity - a criterion popularly used for paraphrase detection methods with input vector similarity (Mihalcca et al., 2006; Milajevs et al., 2014; Fernando and Stevenson, 2008). The resulting objective is a weighted sum of $L_d$, loss for paraphrase detection, and $L_t$, loss for the target task:

$$L_{total} = L_t + \beta L_d \tag{2}$$
$$\text{where}$$

$$L_d = 1 - cos(emb_x, emb_p) = 1 - \frac{emb_x \cdot emb_p}{||emb_x||||emb_p||}$$

and $\beta$ is a hyperparameter for the weighted sum.

## 5.3 Multitask Paraphrase Generation and Detection Model

We propose a combination of both models where we learn both paraphrase generation and detection

as ancillary tasks. The resulting objective is a weighted sum of $L_t, L_g, L_d$:

$$L_{total} = L_t + \alpha(L_g + \beta L_d) \tag{3}$$

where $\alpha, \beta$ are hyperparameters for the weighted sums. We hope to gain both advantages of ParaGen and ParaDetect by summing their objectives.

## 6 Experiments

We evaluate the proposed models over state-of-the-art methods and above existing methods of generalization, on two paraphrase-annotated datasets (emrQA, Overnight) and one that is automatically augmented with noisy paraphrases (CzEng 1.6).

### 6.1 Experiments with Paraphrase Annotated Datasets

We evaluate the proposed models on emrQA and Overnight, with the target task being semantic parsing - mapping English utterances to logical forms (structured representations that uniquely and exactly capture natural language meanings (Fig 1)). We train/test split emrQA with both "naive" and "realistic" (Section 4) schemes, and create four distinct splits for each scheme for fair model evaluation; Overnight has officially released train/test sets (unlike emrQA) so we use the official splits (that are "naive") for comparison with previous work.

**Accuracy Metric**

Our accuracy metric is "exact match" - which only considers model outputs that are identical to the labeled ones as correct. We mention this because "denotation accuracy" - which considers logical forms that return the label answer from the database as correct- has been used in several works on the Overnight dataset. However, there exist many instances in Overnight that can fool denotation accuracy.

In Overnight, there are many quantity-related questions; denotation accuracy can often consider model outputs of quantity-related questions right by chance (Table 2). For example, models often wrongly interpret "less than or equal to $x$" as "$< x$", but this could be considered correct if the database does not contain entries that are exactly $x$ in time, amount, etc (Table 2). For example, in Table 2, given a question "venue of at most two article", the correct gold logical form should contain "$<=$". However, if the database does not contain any venue with exactly two articles, a false positivel logical form that contains "$<$" instead of "$<=$" can

| Domain | Example Question | Gold Logical Form | False Positive Logical Form[*] |
|---|---|---|---|
| Publications | venue of at most two article | (listValue (countComparative (getProperty (singleton en.venue) (string !type)) (reverse (string venue))(string $\leq$)(number 2) (getProperty (en.article) (string !type)))) | (listValue (countComparative (getProperty (singleton en.venue) (string !type)) (reverse (string venue))(string $<$)(number 2) (getProperty (en.article) (string !type)))) |
| Recipes | show me recipes that could be used for one or two meals | (listValue (countComparative (getProperty (singleton en.recipe) (string !type)) (string meal) (string $\leq$) (number 2) (getProperty (en.meal) (string !type)))) | (listValue (countComparative (getProperty (singleton en.recipe) (string !type)) (string meal) (string $\leq$) (number 2) (getProperty (en.meal) (string !type)))) |

Table 2: Example quantitative questions in overnight prone to false positive logical forms under denotation match.

count correct under denotation accuracy. While hard to quantify, many questions in overnight are quantitative, including words such as "at most", "less than", "more than". [2]

Because of such a property, we consider exact match accuracy to be fairer than denotation match accuracy, and used it as our metric; the false positives pointed above cannot happen under exact match accuracy, since it only counts output exactly same as the gold logical form as correct. We also note that there is little worry of such an issue in emrQA, since questions rarely ask for quantitative information.

### 6.1.1 Methods for Comparison

To adequately judge the effect of joint paraphrase learning, we use seq2seq methods that have been established as State-of-the-Art for each dataset as the backbone baseline; proposed joint paraphrase learning is added on top of these backbones. **The same paraphrase augmented dataset is used for the baselines and our proposed models**, since the purpose is to evaluate the effectiveness of our proposed auxiliary objectives.

**Seq2Seq SOTA's** No previous work exists on semantic parsing for emrQA; thus, we establish the first competitive baseline with the copy mechanism (Gu et al., 2016) added on the backbone seq2seq described in Section 5, for copying of medical entities (e.g. *"leukemia"*). For Overnight, we implemented Jia and Liang (2016)'s model as baseline.

**Paraphrase-based Generalization Methods** Our primary goal is to show that active leveraging of paraphrase augmented data in the model gives additional benefits. Thus, we compare our proposed models with Seq2Seq baselines (defined above) on paraphrase-augmented datasets (each input instance in emrQA and Overnight is a paraphrase

of some other instance in the dataset). This comparison proves the effectiveness of the proposed models beyond data augmentation.

We also compare our models with existing paraphrase-based generalization methods that can be used under seq2seq like Gated Average Recurrent Networks (GRAN) (Wieting and Gimpel, 2017) - a GRU with an additional averaging gate - that learn paraphrastic sentence embeddings.

The authors reported that pre-training with their method resulted in performance boost in transfer learning on SemEval tasks. To compare our methods with pre-training via GRAN, we replace the encoder of our baseline seq2seq with a GRAN encoder pre-trained on our tasks' training set, with the GRAN encoder's parameters not frozen.

We also compare with BERT (Devlin et al., 2018) (shown to be powerful in many NLP tasks) fine-tuned on paraphrase detection, which we framed as a sentence pair classification task into paraphrase/ non-paraphrase, applying the procedure in Devlin et al. (2018). For fine-tuning, we constructed the training set with all the paraphrase pairs in the original corpus and added non-paraphrase pairs sampled by the same number. Respectively for emrQA and Overnight, Clinical-BERT (Alsentzer et al., 2019) and 12-layer base BERT (English Wikipedia) were used as base; on both datasets, BERT was fine-tuned well enough to identify paraphrase with around 85% accuracy. For comparison, we took sentence embeddings from the fine-tuned BERT and replaced the encoder with it. We could not compare with end-to-end BERT models, because to our knowledge, no such prior work on semantic parsing exists.

**Pre-trained Word Embeddings.** Since pre-trained word embeddings are known to help generalization, the idea is to evaluate the contributions of the proposed paraphrase model over using standard methods to ensure generalization. We hypothesize two scenarios: (1) when pre-trained embeddings are available for large-scale corpus beyond train-

---

[2]More examples of quantity-related questions that can fool denotation accuracy can be found here: `https://github.com/ysu1989/CrossSemparse/blob/master/data/overnight/recipes/recipes.paraphrases.test.examples`

| Method | emrQA *"naive"* split (random split) | emrQA *"realistic"* split (unseen paraphrases only in test set) |
|---|---|---|
| Baseline: Seq2seq with copy | 85.24% | 54.65% |
| Paraphrase Generation (ParaGen) | 85.87% | 61.97 |
| Paraphrase Detection (ParaDetect) | 85.37% | 62.04% |
| ParaGen + ParaDetect | **86.55%** | **63.75%** |

Table 3: Results on semantic parsing for the emrQA dataset, averaged across four splits.

| Method / Domain | Basketball | Blocks | Calendar | Publications | Recipes | Restaurants | Housing | SocialNetwork |
|---|---|---|---|---|---|---|---|---|
| Baseline: Seq2seq with copy | 82.8% | 39.3% | **59.5%** | 60.2% | 75.0% | 53.3% | 47.1% | 67.6% |
| Paraphrase Generation (ParaGen) | 82.09% | 40.9% | 54.8% | 59.6% | **75.5%** | **53.9%** | **49.2%** | **68.3%** |
| Paraphrase Detection (ParaDetect) | **83.8%** | **42.4%** | 54.2% | 60.9% | 74.5% | 51.5% | 44.4% | **68.3%** |
| ParaGen + ParaDetect | 82.6% | 38.6% | 56.5% | **63.4%** | 70.4% | 52.4% | 45.5% | 67.1% |
| Simple Seq2Seq (Damonte et al.) | 69.6% | 25.1% | 43.5% | 32.9% | 58.3% | 37.3% | 29.6% | 51.2% |
| Transfer Learning (Damonte et al.) | 71.1% | 25.1% | 48.8% | 40.4% | 63.4% | 39.2% | 38.1% | 54.5% |

Table 4: Results on semantic parsing on all domains of the Overnight dataset.

| Method | SP emrQA | SP Overnight (*Publication*) | NMT Eng→Czech |
|---|---|---|---|
| Baseline: Seq2seq with Copy[*] | 54.65% | 60.2 % | 42.77 |
| Baseline + Corpus Word2Vec | 27.66% | 57.1 % | N/A |
| Baseline + Large-Scale Word2Vec | **67.57%** | 44.1% | 42.23 |
| BERT | 52.48% | 26.1% | N/A |
| GRAN | 58.25% | 58.6% | N/A |
| Paraphrase Generation (ParaGen) | 61.97% | 59.6% | **44.29** |
| ParaGen + Corpus Word2Vec | 51.14% | 60.25% | N/A |
| ParaGen + Large-scale Word2Vec | 64.86% | 39.8% | 43.76 |
| Paraphrase Detection (ParaDetect) | 62.04% | 60.9% | 41.77 |
| ParaDetect + Corpus Word2Vec | 46.92% | 57.8% | N/A |
| ParaDetect + Large-scale Word2Vec | 63.02% | 56.5% | 43.90 |
| Para(Gen+Detect) | **63.75%** | **63.4%** | 40.72 |
| Para(Gen+Detect) + Corpus Word2Vec | 53.04% | 60.2% | N/A |
| Para(Gen+Detect) + Large-scale Word2Vec | 66.67% | 51.55% | 41.38 |

Table 5: Results on semantic parsing (SP) for the emrQA dataset ("realistic" split scheme, averaged over 4 splits), Overnight and neural machine translation (NMT) for EngCzech translation. Metrics are exact match and BLEU for respective the first two and the third column.*For neural machine translation, Nematus was used as baseline. Unseen Word acc. denotes the accuracy over validation inputs with tokens that never appeared during training.

ing data (2) when only corpus-trained embeddings are available. As large-scale embeddings, we use clinical word2Vec (Mikolov et al., 2013) trained on all i2b2 (Uzuner et al., 2011) datasets for emrQA, and officially released general English word2vec for Overnight.

### 6.1.2 Results

**emrQA.** For emrQA (Table 3), we can see that the proposed models outperform the baseline under both split schemes, but with a significant gap under the "realistic" split; this shows that our models are capable of robustly generalizing to unseen syntactic variants. We further compare our models with the different generalization methods mentioned (Table 5). ParaGen + ParaDetect is overwhelmingly dominant over other methods When large-scale corpus word embeddings are not available.

In emrQA, there were 338 test inputs with words that never appear during training (such as "considered" in 2nd example of emrQA's Substitution paraphrase in Table 1). These inputs largely determined model performance, with overall accuracy being proportional to accuracy on these. Especially, ParaGen could not capture the topic of the ques-

tion (e.g. medical evaluation, treatment, etc) when specific words were replaced with more general ones (e.g. "diagnosed for" → "considered for"). ParaDetect's error usually occured in mistakenly copying entities.

**Overnight** Across 7 out of 8 domains of Overnight, the best performing model (ParaGen) outperformed baseline up to 3.2% (*Publications*) with 1.6% boost on average (Table 4). We also report results from Damonte et al. (2019), which is an existing work on Overnight with exact match accuracy. With our implementation of Jia and Liang (2016), we achieved a baseline higher than both of the baseline and proposed methods of Damonte et al. (2019). Results across all 8 domains is in Table 4. We further compare our models with different generalization methods. Word2vec was not effective, as in Su and Yan (2017), and pre-training with BERT and GRAN were less effective than Para(Gen+Detect).

**Discussion** Proposed models produced pronounced improvements on emrQA where paraphrases express the multiple ways a physician may phrase information needs. "Has the patient ever been considered for |problem|", "any |problem|

history" involve matching general semantics to that of clinical sub-language. But "considered for" has a broad meaning in the general domain; it is synonymous to "seen for, diagnosed with", collocated with a |clinical problem|. Overnight's paraphrases are open-domain ("which recipes require milk", "which recipes need milk") or require quantitative knowledge ("person that is author of at most two articles", "author of one or two articles" require knowing that there is only "one" between zero and two). This is different from identifying a sub-language meaning of a general phrase.

While joint paraphrase learning cannot learn actual knowledge of a domain (such as quantitative knowledge), it is useful in identifying meanings of general-sense phrases in a specific domain sub-language, that is much needed in clinical settings.

### 6.2 Experiments with Automated Noisy Augmentation

We noisily augmented a subset of CzEng 1.6 with ParaNMT-50M (Wieting and Gimpel, 2018), for training and evaluation on machine translation from English to Czech; because the authors released paraphrases of the English instances of CzEng 1.6 generated from it, we directly used them. We chose the *subtitles* domain from CzEng 1.6 to cover the most open-domain language, which was relatively less covered in the other two datasets (because Overnight has specific domain-specific questions for each domain); we randomly chose 33.33 thousand utterances from CzEng 1.6 *subtitles* and augmented each utterance with 3 more paraphrases. Among the four paraphrases in each group, we randomly assigned one to the test split and the rest to training; the training set consists of roughly 0.1M instances.

We use a state-of-the-art seq2seq model, Nematus (Sennrich et al., 2017), the winning solution for WMT 2017 (one of whose training corpora was CzEng 1.6), as the backbone baseline. The four models were evaluated with and without initialization with general English Word2vec of encoder and decoder parameters. We report the BLEU of all four models in Table 5; we achieved improvement in BLEU by 1.5 in comparison to the baseline, with ParaGen. We further note that the use of Word2vec actually harmed performance.

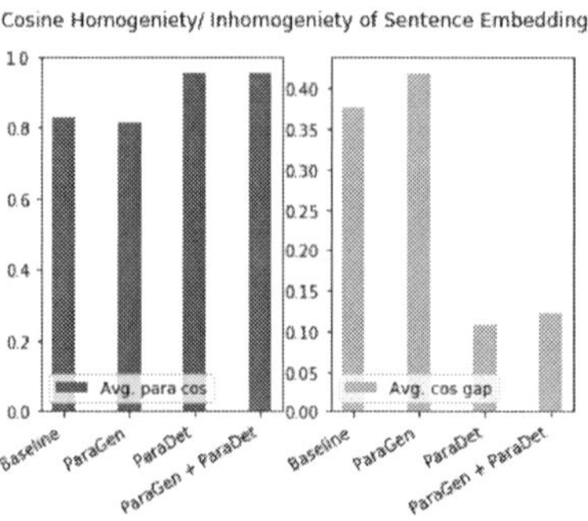


Figure 3: Results on cosine similarity between test question pairs in emrQA. Blue: homogeneity of paraphrases; orange: nonhomogeneity of non-paraphrases.

## 7  Discussion: Cosine Distance Analysis (emrQA)

To understand the contribution of the proposed paraphrase models, we study the cosine similarity between embeddings of sentence pairs, a general metric in textual similarity and paraphrase detection (Agirre et al., 2016; Fern and Stevenson) in Figure 3. We do this by calculating the similarity between the last hidden state of the encoder for a pair of input utterances in the test set, for the four splits of emrQA's "realistic" splitting scheme. We calculate two metrics: (1) the average cosine similarity between pairs of paraphrase utterances (*Avg. para cos*, blue bar in Fig 4) and (2) the average difference between cosine similarity of paraphrase pairs and that of non-paraphrase pairs (*Avg. cos gap*, orange bar in Fig 4). They respectively quantify (1) how *homogenously* paraphrase utterances are embedded as vectors, and (2) how *nonhomogeneously* non-paraphrase utterances are embedded; *high* numbers in both quantities are ideal, if our models behave as intended in the methods section. We observed that ParaDetect achieves noticeably the highest *Avg. para cos*, and ParaGen the highest *Avg. cos gap*; ParaGen + ParaDetect shows something in between the two but closer to ParaDetect. These cosine statistics of embeddings seem to be indicative of model performance. ParaGen + ParaDetect, which embeds both paraphrases homogenously and non-paraphrases nonhomogenously, performs the best in terms of exact match accuracy; the other two models also achieve higher performance than baseline, with much higher *Avg. para cos* and *Avg. cos gap* than baseline.

## 8 Conclusion

We presented a new general seq2seq framework where the main task is trained together with a paraphrase-learning objective to enhance model generalization. We also introduced new splitting schemes that reflect realistic evaluation for practical use. Our proposed approaches outperform the state-of-the-art across three datasets across diverse domains and tasks.

## References


Eneko Agirre, Carmen Banea, Daniel Cer, Mona Diab, Aitor Gonzalez-Agirre, Rada Mihalcea, German Rigau, and Janyce Wiebe. 2016. Semeval-2016 task 1: Semantic textual similarity, monolingual and cross-lingual evaluation. In *Proceedings of the 10th International Workshop on Semantic Evaluation (SemEval-2016)*, pages 497–511, San Diego, California.

Emily Alsentzer, John R. Murphy, Willie Boag, Wei-Hung Weng, Di Jin, Tristan Naumann, and Matthew B. A. McDermott. 2019. Publicly available clinical BERT embeddings. *CoRR*, abs/1904.03323.

Yonatan Belinkov and Yonatan Bisk. 2017. Synthetic and natural noise both break neural machine translation. *arXiv preprint arXiv:1711.02173*.

Jonathan Berant and Percy Liang. 2014. Semantic parsing via paraphrasing. In *Proceedings of the 52nd Annual Meeting of the Association for Computational Linguistics (Volume 1: Long Papers)*, pages 1415–1425, Baltimore, Maryland. Association for Computational Linguistics.

Rahul Bhagat, Eduard Hovy, and Siddharth Patwardhan. 2009. Acquiring paraphrases from text corpora. In *Proceedings of the Fifth International Conference on Knowledge Capture*, K-CAP '09, pages 161–168, New York, NY, USA. ACM.

Rahul Bhagat and Eduard H. Hovy. 2013. What is a paraphrase? *Computational Linguistics*, 39:463–472.

Ondřej Bojar, Ondřej Dušek, Tom Kocmi, Jindřich Libovický, Michal Novák, Martin Popel, Roman Sudarikov, and Dušan Variš. 2016. CzEng 1.6: Enlarged Czech-English Parallel Corpus with Processing Tools Dockered. In *Text, Speech, and Dialogue: 19th International Conference, TSD 2016*, number 9924 in Lecture Notes in Computer Science, pages 231–238, Cham / Heidelberg / New York / Dordrecht / London. Masaryk University, Springer International Publishing.

Antoine Bordes, Jason Weston, and Nicolas Usunier. 2014. Open question answering with weakly supervised embedding models. In *Proceedings of the 2014th European Conference on Machine Learning and Knowledge Discovery in Databases - Volume Part I*, ECMLPKDD'14, pages 165–180, Berlin, Heidelberg. Springer-Verlag.

Chris Callison-Burch, Philipp Koehn, and Miles Osborne. 2006. Improved statistical machine translation using paraphrases. In *Proceedings of the Main Conference on Human Language Technology Conference of the North American Chapter of the Association of Computational Linguistics*, HLT-NAACL '06, pages 17–24, Stroudsburg, PA, USA. Association for Computational Linguistics.

Marco Damonte, Rahul Goel, and Tagyoung Chung. 2019. Practical semantic parsing for spoken language understanding. *CoRR*, abs/1903.04521.

Jacob Devlin, Ming-Wei Chang, Kenton Lee, and Kristina Toutanova. 2018. Bert: Pre-training of deep bidirectional transformers for language understanding.

Li Dong, Jonathan Mallinson, Siva Reddy, and Mirella Lapata. 2017. Learning to paraphrase for question answering. In *Proceedings of the 2017 Conference on Empirical Methods in Natural Language Processing*, pages 875–886, Copenhagen, Denmark. Association for Computational Linguistics.

Li Dong, Furu Wei, Ming Zhou, and Ke Xu. 2015. Question answering over Freebase with multi-column convolutional neural networks. In *Proceedings of the 53rd Annual Meeting of the Association for Computational Linguistics and the 7th International Joint Conference on Natural Language Processing (Volume 1: Long Papers)*, pages 260–269, Beijing, China. Association for Computational Linguistics.

Allyson Ettinger, Rao Sudha, Daumé Hal, and M. Bender Emily. 2017. Towards linguistically generalizable nlp systems: A workshop and shared task. *ArXiv*, abs/1711.01505.

Anthony Fader, Luke Zettlemoyer, and Oren Etzioni. 2013a. Paraphrase-driven learning for open question answering. In *Proceedings of the 51st Annual Meeting of the Association for Computational Linguistics (Volume 1: Long Papers)*, pages 1608–1618, Sofia, Bulgaria. Association for Computational Linguistics.

Anthony Fader, Luke S. Zettlemoyer, and Oren Etzioni. 2013b. Paraphrase-driven learning for open question answering. In *ACL*.

Samuel Fern and Mark Stevenson. A semantic similarity approach to paraphrase detection.

Samuel Fernando and Mark Stevenson. 2008. A semantic similarity approach to paraphrase detection. In *Proceedings of the 11th Annual Research Colloquium of the UK Special Interest Group for Computational Linguistics*, pages 45–52.

Ian.J Goodfellow, Jonathon Shlens, and Christian Szegedy. 2014. Explaining and harnessing adversarial examples. *CoRR*, abs/1412.6572.

Jiatao Gu, Zhengdong Lu, Hang Li, and Victor O.K. Li. 2016. Incorporating copying mechanism in sequence-to-sequence learning. In *Proceedings of the 54th Annual Meeting of the Association for Computational Linguistics (Volume 1: Long Papers)*, pages 1631–1640, Berlin, Germany. Association for Computational Linguistics.

Mohit Iyyer, , John Wieting, Kevin Gimpel, and Luke S. Zettlemoyer. 2018. Adversarial example generation with syntactically controlled paraphrase networks. In *NAACL-HLT*.

Robin Jia and Percy Liang. 2016. Data recombination for neural semantic parsing. In *Proceedings of the 54th Annual Meeting of the Association for Computational Linguistics (Volume 1: Long Papers)*, pages 12–22, Berlin, Germany. Association for Computational Linguistics.

Robin Jia and Percy Liang. 2017. Adversarial examples for evaluating reading comprehension systems. *arXiv preprint arXiv:1707.07328*.

Minh-Thang Luong, Hieu Pham, and Christopher D Manning. 2015. Effective approaches to attention-based neural machine translation. *arXiv preprint arXiv:1508.04025*.

Rada Mihalcea, Courtney Corley, and Carlo Strapparava. 2006. Corpus-based and knowledge-based measures of text semantic similarity. In *Proceedings of the 21st National Conference on Artificial Intelligence - Volume 1*, AAAI'06, pages 775–780. AAAI Press.

Tomas Mikolov, Ilya Sutskever, Kai Chen, Greg S Corrado, and Jeff Dean. 2013. Distributed representations of words and phrases and their compositionality. In *Advances in neural information processing systems*, pages 3111–3119.

Dmitrijs Milajevs, Dimitri Kartsaklis, Mehrnoosh Sadrzadeh, and Matthew Purver. 2014. Evaluating neural word representations in tensor-based compositional settings. In *Proceedings of the 2014 Conference on Empirical Methods in Natural Language Processing (EMNLP)*, pages 708–719, Doha, Qatar. Association for Computational Linguistics.

Jeff Mitchell, Pasquale Minervini, Pontus Stenetorp, and Sebastian Riedel. 2018. Extrapolation in nlp. *arXiv preprint arXiv:1805.06648*.

Anusri Pampari, Preethi Raghavan, Jennifer Liang, and Jian Peng. 2018. emrQA: A large corpus for question answering on electronic medical records. In *Proceedings of the 2018 Conference on Empirical Methods in Natural Language Processing*, pages 2357–2368, Brussels, Belgium. Association for Computational Linguistics.

Rico Sennrich, Orhan Firat, Kyunghyun Cho, Alexandra Birch, Barry Haddow, Julian Hitschler, Marcin Junczys-Dowmunt, Samuel Läubli, Antonio Valerio Miceli Barone, Jozef Mokry, and Maria Nadejde. 2017. Nematus: a toolkit for neural machine translation. In *EACL*.

Minjoon Seo, Aniruddha Kembhavi, Ali Farhadi, and Hananneh Hajishirzi. 2017. Bidirectional attention flow for machine comprehension. In *International Conference on Learning Representations*.

Nitish Srivastava, Geoffrey Hinton, Alex Krizhevsky, Ilya Sutskever, and Ruslan Salakhutdinov. 2014. Dropout: a simple way to prevent neural networks from overfitting. *The Journal of Machine Learning Research*, 15(1):1929–1958.

Yu Su and Xifeng Yan. 2017. Cross-domain semantic parsing via paraphrasing. In *Proceedings of the 2017 Conference on Empirical Methods in Natural Language Processing*, pages 1235–1246, Copenhagen, Denmark. Association for Computational Linguistics.

Ilya Sutskever, Oriol Vinyals, and Quoc V Le. 2014. Sequence to sequence learning with neural networks. In Z. Ghahramani, M. Welling, C. Cortes, N. D. Lawrence, and K. Q. Weinberger, editors, *Advances in Neural Information Processing Systems 27*, pages 3104–3112. Curran Associates, Inc.

Özlem Uzuner, Brett R South, Shuying Shen, and Scott L DuVall. 2011. 2010 i2b2/va challenge on concepts, assertions, and relations in clinical text. *Journal of the American Medical Informatics Association*, 18(5):552–556.

Yushi Wang, Jonathan Berant, and Percy Liang. 2015. Building a semantic parser overnight. In *Proceedings of the 53rd Annual Meeting of the Association for Computational Linguistics and the 7th International Joint Conference on Natural Language Processing (Volume 1: Long Papers)*, pages 1332–1342, Beijing, China. Association for Computational Linguistics.

John Wieting and Kevin Gimpel. 2017. Revisiting recurrent networks for paraphrastic sentence embeddings. *Proceedings of the 55th Annual Meeting of the Association for Computational Linguistics (Volume 1: Long Papers)*.

John Wieting and Kevin Gimpel. 2018. ParaNMT-50M: Pushing the limits of paraphrastic sentence embeddings with millions of machine translations. In *Proceedings of the 56th Annual Meeting of the Association for Computational Linguistics (Volume 1: Long Papers)*, pages 451–462, Melbourne, Australia. Association for Computational Linguistics.

# Appendices

## A   More Details on Types of Paraphrases

We explain on the syntactic variation and synonymous substitution types of paraphrases in more detail. While syntactic variant paraphrases can be similarly identified (by switch of active/ passive tenses or ordering of clauses in Table 1), synonymous substitution paraphrases show different fashion of assumed knowledge across domains/ datasets. emrQA(Pampari et al.)'s paraphrases represent the multiple ways a physician may phrase their information needs; the substitution paraphrases acknowledge the clinical sublanguage of equating "considered for" with "seen for, diagnosed with" when collocated with a |clinical problem|. In overnight (Wang et al.), many substitution paraphrases are regarding quantitative knowledge., while hard to exactly quantify the proportion. While some are easier to identify ("more than two" $\equiv$ "greater than two"), others involve some numerical knowledge that models trained on non-numerical benchmark corpora may lack ("at least two" $\equiv$ "one or two") - for example, that there is only "one" between "zero" and "two".

## B    Implementation and Training Details

### B.1    Fine-tuning BERT for Paraphrase Detection

We chose learning rate among $\{2e-5, 3e-5, 5e-5\}$, and trained for 5 epochs, stopping early at the highest validation accuracy.

### B.2    Hyperparameter Selection

Hyperparameters consist of learning rate and $\alpha, \beta$ from Section 5. They were grid-searched iteratively; first, learning rate for the baseline model was grid-searched, and then $\alpha, \beta$ for each of the proposed models were grid-searched, with the learning rate fixed to what was found for the baseline. Finally, each of the proposed models' learning rates were grid-searched, with $\alpha, \beta$ fixed. emrQA's hyperparmeters were selected among $\alpha \in \{1, 0.1, 0.01\}, \beta \in \{1.25, 1, 0.75, 0.5\}$, learning rate $\in \{5e - 4, 1e - 3, 1.5e - 3\}$; Overnight's hyperparameters among $\alpha \in \{1, 0.1, 0.01\}, \beta \in \{1.25, 1, 0.75, 0.5\}$, learning rate $\in \{1e - 4, 3e - 4, 5e - 4\}$; Finally, CzEng 1.6's were among $\alpha \in \{1, 0.1, 0.01\}, \beta \in \{1.25, 1, 0.75, 0.5\}$, learning rate $\in \{1e - 4, 3e - 4, 5e - 4, 7.5e - 4\}$.

We also note that for each of emrQA, Overnight, and CzEng 1.6, models were trained up to 20, 50, and 100 epochs with early stopping at the epoch that returns best validation accuracy.

### B.3    Implementation Details

All code was implemented with PyTorch. Average runtime of the experiments for was 1.5~2 hours per run for emrQA, and ~30 minutes for Overnight.

# On the diminishing return of labeling clinical reports


**Jean-Baptiste Lamare**
jblamare@enlitic.com

**Tobi Olatunji**
tobi@enlitic.com

**Li Yao**
li@enlitic.com



## Abstract

Ample evidence suggests that better machine learning models may be steadily obtained by training on increasingly larger datasets on natural language processing (NLP) problems from non-medical domains. Whether the same holds true for medical NLP has by far not been thoroughly investigated. This work shows that this is indeed not always the case. We reveal the somehow counter-intuitive observation that performant medical NLP models may be obtained with small amount of labeled data, quite the opposite to the common belief, most likely due to the domain specificity of the problem. We show quantitatively the effect of training data size on a fixed test set composed of two of the largest public chest x-ray radiology report datasets on the task of abnormality classification. The trained models not only make use of the training data efficiently, but also outperform the current state-of-the-art rule-based systems by a significant margin.


## 1 Introduction

It is commonly believed that neural network classifier performance increases as more data with labels are provided, if its capacity is properly optimized and regularized (Banko and Brill, 2001a). In natural language processing (NLP), pretraining on large TB-scale text corpora has become the standard practice in recent years with the emergence of BERT (Devlin et al., 2018) and GPT-2 (Radford et al., 2019), before being fine-tuned on task-specific targets. Furthermore, variants of top deep leanirng (DL) architectures have dominated several language task benchmarks due to their superior computational scalability and statistical capacity (Rajpurkar et al., 2017). Modern neural networks typically employ a large number of parameters, offering large capacity and flexibility in capturing highly non-linear linguistic phenomena. As a model family with low bias and high variance,

it naturally requires much more data to avoid the pitfall of overfitting.

The success of billion-parameter DL models trained on billion-word datasets have drastically transformed the landscape of NLP. Does the same trend hold true in the specific domain of medicine? After all, it is reasonable to expect a significant syntactic and semantic gap between everyday conversations (twitter feeds, news articles, blog posts) and formal medical vocabulary spoken or written in the context of clinical medicine. In fact, it typically requires decades of specialized medical training to excel in this highly demanding field. Such specialization is thus expected for any machine learning model that is trained to perform medical tasks, whether it is information retrieval (Goeuriot et al., 2016), conversational agent (Laranjo et al., 2018), or disease extraction and classification (Chen et al., 2018).

This work investigates the impact of corpus size on the performance of state-of-the-art DL models on multi-label medical report classification tasks. We empirically demonstrate some of the unique properties of the medical language in clinical reports and how such domain-specific features lead to a surprisingly different scaling behavior as the training data size increases. Our main results on two public chest x-ray radiology report datasets consistently suggest that some of the classification tasks do not require copious amount of labeled data to achieve good performance, mostly due to the limited linguistic variation in its domain. Although per category analyses reveal slight variations, this phenomenon is consistently demonstrated across four DL model families presented. Performance between 6,000 and 30,000 reports remain counter-intuitively comparable, demonstrating diminishing returns in labeling effort. In addition, we show that, with a relatively small amount of data, DL models outperform both our private and state-of-




*Proceedings of the 3rd Clinical Natural Language Processing Workshop*, pages 280–290
November 19, 2020. ©2020 Association for Computational Linguistics

the-art (SOTA) public ruled-based systems by a large margin.

## 2 Related work

**Medical computer vision (CV)** Despite the obvious distinction between medical reports and medical images, the two modalities typically appear hand-in-hand in clinical environment. Diagnostic impression and recommendation of imaging studies are typically rendered in the format of structured and unstructured texts. For such reason, reports have become a popular and inexpensive way to derive large amount of labels for machine learning CV tasks at scale (Attaluri et al., 2018; Olatunji et al., 2019; Olatunji and Yao, 2019). In fact, labels obtained this way have been widely used to form large training set for fundamental CV tasks such as triage, detection and segmentation in Yao et al. (2017, 2018, 2019). Therefore, accurate medical NLP brings significant benefit to the development of CV models as a whole.

**Non-medical NLP** The early work of Banko and Brill (2001b) demonstrates a linear performance gain of an NLP disambiguation task when doubling the amount of training corpus on simple machine learning (ML) linear classifiers. Recent NLP advance pushes the envelop much further by leveraging web-scale data – for instance, the Common Crawl project [1] that produces 20TB of textual data from the Internet each month. To cope with such a scale, large models with billions of parameters based on the variants of BERT (Devlin et al., 2018), MT-DNN (Liu et al., 2019b), GPT-2 (Radford et al., 2019), XL-Net (Yang et al., 2019) have emerged with sometimes near-human performance on selected language tasks. It is commonly recognized that better performance can be achieved by training larger models on larger datasets.

**Non-ML medical NLP** Although traditional NLP performance has improved on medical tasks over time, it doesn't lend itself to the scale of significant performance improvements seen with models trained on datasets several terabytes in size (Lee et al., 2019b). Results shown in a 1999 paper (Taira and Soderland, 1999) on statistical NLP for medical reports, a 2006 paper (Meystre and Haug, 2006) extracting predefined problems from clinical notes, a 2013 paper mining FDA drug labels (Li et al., 2013), and a 2019 dataset using Chexpert

labeler (Irvin et al., 2019) demonstrate gradual performance improvements that still reflect the high precision, low recall phenomenon observed with non-ML medical NLP tools.

**ML medical NLP** Nonetheless, machine learning based NLP models have been explored where a reasonable amount of electronic medical records (EMR) are obtained privately. Chen et al. (2018) uses a convolutional neural network (CNN) trained on 2500 thoracic computed tomography (CT) reports to identify pulmonary embolism findings with high AUCs. Lee et al. (2019a) uses a corpus of 3032 musculoskeletal x-ray reports to train a recurrent neural network (RNN) to identify fracture and non-fracture cases with high precision and recall. The work from Rajkomar et al. (2018) represents one of the largest studies on EMR where free-text notes from doctors, nurses and other providers from 216K patients are used to predict mortality, readmission, and length of hospital stay. Liu et al. (2019a) uses hundreds of thousands of chest x-ray reports, but focuses on the task of report generation instead of classification.

**Corpus Size** Roberts (2016) evaluates the impact of combining 6 clinical and non-clinical corpora on similarity of word embeddings in the clinical domain. Results showed task-dependent performance variations. A study from Ahmed and Mehler (2018) on NER in a low resource language showed improved performance when 3 datasets were combined. In line with the dominant trend, Banko and Brill (2001a) applied machine learning techniques to the task of confusion set disambiguation, using three orders of magnitude more training data than previously been applied to the problem. They significantly reduced the error rate simply by adding more training data. Even with a billion words, the learners continued to benefit from additional training data. In contrast, Curran and Osborne (2002) confronts this claim showing that although convergence behaviour on unigram probability estimates improves when using up to one billion words, for some words, no such convergence occurs.

In contrast to the aforementioned studies, this work focuses on analyzing the comparative performance of NLP classifiers on radiology reports in a multi-class setting with respect to different amounts of training data.

---

[1] http://commoncrawl.org

# 3 Experiments

The primary goal of this study is to empirically examine the impact of increasing and decreasing the size of the training data to the quality of DL models produced, and to compare their performance with state-of-the-art rule-based methods. Thus in all following experiments, we freeze the test set while using different sizes of training and validation set to tune the DL models. In particular, we establish incrementally bigger training data by randomly sampling a larger percentage from the entire training set. As a baseline for performance comparison, we also introduce two rule-based classifiers whose performance is independent of the training data sizes.

## 3.1 Dataset

**Data**  Our data consists of several datasets coming from different international sources, both public and private. On the public side, we use a subset of the MIMIC-CXR dataset (Johnson et al., 2019), a large dataset of 377,110 chest x-rays associated with 227,827 imaging studies and corresponding radiology reports. The reports are also provided with labels obtained with the CheXpert labeling tool (Irvin et al., 2019). We also incorporate the OpenI dataset (Demner-Fushman et al., 2012), a collection of 7,470 chest x-rays with 3,955 radiology reports. On the private side, we add about 21,000 reports from our in-house chest x-ray datasets as additional training set.

**Splits**  We only use public datasets to create the test set. First we take the original MIMIC-CXR test split. In addition, we randomly sample half of the OpenI dataset to be used in the test split. We then use the remaining 33,000 reports for training and validation, randomly sampling 10% of it for validation and leaving about 30,000 reports for training. The number of reports per split and provenance are available in table 1.

**Labels**  A team of experts manually provided labels from scratch on the full train/validation/test dataset. Each report was labeled by a single expert, following a private labeling scheme. We also modified the Chexpert labeling scheme to align with label definitions and labeling guidelines used by our team of experts. We merged *Consolidation* and *Pneumonia* reflecting the significant visual overlap between both labels, we excluded *Edema*, *Cardiomegaly* and *No Finding*. These modifications make our and Chexpert's labeling schemes comparable. We show in Table 2 the label counts for all of the abnormalities in the training and test sets.

## 3.2 Training

**DL models**  We train four types of NLP multi-label classifiers, including three relatively small architectures without pretraining and a bigger pretrained BERT model:

- Bidirectional LSTM with attention and dropout. We use word embeddings of size 128 and 128 units.

- CNN (Kim, 2014) following the cited architecture with embedding size 128, 128 filters, and kernel sizes 3, 4 and 5.

- RCNN (Lai et al., 2015) also with embeddings of size 128 and 128 units.

- BERT (Devlin et al., 2018), with the pretrained weights from BioBERT (Lee et al., 2019b)

All models were trained with the Adam optimizer for 20 epochs, with early stopping and a learning rate of 1e-3 except for BERT which had a 5e-5 learning rate (default values). Before training, reports were cleaned by removing headers and footers using keywords. For non-BERT models, reports were preprocessed with the NLTK tokenizer [2], while for BERT we used the original WordPiece tokenizer (Wu et al., 2016).

**Non-DL rule-based medical NLP baselines**  Domain-specific heavily-engineered hand-crafted rule-based NLP tools yield binary outputs for the presence (1) or absence (0) of abnormalities (Olatunji et al., 2019) (Hassanpour and Langlotz, 2016) (Attaluri et al., 2018). SOTA tools typically include additional capabilities that express the associated degree of uncertainty in the report. (Peng et al., 2018), (Rajpurkar et al., 2017) (Savova et al., 2010). This is primarily driven by the high cost of collecting expert-level human annotations. Bootstrapping labels from radiology reports has therefore gained significant attention in recent years. As illustrated in (Olatunji et al., 2019), these hand-crafted tools generally suffer from low recall, a problem we promptly address. Our domain-specific rule-based NLP tool automatically extracts labels from reports in 3 main steps – extraction,

---

[2] https://www.nltk.org/

| Source | Training | Validation | Testing | Total per source |
|---|---|---|---|---|
| MIMIC-CXR | 9,349 | 1,039 | 3,088 | 13,476 |
| OpenI | 1,676 | 186 | 1,862 | 3,724 |
| Private data | 18,900 | 2,100 | 0 | 21,000 |
| Total per split | 29,925 | 3,325 | 4,950 | 38,200 |

Table 1: Number of reports per source and split in the full dataset. The ablation sampling was then done with random sampling out of the training/validation set while the test set is frozen.

| | Training | | Test-MIMIC | | Test-OpenI | |
|---|---|---|---|---|---|---|
| | + | - | + | - | + | - |
| atelectasis | 6,804 | 23,121 | 1,062 | 2,026 | 173 | 1,689 |
| consolidation/pneumonia | 7,178 | 22,747 | 721 | 2,367 | 115 | 1,747 |
| enlarged cardiomediastinum | 5,100 | 24,825 | 1,196 | 1,892 | 215 | 1,647 |
| fracture | 1,857 | 28,068 | 182 | 2,906 | 53 | 1,809 |
| lung lesion | 2,875 | 27,050 | 215 | 2,873 | 252 | 1,610 |
| lung opacity | 10,581 | 19,344 | 851 | 2,237 | 730 | 1,132 |
| pleural effusion | 6,582 | 23,343 | 1,293 | 1,795 | 90 | 1,772 |
| pmneumothorax | 1,057 | 28,868 | 90 | 2,998 | 12 | 1,850 |
| pleural other | 1,987 | 27,938 | 194 | 2,894 | 34 | 1,828 |
| support devices | 9,789 | 20,136 | 1,278 | 1,810 | 169 | 1,693 |

Table 2: Label counts for all 10 of the selected abnormalities

classification and aggregation– similar to Chexpert (Irvin et al., 2019). Classification (Negation and Uncertainty detection) rules were also designed on the universal dependency parse of the report. We, however pursue alternate strategies for mention extraction, negation, uncertainty detection and aggregation that yield high recall and comparable precision, like Olatunji and Yao (2019).

**Evaluation metric**   Unlike rule-based non-DL methods that predict directly a discrete output for each abnormality (e.g., 1 for existence and 0 for absence), DL models output a continuous score indicating the probability of its presence. Typically one needs to decide on binarization threshold to convert DL outputs to discrete decisions which requires additional domain or application specific prior, especially in the field of medical diagnosis where true positives and false negatives are associated with different risk factors. Without such information a priori, one could still use threshold-independent metrics to evaluate model performance. Therefore, for this work, we choose precision recall curve (PRC) and area under precision recall curve (AUC-PR). Recall is equivalent to the standard sensitivity metric in medicine. Precision is more sensitive to false positives than the commonly used specificity when there are large amount of easy-to-classify negatives.

## 4   Results

### 4.1   Global Results Analysis

A quantitative summary using the AUC-PR can be found in table 3 for all four DL models. We also show some of the Precision-Recall curves as well as the rule-based baselines in Figure 1. Contrary to the general trend of performance increase with dataset size, the results demonstrate an interesting phenomenon. Despite the fact that the full dataset size is 30,000, by no means comparable to datasets with billions of tokens, 4 different model architectures (CNN, RNN, RCNN, BioBERT) achieve over 0.94 overall AUC-PR on the MIMIC test set, outperforming SOTA held by domain-specific handcrafted rule-based systems. As seen in Table 3, performance remains comparable as dataset size drops from 100% to about 20% where AUC-PRs drop below 0.90, at which point DL algorithms start to approach the performance of domain specific rule-based tools.

This is counter-intuitive. Without rigorously investigating the effect of dataset size, dominant rule-based systems and ML benchmarks seem to suggest medical NLP is a more difficult task. Our findings suggest otherwise. Additionally, a 2001 study (Campbell and Johnson, 2001) comparing syntactic complexity in medical and non-medical corpora shows that the syntax of medical language shows less variation than non-medical language and is likely simpler.

Our experiments demonstrate that with only about 6000 reports (20% of the data), multiple DL model architectures achieve and sustain micro AUC-PR over 0.90 across multiple label categories while surpasses the non-DL SOTA baselines.

On the OpenI test set, results are slightly worse across the board for DL but still conform to the general trend. It is important to note that performance of the rule based method remains fairly consistent despite the obvious drop in DL performance. This highlights one of the uncelebrated strengths of non-ML medical NLP.

### 4.2  Per Category Analysis

In Figures 2, 3, 4 and 5, we show the Precision-Recall curves with different model architectures and dataset sizes for 8 of the 10 labels due to space limitation. The two labels that we do not show are *Enlarged Cardiomediastinum* and *Pleural Effusion* which are two of the best performing labels, with AUC-PRs of 0.92 and 0.97 respectively with BERT and 2% of the data. A critical look at per category analysis as presented in the different graphs reveals a trend consistent with our intution about the problem. AUC-PR is poor below 5% of the data for categories like *Lung Lesion* (nodules), *Pneumothorax, Consolidation, Pleural Other*, and *Fracture* perform poorly while being relatively higher for other categories. This contrasts with performance on categories like *Support Devices, Lung Opacity* and *Atelectasis*. This trend reflects the ease with which the models are able to understand these concepts and disambiguate them. There are a number of possible explanations for these trends with some examples in Table 4 below.

- These hard categories are typically described syntactically and semantically with a lot of uncertainty or hedging in reports, making it difficult to determine if the concept is being affirmed or negated. The reporting radiologists is unclear as to if the abnormality in question is present or absent. The report typically requests further confirmatory investigations.

- These hard categories reflect the inherent difficulty with visually identifying these cate-

gories on an image. For example, a *Pneumothorax* is typically small and located in the crowded lung apex area. *Lung lesions* exist on a spectrum from focal to diffuse or multifocal, making their descriptions less consistent in reports.

- Some specific categories are commonly conflated because of significant visual similarity. A known pair that reflects this phenomenon is *Collapse/Consolidation*. This expression is very common in reports.

- *Pleural Other* is a catch-all category for an unspecified number of abnormalities involving the pleural cavity. There may not be sufficient examples of each of the patterns. This pattern stays consistent even when trained with the fine-tuned BioBERT model. Vague problem definition caps the performance of even the best DL models.

- *Fracture* also represents the combination of a wide range of syntactically inconsistent abnormalities ranging from gross rib to subtle senile or pathologic spine fractures. A more precise definition (for example disambiguating fracture types) may likely improve performance on this label.

### 4.3  Effect of model architecture and pretraining

Figure 6 shows the comparison of the model performance across all four architectures on 5% of the data and the full dataset. Across the selected model architectures, performance is comparable at 100% of the data. As training dataset shrinks, important distinctions begin to emerge. The intuition here is that the maxpooling in the CNNs (CNN, RCNN) serve as efficient keyword detectors even with small data, whereas the LSTM, despite the attention mechanism, struggles to match this performance because it requires a lot more data to learn how to identify important keywords from the entire sequence in the forward and backward directions. The RCNN outperforms the CNN because of the additional recurrence on top of pooling capabilities. BioBERT however holds steady over 0.90 even at 2% of the data. This pattern reflects the extensive clinical, but also English knowledge contained in the BioBERT model carried over from pretraining tasks on large clinical corpus. The

| Training data | Test-MIMIC | | | | Test-OpenI | | | |
| Percentage | RNN | CNN | RCNN | BERT | RNN | CNN | RCNN | BERT |
|---|---|---|---|---|---|---|---|---|
| 1% | 0.562 | 0.650 | 0.717 | 0.878 | 0.332 | 0.461 | 0.543 | 0.788 |
| 2% | 0.653 | 0.745 | 0.821 | 0.920 | 0.423 | 0.530 | 0.677 | 0.900 |
| 5% | 0.693 | 0.874 | 0.902 | 0.918 | 0.492 | 0.749 | 0.865 | 0.905 |
| 10% | 0.819 | 0.925 | 0.928 | 0.933 | 0.653 | 0.875 | 0.916 | 0.928 |
| 20% | 0.902 | 0.940 | 0.937 | 0.928 | 0.852 | 0.924 | 0.926 | 0.929 |
| 50% | 0.938 | 0.948 | 0.946 | 0.944 | 0.914 | 0.928 | 0.938 | 0.942 |
| 100% | 0.941 | 0.948 | 0.950 | 0.949 | 0.927 | 0.937 | 0.950 | 0.956 |

Table 3: AUC-PR evolution on the test sets with different dataset sizes

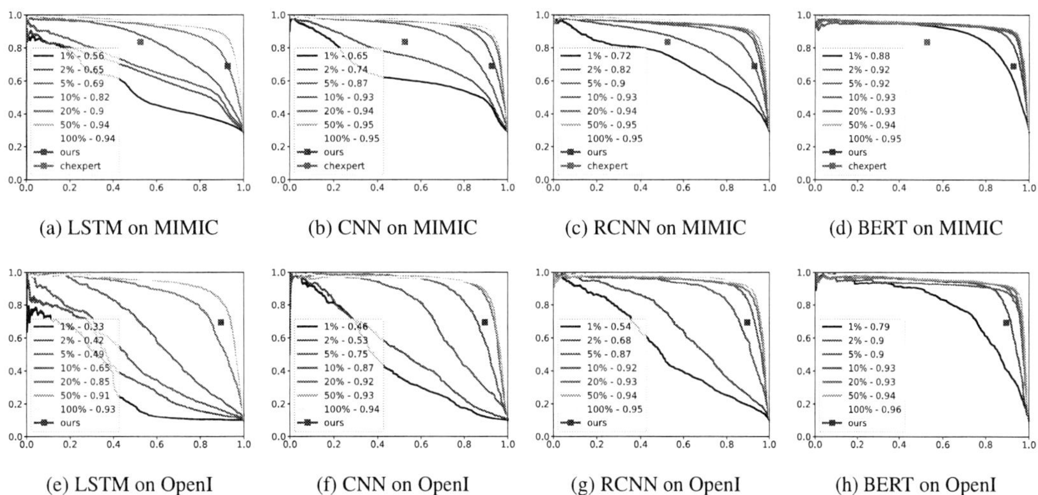

(a) LSTM on MIMIC  (b) CNN on MIMIC  (c) RCNN on MIMIC  (d) BERT on MIMIC

(e) LSTM on OpenI  (f) CNN on OpenI  (g) RCNN on OpenI  (h) BERT on OpenI

Figure 1: PR curves on MIMIC (first row) and OpenI (second row) test sets with different data sizes and comparison with rule-based performance. As commonly shown, the y axis is Precision while the x axis is Recall.

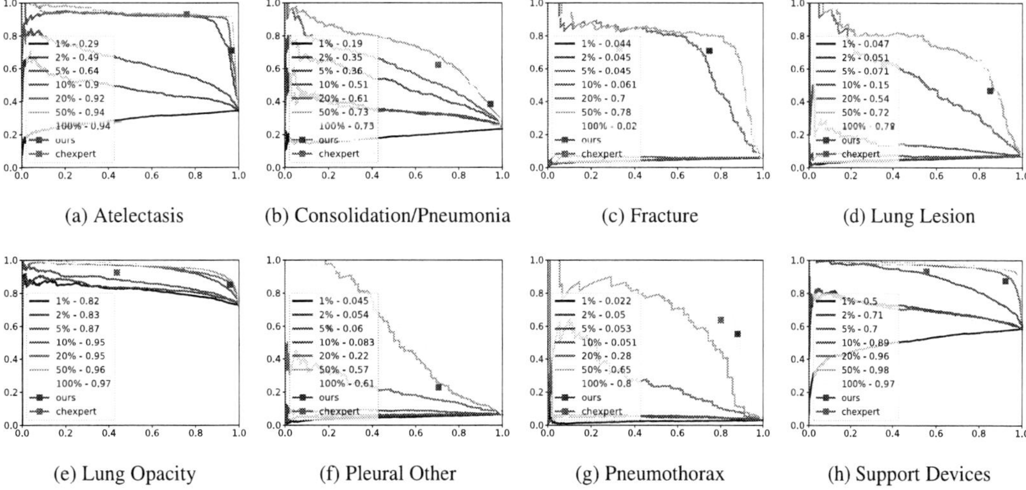

(a) Atelectasis  (b) Consolidation/Pneumonia  (c) Fracture  (d) Lung Lesion

(e) Lung Opacity  (f) Pleural Other  (g) Pneumothorax  (h) Support Devices

Figure 2: LSTM per-label PR curves on MIMIC test set with different data sizes and comparison with rule-based performance. As commonly shown, the y axis is Precision while the x axis is Recall. We can clearly see the distinction between easy labels and more difficult ones. However, the easiness depends not only on the label itself, but also on how many positive examples exist in the dataset. Finally, we can also notice that with 20% of the data, the LSTM model outperforms the rule-based baseline for most labels.

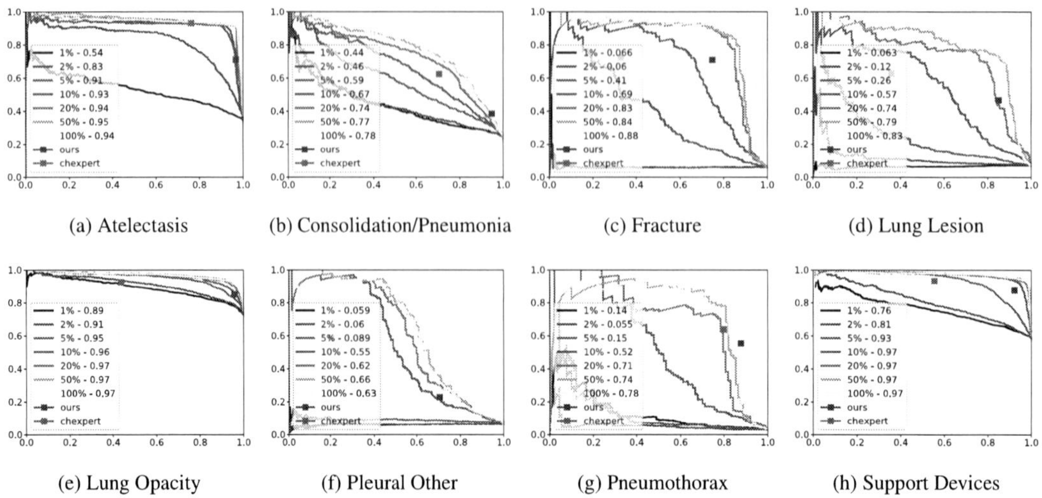

(a) Atelectasis     (b) Consolidation/Pneumonia     (c) Fracture     (d) Lung Lesion

(e) Lung Opacity     (f) Pleural Other     (g) Pneumothorax     (h) Support Devices

Figure 3: CNN per-label PR curves on MIMIC test set with different data sizes and comparison with rule-based performance. As commonly shown, the y axis is Precision while the x axis is Recall. The results are similar to the LSTM, except that the CNN model seems to be able to learn from a small amount of data with more confidence. This is probably due to the ability of the model to focus on keywords through the max pooling operation.

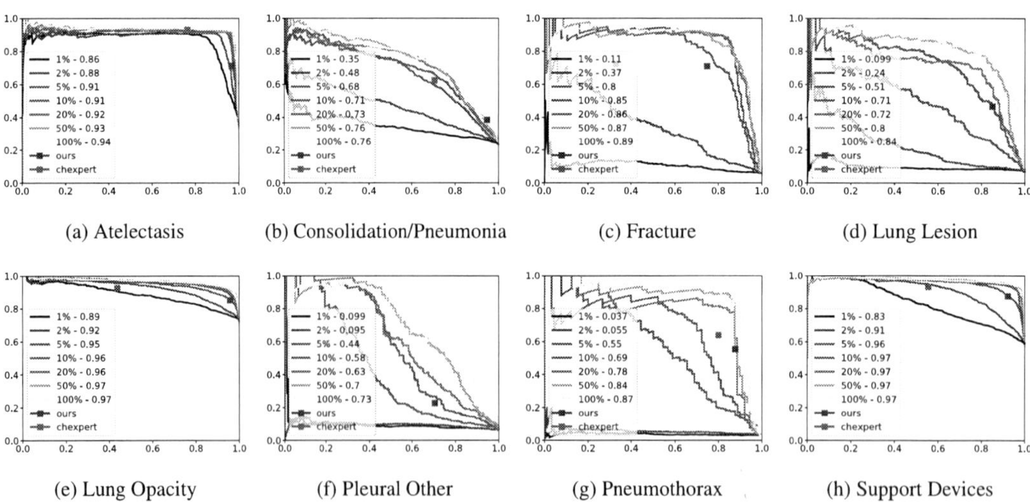

(a) Atelectasis     (b) Consolidation/Pneumonia     (c) Fracture     (d) Lung Lesion

(e) Lung Opacity     (f) Pleural Other     (g) Pneumothorax     (h) Support Devices

Figure 4: RCNN per-label PR curves on MIMIC test set with different data sizes and comparison with rule-based performance. As commonly shown, the y axis is Precision while the x axis is Recall. Just like the previous models, the RCNN outperforms the rule-base baseline with 20% of the data, and obtains a better performance than other models with a small amount of labels.

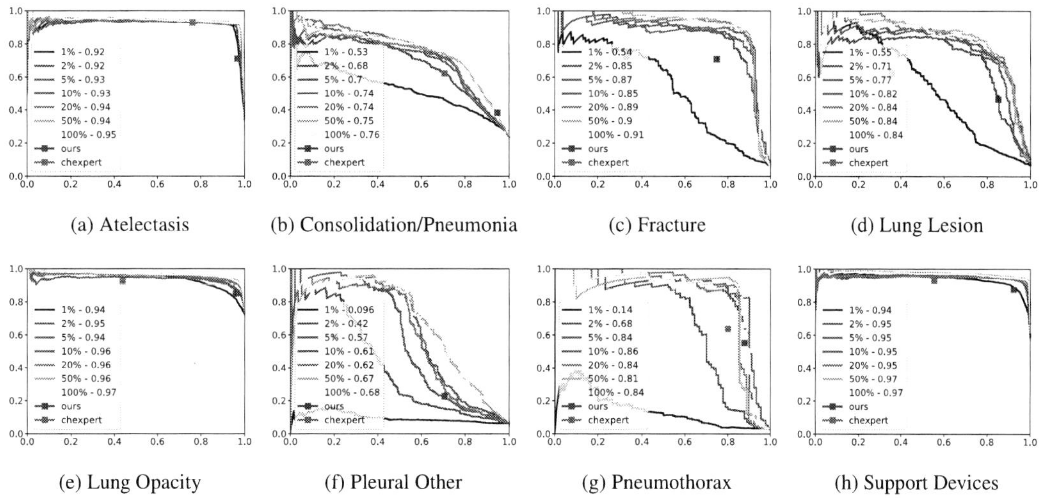

(a) Atelectasis  (b) Consolidation/Pneumonia  (c) Fracture  (d) Lung Lesion

(e) Lung Opacity  (f) Pleural Other  (g) Pneumothorax  (h) Support Devices

Figure 5: BERT per-label PR curves on MIMIC test set with different data sizes and comparison with rule-based performance. As commonly shown, the y axis is Precision while the x axis is Recall. We see here the power of the model size, architecture and pretraining. BERT learns even faster than all of the previous models and outperforms the rule-base baseline with often less than 10% of the data.

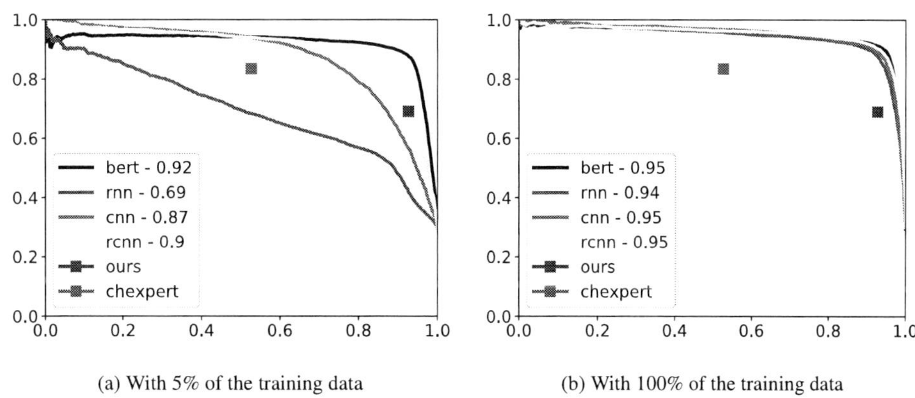

(a) With 5% of the training data  (b) With 100% of the training data

Figure 6: PR curves on the MIMIC test set for each model and comparison with rule-based performance

knowledge proves useful even at 1% of the data where the RNN, trained from scratch, does slightly better than a coin toss on MIMIC, and far worse on OpenI.

### 4.4 Effect of the ratio of positive reports

The number of reports itself is not the unique influence on the performance of the model. As we discussed previously, it also heavily depends on the labels and their definition, as well as the model architecture and its pretraining. We tackle in this paragraph another important element, the ratio of positive reports for each label. Labeling 6,000 reports will not help the model if all of them are negative for the label we are interested in. Figure 7

shows a different take on the curves that we have previously shown. Instead of highlighting the impact of the number of reports on the performance of the model, we plot instead the impact of the number of positive reports for each label. This is particularly important because each label having its own definition means that: i) the labels are not equally likely to be present in a random subset of the data and ii) they may not need the same amount of training data, depending on their difficulty. Figure 7 shows once again that some labels are more difficult than others. Additionally, some labels require a smaller amount of data for the performance to converge. However, these curves allow us to quantitatively conclude that for this task, 600 positive

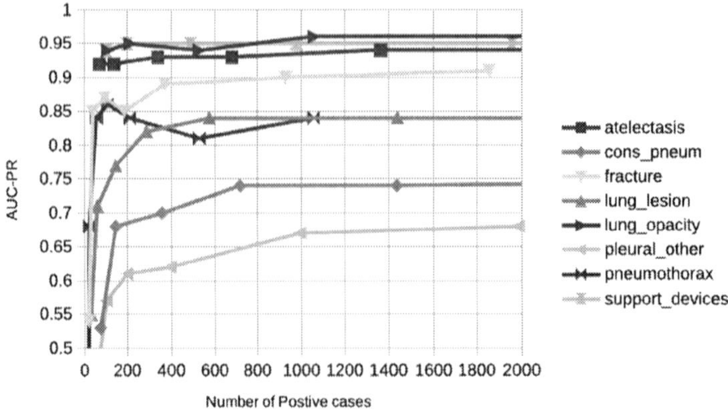

Figure 7: AUC-PR curves of the BioBERT model with increasing number of positive cases for each label. The right side of the curves are cropped in order to focus on the area of change.

| |
|---|
| Two focal areas of subsegmental **collapse/consolidation** in the left upper lobe most likely infective in nature rather than pulmonary embolus or inhaled foreign body. |
| There is a small calcific opacity at the right pulmonary subapical area which is consistent with a granuloma. There is pleural thickening at the lateral aspect of the basal right hemithorax. There is no current evidence of pleural effusion and there is no consolidation. |
| 9-mm opacity just to the right of the trachea is probably a vessel on-end, although could also be a nodule. There may be a trace right pleural effusion on the lateral view. No large pleural effusion or pneumothorax. |

Table 4: Report examples from the training set used in this study. They are reports dictated by radiologists and transcribed thereafter by technicians. All reports refer to chest x-rays studies.

reports per label seems to lead to an early performance saturation regardless of abnormality types. Adding more positive cases beyond this boundary leads to diminishing returns.

### 4.5 Generalization to other tasks

Finally, we want to mention some limitations to our conclusions. While we believe that these findings hold true for any kind of classification on radiology reports (not just chest X-ray), radiology reports only represent a subset of the clinical text data. They are written with a clear objective in mind, sometimes using templates and thus resulting in a smaller vocabulary than random free text. Additionally, if the task was Named Entity Recognition (NER) instead of classification for example, then the results might be slightly different. However, we believe that the main reason behind our findings lies in the uniqueness of clinical data. Clinical data is based on well defined and documented knowledge and experience, therefore containing highly templated syntactic and semantic patterns compared with casual conversations. Due to this nature, we think that our conclusions would still be valid to a large extent in a different clinical NLP context provided that the choice of pretraining and finetuning methods is appropriate.

## 5  Conclusion

The intuition from low resource languages and the general non-medical domain suggests sustained performance improvement with larger datasets. We seek to answer the lingering question about how much data is considered as sufficient in classifying clinical texts and show that the necessary corpus size varies with the complexity of the specific category but to a far less degree than what has been previously thought. With less than 6,000 labeled reports, DL models are able to yield comparable performance with using 30,000 reports on a multilabel classification problem, demonstrating the counter-intuitive effect of diminishing returns from expert labeling efforts.

## References

Sajawel Ahmed and Alexander Mehler. 2018. Resource-size matters: Improving neural named entity recognition with optimized large corpora. In *2018 17th IEEE International Conference on Machine Learning and Applications (ICMLA)*, pages 919–924. IEEE.

Nithya Attaluri, Ahmed Nasir, Carolynne Powe, Harold Racz, Ben Covington, Li Yao, Jordan Prosky, Eric Poblenz, Tobi Olatunji, and Kevin Lyman. 2018. Efficient and accurate abnormality mining from radiology reports with customized false positive reduction. *arXiv preprint arXiv:1810.00967.*

Michele Banko and Eric Brill. 2001a. Mitigating the paucity-of-data problem: Exploring the effect of training corpus size on classifier performance for natural language processing. In *Proceedings of the first international conference on Human language technology research*, pages 1–5. Association for Computational Linguistics.

Michele Banko and Eric Brill. 2001b. Scaling to very very large corpora for natural language disambiguation. In *Proceedings of the 39th Annual Meeting on Association for Computational Linguistics*, ACL '01, page 26–33, USA. Association for Computational Linguistics.

David A Campbell and Stephen B Johnson. 2001. Comparing syntactic complexity in medical and non-medical corpora. In *Proceedings of the AMIA Symposium*, page 90. American Medical Informatics Association.

Matthew C Chen, Robyn L Ball, Lingyao Yang, Nathaniel Moradzadeh, Brian E Chapman, David B Larson, Curtis P Langlotz, Timothy J Amrhein, and Matthew P Lungren. 2018. Deep learning to classify radiology free-text reports. *Radiology*, 286(3):845–852.

James R Curran and Miles Osborne. 2002. A very very large corpus doesn't always yield reliable estimates. In *proceedings of the 6th conference on Natural language learning-Volume 20*, pages 1–6. Association for Computational Linguistics.

Dina Demner-Fushman, Sameer Antani, Matthew Simpson, and George R Thoma. 2012. Design and development of a multimodal biomedical information retrieval system. *Journal of Computing Science and Engineering*, 6(2):168–177.

Jacob Devlin, Ming-Wei Chang, Kenton Lee, and Kristina Toutanova. 2018. Bert: Pre-training of deep bidirectional transformers for language understanding. *arXiv preprint arXiv:1810.04805.*

Lorraine Goeuriot, Gareth JF Jones, Liadh Kelly, Henning Müller, and Justin Zobel. 2016. Medical information retrieval: introduction to the special issue. *Information Retrieval Journal*, 19(1-2):1–5.

Saeed Hassanpour and Curtis P Langlotz. 2016. Information extraction from multi-institutional radiology reports. *Artificial intelligence in medicine*, 66:29–39.

Jeremy Irvin, Pranav Rajpurkar, Michael Ko, Yifan Yu, Silviana Ciurea-Ilcus, Chris Chute, Henrik Marklund, Behzad Haghgoo, Robyn Ball, Katie Shpanskaya, et al. 2019. Chexpert: A large chest radiograph dataset with uncertainty labels and expert comparison. In *Thirty-Third AAAI Conference on Artificial Intelligence.*

Alistair EW Johnson, Tom J Pollard, Seth Berkowitz, Nathaniel R Greenbaum, Matthew P Lungren, Chih-ying Deng, Roger G Mark, and Steven Horng. 2019. Mimic-cxr: A large publicly available database of labeled chest radiographs. *arXiv preprint arXiv:1901.07042.*

Yoon Kim. 2014. Convolutional neural networks for sentence classification. *CoRR*, abs/1408.5882.

Siwei Lai, Liheng Xu, Kang Liu, and Jun Zhao. 2015. Recurrent convolutional neural networks for text classification.

Liliana Laranjo, Adam G Dunn, Huong Ly Tong, Ahmet Baki Kocaballi, Jessica Chen, Rabia Bashir, Didi Surian, Blanca Gallego, Farah Magrabi, Annie YS Lau, et al. 2018. Conversational agents in healthcare: a systematic review. *Journal of the American Medical Informatics Association*, 25(9):1248–1258.

Changhwan Lee, Yeesuk Kim, Young Soo Kim, and Jongseong Jang. 2019a. Automatic disease annotation from radiology reports using artificial intelligence implemented by a recurrent neural network. *American Journal of Roentgenology*, 212(4):734–740.

Jinhyuk Lee, Wonjin Yoon, Sungdong Kim, Donghyeon Kim, Sunkyu Kim, Chan Ho So, and Jaewoo Kang. 2019b. BioBERT: a pre-trained biomedical language representation model for biomedical text mining. *Bioinformatics.*

Qi Li, Louise Deleger, Todd Lingren, Haijun Zhai, Megan Kaiser, Laura Stoutenborough, Anil G Jegga, Kevin Bretonnel Cohen, and Imre Solti. 2013. Mining fda drug labels for medical conditions. *BMC medical informatics and decision making*, 13(1):53.

Guanxiong Liu, Tzu-Ming Harry Hsu, Matthew McDermott, Willie Boag, Wei-Hung Weng, Peter Szolovits, and Marzyeh Ghassemi. 2019a. Clinically accurate chest x-ray report generation. *arXiv preprint arXiv:1904.02633.*

Xiaodong Liu, Pengcheng He, Weizhu Chen, and Jianfeng Gao. 2019b. Multi-task deep neural networks for natural language understanding. *arXiv preprint arXiv:1901.11504.*

Stéphane Meystre and Peter J Haug. 2006. Natural language processing to extract medical problems from electronic clinical documents: performance evaluation. *Journal of biomedical informatics*, 39(6):589–599.

Tobi Olatunji and Li Yao. 2019. Learning to estimate label uncertainty for automatic radiology report parsing. *arXiv preprint arXiv:1910.00673.*

Tobi Olatunji, Li Yao, Ben Covington, Alexander Rhodes, and Anthony Upton. 2019. Caveats in generating medical imaging labels from radiology reports. *arXiv preprint arXiv:1905.02283*.

Yifan Peng, Xiaosong Wang, Le Lu, Mohammadhadi Bagheri, Ronald Summers, and Zhiyong Lu. 2018. Negbio: a high-performance tool for negation and uncertainty detection in radiology reports. *AMIA Summits on Translational Science Proceedings*, 2017:188.

Alec Radford, Jeffrey Wu, Rewon Child, David Luan, Dario Amodei, and Ilya Sutskever. 2019. Language models are unsupervised multitask learners. *OpenAI Blog*, 1(8):9.

Alvin Rajkomar, Eyal Oren, Kai Chen, Andrew M Dai, Nissan Hajaj, Michaela Hardt, Peter J Liu, Xiaobing Liu, Jake Marcus, Mimi Sun, et al. 2018. Scalable and accurate deep learning with electronic health records. *NPJ Digital Medicine*, 1(1):18.

Pranav Rajpurkar, Jeremy Irvin, Kaylie Zhu, Brandon Yang, Hershel Mehta, Tony Duan, Daisy Ding, Aarti Bagul, Curtis P. Langlotz, Katie Shpanskaya, Matthew P. Lungren, and Andrew Y. Ng. 2017. Chexnet: Radiologist-level pneumonia detection on chest x-rays with deep learning. *arXiv preprint arXiv:1711.05225*.

Kirk Roberts. 2016. Assessing the corpus size vs. similarity trade-off for word embeddings in clinical nlp. In *Proceedings of the Clinical Natural Language Processing Workshop (ClinicalNLP)*, pages 54–63.

Guergana K Savova, James J Masanz, Philip V Ogren, Jiaping Zheng, Sunghwan Sohn, Karin C Kipper-Schuler, and Christopher G Chute. 2010. Mayo clinical text analysis and knowledge extraction system (ctakes): architecture, component evaluation and applications. *Journal of the American Medical Informatics Association*, 17(5):507–513.

Ricky K Taira and Stephen G Soderland. 1999. A statistical natural language processor for medical reports. In *Proceedings of the AMIA Symposium*, page 970. American Medical Informatics Association.

Yonghui Wu, Mike Schuster, Zhifeng Chen, Quoc V. Le, Mohammad Norouzi, Wolfgang Macherey, Maxim Krikun, Yuan Cao, Qin Gao, Klaus Macherey, Jeff Klingner, Apurva Shah, Melvin Johnson, Xiaobing Liu, Lukasz Kaiser, Stephan Gouws, Yoshikiyo Kato, Taku Kudo, Hideto Kazawa, Keith Stevens, George Kurian, Nishant Patil, Wei Wang, Cliff Young, Jason Smith, Jason Riesa, Alex Rudnick, Oriol Vinyals, Greg Corrado, Macduff Hughes, and Jeffrey Dean. 2016. Google's neural machine translation system: Bridging the gap between human and machine translation. *CoRR*, abs/1609.08144.

Zhilin Yang, Zihang Dai, Yiming Yang, Jaime Carbonell, Russ R Salakhutdinov, and Quoc V Le. 2019. Xlnet: Generalized autoregressive pretraining for language understanding. In *Advances in neural information processing systems*, pages 5754–5764.

Li Yao, Eric Poblenz, Dmitry Dagunts, Ben Covington, Devon Bernard, and Kevin Lyman. 2017. Learning to diagnose from scratch by exploiting dependencies among labels. *arXiv preprint arXiv:1710.10501*.

Li Yao, Jordan Prosky, Ben Covington, and Kevin Lyman. 2019. A strong baseline for domain adaptation and generalization in medical imaging. *arXiv preprint arXiv:1904.01638*.

Li Yao, Jordan Prosky, Eric Poblenz, Ben Covington, and Kevin Lyman. 2018. Weakly supervised medical diagnosis and localization from multiple resolutions. *arXiv preprint arXiv:1803.07703*.

# The Chilean Waiting List Corpus: a new resource for clinical Named Entity Recognition in Spanish


**Pablo Báez[1], Fabián Villena[1,2], Matías Rojas[3], Manuel Durán[1], and Jocelyn Dunstan[1,2]**

[1]Center for Medical Informatics and Telemedicine, University of Chile.
[2]Center for Mathematical Modeling, University of Chile.
[3]Department of Computer Sciences, University of Chile.
{pablobaez,manuel.duran,matias.rojas.g}@ug.uchile.cl
{fabian.villena,jdunstan}@uchile.cl



## Abstract

In this work we describe the Waiting List Corpus consisting of de-identified referrals for several specialty consultations from the waiting list in Chilean public hospitals. A subset of 900 referrals was manually annotated with 9,029 entities, 385 attributes, and 284 pairs of relations with clinical relevance. A trained medical doctor annotated these referrals, and then together with other three researchers, consolidated each of the annotations. The annotated corpus has nested entities, with 32.2% of entities embedded in other entities. We use this annotated corpus to obtain preliminary results for Named Entity Recognition (NER). The best results were achieved by using a biLSTM-CRF architecture using word embeddings trained over Spanish Wikipedia together with clinical embeddings computed by the group. NER models applied to this corpus can leverage statistics of diseases and pending procedures within this waiting list. This work constitutes the first annotated corpus using clinical narratives from Chile, and one of the few for the Spanish language. The annotated corpus, the clinical word embeddings, and the annotation guidelines are freely released to the research community.


## 1 Introduction

The analysis of clinical text has particular challenges due to the extensive use of non-standardized abbreviations, the variability of the clinical language across medical specialties and health professionals, and its restricted availability for privacy reasons, to mention some (Dalianis, 2018). Given that most text resources are available for the English language (Névéol et al., 2018), focusing on clinical text in Spanish represents an opportunity to gather efforts on its development.

A common task in Natural Language Processing (NLP) is Named Entity Recognition (NER), which aims to automatically identify essential pieces of information (entities) in a text written in natural language. In the general domain, NER was first defined to identify personal names, organizations, and locations (Chinchor and Robinson, 1997), to then be extended to a variety of entities depending on the particular application. Nowadays, the best results for the original 2003 NER task (Sang and De Meulder, 2003) are self-attention networks (Baevski et al., 2019), differentiable neural architecture search methods (Jiang et al., 2019), and LSTM-CRF enriched with ELMo, BERT, and Flair contextual embeddings (Straková et al., 2019).

In the context of clinical NLP, NER is commonly used for the identification of diseases, body parts, or medications (Dalianis, 2018). The automatic extraction of this information allows, for example, the detection of risk factors on discharge records (Uzuner et al., 2008), personal information (Lange et al., 2019), frequencies and doses of drugs (Uzuner et al., 2010a), or the leverage of epidemiological information on the existence of diseases (Lott et al., 2018).

Human-annotated clinical corpora are costly, but they are necessary for at least three reasons: 1) the annotation procedure focuses and clarifies the requirements of a computational algorithm, 2) it provides data for resolving NLP tasks, and 3) it provides a benchmark against which to evaluate the results obtained by computational models (Roberts et al., 2007).

In practice, the manual annotation process implies that the annotator, with expertise in a subject previously discussed and defined as appropriate, reviews the corpus. Following guidelines and an annotation scheme, he or she selects a text segment in the document and assigns it to an entity type and, if appropriate, adds an attribute or relation to connect the segment to another entity.

### 1.1 The Chilean waiting list as the case study

In Chile, the public healthcare system covers 75% of the population (Fondo Nacional de Salud, 2013).




*Proceedings of the 3rd Clinical Natural Language Processing Workshop*, pages 291–300
November 19, 2020. ©2020 Association for Computational Linguistics

The high demand for a visit to a specialist within this system, which requires a referral from a general practitioner, is handled by a Waiting List (WL) (Ministerio de Salud de Chile, 2011b). This is divided into "GES" (acronyms in Spanish for Explicit Health Guarantees), which covers 80 prioritized health conditions (Ministerio de Salud de Chile, 2004), and the "non-GES", which covers the remaining consultations. During 2016, about 22,500 patients died while waiting for their first consultation with a specialist, and 2,358 died before the surgery they needed. In 2017, there were 1,661,826 persons in the non-GES WL pending for a specialist's appointment, with an average waiting time above 400 days (Estay et al., 2017).

Under this scenario, it is essential to develop automated systems that allow the analysis of this non-GES WL, to both improve the management of patients that should be prioritized as well as the secondary use of the information. Tasks that can be achieved with a working NER model include the prioritization of patients, the selection of cases that can be solved by telemedicine, the estimated number of people who present more than one disease (comorbidity), or that take more than one medication (polypharmacy), statistics of the pending procedures, or the family background of diseases when mentioned.

Every public health institution in Chile uploads weekly spreadsheets with non-GES WL cases que contiene informacion sobre las interconsultas. The referrals contain the personal information of the patient, the referring and admitting healthcare providers, the medical specialty, and in the form of unstructured text the suspected diagnosis (Ministerio de Salud de Chile, 2011b). Villena and Dunstan (2019) examined the unstructured data in this WL, using word clouds to visualize the weighted word frequency by medical specialty. Although this methodology is informative, it is necessary to advance in the automatic detection of diseases within these referrals to improve their clinical management and support epidemiological studies, which is also one of the main motivations to create an annotated *corpus*. Apart from the clinical relevance, choosing the non-GES WL is also practical since it can be accessed through Transparency Law, a country-wide initiative for better access to data (Ministerio Secretaría General de la Presidencia, 2008). Data comes de-identified from the origin and does not require ethics committee approval as it is public information (Martinez et al., 2019). The public character of these referrals makes it possible to use them in shared tasks or to share them with the research community.

## 1.2 Related annotated corpora

In terms of linguistic resources using clinical text in Spanish, publications from Spain are predominant, such as the work of Oronoz et al. (2013) that annotated disease, drug, and substance in medical records. The same group published a corpus afterward for adverse drug reactions (Oronoz et al., 2015). For negation, there are the works of Cruz Diaz et al. (2017) using anamnesis and radiology reports, Marimon et al. (2017) using clinical reports from a hospital in Barcelona, and Lima et al. (2020) who released a biomedical corpus annotated with negation and uncertainty. From Spanish-speaking countries besides Spain, and to the best of our knowledge, the only published work is by Cotik et al. (2017) in Argentina for the annotation of clinical findings, body parts, negation, temporal terms, and abbreviations in radiology reports. Some of the work done on biomedical texts is also noteworthy; Moreno-Sandoval and Campillos-Llanos (2013) annotated Part-of-Speech in biomedical documents written in Spanish, Japanese, and Arabic,Krallinger et al. (2015) annotated PubMed abstracts in Spanish with chemicals and drugs. More recently, Campillos-Llanos (2019) created a medical lexicon by mapping words to the Unified Medical Language System (UMLS) identifiers. Spanish is one of the most widely spoken languages globally, but there is a lack of language resources. Machine understanding of clinical texts requires dealing with a non-standardized use of the language, mainly due to the heavy use of abbreviations, local jargon, and a large presence of spelling errors. Creating clinical resources from different Spanish-speaking countries will allow us to estimate the variability of medical language. This comparison is especially useful when measured over real clinical narratives compared to biomedical literature due to its significantly different properties.

## 2 The Waiting List Corpus

During 2018, we requested the non-GES WL from the 29 health services in the country through Transparency Law (Ministerio Secretaría General de la Presidencia, 2008). These requests were answered positively by 23 of the health services and sent WL datasets for years between 2008 and 2018.

As a result, the group has 5,176,858 referrals, originated at the 40 medical and 11 dental specialties defined in the Chilean regulation (Ministerio de Salud de Chile, 2011b). The specialties with more referrals are ophthalmology (14.49%), traumatology (9.44%), and otorhinolaryngology (7.53%). The distribution between medical and dental referrals is 83% versus 11%, and 6% of the referrals have missing values in the specialty attribute.

Considering only the reasons for referral (written in free-text), we have 994,946 different diagnoses. A random subset of these diagnoses was selected for annotation, with the criterion of selecting those with more than 100 characters. Using this condition, we reduce the corpus to 107,235 unique candidates. Moreover, we removed diagnoses with text imperfections (such as a clear cut at the end of the referral or a text encoding error) or without extra text information (an exact copy of an ICD-10 diagnosis). After filtering, one of the managers inspected each of the remaining diagnoses to ensure that they fully met the conditions. Even though the referrals come de-identified from the source, this person also checked for any personal information.

## 3 Annotation scheme

Four annotators (three medical students and one medical doctor) were selected for the initial stage of the annotation process, who were permanently supported by three project managers. The choice of annotators and their background is a significant factor. Roberts et al. (2009) describe how clinically trained annotators are better than linguists and computer scientists at annotating clinical text with semantic relationships. It is common to collect annotations from workers with advanced medical training, either as general practitioners, researchers with training on general medicine, or final-year medical students (Koeling et al., 2011). We worked here with three third-year medical students, whose annotations contributed to the improvement of the annotation guidelines.

The annotation process involved three stages as shown in Figure 1. In the first stage, a test version of the annotation guidelines was written, with an in-depth study of other available guidelines for similar entities, such as those published by Mota et al. (2018) and Intxaurrondo et al. (2018). These guidelines were evaluated during the annotation of 25 referrals, followed by the curation of a reference.

In the second stage, the three medical students annotated 50 identical referrals in weekly annotation rounds for three weeks. In an iterative improvement process, the medical students were retrained after each round of annotation. At this point, the guidelines were further modified to clarify the task and improve consistency. At the end of this stage, the first accepted version of the guidelines was established and released.

In stage three, a medical doctor joined the group (namely *senior annotator*) and was asked to annotate the same 150 referrals done by the students independently. Each referral was compared with the previous annotations, with the aim that the analysis and discussion process to find consensus on annotations helped strengthen the senior annotator's training. Recruiting medical doctors to invest time

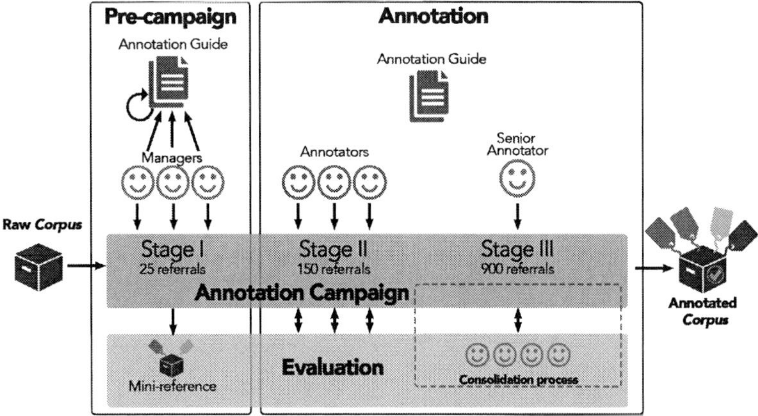


Figure 1: Annotation stages for the creation of annotation guidelines, the training of the senior annotator, and the production stage where 900 referrals were consolidated. Figure adapted from Fort (2016).

on the annotation task is a challenge. Therefore, the option of training non-expert annotators such as students, is often considered. However, the annotation of some complex entities, by definition or extension, may lead to low agreement among non-expert annotators impacting the overall agreement as well (Lewinski et al., 2017). We addressed this situation by implementing a pre-annotation stage of straightforward entities, such as abbreviations and body parts, done by medical students. Thus, the senior annotator could focus on entities, attributes, and relations that required higher clinical expertise.

For the consolidation process, we decided to have each annotation revised by a team of four researchers, including the senior annotator, a dentist, the postdoc that created the annotation guidelines, and the principal investigator. This means that once a batch of 150 referrals was fully annotated, the three managers and the senior annotator analyzed and discussed the annotations one by one until an agreement was reached. When consolidated, the referrals became part of the ground truth. In the beginning, the consolidation of 150 referrals took around 6 hours, but by round 4, the time was reduced to approximately 3 hours. It is important to note that we did not use automatic pre-annotation methods: each of the referrals was manually annotated from scratch. We used this time-consuming approach to compensate for the absence of a second senior annotator.

## 3.1 Annotation guidelines

A document with the guidelines for annotators was created by the managers, which was a result of a literature review and their annotation during Stage I (Mota et al., 2018; Uzuner et al., 2010b, 2011; Névéol et al., 2011; Intxaurrondo et al., 2018; Skeppstedt et al., 2014). The Unified Medical Language System (UMLS) was used to define the entity names and dependencies and resolve disagreements and uncertainties.

The guidelines were initially designed to instruct medical students and were later improved by the feedback given by the senior annotator. In the current version, the guidelines starts with a brief introduction to clinical NLP and instructions to initiate a session in the platform and perform the annotation using BRAT (BRAT Rapid Annotation Tool). This is always complemented with a face-to-face meeting with the annotators.

The guidelines are under constant update when

the need for clarification or further example cases emerges from the consolidation process. The current version of the annotation guidelines (in Spanish) is freely available [1].

The annotated entities and attributes are described in Table 1. The choice of entities was based on literature revision and our interest within this corpus. For example, the referrals are from a waiting list, and we were interested in describing how many procedures were pending. Moreover, it was important for us to distinguish between laboratory, diagnostic or therapeutic procedures. We are also interested in mining the family history of diseases, and therefore, we included entities, attributes, and relations *ad hoc* with this goal. The corpus was for example, enriched with the *has* relation between family members and disease, and to connect diagnostic procedures and laboratory or test results.

|  | Entity | Attribute |
|---|---|---|
| Finding | Laboratory or Test Result | |
| | Sign or Symptom | Negated |
| Procedure | Laboratory Procedure | |
| | Diagnostic Procedure | Pending |
| | Therapeutic Procedure | |
| | Family Member | Maternal Paternal |
| | Disease | Negated IFB |
| | Body Part | |
| | Medication | |
| | Abbreviation | |

Table 1: Description of the entities and attributes we are annotating in the corpus. IFB: Implicit Family Background

For all the entities, the rules were classified into four types: (i) general, which are suitable for positive and negative rules, (ii) positive, what has to be annotated, (iii) negative, what should not be annotated and (iv) multi-word, when to consider multiple tokens in an entity. Two general rules were then explained, which are not to include punctuation and white spaces at the end of entities and to annotate even if grammatical errors are found, as long as the meaning is understood. Afterward, the entity was briefly defined, followed by positive, negative and multi-word rules, each of them supported by several examples. The text was complemented with diagrams constructed from screenshots of the platform.

For the case of attributes, there were four types: negated (for sign/symptoms and diseases), pend-

---

ing (for procedures), maternal or paternal (for family member), and implicit family background (for diseases). The corresponding entities were annotated with the label, without including the token(s) used to express the attribute (e.g., in "waiting for surgery", the entity "surgery" is annotated as a therapeutic procedure with the pending attribute). We included implicit family background to consider expressions such as *there is a family history of cancer* without specifying which family member(s) present the disease. Finally, relations were used to connect certain entities. Following the previous example, the entity *cancer* should be connected to the entity that carries family member information when corresponding.

An example of an annotated referral is shown in Fig. 2. In this referral, one can see three relations between diseases and family members. Additionally, we observe nested entities in *cancer de colon* (colon cancer) and *cancer de recto* (rectal cancer). In both cases, there is a body part contained in a longer disease entity. Section 4 describes nested entities within this corpus.

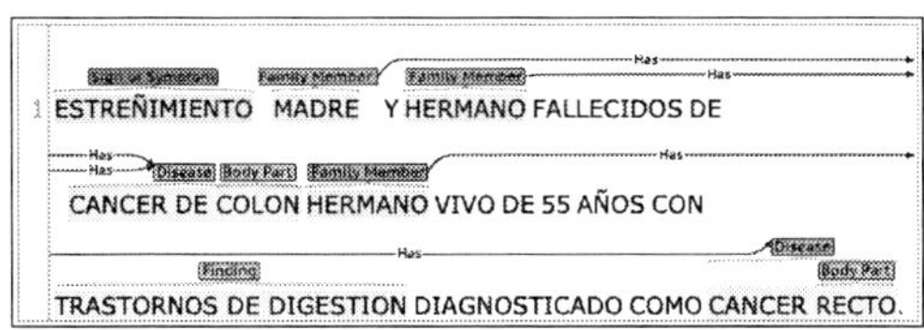


Figure 2: An example of an annotated referral using BRAT Rapid Annotation Tool. This can be translated into English as follows: "Constipation deceased mother and brother of colon cancer living brother aged 55 with digestive disorders diagnosed as rectal cancer"

## 3.2 Inter-annotator agreement

The difficulty of the task was assessed by calculating the inter-annotator agreement during Stages I and II (Fort, 2016). In particular, we used the F1-Score to compare pairs of annotations (Hripcsak and Rothschild, 2005). The F1-Scores can be "strict" and "relaxed". In the strict case, the annotation is required to match exactly in entity and tokens selected, while in the relaxed case, the annotation is required to have the same class. However, there may be a partial match in the entity length, with an overlap of tokens. As an example, for the expression "breast cancer" if an annotator A marks only "cancer" as a disease, and annotator B decides to select the full expression "breast cancer" as disease, using the strict metric there would be

no agreement between A and B. In contrast, with the relaxed metric there would be agreement since both annotators include the word "cancer".

We calculated the inter-annotator agreement between pairs, considering the three medical students and the ground truth. Figure 3 shows the F1 strict and relaxed for every pair in 150 referrals.

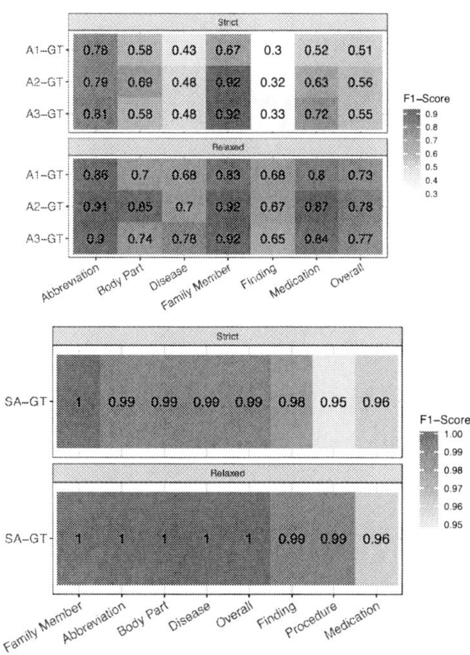

Figure 3: F1-score (strict and relaxed). Top: Every medical student (A1, A2 and A3) compared with the ground truth and calculated over the first 150 referrals. Bottom: Comparison between the senior annotator and the ground truth for the referrals 1-150.

As mentioned before, the senior annotator carries out the first version of the annotations. The referrals are then consolidated by the three managers and the senior annotator. Both the time required and the number of editions during the consolidation process decrease as several rounds of annotation are achieved. Figure 3 (bottom) shows the comparison between the senior annotator and the ground truth over 150 referrals (referrals 1-150 in the corpus).

## 4 Results

### 4.1 Annotated corpus statistics

The corpus consists of 900 referrals, with 1,912 sentences, 36,157 tokens, and a vocabulary size of 7,980 tokens. Each diagnosis has a mean of 40 [37 - 42 CI 95 %] tokens, normally distributed across the diagnoses. The medical specialties more often annotated are traumatology (16.64%), gynecology (8.85%) and pediatrics (7.02%). The ratio between medical and dental specialties is 88:12. The annotated corpus is freely available[2].

A total of 9,029 entities were annotated and the distribution per entity type and document (referral) is shown in Fig. 4. In terms of the annotated attributes and relations, they are much less in number than entities. For the attributes, we have 256 negated, 126 pending, 2 implicit family background, and 1 maternal. For relations, we have 284 pairs of relations.

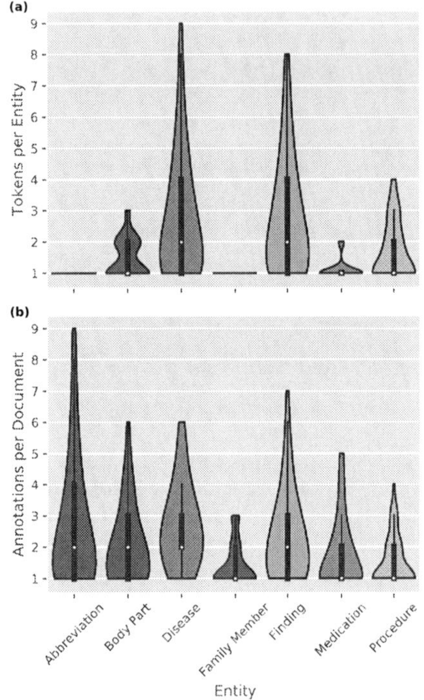


Figure 4: Frequency distribution and median (white point) of (a) tokens per entity across the corpus, and (b) annotated entities per document.

As previously mentioned, this corpus has nested entities, which are entities embedded in other entities (Finkel and Manning, 2009). For example, in Figure 2, the body part *colon* is nested inside the disease entity *cancer de colon*. Figure 5 illustrates this fact, with numbers indicating how many times the entity in the row is nested in the entity in the column. Please note that this matrix is not symmetric, as it is much more common to find, for example,

an abbreviation in a finding (287 times) than a finding in an abbreviation (91). Besides, when nested annotations have the same length, we count them as embedded one into each other for both entities. An example of that is *HTA* (*high blood pressure*), which is both a disease and an abbreviation.

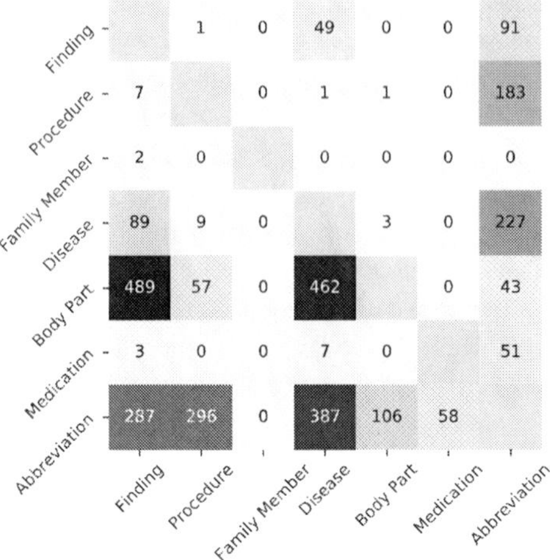


Figure 5: Characterization of nested entities. The numbers indicate how many times the entity in the row is embedded in the entity in the column.

### 4.2 Preliminary NER models

BRAT annotation generates a file in *standoff* format[3] for each referral. This file follows a basic structure with three columns containing: an ID per annotation and its consecutive order of appearance, the entity type with the indexes for the beginning and end characters of the annotation, and the character string that constitute that entity.

These files can be converted to the *CoNLL* format[4] (Furrer et al., 2019), which is widely used in the NLP community. Unfortunately, this format does not support nested entities, therefore we have to choose which nested entity to use (commonly the longest). When a token is annotated with two entities, *HTA* for example, to translate it to *CoNLL* format we have to keep one of the two arbitrarily.

For the preliminary results shown here, we decided to focus on three specific entities. Disease, because its recognition is a task of enormous clinical relevance. Medication, since medical doc-

[2]http://doi.org/10.5281/zenodo.3926705

[3]http://2011.bionlp-st.org/home/file-formats
[4]https://github.com/spyysalo/standoff2conll

tors sometimes prescribe the active component and other the commercial brand, we wanted to explore how well the different tested models deal with that. Finally, abbreviations were chosen since they are widespread in the corpus and are morphologically distinctive.

We compared the performance of a multiclass model (where nested entities are lost) with three models for each entity (where all entities are retained, no matter if they are nested or nesting an entity). As a baseline, we used the Flair Framework, a biLSTM-CRF architecture that creates contextual embeddings for each word. This approach was the state-of-the-art for the NER CoNNL03 task in English and German (Akbik et al., 2018). This architecture is easy to implement as code and pre-trained language models are available to the community[5].

For the embedding layer, we compared Flair embeddings pre-trained over Wikipedia in Spanish with those enhanced by domain-specific embeddings. The latest were trained over a clinical corpus composed by the unannotated Waiting List Corpus described in Section 2 plus referrals collected by the group for another project. The vocabulary size of this corpus is 57,112 tokens. These clinical embeddings can be downloaded from here[6]. Furthermore, the two embeddings were not left static, so the weights were updated during the training stage.

The grid-search method from Flair was used to tune the hyperparameters: a learning rate of 0.1, batch size of 32, 100 epochs, LSTM hidden size of 256 and dropout 0.1864. The models were tested ten times with different initialization parameters.

The results were expressed as mean and standard deviation (SD). Table 2 shows the results for the multiclass model where nested entities are lost, while Table 3 shows the results of three different NER models, one for each of the entities.

As expected, multiple models outperform a multiclass model where nested entities are lost. In terms of the embedding layer's choice, models with added clinical embeddings have a better performance than those using the Spanish Wikipedia Flair embeddings alone. Nevertheless, it is interesting the small difference between the two for the recognition of abbreviations. This is probably due to the different sizes of both corpora, where the training corpus for the Flair embedding is significantly larger, but also the fact that the embeddings are dynamically tuned during training. The most significant improvement of adding clinical embeddings is observed in the medication entity, which is also the one with fewer training examples. Finally, abbreviations are indeed the most manageable entities to learn, with an F1-score of 0.92.

## 5 Conclusions and future work

There is a lack of language resources for the Spanish language in the clinical domain, and the work presented here constitutes the first annotated corpus using Chilean narratives. We believe that projects like ours help filling the gap with respect to clinical NLP done in English. This paper shares 900 annotated referrals, the annotation guidelines, clinical word embeddings, and the code used to generate the results presented here.

In terms of developing NER models trained on this corpus, future work includes improving the recall for disease and medication, due to the importance of identifying these entities, and dealing with nested NER, for which there is a variety

[5]https://github.com/zalandoresearch/flair
[6]http://doi.org/10.5281/zenodo.3924799

| Entity | # of test entities | Pre-trained embbedings | | | Pre-trained + clinical embeddings | | |
|---|---|---|---|---|---|---|---|
| | | Precision | Recall | F1-Score | Precision | Recall | F1-Score |
| Abbreviations | 457 | 0.85 (0.012) | 0.91 (0.014) | 0.88 (0.004) | 0.86 (0.01) | 0.92 (0.013) | 0.89 (0.005) |
| Disease | 403 | 0.73 (0.034) | 0.65 (0.023) | 0.69 (0.008) | 0.75 (0.013) | 0.71 (0.015) | 0.73 (0.01) |
| Medication | 44 | 0.68 (0.05) | 0.59 (0.032) | 0.63 (0.021) | 0.74 (0.047) | 0.72 (0.036) | 0.73 (0.036) |

Table 2: Multiclass model where nested entities are lost. Data shown are mean (SD).

| Entity | # of test entities | Pre-trained embbedings | | | Pre-trained + clinical embeddings | | |
|---|---|---|---|---|---|---|---|
| | | Precision | Recall | F1-Score | Precision | Recall | F1-Score |
| Abbreviations | 507 | 0.92 (0.004) | 0.92 (0.007) | 0.92 (0.004) | 0.91 (0.002) | 0.93 (0.003) | 0.92 (0.002) |
| Disease | 456 | 0.76 (0.008) | 0.65 (0.009) | 0.70 (0.004) | 0.79 (0.004) | 0.75 (0.009) | 0.77 (0.005) |
| Medication | 53 | 0.71 (0.02) | 0.50 (0.032) | 0.58 (0.026) | 0.79 (0.038) | 0.71 (0.016) | 0.75 (0.024) |

Table 3: Multiple models for each entity. All entities are retained. Data shown are mean (SD).

of approaches as summarized in (Dadas and Protasiewicz, 2020). Besides, our annotated corpus has hierarchical entities (for example, test result and sign/symptom are part of the entity finding). We plan to investigate the hierarchical nested NER using architectures as in Marinho *et al.*(Marinho et al., 2019). Finally, our corpus has attributes and relations which we have not addressed yet. Once we have a higher amount of annotated referrals, we plan to host a shared task to advance this corpus's multiple challenges.

One of our goals working on this corpus and training NER models is to recognize diseases within this waiting list automatically. In particular, telemedicine has been posed as one of the solutions to decrease the waiting times in the Chilean public healthcare sector (Ministerio de Salud de Chile, 2011a). To correctly estimate the effect, one needs to summarize the suspected diagnoses and check which of them are eligible for telemedicine consultations. Furthermore, diseases that need to be examined rapidly could be prioritized using an automatic detection of diseases.

Part of the group's expertise is in the genetic components of diseases. For that reason, we want to explore the possible risk factors (genetic or environmental), which could be obtained from the mentions of the patients' family history and habits. In this regard, we pay special attention to identifying relations between family members and diseases, with maternal and paternal components labeled. This corpus is not particularly rich in those entities. However, we are starting to collaborate with a cancer center, and we plan to translate the know-how from this annotated corpus to future projects in that direction.

## Acknowledgements

This work was funded by CMM-ANID AFB 170001. Also, PB receives support from U-INICIA VID 2019 UI-004/19 and ICM P09-015F, and JD from the cost center 570111 - CIMT-CORFO. We want to thank Leonardo Campillos-Llanos for his constructive comments on the manuscript and overall support. We also acknowledge the help received from Martin Krallinger, Aureliè Neveol, Felipe Bravo, and Karen Fört. Finally, we are very grateful to reviewers for their helpful comments.

## References


Alan Akbik, Duncan Blythe, and Roland Vollgraf. 2018. Contextual string embeddings for sequence labeling. In *COLING 2018, 27th International Conference on Computational Linguistics*, pages 1638–1649.

Alexei Baevski, Sergey Edunov, Yinhan Liu, Luke Zettlemoyer, and Michael Auli. 2019. Cloze-driven pretraining of self-attention networks. *arXiv preprint arXiv:1903.07785*.

Leonardo Campillos-Llanos. 2019. First steps towards building a medical lexicon for spanish with linguistic and semantic information. In *Proceedings of the 18th BioNLP Workshop and Shared Task*, pages 152–164.

Nancy Chinchor and Patricia Robinson. 1997. Muc-7 named entity task definition. In *Proceedings of the 7th Conference on Message Understanding*, volume 29, pages 1–21.

Viviana Cotik, Darío Filippo, Roland Roller, Hans Uszkoreit, and Feiyu Xu. 2017. Annotation of entities and relations in spanish radiology reports. In *RANLP*, pages 177–184.

Noa P Cruz Diaz, Roser Morante, Manuel J Mana López, Jacinto Mata Vázquez, and Carlos L Parra Calderón. 2017. Annotating negation in spanish clinical texts. In *Proceedings of the workshop computational semantics beyond events and roles*, pages 53–58.

Sławomir Dadas and Jarosław Protasiewicz. 2020. A bidirectional iterative algorithm for nested named entity recognition. *IEEE Access*, 8:135091–135102.

Hercules Dalianis. 2018. *Clinical text mining: Secondary use of electronic patient records*. Springer Nature.

Roberto Estay, Cristóbal Cuadrado, Francisca Crispi, Fernando González, Francisco Alvarado, and Natalia Cabrera. 2017. Desde el conflicto de listas de espera, hacia el fortalecimiento de los prestadores públicos de salud: Una propuesta para chile. *Cuadernos Médico Sociales*, 57(1).

Jenny Rose Finkel and Christopher D Manning. 2009. Nested named entity recognition. In *Proceedings of the 2009 conference on empirical methods in natural language processing*, pages 141–150.

Fondo Nacional de Salud. 2013. Población Inscrita en FONASA, `https://public.tableau.com/views/Poblacion2002-2020/INEeInscritos`. Technical report.

Karën Fort. 2016. *Collaborative Annotation for Reliable Natural Language Processing: Technical and Sociological Aspects*. John Wiley & Sons.

Lenz Furrer, Joseph Cornelius, and Fabio Rinaldi. 2019. Uzh@ craft-st: a sequence-labeling approach to concept recognition. In *Proceedings of The 5th Workshop on BioNLP Open Shared Tasks*, pages 185–195.

George Hripcsak and Adam S Rothschild. 2005. Agreement, the f-measure, and reliability in information retrieval. *Journal of the American Medical Informatics Association*, 12(3):296–298.

Ander Intxaurrondo, Juan Carlos de la Torre, H Rodriguez Betanco, Montserrat Marimon, Jose Antonio Lopez-Martin, Aitor Gonzalez-Agirre, J Santamaría, Marta Villegas, and Martin Krallinger. 2018. Resources, guidelines and annotations for the recognition, definition resolution and concept normalization of spanish clinical abbreviations: the barr2 corpus. In *SEPLN*.

Yufan Jiang, Chi Hu, Tong Xiao, Chunliang Zhang, and Jingbo Zhu. 2019. Improved differentiable architecture search for language modeling and named entity recognition. In *Proceedings of the 2019 Conference on Empirical Methods in Natural Language Processing and the 9th International Joint Conference on Natural Language Processing (EMNLP-IJCNLP)*, pages 3576–3581.

Rob Koeling, John Carroll, Rosemary Tate, and Amanda Nicholson. 2011. Annotating a corpus of clinical text records for learning to recognize symptoms automatically. In *Proceedings of LOUHI 2011 Third International Workshop on Health Document Text Mining and Information Analysis. CEUR Workshop Proceedings*, pages 43–50.

Martin Krallinger, Obdulia Rabal, Florian Leitner, Miguel Vazquez, David Salgado, Zhiyong Lu, Robert Leaman, Yanan Lu, Donghong Ji, Daniel M Lowe, et al. 2015. The chemdner corpus of chemicals and drugs and its annotation principles. *Journal of cheminformatics*, 7(1):1–17.

Lukas Lange, Heike Adel, and Jannik Strötgen. 2019. NLNDE: The neither language-nor-domain-experts' way of Spanish medical document de-identification. *CEUR Workshop Proceedings*, 2421:671–678.

Nastassja A Lewinski, Ivan Jimenez, and Bridget T McInnes. 2017. An annotated corpus with nanomedicine and pharmacokinetic parameters. *International journal of nanomedicine*, 12:7519.

Salvador Lima, Naiara Perez, Montse Cuadros, and German Rigau. 2020. Nubes: A corpus of negation and uncertainty in spanish clinical texts. *arXiv preprint arXiv:2004.01092*.

Jason P Lott, Denise M Boudreau, Ray L Barnhill, Martin A Weinstock, Eleanor Knopp, Michael W Piepkorn, David E Elder, Steven R Knezevich, Andrew Baer, Anna NA Tosteson, et al. 2018. Population-based analysis of histologically confirmed melanocytic proliferations using natural language processing. *JAMA dermatology*, 154(1):24–29.

Montserrat Marimon, Jorge Vivaldi, and Núria Bel Rafecas. 2017. annotation of negation in the iula spanish clinical record corpus. *Blanco E, Morante R, Saurí R, editors. SemBEaR 2017. Computational Semantics Beyond Events and Roles; 2017 Apr 4; Valencia, Spain. Stroudsburg (PA): ACL; 2017. p. 43-52.*

Zita Marinho, Alfonso Mendes, Sebastiao Miranda, and David Nogueira. 2019. Hierarchical nested named entity recognition. In *Proceedings of the 2nd Clinical Natural Language Processing Workshop*, pages 28–34.

Diego A Martinez, Haoxiang Zhang, Magdalena Bastias, Felipe Feijoo, Jeremiah Hinson, Rodrigo Martinez, Jocelyn Dunstan, Scott Levin, and Diana Prieto. 2019. Prolonged wait time is associated with increased mortality for chilean waiting list patients with non-prioritized conditions. *BMC public health*, 19(1):233.

Ministerio de Salud de Chile. 2004. Ley 19.966, `https://www.leychile.cl/navegar?idnorma=229834`.

Ministerio de Salud de Chile. 2011a. Estrategia Nacional de Salud para el cumplimiento de los Objetivos Sanitarios de la Década 2010-2020.

Ministerio de Salud de Chile. 2011b. Norma Técnica Para El Registro De Las Listas De Espera, `www.supersalud.gob.cl/664/w3-propertyvalue-6249.html`.

Ministerio Secretaría General de la Presidencia. 2008. Ley 20.285, `https://www.leychile.cl/navegar?idnorma=276363&idparte=`.

Antonio Moreno-Sandoval and Leonardo Campillos-Llanos. 2013. Design and annotation of multimedica–a multilingual text corpus of the biomedical domain. *Procedia-Social and Behavioral Sciences*, 95:33–39.

Enrique Mota, Nelson Martín, Ángel Moreno, Elvira Ferrete, Jesús Santamaría, Montserrat Marimon, Ander Intxaurrondo, Aitor González-Agirre, Marta Villegas, and Martin Krallinger. 2018. Guías de anotación de información de salud protegida.

Aurélie Névéol, Hercules Dalianis, Sumithra Velupillai, Guergana Savova, and Pierre Zweigenbaum. 2018. Clinical natural language processing in languages other than english: opportunities and challenges. *Journal of biomedical semantics*, 9(1):12.

Aurélie Névéol, Rezarta Islamaj Doğan, and Zhiyong Lu. 2011. Semi-automatic semantic annotation of pubmed queries: a study on quality, efficiency, satisfaction. *Journal of biomedical informatics*, 44(2):310–318.

Maite Oronoz, Arantza Casillas, Koldo Gojenola, and Alicia Perez. 2013. Automatic annotation of medical records in spanish with disease, drug and substance names. In *Iberoamerican Congress on Pattern Recognition*, pages 536–543. Springer.

Maite Oronoz, Koldo Gojenola, Alicia Pérez, Arantza Díaz de Ilarraza, and Arantza Casillas. 2015. On the creation of a clinical gold standard corpus in spanish: Mining adverse drug reactions. *Journal of biomedical informatics*, 56:318–332.

Angus Roberts, Robert Gaizauskas, Mark Hepple, Neil Davis, George Demetriou, Yikun Guo, Jay Subbarao Kola, Ian Roberts, Andrea Setzer, Archana Tapuria, et al. 2007. The clef corpus: semantic annotation of clinical text. In *AMIA Annual Symposium Proceedings*, volume 2007, page 625. American Medical Informatics Association.

Angus Roberts, Robert Gaizauskas, Mark Hepple, George Demetriou, Yikun Guo, Ian Roberts, and Andrea Setzer. 2009. Building a semantically annotated corpus of clinical texts. *Journal of biomedical informatics*, 42(5):950–966.

Erik F Sang and Fien De Meulder. 2003. Introduction to the conll-2003 shared task: Language-independent named entity recognition. *arXiv preprint cs/0306050*.

Maria Skeppstedt, Maria Kvist, Gunnar H Nilsson, and Hercules Dalianis. 2014. Automatic recognition of disorders, findings, pharmaceuticals and body structures from clinical text: An annotation and machine learning study. *Journal of biomedical informatics*, 49:148–158.

Jana Straková, Milan Straka, and Jan Hajič. 2019. Neural architectures for nested ner through linearization. *arXiv preprint arXiv:1908.06926*.

Özlem Uzuner, Ira Goldstein, Yuan Luo, and Isaac Kohane. 2008. Identifying patient smoking status from medical discharge records. *Journal of the American Medical Informatics Association*, 15(1):14–24.

Özlem Uzuner, Imre Solti, and Eithon Cadag. 2010a. Extracting medication information from clinical text. *Journal of the American Medical Informatics Association*, 17(5):514–518.

Özlem Uzuner, Imre Solti, Fei Xia, and Eithon Cadag. 2010b. Community annotation experiment for ground truth generation for the i2b2 medication challenge. *Journal of the American Medical Informatics Association*, 17(5):519–523.

Özlem Uzuner, Brett R South, Shuying Shen, and Scott L DuVall. 2011. 2010 i2b2/va challenge on concepts, assertions, and relations in clinical text. *Journal of the American Medical Informatics Association*, 18(5):552–556.

Fabián Villena and Jocelyn Dunstan. 2019. Obtención automática de palabras clave en textos clínicos: una aplicación de procesamiento del lenguaje natural a datos masivos de sospecha diagnóstica en chile. *Revista médica de Chile*, 147(10):1229–1238.

# Exploring Text Specific and Blackbox Fairness Algorithms in Multimodal Clinical NLP

John Chen[1,2], Ian Berlot-Attwell [1,2], Safwan Hossain [1,2], Xindi Wang [2,3], Frank Rudzicz [1,2,4]

[1] University of Toronto, [2] Vector Institute, [3] University of Western Ontario, [4] St. Michael's Hospital

{johnc, ianberlot, hossa120, frank }@cs.toronto.edu

xwang842@uwo.ca

## Abstract

Clinical machine learning is increasingly multimodal, collected in both structured tabular formats and unstructured forms such as free text. We propose a novel task of exploring *fairness* on a multimodal clinical dataset, adopting *equalized odds* for the downstream medical prediction tasks. To this end, we investigate a modality-agnostic fairness algorithm - equalized odds post processing - and compare it to a text-specific fairness algorithm: debiased clinical word embeddings. Despite the fact that debiased word embeddings do not explicitly address equalized odds of protected groups, we show that a text-specific approach to fairness may simultaneously achieve a good balance of performance *and* classical notions of fairness. We hope that our paper inspires future contributions at the critical intersection of clinical NLP and fairness. The full source code is available here: `https://github.com/johntiger1/multimodal_fairness`

## 1 Introduction

Natural language processing is increasingly leveraged in sensitive domains like healthcare. For such critical tasks, the need to prevent discrimination and bias is imperative. Indeed, ensuring equality of health outcomes across different groups has long been a guiding principle of modern health care systems (Culyer and Wagstaff, 1993). Moreover, medical data presents a unique opportunity to work with different *modalities*, specifically *text* (e.g., patient narratives, admission notes, and discharge summaries) and numerical or categorical data (often denoted *tabular* data, e.g., clinical measurements such as blood pressure, weight, or demographic information like ethnicity). Multi-modal data is not only reflective of many real-world settings, but machine learning models which leverage both structured and unstructured data often achieve greater performance than their individual

constituents (Horng et al., 2017). While prior work studied fairness in the text and tabular modalities in isolation, there is little work on applying notions of algorithmic fairness in the broader multimodal setting (Zhang et al., 2020; Chen et al., 2018).

Our work brings a novel perspective towards studying fairness algorithms for models which operate on *both* text and tabular data, in this case applied to the MIMIC-III clinical dataset (MIMIC-III) (Johnson et al., 2016). We evaluate two fairness algorithms: equalized-odds through post-processing, which is agnostic to the underlying classifier, and word embedding debiasing which is a text-specific technique. We show that ensembling classifiers trained on structured and unstructured data, along with the aforementioned fairness algorithms, can both improve performance and mitigate unfairness relative to their constituent components. We also achieve strong results on several MIMIC-III clinical benchmark prediction tasks using a dual modality ensemble; these results may be of broader interest in clinical machine learning (Harutyunyan et al., 2019; Khadanga et al., 2019).

## 2 Background

### 2.1 Combining Text and Tabular Data in Clinical Machine Learning

Prior work has shown that combining unstructured text with vital sign time series data improves performance on clinical prediction tasks. Horng et al. (2017) showed that augmenting an SVM with text information in addition to vital signs data improved retrospective sepsis detection. Akbilgic et al. (2019) showed that using a text-based risk score improves performance on prediction of death after surgery for a pediatric dataset. Closest to our work, Khadanga et al. (2019) introduced a joint-modality neural network which outperforms single-modality neural networks on several benchmark



*Proceedings of the 3rd Clinical Natural Language Processing Workshop*, pages 301–312
November 19, 2020. ©2020 Association for Computational Linguistics

prediction tasks for MIMIC-III.

## 2.2 Classical fairness metrics

Many algorithmic fairness notions fall into one of two broad categories: individual fairness enforcing fairness across individual samples, and group fairness seeking fairness across protected groups (e.g. race or gender). We focus on a popular group-level fairness metric: *Equalized Odds* (EO) (Hardt et al., 2016). Instead of arguing that average classification probability should be equal across all groups (also known as *Demographic Parity*) – which may be unfair if the underlying group-specific base rates are unequal – EO allows for classification probabilities to differ across groups only through the underlying ground truth. Formally, a binary classifier $\hat{Y}$ satisfies EO for a set of groups $\mathcal{S}$ if, for ground truth $Y$ and group membership $A$:

$$\Pr(\hat{Y} = 1 \mid Y = y, A = a) = \Pr(\hat{Y} = 1 \mid Y = y, A = a')$$
$$\forall y \in \{0, 1\}, \forall a, a' \in \mathcal{S}$$

In short, the true positive (TP) and true negative (TN) rates should be equal across groups.

## 2.3 Equalized Odds Post Processing

Hardt et al. (2016) proposed a model-agnostic post-processing algorithm that minimizes this group specific error discrepancy while considering performance. Briefly, the post-processing algorithm determines group-specific random thresholds based on the intersection of group-specific ROC curves. The multi-modality of our underlying data and the importance of privacy concerns in the clinical setting make post-processing especially attractive as it allows fairness to be achieved agnostic to the inner workings of the base classifier.

## 2.4 Debiasing word embeddings

Pretrained word embeddings encode the societal biases of the underlying text on which they are trained, including gender roles and racial stereotypes (Bolukbasi et al., 2016; Zhao et al., 2018; Manzini et al., 2019). Recent work has attempted to mitigate this bias in context-free embeddings while preserving the utility of the embeddings. Bolukbasi et al. (2016) analyzed gender subspaces by comparing distances between word vectors with pairs of gender-specific words to remove bias from gender-neutral words. Manzini et al. (2019) extended this work to the multi-class setting, enabling debiasing in race and religion. Concurrent to their work, (Ravfogel et al., 2020) propose iterative null space

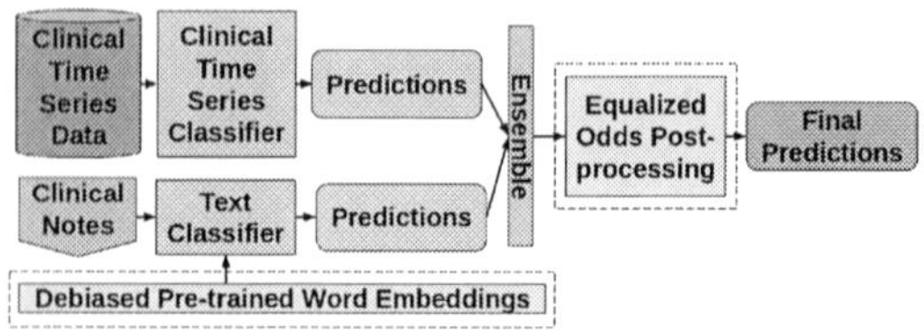


Figure 1: Experimental setup and ensemble architecture. Fairness approaches are indicated in dotted boxes.

projection as a technique to hide information about protected attributes by casting it into the null space of the classifier. Following the recent popularity of BERT and ELMo, Liang et al. (2020) consider extending debiasing to sentence-level, contextualized representations.

## 3 Experimental Setup

### 3.1 Clinical Prediction Tasks

MIMIC-III contains deidentified health data associated with 60,000 intensive care unit (ICU) admissions (Johnson et al., 2016). It contains both unstructured textual data (in the form of clinical notes) and structured data (in the form of clinical time series data and demographic, insurance, and other related meta-data). We focus on two benchmark binary prediction tasks for ICU stays previously proposed by Harutyunyan et al. (2019): in-hospital mortality prediction (IHM), which aims to predict mortality based on the first 48 hours of a patient's ICU stay, and phenotyping, which aims to retrospectively predict the acute-care conditions that impacted the patient. Following Khadanga et al. (2019) we extend the prediction tasks to leverage clinical text linked to their ICU stay. For both tasks the classes are higly imbalanced: in the IHM task only 13.1% of training examples are positive, and the relative imbalance of the labels in the phenotyping class can be seen in Figure 2. To account for the label imbalance we evaluate performance using AUC ROC and AUC PRC. More details can be found in Appendix A.

### 3.2 Fairness Definition

Next, we consider how we can extend a definition of fairness to this multimodal task. Following work by Zhang et al. (2020) in the single-modality setting, we examine True Positive and True Negative rates on our clinical prediction task between different protected groups. Attempting to equalize these rates corresponds to satisfying *Equalized*

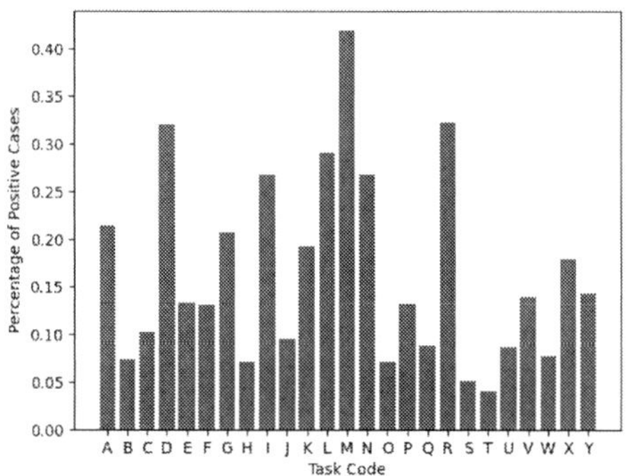

Figure 2: Percentage of positive train cases for each of the 25 phenotyping tasks. The critical care conditions corresponding to the task codes can be found in Table 3 of the Appendix

| Sensitive Group | Train Count | Test Count | % of Test |
|---|---|---|---|
| F | 7940 | 1415 | 44.0 % |
| M | 9708 | 1778 | 56.0 % |
| ASIAN | 408 | 60 | 1.9 % |
| BLACK | 1658 | 285 | 8.9 % |
| HISPANIC | 521 | 107 | 3.3 % |
| OTHER | 2655 | 459 | 14.4 % |
| WHITE | 12406 | 2282 | 71.5 % |
| Government | 356 | 74 | 2.3 % |
| Medicaid | 1362 | 205 | 6.4 % |
| Medicare | 9857 | 1757 | 55.0 % |
| Private | 4946 | 932 | 29.2 % |
| Self Pay | 133 | 33 | 1.0 % |
| UNKNOWN | 994 | 192 | 6.1 % |

Table 1: Distribution of sensitive-attributes over train and test data for the In-Hospital Mortality task

*Odds.* EO satisfies many desiderata within clinical settings, and has been used in previous clinical fairness work (Pfohl et al., 2019a; Garb, 1997; Pfohl et al., 2019b). While EO does not explicitly incorporate the *multimodality* of our data, it accurately emphasizes the importance of the *downstream* clinical prediction task on the protected groups. Nonetheless, we acknowledge that EO alone is insufficient for practical deployment; naïve application can result in unacceptable performance losses and thus consultations with physicians and stakeholders must be held (Rajkomar et al., 2018).

### 3.3 Classification Models

We provide brief descriptions below with details available in Appendix B.

- **Structured Data Model:** Following Harutyunyan et al. (2019), we use a channel-wise bidirectional Long Short Term Memory network (bi-LSTM).

- **Unstructured Textual Data:** We use a CNN encoder to extract the semantic features from clinical notes. Importantly, we experiment with training word embeddings from scratch and utilizing pre-trained BioWordVec embeddings (Zhang et al., 2019).

- **Ensemble:** We perform logistic regression on the output binary classification probabilities from the previous models.

## 4 Fairness Setup

### 4.1 Sensitive groups

Recall that EO explicitly ensures fairness with respect to sensitive groups while debiasing implicitly depends upon it. Leveraging the demographic data in MIMIC-III, we consider ethnicity (divided into Asian, Black, Hispanic, White and other), biological sex (divided into male and female), and insurance type (divided into government, medicare, medicaid, self-pay, private, and unknown). With the exception of biological sex, the sensitive groups are highly imbalanced (see Table 1). Note that insurance-type has been shown to be a proxy for socioeconomic status (SES) (Chen et al., 2019).

### 4.2 Equalized Odds Post-Processing

We apply our equalized-odds post processing algorithm on the predictions of the trained single-modality classifiers (physiological signal LSTM model as well as text-only CNN model) as well as the trained ensemble classifier. Note that we apply EO postprocessing only once for each experiment: either on the outputs of the single-modality model, or on the ensemble predictions. The fairness approaches are mutually exclusive: we do not consider applying EO postprocessing together with debiased word embeddings. We consider using both soft prediction scores (interpretable as probabilities) as well as thresholded hard predictions as input to the post-processing algorithm. These choices impact the fairness performance trade-off as discussed further in Section 5.

### 4.3 Socially Debiased Clinical Word Embeddings

While clinically pre-trained word embeddings may improve downstream task performance, they are not immune from societal bias (Khattak et al., 2019). We socially debias these clinical word embeddings following Manzini et al. (2019). We manually select sets of social-specific words (see Appendix C) to identify the fairness-relevant social bias subspace. Formally, having identified the basis vectors $\{b_1, b_2, ..., b_n\}$ of the social bias subspace $\mathcal{B}$, we can find the projection $w_B$ of a word embedding $w$:

$$w_{\mathcal{B}} = \sum_{i=1}^{n} \langle w, b_i \rangle b_i$$

Next we apply hard debiasing, which will remove bias from existing word embeddings by subtracting $w_B$, their component in this fairness subspace. This yields $w'$, our socially debiased word embedding:

$$w' = \frac{w - w_B}{\|w - w_B\|}$$

We consider debiasing with respect to race and gender. The race debiased embeddings are re-used for insurance tasks as empiric research has indicated that the use of proxy groups in fairness can be effective (Gupta et al., 2018) and SES is strongly related to race (Williams et al., 2016).

## 5 Results and Analysis

|  | IHM | | Phenotyping | |
| --- | --- | --- | --- | --- |
|  | AUC PRC | AUC ROC | Macro AUCROC | Overall AUCROC |
| Harutyunyan et. al (2019) – No Text | 0.515 | 0.862 | 0.776 | 0.825 |
| Khadanga et. al (2019) – Ensemble | 0.525 | 0.865 | – | – |
| Ours – Text Only | 0.472 | 0.815 | 0.766 | 0.829 |
| Ours – Text Only + BioWordVec | 0.489 | 0.841 | 0.771 | 0.837 |
| Ours – Ensemble | **0.582** | 0.880 | 0.822 | 0.861 |
| Ours – Ensemble + BioWordVec | **0.582** | **0.886** | **0.829** | **0.870** |

Table 2: Leveraging clinical pretrained word embeddings improves performance compared to training word embeddings from scratch in the text-only model. Ensembling the text-only model with the clinical time series classifier improves performance further.

### 5.1 Ensembling clinical word embeddings with structured data improves performance

Empirically, we observe superior performance to prior literature on a suite of clinical prediction tasks in Table 2; more tasks are evaluated in Appendix Table A. Full hyperparameter settings and code for reproducibility can be found here [1]. The ensemble model outperforms both constituent classifiers (AUC plot on Figure 3). This holds even when fairness/debiasing techniques are applied, emphasizing the overall effectiveness of leveraging multi-modal data. However, the ensemble's improvements in performance do not directly translate to improvements in fairness; see the True Positive (TP) graph in Figure 3, where the maximum TP gap remains consistent under the ensemble.

### 5.2 Debiased word embeddings and the fairness performance trade-off

Improving fairness usually comes at the cost of reduced performance (Menon and Williamson, 2018). Indeed, across all tasks, fairness groups and classifiers, we observe the group-specific disparities of TP and TN rates generally diminish when equalized odds post-processing is used (see Appendix F for additional results). However, this post-processing also leads to a degradation in the AUC. Note that we apply EO-post processing on hard (thresholded) predictions of the classifiers. If instead *soft* prediction scores are used as inputs to the post-processing step, both the performance degradation and the fairness improvement are softened (Hardt et al., 2016).

Generally, word embedding debiasing (WED) also helps reduce TP/TN discrepancies, although not to the same extent as EO postprocessing. Remarkably, in certain tasks, WED also yields a performance improvement, even compared to the fairness-free, unconstrained ensemble classifier. In particular, for the AUC graph in Figure 3, leveraging debiased word embeddings improves the performance of the ensemble; at the same time, the TP and TN group discrepancy ranges are improved. However, we stress that this outcome was not consistently observed and further investigation is warranted.

We emphasize that EO and WED serve different purposes with different motivations. While EO explicitly seeks to minimize the TP/TN range

---

[1] `https://github.com/johntiger1/multimodal_fairness/clinicalnlp`

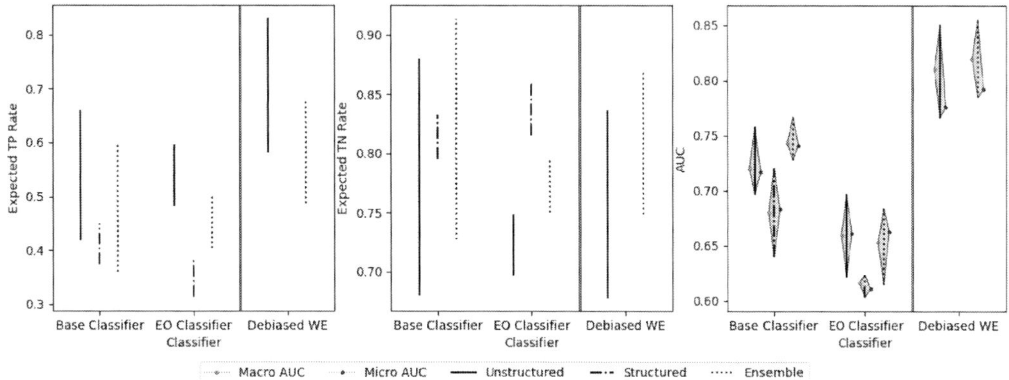


Figure 3: Plots of TP Rate, TN Rate, and AUC on phenotyping task M for groups defined by sensitive attribute of race. Each vertical black line represents a classifier (line style indicating modality); the length of the line represents the range of scores over fairness groups. In the TP/TN graphs, a shorter line represents better fairness; there is less discrepancy between the maximum and minimum group-specific TP/TN rates. In the AUC graph (far right), the higher the vertical position of the line, the better the performance. EO is effective at reducing the spread in TP/TN rates for the ensemble classifier (first two graphs) at the cost of performance (far right) graph. Meanwhile, debiased word embeddings both improves fairness, reducing the length of the line in the first two graphs, while achieving superior performance in AUC graph

between sensitive groups (reflected in its performance on the first two plots in Figure 3), WED seeks to neutralize text-specific bias in the word-embeddings. Despite the difference in goals, and despite operating only on the text-modality of the dataset, WED is still able to reduce the group-specific TP/TN range; recent work on *proxy fairness* in text has shown that indirect correlation between bias in text and protected attributes may be useful in achieving parity (Romanov et al., 2019).

Although WED demonstrate some good properties with respect to both fairness and performance for our specific dataset and task, we caution that they represent only one approach to fairness in NLP (Blodgett et al., 2020). Indeed, WED suffers from shortcomings related to intersectional fairness (Gonen and Goldberg, 2019), and we encourage further discussion into concretely defining fair, real-world NLP tasks and developing novel algorithms.

Our results highlight the important role practitioners and stakeholders play in algorithmic fairness on clinical applications. The trade-off between performance and fairness, whether between the soft and hard labels used for EO, or between EO and debiased word embeddings, must be balanced based on numerous real world factors.

## 6 Discussion

In this paper, we propose a novel multimodal fairness task for the MIMIC-III dataset, based on equalized odds. We provide two baselines: a classifier-agnostic fairness algorithm (equalized odds post-processing) and a text-specific fairness algorithm (debiased word embeddings). We observe that both methods generally follow the fairness performance tradeoff seen in single-modality tasks. EO is more effective at reducing the disparities in group-specific error rates while word-embedding debiasing has better performance. Future work can consider more generalized notions of fairness such as preferences-based frameworks, or extend text-specific fairness to contextualized word embeddings (Hossain et al., 2020; Zhang et al., 2020). Further analysis of the fairness performance trade-off, especially in multimodal settings, will facilitate equitable decision making in the clinical domain.

## 7 Acknowledgements


We would like to acknowledge Vector Institute for office and compute resources. We would also like to thank Matt Gardner for his help with answering questions when using AllenNLP (Gardner et al., 2017). John Chen and Safwan Hossain are funded by an Ontario Graduate Scholarship and a Vector Institute Research Grant. Ian Berlot-Attwell is funded by a Canada Graduate Scholarships-Master's, and a Vector Institute Research Grant. Frank Rudzicz is supported by a CIFAR Chair in AI.

## References

Oguz Akbilgic, Ramin Homayouni, Kevin Heinrich, Max Raymond Langham, and Robert Lowell Davis. 2019. Unstructured text in EMR improves prediction of death after surgery in children. In *Informatics*, volume 6, page 4. Multidisciplinary Digital Publishing Institute.

Su Lin Blodgett, Solon Barocas, Hal Daumé III, and Hanna Wallach. 2020. Language (technology) is power: A critical survey of" bias" in nlp. *arXiv preprint arXiv:2005.14050*.

Tolga Bolukbasi, Kai-Wei Chang, James Zou, Venkatesh Saligrama, and Adam Tauman Kalai. 2016. Man is to computer programmer as woman is to homemaker? Debiasing word embeddings. In *NIPS*.

I. Y. Chen, P. Szolovits, and M. Ghassemi. 2019. Can AI Help Reduce Disparities in General Medical and Mental Health Care? *AMA J Ethics*, 21(2):167–179.

Irene Chen, Fredrik D Johansson, and David Sontag. 2018. Why is my classifier discriminatory? In *Advances in Neural Information Processing Systems*, pages 3539–3550.

AJ Culyer and A Wagstaff. 1993. Equity and equality in health and health care. *Journal of health economics*, 12(4):431–457.

Howard N. Garb. 1997. Race bias, social class bias, and gender bias in clinical judgment. *Clinical Psychology: Science and Practice*, 4(2):99–120.

Matt Gardner, Joel Grus, Mark Neumann, Oyvind Tafjord, Pradeep Dasigi, Nelson F. Liu, Matthew Peters, Michael Schmitz, and Luke S. Zettlemoyer. 2017. Allennlp: A deep semantic natural language processing platform.

Hila Gonen and Yoav Goldberg. 2019. Lipstick on a pig: Debiasing methods cover up systematic gender biases in word embeddings but do not remove them. In *Proceedings of the 2019 Conference of the North American Chapter of the Association for Computational Linguistics: Human Language Technologies, Volume 1 (Long and Short Papers)*, pages 609–614.

Maya R. Gupta, Andrew Cotter, Mahdi Milani Fard, and Serena Wang. 2018. Proxy fairness. *CoRR*, abs/1806.11212.

Moritz Hardt, Eric Price, Eric Price, and Nati Srebro. 2016. Equality of opportunity in supervised learning. In D. D. Lee, M. Sugiyama, U. V. Luxburg, I. Guyon, and R. Garnett, editors, *Advances in Neural Information Processing Systems 29*, pages 3315–3323. Curran Associates, Inc.

Hrayr Harutyunyan, Hrant Khachatrian, David C. Kale, Greg Ver Steeg, and Aram Galstyan. 2019. Multitask learning and benchmarking with clinical time series data. *Scientific Data*, 6(1):96.

Steven Horng, David A Sontag, Yoni Halpern, Yacine Jernite, Nathan I Shapiro, and Larry A Nathanson. 2017. Creating an automated trigger for sepsis clinical decision support at emergency department triage using machine learning. *PloS one*, 12(4).

Safwan Hossain, Andjela Mladenovic, and Nisarg Shah. 2020. Designing fairly fair classifiers via economic fairness notions. In *Proceedings of The Web Conference 2020*, pages 1559–1569.

Alistair Johnson, Tom Pollard, Lu Shen, Li-wei Lehman, Mengling Feng, Mohammad Ghassemi, Benjamin Moody, Peter Szolovits, Leo Celi, and Roger Mark. 2016. MIMIC-III, a freely accessible critical care database. *Scientific Data*, 3:160035.

Swaraj Khadanga, Karan Aggarwal, Shafiq Joty, and Jaideep Srivastava. 2019. Using clinical notes with time series data for icu management. *arXiv preprint arXiv:1909.09702*.

Faiza Khan Khattak, Serena Jeblee, Chloé Pou-Prom, Mohamed Abdalla, Christopher Meaney, and Frank Rudzicz. 2019. A survey of word embeddings for clinical text. *Journal of Biomedical Informatics: X*, page 100057.

Yoon Kim. 2014. Convolutional neural networks for sentence classification. *arXiv preprint arXiv:1408.5882*.

Paul Pu Liang, Irene Mengze Li, Emily Zheng, Yao Chong Lim, Ruslan Salakhutdinov, and Louis-Philippe Morency. 2020. Towards debiasing sentence representations. *arXiv preprint arXiv:2007.08100*.

Thomas Manzini, Lim Yao Chong, Alan W Black, and Yulia Tsvetkov. 2019. Black is to criminal as caucasian is to police: Detecting and removing multiclass bias in word embeddings. In *Proceedings of the 2019 Conference of the North American Chapter of the Association for Computational Linguistics: Human Language Technologies, Volume 1 (Long and Short Papers)*, pages 615–621, Minneapolis, Minnesota. Association for Computational Linguistics.

Aditya Krishna Menon and Robert C Williamson. 2018. The cost of fairness in binary classification. In *Proceedings of the 1st Conference on Fairness, Accountability and Transparency*, volume 81 of *Proceedings of Machine Learning Research*, pages 107–118, New York, NY, USA. PMLR.

F. Pedregosa, G. Varoquaux, A. Gramfort, V. Michel, B. Thirion, O. Grisel, M. Blondel, P. Prettenhofer, R. Weiss, V. Dubourg, J. Vanderplas, A. Passos, D. Cournapeau, M. Brucher, M. Perrot, and E. Duchesnay. 2011. Scikit-learn: Machine learning in Python. *Journal of Machine Learning Research*, 12:2825–2830.

Stephen Pfohl, Ben Marafino, Adrien Coulet, Fatima Rodriguez, Latha Palaniappan, and Nigam H. Shah. 2019a. Creating fair models of atherosclerotic cardiovascular disease risk. In *Proceedings of the 2019 AAAI/ACM Conference on AI, Ethics, and Society*, AIES '19, page 271–278, New York, NY, USA. Association for Computing Machinery.

Stephen R. Pfohl, Tony Duan, Daisy Yi Ding, and Nigam H. Shah. 2019b. Counterfactual reasoning for fair clinical risk prediction. In *Proceedings of the 4th Machine Learning for Healthcare Conference*, volume 106 of *Proceedings of Machine Learning Research*, pages 325–358, Ann Arbor, Michigan. PMLR.

Alvin Rajkomar, Michaela Hardt, Michael D. Howell, Greg Corrado, and Marshall H. Chin. 2018. Ensuring fairness in machine learning to advance health equity. *Annals of Internal Medicine*, 169(12):866–872.

Shauli Ravfogel, Yanai Elazar, Hila Gonen, Michael Twiton, and Yoav Goldberg. 2020. Null it out: Guarding protected attributes by iterative nullspace projection. *arXiv preprint arXiv:2004.07667*.

Alexey Romanov, Maria De-Arteaga, Hanna Wallach, Jennifer Chayes, Christian Borgs, Alexandra Chouldechova, Sahin Geyik, Krishnaram Kenthapadi, Anna Rumshisky, and Adam Kalai. 2019. What's in a name? reducing bias in bios without access to protected attributes. In *Proceedings of the 2019 Conference of the North American Chapter of the Association for Computational Linguistics: Human Language Technologies, Volume 1 (Long and Short Papers)*, pages 4187–4195.

David R. Williams, Naomi Priest, and Norman B. Anderson. 2016. Understanding associations among race, socioeconomic status, and health: Patterns and prospects. *Health psychology : official journal of the Division of Health Psychology, American Psychological Association*, 35(4):407–411. 27018733[pmid].

Haoran Zhang, Amy X. Lu, Mohamed Abdalla, Matthew McDermott, and Marzyeh Ghassemi. 2020. Hurtful words: Quantifying biases in clinical contextual word embeddings. In *Proceedings of the ACM Conference on Health, Inference, and Learning*, CHIL '20, page 110–120, New York, NY, USA. Association for Computing Machinery.

Ye Zhang and Byron Wallace. 2015. A sensitivity analysis of (and practitioners' guide to) convolutional neural networks for sentence classification. *arXiv preprint arXiv:1510.03820*.

Yijia Zhang, Qingyu Chen, Zhihao Yang, Hongfei Lin, and Zhiyong Lu. 2019. Biowordvec, improving biomedical word embeddings with subword information and mesh. *Scientific data*, 6(1):1–9.

Jieyu Zhao, Yichao Zhou, Zeyu Li, Wei Wang, and Kai-Wei Chang. 2018. Learning gender-neutral word embeddings. In *Proceedings of the 2018 Conference on Empirical Methods in Natural Language Processing*, pages 4847–4853, Brussels, Belgium. Association for Computational Linguistics.

# A  Details on Clinical Prediction Tasks

## A.1  Defining the Multimodal MIMIC-III Benchmark Prediction Tasks

Existing work by (Harutyunyan et al., 2019) previously defined four benchmark clinical prediction tasks on ICU stays information from the large MIMIC-III database.  They produce a derived dataset, focusing on 17 timeseries clinical features, without text. The goal is predict the task specific outcome (mortality, phenotyping, decompensation, length-of-stay) for the given ICU stay. We utilize their derived dataset directly, which provides training and test examples for all four tasks, but join the derived dataset back with the original to obtain linked clinical text. We make the key choice that we drop examples without *relevant* (i.e. no causal leakage) extracted clinical notes, as in (Khadanga et al., 2019). Thus, we concretely define the Combined Modality MIMIC-III Benchmark Prediction Task as extending the benchmark clinical prediction task by (Harutyunyan et al., 2019) to include linked clinical text. If there are no notes associated with an example, then we remove this instance from the task. Note that we also drop ICU stays which only have unusable notes due to causal leakage; for instance death reports for mortality prediction.

## A.2  Note extraction

To extract relevant notes, we build a mapping from the derived dataset provided by (Harutyunyan et al., 2019) and the MIMIC-III database. For each training and test instance in each task, we find the clinical notes in the MIMIC-III database. For the IHM task, if we do not find any notes within the first 48 hours of their stay, we drop the patient, since there is no *relevant* textual information. Note that this is consistent with the original task formulation by (Harutyunyan et al., 2019) of in-hospital mortality prediction using at most the first 48 hours of clinical data. Furthermore, this follows (Khadanga et al., 2019).

For the phenotyping task, which is not covered by (Khadanga et al., 2019), we relax this time condition. In the original formulation of the task, phenotyping is a *retrospective* multilabel multiclass classification task, meaning that all vital signs data associated with the ICU stay is provided and can be used by the model. Therefore, we only drop the patient if there are no notes for the entire ICU stay.

## A.3  Preprocessing

We use the same preprocessing as in (Khadanga et al., 2019), finding it to be mildly beneficial for performance.

## A.4  Cohort statistics

In the medical literature, *cohort selection* is the process of selecting the population of patients for inclusion in a study. These patients will then provide the training instances for the clinical prediction task. We report the cohort statistics for our binary clinical prediction multimodal tasks.

### A.4.1  In-Hospital Mortality

| Sensitive Group | Train Count | Test Count | % of Test |
|---|---|---|---|
| F | 7940 | 1415 | 44.0 % |
| M | 9708 | 1778 | 56.0 % |
| ASIAN | 408 | 60 | 1.9 % |
| BLACK | 1658 | 285 | 8.9 % |
| HISPANIC | 521 | 107 | 3.3 % |
| OTHER | 2655 | 459 | 14.4 % |
| WHITE | 12406 | 2282 | 71.5 % |
| Government | 356 | 74 | 2.3 % |
| Medicaid | 1362 | 205 | 6.4 % |
| Medicare | 9857 | 1757 | 55.0 % |
| Private | 4946 | 932 | 29.2 % |
| Self Pay | 133 | 33 | 1.0 % |
| UNKNOWN | 994 | 192 | 6.1 % |

### A.4.2  Phenotyping

| Sensitive Group | Train Count | Test Count | % of Test |
|---|---|---|---|
| F | 15638 | 2750 | 44% |
| M | 19803 | 3504 | 56% |
| ASIAN | 826 | 133 | 2.1 % |
| BLACK | 3378 | 575 | 9.1 % |
| HISPANIC | 1158 | 206 | 3.3 % |
| OTHER | 5004 | 854 | 13.7 % |
| WHITE | 25075 | 4486 | 71.7 % |
| Government | 845 | 150 | 2.4 % |
| Medicaid | 2850 | 433 | 6.9 % |
| Medicare | 18702 | 3298 | 52.7 % |
| Private | 10784 | 1923 | 30.7 % |
| Self Pay | 380 | 73 | 1.2 % |
| UNKNOWN | 1880 | 377 | 6.0 % |

## A.5  Task Statistics

### A.5.1  In-Hospital Mortality

| Label | Train Set Count | Test Set Count |
|---|---|---|
| 0 | 15337 | 2829 |
| 1 | 2311 | 364 |

### A.5.2 Phenotyping

Plots of the prevalance of the 25 critical care conditions can be found in Figures 4 and 2 for the test and train sets respectively, a legend that doubles as the full list of phenotyping tasks is available in Table 3.

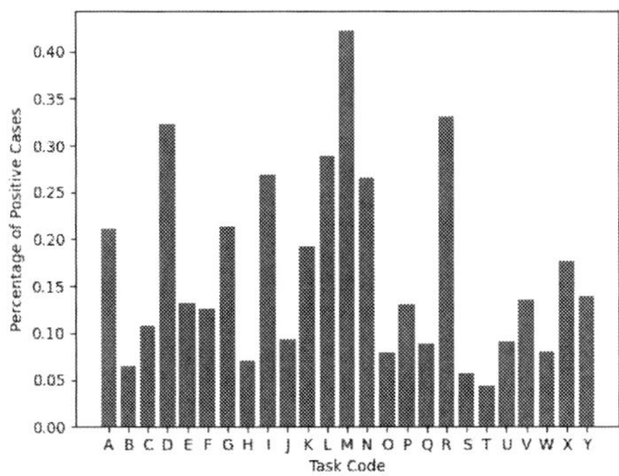

Figure 4: Percentage of positive test cases for each of the 25 phenotyping tasks

## B  Model Details

### B.1  Structured Data Model

We use the baseline developed by Harutyunyan et al. (2019). The structured data model takes as input a time-series of 17 clinical variables, which are extracted features for the benchmark tasks introduced in the same paper. The model is a channel-wise LSTM where each clinical variable is transcoded by a bidirectional LSTM, concatenated with the other transcoded sequences and passed to a final LSTM for prediction.

### B.2  Unstructured Data Model

We implement a simple CNN-based encoder (Kim, 2014; Zhang and Wallace, 2015) to process the clinical notes and produce a task-specific prediction. We experiment with various settings including model architecture, word embedding dimension, preprocessing, varying the maximum number of tokens, L2 regularization and batch size. Below, we report the final hyperparameters and settings used to generate all plots and reported throughout.

Our CNNEncoder is built using the AllenNLP framework (Gardner et al., 2017). We use 1D kernel ($n$ gram) filter sizes of 2, 3 and 5, learning 5 filters for each filter size. Convolution is done on word embedding representations of the input, across $n$-gram windows of the sequence, and are

| Code | Task |
| --- | --- |
| A | Acute and unspecified renal failure |
| B | Acute cerebrovascular disease |
| C | Acute myocardial infarction |
| D | Cardiac dysrhythmias |
| E | Chronic kidney disease |
| F | Chronic obstructive pulmonary disease and bronchiectasis |
| G | Complications of surgical procedures or medical care |
| H | Conduction disorders |
| I | Congestive heart failure |
| J | Coronary atherosclerosis and other heart disease |
| K | Diabetes mellitus with complications |
| L | Diabetes mellitus without complication |
| M | Disorders of lipid metabolism |
| N | Essential hypertension |
| O | Fluid and electrolyte disorders |
| P | Gastrointestinal hemorrhage |
| Q | Hypertension with complications and secondary hypertension |
| R | nonhypertensive |
| S | Other liver diseases |
| T | Other lower respiratory disease |
| U | Other upper respiratory disease |
| V | Pleurisy |
| W | Pneumonia (except that caused by tuberculosis or sexually transmitted disease) |
| X | pneumothorax |
| Y | pulmonary collapse |

Table 3: List of critical care conditions in the phenotyping task, and their corresponding alphabetic codes.

pooled before being combined. The CNNEncoder produces a single fixed size vector, and we use a simple linear layer on top to perform the classification.

For all multimodal tasks, we limit the maximum number of tokens input to 1536, taking the most recent notes first (taking care to avoid causal leakage as described in 3.1), and apply preprocessing as in (Khadanga et al., 2019). For the decompensation task, we subsample the number of training instances due to engineering and efficiency reasons. From 2 million possible training instances, we sample 50 000 examples, with weighting to balance the number of positive and negatively training instances in a 50/50 split.

We train for up to 50 epochs, using Adam optimizer with learning rate set to 0.001. When we use pretrained word embeddings (either debiased or not), we do not finetune or update them. We do not use any L2 regularization or dropout, instead employing early stopping with patience of 5 epochs, using validation loss as the stopping criterion. We use batch size 256. Training is completed on 1 NVIDIA Titan Xp with 12 GB of memory.

### B.3 Ensemble Model

We use scikit-learn (Pedregosa et al., 2011) with the default setting of L2 regularization with $C = 1$

## C  Sets of social-specific Words

### C.1  Sets of Gender-specific Words

- {"he", "she"}
- {"his", "hers"}
- {"son", "daughter"}
- {"father", "mother"}
- {"male", "female"}
- {"boy", "girl"}
- {"uncle", "aunt"}

### C.2  Sets of Racial-specific Words

- {"black", "caucasian", "asian", "hispanics"}
- {"african", "caucasian", "asian", "hispanics"}
- {"black", "white", "asian", "hispanics"}
- {"africa", "america", "asia", "hispanics"}
- {"africa", "america", "china", "hispanics"}
- {"africa", "europe", "asia", "hispanics"}

- {"black", "caucasian", "asian", "latino"}
- {"african", "caucasian", "asian", "latino"}
- {"black", "white", "asian", "latino"}
- {"africa", "america", "asia", "latino"}
- {"africa", "america", "china", "latino"}
- {"africa", "europe", "asia", "latino"}
- {"black", "caucasian", "asian", "spanish"}
- {"african", "caucasian", "asian", "spanish"}
- {"black", "white", "asian", "spanish"}
- {"africa", "america", "asia", "spanish"}
- {"africa", "america", "china", "spanish"}
- {"africa", "europe", "asia", "spanish"}

## D  Hard Debiasing

Hard debiasing is a debiasing algorithm which involves two steps: neutralize and equalize. Neutralization ensures that all the social-neural words in the social subspace do not contain bias (e.g. doctors and nurses). Equalization forces that social-specific words are equidistant to all words in each equality set (e.g. the bias components in man and woman are in opposite directions but with same magnitude) (Bolukbasi et al., 2016; Manzini et al., 2019). Following Manzini et al. (2019), hard debiasing is formulated as follows: given a bias social subspace $\mathcal{B}$ spanned by the vectors $\{b_1, b_2, ..., b_n\}$, the embedding of a word in this subspace is:

$$w_{\mathcal{B}} = \sum_{i=1}^{n} \langle w, b_i \rangle b_i$$

To neutralize, each word $w \in N$, where $N$ is the set of social-neural words, remove the bias components from the word and the re-embedded word $\vec{w}$ is obtained as:

$$\vec{w} = \frac{w - w_{\mathcal{B}}}{\| w - w_{\mathcal{B}} \|}$$

To equalize, for an equality set $E$, let $\mu$ be the mean embeddings of the equlity set $E$, which is defined as:

$$\mu = \frac{w}{E} \sum_{w \in E}$$

For each word $w \in E$, the equalization is defined as:

$$\hat{w} = (\mu - \mu_{\mathcal{B}}) + \sqrt{1 - \| \mu - \mu_{\mathcal{B}} \|^2} \frac{w - w_{\mathcal{B}}}{\| w - w_{\mathcal{B}} \|}$$

When doing racial debiasing, we divide ethnicity into groups: White, Black, Asian, and Hispanics. We do not contain the "other" group as it hard to define social-specific sets and analogies for "other".

## E  Phenotyping Task

In Figure 3 we plot performance and fairness for the phenotyping task, specifically the detection of disorders of lipid metabolism. This task was selected as it is the phenotyping task with the most balanced labels with 16855 negative instances and 12239 positive instances in the training data. Thus, it should be more amenable to EO postprocessing. As expected we see that EO postprocessing succeeds in reducing the TP/TN ranges at the cost of AUC. We also again see that ensembling improves performance both before and after postprocessing. For this task specifically we observe that using debiased word embeddings improves AUC compared to the non-debiased word embeddings.

## F  Full Results

Our experiment universe consisted of the cross product between choice of protected attribute (gender, ethnicity, insurance status), task (phenotyping, in-hospital mortality prediction, decompensation), hard vs soft EO postprocessing and word embedding vs debiased word embedding.

### F.1  Fairness/Performance on the In-Hospital Mortality Task

We provide a more detailed set of graphs for an in-hospital mortality prediction task, where we used hard EO postprocessing on protected groups defined by insurance status. We illustrate the TP/TN/AUC metrics for each protected group in Figure 5.

In this task configuration, as well as the task configuration in Figure 3 EO postprocessing is applied to hard classification of the three classifiers in the Base Classifier column, to produce the EO Classifier column. The Debiased Word Embedding (WE) column contains an unstructured classifier using word embeddings debiased for 4 ethnicities, and an ensemble created by merging the aforementioned classifier with the structured base classifier. We utilize debiasing on ethnicity type as a proxy for insurance status, as mentioned in the Discussion.

Note that EO post-processing sometimes *worsens* the TP/TN spread, as in the TP graph for the structured classifier. We therefore qualify our EO

results by noting the limitations of our real-world dataset, which include significant group and label imbalance and non-binary group labels, all of which impact the results of EO post-processing (see Appendix A.4).

Finally, on this task configuration, we observe that debiased word embeddings are not a panacea. We note that WED has slightly worsened the TP gap, and does not offer a clear cut performance improvement as on the phenotyping task M. Therefore, further research is needed to explore when and why debiased word embeddings may simultaneously improve fairness and performance. Ultimately, domain expertise and focus on the downstream impact on the patient experience will be critical for leveraging any of these fair machine learning models in clinical applications.

### F.2  Full table of results

The performance for all model and tasks tried can be found in Table 4. Note that debiased word embeddings can improve the performance (micro and macro AUC), even compared to an unconstrained classifier using clinically relevant BioWordVec embeddings.

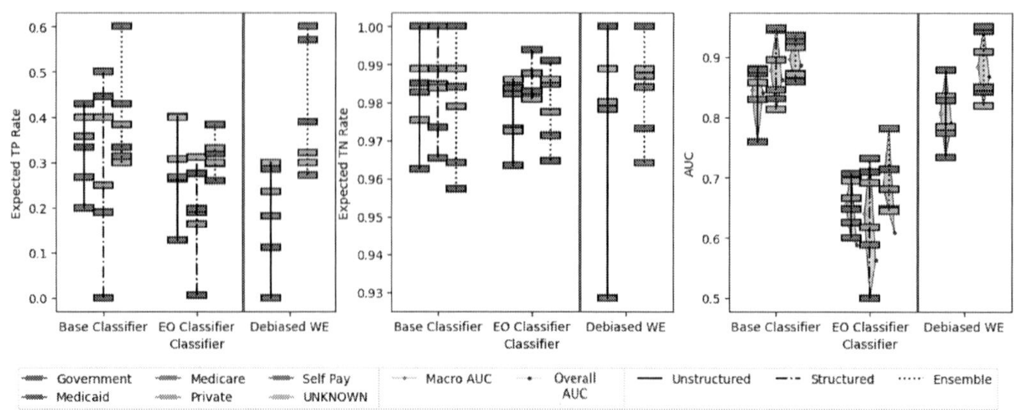



Figure 5: Plot of Fairness and Performance on the in-hospital mortality task. Note that debiased word embeddings slightly worsen the TP gap in this task (left most graph), while improving the TN gap (middle graph). EO reduces both gaps, at a major cost in performance (right most graph).

| | IHM | | Phenotyping | | Decompen. | |
|---|---|---|---|---|---|---|
| | AUC PRC | AUC ROC | Macro AUC ROC | Micro AUC ROC | AUC PRC | AUC ROC |
| Harutyunyan et. al (2019) – No Text | 0.515 | 0.862 | 0.776 | 0.825 | 0.344 | 0.911 |
| Khadanga et. al (2019) – Ensemble | 0.525 | 0.865 | – | – | 0.345 | 0.907 |
| Ours – Text Only | 0.472 | 0.815 | 0.766 | 0.829 | 0.235 | 0.867 |
| Ours – Text Only + BioWordVec | 0.489 | 0.841 | 0.771 | 0.837 | 0.225 | 0.879 |
| Ours – Text Only + BioWordVec + Debiasing | 0.392 | 0.790 | 0.831 | 0.874 | 0.265 | 0.331 |
| Ours – Ensemble | **0.582** | 0.880 | 0.822 | 0.861 | 0.399 | 0.917 |
| Ours – Ensemble + BioWordVec | **0.582** | **0.886** | 0.829 | 0.870 | **0.404** | **0.920** |
| Ours – Ensemble + BioWordVec + Debiasing | 0.539 | 0.870 | **0.854** | **0.888** | 0.405 | 0.922 |

Table 4: Leveraging clinical pretrained word embeddings improves performance compared to training word embeddings from scratch in the text-only model. Ensembling the text-only model with the clinical time series classifier improves performance further. As with Khadanga et al. (2019), our results are not directly comparable with Harutyunyan et al. (2019) since we ignore patients without any clinical notes.

**Association for Computational Linguistics**
209 N. Eighth Street
Stroudsburg, Pennsylvania 18360

ISBN 978-1-7138-1989-9